THE PROSE READER

*Essays for Thinking,
Reading, and Writing*

FOURTH EDITION

Kim Flachmann
Michael Flachmann

California State University
Bakersfield

Prentice Hall, Upper Saddle River, New Jersey 07458

Library of Congress Cataloging- in Publication Data

The prose reader : essays for thinking, reading, and writing /
[compiled by] Kim Flachmann, Michael Flachmann.— 4th ed.
    p.   cm.
Includes bibliographical references and index.
ISBN 0–13–190760–3
    1. College readers.   2. English language—Rhetoric.   3. Critical
thinking.   I. Flachmann, Kim.   II. Flachmann, Michael.
PE1417.P847   1995
808´.0427—dc20   95–4778
                                                       CIP

Acquisition editor: Alison Reeves
Development editor: Kara Hado
Project manager: Maureen Richardson
Manufacturing buyer: Lynn Pearlman
Cover design: Carole Anson
Cover art: Braque, Georges. L'Estaque, 1906. Musee
National d'Art Moderne, Paris. Courtesy of Giraudon/Art
Resource, New York

Printed in the United States of America

10 9 8 7 6 5 4

ISBN 0-13-190760-3
ISBN 0-13-197898-5 (Instructor's Edition)

Prentice-Hall International (UK) Limited, London
Prentice-Hall of Australia Pty. Limited, Sydney
Prentice-Hall Canada Inc., Toronto
Prentice-Hall Hispanoamericana, S.A., Mexico
Prentice-Hall of India Private Limited, New Delhi
Prentice-Hall of Japan, Inc., Tokyo
Simon & Schuster Asia Pte. Ltd., Singapore
Editora Prentice-Hall do Brasil, Ltd., Rio de Janeiro

For Our Students

Rhetorical
Table of Contents

The description of a simple, comforting ritual—the putting up of a front-porch swing in early summer—confirms the value of ceremony in the life of a small town.

■

2 Narration: *Telling a Story*   100

--- ∎

3 Example: *Illustrating Ideas* 154

7 Definition: *Limiting the Frame of Reference*   388

---

8 Cause/Effect   *Tracing Reasons and Results*   444

10 Documented Essays: *Reading and Writing from Sources* 589

---

11 Essays on Thinking, Reading, and Writing   634

Thematic
Table of Contents

BEHAVIORAL SCIENCE

WRITING

Preface to the Instructor

The Prose Reader is based on the assumption that lucid writing follows lucid thinking, whereas poor written work is almost inevitably the product of foggy, irrational thought processes. As a result, our primary purpose in this book, as in the first three editions, is to help students *think* more clearly and logically—both in their minds and on paper.

Reading and writing are companion activities that involve students in the creation of thought and meaning—either as readers interpreting a text or as writers constructing one. Clear thinking, then, is the pivotal point that joins together these two efforts. Although studying the rhetorical strategies presented in *The Prose Reader* is certainly not the only way to approach writing, it is a productive means of helping students improve their abilities to think, read, and write on progressively more sophisticated levels.

The symbiosis we envision among thinking, reading, and writing is represented in this text by the following hierarchy of cognitive levels:

1. *Literal, characterized by a basic understanding of words and their meanings;*
2. *Interpretive, consisting of a knowledge of linear connections between ideas and an ability to make valid inferences based on those ideas; and*
3. *Critical, the highest level, distinguished by the systematic investigation of complex ideas and by the analysis of their relationship to the world around us.*

WHAT REMAINS THE SAME

The Prose Reader is organized according to the belief that our mental abilities are generally sequential. In other words, students cannot read or write analytically before they are able to perform well on the literal and interpretive levels. Accordingly, the book progresses from selections that require predominantly literal skills, *description, narration, and example,*

through readings involving more interpretation,

process analysis, division/classification, comparison/contrast, and definition,

to essays that demand a high degree of analytical thought,

cause/effect, and argument/persuasion.

Depending on the caliber of your students and your prescribed curriculum, these rhetorical modes can, of course, be studied in any order. In the Rhetorical Table of Contents, each entry includes a one- or two-sentence synopsis of the selection so you can peruse the list quickly and decide which essays to assign. An alternate Thematic Table of Contents lists selections by academic discipline, responding to recent nationwide attempts to integrate reading and writing in content areas other than English through "Writing Across the Curriculum."

▶ *The chapter introductions are filled with several types of useful information about each rhetorical mode.*

Each of the nine rhetorical divisions in the text is introduced by an explanation of how to think, read, and write in that particular mode. These introductions also contain a sample student paragraph and a complete student essay that illustrate each rhetorical pattern and help bridge the sometimes formidable gap between student and professional writing.

After each essay, the student writer has provided a thorough analysis of the experience, explaining the most enjoyable, exasperating, or noteworthy aspects of writing that particular essay. (We have found that this combination of student essays and commentaries makes the professional selections easier for students to read and more accessible as models of thinking and writing.) Although each chapter focuses on one particular rhetorical strategy, students are continually encouraged to examine ways in which other modes help support each writer's main intentions.

▶ *As in earlier editions, the essays in* The Prose Reader *continue to represent a wide range of topics.*

These subjects include discrimination, ethnic identity, job opportunities, aging, education, sports, women's roles, prison life, time management, AIDS, immigration, physical handicaps, and the writing process itself.

The essays were selected on the basis of five important criteria: (1) high interest level, (2) currency in the field, (3) moderate length, (4) readability, and (5) broad subject variety.

Together, these essays portray the universality of human experience as expressed through the viewpoints of men and women, many different ethnic and racial groups, and a variety of ages and social classes.

► *The Argument and Persuasion chapter (Chapter 9) covers topics such as religion's place in public schools, affirmative action, gun control, and immigration, and it includes two sets of opposing-viewpoint essays on freedom of the press and the effects of TV.*

The essays in this chapter are particularly useful for helping your students refine their critical thinking skills in preparation for longer, more sustained papers on a single topic. The first five essays in this chapter encourage students to wrestle with provocative issues that make a difference in how we all live. Then, the two sets of opposing viewpoint essays help the students see coherent arguments at work from two different perspectives on a single issue.

► *"Documented Essays: Reading and Writing from Sources" (Chapter 10) features academic writing throughout the college curriculum in the form of research papers on group violence and Latina health.*

These essays demonstrate the two most common documentation styles—Modern Language Association (MLA) and American Psychological Association (APA). By including documented essays, we intend to clarify some of the mysteries connected with research and documentation; we have also tried to provide interesting material for creating more elaborate writing assignments in accord with your own specific course goals. In addition, we offer a full range of apparatus for these selections, including a list of

Further Reading on each subject and suggested topics for longer, more sophisticated essays and research papers.

▶ *The book ends with our popular chapter called "Thinking, Reading, and Writing."*

This section includes essays on listening, reading fiction, understanding the process of writing, writing with style, and composing on the computer. In addition to demonstrating all the rhetorical modes at work, these essays provide a strong conclusion to the theoretical framework of this text, which focuses intently on the interrelationships among thinking, reading, and writing.

▶ *Because our own experience suggests that students often produce their best writing when they are personally involved in the topics of the essays they read and in the human drama surrounding those essays, we precede each selection with thorough biographical information on the author and provocative prereading questions on the subject of the essay.*

The biographies explain the real experiences from which an essay emerged, and the prereading questions ("Preparing to Read") help students focus on the purpose, audience, and subject of the essay. The prereading questions also foreshadow the questions and writing assignments that follow each selection. Personalizing this preliminary material encourages students to identify with both the writer of the essay and the essay's subject matter—and thus engages the students' attention and energizes their response to the selections they read.

▶ *The questions at the end of each selection are designed to help students move sequentially from various literal-level responses to interpretation and analysis.*

Five different types of questions are furnished for each essay:

1. *"Understanding Details," questions that test the students' literal and interpretive understanding of what they have read;*
2. *"Analyzing Meaning," questions that require students to analyze various aspects of the essay;*

3. *"Discovering Rhetorical Strategies," questions that investigate the author's rhetorical plan in constructing the essay;*
4. *"Making Connections," questions that ask students to find thematic and rhetorical connections among essays they have read; and*
5. *"Ideas for Discussion/Writing," exercises that supply writing and discussion topics for use inside or outside the classroom.*

These questions deliberately examine both the form and the content of the essays so that your students can cultivate a similar balance in their own writing.

▶ *The writing assignments are preceded by Preparing to Write questions designed to encourage students to express their feelings, thoughts, observations, and opinions on various topics.*

Questions about their own ideas and experiences help students produce writing that corresponds as closely as possible to the way they think.

▶ *The writing assignments themselves seek to involve the students in realistic situations by providing a specific purpose and audience for each essay topic.*

In this manner, student writers are drawn into rhetorical scenes that carefully focus their responses to a variety of questions or problems.

▶ *The book concludes with a glossary of composition terms (along with examples and page references from the text) and an index of authors and titles.*

WHAT IS NEW

We have made several changes in the fourth edition of *The Prose Reader* that represent the responses of reviewers from many different types of colleges and universities all over the United States:

▶ *We have expanded the rhetorical introductions, including more specific instruction on writing each type of essay, a new section focusing on each rhetorical mode as a way of thinking, and additional material introducing and explaining the student essays.*

▸ *The fourth edition of* The Prose Reader *contains fifteen new essays. We have updated some of the selections, added new authors, and introduced new topics, such as growing up, the logistics of job interviews, work and motherhood, male and female identity, writing, personal identity, immigration, TV, the media, and Latina health.*

▸ *Since multicultural and women's issues have always been well represented in* The Prose Reader, *this edition continues to make a commitment to cultural and sexual diversity by including many new essays by women and ethnic-minority authors, among them Maya Angelou, Barbara Ehrenreich, Gloria Steinem, Rita Mae Brown, Alice Walker, and Peter Salins.*

▸ *We have replaced both sets of pro/con essays to make them more timely and accessible to our students today. The topics covered are freedom of the press and the relationship between TV and violence.*

▸ *We have included a documented essay in Chapter 10 on an important new issue in the health care debate. We now offer documented essays on group violence and Latina health, which demonstrate both the MLA and the APA documentation styles.*

▸ *We have expanded the number of questions after each essay, including a new set of questions entitled "Making Connections," which ask students to draw conclusions and recognize thematic and rhetorical relationships they may not have seen before among various essays in this book.*

WHAT SUPPLEMENTS ARE AVAILABLE

Available with *The Prose Reader* is a thorough **Annotated Instructor's Edition** designed to help make your life in the classroom a little easier. We have filled the margins of the AIE with many different kinds of supplementary material, including background information about each essay, definitions of terms that may be unfamiliar to your students, a list of related readings from this text that can be taught profitably with each other, a list of related videos from the *ABC News/Prentice Hall Video Library,* innovative teaching ideas, provocative quotations, specific answers to the questions that follow each selection, additional essay topics, and instructor comments on teaching in different rhetorical modes.

In addition to the *Annotated Instructor's Edition,* we have created a new supplement that combines the **Instructor's Resource Manual** and the **Quiz Book**. In it, we identify and discuss some of the most widely used theoretical approaches to the teaching of composition; we then offer innovative options for organizing your course, specific suggestions for the first day of class, a summary of the advantages and disadvantages of using different teaching strategies, and several successful techniques for responding to student writing. Next, we provide two objective quizzes for each essay to help you monitor your students' mastery of a selection's vocabulary and content. This supplement ends with some additional professional essays (two opposing viewpoint essays and one documented essay), a series of student essays (one for each rhetorical strategy featured in the text) followed by the student writer's comments, and an annotated bibliography of books about thinking, reading, and writing.

An exciting new supplement available with this edition of *The Prose Reader* is a **computer disk (3^1/$_2$" IBM and Macintosh format)** that contains all the quizzes from the *Instructor's Resource with Quiz Book.* These quizzes can be copied onto other disks or printed directly from the master disk for your students to work with. This computer disk will be especially useful in colleges and universities that have computer classrooms for their composition courses; in addition, students can take individual copies of the disk with them to complete their assignments off campus.

Also available with *The Prose Reader* is the complete *ABC News/Prentice Hall Video Library*, which is a series of nine video clips (from four to twelve minutes long) on such provocative subjects as teens and prejudice, Prozac, and political correctness on college campuses. In the margins of the *Annotated Instructor's Edition*, we list videos from this collection that can effectively be taught with certain essays in the text.

This entire instructional package, available to you free of charge, is intended to help your students discover what they want to say and to prompt them to shape their ideas into a coherent form, thereby encouraging their intelligent involvement in the complex and exciting world around them.

ACKNOWLEDGMENTS

We are pleased to acknowledge the kind assistance and support of a number of people who have helped us put together this fourth edition of *The Prose Reader*. For creative and editorial guidance at Prentice Hall, we thank Alison Reeves, Executive Editor; Kara Hado, Assistant Editor; and Maureen Richardson, Project Manager.

For reviews of the manuscript at various stages of completion, we are grateful to Janice Jones, Kent State University, Kent, Ohio; Lyle W. Morgan II, Pittsburgh State University, Pittsburgh, Pennsylvania; Carolyn D. Coward, Shelby State Community College, Memphis, Tennessee; Teresa Purvis, Lansing Community College, Lansing, Michigan; Gena E. Christopher, Jacksonville State University, Jacksonville, Florida; Donnie Yeilding, Central Texas College, Killeen, Texas; Steve Katz, State Technical Institute, Memphis, Tennessee; Craig Howard White, University of Houston, Clear Lake, Houston, Texas; Judith Dan, Boston University, Boston, Massachusetts; Arlie R. Peck, University of Rio Grande, Rio Grande, Ohio; Barbara Smith, Iona College, New Rochelle, New York; Vermell Blanding, Hostos Community College, Bronx, New York; Nancy G. Wright, Austin Peay State University, Clarksville, Tennessee; Paula Miller, Azusa Pacific University, Azusa, California; Paul Kistel, Pierce College, Tacoma, Washington; Christopher Belcher, Community College of Allegheny County, Pittsburgh, Pennsylvania; Helen F. Maxon, Southwestern Oklahoma State University, Oklahoma City, Oklahoma; Geoffrey C. Goodale, University of Massachusetts at Boston, Boston, Massachusetts; Martha Bergeron, Vance-Granville Community College, Henderson, North Carolina; Jan LaFever, Friends University, Wichita, Kansas; Virginia Leonard, West Liberty State College, Wichita, Kansas; Melissa A. Bruner, Southwestern Oklahoma State University, West Liberty, Virginia; James Zarzana, Southwest State University, Marshall, Minnesota; Terrence Burke, Cuyahoga Community College, Cleveland, Ohio; Ellen Dugan-Barrette, Brescia College, Owensboro,

Kentucky; Lewis Emond, Dean Junior College, Franklin, Massachusetts; Jay Jernigan, Eastern Michigan University, Ypsilanti, Michigan; Nellie McCrory, Gaston College, Dallas, North Carolina; Leslie Shipp, Clark County Community College, Henderson, Nevada; and William F. Sutlife, Community College of Allegheny County, Monroeville, Pennsylvania, and for student essays and writing samples, we thank Rosa Marie Augustine, Donel Crow, Dawn Dobie, Gloria Dumler, Jeff Hicks, Julie Anne Judd, Judi Koch, Dawn McKee, Paul Newberry, Joanne Silva-Newberry, JoAnn Slate, Peggy Stuckey, and Jan Titus.

Several writing instructors across the United States have been kind enough to help shape the fourth edition of *The Prose Reader* by responding to specific questions about their teaching experiences with the book: Charles Bordogna, Bergen Community College, Paramus, New Jersey; Mary G. Marshall and Eileen M. Ward, College of DuPage, Glen Ellyn, Illinois; Michael J. Huntington and Judith C. Kohl, Dutchess Community College, Poughkeepsie, New York; Ted Johnston, El Paso County Community College, El Paso, Texas; Koala C. Hartnett, Rick James Mazza, and William H. Sherman, Fairmont State College, Fairmont, West Virginia; Miriam Dick and Betty Krasne, Mercy College, Dobbs Ferry, New York; Elvis Clark, Mineral Area College, Flat River, Missouri; Dayna Spencer, Pittsburg State University, Pittsburg, Kansas; James A. Zarzana, Southwest State University, Marshall, Minnesota; Susan Reinhart Schneling and Trudy Vanderback, Vincennes University, Vincennes, Indiana; Carmen Wong, Virginia Commonwealth University, Richmond, Virginia; and John W. Hattman and Virginia E. Leonard, West Liberty State College, West Liberty, West Virginia. We want to extend special thanks to Sandra R. Woods, Fairmont State College, whose students' comments on the second edition were exceptionally valuable to us in making decisions for this edition.

We are also grateful to the following professors from our university who have offered useful advice about the book: Mary Allen, Charles Bicak, Ken Gobalet, Richard Graves, Bob Horton, Bruce Jones, Gary Kessler, Richard Noel, Warren Paap, Norman Prigge, Phil Silverman, and Jerry Stanley of the Writing Across the Curriculum Program; and Sophia Adjaye, Ed Barton, Lynette Betty, Robert Carlisle, Lorna Clymer, Bonnie Greene, Solomon

Iyasere, Victor Lasseter, Jeff Mc Mahon, Char Myers, Susan Stone, and Emily Thiroux of the English and Communications Department at California State University, Bakersfield.

In preparing our *Annotated Instructor's Edition*, we owe special gratitude to the following writing instructors who have contributed their favorite techniques for teaching various rhetorical strategies: Mary P. Boyles, Pembroke State University; Terrence W. Burke, Cuyahoga Community College; Mary Lou Conlin, Cuyahoga Community College; Ellen Dugan-Barrette, Brescia College; Janet Eber, County College of Morris; Louis Emond, Dean Junior College; Peter Harris, West Virginia Institute of Technology, Montgomery; Jay Jernigan, Eastern Michigan University; Judith C. Kohl, Dutchess Community College; Joanne H. McCarthy, Tacoma Community College; Anthony McCrann, Peru State College; Nellie McCrory, Gaston College; Alan Price, Peru State University—Hazelton; Patricia A. Ross, Moorpark College; Leslie Shipp, Clark County Community College; Rodney Simard, California State University, San Bernadino; Elizabeth Wahlquist, Brigham Young University; John White, California State University, Fullerton; and Ted Wise, Porterville College. We also want to thank our graduate students and teaching assistants for suggesting instructional material to supplement the student text and for class-testing some of it as we were writing. Last, we are grateful to Julie Denny, Jill Kleiss, Patti Bartlett, Reza Azarmsa, Asad Dadarkar, Bob and Kris Nahama, Mandy Fischer, and Eric Blomberg for special contributions they each made to the book.

Very special thanks are due to Kathryn Benander, who served as a research and editorial assistant throughout the entire project; to Sue Keintz, who assisted us on the new *Instructor's Resource Manual with Quiz Book*; and to Mette Nielsen, who supported our efforts on this text in many important ways.

Our final and most important debt is to our students, who have taught us so much over the years about the writing process.

Preface to the Student

Accurate thinking is the beginning and fountain of writing.
—Horace

THE PURPOSE OF THIS TEXT

Have you ever had trouble expressing your thoughts? If so, you're not alone. Many people have this difficulty—especially when they are asked to write their thoughts down.

The good news is that this "ailment" can be cured. We've learned over the years that the more clearly students think about the world around them, the more easily they can express their ideas through written and spoken language. As a result, this textbook intends to improve your writing by helping you think clearly, logically, and critically about important ideas and issues that exist in our world today. You will learn to reason, read, and write about your environment in increasingly complex ways, moving steadily from a simple, literal understanding of topics to interpretation and analysis. Inspired by well-crafted prose models and guided by carefully worded questions, you can actually raise the level of your thinking skills while improving your reading and writing abilities.

The Prose Reader is organized on the assumption that as a college student you should be able to think, read, and write on three increasingly difficult levels:

1. *Literal, which involves a basic understanding of a selection and the ability to repeat or restate the material;*
2. *Interpretive, which requires you to make associations and draw inferences from information in your reading; and*
3. *Analytical or critical, which invites you to systematically separate, explain, evaluate, and reassemble various important ideas discovered in your reading.*

For example, students with a literal grasp of an essay would be able to understand the words on the page, cite details from the selection, and paraphrase certain sections of the essay. Students equipped with interpretive skills will see implicit relationships within a selection (such as comparison/contrast or cause/effect), make inferences from information that is supplied, and comprehend the intricacies of figurative language. Finally, students functioning analytically will be able to summarize and explain difficult concepts and generate plausible hypotheses from a series of related ideas. In short, this book leads you systematically toward higher levels of thinking and writing.

In order to stimulate your thinking on all levels, this text encourages you to participate in the making of meaning—as both a reader and a writer. As a reader, you have a responsibility to work with the author of each essay to help create sense out of the words on the page; as a writer, you must be conscious enough of your audience so that they perceive your intended purpose clearly and precisely through the ideas, opinions, and details that you provide. Because of this unique relationship, we envision reading and writing as companion acts in which writer and reader are partners in the development of meaning.

To demonstrate this vital interrelationship between reader and writer, our text provides you with prose models that are intended to inspire your own thinking and writing. In the introduction to each chapter, we include a student paragraph and a student essay that feature the particular rhetorical strategy under discussion. The essay is highlighted by annotations and by underlining to illustrate how to write that type of essay and to help bridge the gap between student writing and the professional selections in the text. After each essay, the student writer has drafted a personal note with some useful advice about generating that particular type of essay. The essays that follow each chapter introduction, selected from a wide variety of well-known contemporary authors, are intended to encourage you to improve your writing through a partnership with some of the best examples of professional prose available today. Just as musicians and athletes richly benefit from studying the techniques of the foremost people in their fields, you will, we hope, grow in spirit and language use from your collaborative work with the writers in this collection.

HOW TO USE THIS TEXT

The Prose Reader contains essays representing the four main purposes of writing:

Description
Narration
Exposition
Persuasion

Our primary focus within this framework is on exposition (which means "explanation"), because you will need to master this type of verbal expression to succeed in both the academic and the professional worlds. Although the essays in this text can be read in any order, we begin with

description

because it is a basic technique that often appears in other forms of discourse. We then move to

narration, or storytelling,

and next to the six traditional expository strategies:

example
process analysis
division/classification
comparison/contrast
definition
cause/effect

The text continues with an expanded chapter on

argument and persuasion,

including two sets of opposing viewpoint essays. Chapter 10 discusses and presents

documented research papers,

and the anthology concludes with selections about thinking, reading, and writing.

"Pure" rhetorical types rarely exist, of course, and when they do, the result often seems artificial. Therefore, although each essay in this collection focuses on a single rhetorical mode as its primary strategy, other strategies are always at work in it. These selections concentrate on one primary technique at a time in much the same way a well-arranged photograph highlights a certain visual detail, though many other elements function in the background to make the picture an organic whole.

Each chapter begins with an explanation of a single rhetorical technique. These explanations are divided into six sections that move from the effect of this technique on our daily lives to its integral role in the writing process. The first section catalogs the use of each rhetorical mode in our lives. The second section, "Defining _____ " (e.g., "Defining Description"), offers a working definition of the technique and a sample/student paragraph so that we all have the same fundamental understanding of the term. A third section, entitled "Thinking Critically by Using _____," introduces each rhetorical mode as a pattern of thought that helps us organize and more fully understand our experiences. A fourth section, called "Reading and Writing _____ Essays" (e.g., "Reading and Writing Descriptive Essays"), explains the processes of reading and writing an essay in each rhetorical mode, and a fifth section presents an annotated student essay showing this particular rhetorical method "at work," followed by comments from the student writer. The last part offers some final comments on each rhetorical strategy.

Before each reading selection, we have designed some material to focus your attention on a particular writer and topic before you begin reading the essay. This "prereading" segment begins with biographical information about the author and ends with a number of questions to whet your appetite for the essay that follows. This section is intended to help you discover interesting relationships among ideas in your reading and then anticipate various ways of thinking about and analyzing the essay. The prereading questions forecast not only the material in the essay, but also the questions and writing assignments that follow.

The questions following each reading selection are designed as guides for thinking about the essay. These questions are at the heart of the relationship represented in this book among thinking, reading, and writing. They are divided into four interrelated sections that move you smoothly from a literal understanding of what you have just read, to interpretation, and finally to analysis. The first set of questions, "Understanding Details," focuses on the basic facts and opinions in the selection. The second set of questions, "Analyzing Meaning," asks you to explain certain facts and to evaluate various assumptions of the essay in an effort to understand the entire selection on an analytical level. The third set of questions, "Discovering Rhetorical Strategies," guides your thinking on how the author achieved certain effects through word choice, sentence structure, organization of ideas, and selection of details. This third series of questions often requires you to apply to your reading of an essay material you learned about a particular mode of writing in the chapter introduction. And "Making Connections," the fourth group of questions, asks you to identify and process relationships and connections that you may not have noticed before between this essay and others in the book.

The final section of questions consists of three "Ideas for Discussion/Writing." These topics are preceded by "prewriting" questions to help you generate new ideas. Most of the Discussion/Writing topics specify a purpose (a definite reason for writing the essay) and an audience (an identifiable person or group of people you should address in your essay) so that you can focus your work as precisely as possible. These assignments outline realistic scenes and roles for you to play in those scenes so that, as you write, your relationship to your subject and audience will be clear and precise.

The word *essay* (which comes from the Old French *essai*, meaning a "try" or an "attempt") is an appropriate label for these writing assignments, because they all ask you to grapple with an idea or problem and then try to give shape to your conclusions in some effective manner. Such "exercises" can be equated with the development of athletic ability in sports: The essay itself demonstrates that you can put together all the various skills you have learned; it proves that you can actually play the sport. After you have studied the different techniques at work in a reading selection, a specific essay assignment lets you practice them all in unison and allows you to discover for yourself even more secrets about the intricate details of effective communication.

Introduction

Thinking, Reading, and Writing

Reading and writing are companion activities that involve students in the creation of thought and meaning—either as readers interpreting a text or as writers constructing one. Clear thinking, then, is the pivotal point that joins together these two efforts. Although studying the rhetorical strategies presented in *The Prose Reader* is certainly not the only way to approach writing, it does provide a productive means of helping students improve their abilities to think, read, and write on progressively more sophisticated levels.

Actually, we can improve the way we think, read, and write by exercising our brains on three sequential levels:

1. The literal level is the foundation of all human understanding; it entails knowing the meanings of words—individually and in relation to one another. In order for someone to comprehend the sentence "You must exercise your brain to reach your full mental potential" on the literal level, for example, that person would have to know the definitions of all the words in the sentence and understand the way those words work together to make meaning.

2. Interpretation requires the ability to make associations between details, draw inferences from pieces of information, and reach conclusions about the material. An interpretive understanding of the sample sentence in level 1 might be translated into the following thoughts: "Exercising the brain sounds a bit like exercising the body. I wonder if there's any correlation between the two. If the brain must be exercised, it is probably made up of muscles, much as the body is." None of these particular "thoughts" is made explicit in the sentence, but each is suggested in one way or another.

3. *Thinking, reading, and writing critically,* the most sophisticated form of rational abilities, involves a type of mental activity that is crucial for successful academic and professional work. A critical analysis of our sample sentence might proceed in the following way: "This sentence is talking to me. It actually addresses me with the word *you.* I wonder what *my* mental potential is. Will I be able to reach it? Will I know when I attain it? Will I be comfortable with it? I certainly want to reach this potential, whatever it is. Reaching it will undoubtedly help me succeed scholastically and professionally. The brain is obviously an important tool for helping me achieve my goals in life, so I want to take every opportunity I have to develop and maintain this part of my body." Students who can take an issue or idea apart in this fashion and understand its various components more thoroughly after reassembling them are rewarded intrinsically with a clearer knowledge of life's complexities and the ability to generate creative, useful ideas. They are also rewarded extrinsically with good grades and are more likely to earn responsible jobs with higher pay, because their understanding of the world around them is perceptive and they are able to apply this understanding effectively to their professional and personal lives.

In this textbook, you will learn to think critically by reading essays written by intelligent, interesting authors and by writing your own essays on a variety of topics. The next several pages offer guidelines for approaching the thinking, reading, and writing assignments in this book. These suggestions should also be useful to you in your other courses.

THINKING CRITICALLY

Recent psychological studies have shown that "thinking" and "feeling" are complementary operations. All of us have feelings that are automatic and instinctive. To feel pride after winning first place at a track meet, for example, or to feel anger at a spiteful friend is not behavior we have to study and master; such emotions come naturally to human beings. Thinking, on the other hand, is much less spontaneous than feeling; research suggests that study and practice are required for sustained mental development.

Thinking critically involves grappling with the ideas, issues, and problems that surround you in your immediate environment and in the world at large. It does not necessarily entail finding fault, which you might naturally associate with the word *critical*, but rather suggests continually questioning and analyzing the world around you. Thinking critically is the highest form of mental activity that human beings engage in; it is the source of success in college and in our professional and personal lives. Fortunately, all of us can learn how to think more critically.

Critical thinking means taking apart an issue, idea, or problem; examining its various parts; and reassembling the topic with a fuller understanding of its intricacies. Implied in this explanation is the ability to see the topic from one or more new perspectives. Using your mind in this way will help you find solutions to difficult problems, design creative plans of action, and ultimately live a life consistent with your opinions on important issues that we all must confront on a daily basis.

Since critical or analytical thinking is one of the highest forms of mental activity, it requires a great deal of concentration and practice. Once you have actually felt how your mind works and processes information at this level, however, re-creating the experience is somewhat like riding a bicycle: you will be able to do it naturally, easily, and gracefully whenever you want to.

Our initial goal, then, is to help you think critically when you are required to do so in school, on the job, or in any other area of your life. If this form of thinking becomes a part of your daily routine, you will quite naturally be able to call upon it whenever you need it.

Working with the rhetorical modes is an effective way to achieve this goal. With some guidance, each rhetorical pattern can provide you with a mental workout to prepare you for writing and critical thinking in the same way that physical exercises warm you up for various sports. Just as in the rest of the body, the more exercise the brain gets, the more flexible it becomes and the higher the levels of thought it can attain. Through these various guided thinking exercises, you can systematically strengthen your ability to think analytically.

As you move through the following chapters, we will ask you to isolate each rhetorical mode—much like isolating your abs, thighs, and biceps in a weight-lifting workout—so that you can concentrate on these thinking patterns one at a time. Each rhetorical pattern we study will suggest slightly different ways of seeing the world, processing information, and solving problems. Each offers important ways of thinking and making sense of our immediate environment and the larger world around us. Looking closely at rhetorical modes or specific patterns of thought helps us discover how our minds work. In the same fashion, becoming more intricately aware of our thought patterns lets us improve our basic thinking skills as well as our reading and writing abilities. Thinking critically helps us discover fresh insights into old ideas, generate new thoughts, and see connections between related issues. It is an energizing mental activity that puts us in control of our lives and our environment rather than leaving us at the mercy of our surroundings.

Each chapter introduction provides three exercises specifically designed to help you focus in isolation on a particular pattern of thought. While you are attempting to learn what each pattern feels like in your head, use your imagination to play with these exercises on as many different levels as possible.

When you practice each of the rhetorical patterns of thought, you should be aware of building on your previous thinking skills. As the book progresses, the rhetorical modes become more complex and require a higher degree of concentration and effort. Throughout the book, therefore, you should keep in mind that ultimately you want to let these skills accumulate into a full-powered, well-developed ability to process the world around you—including reading, writing, seeing, and feeling—on the most advanced analytical level you can master.

READING CRITICALLY

Reading critically begins with developing a natural curiosity about an essay and nurturing that curiosity throughout the reading process. To learn as much as you can from an essay, you should first study any preliminary material you can find, then read the essay to get a general overview of its main ideas, and finally read the selection again to achieve a deeper understanding of its intent. The three phases of the reading process explained below—preparing to read, reading, and rereading—will help you develop this "natural curiosity" so you can approach any reading assignment with an active, inquiring mind; they should occur cyclically as you read each essay.

Preparing to Read

Focusing your attention is an important first stage in both the reading and the writing processes. In fact, learning as much as you can about an essay and its "context" (the circumstances surrounding its development) before you begin reading can help you move through the essay with an energetic, active mind and then reach some degree of analysis before writing on the assigned topics. In particular, knowing where an essay was first published, studying the writer's background, and doing some preliminary thinking on the subject of a reading selection will help you understand the writer's ideas and form some valid opinions of your own.

As you approach any essay, you should concentrate on four specific areas that will begin to give you an overview of the material you are about to read. We use an essay by Lewis Thomas to demonstrate these techniques.

1. Title. A close look at the title will usually provide important clues about the author's attitude toward the topic, the author's stand on an issue, or the mood of an essay. It can also furnish you with a sense of audience and purpose.

To Err Is Human

From this title, for example, we might infer that the author will discuss errors, human nature, and the extent to which mistakes influence human behavior. The title is half of a well-known proverbial quotation (Alexander Pope's "To err is human, to forgive, divine"), so we might speculate further that the author has written an essay intended for a well-read audience interested in the relationship between errors and humanity. After reading only four words of the essay—its title—you already have a good deal of information about the subject, its audience, and the author's attitude toward both.

2. Synopsis. The Rhetorical Table of Contents in this text contains a synopsis of each essay, very much like the following, so that you can find out more specific details about its contents before you begin reading.

> Physician Lewis Thomas explains how we can profit from our mistakes—especially if we trust human nature. Perhaps someday, he says, we can apply this same principle to the computer and magnify the advantages of these errors.

From this synopsis, we learn that Thomas's essay will be an analysis of human errors and of the way we can benefit from those errors. The synopsis also tells us the computer has the potential to magnify the value of our errors.

3. Biography. Learning as much as you can about the author of an essay will generally stimulate your interest in the material and help you achieve a deeper understanding of the issues to be discussed. From the biographies in this book, you can learn, for example, whether a writer is young or old, conservative or liberal, open- or close-minded. You might also discover if the essay was written at the beginning, middle, or end of the author's career or how well versed the writer is on the topic. Such information will invariably provide a deeper, more thorough understanding of a selection's ideas, audience, and logical structure.

LEWIS THOMAS   (1913 –   )

Lewis Thomas is a physician who is currently president emeritus of the Sloan-Kettering Cancer Center and scholar-in-residence at the Cornell University Medical Center in New York City. A graduate of Princeton University and Harvard Medical School, he was formerly head of pathology and dean of the New York University–Bellevue Medical Center and dean of the Yale Medical School. In addition to having written over two hundred scientific papers on virology and immunology, he has authored many popular scientific essays, some of which have been collected in *Lives of a Cell* (1974), *The Medusa and the Snail* (1979), *Late Night Thoughts on Listening to Mahler's Ninth Symphony* (1983), and *Etcetera, Etcetera* (1990). The memoirs of his distinguished career have been published in *The Youngest Science: Notes of a Medicine Watcher* (1983). Thomas likes to refer to his essays as "experiments in thought": "Although I usually think I know what I'm going to be writing about, what I'm going to say, most of the time it doesn't happen that way at all. At some point I get misled down a garden path. I get surprised by an idea that I hadn't anticipated getting, which is a little bit like being in a laboratory."

As this information indicates, Thomas is a prominent physician who has published widely on scientific topics. We know that he considers his essays "experiments in thought," which makes us expect a relaxed, spontaneous treatment of his subjects. From this biography, we can also infer that he is a leader in the medical world and that, because of the positions he has held, he is well respected in his professional life. Last, we can speculate that he has a clear sense of his audience because he is able to present difficult concepts in clear, everyday language.

4. Preparing to read. One other type of preliminary material will broaden your overview of the topic and enable you to approach the essay with an active, thoughtful mind. The

"Preparing to Read" sections following the biographies are intended to focus your attention and stimulate your curiosity before you begin the essay. They will also get you ready to form your own opinions on the essay and its topic as you read. Keeping a journal to respond to these questions is an excellent idea, because you will then have a record of your thoughts on various topics related to the reading selection that follows.

Preparing to Read

The following essay, which originally appeared in the *New England Journal of Medicine* (January 1976), illustrates the clarity and ease with which Thomas explains complex scientific topics. As you prepare to read this essay, take a few moments to think about the role mistakes play in our lives: What are some memorable mistakes you have made in your life? Did you learn anything important from any of these errors? Do you make more or fewer mistakes than other people you know? Do you see any advantages to making mistakes? Any disadvantages?

Discovering where, why, and how an essay was first written will provide you with a context for the material you are about to read: Why did the author write this selection? Where was it first published? Who was the author's original audience? This type of information enables you to understand the circumstances surrounding the development of the selection and to identify any topical or historical references the author makes. All the selections in this textbook were published elsewhere first—in another book, a journal, or a magazine. Some are excerpts from longer works. The author's original audience, therefore, consisted of the readers of that particular publication.

From the sample "Preparing to Read" material, we learn that Thomas's essay "To Err Is Human" was originally published in the *New England Journal of Medicine*, a prestigious periodical read principally by members of the scientific community. Written early in 1976, the article plays upon its audience's growing fascination with computers and with the limits of artificial intelligence—subjects just as timely today as they were in the mid–1970s.

The questions here prompt you to consider your own ideas, opinions, or experiences in order to help you generate thoughts on the topic of errors in our lives. These questions are, ideally, the last step in preparing yourself for the active role you should play as a reader.

Reading

People read essays in books, newspapers, magazines, and journals for a great variety of reasons. One reader may want to be stimulated intellectually, whereas another seeks relaxation; one person reads to keep up with the latest developments in his or her profession, whereas the next wants to learn why a certain event happened or how something can be done; some people read in order to be challenged by new ideas, whereas others find comfort principally in printed material that supports their own moral, social, or political opinions. The essays in this textbook variously fulfill all these expectations. They have been chosen, however, not only for these reasons, but for an additional, broader purpose: Reading them can help make you a better writer.

Every time you read an essay in this book, you will also be preparing to write your own essay concentrating on the same rhetorical pattern. For this reason, as you read you should pay careful attention to both the content (subject matter) and the form (language, sentence structure, organization, and development of ideas) of each essay. You will also see how effectively experienced writers use particular rhetorical modes (or patterns of thought) to organize and communicate their ideas. Each essay in this collection features one dominant pattern that is generally supported by several others. In fact, the more aware you are of each author's writing techniques, the more rapidly your own writing process will mature and improve.

The questions before and after each essay teach you a way of reading that can help you discover the relationship of a writer's ideas to one another as well as to your own ideas. These questions can also help clarify for you the connection between the writer's topic, his or her style or manner of expression, and your own composing process. In other words, the questions are designed to help you understand and generate ideas, then discover various choices the writers make in composing their essays, and finally realize the freedom you have to make related choices in your own writing. Such an approach to the process of reading takes reading and writing out of the realm of mystical creation and places them in the realistic world of the possible; a process of this sort takes some of the mystery out of reading and writing and makes them manageable tasks at which anyone can become proficient.

Three general guidelines, each of which is explained below in detail, will help you develop your own system for reading and responding to what you have read:

1. *Read the essay to get an overall sense of it.*
2. *Summarize the essay.*
3. *Read the questions and assignments that follow the essay.*

Guideline 1. First, read the essay to get an overall sense of it in relation to its title, purpose, audience, author, and publication information. Write (in the margins, on a separate piece of paper, or in a journal) your initial reactions, comments, and personal associations.

To illustrate, on the following pages is the Thomas essay with a student's comments in the margins, showing how the student reacted to the essay upon reading it for the first time.

LEWIS THOMAS (1913 –   )

To Err Is Human

Boy is this true!

Everyone must have had at least one 1
personal experience with a computer error
by this time. Bank balances are suddenly
reported to have jumped from $379 into
the millions, appeals for charitable contributions are mailed over and over to people
with crazy sounding names at your address, *Last spring*
department stores send the wrong bills, *this hap-*
utility companies write that they're turning *pened to me.*
everything off, that sort of thing. If you
manage to get in touch with someone and
complain, you then get instantaneously
typed, guilty letters from the same computer, saying, "Our computer was in error, and
exactly an adjustment is being made in your
account."

These are supposed to be the sheerest, 2
blindest accidents. Mistakes are not
believed to be part of the normal behavior
of a good machine. If things go wrong, it
How can it must be a personal, human error, the result
be? of fingering, tampering, a button getting
stuck, someone hitting the wrong key. The
computer, at its normal best, is infallible.

I wonder whether this can be true. 3
After all, the whole point of computers is
that they represent an extension of the
human brain, vastly improved upon but *In what*
nonetheless human, superhuman maybe. *way?*

11

A good computer can think clearly and quickly enough to beat you at chess, and some of them have even been programmed to write obscure verse. They can do anything we can do, and more besides. *Can this be proven?*

It is not yet known whether a computer has its own consciousness, and it would be hard to find out about this. When you walk into one of those great halls now built for the huge machines, and stand listening, it is easy to imagine that the faint, distant noises are the sound of thinking, and the turning of the spools gives them the look of wild creatures rolling their eyes in the effort to concentrate, choking with information. <u>But real thinking, and dreaming, are other matters</u>. *4 / expected this essay to be so much more stuffy than it is. / can even understand it.*

In what way?

On the other hand, the evidences of something like an *unconscious*, equivalent to ours, are all around, in every mail. As extensions of the human brain, they have been constructed with the same property of error, spontaneous, uncontrolled, and rich in possibilities. *5 good, clear comparison for the general reader*

<u>Mistakes are at the very base of human thought</u>, embedded there, feeding the structure like <u>root nodules</u>. If we were not provided with the knack of being wrong, we could never get anything useful done. *6 / don't understand this*

so true

great image

We think our way along by choosing between right and wrong alternatives, and the wrong choices have to be made as frequently as the right ones. We get along in life this way. We are built to make mistakes, coded for error. *I agree! This is how we learn*

We learn, as we say, <u>by "trial and error."</u> Why do we always say that? Why not "trial and rightness" or "trial and triumph"? The old phrase puts it that way *7 ?*

because that is, in real life, the way it is done.

8

A good laboratory, like a good bank or a corporation or government, has to run like a computer. Almost everything is done flawlessly, by the book, and all the numbers add up to the predicted sums. The days go by. And then, if it is a <u>lucky</u> day, and a <u>lucky</u> laboratory, somebody makes a <u>mistake</u>: the wrong buffer, something in one of the blanks, a decimal misplaced in reading counts, the warm room off by a degree and a half, a mouse out of his box, or just a mis-reading of the day's protocol. Whatever, when the results come in, something is obviously screwed up, and <u>then the action can begin</u>.

9

The misreading is not the important error; <u>it opens the way</u>. The next step is the crucial one. If the investigator can bring himself to say, "But even so, look at that!" then the new finding, whatever it is, is ready for snatching. What is needed, for progress to be made, is <u>the move based on error</u>.

10

Whenever new kinds of thinking are about to be accomplished, or new varieties of music, there has to be an argument beforehand. With two sides debating in the same mind, haranguing, there is an amiable understanding that one is right and the other wrong. Sooner or later the thing is settled, but there can be no action at all if there are not the two sides, and the argument. <u>The hope is in the faculty of wrongness</u>, the tendency toward error. The capacity to leap across mountains of information to land lightly on the wrong side represents the highest of human endowments.

Another effective comparison for the general reader

Isn't this a contradiction?

What?

aha!

interesting idea

I believe Thomas here because of his background.

13

Could this be related to the human ability to think critically?

It may be that this is a uniquely human gift, perhaps even stipulated in our genetic instructions. Other creatures do not seem to have DNA sequences for making mistakes as a routine part of daily living, certainly not for programmed error as a guide for action. [11]

We are at our human finest, <u>dancing with our minds</u>, when there are more choices than two. Sometimes there are ten, even twenty different ways to go, all but one bound to be wrong, and the richness of selection in such situations can lift us onto totally new ground. This process is called exploration and is based on human fallibility. If we had only a single center in our brains, capable of responding only when a correct decision was to be made, instead of the jumble of different, credulous, easily conned clusters of neurones that provide for being flung off into blind alleys, up trees, down dead ends, out into blue sky, along wrong turnings, around bends, we could only stay the way we are today, stuck fast. [12]

Nice mental image

Yes, but this is so frustrating

This is a great sentence — it has a lot of feeling

<u>The lower animals do not have this splendid freedom</u>. They are limited, most of them, to absolute infallibility. Cats, for all their good side, never make mistakes. <u>I have never seen a maladroit, clumsy, or blundering cat</u>. Dogs are sometimes fallible, occasionally able to make charming minor mistakes, but they get this way by trying to mimic their masters. <u>Fish are flawless in everything they do</u>. Individual cells in a tissue are mindless machines, perfect in their performance, as absolutely inhuman as bees. [13]

I love the phrase "splendid freedom"

see ¶ 11

look up "maladroit"

I never thought of mistakes this way

I like this idea

We should have this in mind as we become dependent on more complex computers for the arrangement of our affairs. [14]

Give the computers their heads, I say; let them go their way. If we can learn to do this, turning our heads to one side and wincing while the work proceeds, the possibilities for the future of mankind, and computerkind, are limitless. <u>Your average good computer can make calculations in an instant which would take a lifetime of slide rules for any of us.</u> Think of what we could gain from the near infinity of precise, <u>machine-made miscomputation</u> which is now so easily within our grasp. We would begin the solving of some of our hardest problems. How, for instance, should we go about organizing ourselves for social living on a planetary scale, now that we have become, as a plain fact of life, a single community? We can assume, as a working hypothesis, that all the right ways of doing this are unworkable. What we need, then, for moving ahead, is a set of wrong alternatives much longer and more interesting than the short list of mistaken courses that any of us can think up right now. We need, in fact, an infinite list, and when it is printed out we need the computer to turn on itself and select, at random, the next way to go. If it is a big enough mistake, we could find ourselves on a new level, stunned, out in the clear, ready to move again.

[margin left:] Thomas makes our technology sound really exciting

[margin left:] We need to program computers to make deliberate mistakes so they can help our natural human tendency to learn thru error

[margin left:] Not a contradiction after all.

[margin right:] so true

[margin right:] yes

[margin right:] So mistakes have value!

Guideline 2. After you have read the essay for the first time, summarize its main ideas in some fashion. The form of this task might be anything from a drawing of the main ideas as they relate to one another to a succinct summary. You could draw a graph or map of the topics in the essay (in much the same way that a person would draw a map of an area for someone unfamiliar with a particular route); outline the ideas to get an overview of the piece; or summarize the ideas to check your understanding of the main points of the selection. Any of these tasks can be completed from your original notes and underlining. Each will give you a slightly more thorough understanding of what you have read.

Guideline 3. Next, read the questions and assignments following the essay to help focus your thinking for the second reading. Don't answer the questions at this time; just read them to make sure you are picking up the main ideas from the selection and thinking about relevant connections among those ideas.

Rereading

Following your initial reading, read the essay again, concentrating this time on how the author achieved his or her purpose. The temptation to skip this stage of the reading process is often powerful, but this second reading is crucial to your development as a critical reader in all of your courses. This second reading could be compared to seeing a good movie for the second time: The first viewing would provide you with a general understanding of the plot, the characters, the setting, and the overall artistic accomplishment of the director; during the second viewing, however, you would undoubtedly notice many more details and see their specific contributions to the artistic whole. Similarly, the second reading of an essay allows a much deeper understanding of the work under consideration and prepares you to analyze the writer's ideas.

You should also be prepared to do some detective work at this point and look closely at the assumptions the essay is based on: For example, how does the writer move from idea to idea in the essay? What hidden assertions lie behind these ideas? Do you agree or disagree with these assertions? Your assessment of these unspoken assumptions will often play a major role in your critical response to an essay. In the case of Thomas's essay, do you accept the unspoken connection he makes between the workings of the human brain and the computer? What parts of the essay hinge upon your acceptance of this connection? What other assumptions are fundamental to Thomas's reasoning? If you accept his thinking along the way, you are more likely to agree with the general flow of Thomas's essay. If you discover a flaw in his premises or assumptions, your acceptance of his argument will start to break down.

Next, answer the questions that follow the essay. The "Understanding Details" questions will help you understand and remember what you have read on both the literal and the interpretive levels. Some of the questions ask you to restate various important points the author makes (literal); others help you see relationships between the different ideas presented (interpretive).

Understanding Details

Literal 1. According to Thomas, in what ways are computers and humans similar? In what ways are they different?

Lit/Interp 2. In what ways do we learn by "trial and error"? Why is this a useful way to learn?

Interpretive 3. What does Thomas mean by the statement, "If we were not provided with the knack of being wrong, we could never get anything useful done" (paragraph 6)?

Interpretive 4. According to Thomas, in what important way do humans and "lower" animals differ? What does this comparison have to do with Thomas's main line of reasoning?

The "Analyzing Meaning" questions require you to analyze and evaluate some of the writer's ideas in order to form valid opinions of your own. These questions demand a higher level of thought than the previous set and help you prepare more specifically for the discussion/writing assignments that follow the questions.

Analyzing Meaning

Analytical 1. What is Thomas's main point in this essay? How do the references to computers help him make this point?

Analytical 2. In paragraph 10, Thomas explains that an argument must precede the beginning of something new and different. Do you think this is an accurate observation? Explain your answer.

| Analytical | 3. Why does Thomas perceive human error as such a positive quality? What does "exploration" have to do with this quality (paragraph 12)? |
| Analytical | 4. What could we gain from "the near infinity of precise, machine-made miscomputation" (paragraph 14)? In what ways would our civilization advance? |

The "Discovering Rhetorical Strategies" questions ask you to look closely at what strategies the writer uses to develop his or her thesis and how those strategies work. The questions address features of the writer's composing process such as word choice, use of detail, transitions, statement of purpose, organization of ideas, sentence structure, and paragraph development. The intent of these questions is to raise various elements of the composing process to the conscious level so you can use them in creating your own essays. If you are able to understand and describe what choices a writer makes to create certain effects in his or her prose, you are more likely to be able to perceive the range of choices available to you as you write and to be aware of your ability to control your readers' thoughts and feelings.

Discovering Rhetorical Strategies

1. Thomas begins his essay with a list of experiences most of us have had at one time or another. Do you find this an effective beginning? Why or why not?

2. Which main points in his essay does Thomas develop in most detail? Why do you think he chooses to develop these points so thoroughly?

3. Explain the simile Thomas uses in paragraph 6: "Mistakes are at the very base of human thought, embedded there, feeding the structure like root nodules." Is this comparison between "mistakes" and "root modules" useful in this context? Why or why not? Find another simile or metaphor in this essay, and explain how it works.

> 4. What principal rhetorical strategies does Thomas use to make his point? Give examples of each from the essay.

A final set of questions, "Making Connections," asks you to consider the essay you have just read in reference to other essays in the book. Your instructor will assign these questions according to the essays you have read. The questions may have you compare the writers' treatment of an idea, the authors' style of writing, the difference in their opinions, or the similarities between their views of the world. Such questions will help you see connections in your own life—not only in your reading and your immediate environment, but also in the larger world around you. These questions, in particular, encourage you to move from specific references in the selections to a broader range of issues and circumstances that affect your daily life.

Making Connections

1. Kimberly Wozencraft ("Notes from the Country Club") and Judith Wallerstein and Sandra Blakeslee ("Second Chances for Children of Divorce") refer both directly and indirectly to learning from mistakes. Would Lewis Thomas agree with their approach to this topic? In what ways do these authors think alike about the benefits of making errors? In what ways do they differ on the topic? Explain your answer.

2. Lewis Thomas and William Zinsser ("Writing with a Word Processor") both discuss the usefulness of computers. In what ways do their ideas complement each other? In what ways do they differ?

3. According to Thomas, humans are complex organisms with a great deal of untapped potential. Jane Goodall ("The Mind of the Chimpanzee") and William Golding ("Thinking as a Hobby") also comment on the uniqueness of human beings. In what ways do these three writers agree or disagree with each other on the intelligence and resourcefulness of human beings? To what extent would each author argue that humans use their mental capacities wisely and completely? Explain your answer.

Because checklists can provide a helpful method of reviewing important information, we offer here a series of questions that represent the three stages of reading just discussed. All these guidelines can be generalized into a checklist for reading any academic assignment in any discipline.

Reading Inventory

Preparing to Read

Title

1. What can I infer from the title of the essay about the author's attitude toward the subject or the general tone of the essay?
2. Who do I think is the author's audience? What is the principal purpose of the essay?

Synopsis

3. What is the general subject of the essay?
4. What is the author's approach to the subject?

Biography

5. What do I know about the author's age, political stance, general beliefs?
6. How qualified is the author to write on this subject?
7. When did the author write the essay? Under what conditions? In what context?
8. Why did the author write this selection?
9. Where was the essay first published?

Content

10. What would I like to learn about this topic?
11. What are some of my opinions on this subject?

Reading

1. What are my initial reactions, comments, and personal associations in reference to the ideas in this essay?
2. Did I summarize the essay's main ideas?
3. Did I read the questions and assignments following the essay?

Rereading

1. How does the author achieve his or her purpose in this essay?

2. What assumptions underlie the author's reasoning?

3. Do I have a clear literal understanding of this essay? What words do I need to look up in a dictionary? What do these words mean—by themselves and in their respective sentences?

4. Do I have a solid interpretive understanding of this essay? Do I understand the relationship among ideas? What conclusions can I draw from this essay?

5. Do I have an accurate analytical understanding of this essay? Which ideas can I take apart, examine, and put back together again? What is my evaluation of this material?

6. Do I understand the rhetorical strategies the writer uses and the way they work? Can I explain the effects of these strategies?

WRITING CRITICALLY

The last stage of responding to the reading selections in this text offers you various "Ideas for Discussion/Writing" that will allow you to demonstrate the different skills you have learned in each chapter. You will be most successful if you envision each writing experience as an organic process that follows a natural cycle of prewriting, writing, and rewriting.

Preparing to Write

The prewriting phase involves exploring a subject, generating ideas, selecting and narrowing a topic, analyzing an audience, and developing a purpose. Preceding the writing assignments are "Preparing to Write" questions you should respond to before trying to structure your thoughts into a coherent essay. These questions will assist you in generating new thoughts on the topics and may even stimulate new approaches to old ideas. Keeping a journal to respond to these questions is an excellent technique, because you will then have a record of your opinions on various topics related to the writing assignments that follow. No matter what format you use to answer these questions, the activity of prewriting generally continues in various forms throughout the writing process.

Preparing to Write

Write freely about an important mistake you have made: How did the mistake make you feel? What (if anything) did you learn from this mistake? What did you fail to learn that you should have learned? Did this mistake have any positive impact on your life? What were its negative consequences? How crucial are mistakes in our lives?

Responses to these questions can be prompted by a number of different "invention" techniques and carried out by you individually, with another student, in small groups, or as a class project. Invention strategies can help you generate responses to these questions and discover related ideas through the various stages of writing your papers. Because you will undoubtedly vary your approach to different assignments, you should be familiar with the following choices available to you:

Brainstorming. The basis of brainstorming is free association. Ideally, you should get a group of students together and bounce ideas, words, and thoughts off one another until they begin to cluster around related topics. If you don't have a group of students handy, brainstorm by yourself or with a friend. In a group of students or with a friend, the exchange of thoughts usually starts orally but should transfer to paper when your ideas begin to fall into related categories. When you brainstorm by yourself, however, you should write down everything that comes to mind. The act of recording your ideas in this case becomes a catalyst for other thoughts; you are essentially setting up a dialogue with yourself on paper. Then, keep writing down words and phrases that occur to you until they begin to fall into logical subdivisions or until you stop generating new ideas.

Freewriting. Freewriting means writing to discover what you want to say. Set a time limit of about ten minutes, and just write by free association. Write about what you are seeing, feeling, touching, thinking; write about having nothing to say; recopy the sentence you just wrote—anything. Just keep writing on paper, on a typewriter, or on a computer. After you have generated some material, locate an idea that is central to your writing assignment, put it at the top of another page, and start freewriting again, letting your thoughts take shape around this central idea. This second type of preparation is called *focused freewriting* and is especially valuable when you already have a specific topic.

Journal Entries. Journal entries are much like freewriting, except you have some sense of an audience—probably either your instructor or yourself. In a journal, anything goes. You can respond to the "Preparing to Write" questions, jot down thoughts, paste up articles that spark your interest, write sections of dialogue, draft letters (the kind you never send), record dreams, or make lists. The possibilities are unlimited. An excellent way of practicing writing, the process of keeping a journal is also a wonderful means of dealing with new ideas—a way of fixing them in your mind and making them yours.

Direct Questions. This technique involves asking a series of questions useful in any writing situation to generate ideas, arrange thoughts, or revise prose. One example of this strategy is to use the inquiries journalists rely on to check the coverage in their articles:

Who:	*Who played the game?*
	Who won the game?
What:	*What kind of game was it?*
	What happened in the game?
Why:	*Why was the game played?*
Where:	*Where was the game played?*
When:	*When was the game played?*
How:	*How was the game played?*

If you ask yourself extended questions of this sort on a specific topic, you will begin to produce thoughts and details that will undoubtedly be useful to you in the writing assignments that follow.

Clustering. Clustering is a method of drawing or mapping your ideas as fast as they come into your mind. Put a word, phrase, or sentence in a circle in the center of a blank page. Then, put every new idea that comes to you in a circle and show its relationship to a previous thought by drawing a line to the circle containing the previous idea. You will probably reach a natural stopping point for this exercise in two to three minutes.

Although you can generate ideas in a number of different ways, the main principle behind the "Preparing to Write" questions in this text is to encourage you to do what is called *expressive writing* before you tackle any writing assignment. This is writing based on your feelings, thoughts, experiences, observations, and opinions. The process of answering questions about your own ideas and experiences makes you "think on paper," encouraging you to surround yourself with your own thoughts and opinions. From this reservoir, you can then choose the ideas you want to develop into an essay and begin writing about them one at a time.

As you use various prewriting techniques to generate responses to the "Preparing to Write" questions, you should know that these responses can (and probably will) appear in many different forms. You can express yourself in lists, outlines, random notes, sentences and paragraphs, charts, graphs, or pictures—whatever keeps the thoughts flowing smoothly and productively. One of our students used a combination of brainstorming and clustering to generate the following thoughts in response to the prewriting exercise following the Thomas essay:

Brainstorming

Mistakes:
- *happen when I'm in a hurry*
- *make me feel stupid*
- *love*
- *relationships*
- *trip back East*
    - *pride*
    - *going in circles*
- *Bob*
- *learned a lot about people*
- *people aren't what they seem*
- *getting back on track*
- *parents*
- *corrections*
- *learning from mistakes*
    - *I am a better person*
    - *my values are clear*

- *mistakes help us change*
  - *painful*
  - *helpful*
  - *valuable*

Clustering

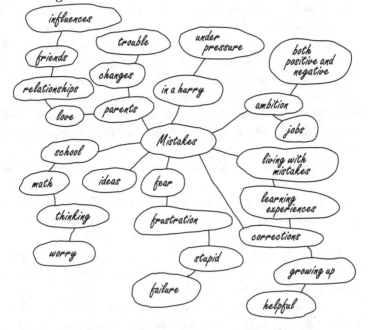

From the free-flowing thoughts you generate, you next need to decide what to write about and how to limit your subject to a manageable length. Our student writer chose topic 2 from the "Choosing a Topic" list after the essay (see page 28). Her initial responses to the prewriting questions helped her decide to write on "A Time I Got Lost." She then generated more focused ideas and opinions in the form of a journal entry. It is printed here just as she wrote it, errors and all.

Journal Entry

The craziest mistake I think I ever made was on a trip I took recently—I was heading to the east coast from California and reached Durham, North Carolina. I was so excited because I was going to get to see the Atlantic Ocean for the first time in my life and Durham was one of my last towns before I reached the sea. In Durham I was going to have to change from a northeast direction to due east.

When I got there the highway was under construction. I took the detour, but got all skrewed up till I realized that I had gone the wrong direction. By this time I was lost somewhere in downtown Durham and didn't know which way was east. I stoped and asked a guy at a gas station and he explained how to get back on the east-bound highway. The way was through the middle of town. By the time I got to where I was supposed to turn right I could only turn left. So I started left and then realized I couldn't turn back the other way! I made a couple of other stops after that, and one jerk told me I "just couldn't get there from here." Eventually I found a truck driver heading toward the same eastbound highway, and he told me to follow him. An hour and forty minutes after reaching Durham's city limits I finally managed to leave going east. I felt as if I had spent an entire month there!

The thing I learned from this was just how egocentric I am. I would not have made this error if I had not been so damn cocky about my sense of direction. My mistake was made worse because I got flustered and didn't listen to the directions clearly. I find that the reason I most often make a mistake is because I don't listen carefully to instructions. This has been a problem all my life.

After I got over feeling really dum I decided this kind of thing was not going to happen again. It was too much a waste of time and gas, so I was going to be more careful of road signs and directions.

This all turned out to be a positive experience though. I learned that there are lots of friendly, helpful people. It was kind of reassuring to know that other folks would help you if you just asked.

I feel this and other mistakes are crucial not only to my life but to personal growth in general. It is the making of mistakes that helps people learn where they are misdirecting their energies. I think mistakes can help all of us learn to be more careful about some part of our lives. This is why mistakes are crucial. Otherwise, we would continue in the same old rut and never improve.

This entry served as the foundation upon which the student built her essay. Her next step was to consider *audience* and *purpose* (which are usually specified in the writing assignments in this text). The first of these features identifies the person or group of people you will address in your essay. The second is a declaration of your principal reason for writing the essay, which usually takes the form of a thesis statement (the statement of purpose or the controlling idea of an essay). Together these pieces of information consciously or subconsciously help you make most of the decisions you are faced with as you write: what words to choose, what sentence structures to use, what order to present ideas in, which topics to develop, and which to summarize. Without a doubt, the more you know about your audience (age, educational background, likes, dislikes, biases, political persuasion, and social status) and your purpose (to inform, persuade, and/or entertain), the easier the writing task will be. In the rough draft and final draft of the essay in the section that follows, the student knew she was writing to a senior English class at her old high school in order to convince them that mistakes can be positive factors in their lives. This clear sense of audience and purpose helped her realize she should use fairly advanced vocabulary, call upon a variety of sentence structures, and organize her ideas chronologically to make her point most effectively to her intended audience.

At this stage of the writing process, some people benefit from assembling their ideas in the form of an outline. Others use an outline as a check on their logic and organization after the first draft has been written. Whether your outlines are informal (a simple list) or highly structured, they can help you visualize the logical relationship of your ideas to each other. We recommend using your outline throughout the prewriting and writing stages to ensure that your work will be carefully and tightly organized.

Writing

The writing stage asks you to draft an essay based upon the prewriting material you have assembled. Because you have already made the important preliminary decisions regarding your topic, your audience, and your purpose, the task of actually writing the essay should follow naturally. (Notice we did not say this task should necessarily be easy—just natural.) At this stage, you should look upon your essay as a way of solving a problem or answering a question: The problem/question is posed in your writing assignment, and the solution/answer is your essay. The three "Choosing a Topic" assignments that follow the prewriting questions in the text require you to consider issues related to the essay you just read. Although they typically ask you to focus on one rhetorical pattern, they draw on many rhetorical strategies (as do all writing assignments in the text) and require you to support your statements with concrete examples. These assignments refer to the Lewis Thomas essay and emphasize the use of example, his dominant rhetorical strategy.

Choosing a Topic

1. You have decided to write an editorial for your local newspaper concerning the impact of computers on our lives. Cite specific experiences you have had with computers to help make your main point.

2. You have been invited back to your high school to make a speech to a senior English class about how people can learn from their mistakes. Write your speech in the form of an essay explaining what you learned from a crucial mistake you have made. Use examples to show these students that mistakes can be positive factors in their lives.

3. In an essay for your writing class, explain one specific human quality. Use Thomas's essay as a model. Cite examples to support your explanation.

The following essay is our student's first-draft response to topic 2. After writing her journal entry, the student drafted a tentative thesis statement: "I know there are positive attitudes that can come from making a mistake because I recently had an opportunity to learn some valuable lessons in this way." This statement helped the student writer further develop and organize her ideas as she focused finally on one well-chosen example to illustrate her thesis. At this point, the thesis is simply the controlling idea around which the other topics take shape; it is often revised several times before the final draft.

First Draft: A Time I Got Lost

Parents and teachers frequently pressure us to avoid committing errors. Meanwhile, our friends laugh at us when we make mistakes. With all these different messages, it is hard for us to think of mistakes as positive events. But if any of you take the time to think about what you have learned from mistakes, I bet you will realize all the good things that have come from these events. I know there are positive attitudes that can come from making a mistake because I recently had an opportunity to learn some valuable lessons in this way.

While traveling back east this last summer, I made the mistake of turning west on an interstate detour in order to reach the Atlantic Ocean. The adventure took me into the heart of Durham, North Carolina, where I got totally lost. I had to get directions several times until two hours later I was going in the right direction. As I was driving out of town, I realized that although I had made a dumb mistake, I had learned a great deal. Overall, the detour was actually a positive experience.

The first thing I remember thinking after I had gotten my wits together was that I had definitely learned something from making the mistake. I had the opportunity to see a new city, filled with new people—3,000 miles from my own hometown, but very much like it. I also became aware that the beach is not always toward the west, as it is in California. The entire experience was like getting a geography lesson firsthand.

As this pleasant feeling began to grow, I came to another realization. I was aware of how important other people can be in making a mistake into a positive experience. My first reaction was "Oh no, someone is going to know I made a mistake!" But the amazing part about this mistake was how supportive everyone was. The townspeople had been entirely willing to help someone they did not know. This mistake helped me to learn that people tend to be nicer than I had imagined.

The final lesson I learned from getting lost in Durham was how to be more cautious about my actions so as not to repeat the same mistake. It was this internalization of all the information I gleaned from making the mistake that I see as the most positive part of the experience. I realized that in order to avoid such situations in the future I would have to be less egocentric in my decisions and more willing to listen to directions from other people. I needed to learn that my set way of doing things was not always the best way. If I had not made the mistake, I would not have been aware of my other options.

By making this mistake I learned that there is a more comprehensive manner of looking at the world. In the future, if we could all stop after making a mistake and ask ourselves, "What can I learn from this?" we would be less critical of ourselves and have a great many more positive experiences. If I were not able to make mistakes, I would probably not be able to expand my knowledge of my environment, my understanding of people, and my choice of various actions.

Rewriting

The rewriting stage includes revising, editing, and proofreading. The first of these activities, *revising*, actually takes place during the entire writing process as you change words, recast sentences, and move whole paragraphs from one place to another. Making these linguistic and organizational choices means you will also be constantly adjusting your content to your purpose (what you want to accomplish) and your audience (the readers) in much the same way you alter your speech to communicate more effectively in response to the gestures, eye movements, or facial expressions of your listener. Revising is literally the act of "reseeing" your essay, looking at it through your readers' eyes to determine whether or not it achieves its purpose. As you revise, you should consider matters of both content and form. *In content*, do you have an interesting, thought-provoking title for your essay? Do you think your thesis statement will be clear to your audience? Does your introduction capture readers' attention? Is your treatment of your topic consistent throughout the essay? Do you support your assertions with specific examples? Does your conclusion sum up your main points? *In form*, is your essay organized effectively? Do you use a variety of rhetorical strategies? Are your sentence structure and vocabulary varied and interesting?

If you compose on a word processor, you will certainly reap the benefits of it as you revise. Word processors remove much of the drudgery of rewriting and retyping your drafts. On a typewriter, you may not make as many major revisions as necessary because of the length of time needed to retype the material. Word processors allow you to move paragraphs or whole sections of your paper from one position to another by pressing a few keys. Without the manual labor of cutting and pasting, you can immediately see if the new organization will improve the logic and coherence of your paper. You may then remove repetitions or insert words and sentences that will refine the transitions between sections.

You should also consider the value of the graphic design options available on computer software, because the way you present your papers generally affects how your instructor evaluates them. If they are clearly laid out without coffee stains or paw prints from your dog, you have a better chance of being taken seriously than if they are sloppily done. A computer can help in this regard, giving you access to boldface type, italics, boxes, bullets, and graphs of all sorts and letting you make a new copy if you do have an unexpected encounter with a coffee cup or a dog.

Editing entails correcting mistakes in your writing so that your final draft conforms to the conventions of standard written English. Correct punctuation, spelling, and mechanics will help you make your points and will encourage your readers to move smoothly through your essay from topic to topic. At this stage, you should be concerned about such matters as whether your sentences are complete, whether your punctuation is correct and effective, whether you have followed conventional rules for using mechanics, and whether the words in your essay are spelled correctly.

Proofreading involves reading over your entire essay, slowly and carefully, to make certain you have not allowed any errors to slip into your draft. (Most college instructors don't look upon errors as kindly as Thomas does.) In general, good writers try to let some time elapse between writing the final draft and proofreading it (at least a few hours, perhaps a day or so). Otherwise, they find themselves proofreading their thoughts rather than their words. Some writers even profit from proofreading their papers backward—a technique that allows them to focus on individual words and phrases rather than on entire sentences.

Because many writers work well with checklists, we present here a set of guidelines that will help you review the entire writing process.

Writing Inventory

Preparing to Write

1. Have I explored the prewriting questions through brainstorming, freewriting, journal entries, direct questions, or clustering?
2. Do I understand my topic or assignment?
3. Have I narrowed my topic adequately?
4. Do I have a specific audience for my essay? Do I know their likes and dislikes? Their educational level? Their knowledge about the topic?
5. Do I have a clear and precise purpose for my essay?

Writing

1. Can I express my topic as a problem or question?
2. Is my essay a solution or an answer to that problem or question?

Rewriting

Revising the Content

1. Does my essay have a clear, interesting title?
2. Will my statement of purpose (or thesis) be clear to my audience?
3. Will the introduction make my audience want to read the rest of my essay?

4. Do I pursue my topic consistently throughout the essay?
5. Have I included enough details to prove my main points?
6. Does my conclusion sum up my central points?
7. Will I accomplish my purpose with this audience?

Revising the Form

1. Have I organized my ideas as effectively as possible for this audience?
2. Do I use appropriate rhetorical strategies to support my main point?
3. Is my sentence structure varied and interesting?
4. Is my vocabulary appropriate for my topic, my purpose, and my audience?
5. Do I present my essay as effectively as possible, including useful graphic design techniques on the computer, if appropriate?

Editing and Proofreading

1. Have I written complete sentences throughout my essay?
2. Have I used punctuation correctly and effectively (check especially the use of commas, colons, and semicolons)?
3. Have I followed conventional rules for mechanics (capitalization, underlining or italics, abbreviations, and numbers)?
4. Are all the words in my essay spelled correctly? (Use a dictionary when in doubt.)

Following is the student's revised draft of her essay on making mistakes in life. The final draft of this typical freshman essay (written to high school seniors, as the assignment specifies) represents the entire writing process at work. We have made notes in the margin to highlight various effective elements in her essay, and we have underlined substantial changes in words and phrases from earlier drafts.

Mistakes and Maturity

Rapport with audience and point of view established	Parents and teachers frequently harp on us to correct our errors. Meanwhile, our friends laugh at us when we make mistakes. With all these negative messages, most of us have a	Catchy title; good change from first draft

hard time believing that problems can be positive experiences. But if we take the time to think about what we have learned from various blunders, we will realize all the good that has come from these events. I know making mistakes can have positive results because I recently learned several valuable lessons from one unforgettable experience.

Clear, stimulating introduction for high school seniors

Revised thesis statement

While I was traveling on the east coast last summer, I made the mistake of turning west on an interstate detour in an attempt to reach the Atlantic Ocean. This adventure took me into the center of Durham, North Carolina, where I became totally lost, bewildered, and angry at myself. I had to ask for directions several times until two hours later, when I finally found the correct highway toward the ocean. As I was driving out of town, I realized that although I had made a "dumb" mistake, I had actually learned a great deal. Overall, my adventure had been quite positive.

Good brief summary of complex experience (see notes from Preparing to Write)

Background information

Good details

The first insight I remember having after my wits returned was that I had definitely learned more about United States geography from making this mistake. I had become intimately acquainted with a town 3,000 miles from home that greatly resembled my own city, and I had become aware that the beach is not always toward the west, as it is in California. I had also met some pleasant strangers. Looking at my

First topic (Topics are in chronological order)

Adequate number of examples

Nice close to this paragraph

confusion as a learning experience encouraged me to have positive feelings about the mistake.

Second topic

As I relaxed and let this happy feeling grow, I came to another realization. I became aware of how important other people can be in turning a mistake into a positive event. Although my first reaction had been "Oh, no! Someone is going to know I'm lost," I was amazed by how supportive other people were during my panic and embarrassment.

Clear explanation with details

From an old man swinging on his front porch to an elementary school boy crossing the street with his bright blue backpack, I found that the townspeople of Durham were entirely willing to help someone they did not even know. I realized

Good summary statement

that people in general are nicer than I had previously thought.

Third topic

The final lesson I learned from making this mistake was how to be more cautious about my future decisions. This insight was, in fact, the most positive part of the entire experience. What I realized I must do to prevent similar errors in the

Specific details

future was to relax, not be so bull-headed in my decisions, and be more willing to listen to directions from other people. I might never have had these positive realizations if I had not made this mistake.

Clear transition statement

Thus, by driving in circles for two hours, I developed a more comprehensive way of looking at the world. If I were unable to make

mistakes, I probably would not have
had this chance to learn about my
environment, improve my impressions
of strangers, and reconsider the
egocentric way in which I act in
certain situations. Perhaps there's
a lesson here for all of us.

Good summary of three topics without being repetitive

Concluding statement applicable to all readers

Instead of criticizing ourselves
unduly, if each one of us could
pause after we make an error and
ask, "How can I profit from this?,"
we would realize that mistakes can
often be turned into positive
events that will help us become
more confident and mature.

Nicely focused concluding remark

As these various drafts of the student paper indicate, the essay assignments in this book encourage you to transfer to your own writing your understanding of how form and content work together. If you use the short-answer questions after each reading selection as a guide, the writing assignments will help you learn how to give shape to your own ideas and to gain control of your readers' thoughts and feelings. In essence, they help you recognize the power you have through language over your life and your environment.

CONCLUSION

As you approach the essays in this text, remember that both reading and writing function most efficiently as processes of discovery. Through them, you educate and expand your own mind and the minds of your readers. They can provide a powerful means of discovering new information or clarifying what you already know. Reading and writing lead to understanding. And just as you can discover how to read through writing, so too can you become more aware of the details of the writing process through reading. We hope your time spent with this book is both pleasant and profitable as you refine your ability to discover and express effectively the good ideas within yourself.

1

Description

Exploring Through the Senses

All of us use description in our daily lives. We might, for example, try to convey the horrors of a recent history exam to our parents, or help a friend visualize someone we met on vacation, or describe an automobile accident for a police report. Whatever our specific purpose, description is fundamental to the act of communication: We give and receive descriptions constantly, and our lives are continually affected by this simple yet important rhetorical technique.

DEFINING DESCRIPTION

Description may be defined as the act of capturing people, places, events, objects, and feelings in words so that a reader (or listener) can visualize and respond to them. Unlike narration, which traditionally presents events in a clear time sequence, description essentially suspends its objects in time, making them exempt from such limits of chronology. Narration tells a story, while pure description contains no action or time. Description is one of our primary forms of self-expression; it paints a verbal picture that helps the reader understand or share a sensory experience through the process of "showing" rather than "telling." *Telling* your friends, for example, that "the campgrounds were filled with friendly, happy activities" is not as engaging as *showing* them by saying, "The campgrounds were alive with the smell of spicy baked beans, the sound of high-pitched laughter, and the sight of happy families sharing the warmth of a fire." Showing your readers helps them understand your experience through as many senses as possible.

Descriptions range between extremes: (1) totally objective reports (with no trace of opinions or feelings), such as we might find in a dictionary or an encyclopedia, and (2) very subjective accounts, which focus almost exclusively on personal impressions. The same horse, for instance, might be described by one writer as "a large, solid-hoofed herbivorous mammal having a long mane and a tail" (objective) and by another as "a magnificent and spirited beast flaring its nostrils in search of adventure" (subjective). Most descriptive writing, however, falls somewhere between these two extremes: "a large, four-legged beast in search of adventure."

Objective description is principally characterized by its impartial, precise, and emotionless tone. Found most prominently in technical and scientific writing, such accounts might include a description of equipment to be used in a chemistry experiment, the results of a market survey for a particular consumer product, or a medical appraisal of a heart patient's physical symptoms. In situations like these, accurate, unbiased, and easily understandable accounts are of the utmost importance.

Subjective description, in contrast, is intentionally created to produce a particular response in the reader or listener. Focusing on feelings rather than on raw data, it tries to activate as many senses as possible, thereby leading the audience to a specific conclusion or state of mind. Examples of subjective descriptions are a parent's disapproving comments about one of your friends, a professor's glowing analysis of your most recent "A" paper, or a basketball coach's critique of the team's losing effort in last night's big game.

In most situations, the degree of subjectivity or objectivity in a descriptive passage depends to a large extent upon the writer's purpose and intended audience. In the case of the heart patient mentioned above, the person's physician might present the case in a formal, scientific way to a group of medical colleagues; in a personal, sympathetic way to the invalid's spouse; and in financial terms to a number of potential contributors in order to solicit funds for heart disease research.

The following paragraph describes one student's fond memories of visiting "the farm." As you read it, notice the writer's use of subjective description to communicate to her readers the multitude of contradictory feelings she connects with this rural retreat.

The shrill scream of the alarm shatters a dream. This is the last day of my visit to the place I call "the farm," an old ramshackle house in the country owned by one of my aunts. I want to go out once more in the peace of the early morning, walk in the crisp and chilly hour, and breathe the sweet air. My body feels jarred as my feet hit the hard-packed clay dirt. I tune out my stiff muscles and cold arms and legs and instead focus on two herons playing hopscotch on the canal bank: Every few yards I walk toward them, they fly one over the other an almost equal distance away from me. A killdeer with its piercing crystalline cry dips its body as it flies low over the water, the tip of its wing leaving a ring to reverberate outward. The damp earth has a strong, rich, musky scent. To the east, dust rises, and for the first time I hear the clanking and straining of a tractor as it harrows smooth the soil before planting. A crop duster rises close by just as it cuts off its release of spray, the acrid taste of chemical filtering down through the air. As the birds chatter and peck at the fields, I reluctantly return to my life in the city.

THINKING CRITICALLY BY USING DESCRIPTION

Each rhetorical mode in this book gives us new insight into the process of thinking by providing different options for arranging our thoughts and our experiences. The more we know about these options, the more conscious we become of how our minds operate and the better chance we have to improve and refine our thinking skills. (For a more thorough definition of the term "rhetorical mode," see the glossary at the end of this book.)

As you examine description as a way of thinking, consider it in isolation for a moment—away from the other rhetorical modes. Think of it as a muscle you can isolate and strengthen on its own in a weight-training program before you ask it to perform together with other muscles. By isolating description, you will learn more readily what it entails and how it functions as a critical thinking tool. In the process, you will also strengthen your knowledge of how to recognize and use description more effectively in your reading, in your writing, and in your daily life.

Just as you exercise to strengthen muscles, so too will you benefit from doing exercises to improve your skill in using descriptive techniques. As you have learned, description depends to a great extent on the keenness of your senses. So as you prepare to read and write descriptive essays, do the following tasks so that you can first learn what the process of description feels like in your own head. Really use your imagination to play with these exercises on as many different levels as possible. Also write when you are asked to do so. The combination of thinking and writing is often especially useful when we practice our thinking skills.

1. Make a list of five descriptive words you would use to trigger each of the following senses: taste, sight, hearing, touch, and smell.
2. Find a picture of a person, an animal, a bouquet of flowers, a sunset, or some other still-life portrait. List words you would use to describe this picture to a classmate. Then, list a few similes and metaphors that actually describe this still-life. How would your description differ if you were seeing the subject in real life rather than in a picture?
3. Choose an unusual object and brainstorm about its physical characteristics. Then, brainstorm about the emotions this object evokes. Why is this object so unusual or special? Compare your two brainstorming results and draw some conclusions about their differences.

READING AND WRITING DESCRIPTIVE ESSAYS

All good descriptions share four fundamental qualities: (1) an accurate sense of audience (who the readers are) and purpose (why the essay was written), (2) a clear vision of the object being described, (3) a careful selection of details that help communicate the author's vision, and (4) a consistent point of view or perspective from which a writer composes. The dominant impression or main effect the writer wishes to leave with a specific audience dictates virtually all of the verbal choices in a descriptive essay. Although description is featured in this chapter, you should also pay close attention to how other rhetorical strategies (such as example, division/classification, and cause/effect) can effectively support the dominant impression.

How to Read a Descriptive Essay

Preparing to Read. As you approach the reading selections in this chapter, you should focus first on the author's title and try to make some initial assumptions about the essay that follows: Does Ray Bradbury reveal his attitude toward his subject in the title "Summer Rituals"? Can you guess what the general mood of Kimberly Wozencraft's "Notes from the Country Club" will be? Then, scan the essay to discover its audience and purpose: What do you think John McPhee's purpose is in "The Pines"? Whom is Malcolm Cowley addressing in "The View from 80"? You should also read the synopsis of each essay in the Rhetorical Table of Contents (on pages v–xiv); these brief summaries will provide you with helpful information at this point in the reading process.

Next, learn as much as you can about the author and the conditions under which the essay was composed, information that is provided in the biographical statement before each essay. For a descriptive essay, the conditions under which the author wrote the essay, coupled with his or her purpose, can be very revealing: Can you determine when Amy Tan's piece was written? Does it describe the narrator's life now or in the past? When and under what conditions did Kimberly Wozencraft write "Notes from the Country Club"? What was her intention in writing the essay? Learning where the essay was first published will also give you valuable information about its audience.

Last, before you begin to read, try to do some brainstorming on the essay's title. In this chapter, respond to the Preparing to Read questions before each essay, which ask you to begin thinking and writing about the topic under consideration. Then, pose your own questions: What are some of the most important rituals in your life (Bradbury)? How do you envision your favorite retreat (Tan)? What would you like to learn from Cowley about the joys and frustrations of being eighty years old?

Reading. As you read each essay for the first time, jot down your initial reactions to it, and try to make connections and see relationships among the author's biography; the essay's title, purpose, and audience; and the synopsis. In this way, you will create a context or framework for your reading. See if you can figure out, for example, what Bradbury is implying about rituals in general in his essay "Summer Rituals" or why Wozencraft wrote an essay about her experiences in prison. Try to discover what the relationship is between purpose, audience, and publication information in Cowley's essay.

Also determine at this point if the author's treatment of his or her subject is predominantly objective (generally free of emotion) or subjective (heavily charged with emotion). Or perhaps the essay falls somewhere between these two extremes.

In addition, make sure you have a general sense of the dominant impression each author is trying to convey. Such an initial approach to reading these descriptive selections will give you a foundation upon which to analyze the material during your second, more in-depth reading.

Finally, at the end of your first reading, take a look at the questions after each essay to make certain you can answer them. This material will guide your rereading.

Rereading. As you reread these descriptive essays, you should be discovering exactly what the essay's dominant impression is and how the author created it. Notice each author's careful selection of details and the way in which these details come together to leave you with this impression. Also try to determine how certain details add to and detract from that dominant impression and how the writer's point of view affects it: How does McPhee create a sense of complacency in "The Pines"? How does Wozencraft enable us to identify with her prison experiences when we have never been in prison?

Try to find during this reading other rhetorical modes that support the description. Although the essays in this chapter describe various persons, places, or objects, all of the authors call upon other rhetorical strategies (especially example and comparison/contrast) to communicate their descriptions. How do these various rhetorical strategies work together in each essay to create a coherent whole?

Finally, answering the questions after each essay will check your understanding of the author's main points and help you think critically about the essay in preparing for the discussion/writing assignments that follow.

For an inventory of the reading process, you may want to review the checklists on pages 20–21 of the Introduction.

How to Write a Descriptive Essay

Preparing to Write. Before you choose a writing assignment, use the prewriting questions that follow each essay to help you discover your own ideas and opinions about the general topic of the essay. Next, choose an assignment or read the one assigned to you. Then, just as you do when you read an essay, you should determine the audience and purpose for your description (if these are not specified for you in the assignment). To whom are you writing? And why? Will an impartial, objective report be appropriate, or should you present a more emotional, subjective account to accomplish your task? In assessing your audience, you need to determine what they do and do not know about your topic. This information will help you make decisions about what you are going to say and how you will say it. Your purpose will be defined by what you intend your audience to know, think, or believe after they have read your descriptive essay. Do you want them to make up their own minds about summer rituals or old age, for example, based on an objective presentation of data, or do you hope to sway their opinions through a more subjective display of information? Or perhaps you will decide to blend the two techniques, combining facts and opinions, in order to achieve the impression of personal certainty based on objective evidence. What dominant impression do you want to leave with your audience? As you might suspect, decisions regarding audience and purpose are as important to writing descriptions as they are to reading descriptions and will shape your descriptive essay from start to finish.

The second quality of good description concerns the object of your analysis and the clarity with which you present it to the reader. Whenever possible, you should thoroughly investigate the person, place, moment, or feeling you wish to describe, paying particular attention to its effect upon each of your five senses. What can you see, smell, hear, taste, and touch as you examine it? If you want to describe your house, for example, begin by asking yourself a series of pertinent questions: How big is the house? What color is it? How many exterior doors does the house have? How many interior doors? Are any of the rooms wallpapered? If so, what are the color and texture of that wallpaper? How many different shades of paint cover the walls? Which rooms have constant noises (from clocks and other mechanical devices)? Are the kitchen appliances hot or cold to the touch? What is the quietest room in the house? The noisiest? What smells do you notice in the laundry? In the kitchen? In the basement? Most important, do any of these sensory questions trigger particular childhood memories? Although you will probably not use all of these details in your descriptive essay, the process of generating and answering such detailed questions will help reacquaint you with the object of your description as it also assists you in designing and focusing your paper. To help you generate some of these ideas, you may want to review the prewriting techniques introduced on pages 21–23.

Writing. As you write, you must select the details of your description with great care and precision so that you leave your reader with a specific impression. If, for instance, you want your audience to feel the warmth and comfort of your home, you might concentrate on describing the plush carpets, the big upholstered chairs, the inviting scent of hot apple cider, and the crackling fire. If, on the other hand, you want to gain your audience's sympathy, you might prefer to focus on the sparse austerity of your home environment: the bare walls, the quietness, the lack of color and decoration, the dim lighting, and the frigid temperature. You also want to make sure you omit unrelated ideas, like a conversation between your parents you accidentally overheard. Your careful choice of details will help control your audience's reaction.

To make your impression even more vivid, you might use figurative language to fill out your descriptions. Using words "figuratively" means using them imaginatively rather than literally. The two most popular forms of figurative language are *simile* and *metaphor*. A *simile* is a comparison between two dissimilar objects or ideas introduced by *like* or *as*: "The rocking chairs sounded like crickets" (Bradbury). A *metaphor* is an implied comparison between two dissimilar objects or ideas that is not introduced by *like* or *as*: "Life for younger persons is still a battle royal of each against each" (Cowley). Besides enlivening your writing, figurative language helps your readers understand objects, feelings, and ideas that are complex or obscure by comparing them with things that are more familiar.

The last important quality of an effective descriptive essay is point of view, your physical perspective on your subject.

Because the organization of your essay depends on your point of view, you need to choose a specific angle from which to approach your description. If you verbally jump around your home, referring first to a picture on the wall in your bedroom, next to the microwave in the kitchen, and then to the quilt on your bed, no reasonable audience will be able to follow your description. Nor will they want to. If, however, you move from room to room in some logical, sequential way, always focusing on the details you want your readers to know, you will be helping your audience form a clear, memorable impression of your home. Your vision will become their vision. In other words, your point of view plays a part in determining the organization of your description. Working spatially, you could move from side to side (from one wall to another in the rooms we have discussed), from top to bottom (from ceiling to floor), or from far to near (from the farthest to the closest point in a room), or you might progress from large to small objects, from uninteresting to interesting, or from funny to serious. Whatever plan you choose should help you accomplish your purpose with your particular audience.

Rewriting. As you reread each of your descriptive essays, play the role of your audience and try to determine what dominant impression you receive by the end of your reading.

Do you communicate the dominant impression you want to convey?
Do you have a clear point of view on your subject?
How does the essay make you feel?
What does it make you think about?
Which senses does it stimulate?
Do you use similes or metaphors when appropriate?
Are you "showing" rather than "telling" in your description?
Which sections of the essay are most effective?
What could you do to make the weaker sections more effective?
Could you, for example, add more detailed information, reorganize some of the essay, or omit irrelevant material?

For additional suggestions on the writing process, you may want to consult the checklists on pages 32–33 of the Introduction.

STUDENT ESSAY: DESCRIPTION AT WORK

In the following essay, a student relives some of her childhood memories through a subjective description of her grandmother's house. As you read it, pay particular attention to the different types of sensual details the student writer chooses in order to communicate to readers her dominant impression of her grandmother's home. Notice also her use of carefully chosen details to "show" rather than "tell" us about her childhood reminiscences, especially her comparisons, which make the memory as vivid for the reader as it is for the writer.

Grandma's House

Writer's point of view or perspective

My most vivid childhood memories are set in my Grandma Goodlink's house, a curious blend of familiar and mysterious treasures. Grandma lived at the end of a dead-end street, in the same house she had lived in since the first day of her marriage. That was half a century and thirteen children ago. A set of crumbly steps made of concrete mixed with gravel led up to her front door. I remember a big gap between the house and the steps, as if someone had not pushed them up close enough to the house. Anyone who looked into the gap could see old toys and books that had fallen into the crack behind the steps and had remained there, forever irretrievable.

Dominant impression

Comparison (simile)

Sight

Only a hook-type lock on the front door protected Grandma's many beautiful antiques. Her living room was set up like a church or schoolroom, with an old purple velvet couch against the far wall and two chairs immediately in front of the couch facing the same direction. One-half of the couch was always buried in old clothes, magazines, and newspapers, and a lone shoe sat atop the pile, a finishing touch to some bizarre modern sculpture. To one side was

Sight

Comparison (simile)

Sight

Comparison (metaphor)

46

an aged and tuneless upright piano with **Sound**
yellowed keys. The ivory overlay was miss- **Sight**
Sight ing so that the wood underneath showed
through, and many of the keys made only a
Sound muffled and frustrating thump, no matter
how hard I pressed them. On the wall facing the piano was the room's only window,
draped with yellowed lace curtains. **Sight**
Grandma always left that window open. I
Smell remember sitting near it, smelling the rain
while the curtains tickled my face. **Touch**

For no apparent reason, an old curtain **Sight**
hung in the door between the kitchen and
the living room. In the kitchen, a large
Formica-topped table always held at least a
half-dozen varieties of homemade jelly, as **Taste**
well as a loaf of bread, gooseberry pies or
cherry pies with the pits left in, boxes of
cereal, and anything else not requiring re-
Compari- frigeration, as if the table served as a small,
son (simile) portable pantry. Grandma's kitchen always
Smell smelled of toast, and I often wondered—
and still do—if she lived entirely on toast.
A hole had eaten through the kitchen **Sight**
floor, not just the warped yellow linoleum,
but all the way through the floor itself. My
sisters and I never wanted to take a bath at
Grandma's house, because we discovered
that anyone who lay on the floor on his
stomach and put one eye to the hole could
see the bathtub, which was kept in the
musty basement because the upstairs bath- **Smell**
Sight room was too small.

The back bedroom was near the kitchen
and adjacent to the basement stairs. I once
heard one of my aunts call that room a fire-
trap, and indeed it was. The room was
wallpapered with the old newspapers **Sight**
Grandma liked to collect, and the bed was
Sight stacked high with my mother's and aunts'

old clothes. There was no space between the furniture in that room, only a narrow path against one wall leading to the bed. A sideboard was shoved against the opposite wall; a sewing table was pushed up against the sideboard; a short chest of drawers lay against the sewing table; and so on. But no one could identify these pieces of forgotten furniture without digging through the sewing patterns, half-made dresses, dishes, and books. Any outsider would just think this was a part of the room where the floor had been raised to about waist-level, so thoroughly was the mass of furniture hidden.

Sight

Stepping off Grandma's sloping back porch was <u>like stepping into an enchanted forest</u>. The grass and weeds were hip-level, with a tiny dirt path leading to nowhere, <u>as if it had lost its way in the jungle</u>. A <u>fancy white fence</u>, courtesy of the neighbors, bordered the yard in back and vainly attempted to hold in the <u>gooseberries, raspberries, and blackberries</u> that grew wildly along the side of <u>Grandma's yard. Huge crabapple, cherry, and walnut trees</u> shaded the house and hid the sky. I used to stand under them and look up, pretending to be deep in a magic forest. The ground was <u>cool and damp</u> under my bare feet, even in the middle of the day, and my head would fill with the <u>sweet fragrance of mixed spring flowers</u> and the <u>throaty cooing of doves</u> I could never find but could always hear. But, before long, the wind would shift, and the <u>musty aroma of petroleum</u> from a nearby refinery would jerk me back to reality.

Compari-son (simile)

Compari-son (simile)

Sight

Sight

Sight

Touch

Smell

Sound

Smell

Grandma's house is indeed a place for memories. Just as her decaying concrete steps store the treasures of many lost childhoods, <u>her house still stands, guarding the memories of generations of children and grandchildren.</u>

Dominant impression rephrased

48

Student Writer's Comments

Writing this descriptive essay was easy and enjoyable for me—once I got started. I decided to write about my grandmother's house because I knew it so well, but I had trouble coming up with the impression I wanted to convey to my readers. I have so many recollections of this place I didn't know which set of memories would be most interesting to others. So I began by brainstorming, forcing myself to think of images from all five senses.

After I had accumulated plenty of images, which triggered other memories I had completely forgotten, I began to write. I organized my essay spatially as if I were walking through Grandma's house room by room. But I let my senses lead the way. Before I started writing, I had no idea how many paragraphs I would have, but as I meandered through the house recording my memories of sights, smells, sounds, tastes, and textures, I ended up writing one paragraph on each room, plus one for the yard. For this assignment, I wrote the three paragraphs about the inside of the house first; then, the introduction started to take shape in my head, so I got it down; and last, I wrote the paragraph on the backyard and my conclusion. Finally, my "dominant impression" came to me: This is a house that guards the memories of many generations. My grandmother has always lived in this house, and my mother has her own set of memories associated with this place too.

This focus for my paper made the revising process fairly easy, as I worked on the entire essay with a specific purpose in mind. Previously, my biggest problem had been that I had too many scattered memories and realized I had to be more selective. Once I had my dominant impression, I knew which images to keep and which to drop from my draft. Also, as I reworked my essay, I looked for ways to make my description more exciting and vivid for the reader—as if he or she were right there with me. To accomplish this, I explained some special features of my grandma's house by comparing them with items the reader would most likely be familiar with. I also worked, at this point, on making one paragraph flow into another by adding transitions that move the reader smoothly from one group of ideas to the next. "Only a hook-type lock on the front door" got my readers into the living room. The old curtain between the kitchen and the living room moved my essay out of the living room and into the kitchen. I started my third paragraph about the indoors by saying "The back bedroom was near the kitchen and adjacent to the basement stairs" so my readers could get their bearings in relation to other parts of the house they had already been introduced to. Finally, I was content that my essay was a clear, accurate description of my view of my grandma's house. My brother might have a completely different set of memories, but this was my version of a single generation of impressions organized, finally, into one coherent essay.

SOME FINAL THOUGHTS ON DESCRIPTION

Because description is one of the most basic forms of verbal communication, you will find descriptive passages in most of the reading selections throughout this textbook. Description provides us with the means to capture our audience's attention and clarify certain points in all of our writing. The examples chosen for the following section, however, are predominantly descriptive—the main purpose in each being to involve the readers' senses as vividly as possible. As you read through each of these essays, try to determine its intended audience and purpose, the object of the description, the extent to which details are included or excluded, and the author's point of view. Equipped with these four areas of reference, you can become an increasingly sophisticated reader and writer of descriptive prose.

RAY BRADBURY   (1920 –   )

■ ■ ■

Summer Rituals

Ray Bradbury is one of America's best-known and most loved writers of science fiction. His extensive publications include such popular novels as *The Martian Chronicles* (1950), *The Illustrated Man* (1951), *Fahrenheit 451* (1953), *Dandelion Wine* (1957), and *Something Wicked This Way Comes* (1962). He has also written dozens of short stories, poems, essays, plays, and radio and movie scripts (including the screenplay of John Huston's film version of *Moby Dick*). As a child, he escaped his strict Baptist upbringing through a steady diet of Jules Verne, H.G. Wells, and Edgar Rice Burroughs, along with Buck Rogers and Prince Valiant comic books: "I was a sucker for lies, beautiful, fabulous lies, which instruct us to better our lives as a result, but which don't tell the truth." A frequent theme in his many novels is the impact of science on humanity: "My stories are intended," he claims, "as much to forecast how to prevent dooms, as to predict them." Bradbury's more recent publications include *The Last Circus* (1981), *The Complete Poems of Ray Bradbury* (1982), *The Love Affair* (1983), *Dinosaur Tales* (1983), *A Memory for Murder* (1984), *Forever and the Earth* (1984), *Death Is a Lonely Business* (1985), *The Toynbee Convector* (1989), and *A Day in the Life of Hollywood* (1992). The author lives in Cheviot Hills, California, where he enjoys painting and making ceramics.

Preparing to Read

"Summer Rituals," an excerpt from *Dandelion Wine*, describes the comfortable ceremony of putting up a front-porch swing in early summer. Focusing on the perceptions of Douglas, a young boy, the essay clearly sets forth the familiar yet deeply significant rhythms of life in a small town. Before you read this selection, take a few moments to consider the value of ritual in your own life: Can you think of any activities that you and your family have elevated to the level of ceremonial importance? What about holidays?

Birthdays? Sporting events? Spring cleaning? When do these activities take place? Do the same people participate in them every year? Why do you repeat these rituals? What purpose do they have for you? For others whom you know? For society in general?

Y es, summer was rituals, each with its natural time and place. 1
The ritual of lemonade or ice-tea making, the ritual of
wine, shoes, or no shoes, and at last, swiftly following the
others, with quiet dignity, the ritual of the front-porch swing.

On the third day of summer in the late afternoon Grandfather 2
reappeared from the front door to gaze serenely at the two empty
eye rings in the ceiling of the porch. Moving to the geranium-
pot-lined rail like Ahab surveying the mild mild day and the
mild-looking sky, he wet his finger to test the wind, and shucked
his coat to see how shirt sleeves felt in the westering hours. He
acknowledged the salutes of other captains on yet other flowered
porches, out themselves to discern the gentle ground swell of
weather, oblivious to their wives chirping or snapping like
fuzzball hand dogs hidden behind black porch screens.

"All right, Douglas, let's set it up." 3

In the garage they found, dusted, and carried forth the how- 4
dah, as it were, for the quiet summer-night festivals, the swing
chair which Grandpa chained to the porch-ceiling eyelets.

Douglas, being lighter, was first to sit in the swing. Then, after a 5
moment, Grandfather gingerly settled his pontifical weight beside
the boy. Thus they sat, smiling at each other, nodding, as they
swung silently back and forth, back and forth.

Ten minutes later Grandma appeared with water buckets and 6
brooms to wash down and sweep off the porch. Other chairs,
rockers and straight-backs, were summoned from the house.

"Always like to start sitting early in the season," said Grandpa, 7
"before the mosquitoes thicken."

About seven o'clock you could hear the chairs scraping back 8
from the tables, someone experimenting with a yellow-toothed
piano, if you stood outside the dining-room window and listened. Matches being struck, the first dishes bubbling in the suds
and tinkling on the wall racks, somewhere, faintly, a phonograph
playing. And then as the evening changed the hour, at house after

house on the twilight streets, under the immense oaks and elms, on shady porches, people would begin to appear, like those figures who tell good or bad weather in rain-or-shine clocks.

Uncle Bert, perhaps Grandfather, then Father, and some of the 9 cousins; the men all coming out first into the syrupy evening, blowing smoke, leaving the women's voices behind in the cooling-warm kitchen to set their universe aright. Then the first male voices under the porch brim, the feet up, the boys fringed on the worn steps or wooden rails where sometime during the evening something, a boy or a geranium pot, would fall off.

At last, like ghosts hovering momentarily behind the door 10 screen, Grandma, Great-grandma, and Mother would appear, and the men would shift, move, and offer seats. The women carried varieties of fans with them, folded newspapers, bamboo whisks, or perfumed kerchiefs, to start the air moving about their faces as they talked.

What they talked of all evening long, no one remembered next 11 day. It wasn't important to anyone what the adults talked about; it was only important that the sounds came and went over the delicate ferns that bordered the porch on three sides; it was only important that the darkness filled the town like black water being poured over the houses, and that the cigars glowed and that the conversations went on, and on. The female gossip moved out, disturbing the first mosquitoes so they danced in frenzies on the air. The male voices invaded the old house timbers; if you closed your eyes and put your head down against the floor boards you could hear the men's voices rumbling like a distant, political earthquake, constant, unceasing, rising or falling a pitch.

Douglas sprawled back on the dry porch planks, completely 12 contented and reassured by these voices, which would speak on through eternity, flow in a stream of murmurings over his body, over his closed eyelids, into his drowsy ears, for all time. The rocking chairs sounded like crickets, the crickets sounded like rocking chairs, and the moss-covered rain barrel by the dining-room window produced another generation of mosquitoes to provide a topic of conversation through endless summers ahead.

Sitting on the summer-night porch was so good, so easy and 13 so reassuring that it could never be done away with. These were rituals that were right and lasting; the lighting of pipes, the pale hands that moved knitting needles in the dimness, the eating of foil-wrapped, chill Eskimo Pies, the coming and going of all the people. For at some time or other during the evening, everyone visited here; the neighbors down the way, the people across the street; Miss Fern and Miss Roberta humming by in their electric runabout, giving Tom or Douglas a ride around the block and then coming up to sit down and fan away the fever in their cheeks; or Mr. Jonas, the junkman, having left his horse and wagon hidden in the alley, and ripe to bursting with words, would come up the steps looking as fresh as if his talk had never been said before, and somehow it never had. And last of all, the children, who had been off squinting their way through a last hide-and-seek or kick-the-can, panting, glowing, would sickle quietly back like boomerangs along the soundless lawn, to sink beneath the talking talking talking of the porch voices which would weigh and gentle them down. . . .

Oh, the luxury of lying in the fern night and the grass night 14 and the night of susurrant, slumbrous voices weaving the dark together. The grownups had forgotten he was there, so still, so quiet Douglas lay, noting the plans they were making for his and their own futures. And the voices chanted, drifted, in moonlit clouds of cigarette smoke while the moths, like late appleblossoms come alive, tapped faintly about the far street lights, and the voices moved on into the coming years. . . .

UNDERSTANDING DETAILS

1. What are the main similarities and differences between Douglas and Grandfather in this essay? How are their views of the world the same? How are their views different?

2. From the scattered details you have read in this essay, describe Douglas's house. How large do you think the front porch is? What color is the house? How many trees and shrubs surround it? What part of your description is based on facts in the essay? What part comes from inferences you have made on your own?

3. How do the men differ from the women in this excerpt? Divide a piece of paper into two columns; then list as many qualities of each gender as you can find. (For example, the narrator hears the men's voices "rumbling" like an "earthquake";

in contrast, the women move like "ghosts," their gossip "disturbing the . . . mosquitoes.") What other descriptive differences can you find between the men and women? What conclusions can you draw from these differences?

4. How did the conversation blend with the surroundings in Bradbury's description?

ANALYZING MEANING

1. A "ritual" may be briefly defined as "a customarily repeated act that expresses a system of values." Using this definition, explain why the ritual of the front-porch swing is important to Douglas's family. What feelings or implicit values lie behind this particular ritual?

2. What other rituals are mentioned in this essay? How are they related to the front-porch swing? To summer? To Douglas and his family?

3. Bradbury helps us feel the comfort, warmth, and familiarity of the scene depicted in this essay through the use of a number of original descriptive details: for example, "summer-night festivals," "yellow-toothed piano," "rain-or-shine clocks," "syrupy evening," and "foil-wrapped, chill Eskimo Pies." Find at least five other descriptive words or phrases, and explain how each enables us to identify with the characters and situations in this story. Which of the five senses does each of these details arouse in the reader?

4. In what ways do you think Douglas was "completely contented and reassured" (paragraph 12) by the voices around him? Why did Douglas feel this contentment would last "for all time" (paragraph 12)?

DISCOVERING RHETORICAL STRATEGIES

1. Some of the author's sentences are very long and involved, whereas others are quite short. What effects do these changes in sentence length have on you as a reader? Give a specific example of a shift in length from one sentence to another and explain its effect.

2. This descriptive essay is filled with many interesting similes (comparisons using the words *like* or *as*) and metaphors (com-

parisons without *like* or *as*). For example, Grandfather standing on the front porch looks *like* Ahab, the possessed sea captain from Herman Melville's epic novel *Moby Dick* (paragraph 2). Later, Bradbury uses a metaphor to focus his readers on "the night of susurrant, slumbrous voices weaving the dark together" (paragraph 14). Find at least one other comparison, either a simile or a metaphor, and explain how it works within the context of its sentence or paragraph. What type of comparison is being made (a simile or a metaphor)? What do we learn about the object being described (for example, Grandfather or the night) through its association with the other reference (Ahab or voices weaving the dark together)?

3. What is the point of view of the author in this selection? Would the essay be more effective if it were reported from the standpoint of Douglas? Of Grandfather? Of the women? Why or why not? How does the author's point of view help Bradbury organize his description? Should the fact that Bradbury's middle name is Douglas have any bearing on our interpretation of this story?

4. Although Bradbury draws mainly on description to write this essay, what other rhetorical strategies work together to help the reader grasp the full effect of "Summer Rituals"? Give examples of each strategy.

MAKING CONNECTIONS

1. For Douglas, hanging the porch swing was an important yearly ritual. What rituals can you find in the childhoods of Russell Baker ("The Saturday Evening Post") and/or Eudora Welty ("Listening")? What specific meanings did these rituals have within each author's family?

2. Compare and contrast Bradbury's neighborhood with that of Robert Ramirez ("The Barrio"). Which neighborhood would you feel most comfortable in? Why would you feel comfortable there?

3. Which author's relationship with his parents was most like your own: Ray Bradbury's, Amy Tan's ("The Joy Luck Club"), or Russell Baker's ("The Saturday Evening Post")? How did each of these children relate differently to his or her parents?

IDEAS FOR DISCUSSION/WRITING

Preparing to Write

List some of the most important rituals in your life: How many times a year do these rituals occur? What purpose do they serve? How do rituals help create a strong social framework in your life? In your friends' lives? In society in general?

Choosing a Topic

1. Write a descriptive essay about a ritual that is significant in your life, addressing it to someone who has never experienced that particular activity. Include the people involved and the setting. Try to use all five senses in your description.
2. Choose a ritual that is part of your family life, and write an essay describing your feelings about this ceremonial event. Address it to someone outside your family. Use similes and metaphors to make your description as vivid as possible.
3. Explain to someone visiting the United States for the first time the value of a particular tradition in American society. Then, help this person understand the importance of that tradition in your life.

AMY TAN (1952 – 1967)

■ ■ ■

The Joy Luck Club

In a very short time, Amy Tan has established herself as one of the foremost Chinese-American writers. Her first novel, *The Joy Luck Club* (1989), which was praised as "brilliant . . . a jewel of a book" by the *New York Times Book Review*, focuses on the lives of four Chinese women in pre-1949 China and their American-born daughters in modern-day California. Through a series of vignettes, Tan weaves together the dreams and sorrows of these mothers and daughters as they confront oppression in China and equally difficult cultural challenges in the new world of the United States. Like the protagonists in *The Joy Luck Club*, Tan's parents, a Baptist minister and a licensed vocational nurse, emigrated to America shortly before Tan's birth. She showed an early talent for writing when, at age eight, she won an essay contest (and a transistor radio) with a paper entitled "Why I Love the Library." Following the tremendous success of her first novel, Tan apparently had great difficulty writing her second book, *The Kitchen God's Wife* (1991). As she was working on it, she began grinding her teeth, which resulted in two broken molars and a sizable dental bill. "I am glad that I shall never again have to write a second book," the author has confessed. "Actually, I cannot recall any writer—with or without a splashy debut—who said the second book came easily." Her latest book, *The Moon Lady* (1992), was followed by a successful film version of *The Joy Luck Club* (1993).

Preparing to Read

In the following selection, excerpted from the beginning of *The Joy Luck Club*, Tan describes how the club began amid the horror and devastation of Japan's conquest of the Kweilin area of China during the 1930s. As you prepare to read Tan's description, take a few moments to think about a place that is particularly meaningful in your life: What physical characteristics does this place have?

Do you remember it as pleasant or unpleasant? Are you happy or sad when you think about it? What are some sights, smells, tastes, sounds, or textures you associate with this place? Did you ever feel trapped or confined there? If so, how did you escape?

---

y mother started the San Francisco version of the Joy 1 Luck Club in 1949, two years before I was born. This was the year my mother and father left China with one stiff leather trunk filled only with fancy silk dresses. There was no time to pack anything else, my mother had explained to my father after they boarded the boat. Still his hands swam frantically between the slippery silks, looking for his cotton shirts and wool pants.

When they arrived in San Francisco, my father made her hide 2 those shiny clothes. She wore the same brown-checked Chinese dress until the Refugee Welcome Society gave her two hand-me-down dresses, all too large in sizes for American women. The society was composed of a group of white-haired American missionary ladies from the First Chinese Baptist Church. And because of their gifts, my parents could not refuse their invitation to join the church. Nor could they ignore the old ladies' practical advice to improve their English through Bible study class on Wednesday nights and, later, through choir practice on Saturday mornings. This was how my parents met the Hsus, the Jongs, and the St. Clairs. My mother could sense that the women of these families also had unspeakable tragedies they had left behind in China and hopes they couldn't begin to express in their fragile English. Or at least, my mother recognized the numbness in these women's faces. And she saw how quickly their eyes moved when she told them her idea for the Joy Luck Club.

Joy Luck was an idea my mother remembered from the days of 3 her first marriage in Kweilin, before the Japanese came. That's why I think of Joy Luck as her Kweilin story. It was the story she would always tell me when she was bored, when there was nothing to do, when every bowl had been washed and the Formica table had been wiped down twice, when my father sat reading the newspaper and smoking one Pall Mall cigarette after another, a warning not to disturb him. This is when my mother would take out a box of old ski sweaters sent to us by unseen relatives from Vancouver. She would snip the bottom of a sweater and pull out a kinky thread of yarn, anchoring it to a piece of cardboard. And as she began to roll with one sweeping rhythm, she would start her story. Over the years, she told me the same story, except for the ending, which grew darker, casting long shadows into her life, and eventually into mine.

"I dreamed about Kweilin before I ever saw it," my mother [4] began, speaking Chinese. "I dreamed of jagged peaks lining a curving river, with magic moss greening the banks. At the tops of these peaks were white mists. And if you could float down this river and eat the moss for food, you would be strong enough to climb the peak. If you slipped, you would only fall into a bed of soft moss and laugh. And once you reached the top, you would be able to see everything and feel such happiness it would be enough to never have worries in your life ever again.

"In China, everybody dreamed about Kweilin. And when I ar- [5] rived, I realized how shabby my dreams were, how poor my thoughts. When I saw the hills, I laughed and shuddered at the same time. The peaks looked like giant fried fish heads trying to jump out of a vat of oil. Behind each hill, I could see shadows of another fish, and then another and another. And then the clouds would move just a little and the hills would suddenly become monstrous elephants marching slowly toward me! Can you see this? And at the root of the hill were secret caves. Inside grew hanging rock gardens in the shapes and colors of cabbage, winter melons, turnips, and onions. These were things so strange and beautiful you can't ever imagine them.

"But I didn't come to Kweilin to see how beautiful it was. The [6] man who was my husband brought me and our two babies to Kweilin because he thought we would be safe. He was an officer with the Kuomintang, and after he put us down in a small room in a two-story house, he went off to the northwest, to Chungking.

"We knew the Japanese were winning, even when the newspa- [7] pers said they were not. Every day, every hour, thousands of people poured into the city, crowding the sidewalks, looking for places to live. They came from the East, West, North, and South. They were rich and poor, Shanghainese, Cantonese, northerners, and not just Chinese, but foreigners and missionaries of every religion. And there was, of course, the Kuomintang and their army officers who thought they were top level to everyone else.

"We were a city of leftovers mixed together. If it hadn't been 8 for the Japanese, there would have been plenty of reason for fighting to break out among these different people. Can you see it? Shanghai people with north-water peasants, bankers with barbers, rickshaw pullers with Burma refugees. Everybody looked down on someone else. It didn't matter that everybody shared the same sidewalk to spit on and suffered the same fast-moving diarrhea. We all had the same stink, but everybody complained someone else smelled the worst. Me? Oh, I hated the American air force officers who said habba-habba sounds to make my face turn red. But the worst were the northern peasants who emptied their noses into their hands and pushed people around and gave everybody their dirty diseases.

"So you can see how quickly Kweilin lost its beauty for me. I 9 no longer climbed the peaks to say, How lovely are these hills! I only wondered which hills the Japanese had reached. I sat in the dark corners of my house with a baby under each arm, waiting with nervous feet. When the sirens cried out to warn us of bombers, my neighbors and I jumped to our feet and scurried to the deep caves to hide like wild animals. But you can't stay in the dark for so long. Something inside of you starts to fade and you become like a starving person, crazy-hungry for light. Outside I could hear the bombing. Boom! Boom! And then the sound of raining rocks. And inside I was no longer hungry for the cabbage or the turnips of the hanging rock garden. I could only see the dripping bowels of an ancient hill that might collapse on top of me. Can you imagine how it is, to want to be neither inside nor outside, to want to be nowhere and disappear?

"So when the bombing sounds grew farther away, we would 10 come back out like newborn kittens scratching our way back to the city. And always, I would be amazed to find the hills against the burning sky had not been torn apart.

"I thought up Joy Luck on a summer night that was so hot 11 even the moths fainted to the ground, their wings were so heavy with the damp heat. Every place was so crowded there was no room for fresh air. Unbearable smells from the sewers rose up to my second-story window and the stink had nowhere else to go but into my nose. At all hours of the night and day, I heard screaming sounds. I didn't know if it was a peasant slitting the throat of a runaway pig or an officer beating a half-dead peasant for lying in his way on the sidewalk. I didn't go to the window to find out. What use would it have been? And that's when I thought I needed something to do to help me move.

"My idea was to have a gathering of four women, one for each 12
corner of my mah jong table. I knew which women I wanted to ask. They were all young like me, with wishful faces. One was an army officer's wife, like myself. Another was a girl with very fine manners from a rich family in Shanghai. She had escaped with only a little money. And there was a girl from Nanking who had the blackest hair I have ever seen. She came from a low-class family, but she was pretty and pleasant and had married well, to an old man who died and left her with a better life.

"Each week one of us would host a party to raise money and 13
to raise our spirits. The hostess had to serve special *dyansyin* foods to bring good fortune of all kinds—dumplings shaped like silver money ingots, long rice noodles for long life, boiled peanuts for conceiving sons, and of course, many good-luck oranges for a plentiful, sweet life.

"What fine food we treated ourselves to with our meager al- 14
lowances! We didn't notice that the dumplings were stuffed mostly with stringy squash and that the oranges were spotted with wormy holes. We ate sparingly, not as if we didn't have enough, but to protest how we could not eat another bite, we had already bloated ourselves from earlier in the day. We knew we had luxuries few people could afford. We were the lucky ones.

"After filling our stomachs, we would then fill a bowl with 15
money and put it where everyone could see. Then we would sit down at the mah jong table. My table was from my family and was of a very fragrant red wood, not what you call rosewood, but *hong mu*, which is so fine there's no English word for it. The table had a very thick pad, so that when the mah jong *pai* were spilled onto the table the only sound was of ivory tiles washing against one another.

"Once we started to play, nobody could speak, except to say 16
'*Pung!*' or '*Chr!*' when taking a tile. We had to play with serious-ness and think of nothing else but adding to our happiness through winning. But after sixteen rounds, we would again feast, this time to celebrate our good fortune. And then we would talk into the night until the morning, saying stories about good times in the past and good times yet to come.

"Oh, what good stories! Stories spilling out all over the place! 17
We almost laughed to death. A rooster that ran into the house
screeching on top of dinner bowls, the same bowls that held him
quietly in pieces the next day! And one about a girl who wrote
love letters for two friends who loved the same man. And a silly
foreign lady who fainted on a toilet when firecrackers went off
next to her.

"People thought we were wrong to serve banquets every 18
week while many people in the city were starving, eating rats
and, later, the garbage that the poorest rats used to feed on.
Others thought we were possessed by demons—to celebrate
when even within our own families we had lost generations,
had lost homes and fortunes, and were separated, husband from
wife, brother from sister, daughter from mother. Hnnnh! How
could we laugh, people asked.

"It's not that we had no heart or eyes for pain. We were all 19
afraid. We all had our miseries. But to despair was to wish back
for something already lost. Or to prolong what was already unbearable. How much can you wish for a favorite warm coat that
hangs in the closet of a house that burned down with your
mother and father inside of it? How long can you see in your
mind arms and legs hanging from telephone wires and starving
dogs running down the streets with half-chewed hands dangling
from their jaws? What was worse, we asked among ourselves, to
sit and wait for our own deaths with proper somber faces? Or to
choose our own happiness?

"So we decided to hold parties and pretend each week had 20
become the new year. Each week we could forget past wrongs
done to us. We weren't allowed to think a bad thought. We
feasted, we laughed, we played games, lost and won, we told the
best stories. And each week, we could hope to be lucky. That
hope was our only joy. And that's how we came to call our little
parties Joy Luck."

My mother used to end the story on a happy note, bragging 21
about her skill at the game. "I won many times and was so lucky
the others teased that I had learned the trick of a clever thief," she
said. "I won tens of thousands of *yuan*. But I wasn't rich. No. By
then paper money had become worthless. Even toilet paper was
worth more. And that made us laugh harder, to think a thousand-
yuan note wasn't even good enough to rub on our bottoms."

UNDERSTANDING DETAILS

1. What is the Joy Luck Club and why was it formed?
2. List two sights, two smells, two tastes, two sounds, and two textures that Tan's mother recalls in her Kweilin story. How are these senses used throughout the story? How do these sensual details help the reader experience the place described by the author?
3. In what ways did Kweilin lose its beauty for the narrator's mother?
4. How are joy and luck related to the naming of the "Joy Luck Club"?

ANALYZING MEANING

1. Why does Kweilin hold a special meaning for the narrator's mother? Did it keep its positive associations in her memory? Explain your answer.
2. What significance did the varieties of food and the process of eating have at the Joy Luck Club meetings?
3. Why do you think the ending of the narrator's mother's Kweilin story "grew darker" (paragraph 3) over the years?
4. Why did the narrator's mother "want to be neither inside nor outside . . . to be nowhere and disappear" (paragraph 9)? Why did this state of mind appeal to her occasionally?

DISCOVERING RHETORICAL STRATEGIES

1. This descriptive essay contains two different voices. How do we know which voice is speaking/writing? What special characteristics does each voice have?
2. Using vivid details throughout her description, the narrator's mother engages our senses as often as possible. Look, for example, at the following sentences: "So when the bombing sounds grew farther away, we would come back out like newborn kittens scratching our way back to the city. And always, I would be amazed to find the hills against the burning sky had not been torn apart" (paragraph 10). These sentences stimulate our senses of hearing ("bombing sounds"), seeing ("the hills," "the burning sky"), and touching ("scratching"). Reread paragraph 9. Then, list in one column all the senses mentioned and, in another, the words that arouse those senses.

3. How does Tan use words and details to change the tone of her writing at key points in this excerpt?
4. Although this essay moves forward predominantly through description, what other traditional rhetorical modes support Tan's dominant impression? Give examples of each of these modes in the essay.

MAKING CONNECTIONS

1. If Amy Tan, Alleen Pace Nilsen ("Sexism in English: A 1990s Update"), and/or Judy Brady ("Why I Want a Wife") were having a conversation about women's roles in society, which person would you probably agree with most? Explain your answer.
2. Amy Tan and Lewis Sawaquat ("For My Indian Daughter") both went through diverse cultural experiences within American society. How did each of these authors use their cultural experiences to develop their own identities?
3. How is the narrator's relationship with her mother different from the typical non-Western mother–daughter relationships described in Germaine Greer's "A Child Is Born"?

IDEAS FOR DISCUSSION/WRITING

Preparing to Write

Write freely for a few minutes about a place that is special to you: What are some of the strongest memories of the sights, smells, tastes, sounds, and textures you associate with this place? Who else is involved with this place? What are your feelings about this place?

Choosing a Topic

1. Based on your sensory memories, write a descriptive essay about this special place for a friend of yours who has never been there. Decide on a specific impression you want to communicate to your friend and a perspective that will help create that impression.
2. Describe for your classmates your favorite game. How many can play? What are the rules? When is the game most exciting? Why do you like this game?
3. Using your imagination, travel back in time to a particular moment or event in your past. Write an essay describing in de-

tail what you were seeing, smelling, tasting, hearing, and touching at that time in your life. Where were you? How old were you? What was happening at this precise moment in your past? What exactly were you doing? How did you feel while you were engaged in this activity? Who else was in the scene with you? Did you feel safe? Secure? Happy? Sad? Anxious to escape?

JOHN MCPHEE   (1931 –   )

■ ■ ■

The Pines

The range of subjects investigated by author John McPhee is quite astounding. In his twenty books and numerous articles, he has written about sports, food, art, geology, geography, science, history, education, and a variety of other topics. One of the most famous of these "non-fictional, book-length narratives," as he calls them, is *A Sense of Where You Are* (1965), a study of former basketball great Bill Bradley; another is *Levels of the Game* (1969), a chronicle of the epic 1968 U.S. Open semifinal tennis match between Arthur Ashe and Clark Graebner. Most of McPhee's essays have appeared first in the *New Yorker*, a prestigious literary magazine for which he has been a staff writer since 1965. His more recent publications include *In Suspect Terrain* (1983), *La Place de la Concorde Suisse* (1984), *Table of Contents* (1985), *Rising from the Plains* (1986), *The Control of Nature* (1989), *Looking for a Ship* (1990), and *Assembling California* (1993). "What all these pieces of writing have in common," according to the author, "is that they are about real people and real places. All the different topics are just milieus in which to sketch people and places." McPhee lives in New Jersey near Princeton University, where he teaches a seminar entitled "The Literature of Fact." His hobbies include going on long bike rides, fishing for shad and pickerel, and skiing.

Preparing to Read

The following essay, "The Pines," is a small section from a longer piece called *The Pine Barrens* (1968), which describes a remote wilderness in southern New Jersey. Like many of McPhee's narrative essays, "The Pines" is structured around a single colorful character—in this case, Fred Brown, a talkative backwoods native whose simple surroundings and quaint mannerisms speak well for the solitary life. In contrast, Brown's friend Bill Wasovwich is almost painfully shy; he is a person (like McPhee himself, some critics tell us) who speaks little, listens intently, and observes the world around him with great care. Both men worry openly about the encroaching civilization that threatens their unique way of life. As you prepare to read this essay, think for a moment about the different types of people you know: Do you have talkative friends? Quiet friends? Which type of person is most appealing to you? Which type are you? Have you ever lived in the woods? What are the principal advantages of living in a rural environment rather than in a big city? What are the disadvantages?

F red Brown's house is on an unpaved road that curves along 1 the edge of a wide cranberry bog. What attracted me to it was the pump that stands in his yard. It was something of a wonder that I noticed the pump, because there were, among other things, eight automobiles in the yard, two of them on their sides and one of them upside down, all ten years old or older. Around the cars were old refrigerators, vacuum cleaners, partly dismantled radios, cathode-ray tubes, a short wooden ski, a large wooden mallet, dozens of cranberry picker's boxes, many tires, an orange crate dated 1946, a cord or so of firewood, mandolins, engine heads, and maybe a thousand other things. The house itself, two stories high, was covered with tarpaper that was peeling away in some places, revealing its original shingles, made of Atlantic white cedar from the stream courses of the surrounding forest. I called out to ask if anyone was home, and a voice inside called back, "Come in. Come in. Come on the hell in."

I walked through a vestibule that had a dirt floor, stepped up 2 into a kitchen, and went on into another room that had several overstuffed chairs in it and a porcelain-topped table, where Fred Brown was seated, eating a pork chop. He was dressed in a white sleeveless shirt, ankle-top shoes, and undershorts. He gave me a cheerful greeting and, without asking why I had come or what I wanted, picked up a pair of khaki trousers that had been tossed onto one of the overstuffed chairs and asked me to sit down. He set the trousers on another chair, and he apologized for being in the middle of his breakfast, explaining that he seldom drank much but the night before he had had a few drinks and this had caused his day to start slowly. "I don't know what's the matter with me, but there's got to be something the matter with me, because drink don't agree with me anymore," he said. He had a raw onion in one hand, and while he talked he shaved slices from the onion and ate them between bites of the chop. He was a muscular and well-built man, with short, bristly white hair, and he had bright, fast-moving eyes in a wide-open face. His legs were trim and strong, with large muscles in the calves. I guessed that he was about sixty, and for a man of sixty he seemed to be in remarkably good shape. He was actually seventy-nine. "My rule is: Never eat except when you're hungry," he said, and he ate another slice of the onion.

In a straight-backed chair near the doorway to the kitchen sat a young man with long black hair, who wore a visored red leather cap that had darkened with age. His shirt was coarse-woven and had eyelets down a V neck that was laced with a thong. His trousers were made of canvas, and he was wearing gum boots. His arms were folded, his legs were stretched out, he had one ankle over the other, and as he sat there he appeared to be sighting carefully past his feet, as if his toes were the outer frame of a gunsight and he could see some sort of target in the floor. When I had entered, I had said hello to him, and he had nodded without looking up. He had a long, straight nose and high cheekbones, in a deeply tanned face that was, somehow, gaunt. I had no idea whether he was shy or hostile. Eventually, when I came to know him, I found him to be as shy a person as I have ever had a chance to know. His name is Bill Wasovwich, and he lives alone in a cabin about half a mile from Fred. First his father, then his mother left him when he was a young boy, and he grew up depending on the help of various people in the pines. One of them, a cranberry grower, employs him and has given him some acreage, in which Bill is building a small cranberry bog of his own, "turfing it out" by hand. When he is not working in the bogs, he goes roaming, as he puts it, setting out cross-country on long, looping journeys, hiking about thirty miles in a typical day, in search of what he calls "events"—surprising a buck, or a gray fox, or perhaps a poacher or a man with a still. Almost no one who is not native to the pines could do this, for the woods have an undulating sameness, and the understory—huckleberries, sheep laurel, sweet fern, high-bush blueberry—is often so dense that a wanderer can walk in a fairly tight circle and think that he is moving in a straight line. State forest rangers spend a good part of their time finding hikers and hunters, some of whom have vanished for days. In his long, path-

less journeys, Bill always emerges from the woods near his cabin—
and about when he plans to. In the fall, when thousands of
hunters come into the pines, he sometimes works as a guide. In
the evenings, or in the daytime when he is not working or roaming, he goes to Fred Brown's house and sits there for hours. The
old man is a widower whose seven children are long since gone
from Hog Wallow, and he is as expansively talkative and worldly as
the young one is withdrawn and wild. Although there are fifty-
three years between their ages, it is obviously fortunate for each of
them to be the other's neighbor.

That first morning, while Bill went on looking at his out- 4
stretched toes, Fred got up from the table, put on his pants, and
said he was going to cook me a pork chop, because I looked
hungry and ought to eat something. It was about noon, and I was
even hungrier than I may have looked, so I gratefully accepted
his offer, which was a considerable one. There are two or three
small general stores in the pines, but for anything as fragile as a
fresh pork chop it is necessary to make a round trip from Fred's
place of about fifty miles. Fred went into the kitchen and
dropped a chop into a frying pan that was crackling with hot
grease. He has a fairly new four-burner stove that uses bottled
gas. He keeps water in a large bowl on a table in the kitchen and
ladles some when he wants it. While he cooked the meat, he
looked out a window through a stand of pitch pines and into the
cranberry bog. "I saw a big buck out here last night with velvet
on his horns," he said. "Them horns is soft when they're in velvet." On a nail high on one wall of the room that Bill and I were
sitting in was a large meat cleaver. Next to it was a billy club. The
wall itself was papered in a flower pattern, and the wallpaper continued out across the ceiling and down the three other walls,
lending the room something of the appearance of the inside of a
gift box. In some parts of the ceiling, the paper had come loose.
"I didn't paper this year," Fred said. "For the last couple months,
I've had sinus." The floor was covered with old rugs. They had
been put down in random pieces, and in some places as many as
six layers were stacked up. In winter, when the temperature approaches zero, the worst cold comes through the floor. The only
source of heat in the house is a wood-burning stove in the main
room. There were seven calendars on the walls, all current and
none with pictures of nudes. Fading into pastel on one wall was a

rotogravure photograph of President and Mrs. Eisenhower. A framed poem read:

> God hath not promised
> Sun without rain
> Joy without sorrow
> Peace without pain.

Noticing my interest in all this, Fred reached into a drawer and showed me what appeared to be a postcard. On it was a photograph of a woman, and Fred said with a straight face that she was his present girl, adding that he meets her regularly under a juniper tree on a road farther south in the pines. The woman, whose appearance suggested strongly that she had never been within a great many miles of the Pine Barrens, was wearing nothing at all.

I asked Fred what all those cars were doing in his yard, and he said that one of them was in running condition and the rest were its predecessors. The working vehicle was a 1956 Mercury. Each of the seven others had at one time or another been his best car, and each, in turn, had lain down like a sick animal and had died right there in the yard, unless it had been towed home after a mishap elsewhere in the pines. Fred recited, with affection, the history of each car. Of one old Ford, for example, he said, "I upset that up to Speedwell in the creek." And of an even older car, a station wagon, he said, "I busted that one up in the snow. I met a car on a little hill, and hit the brake, and hit a tree." One of the cars had met its end at a narrow bridge about four miles from Hog Wallow, where Fred had hit a state trooper, head on.

The pork was delicious and almost crisp. Fred gave me a potato with it, and a pitcher of melted grease from the frying pan to pour over the potato. He also handed me a loaf of bread and a dish of margarine, saying, "Here's your bread. You can have one piece or two. Whatever you want."

Fred apologized for not having a phone, after I asked where I would have to go to make a call, later on. He said, "I don't have no phone because I don't have no electric. If I had electric, I would have had a phone in here a long time ago." He uses a kerosene lamp, a propane lamp, and two flashlights.

He asked where I was going, and I said that I had no particular destination, explaining that I was in the pines because I found it

71

hard to believe that so much unbroken forest could still exist so near the big Eastern cities, and I wanted to see it while it was still there. "Is that so?" he said, three times. Like many people in the pines, he often says things three times. "Is that so? Is *that* so?"

I asked him what he thought of a plan that has been developed   10 by Burlington and Ocean Counties to create a supersonic jetport in the pines, connected by a spur of the Garden State Parkway to a new city of two hundred and fifty thousand people, also in the pines.

"They've been talking about that for three years, and they've   11 never given up," Fred said.

"It'd be the end of these woods," Bill said. This was the first   12 time I heard Bill speak. I had been there for an hour, and he had not said a word. Without looking up, he said again, "It'd be the end of these woods, I can tell you that."

Fred said, "They could build ten jetports around me. I wouldn't   13 give a damn."

"You ain't going to be around very long," Bill said to him. "It   14 would be the end of these woods."

Fred took that as a fact, and not as an insult. "Yes, it would be   15 the end of these woods," he said. "But there'd be people here you could do business with."

Bill said, "There ain't no place like this left in the country, I   16 don't believe—and I travelled around a little bit, too."

Eventually, I made the request I had intended to make when I   17 walked in the door. "Could I have some water?" I said to Fred. "I have a jerry can and I'd like to fill it at the pump."

"Hell, yes," he said. "That isn't my water. That's God's water.   18 That right, Bill?"

"I *guess* so," Bill said, without looking up. "It's good water, I   19 can tell you that."

"That's God's water," Fred said again. "Take all you want."   20

UNDERSTANDING DETAILS

1. What attracted McPhee to Fred Brown's house? In what ways is this object representative of Fred's yard? Of Fred's life?
2. What other things are in Fred's front yard? What does this collection of junk say about Fred and his lifestyle?
3. In paragraph 3, McPhee comments that, despite the wide difference in age between Fred and Bill, "it is obviously fortunate

for each of them to be the other's neighbor." In what ways do the two characters need each other?

4. Describe in your own words the inside of Fred's house. Which details does McPhee stress in his description? Why does he focus on these and not on others?

ANALYZING MEANING

1. Why is McPhee visiting "the pines"? What do you think his opinion of "the pines" is? What specific references reveal his opinions?

2. Why does Bill go "roaming"? What do you think the purpose of these journeys is?

3. Why does Bill believe a jetport would be "the end of these woods" (paragraph 12)? Why do you think these were the first words Bill had spoken since the author arrived? Explain your answer.

4. Why do you think McPhee ends this piece with several references to God? How does the dialogue about "God's water" help us understand Fred and Bill even more specifically?

DISCOVERING RHETORICAL STRATEGIES

1. Which senses does McPhee concentrate on most in this description? Choose one paragraph to analyze. In one column, write down all the senses the description arouses; in another, record the words and phrases that activate these senses.

2. What "tone" or "mood" is McPhee trying to create in this excerpt? Is he successful? Explain your answer.

3. What is the author's "point of view" in this essay? How would the method of description change if the story were told from Fred's vantage point? From Bill's? How does this particular point of view help the author organize his description?

4. McPhee relies heavily on description to make his point. What other rhetorical modes support this narrative essay? Give examples of each of these modes from the essay.

MAKING CONNECTIONS

1. How does the friendship between Fred and Bill described in McPhee's essay differ from friendships in Robert Ramirez's

"The Barrio" and/or Kimberly Wozencraft's "Notes from the Country Club"? Which friendships are stronger in your opinion? Explain your answer.

2. Compare and contrast McPhee's concern about preserving the environment with the feelings of Jane Goodall ("The Mind of the Chimpanzee"). How are they similar? How are they different?

3. In McPhee's essay, how does Fred Brown feel about the uses and abuses of technology? Would Carl Cannon ("Honey, I Warped the Kids") or John Leonard ("Why Blame TV?") agree with him? Explain your answer.

IDEAS FOR DISCUSSION/WRITING

Preparing to Write

Write freely about someone you know who represents a specific personality "type": What distinguishes this type from other types you know? What do people of this type have in common? What are their looks, values, needs, desires, living conditions, and so on? What do you have in common with the type of person you have just described? How are you different?

Choosing a Topic

1. Give a name (either real or fictitious) to the person you have just described in the prewriting exercise, and write an essay depicting the house, apartment, or room in which this person lives. Try to make your description as vivid and as well organized as McPhee's portrait of Fred Brown. Imagine that the audience for your description is someone who has never met this person and has never seen where the person lives.

2. Write an essay describing for your classmates some of the "junk" you have collected over the years. Why are certain items junk to some people and treasures to others? What makes the things you are describing special to you?

3. Describe the inside of your house, apartment, or room, explaining to your class what the decorations say about you as a person. If someone in your class were to see where you live, could he or she make any accurate deductions about your political, social, or moral values based upon the contents and arrangement of the place you call "home"?

KIMBERLY WOZENCRAFT (1954 –   )

■ ■ ■

Notes from the Country Club

Kimberly Wozencraft grew up in Dallas, Texas, and dropped out of college when she was twenty-one to become a police officer. Her first assignment, prior to training at the police academy, was a street-level undercover narcotics investigation. Like many narcotics agents, Wozencraft became addicted to drugs, which impaired her judgment and resulted in a 1981 conviction for violating the civil rights of a reputed child pornographer. After serving an eighteen-month sentence in the Federal Correctional Institution at Lexington, Kentucky, she moved to New York City, where she has lived since her release. She holds a Master of Fine Arts degree from Columbia University, and her essays, poems, and short stories have appeared in a variety of magazines, including *Northwest Review, Quarto, Big Wednesday*, and *Witness*. Her first novel, *Rush*, was made into a movie in 1992.

Preparing to Read

Originally published in *Witness*, "Notes from the Country Club" was selected for inclusion in *The Best American Essays of 1988*, edited by Annie Dillard. Through carefully constructed prose, the author describes her prison environment and the anxiety caused by living for more than a year in such an alien, difficult place. As you prepare to read this essay, take a moment to think about your own behavior in difficult situations: What kind of person do you become? How do you act toward other people? How is this behavior different from the way you usually act? How do you know when you're in a difficult situation? What do you generally do to relieve the tension?

T hey had the Haitians up the hill, in the "camp" section 1
where they used to keep the minimum security cases.
The authorities were concerned that some of the
Haitians might be diseased, so they kept them isolated from the

main coed prison population by lodging them in the big square brick building surrounded by eight-foot chain-link with concertina wire on top. We were not yet familiar with the acronym AIDS.

One or two of the Haitians had drums, and in the evenings when the rest of us were in the Big Yard, the drum rhythms carried over the bluegrass to where we were playing gin or tennis or softball or just hanging out waiting for dark. When they really got going some of them would dance and sing. Their music was rhythmic and beautiful, and it made me think of freedom. 2

There were Cubans loose in the population, spattering their guttural Spanish in streams around the rectangular courtyard, called Central Park, at the center of the prison compound. These were Castro's Boat People, guilty of no crime in this country, but requiring sponsors before they could walk the streets as free people. 3

Walking around the perimeter of Central Park was like taking a trip in microcosm across the United States. Moving leftward from the main entrance, strolling along under the archway that covers the wide sidewalk, you passed the doorway to the Women's Unit, where I lived, and it was how I imagined Harlem to be. There was a white face here and there, but by far most of them were black. Ghetto blasters thunked out rhythms in the sticky evening air, and folks leaned against the window sills, smoking, drinking Cokes, slinking and nodding. Every once in a while a joint was passed around, and always there was somebody pinning, checking for hacks on patrol. 4

Past Women's Unit was the metal door to the Big Yard, the main recreation area of three or four acres, two sides blocked by the building, two sides fenced in the usual way—chain-link and concertina wire. 5

Past the Big Yard you entered the Blue Ridge Mountains, a sloping grassy area on the edge of Central Park, where the locals, people from Kentucky, Tennessee, and the surrounding environs, sat around playing guitars and singing, and every once in a while passing around a quart of hooch. They make it from grapefruit juice and a bit of yeast smuggled out of the kitchen. Some of the inmates who worked in Cable would bring out pieces of a black foam rubber substance and wrap it around empty Cremora jars to make thermos jugs of sorts. They would mix the grapefruit juice 6 and yeast in the containers and stash them in some out-of-the-way spot for a few weeks until presto! you had hooch, bitter and tart and sweet all at once, only mildly alcoholic, but entirely suitable for evening cocktails in Central Park.

Next, at the corner, was the Commissary, a tiny store tucked 7 inside the entrance to Veritas, the second women's unit. It wasn't much more than a few shelves behind a wall of Plexiglas, with a constant line of inmates spilling out of the doorway. They sold packaged chips, cookies, pens and writing paper, toiletries, some fresh fruit, and the ever-popular ice cream, sold only in pints. You had to eat the entire pint as soon as you bought it, or else watch it melt, because there weren't any refrigerators. Inmates were assigned one shopping night per week, allowed to buy no more than seventy-five dollars' worth of goods per month, and were permitted to pick up a ten-dollar roll of quarters if they had enough money in their prison account. Quarters were the basic spending unit in the prison; possession of paper money was a shippable offense. There were vending machines stocked with junk food and soda, and they were supposedly what the quarters were to be used for. But we gambled, we bought salami or fried chicken sneaked out by the food service workers, and of course people sold booze and drugs. The beggars stood just outside the Commissary door. Mostly they were Cubans, saying, "Oyez! Mira! Mira! Hey, Poppy, one quarter for me. One cigarette for me, Poppy?"

There was one Cuban whom I was specially fond of. His name 8 was Shorty. The name said it. He was only about five-two, and he looked just like Mick Jagger. I met him in Segregation, an isolated section of tiny cells where prisoners were locked up for having violated some institutional rule or another. They tossed me in there the day I arrived; again the authorities were concerned, supposedly for my safety. I was a police woman before I became a convict, and they weren't too sure that the other inmates would like that. Shorty saved me a lot of grief when I went into Seg. It didn't matter if you were male or female there, you got stripped and handed a tee shirt, a pair of boxer shorts and a set of Peter Pans—green canvas shoes with thin rubber soles designed to prevent you from running away. As if you could get past three steel doors and a couple of hacks just to start with. When I was marched down the hall between the cells the guys started

77

whistling and hooting and they didn't shut up even after I was locked down. They kept right on screaming until finally I yelled out, "Yo no comprendo!" and they all moaned and said, "Another . . . Cuban," and finally got quiet. Shorty was directly across from me, I could see his eyes through the rectangular slot in my cell door. He rattled off a paragraph or two of Spanish, all of which was lost on me, and I said quietly, "Yo no comprendo bien español. Yo soy de Texas, yo hablo inglés?" I could tell he was smiling by the squint of his eyes, and he just said, "Bueno." When the hacks came around to take us out for our mandatory hour of recreation, which consisted of standing around in the Rec area while two guys shot a game of pool on the balcony above the gym, Shorty slipped his hand into mine and smiled up at me until the hack told him to cut it out. He knew enough English to tell the others in Seg that I was not really Spanish, but he kept quiet about it, and they left me alone.

Beyond the Commissary, near the door to the dining hall, was   9
East St. Louis. The prison had a big portable stereo system which they rolled out a few times a week so that an inmate could play at being a disc jockey. They had a good-sized collection of albums and there was usually some decent jazz blasting out of there. Sometimes people danced, unless there were uptight hacks on duty to tell them not to.

California was next. It was a laid back kind of corner near the   10
doors to two of the men's units. People stood around and smoked hash or grass or did whatever drugs happened to be available and there was sometimes a sort of slow-motion game of handball going on. If you wanted drugs, this was the place to come.

If you kept walking, you would arrive at the Power Station, the   11
other southern corner where the politicos-gone-wrong congregated. It might seem odd at first to see these middle-aged government mavens standing around in their Lacoste sport shirts and Sans-a-belt slacks, smoking pipes or cigars and waving their arms to emphasize some point or other. They kept pretty much to themselves and ate together at the big round tables in the cafeteria, sipping cherry Kool-Aid and pretending it was Cabernet Sauvignon.

That's something else you had to deal with—the food. It was   12
worse than elementary school steam table fare. By the time they finished cooking it, it was tasteless, colorless, and nutritionless.

The first meal I took in the dining room was lunch. As I walked toward the entry, a tubby fellow was walking out, staggering really, rolling his eyes as though he were dizzy. He stopped and leaned over, and I heard someone yell, "Watch out, he's gonna puke!" I ducked inside so as to miss the spectacle. They were serving some rubbery, faint pink slabs that were supposed to be ham, but I didn't even bother to taste mine. I just slapped at it a few times to watch the fork bounce off and then ate my potatoes and went back to the unit.

Shortly after that I claimed that I was Jewish, having gotten the word from a friendly New York lawyer who was in for faking some of his clients' immigration papers. The kosher line was the only way to get a decent meal in there. In fact, for a long time they had a Jewish baker from Philadelphia locked up, and he made some truly delicious cream puffs for dessert. They sold for seventy-five cents on the black market, but once I had established myself in the Jewish community I got them as part of my regular fare. They fed us a great deal of peanut butter on the kosher line; every time the "goyim" got meat, we got peanut butter, but that was all right with me. Eventually I was asked to light the candles at the Friday evening services, since none of the real Jewish women bothered to attend. I have to admit that most of the members of our little prison congregation were genuine *alter kokers*, but some of them were amusing. And I enjoyed learning first hand about Judaism. The services were usually very quiet, and the music, the ancient intoning songs, fortified me against the screeching pop-rock vocal assaults that were a constant in the Women's Unit. I learned to think of myself as the *shabot shiksa*, and before my time was up, even the rabbi seemed to accept me. 13

I suppose it was quite natural that the Italians assembled just "down the street" from the offending ex-senators, judges, and power brokers. Just to the left of the main entrance. The first night I made the tour, a guy came out of the shadows near the building and whispered to me. "What do you need, sweetheart? What do you want, I can get it. My friend Ahmad over there, he's very rich, and he wants to buy you things. What'll it be, you want some smoke, a few ludes, vodka, cigarettes, maybe some kosher salami fresh from the kitchen? What would you like?" I just stared at him. The only thing I wanted at that moment was out, and even Ahmad's millions, if they existed at all, couldn't do 14 that. The truth is, every guy I met in there claimed to be wealthy, to have been locked up for some major financial crime. Had I taken all of them up on their offers of limousines to pick me up at the front gate when I was released and take me to the airport for a ride home in a private Lear jet, I would have needed my own personal cop out front just to direct traffic.

Ahmad's Italian promoter eventually got popped for zinging the cooking teacher one afternoon on the counter in the home economics classroom, right next to the new Cuisinart. The assistant warden walked in on the young lovebirds, and before the week was up, even the Cubans were walking around singing about it. They had a whole song down, to the tune of "Borracho Me Acosté a Noche." — 15

At the end of the tour, you would find the jaded New Yorkers, sitting at a picnic table or two in the middle of the park, playing gin or poker and bragging about their days on Madison Avenue and Wall Street, lamenting the scarcity of good deli, even on the kosher line, and planning where they would take their first real meal upon release. — 16

If you think federal correctional institutions are about the business of rehabilitation, drop by for an orientation session one day. There at the front of the classroom, confronting rows of mostly black faces, will be the warden, or the assistant warden, or the prison shrink, pacing back and forth in front of the blackboard and asking the class, "Why do you think you're here?" This gets a general grumble, a few short, choked laughs. Some well-meaning soul always says it—rehabilitation. — 17

"Nonsense!" the lecturer will say. "There are several reasons for locking people up. Number one is incapacitation. If you're in here, you can't be out there doing crime. Secondly, there is deterrence. Other people who are thinking about doing crime see that we lock people up for it and maybe they think twice. But the real reason you are here is to be punished. Plain and simple. You done wrong, now you got to pay for it. Rehabilitation ain't even part of the picture. So don't be looking to us to rehabilitate you. Only person can rehabilitate you is you. If you feel like it, go for it, but leave us out. We don't want to play that game." — 18

So that's it. You're there to do time. I have no misgivings about why I went to prison. I deserved it. I was a cop, I got strung out on cocaine, I violated the rights of a pornographer. My own drug — 19 use as an undercover narcotics agent was a significant factor in my crime. But I did it and I deserved to be punished. Most of the people I met in Lexington, though, were in for drugs, and the majority of them hadn't done anything more than sell an ounce of cocaine or a pound of pot to some apostle of the law.

It seems lately that almost every time I look at the *New York* 20 *Times* op-ed page, there is something about the drug problem. I have arrested people for drugs, and I have had a drug problem myself. I have seen how at least one federal correctional institution functions. It does not appear that the practice of locking people up for possession or distribution of an insignificant quantity of a controlled substance makes any difference at all in the amount of drug use that occurs in the United States. The drug laws are merely another convenient source of political rhetoric for aspiring officeholders. Politicians know that an antidrug stance is an easy way to get votes from parents who are terrified that their children might wind up as addicts. I do not advocate drug use. Yet, having seen the criminal justice system from several angles, as a police officer, a court bailiff, a defendant, and a prisoner, I am convinced that prison is not the answer to the drug problem, or for that matter to many other white-collar crimes. If the taxpayers knew how their dollars were being spent inside some prisons, they might actually scream out loud.

There were roughly 1,800 men and women locked up in Lex, at 21 a ratio of approximately three men to every woman, and it did get warm in the summertime. To keep us tranquil they devised some rather peculiar little amusements. One evening I heard a commotion on the steps at the edge of Central Park and looked over to see a rec specialist with three big cardboard boxes set up on the plaza, marked 1, 2, and 3. There were a couple of hundred inmates sitting at the bottom of the steps. Dennis, the rec specialist, was conducting his own version of the television game show *Let's Make a Deal!* Under one of the boxes was a case of soda, under another was a racquetball glove, and under a third was a fly swatter. The captive contestant picked door number 2, which turned out to contain the fly swatter, to my way of thinking the best prize there. Fly swatters were virtually impossible to get through approved channels, and therefore cost as much as two packs of cigarettes on the black market.

Then there was the Annual Fashion Show, where ten or 22 twenty inmates had special packages of clothing sent in, only for the one evening, and modeled them on stage while the baddest drag queen in the compound moderated and everyone else ooohed and aahhed. They looked good up there on stage in Christian Dior and Ralph Lauren instead of the usual fatigue pants and white tee shirts. And if such activities did little to pre-pare inmates for a productive return to society, well, at least they contributed to the fantasyland aura that made Lexington such an unusual place.

I worked in Landscape, exiting the rear gate of the compound   23 each weekday morning at about nine after getting a half-hearted frisk from one of the hacks on duty. I would climb on my tractor to drive to the staff apartment complex and pull weeds or mow the lawn. Landscape had its prerogatives. We raided the gardens regularly and at least got to taste fresh vegetables from time to time. I had never eaten raw corn before, but it could not have tasted better. We also brought in a goodly supply of real vodka, and a bit of hash now and then, for parties in our rooms after lights out. One guy strapped a six-pack of Budweiser to his arms with masking tape and then put on his prison-issue Army field jacket. When he got to the rear gate, he raised his arms straight out at shoulder level, per instructions, and the hack patted down his torso and legs, never bothering to check his arms. The inmate had been counting on that. He smiled at the hack and walked back to his room, a six-pack richer.

I was fortunate to be working Landscape at the same time as   24 Horace, a fellow who had actually lived in the city of Lexington before he was locked up. His friends made regular deliveries of assorted contraband, which they would stash near a huge elm tree near the outer stone fence of the reservation. Horace would drive his tractor over, make the pickup, and the rest of us would carry it, concealed, through the back gate when we went back inside for lunch or at the end of the day. "Contraband" included every-thing from drugs to blue eye shadow. The assistant warden be-lieved that female inmates should wear no cosmetics other than what she herself used—a bit of mascara and a light shade of lip-stick. I have never been a plaything of Fashion, but I did what I could to help the other women prisoners in their never-ending quest for that Cover Girl look.

You could depend on the fact that most of the hacks would   25 rather have been somewhere else, and most of them really didn't care *what* the inmates did, as long as it didn't cause any commotion. Of course, there were a few you had to look out for. The captain in charge of security was one of them. We tried a little experiment once, after having observed that any time he saw someone laughing, he took immediate steps to make the inmate and everyone around him acutely miserable. Whenever we saw him in the area, we immediately assumed expressions of intense unhappiness, even of despair. Seeing no chance to make anyone more miserable than they already appeared to be, the captain left us alone.

Almost all of the female hacks, and a good number of the 26 males, had outrageously large derrières, a condition we inmates referred to as "the federal ass." This condition may have resulted from the fact that most of them appeared, as one inmate succinctly described it, simply to be "putting in their forty a week to stay on the government teat." Employment was not an easy thing to find in Kentucky.

Despite the fact that Lexington is known as a "country club" 27 prison, I must admit that I counted days. From the first moment that I was in, I kept track of how many more times I would have to watch the sun sink behind eight feet of chain-link, of how many more days I would have to spend eating, working, playing and sleeping according to the dictates of a "higher authority." I don't think I can claim that I was rehabilitated. If anything I underwent a process of dehabilitation. What I learned was what Jessica Mitford tried to tell people many years ago in her book *Kind and Usual Punishment*. Prison is a business, no different from manufacturing tires or selling real estate. It keeps people employed and it provides cheap labor for NASA, the U.S. Postal Service, and other governmental or quasi-governmental agencies. For a short time, before I was employed in Landscape, I worked as a finisher of canvas mailbags, lacing white rope through metal eyelets around the top of the bags and attaching clamps to the ropes. I made one dollar and fourteen cents for every one hundred that I did. If I worked very hard, I could do almost two hundred a day.

It's not about justice. If you think it's about justice, look at 28 the newspapers and notice who walks. Not the little guys, the guys doing a tiny bit of dealing, or sniggling a little on their income tax, or the woman who pulls a stunt with welfare checks because her husband has skipped out and she has no other way to feed her kids. I do not say that these things are right. But the process of selective prosecution, the "making" of cases by D.A.s and police departments, and the presence of some largely unenforceable statutes currently on the books (it is the reality of "compliance": no law can be forced on a public which chooses to ignore it, hence, selective prosecution) make for a criminal justice system which cannot realistically function in a fair and equitable manner. Criminal justice—I cannot decide if it is the ultimate oxymoron or a truly accurate description of the law enforcement process in America.

In my police undercover capacity, I have sat across the table 29 from an armed robber who said, "My philosophy of life is slit thy neighbor's throat and pimp his kids." I believe that the human animals who maim and kill people should be dealt with, as they say, swiftly and surely. But this business of locking people up, at enormous cost, for minor, nonviolent offenses does not truly or effectively serve the interest of the people. It serves only to promote the wasteful aspects of the federal prison system, a system that gulps down tax dollars and spews up *Let's Make a Deal!*

I think about Lexington almost daily. I will be walking up 30 Broadway to shop for groceries, or maybe riding my bike in the original Central Park and suddenly I'm wondering who's in there now, at this very moment, and for what inane violations, and what they are doing. Is it chow time, is the Big Yard open, is some inmate on stage in the auditorium singing "As Time Goes By" in a talent show? It is not a fond reminiscence, or a desire to be back in the Land of No Decisions. It is an awareness of the waste. The waste of tax dollars, yes, but taxpayers are used to that. It is the unnecessary trashing of lives that leaves me uneasy. The splitting of families, the enforced monotony, the programs which purport to prepare an inmate for re-entry into society but which actually succeed only in occupying a few more hours of the inmate's time behind the walls. The nonviolent offenders, such as small-time drug dealers and the economically deprived who were driven to crime out of desperation, could remain in society under less costly supervision, still undergoing "punishment" for their crime, but at least contributing to rather than draining the resources of society.

Horace, who was not a subtle sort of fellow, had some tee shirts 31 made up. They were delivered by our usual supplier out in

Landscape, and we wore them back in over our regular clothes. The hacks tilted their heads when they noticed, but said nothing. On the front of each shirt was an outline of the state of Kentucky, and above the northwest corner of the state were the words "Visit Beautiful Kentucky!" Inside the state boundary were:

- Free *A*ccommodations
- Complimentary Meals
- Management Holds Calls
- Recreational Exercise

In small letters just outside the southwest corner of the state was: "Length of Stay Requirement." And in big letters across the bottom:

Take Time to Do Time

F.C.I. Lexington

I gave mine away on the day I finished my sentence. It is a   32
time-honored tradition to leave some of your belongings to friends who have to stay behind when you are released. But you must never leave shoes. Legend has it that if you do, you will come back to wear them again.

UNDERSTANDING DETAILS

1. Draw Lexington prison and put the names on the sections of the facility. Then, describe each section in your own words.
2. Why was walking around the outside of Central Park "like taking a trip in microcosm across the United States" (paragraph 4)? Give examples to explain your answer.
3. Why was Wozencraft especially fond of Shorty? What secret did they share at the beginning of the author's prison term?
4. Does the author feel she had been unfairly punished by being sent to prison? What had she done wrong?

ANALYZING MEANING

1. What was Wozencraft's attitude toward other people in Lexington prison? Why do you think she felt this way? What types of relationships did she have with inmates and staff members?

2. Why does the author say, "If the taxpayers knew how their dollars were being spent inside some prisons, they might actually scream out loud" (paragraph 20)? What exactly is she referring to? What is she implying? Give some examples.
3. Why do you think Lexington is known as a "country club" prison? What features of the prison might have brought about its nickname?
4. Wozencraft feels strongly that people who perform minor, nonviolent crimes should not be put in prison. Why does she feel this way? Who should be locked up according to the author? From her point of view, how does rehabilitation take place?

DISCOVERING RHETORICAL STRATEGIES

1. This essay is organized predominantly as a clockwise tour of Lexington prison. How and when does Wozencraft introduce the facts about her own imprisonment and her opinions about the current American system of justice? Explain in as much detail as you can the effect of integrating the guided tour and the related facts and opinions.
2. Wozencraft uses specific prison jargon throughout this essay. In what way does this jargon add to or detract from the essay? What effect would the essay have without this jargon?
3. Wozencraft ends her essay with an explanation of "a time-honored tradition." Is this an effective ending for the piece? Why or why not?
4. Though spatial description is the dominant rhetorical strategy the author uses in this essay to accomplish her purpose, what other strategies help make the essay effective? Give examples of these strategies.

MAKING CONNECTIONS

1. If Kimberly Wozencraft, Nancy Gibbs ("When Is It Rape?"), and/or John Langone ("Group Violence") were having a discussion about crime, how would each of these authors define the term? With whom would you agree most? Explain your answer.
2. Amy Tan's narrator ("The Joy Luck Club"), Harold Krents ("Darkness at Noon"), and Harry Edwards ("Triple Tragedy in

Black Society") all feel imprisoned in much the same way Wozencraft does in her essay. In what way is each of these authors "confined?" Have you ever felt imprisoned for any reason? Why? How did you escape?

3. What would Wozencraft, Germaine Greer ("A Child Is Born"), and/or William Ouchi ("Japanese and American Workers: Two Casts of Mind") have to say about the importance of relying on other people to help endure difficult or challenging situations? How much do you rely on friends and relatives in your own life? How comfortable are you with these relationships?

IDEAS FOR DISCUSSION/WRITING

Preparing to Write

Write freely about your memories of a recent difficult or awkward situation in your life: What were the circumstances? What did you do? What did others do? How did you relate to others in this situation? Why was the situation so difficult? How did you get out of it?

Choosing a Topic

1. Write an essay describing for your peers a difficult or awkward situation you have been in recently. Why was it awkward? Explain the specific circumstances so that your classmates can clearly imagine the setting and the difficulty or problem. Then, discuss your reaction to the situation.

2. A friend of yours has just been sentenced to prison for one year. Write a letter to this person describing what you think his or her biggest adjustments will be.

3. Wozencraft describes many problems within the prison system. With these problems in mind, write a letter to the editor of your local newspaper discussing whether prisons actually rehabilitate criminals. Use examples from Wozencraft's essay to help make your point.

MALCOLM COWLEY   (1898 – 1989)

■ ■ ■

The View from 80

Malcolm Cowley had a long and distinguished career as a literary historian, critic, editor, and poet. After receiving his bachelor's degree at Harvard, he served in the American Ambulance Corps during World War I, then pursued graduate studies in literature at the University of Montpellier in France. In 1929, he became associate editor of *The New Republic*, presiding over the magazine's literary department for the next fifteen years. Perhaps his most important book of literary criticism is *Exile's Return* (1934), a study of the "lost generation" of expatriate Americans living in Paris in the 1920s, which included Ernest Hemingway, Ezra Pound, F. Scott Fitzgerald, and Hart Crane. Cowley returned to the same topic in 1973 with *A Second Flowering: Works and Days of the Lost Generation*. He also published editions of such authors as Hemingway, William Faulkner, Nathaniel Hawthorne, Walt Whitman, and Fitzgerald; two collections of his own poetry, *Blue Juniata* (1929) and *The Dry Season* (1941); and numerous other translations, editions, and books of criticism. His most recent publications include *The Flower and the Leaf: A Contemporary Record of American Writing Since 1941* (1985) and *Conversations with Malcolm Cowley* (1986). Asked the secret of his amazing productivity, Cowley replied: "Writers often speak of 'saving their energy,' as if each man were given a nickel's worth of it, which he is at liberty to spend. To me, the mind of the poet resembles Fortunatus' purse: The more spent, the more it supplies."

Preparing to Read

The following essay was originally commissioned by *Life* magazine (1978) for inclusion in a series of articles on aging. Cowley later converted the piece into the first chapter of a book with the same title: *The View from 80* (1980). Through a combination of vivid personal experience and well-researched documentation, the author crafted an essay that helps us experience what life is like for an eighty-year-old man. As you prepare to read Cowley's description of "the country of age," take some time to think about age in general: How many people over the age of sixty do you know? Over the age of seventy? How do they behave? Do you think these older people see themselves in the same way you see them? Do you think they consider themselves "old"? What clues remind them of their advancing age? What events and attitudes remind you of your age? In what ways will you be different than you are now when you reach the age of eighty?

T hey gave me a party on my 80th birthday in August 1978. First there were cards, letters, telegrams, even a cable of congratulation or condolence; then there were gifts, mostly bottles; there was catered food and finally a big cake with, for some reason, two candles (had I gone back to very early childhood?). I blew the candles out a little unsteadily. Amid the applause and clatter I thought about a former custom of the Northern Ojibwas when they lived on the shores of Lake Winnipeg. They were kind to their old people, who remembered and enforced the ancient customs of the tribe, but when an old person became decrepit, it was time for him to go. Sometimes he was simply abandoned, with a little food, on an island in the lake. If he deserved special honor, they held a tribal feast for him. The old man sang a death song and danced, if he could. While he was still singing, his son came from behind and brained him with a tomahawk.

That was quick, it was dignified, and I wonder whether it was any more cruel, essentially, than some of our civilized customs or inadvertencies in disposing of the aged. I believe in rites and ceremonies. I believe in big parties for special occasions such as an 80th birthday. It is a sort of belated bar mitzvah, since the 80-year-old, like a Jewish adolescent, is entering a new stage of life; let him (or her) undergo a *rite de passage*, with toasts and a cantor. Seventy-year-olds, or septuas, have the illusion of being middle-aged, even if they have been pushed back on a shelf. The 80-year-old, the octo, looks at the double-dumpling figure and admits that he is old. The last act has begun, and it will be the test of the play.

To enter the country of age is a new experience, different from what you supposed it to be. Nobody, man or woman, knows the country until he has lived in it and has taken out his citizenship papers. Here is my own report, submitted as a road map and guide to some of the principal monuments.

The new octogenarian feels as strong as ever when he is sitting 4 back in a comfortable chair. He ruminates, he dreams, he remembers. He doesn't want to be disturbed by others. It seems to him that old age is only a costume assumed for those others; the true, the essential self is ageless. In a moment he will rise and go for a ramble in the woods, taking a gun along, or a fishing rod, if it is spring. Then he creaks to his feet, bending forward to keep his balance, and realizes that he will do nothing of the sort. The body and its surroundings have their messages for him, or only one message: "You are old." Here are some of the occasions on which he receives the message:

- when it becomes an achievement to do thoughtfully, step by step, what he once did instinctively
- when his bones ache
- when there are more and more little bottles in the medicine cabinet, with instructions for taking four times a day
- when he fumbles and drops his toothbrush (butterfingers)
- when his face has bumps and wrinkles, so that he cuts himself while shaving (blood on the towel)
- when year by year his feet seem farther from his hands
- when he can't stand on one leg and has trouble pulling on his pants
- when he hesitates on the landing before walking down a flight of stairs
- when he spends more time looking for things misplaced than he spends using them after he (or more often his wife) has found them
- when he falls asleep in the afternoon
- when it becomes harder to bear in mind two things at once
- when a pretty girl passes him in the street and he doesn't turn his head
- when he forgets names, even of people he saw last month ("Now I'm beginning to forget nouns," the poet Conrad Aiken said at 80)
- when he listens hard to jokes and catches everything but the snapper
- when he decides not to drive at night anymore

- when everything takes longer to do—bathing, shaving, getting dressed or undressed—but when time passes quickly, as if he were gathering speed while coasting downhill. The year from 79 to 80 is like a week when he was a boy.

Those are some of the intimate messages. "Put cotton in your ears and pebbles in your shoes," said a gerontologist, a member of that new profession dedicated to alleviating all maladies of old people except the passage of years. "Pull on rubber gloves. Smear Vaseline over your glasses, and there you have it: instant aging." Not quite. His formula omits the messages from the social world, which are louder, in most cases, than those from within. We start by growing old in other people's eyes, then slowly we come to share their judgment. 5

I remember a morning many years ago when I was backing out of the parking lot near the railroad station in Brewster, New York. There was a near collision. The driver of the other car jumped out and started to abuse me; he had his fists ready. Then he looked hard at me and said, "Why, you're an old man." He got back into his car, slammed the door, and drove away, while I stood there fuming. "I'm only 65," I thought. "He wasn't driving carefully. I can still take care of myself in a car, or in a fight, for that matter." 6

My hair was whiter—it may have been in 1974—when a young woman rose and offered me her seat in a Madison Avenue bus. That message was kind and also devastating. "Can't I even stand up?" I thought as I thanked her and declined the seat. But the same thing happened twice the following year, and the second time I gratefully accepted the offer, though with a sense of having diminished myself. "People are right about me," I thought while wondering why all those kind gestures were made by women. Do men now regard themselves as the weaker sex, not called upon to show consideration? All the same it was a relief to sit down and relax. 7

A few days later I wrote a poem, "The Red Wagon," that belongs in the record of aging: 8

> For his birthday they gave him a red express wagon
> with a driver's high seat and a handle that steered.
> His mother pulled him around the yard.

"Giddyap," he said, but she laughed and went off
to wash the breakfast dishes.

"I wanta ride too," his sister said,
and he pulled her to the edge of a hill.
"Now, sister, go home and wait for me,
but first give a push to the wagon."
He climbed again to the high seat,
this time grasping that handle-that-steered.

The red wagon rolled slowly down the slope,
then faster as it passed the schoolhouse
and faster as it passed the store,
the road still dropping away.
Oh, it was fun.
But would it ever stop?
Would the road always go downhill?
The red wagon rolled faster.
Now it was in strange country.
It passed a white house he must have dreamed about,
deep woods he had never seen,
a graveyard where, something told him, his sister
was buried.

Far below
the sun was sinking into a broad plain.

The red wagon rolled faster.
Now he was clutching the seat, not even trying to steer.
Sweat clouded his heavy spectacles.
His white hair streamed in the wind.

Even before he or she is 80, the aging person may undergo an- 9
other identity crisis like that of adolescence. Perhaps there had
also been a middle-aged crisis, the male or the female
menopause, but the rest of adult life he had taken himself for
granted, with his capabilities and failings. Now, when he looks in
the mirror, he asks himself, "Is this really me?"—or he avoids the
mirror out of distress at what it reveals, those bags and wrinkles.
In his new makeup he is called upon to play a new role in a play
that must be improvised. André Gide, that long-lived man of letters, wrote in his journal, "My heart has remained so young that I
have the continual feeling of playing a part, the part of the 70-
year-old that I certainly am; and the infirmities and weaknesses

that remind me of my age act like a prompter, reminding me of my lines when I tend to stray. Then, like the good actor I want to be, I go back into my role, and I pride myself on playing it well."

In his new role the old person will find that he is tempted by   10
new vices, that he receives new compensations (not so widely known), and that he may possibly achieve new virtues. Chief among these is the heroic or merely obstinate refusal to surrender in the face of time. One admires the ships that go down with all flags flying and the captain on the bridge.

Among the vices of age are avarice, untidiness, and vanity,   11
which last takes the form of a craving to be loved or simply admired. Avarice is the worst of those three. Why do so many old persons, men and women alike, insist on hoarding money when they have no prospect of using it and even when they have no heirs? They eat the cheapest food, buy no clothes, and live in a single room when they could afford better lodging. It may be that they regard money as a form of power; there is a comfort in watching it accumulate while other powers are dwindling away. How often we read of an old person found dead in a hovel, on a mattress partly stuffed with bankbooks and stock certificates! The bankbook syndrome, we call it in our family, which has never succumbed.

Untidiness we call the Langley Collyer syndrome. To explain,   12
Langley Collyer was a former concert pianist who lived alone with his 70-year-old brother in a brownstone house on upper Fifth Avenue. The once fashionable neighborhood had become part of Harlem. Homer, the brother, had been an admiralty lawyer, but was now blind and partly paralyzed; Langley played for him and fed him on buns and oranges, which he thought would restore Homer's sight. He never threw away a daily paper because Homer, he said, might want to read them all. He saved other things as well and the house became filled with rubbish from roof to basement. The halls were lined on both sides with bundled newspapers, leaving narrow passageways in which Langley had devised booby traps to catch intruders.

On March 21, 1947, some unnamed person telephoned the   13
police to report that there was a dead body in the Collyer house. The police broke down the front door and found the hall impassable; then they hoisted a ladder to a second-story window. Behind it Homer was lying on the floor in a bathrobe; he had

starved to death. Langley had disappeared. After some delay, the police broke into the basement, chopped a hole in the roof, and began throwing junk out of the house, top and bottom. It was 18 days before they found Langley's body, gnawed by rats. Caught in one of his own booby traps, he had died in a hallway just outside Homer's door. By that time the police had collected, and the Department of Sanitation had hauled away, 120 tons of rubbish, including, besides the newspapers, 14 grand pianos and the parts of a dismantled Model T Ford.

Why do so many old people accumulate junk, not on the scale   14 of Langley Collyer, but still in a dismaying fashion? Their tables are piled high with it, their bureau drawers are stuffed with it, their closet rods bend with the weight of clothes not worn for years. I suppose that the piling up is partly from lethargy and partly from feeling that everything once useful, including their own bodies, should be preserved. Others, though not so many, have such a fear of becoming Langley Collyers that they strive to be painfully neat. Every tool they own is in its place, though it will never be used again; every scrap of paper is filed away in alphabetical order. At last their immoderate neatness becomes another vice of age, if a milder one.

The vanity of older people is an easier weakness to explain,   15 and to condone. With less to look forward to, they yearn for recognition of what they have been: the reigning beauty, the athlete, the soldier, the scholar. It is the beauties who have the hardest time. A portrait of themselves at twenty hangs on the wall, and they try to resemble it by making an extravagant use of creams, powder, and dyes. Being young at heart, they think they are merely revealing their essential persons. The athletes find shelves for their silver trophies, which are polished once a year. Perhaps a letter sweater lies wrapped in a bureau drawer. I remember one evening when a no–longer athlete had guests for dinner and tried to find his sweater. "Oh, that old thing," his wife said. "The moths got into it and I threw it away." The athlete sulked and his guests went home early.

But there are also pleasures of the body, or the mind, that are   16 enjoyed by a greater number of older persons. Those pleasures include some that younger people find hard to appreciate. One of them is simply sitting still, like a snake on a sunwarmed stone, with a delicious feeling of indolence that was seldom attained in earlier years. A leaf flutters down; a cloud moves by inches across the horizon. At such moments the older person, completely relaxed, has become a part of nature—and a living part, with blood coursing through his veins. The future does not exist for him. He thinks, if he thinks at all, that life for younger persons is still a battle royal of each against each, but that now he has nothing more to win or lose. He is not so much above as outside the battle, as if he had assumed the uniform of some small neutral country, perhaps Liechtenstein or Andorra. From a distance he notes that some of the combatants, men or women, are jostling ahead—but why do they fight so hard when the most they can hope for is a longer obituary? He can watch the scrounging and gouging, he can hear the shouts of exultation, the moans of the gravely wounded, and meanwhile he feels secure; nobody will attack him from ambush.

Age has other physical compensations besides the nirvana of dozing in the sun. A few of the simplest needs become a pleasure to satisfy. When an old woman in a nursing home was asked what she really liked to do she answered in one word: "Eat." She might have been speaking for many of her fellows. Meals in a nursing home, however badly cooked, serve as climactic moments of the day. The physical essence of the pensioners is being renewed at an appointed hour; now they can go back to meditating or to watching TV while looking forward to the next meal. They can also look forward to sleep, which has become a definite pleasure, not the mere interruption it once had been. **17**

Here I am thinking of old persons under nursing care. Others ferociously guard their independence, and some of them suffer less than one might expect from being lonely and impoverished. They can be rejoiced by visits and meetings, but they also have company inside their heads. Some of them are busiest when their hands are still. What passes through the minds of many is a stream of persons, images, phrases, and familiar tunes. For some that stream has continued since childhood, but now it is deeper; it is their present and their past combined. At times they conduct silent dialogues with a vanished friend, and these are less tiring— often more rewarding—than spoken conversations. If inner resources are lacking, old persons living alone may seek comfort **18** and a kind of companionship in the bottle. I should judge from the gossip of various neighborhoods that the outer suburbs from Boston to San Diego are full of secretly alcoholic widows. One of those widows, an old friend, was moved from her apartment into a retirement home. She left behind her a closet in which the floor was covered wall to wall with whiskey bottles. "Oh, those empty bottles!" she explained. "They were left by a former tenant."

Not whiskey or cooking sherry but simply giving up is the greatest temptation of age. It is something different from a stoical acceptance of infirmities, which is something to be admired.   19

The givers-up see no reason for working. Sometimes they lie in bed all day when moving about would still be possible, if difficult. I had a friend, a distinguished poet, who surrendered in that fashion. The doctors tried to stir him to action, but he refused to leave his room. Another friend, once a successful artist, stopped painting when his eyes began to fail. His doctor made the mistake of telling him that he suffered from a fatal disease. He then lost interest in everything except the splendid Rolls-Royce, acquired in his prosperous days, that stood in the garage. Daily he wiped the dust from its hood. He couldn't drive it on the road any longer, but he used to sit in the driver's seat, start the motor, then back the Rolls out of the garage and drive it in again, back twenty feet and forward twenty feet; that was his only distraction.   20

I haven't the right to blame those who surrender, not being able to put myself inside their minds or bodies. Often they must have compelling reasons, physical or moral. Not only do they suffer from a variety of ailments, but also they are made to feel that they no longer have a function in the community. Their families and neighbors don't ask them for advice, don't really listen when they speak, don't call on them for efforts. One notes that there are not a few recoveries from apparent senility when that situation changes. If it doesn't change, old persons may decide that efforts are useless. I sympathize with their problems, but the men and women I envy are those who accept old age as a series of challenges.   21

For such persons, every new infirmity is an enemy to be outwitted, an obstacle to be overcome by force of will. They enjoy each little victory over themselves, and sometimes they win a major success. Renoir was one of them. He continued painting, and magnificently, for years after he was crippled by arthritis;   22 the brush had to be strapped to his arm. "You don't need your hand to paint," he said. Goya was another of the unvanquished. At 72 he retired as an official painter of the Spanish court and decided to work only for himself. His later years were those of the famous "black paintings" in which he let his imagination run (and also of the lithographs, then a new technique). At 78 he escaped a reign of terror in Spain by fleeing to Bordeaux. He was deaf and his eyes were failing; in order to work he had to wear several pairs of spectacles, one over another, and then use a magnifying glass; but he was producing splendid work in a totally new style. At 80 he drew an ancient man propped on two sticks, with a mass of white hair and beard hiding his face and with the inscription "I am still learning."

"Eighty years old!" the great Catholic poet Paul Claudel wrote   23
in his journal. "No eyes left, no ears, no teeth, no legs, no wind! And when all is said and done, how astonishingly well one does without them!"

UNDERSTANDING DETAILS

1. Name five ways, according to Cowley, that people begin to realize they are "old." How did Cowley himself learn that he was old?
2. List three vices of old age, and explain them as Cowley sees them.
3. What are three compensations of advancing age? In what ways are these activities pleasurable?
4. What does Cowley mean in paragraph 15 by "the vanity of older people"? How do older people manifest this vanity?

ANALYZING MEANING

1. What does the wagon symbolize in the author's poem about aging (paragraph 8)? What purpose does this poem serve in the essay?
2. For older people, what is the value of the conversations, images, friends, relatives, and melodies that pass through their minds? How might the elderly use these distractions constructively?
3. According to this essay, what qualities characterize those people who "surrender" (paragraph 21) to old age and those who

"accept old age as a series of challenges" (paragraph 21)? Why do you think Cowley has more respect for the latter group?

4. What is Cowley's general attitude toward "the country of age"? Why does he feel that way about this stage of life?

DISCOVERING RHETORICAL STRATEGIES

1. After reading this essay, try to summarize in a single word or phrase Cowley's impressions of old age. How does this dominant impression help the author organize the many different details presented in his essay?

2. Why did Cowley include the reference to the Ojibwas at the end of the first paragraph? What effect does that anecdote have on our sympathies as readers?

3. Cowley uses a number of distinct metaphors in describing old age. He equates being old, for example, with acting out a certain "role" in life. He also portrays aging as a "rite of passage," a "challenge," and an "unfamiliar country" through which we must travel. In what sense is each of these metaphors appropriate? How does each help us understand the process of growing old?

4. Cowley uses language to describe a state of being that most of us are not familiar with yet. What other rhetorical strategies does he call upon to make his descriptive essay effective? Give examples of each.

MAKING CONNECTIONS

1. What are the primary differences between the sexism described by Alleen Pace Nilsen ("Sexism in English: A 1990s Update") and Judy Brady ("Why I Want a Wife"), the racism explained by Lewis Sawaquat ("For My Indian Daughter") and Harry Edwards ("Triple Tragedy in Black Society"), and/or the "ageism" recounted by Malcolm Cowley? Is one of these "isms" more dangerous than the others? Have you ever experienced any of these types of prejudice?

2. Compare and contrast the weaknesses of old age depicted in Cowley's essay with those portrayed by Fred Brown in John McPhee's "The Pines" or by the grandfather in Ray Bradbury's "Summer Rituals." Do you know anyone in his or her eight-

ies? How does that person act? How do you think you will behave when you are that old?

3. How is Cowley's description of the "identity crisis" many older people go through similar to the identity crisis Lewis Sawaquat ("For My Indian Daughter") suffered when he discovered his Native American heritage and Richard Rodriguez ("The Fear of Losing a Culture") went through when he immigrated to America? Have you ever gone through an identity crisis? How did you resolve it? Was your crisis like those described by Cowley, Sawaquat, or Rodriguez in any way?

IDEAS FOR DISCUSSION/WRITING

Preparing to Write

Write freely about your impressions of one or more older people in your life: Who are they? What characteristics do they share? How are they different from each other? Different from you? Similar to you? How do you know they are "old"?

Choosing a Topic

1. Cowley explains at the outset of his essay that "the country of age is a new experience, different from what you supposed it to be. Nobody, man or woman, knows the country until he has lived in it and has taken out his citizenship papers" (paragraph 3). Interview an older person to discover his or her view of "the country of age." Then write an essay for your peers describing that person's opinions.

2. In his essay, Cowley describes the signals he receives from his body and his environment that tell him he is "old." What messages did you receive when you were young that indicated you were a "child"? What messages do you receive now that remind you of your present age? How are these messages different from those you received when you were a child? Describe these signals in a well-developed essay addressed to your classmates.

3. Do you think that Americans treat their aged with enough respect? Explain your answer in detail to an older person. Describe various situations that support your opinion.

2

Narration

Telling a Story

A good story is a powerful method of getting someone's attention. The excitement that accompanies a suspenseful ghost story, a lively anecdote, or a vivid joke easily attests to this effect. In fact, narration is one of the earliest verbal skills we all learn as children, providing us with a convenient, logical, and easily understood means of sharing our thoughts with other people. Storytelling is powerful because it offers us a way of dramatizing our ideas so that others can identify with them.

DEFINING NARRATION

Narration involves telling a story that is often based on personal experience. Stories can be oral or written, real or imaginary, short or long. A good story, however, always has a point or purpose. It can be the dominant mode (as in a novel or short story), supported by other rhetorical strategies, or it can serve the purpose of another rhetorical mode (as in a persuasive essay, a historical survey, or a scientific report).

In its subordinate role, narration can provide examples or explain ideas. If asked why you are attending college, for instance, you might turn to narration to make your answer clear, beginning with a story about your family's hardships in the past. The purpose of telling such a story would be to help your listeners appreciate your need for higher education by encouraging them to understand and identify with your family history.

Unlike description, which generally portrays people, places, and objects in *space*, narration asks the reader to follow a series of actions through a particular *time* sequence. Description often complements the movement of narration, though. People must be depicted, for instance, along with their relationships to one another, before their actions can have any real meaning for us; similarly, places must be described so that we can picture the setting and understand the activities in a specific scene. The organization of the action and the time spent on each episode in a story should be based principally on a writer's analysis of the interests and needs of his or her audience.

To be most effective, narration should prolong the exciting parts of a story and shorten the routine facts that simply move the reader from one episode to another. If you were robbed on your way to work, for example, a good narrative describing the incident would concentrate on the traumatic event itself rather than on such mundane and boring details as what you had for breakfast and what clothes you had put on prior to the attack. Finally, just like description, narration *shows* rather than *tells* its purpose to the audience. The factual statement "I was robbed this morning" could be made much more vivid and dramatic through the addition of some simple narration: "As I was walking to work at 7:30 A.M., a huge and angry-looking man ran up to me, thrust a gun into the middle of my stomach, and took my money, my new wristwatch, all my credit cards, and my pants—leaving me penniless and embarrassed."

The following paragraph written by a student recounts a recent parachuting experience. As you read this narrative, notice especially the writer's use of vivid detail to *show* rather than *tell* her message to the readers.

I have always needed occasional "fixes" of excitement in my life, so when I realized one spring day that I was more than ordinarily bored, I made up my mind to take more than ordinary steps to relieve that boredom. I decided to go parachuting. The next thing I knew, I was stuffed into a claustrophobically small plane with five other terrified people, rolling down a bumpy, rural runway, droning my way to 3,500 feet and an exhilarating experience. Once over the jump area, I waited my turn, stepped onto the strut, held my breath, and then kicked off into the cold, rushing air as my heart pounded heavily. All I could think was, "I hope this damn para-chute opens!" The sensation of falling backward through space was unfamiliar and disconcerting till my chute opened with a loud "pop," momentarily pulling me upward toward the distant sky. After several minutes of floating downward, I landed rudely on the hard ground. Life, I remembered happily, could be awfully exciting. And a month later, when my tailbone had stopped throbbing, I still felt that way.

THINKING CRITICALLY BY USING NARRATION

Rhetorical modes offer us different ways of perceiving reality. Narration is an especially useful tool for sequencing or putting details and information in some kind of logical order, usually chronological. Working with narration helps us see clear sequences separate from all other mental functions.

Practicing exercises in narrative techniques can help you see clear patterns in topics you are writing about. Although narration is usually used in conjunction with other rhetorical modes, we are going to isolate it here so that you can appreciate its specific mechanics separately from other mental activities. If you feel the process of narration in your head, you are more likely to understand exactly what it entails and thus to use it more effectively in reading other essays and in organizing and writing your own essays.

For the best results, we will once again single out narration and do some warm-up exercises to make your sequencing perceptions as accurate and successful as possible. In this way, you will actually learn to feel how your mind works in this particular mode and then be more aware of the thinking strategies available to you in your own reading and writing. As you become more conscious of the mechanics of the individual rhetorical modes, you will naturally become more adept at combining them to accomplish the specific purpose and the related effect you want to create.

The following exercises, which require a combination of thinking and writing skills, will help you practice this particular strategy in isolation. Just as in a physical workout, we will warm up your mental capabilities one by one as if they were muscles that can be developed individually before being used together in harmony.

1. Make a chronological list of the different activities you did yesterday, from waking in the morning to sleeping at night. Randomly pick two events from your day, and treat them as the highlights of your day. Now, write freely for five minutes, explaining the story of your day and emphasizing the importance of these two highlights.
2. Recall an important event that happened to you between the ages of five and ten. Brainstorm about how this event made you feel at the time it happened. Then, brainstorm about how this event makes you feel now. What changes have you discovered in your view of this event?
3. Create a myth or story that illustrates a belief or idea that you think is important. You might begin with a moral that you believe in and then compose a story that "teaches" or demonstrates that moral.

READING AND WRITING NARRATIVE ESSAYS

To read a narrative essay most effectively, you should spend your time concentrating on the writer's main story line and use of details. To create an effective story, you have some important decisions to make before you write and certain variables to control as you actually draft your narrative.

During the prewriting stage, you need to generate ideas and choose a point of view through which your story will be presented. Then, as you write, the preliminary decisions you have made regarding the selection and arrangement of your details (especially important in a narrative) will allow your story to flow more easily. Carefully controlled organization, along with appropriate timing and pacing, can influence your audience's reactions in very powerful ways.

How to Read a Narrative Essay

Preparing to Read. As you prepare to read the narratives in this chapter, try to guess what each title tells you about its essay's topic and about the author's attitude toward that topic: Can you tell, for example, what Lewis Sawaquat feels toward his daughter from his title "For My Indian Daughter" or what George Orwell's attitude is toward the events described in "Shooting an Elephant"? Also, scan the essay and read its synopsis in the

Rhetorical Table of Contents to help you anticipate as much as you can about the author's purpose and audience.

The more you learn from the biography about the author and the circumstances surrounding the composition of a particular essay, the better prepared you will be to read the essay. For a narrative essay, the writer's point of view or perspective toward the story and its characters is especially significant. From the biographies, can you determine Orwell's reason for writing his essay or Maya Angelou's attitude toward Annie Johnson's energy and determination in "New Directions"? What is Russell Baker's opinion of his mother in "The Saturday Evening Post"?

Last, before you begin to read, answer the Preparing to Read questions and then try to generate some of your own inquiries on the general subject of the essay: What do you want to know about being a Native American (Sawaquat)? What childhood experience greatly affected your life (Baker)? What do you think of British Imperialism (Orwell)?

Reading. As you read a narrative essay for the first time, simply follow the story line and try to get a general sense of the narrative and of the author's general purpose. Is Orwell's purpose to make us feel sympathetic or antagonistic toward his role in shooting the elephant? Is Baker trying to encourage us all to be writers or simply to help us understand why he writes? Record your initial reactions to each essay as they occur to you.

Based on the biographical information preceding the essay and on the essay's tone, purpose, and audience, try to create a context for the narrative as you read. How do such details help you understand your reading material more thoroughly? A first reading of this sort, along with a survey of the questions that follow the essay, will help prepare you for a critical understanding of the material when you read it for the second time.

Rereading. As you reread these narrative essays, notice the author's selection and arrangement of details. Why does Orwell organize his story one way and Baker another? What effect does their organization create?

Also, pay attention to the timing and the pacing of the story line. What do the long descriptions of Annie's plans add to Angelou's "New Directions"? What does the quick pace of Keillor's narrative communicate?

In addition, consider at this point what other rhetorical strategies the authors use to support their narratives. Which writers use examples to supplement their stories? Which use definitions? Which use comparisons? Why do they use these strategies?

Finally, when you answer the questions after each essay, you can check your understanding of the material on different levels before you tackle the discussion/writing topics that follow. For a general checklist of reading guidelines, please see pages 20–21 of the Introduction.

How to Write a Narrative Essay

Preparing to Write. First, you should answer the prewriting questions to help you generate thoughts on the subject at hand. Next, as in all writing, you should explore your subject matter and discover as many specific details as possible. (See pages 21–23 of the Introduction for a discussion of prewriting techniques.) Some writers rely on the familiar journalistic checklist of Who, What, When, Where, Why, and How to make sure they cover all aspects of their narrative. If you were using the story of a basketball game at your college to demonstrate the team spirit of your school, for example, you might want to consider telling your readers *who* played in the game and/or *who* attended; *what* happened before, during, and after the game; *when* and *where* it took place; *why* it was being played (or *why* these particular teams were playing each other or *why* the game was especially important); and *how* the winning basket was shot. Freewriting or a combination of freewriting and the journalistic questions is another effective way of getting ideas and story details on paper for use in a first draft.

Once you have generated these ideas, you should always let your purpose and audience ultimately guide your selection of details, but the process of gathering such journalistic information gives you some material from which to choose. You will also need to decide whether to include dialogue in your narrative. Again, the difference here is between *showing* and *telling*: Will your audience benefit from reading what was actually said, word for word, during a discussion, or will a brief description of the conversation be sufficiently effective? In fact, all the choices you make at this stage of the composing process will give you material with which to create emphasis, suspense, conflict, and interest in your subject.

Next, you must decide upon the point of view that will most readily help you achieve your purpose with your specific audience. Point of view includes the (1) person, (2) vantage point, and (3) attitude of your narrator. *Person* refers to who will tell the story: an uninvolved observer, a character in the narrative, or an omniscient (all-seeing) narrator. This initial decision will guide your thoughts on *vantage point*, which is the frame of reference of the narrator: close to the action, far from the action, looking back on the past, or reporting on the present. Finally, your narrator will naturally have an *attitude*, or *personal feeling*, about the subject: accepting, hostile, sarcastic, indifferent, angry, pleased, or any of a number of similar emotions. Once you adopt a certain perspective in a story, you must follow it for the duration of the narrative. This consistency will bring focus and coherence to the story.

Writing. After you have explored your topic and adopted a particular point of view, you need to write a thesis statement and to select and arrange the details of your story coherently so that the narrative has a clear beginning, middle, and end. The most natural way to organize the events of a narrative, of course, is chronologically. In your story about the school basketball game, you would probably narrate the relevant details in the order they occurred (i.e., sequentially, from the beginning of the game to its conclusion). More experienced writers may elect to use flashbacks: An athlete might recall a significant event that happened during the game, or a coach might recollect the contest's turning point. Your most important consideration is that the elements of a story follow some sort of time sequence, aided by the use of clear and logical transitions (e.g., "then," "next," "at this point," "suddenly") that help the reader move smoothly from one event to the next.

Rewriting. As you reread the narrative you have written, pretend you are a reader and make sure you have told the story from the most effective point of view, considering both your purpose and your audience:

Is your purpose (or thesis) clearly stated?

Who is your audience?

Will your readers identify with your narrator?

106

To what extent does this narrator help you achieve your purpose? Is the narrator's attitude appropriate to your subject?

Further, as you reread, make certain you can follow the events of the story as they are related:

Does one event lead naturally to the next?

Are all the events relevant to your purpose?

Will these events interest your audience?

Have you chosen appropriate details to enhance the story?

Do you show rather than tell your message?

For more advice on writing and editing, see pages 32–33.

STUDENT ESSAY: NARRATION AT WORK

The following essay characterizes the writer's mother by telling a story about an unusual family vacation. As you read it, notice that the student writer states her purpose clearly and succinctly in the first paragraph. She then becomes an integral part of her story as she carefully selects examples and details that help convey her thesis.

A Vacation with My Mother

First-person narrator   I had an interesting childhood—not because of where I grew up and not because I ever did anything particularly adventuresome or thrilling. In fact, I don't think my life seemed especially interesting to me at the time. But now, telling friends about my supposedly ordinary childhood, I notice an array of responses ranging from astonishment to hilarity. The source of their surprise and amusement is my mother— gracious, charming, sweet, and totally out of synchronization with the rest of the world. One strange family trip we took when I was eleven captures the essence of her zaniness.

General subject

Specific subject

Thesis statement

My two sets of grandparents lived in Colorado and North Dakota, respectively, and my parents decided we would spend a few weeks driving to those states and seeing all the sights along the relaxed and rambling way. My eight-year-old brother, David, and I had some serious reservations. If Dad had ever had Mom drive him to school, we reasoned, he'd never even consider letting her help drive us anywhere out of town, let alone out of California. If we weren't paying attention, we were as likely to end up at her office or the golf course as we were to arrive at school. Sometimes she'd drop us off at a friend's house to play and then forget where she'd left us. The notion of going on a long trip with her was really unnerving.

How can I explain my mother to a stranger? Have you ever watched reruns of the old *I Love Lucy* with Lucille Ball? I did as a child, and I thought Lucy Ricardo was normal. I lived with somebody a lot like her. Now, Mom wasn't a redhead (not usually, anyway), and Dad wasn't a Cuban nightclub owner, but at home we had the same situation of a loving but bemused husband trying to deal with the off-the-wall logic and enthusiasm of a frequently exasperating wife. We all adored her, but we had to admit it: Mom was a flaky, absent-minded, genuine eccentric.

As the first day of our trip approached, David and I reluctantly said good-bye to all of our friends. Who knew if we'd ever see any of them again? Finally, the moment of our departure arrived, and we loaded suitcases, books, games, some camping gear, and a tent into the car and bravely drove off. We bravely drove off again two hours later after we'd returned home to get the

Margin notes:

Narrator's attitude

Examples

Transition

Narrator's vantage point

Transition

Careful selection of details

purse and traveler's checks that Mom had forgotten.

David and I were always a little nervous when using gas station bathrooms if Mom was driving while Dad napped: "You stand outside the door and play lookout while I go, and I'll stand outside the door and play lookout while you go." I had terrible visions: "Honey, where are the kids?" "What?! Oh, gosh . . . I thought they were being awfully quiet. Uh . . . Idaho?" We were never actually abandoned in a strange city, but we weren't about to take any chances.

On the fourth or fifth night of the trip, we had trouble finding a motel with a vacancy. After driving futilely for an hour, Mom suddenly had a great idea: Why didn't we find a house with a likely-looking back yard and ask if we could pitch our tent there? To her, the scheme was eminently reasonable. Vowing quietly to each other to hide in the back seat if she did it, David and I groaned in anticipated mortification. To our profound relief, Dad vetoed the idea. Mom never could understand our objections. If a strange family showed up on her front doorstep, Mom would have been delighted. She thinks everyone in the world is as nice as she is. We finally found a vacancy in the next town. David and I were thrilled—the place featured bungalows in the shape of Native American tepees.

The Native-American motif must have reminded my parents that we had not yet used the brand-new tent, Coleman stove, portable mattress, and other camping gear we had brought. We headed to a national park the next day and found a campsite by a lake. It took hours to figure out how to get the tent up: It was one of those deluxe

Margin notes: Use of dialogue · Examples · Transition · Passage of time · Example · Transition · Chronological order · Careful selection of details

models with mosquito-net windows, canvas floors, and enough room for three large families to sleep in. It was after dark before we finally got it erected, and the night had turned quite cold. We fixed a hurried campfire dinner (chicken burned on the outside and raw in the middle) and prepared to go to sleep. That was when we realized that Mom had forgotten to bring along some important pieces of equipment—our sleeping bags. The four of us huddled together on our thin mattresses under the carpet from the station-wagon floor. That ended our camping days. Give me a stucco tepee any time.

We drove through several states and saw lots of great sights along the way: the Grand Canyon, Carlsbad Caverns, caves, mountains, waterfalls, even a haunted house. David and I were excited and amazed at all the wonders we found, and Mom was just as enthralled as we were. Her constant pleasure and sense of the world as a beautiful, magical place was infectious. I never realized until I grew up how really childlike—in the best sense of the word— my mother actually is. She is innocent, optimistic, and always ready to be entertained.

Examples (spatial order)

Transition Looking back on that long-past family vacation, I now realize that my childhood was more special because I grew up with a mother who wasn't afraid to try anything and who taught me to look at the world as a series of marvelous opportunities to be explored. What did it matter that she thought England was bordered by Germany? We were never going to try to drive there. So what if she was always leaving her car keys in the refrigerator or some

Narrator's attitude

Examples

Concluding remark
> other equally inexplicable place? In the end,
> we always got where we were going—and
> we generally had a grand time along the
> way.

Student Writer's Comments

I enjoyed writing about this childhood vacation because of all the memories it brought back. I knew I wanted to write a narrative to explain my mother, and the word *zany* immediately popped into my mind. So I knew what my focus was going to be from the outset. My prewriting started in my head as soon as I found this angle. So many thoughts and memories rushed into my head that I couldn't even get to a piece of paper to write them down before I lost some of them. But there were way too many to put into one essay. The hardest part of writing this narrative was trying to decide what material to use and what to leave out. Spending a little more time before writing my first draft proved to be a good investment in this case. I got a clean piece of paper and began freewriting, trying to mold some of my scattered ideas from brainstorming into a coherent, readable form. During this second stage of prewriting, I remembered one special vacation we took that I thought might capture the essence of my mother—and also of my family.

My first draft was about three times the length of this one. My point of view was the innocent participant/observer who came to know and love her mother for her absent-mindedness. I had really developed my thesis from the time I got this writing assignment. And I told my story chronologically except for looking back in the last paragraph when I attempted to analyze the entire experience. I had no trouble *showing* rather than *telling* because all of the details were so vivid to me—as if they had happened yesterday. But that was my downfall. I soon realized that I could not possibly include everything that was on the pages of my first draft.

The process of cranking out my rough draft made my point of view toward life with my mother very clear to me and helped me face the cutting that was ahead of me. I took the raw material of a very lengthy first draft and forced myself to choose the details and examples that best characterized my mother and what life was like growing up under the care of such a lovely but daffy individual. The sense of her being both "lovely" and "daffy" was the insight that helped me the most in revising the content of my essay. I made myself ruthlessly eliminate anything that interfered with the overall effect I was trying to create—from extraneous images and details to words and phrases that didn't contribute to this specific view of my mom.

The final result, according to my classmates, communicated my message clearly and efficiently. The main criticism I got from my class was that I might have cut too much from my first draft. But I think this focused picture with a few highlights conveys my meaning in the best possible way. I offered enough details to *show* rather than *tell* my readers what living with my mother was like, but not too many to bore them. I was also able to take the time in my essay to be humorous now and then ("David and I reluctantly said good-bye to all of our friends. Who knew if we'd ever see any of them again?" and "Give me a stucco tepee any time."), as well as pensive and serious ("I now realize that my childhood was more special because I grew up with a mother who wasn't afraid to try anything and who taught me to look at the world as a series of marvelous opportunities to be explored."). Even though in looking at the essay now I would tamper with a few things, I am generally happy with the final draft. It captures the essence of my mother from my point of view, and it also gave my class a few laughs. Aren't the readers' reactions the ultimate test of a good story?

SOME FINAL THOUGHTS ON NARRATION

Just as with other modes of writing, all decisions regarding narration should be made with a specific purpose and an intended audience constantly in mind. As you will see, each narrative in this section is directed at a clearly defined audience. Notice, as you read, how each writer manipulates the various features of narration so that the readers are simultaneously caught up in the plot and deeply moved to feel, act, think, and believe the writer's personal opinions.

LEWIS SAWAQUAT (1935 –)

■ ■ ■

For My Indian Daughter

Lewis Sawaquat is a Native American who recently retired from his thirty-year job as a surveyor for the Soil Conservation Service of the United States Department of Agriculture. He was born in Harbor Springs, Michigan, where his great-grandfather was the last official "chief" of the region. After finishing high school, Sawaquat entered the army, graduated from Army Survey School, and then completed a tour of duty in Korea. Upon returning to America, he enrolled in the Art Institute of Chicago to study commercial art. Sawaquat now lives in Interlochen, Michigan, where his hobbies include gardening, swimming, and walking in the woods. He also helps support the Native-American Scholarship Program at the Pathfinder's School in his hometown and serves as a pipe carrier and cultural/spiritual adviser to his Ottawa tribe. Now that he is retired, he hopes to write a book entitled *Dreams: The Universal Language*, which will investigate the Native-American approach to dream interpretation. His advice to students using *The Prose Reader* is to "pay attention to life; there's nothing more important to becoming a writer."

Preparing to Read

"For My Indian Daughter" originally appeared in the "My Turn" column of *Newsweek* magazine (September 5, 1983) under the author's former name, Lewis Johnson. In his article, the author speaks eloquently of prejudice, ethnic pride, and growing cultural awareness. Before reading this selection, think for a few minutes about your own heritage: What is your ethnic identity? Are you content with this background? Have you ever gone through an identity crisis? Do you anticipate facing any problems because of your ancestry? If so, how will you handle these problems when they occur?

M y little girl is singing herself to sleep upstairs, her voice   1
mingling with the sounds of the birds outside in the
old maple trees. She is two and I am nearly 50, and I
am very taken with her. She came along late in my life, unexpected and unbidden, a startling gift.

Today at the beach my chubby-legged, brown-skinned daugh-   2
ter ran laughing into the water as fast as she could. My wife and I
laughed watching her, until we heard behind us a low guttural
curse and then an unpleasant voice raised in an imitation war
whoop.

I turned to see a fat man in a bathing suit, white and soft as a   3
grub, as he covered his mouth and prepared to make the Indian
war cry again. He was middle-aged, younger than I, and had three
little children lined up next to him, grinning foolishly. My wife
suggested we leave the beach, and I agreed.

I knew the man was not unusual in his feelings against   4
Indians. His beach behavior might have been socially unacceptable to more civilized whites, but his basic view of Indians is expressed daily in our small town, frequently on the editorial pages
of the county newspaper, as white people speak out against
Indian fishing rights and land rights, saying in essence, "Those
Indians are taking our fish, our land." It doesn't matter to them
that we were here first, that the U.S. Supreme Court has ruled in
our favor. It matters to them that we have something they want,
and they hate us for it. Backlash is the common explanation of
the attacks on Indians, the bumper stickers that say, "Spear an
Indian, Save a Fish," but I know better. The hatred of Indians
goes back to the beginning when white people came to this
country. For me it goes back to my childhood in Harbor
Springs, Mich.

Theft. Harbor Springs is now a summer resort for the very af-   5
fluent, but a hundred years ago it was the Indian village of my
Ottawa ancestors. My grandmother, Anna Showanessy, and other
Indians like her, had their land there taken by treaty, by fraud, by
violence, by theft. They remembered how whites had burned
down the village at Burt Lake in 1900 and pushed the Indians
out. These were the stories in my family.

When I was a boy my mother told me to walk down the alleys   6
in Harbor Springs and not to wear my orange football sweater

out of the house. This way I would not stand out, not be noticed, and not be a target.

I wore my orange sweater anyway and deliberately avoided the 7 alleys. I was the biggest person I knew and wasn't really afraid. But I met my comeuppance when I enlisted in the U.S. Army. One night all the men in my barracks gathered together and, gang-fashion, pulled me into the shower and scrubbed me down with rough brushes used for floors, saying, "We won't have any dirty Indians in our outfit." It is a point of irony that I was cleaner than any of them. Later in Korea I learned how to kill, how to bully, how to hate Koreans. I came out of the war tougher than ever and, strangely, white.

I went to college, got married, lived in La Porte, Ind., worked 8 as a surveyor and raised three boys. I headed Boy Scout groups, never thinking it odd when the Scouts did imitation Indian dances, imitation Indian lore.

One day when I was 35 or thereabouts I heard about an 9 Indian powwow. My father used to attend them and so with great curiosity and a strange joy at discovering a part of my heritage, I decided the thing to do to get ready for this big event was to have my friend make me a spear in his forge. The steel was fine and blue and iridescent. The feathers on the shaft were bright and proud.

In a dusty state fairground in southern Indiana, I found white 10 people dressed as Indians. I learned they were "hobbyists," that is, it was their hobby and leisure pastime to masquerade as Indians on weekends. I felt ridiculous with my spear, and I left.

It was years before I could tell anyone of the embarrassment of 11 this weekend and see any humor in it. But in a way it was that weekend, for all its silliness, that was my awakening. I realized I didn't know who I was. I didn't have an Indian name. I didn't speak the Indian language. I didn't know the Indian customs. Dimly I remembered the Ottawa word for dog, but it was a baby word, *kahgee*, not the full word, *muhkahgee*, which I was later to learn. Even more hazily I remembered a naming ceremony (my own). I remembered legs dancing around me, dust. Where had that been? Who had I been? "Sawaquat," my mother told me when I asked, "where the tree begins to grow."

That was 1968, and I was not the only Indian in the country 12 who was feeling the need to remember who he or she was. There were others. They had powwows, real ones, and eventually I found them. Together we researched our past, a search that for me culminated in the Longest Walk, a march on Washington in 1978. Maybe because I now know what it means to be Indian, it surprises me that others don't. Of course there aren't very many of us left. The chances of an average person knowing an average Indian in an average lifetime are pretty slim.

Circle. Still, I was amused one day when my small, four-year- 13 old neighbor looked at me as I was hoeing in my garden and said, "You aren't a real Indian, are you?" Scotty is little, talkative, likable. Finally I said, "I'm a real Indian." He looked at me for a moment and then said, squinting into the sun, "Then where's your horse and feathers?" The child was simply a smaller, whiter version of my own ignorant self years before. We'd both seen too much TV, that's all. He was not to be blamed. And so, in a way, the moronic man on the beach today is blameless. We come full circle to realize other people are like ourselves, as discomfiting as that may be sometimes.

As I sit in my old chair on my porch, in a light that is fading 14 so the leaves are barely distinguishable against the sky, I can picture my girl asleep upstairs. I would like to prepare her for what's to come, take her each step of the way saying, there's a place to avoid, here's what I know about this, but much of what's before her she must go through alone. She must pass through pain and joy and solitude and community to discover her own inner self that is unlike any other and come through that passage to the place where she sees all people are one, and in so seeing may live her life in a brighter future.

UNDERSTANDING DETAILS

1. What is the principal point of this essay by Sawaquat? How many different stories does the author tell to make this point?
2. What does Sawaquat see as the origin of the hatred of Native Americans in the United States?
3. What does Sawaquat learn from his first powwow (paragraphs 9 and 10)?
4. How does Sawaquat discover his original identity? In what way does this knowledge change him?

ANALYZING MEANING

1. Why does Sawaquat begin this essay with the story about his daughter on the beach? How does the story make you feel?
2. Why do thoughts about his daughter prompt Sawaquat's memories of his own identity crisis? What does the author's identity have to do with his daughter?
3. The author calls paragraphs 5–12 "Theft" and paragraphs 13–14 "Circle." Explain these two subtitles from the author's point of view?
4. Why do you think Sawaquat says that his daughter "must pass through pain and joy and solitude and community to discover her own inner self" (paragraph 14)? To what extent do we all need to do this in our lives?

DISCOVERING RHETORICAL STRATEGIES

1. Sawaquat occasionally uses dialogue to help make his points. What does the dialogue add to the various narratives he cites here?
2. Describe as thoroughly as possible the point of view of Sawaquat's narrator. Include in your answer a discussion of person, vantage point, and attitude.
3. Why do you think Sawaquat divides his essay into three sections? Why do you think he spends most of his time on the second section?
4. Although Sawaquat uses primarily narration to advance his point of view, which other rhetorical strategies help support his essay? Give examples of each.

MAKING CONNECTIONS

1. Compare the concern Lewis Sawaquat has for his daughter with that displayed for Russell Baker ("The Saturday Evening Post") by his mother and/or that for Amy Tan's narrator ("The Joy Luck Club") by her mother. Which parent do you think loves his or her child most? On what do you base this conclusion?
2. How strong is Sawaquat's attachment to his Native-American culture? Contrast the passion of his ethnic identity with that

demonstrated by Alice Walker ("Beauty: When the Other Dancer Is the Self"), Richard Rodriguez ("The Fear of Losing a Culture"), or Shelby Steele ("Affirmative Action: The Price of Preference").

3. What responsibilities, according to Sawaquat, should parents accept regarding the eventual happiness of their children? Would Bill Cosby ("The Baffling Question"), Michael Dorris ("The Broken Cord"), or Barbara Ehrenreich ("Stop Ironing the Diapers") agree with him? Why or why not? To what extent do you agree with Sawaquat?

IDEAS FOR DISCUSSION/WRITING

Preparing to Write

Write freely about your own identity: What is your cultural heritage? How do you fit into your immediate environment? Has your attitude about yourself and your identity changed over the years? Do you know your own inner self? How do you plan to continue learning about yourself?

Choosing a Topic

1. Write a narrative essay that uses one or more stories from your past in order to describe to a group of friends the main features of your identity.

2. Explain to your children (whether real or imaginary) in narrative form some simple but important truths about your heritage. Take care to select your details well, choose an appropriate point of view, and arrange your essay logically so that you keep your readers' interest throughout the essay.

3. Have you recently experienced any social traumas in your life that you would like to prepare someone else for? Write a letter to the person you would like to warn. Use narration to explain the situation, and suggest ways to avoid the negative aspects you encountered.

George Orwell   (1903 – 1950)

Shooting an Elephant

"George Orwell" was the pseudonym of English writer Eric Arthur Blair. Born in India, where his father was a British civil servant, Orwell moved to England in 1907 to attend Eton School, then returned to Burma to serve as an officer in the Indian Imperial Police. From 1927 to 1935, he lived an impoverished existence in Paris and London until his persistence as a writer brought him critical praise. After a series of modestly successful novels, Orwell wrote the classic *Animal Farm* (1945), his best-known work, a prose satire of Stalinism and totalitarianism. Collections of his essays include *Inside the Whale* (1940), *Critical Essays* (1946), and *Shooting an Elephant* (1950). In his later years, ill with tuberculosis, Orwell wrote his darkly horrifying *Nineteen Eighty-Four* (1949), which predicted a world where unorthodox thought is prohibited, love is condemned, and three superpowers control the entire planet.

Preparing to Read

"Shooting an Elephant," an essay from Orwell's collection of the same title, chronicles one of the author's autobiographical experiences as a police officer in Burma in the 1920s. Full of anti-imperialist sentiment, the story uses the death of an elephant as an emblem of Orwell's frustration with his role in England's colonial domination of India. As you prepare to read this essay, take a few moments to consider the many influences that shape your life: What forces have power over you? Have you ever done something you didn't want to do because of these forces? Have you ever been ashamed of the extent to which social or ethical pressures have governed your life? Why did you allow these forces to control you? How did you feel while all this was going on? Can you think of a specific situation in which you resisted these outside forces? What was the result?

In Moulmein, in Lower Burma, I was hated by large numbers 1
of people—the only time in my life that I have been important enough for this to happen to me. I was sub-divisional
police officer of the town, and in an aimless, petty kind of way
anti-European feeling was very bitter. No one had the guts to
raise a riot, but if a European woman went through the bazaars
alone somebody would probably spit betel juice over her dress. As
a police officer I was an obvious target and was baited whenever
it seemed safe to do so. When a nimble Burman tripped me up
on the football field and the referee (another Burman) looked the
other way, the crowd yelled with hideous laughter. This happened
more than once. In the end the sneering yellow faces of young
men that met me everywhere, the insults hooted after me when I
was at a safe distance, got badly on my nerves. The young
Buddhist priests were the worst of all. There were several thousands of them in the town and none of them seemed to have
anything to do except stand on street corners and jeer at
Europeans.

All this was perplexing and upsetting. For at that time I had al- 2
ready made up my mind that imperialism was an evil thing and
the sooner I chucked up my job and got out of it the better.
Theoretically—and secretly, of course—I was all for the Burmese
and all against their oppressors, the British. As for the job I was
doing, I hated it more bitterly than I can perhaps make clear. In a
job like that you see the dirty work of Empire at close quarters.
The wretched prisoners huddling in the stinking cages of the
lock-ups, the grey, cowed faces of the long-term convicts, the
scarred buttocks of the men who had been flogged with bam-
boos—all these oppressed me with an intolerable sense of guilt.
But I could get nothing into perspective. I was young and ill-ed-
ucated and I had had to think out my problems in the utter silence that is imposed on every Englishman in the East. I did not
even know that the British Empire is dying, still less did I know
that it is a great deal better than the younger empires that are
going to supplant it. All I knew was that I was stuck between my
hatred of the empire I served and my rage against the evil-spirited
little beasts who tried to make my job impossible. With one part
of my mind I thought of the British Raj as an unbreakable
tyranny, as something clamped down, *in saecula saeculorum*, upon

the will of prostrate peoples; with another part I thought that the greatest joy in the world would be to drive a bayonet into a Buddhist priest's guts. Feelings like these are the normal by-products of imperialism; ask any Anglo-Indian official, if you can catch him off duty.

One day something happened which in a roundabout way was 3 enlightening. It was a tiny incident in itself, but it gave me a better glimpse than I had had before of the real nature of imperialism—the real motives for which despotic governments act. Early one morning the sub-inspector at a police station at the other end of the town rang me up on the phone and said that an elephant was ravaging the bazaar. Would I please come and do something about it? I did not know what I could do, but I wanted to see what was happening and I got on to a pony and started out. I took my rifle, an old .44 Winchester and much too small to kill an elephant, but I thought the noise might be useful *in terrorem*. Various Burmans stopped me on the way and told me about the elephant's doings. It was not, of course, a wild elephant, but a tame one which had gone "must." It had been chained up, as tame elephants always are when their attack of "must" is due, but on the previous night it had broken its chain and escaped. Its mahout, the only person who could manage it when it was in that state, had set out in pursuit, but had taken the wrong direction and was now twelve hours' journey away, and in the morning the elephant had suddenly reappeared in town. The Burmese population had no weapons and were quite helpless against it. It had already destroyed somebody's bamboo hut, killed a cow and raided some fruit-stalls and devoured the stock; also it had met the municipal rubbish van and, when the driver jumped out and took to his heels, had turned the van over and inflicted violences upon it.

The Burmese sub-inspector and some Indian constables were 4 waiting for me in the quarter where the elephant had been seen. It was a very poor quarter, a labyrinth of squalid bamboo huts, thatched with palm-leaf, winding all over a steep hillside. I remember that it was a cloudy, stuffy morning at the beginning of the rains. We began questioning the people as to where the elephant had gone and, as usual, failed to get any definite information. That is invariably the case in the East; a story always sounds clear enough at a distance, but the nearer you get to the scene of events the vaguer it becomes. Some of the people said that the elephant had gone in one direction, some said that he had gone in another, some professed not even to have heard of any elephant. I had almost made up my mind that the whole story was a pack of lies, when we heard yells a little distance away. There was a loud, scandalized cry of "Go away, child! Go away this instant!" and an old woman with a switch in her hand came round the corner of a hut, violently shooing away a crowd of naked children. Some more women followed, clicking their tongues and exclaiming; evidently there was something that the children ought not to have seen. I rounded the hut and saw a man's dead body sprawling in the mud. He was an Indian, a black Dravidian coolie, almost naked, and he could not have been dead many minutes. The people said that the elephant had come suddenly upon him round the corner of the hut, caught him with its trunk, put its foot on his back and ground him into the earth. This was the rainy season and the ground was soft, and his face had scored a trench a foot deep and a couple of yards long. He was lying on his belly with arms crucified and head sharply twisted to one side. His face was coated with mud, the eyes wide open, the teeth bared and grinning with an expression of unendurable agony. (Never tell me, by the way, that the dead look peaceful. Most of the corpses I have seen looked devilish.) The friction of the great beast's foot had stripped the skin from his back as neatly as one skins a rabbit. As soon as I saw the dead man I sent an orderly to a friend's house nearby to borrow an elephant rifle. I had already sent back the pony, not wanting it to go mad with fright and throw me if it smelt the elephant.

The orderly came back in a few minutes with a rifle and five cartridges, and meanwhile some Burmans had arrived and told us that the elephant was in the paddy fields below, only a few hundred yards away. As I started forward practically the whole population of the quarter flocked out of the houses and followed me. They had seen the rifle and were all shouting excitedly that I was going to shoot the elephant. They had not shown much interest in the elephant when he was merely ravaging their homes, but it was different now that he was going to be shot. It was a bit of fun to them, as it would be to an English crowd; besides they wanted the meat. It made me vaguely uneasy. I had no intention

5

of shooting the elephant—I had merely sent for the rifle to defend myself if necessary—and it is always unnerving to have a crowd following you. I marched down the hill, looking and feeling a fool, with the rifle over my shoulder and an ever-growing army of people jostling at my heels. At the bottom, when you got away from the huts, there was a metalled road and beyond that a miry waste of paddy fields a thousand yards across, not yet ploughed but soggy from the first rains and dotted with coarse grass. The elephant was standing eight yards from the road, his left side towards us. He took not the slightest notice of the crowd's approach. He was tearing up bunches of grass, beating them against his knees to clean them and stuffing them into his mouth.

I had halted on the road. As soon as I saw the elephant I knew 6 with perfect certainty that I ought not to shoot him. It is a serious matter to shoot a working elephant—it is comparable to destroying a huge and costly piece of machinery—and obviously one ought not to do it if it can possibly be avoided. And at that distance, peacefully eating, the elephant looked no more dangerous than a cow. I thought then and I think now that his attack of "must" was already passing off, in which case he would merely wander harmlessly about until the mahout came back and caught him. Moreover, I did not in the least want to shoot him. I decided that I would watch him for a little while to make sure that he did not turn savage again, and then go home.

But at that moment I glanced round at the crowd that had followed me. It was an immense crowd, two thousand at the least and growing every minute. It blocked the road for a long distance on either side. I looked at the sea of yellow faces above the garish clothes—faces all happy and excited over this bit of fun, all certain that the elephant was going to be shot. They were watching me as they would watch a conjurer about to perform a trick. They did not like me, but with the magical rifle in my hands I was momentarily worth watching. And suddenly I realized that I should have to shoot the elephant after all. The people expected it of me and I had got to do it; I could feel their two thousand wills pressing me forward, irresistibly. And it was at this moment, as I stood there with the rifle in my hands, that I first grasped the hollowness, the futility of the white man's dominion in the East. Here was I, the white man with his gun, standing in front of the unarmed native crowd—seemingly the leading actor of the piece; but in reality I was only an absurd puppet pushed to and fro by the will of those yellow faces behind. I perceived in this moment that when the white man turns tyrant it is his own freedom that he destroys. He becomes a sort of hollow, posing dummy, the conventionalized figure of a sahib. For it is the condition of his rule that he shall spend his life in trying to impress the "natives," and so in every crisis he has got to do what the "natives" expect of him. He wears a mask, and his face grows to fit it. I had got to shoot the elephant. I had committed myself to doing it when I sent for the rifle. A sahib has got to act like a sahib, he has got to appear resolute, to know his own mind and do definite things. To come all that way, rifle in hand, with two thousand people marching at my heels, and then to trail feebly away, having done nothing—no, that was impossible. The crowd would laugh at me. And my whole life, every white man's life in the East, was one long struggle not to be laughed at.

But I did not want to shoot the elephant. I watched him beat- 8 ing his bunch of grass against his knees, with that preoccupied grandmotherly air that elephants have. It seemed to me that it would be murder to shoot him. At that age I was not squeamish about killing animals, but I had never shot an elephant and never wanted to. (Somehow it always seems worse to kill a *large* ani-mal.) Besides, there was the beast's owner to be considered. Alive, the elephant was worth at least a hundred pounds; dead, he would only be worth the value of his tusks, five pounds, possibly. But I had got to act quickly. I turned to some experienced-look-ing Burmans who had been there when we arrived, and asked them how the elephant had been behaving. They all said the same thing: he took no notice of you if you left him alone, but he might charge if you went too close to him.

It was perfectly clear to me what I ought to do. I ought to walk 9 up to within, say, twenty-five yards of the elephant and test his be-havior. If he charged, I could shoot; if he took no notice of me, it would be safe to leave him until the mahout came back. But also I knew that I was going to do no such thing. I was a poor shot with a rifle and the ground was soft mud into which one would sink at every step. If the elephant charged and I missed him, I should have about as much chance as a toad under a steam-roller. But even then I was not thinking particularly of my own skin, only of the watchful yellow faces behind. For at that moment, with the crowd watching me, I was not afraid in the ordinary sense, as I would have been if I had been alone. A white man mustn't be frightened in front of "natives"; and so, in general, he isn't frightened. The sole thought in my mind was that if anything went wrong those two thousand Burmans would see me pursued, caught, trampled on and reduced to a grinning corpse like that Indian up the hill. And if that happened it was quite probable that some of them would laugh. That would never do. There was only one alternative. I shoved the cartridges into the magazine and lay down on the road to get a better aim.

The crowd grew very still, and a deep, low, happy sigh, as of 10 people who see the theatre curtain go up at last, breathed from innumerable throats. They were going to have their bit of fun after all. The rifle was a beautiful German thing with cross-hair sights. I did not then know that in shooting an elephant one would shoot to cut an imaginary bar running from ear-hole to ear-hole. I ought, therefore, as the elephant was sideways on, to have aimed straight at his ear-hole; actually I aimed several inches in front of this, thinking the brain would be further forward.

When I pulled the trigger I did not hear the bang or feel the 11 kick—one never does when a shot goes home—but I heard the devilish roar of glee that went up from the crowd. In that instant, in too short a time, one would have thought, even for the bullet to get there, a mysterious, terrible change had come over the elephant. He neither stirred nor fell, but every line of his body had altered. He looked suddenly stricken, shrunken, immensely old, as though the frightful impact of the bullet had paralyzed him without knocking him down. At last, after what seemed a long time—it might have been five seconds, I dare say—he sagged flabbily to his knees. His mouth slobbered. An enormous senility seemed to have settled upon him. One could have imagined him thousands of years old. I fired again into the same spot. At the second shot he did not collapse but climbed with desperate slowness to his feet and stood weakly upright, with legs sagging and head drooping. I fired a third time. That was the shot that did for him. You could see the agony of it jolt his whole body and knock the last remnant of strength from his legs. But in falling he seemed for a moment to rise, for as his hind legs collapsed beneath him he seemed to tower upward like a huge rock toppling, his trunk reaching skywards like a tree. He trumpeted, for the first and only time. And then down he came, his belly towards me, with a crash that seemed to shake the ground even where I lay.

I got up. The Burmans were already racing past me across the   12
mud. It was obvious that the elephant would never rise again, but he was not dead. He was breathing very rhythmically with long rattling gasps, his great mount of a side painfully rising and falling. His mouth was wide open—I could see far down into caverns of pale pink throat. I waited a long time for him to die, but his breathing did not weaken. Finally I fired my two remaining shots into the spot where I thought his heart must be. The thick blood welled out of him like red velvet, but still he did not die. His body did not even jerk when the shots hit him, the tortured breathing continued without a pause. He was dying, very slowly and in great agony, but in some world remote from me where not even a bullet could damage him further. I felt that I had got to put an end to that dreadful noise. It seemed dreadful to see the great beast lying there, powerless to move and yet powerless to die, and not even to be able to finish him. I sent back for my small rifle and poured shot after shot into his heart and down his throat. They seemed to make no impression. The tortured gasps continued as steadily as the ticking of a clock.

In the end I could not stand it any longer and went away. I   13
heard later that it took him half an hour to die. Burmans were bringing *dahs* and baskets even before I left, and I was told they had stripped his body almost to the bones by the afternoon.

Afterwards, of course, there were endless discussions about the   14
shooting of the elephant. The owner was furious, but he was only an Indian and could do nothing. Besides, legally I had done the right thing, for a mad elephant has to be killed, like a mad dog, if its owner fails to control it. Among the Europeans opinion was divided. The older men said I was right, the younger men said it was a damn shame to shoot an elephant for killing a coolie, because an elephant was worth more than any damn Coringhee coolie. And afterwards I was very glad that the coolie had been killed; it put me legally in the right and it gave me a sufficient pretext for shooting the elephant. I often wondered whether any of the others grasped that I had done it solely to avoid looking a fool.

UNDERSTANDING DETAILS

1. Why does Orwell hate his job? According to him, what is the relationship between British imperialism in Burma and the treatment of foreigners?
2. What has the elephant done during its attack of "must"?
3. At what precise moment does Orwell realize he has to shoot the elephant?
4. In your own words, describe the shooting of the elephant from the time the first bullet hits its mark to the actual death.

ANALYZING MEANING

1. Why does the crowd want to see the elephant killed? Why does Orwell feel he has to shoot the animal?
2. In paragraph 7, Orwell says, "And my whole life, every white man's life in the East, was one long struggle not to be laughed at." Why is not being laughed at so important to him (and other imperialists)? What political overtones does this desire to save face carry?
3. The elephant's death is slow and no doubt very painful. What do these details add to the essay? What significance do they have in light of the emotional crisis the author is undergoing?
4. What are the consequences of the elephant's death? Do you think Orwell took the right action? What else could he have done?

DISCOVERING RHETORICAL STRATEGIES

1. From what point of view is Orwell's narrative written? How does this particular point of view help us understand Orwell's attitude toward the experience? How does this point of view help the author accomplish his purpose?
2. Orwell tends to second-guess himself throughout the story. Look, for example, at the following:

> It was perfectly clear to me what I ought to do. I ought to walk up to within, say, twenty-five yards of the elephant and test his behavior. If he charged, I could shoot; if he took no notice of me, it would be safe to leave him until the mahout came back. But also I knew that I was going to do no such thing. [paragraph 9]

Find at least two other such contradictions in the essay. What effect does this verbal strategy have on us as readers?

3. How does Orwell organize the details of this narrative? At what point in the story does the climax occur? When does the passage of time seem slowest to you? How does the author create this change of pace?

4. Although Orwell's essay is primarily narrative, what other rhetorical strategies does he use to make his point? Give examples of each.

MAKING CONNECTIONS

1. How do Orwell and John Langone ("Group Violence") differ in their opinion of mob psychology? How do they agree? Which author do you agree with most?

2. In his essay, Orwell vividly relates the cultural differences between himself and the Burmese citizens he has been sent to govern. How does this cultural gap differ from those described by Germaine Greer ("A Child Is Born") and/or Richard Rodriguez ("The Fear of Losing a Culture")? Which of these cultural gaps is the widest? Explain your answer.

3. Compare and contrast Orwell's insights into power with those expressed by Joyce Carol Oates ("On Boxing") and Gloria Steinem ("The Politics of Muscle"). How addicted to power are Americans today? Explain your answer.

IDEAS FOR DISCUSSION/WRITING

Preparing to Write

Write freely about a time in your life when you were forced to do something you didn't want to do: What were the circumstances? How did you feel? What were the motivating forces for what you did? What were your alternatives? Were you satisfied with the outcome? How do you feel about this experience now?

Choosing a Topic

1. Write a narrative essay telling your classmates about a time you were forced to do something you didn't want to do. Make a special effort to communicate your feelings regarding this experience. Remember to choose your details and point of view with an overall purpose in mind.

2. What is America's system of social classes? Where do you fit into the structure? Does our system allow for mobility? Write a narrative essay for your classmates explaining your under-standing of the American class system. Use yourself and/or a friend as an example.
3. Explain in a coherent essay written for the general public why you think we are all sometimes motivated by forces that work against our better judgment. Refer to the Orwell essay or to experiences of your own to support your explanation.

Maya Angelou   (1928 –   )

■ ■ ■

New Directions

Maya Angelou was born Marguerite Johnson on April 4, 1928, in
St. Louis, Missouri. Nicknamed "Maya" by her brother, she
moved with her family to California; then, at age three, she was
sent to live with her grandmother in Stamps, Arkansas, where she
spent the childhood years later recorded in her autobiographical
novel *I Know Why the Caged Bird Sings* (1970). After a brief marriage, she embarked upon an amazingly prolific career in dance,
drama, and writing. During the past forty years, Angelou has been
at various times a nightclub performer specializing in calypso
songs and dances, an actress, a playwright, a civil-rights activist, a
newspaper editor, a television writer and producer, a poet, and a
screenwriter. She has also written several television specials, including *Three Way Choice* (a five-part miniseries) and *Afro-
Americans in the Arts*, both for PBS. Her most recent work has
included a BBC-TV documentary entitled *Trying to Make It
Home* (1988); a stage production of Errol John's *Moon on a
Rainbow Shawl*, which she directed in London (1988); and three
novels, *I Shall Not Be Moved* (1990), *Lessons in Living* (1993), and
Wouldn't Take Nothing for My Journey Now (1993). A tall, graceful,
and imposing woman, Angelou was once described as conveying
"pride without arrogance, self-esteem without smugness."

Preparing to Read

Taken from Angelou's newest book, *Wouldn't Take Nothing for My
Journey Now*, the following essay describes how Annie Johnson, a
strong and determined woman, found "a new path" in her life.
Before you read this essay, take a moment to think about a time
you changed directions: What were the circumstances surrounding this change? Why did you make the change? What did you
learn from the experience? What alterations would you make if
you followed this path again?

I n 1903 the late Mrs. Annie Johnson of Arkansas found herself 1
with two toddling sons, very little money, a slight ability to
read and add simple numbers. To this picture add a disastrous
marriage and the burdensome fact that Mrs. Johnson was a
Negro.

When she told her husband, Mr. William Johnson, of her dis- 2
satisfaction with their marriage, he conceded that he too found it
to be less than he expected, and had been secretly hoping to leave
and study religion. He added that he thought God was calling
him not only to preach but to do so in Enid, Oklahoma. He did
not tell her that he knew a minister in Enid with whom he could
study and who had a friendly, unmarried daughter. They parted
amicably, Annie keeping the one-room house and William taking
most of the cash to carry himself to Oklahoma.

Annie, over six feet tall, big-boned, decided that she would not 3
go to work as a domestic and leave her "precious babes" to anyone else's care. There was no possibility of being hired at the
town's cotton gin or lumber mill, but maybe there was a way to
make the two factories work for her. In her words, "I looked up
the road I was going and back the way I come, and since I wasn't
satisfied, I decided to step off the road and cut me a new path."
She told herself that she wasn't a fancy cook but that she could
"mix groceries well enough to scare hunger away from a starving
man."

She made her plans meticulously and in secret. One early 4
evening to see if she was ready, she placed stones in two five-gallon
pails and carried them three miles to the cotton gin. She rested a
little, and then, discarding some rocks, she walked in the darkness to
the saw mill five miles farther along the dirt road. On her way back
to her little house and her babies, she dumped the remaining rocks
along the path.

That same night she worked into the early hours boiling 5
chicken and frying ham. She made dough and filled the rolled-
out pastry with meat. At last she went to sleep.

The next morning she left her house carrying the meat pies, 6
lard, an iron brazier, and coals for a fire. Just before lunch she appeared in an empty lot behind the cotton gin. As the dinner
noon bell rang, she dropped the savors into boiling fat and the
aroma rose and floated over to the workers who spilled out of the
gin, covered with white lint, looking like specters.

Most workers had brought their lunches of pinto beans and 7
biscuits or crackers, onions and cans of sardines, but they were
tempted by the hot meat pies which Annie ladled out of the fat.
She wrapped them in newspapers, which soaked up the grease,
and offered them for sale at a nickel each. Although business was
slow, those first days Annie was determined. She balanced her appearances between the two hours of activity.

So, on Monday if she offered hot fresh pies at the cotton gin 8
and sold the remaining cooled-down pies at the lumber mill for
three cents, then on Tuesday she went first to the lumber mill
presenting fresh, just-cooked pies as the lumbermen covered in
sawdust emerged from the mill.

For the next few years, on balmy spring days, blistering sum- 9
mer noons, and cold, wet, and wintry middays, Annie never disappointed her customers, who could count on seeing the tall,
brown-skin woman bent over her brazier, carefully turning the
meat pies. When she felt certain that the workers had become dependent on her, she built a stall between the two hives of industry
and let the men run to her for their lunchtime provisions.

She had indeed stepped from the road which seemed to have 10
been chosen for her and cut herself a brand-new path. In years
that stall became a store where customers could buy cheese, meal,
syrup, cookies, candy, writing tablets, pickles, canned goods, fresh
fruit, soft drinks, coal, oil, and leather soles for worn-out shoes.

Each of us has the right and the responsibility to assess the 11
roads which lie ahead, and those over which we have traveled,
and if the future road looms ominous or unpromising, and the
roads back uninviting, then we need to gather our resolve and,
carrying only the necessary baggage, step off that road into another direction. If the new choice is also unpalatable, without
embarrassment, we must be ready to change that as well.

UNDERSTANDING DETAILS

1. What path is Annie Johnson following that she dislikes? How
   does she change this path?
2. Describe Annie physically and mentally in your own words.
   Use as much detail as possible.
3. Why does Annie carry stones in two five-gallon pails for three
   miles? What is she trying to accomplish?

4. In what ways does Annie's business grow? How does Annie's personality make this growth possible?

ANALYZING MEANING

1. Why do you think Annie succeeds in her business? What are the main ingredients of her success?
2. In what ways are the details at the beginning of this narrative essay typical of the year 1903?
3. What does Angelou mean when she says, "Each of us has the right and the responsibility to assess the roads which lie ahead, and those over which we have traveled" (paragraph 11)? In what way is this message basic to an understanding of the essay?
4. Explain the title of the essay. Cite specific details from the essay in your explanation.

DISCOVERING RHETORICAL STRATEGIES

1. Angelou writes this narrative essay in a fairly formal style, using multisyllable words (*concede* rather than *yield* or *admit*) and the characters' title and names (Mrs. Annie Johnson instead of Annie Johnson). Why do you think Angelou presents her essay in this way? Describe the tone she maintains throughout the essay.
2. The author uses the metaphor of taking a "new road" to describe Annie Johnson's decision. Is this metaphor effective in your opinion? Why or why not?
3. Over what period of time do you think this story took place? How does the author show her readers that time is passing in this narrative essay?
4. Angelou often ends her essays with lessons that she wants the readers to understand. How does her lesson in the last paragraph of this narrative essay affect the story? Does the story itself go with the lesson? How did you respond to having the author tell you what to think at the end of the story?

MAKING CONNECTIONS

1. In Angelou's essay, Annie Johnson cuts "a new path" for herself by selling food to factory workers. Contrast this sudden change in the direction of her life with similar "new paths" taken by

Bill Cosby ("The Baffling Question"), by female weightlifters in Gloria Steinem's "The Politics of Muscle," or by naval pilots in Tom Wolfe's "The Right Stuff." Who do you think had the most difficult transition to make? Explain your answer.

2. If Angelou, Russell Baker ("The Saturday Evening Post"), Jane Goodall ("The Mind of the Chimpanzee"), and Harold Krents ("Darkness at Noon") were having a discussion about the value of persistence and determination in life, which author would argue most strongly for the value of that quality in life? Why? Would you agree?

3. Food is an important ingredient not only in Angelou's essay, but also in those written by Amy Tan ("The Joy Luck Club"), Ray Bradbury ("Summer Rituals"), Kimberly Wozencraft ("Notes From the Country Club"), and Garrison Keillor ("How the Crab Apple Grew"). Which of these most involves the topic of food? Which the least? Which authors use food as a structuring device in their essays?

IDEAS FOR DISCUSSION/WRITING

Preparing to Write

Write freely about all the major changes you have made in your life: Were most of these changes for the best? How did they benefit you? How did they benefit others? Did they hurt anyone? Do you think most people have trouble changing directions in their lives? Why or why not? How might we all improve our attitudes about change?

Choosing a Topic

1. The editor of your school newspaper has asked you to write a narrative essay about an important change you made in your life. The newspaper is running a series of essays about changing directions in life, and the staff has heard that you have a story to tell. Tell your story in essay form to be printed in the school newspaper.

2. Why are major changes so difficult for us to make? Use a narrative essay written for your peers to respond to this question. Use characters to dramatize your answer.

3. Decide on an important truth about life, and then write a narrative essay to support that truth. Make the details as vivid as possible.

RUSSELL BAKER   (1925 –   )

■ ■ ■

The Saturday Evening Post

Russell Baker is one of America's foremost satirists and humorists. Born in Virginia, he grew up in New Jersey and Maryland, graduated from Johns Hopkins University, and then served for two years as a pilot in the U.S. Navy. Following the service, he became a newspaper reporter for the *Baltimore Sun*, which sent him to England as its London correspondent. He subsequently joined the staff of the *New York Times* as a member of its Washington bureau. Since 1962, he has written his widely syndicated "Observer" column in the *Times*, which blends wry humor, a keen interest in language, and biting social commentary about the Washington scene. His books include *An American in Washington* (1961), *No Cause for Panic* (1964), and *Poor Russell's Almanac* (1972), plus two collections of early essays, *So This Is Depravity* (1980) and *The Rescue of Miss Yaskell and Other Pipe Dreams* (1983). *Growing Up* (1982), a best-seller vividly recounting his own childhood, earned him the 1983 Pulitzer Prize for biography. His more recent publications include *The Good Times* (1989), which continues his life story from approximately age twenty until he began working for the *New York Times* in the early 1960s, and *There's a Country in My Cellar: The Best of Russell Baker* (1990), a collection of his newspaper columns.

Preparing to Read

The following skillfully written essay is an excerpt from Baker's autobiography, *Growing Up*. In it, the author recalls enduring memories from his youth that clearly project the experiences and emotions of his coming of age in 1920s rural Virginia. As you prepare to read this selection, think for a moment about some of your own childhood memories: What were your strengths as a child? Your weaknesses? Have these character traits changed as you've matured? How are you like or unlike various members of your family? How do you react to these similarities and/or differences? What are your main goals in life? How do your character traits affect these goals?

I began working in journalism when I was eight years old. It   1
was my mother's idea. She wanted me to "make something" of myself and, after a levelheaded appraisal of my strengths, decided I had better start young if I was to have any chance of keeping up with the competition.

The flaw in my character which she had already spotted was   2
lack of "gumption." My idea of a perfect afternoon was lying in front of the radio rereading my favorite Big Little Book, *Dick Tracy Meets Stooge Viller.* My mother despised inactivity. Seeing me having a good time in repose, she was powerless to hide her disgust. "You've got no more gumption than a bump on a log," she said. " Get out in the kitchen and help Doris do those dirty dishes."

My sister Doris, though two years younger than I, had enough   3
gumption for a dozen people. She positively enjoyed washing dishes, making beds, and cleaning the house. When she was only seven she could carry a piece of short-weighted cheese back to the A & P, threaten the manager with legal action, and come back triumphantly with the full quarter-pound we'd paid for and a few ounces extra thrown in for forgiveness. Doris could have made something of herself if she hadn't been a girl. Because of this defect, however, the best she could hope for was a career as a nurse or schoolteacher, the only work that capable females were considered up to in those days.

This must have saddened my mother, this twist of fate that had   4
allocated all the gumption to the daughter and left her with a son who was content with Dick Tracy and Stooge Viller. If disappointed, though, she wasted no energy on self-pity. She would make me make something of myself whether I wanted to or not. "The Lord helps those who help themselves," she said. That was the way her mind worked.

She was realistic about the difficulty. Having sized up the ma-   5
terial the Lord had given her to mold, she didn't overestimate what she could do with it. She didn't insist that I grow up to be President of the United States.

Fifty years ago parents still asked boys if they wanted to grow   6
up to be President, and asked it not jokingly but seriously. Many

parents who were hardly more than paupers still believed their sons could do it. Abraham Lincoln had done it. We were only sixty-five years from Lincoln. Many a grandfather who walked among us could remember Lincoln's time. Men of grandfatherly age were the worst for asking if you wanted to grow up to be President. A surprising number of little boys said yes and meant it.

I was asked many times myself. No, I would say, I didn't want 7 to grow up to be President. My mother was present during one of these interrogations. An elderly uncle, having posed the usual question and exposed my lack of interest in the Presidency, asked, "Well, what *do* you want to be when you grow up?"

I loved to pick through trash piles and collect empty bottles, 8 tin cans with pretty labels, and discarded magazines. The most desirable job on earth sprang instantly to mind. "I want to be a garbage man," I said.

My uncle smiled, but my mother had seen the first distressing 9 evidence of a bump budding on a log. "Have a little gumption, Russell," she said. Her calling me Russell was a signal of unhappiness. When she approved of me I was always "Buddy."

When I turned eight years old she decided that the job of 10 starting me on the road toward making something of myself could no longer be safely delayed. "Buddy," she said one day, "I want you to come home right after school this afternoon. Somebody's coming and I want you to meet him."

When I burst in that afternoon she was in conference in the 11 parlor with an executive of the Curtis Publishing Company. She introduced me. He bent low from the waist and shook my hand. Was it true as my mother had told him, he asked, that I longed for the opportunity to conquer the world of business?

My mother replied that I was blessed with a rare determina- 12 tion to make something of myself.

"That's right," I whispered. 13

"But have you got the grit, the character, the never-say-quit 14 spirit it takes to succeed in business?"

My mother said I certainly did. 15

"That's right," I said. 16

He eyed me silently for a long pause, as though weighing 17 whether I could be trusted to keep his confidence, then spoke man-to-man. Before taking a crucial step, he said, he wanted to advise me that working for the Curtis Publishing Company placed enormous responsibility on a young man. It was one of the great companies of America. Perhaps the greatest publishing house in the world. I had heard, no doubt, of the *Saturday Evening Post?*

Heard of it? My mother said that everyone in our house had heard of the *Saturday Post* and that I, in fact, read it with religious devotion. 18

Then doubtless, he said, we were also familiar with those two monthly pillars of the magazine world, the *Ladies Home Journal* and the *Country Gentleman.* 19

Indeed we were familiar with them, said my mother. 20

Representing the *Saturday Evening Post* was one of the weightiest honors that could be bestowed in the world of business, he said. He was personally proud of being a part of the great corporation. 21

My mother said he had every right to be. 22

Again he studied me as though debating whether I was worthy of a knighthood. Finally: "Are you trustworthy?" 23

My mother said I was the soul of honesty. 24

"That's right," I said. 25

The caller smiled for the first time. He told me I was a lucky young man. He admired my spunk. Too many young men thought life was all play. Those young men would not go far in this world. Only a young man willing to work and save and keep his face washed and his hair neatly combed could hope to come out on top in a world such as ours. Did I truly and sincerely believe that I was such a young man? 26

"He certainly does," said my mother. 27

"That's right," I said. 28

He said he had been so impressed by what he had seen of me that he was going to make me a representative of the Curtis Publishing Company. On the following Tuesday, he said, thirty freshly printed copies of the *Saturday Evening Post* would be delivered at our door. I would place these magazines, still damp with the ink of the presses, in a handsome canvas bag, sling it over my shoulder, and set forth through the streets to bring the best in journalism, fiction, and cartoons to the American public. 29

He had brought the canvas bag with him. He presented it with reverence fit for a chasuble. He showed me how to drape the sling over my left shoulder and across the chest so that the pouch 30 lay easily accessible to my right hand, allowing the best in journalism, fiction, and cartoons to be swiftly extracted and sold to a citizenry whose happiness and security depended upon us soldiers of the free press.

The following Tuesday I raced home from school, put the can- 31 vas bag over my shoulder, dumped the magazines in, and, tilting to the left to balance their weight on my right hip, embarked on the highway of journalism.

We lived in Belleville, New Jersey, a commuter town at the 32 northern fringe of Newark. It was 1932, the bleakest year of the Depression. My father had died two years before, leaving us with a few pieces of Sears, Roebuck furniture and not much else, and my mother had taken Doris and me to live with one of her younger brothers. This was my Uncle Allen. Uncle Allen had made something of himself by 1932. As salesman for a soft-drink bottler in Newark, he had an income of $30 a week; wore pearl-gray spats, detachable collars, and a three-piece suit; was happily married; and took in threadbare relatives.

With my load of magazines I headed toward Belleville Avenue. 33 That's where the people were. There were two filling stations at the intersection with Union Avenue, as well as an A & P, a fruit stand, a bakery, a barber shop, Zuccarelli's drugstore, and a diner shaped like a railroad car. For several hours I made myself highly visible, shifting position now and then from corner to corner, from shop window to shop window, to make sure everyone could see the heavy black lettering on the canvas bag that said THE SATURDAY EVENING POST. When the angle of the light indicated it was suppertime, I walked back to the house.

"How many did you sell, Buddy?" my mother asked. 34

"None." 35

"Where did you go?" 36

"The corner of Belleville and Union Avenues." 37

"What did you do?" 38

"Stood on the corner waiting for somebody to buy a *Saturday* 39 *Evening Post.*"

"You just stood there?" 40

"Didn't sell a single one." 41

"For God's sake, Russell!" 42

Uncle Allen intervened. "I've been thinking about it for some 43 time," he said, "and I've about decided to take the *Post* regularly.

Put me down as a regular customer." I handed him a magazine and he paid me a nickel. It was the first nickel I earned.

Afterwards my mother instructed me in salesmanship. I would have to ring doorbells, address adults with charming self-confidence, and break down resistance with a sales talk pointing out that no one, no matter how poor, could afford to be without the *Saturday Evening Post* in the home. 44

I told my mother I'd changed my mind about wanting to succeed in the magazine business. 45

"If you think I'm going to raise a good-for-nothing," she replied, "you've got another think coming." She told me to hit the streets with the canvas bag and start ringing doorbells the instant school was out next day. When I objected that I didn't feel any aptitude for salesmanship, she asked how I'd like to lend her my leather belt so she could whack some sense into me. I bowed to superior will and entered journalism with a heavy heart. 46

My mother and I had fought this battle almost as long as I could remember. It probably started even before memory began, when I was a country child in northern Virginia and my mother, dissatisfied with my father's plain workman's life, determined that I would not grow up like him and his people, with calluses on their hands, overalls on their backs, and fourth-grade educations in their heads. She had fancier ideas of life's possibilities. Introducing me to the *Saturday Evening Post*, she was trying to wean me as early as possible from my father's world where men left with their lunch pails at sunup, worked with their hands until the grime ate into the pores, and died with a few sticks of mail-order furniture as their legacy. In my mother's vision of the better life there were desks and white collars, well-pressed suits, evenings of reading and lively talk, and perhaps—if a man were very, very lucky and hit the jackpot, really made something important of himself—perhaps there might be a fantastic salary of $5,000 a year to support a big house and a Buick with a rumble seat and a vacation in Atlantic City. 47

And so I set forth with my sack of magazines. I was afraid of the dogs that snarled behind the doors of potential buyers. I was timid about ringing the doorbells of strangers, relieved when no one came to the door, and scared when someone did. Despite my mother's instructions, I could not deliver an engaging sales pitch. When a door opened I simply asked, "Want to buy a 48

Saturday Evening Post?" In Belleville few persons did. It was a town of 30,000 people, and most weeks I rang a fair majority of its doorbells. But I rarely sold my thirty copies. Some weeks I canvassed the entire town for six days and still had four or five unsold magazines on Monday evening; then I dreaded the coming of Tuesday morning, when a batch of thirty fresh *Saturday Evening Posts* was due at the front door.

"Better get out there and sell the rest of those magazines   49
tonight," my mother would say.

I usually posted myself then at a busy intersection where a traf-   50
fic light controlled commuter flow from Newark. When the light turned red I stood on the curb and shouted my sales pitch at the motorists.

"Want to buy a *Saturday Evening Post?*"   51

One rainy night when car windows were sealed against me I   52
came back soaked and with not a single sale to report. My mother beckoned to Doris.

"Go back down there with Buddy and show him how to sell   53
these magazines," she said.

Brimming with zest, Doris, who was then seven years old, re-   54
turned with me to the corner. She took a magazine from the bag, and when the light turned red she strode to the nearest car and banged her small fist against the closed window. The driver, probably startled at what he took to be a midget assaulting his car, lowered the window to stare, and Doris thrust a *Saturday Evening Post* at him.

"You need this magazine," she piped, "and it only costs a   55
nickel."

Her salesmanship was irresistible. Before the light changed half   56
a dozen times, she disposed of the entire batch. I didn't feel humiliated. To the contrary. I was so happy I decided to give her a treat. Leading her to the vegetable store on Belleville Avenue, I bought three apples, which cost a nickel, and gave her one.

"You shouldn't waste money," she said.   57

"Eat your apple." I bit into mine.   58

"You shouldn't eat before supper," she said. "It'll spoil your ap-   59
petite."

Back at the house that evening, she dutifully reported me for   60
wasting a nickel. Instead of a scolding, I was rewarded with a pat on the back for having the good sense to buy fruit instead of

candy. My mother reached into her bottomless supply of maxims and told Doris, "An apple a day keeps the doctor away."

By the time I was ten I had learned all my mother's maxims by heart. Asking to stay up past normal bedtime, I knew that a refusal would be explained with, "Early to bed and early to rise, makes a man healthy, wealthy, and wise." If I whimpered about having to get up early in the morning, I could depend on her to say, "The early bird gets the worm." 61

The one I most despised was, "If at first you don't succeed, try, try again." This was the battle cry with which she constantly sent me back into the hopeless struggle whenever I moaned that I had rung every doorbell in town and knew there wasn't a single potential buyer left in Belleville that week. After listening to my explanation, she handed me the canvas bag and said, "If at first you don't succeed. . . ." 62

Three years in that job, which I would gladly have quit after the first day except for her insistence, produced at least one valuable result. My mother finally concluded that I would never make something of myself by pursuing a life in business and started considering careers that demanded less competitive zeal. 63

One evening when I was eleven I brought home a short "composition" on my summer vacation which the teacher had graded with an A. Reading it with her own schoolteacher's eye, my mother agreed that it was top-drawer seventh grade prose and complimented me. Nothing more was said about it immediately, but a new idea had taken life in her mind. Halfway through supper she suddenly interrupted the conversation. 64

"Buddy," she said, "maybe you could be a writer." 65

I clasped the idea to my heart. I had never met a writer, had shown no previous urge to write, and hadn't a notion how to become a writer, but I loved stories and thought that making up stories must surely be almost as much fun as reading them. Best of all, though, and what really gladdened my heart, was the ease of the writer's life. Writers did not have to trudge through the town peddling from canvas bags, defending themselves against angry dogs, being rejected by surly strangers. Writers did not have to ring doorbells. So far as I could make out, what writers did couldn't even be classified as work. 66

I was enchanted. Writers didn't have to have any gumption at all. I did not dare tell anybody for fear of being laughed at in the 67 schoolyard, but secretly I decided that what I'd like to be when I grew up was a writer.

UNDERSTANDING DETAILS

1. How does Baker's ideal day differ from that of his sister?
2. According to the author's mother, what is the main flaw in his character? How does this flaw eventually affect his choice of a career?
3. Why does Baker feel he has no "aptitude for salesmanship" (paragraph 46)? What has led him to this conclusion?
4. Which of his mother's maxims does the author dislike the most? Explain his reaction.

ANALYZING MEANING

1. Why does Baker begin this selection with a comparison of his personality and his sister's? What does this comparison have to do with the rest of the essay?
2. Why does the author's mother insist that he work for the *Saturday Evening Post*? What does she think he will gain from the experience? What does he actually learn?
3. What "battle" (paragraph 47) have the author and his mother been fighting for as long as he can remember? Who finally wins this battle?
4. Why is Baker so delighted with the idea of becoming a writer when he grows up? How is this notion compatible with his personality?

DISCOVERING RHETORICAL STRATEGIES

1. How does Baker arrange the details in this excerpt? Why do you think he organizes them in this way? How would a different arrangement have changed the essay?
2. Who do you think is Baker's intended audience? Describe them in detail. How did you come to this conclusion?
3. What is the climax of Baker's narrative? How does he lead up to and develop this climactic moment? What stylistic traits tell us that this is the most exciting point in the story?
4. Besides narration, what other rhetorical strategies does Baker draw on to develop his thesis? Give examples of each of these strategies.

MAKING CONNECTIONS

1. Compare and contrast Baker's insistence on the importance of dedicating oneself to a career with similar sentiments found in essays by Gloria Steinem ("The Politics of Muscle"), Tom Wolfe ("The Right Stuff"), or William Ouchi ("Japanese and American Workers: Two Casts of Mind"). How dedicated do you intend to be to your own future career?

2. How is young Russell Baker's naive conception of a writer's "easy" life different from the views on writing expressed by Paul Roberts ("How to Say Nothing in Five Hundred Words"), Annie Dillard ("When You Write"), or Kurt Vonnegut ("How to Write with Style")? Which of these authors would argue most fervently that writing is "hard" work? How do you feel about the process of writing? Is it easy or hard for you? Explain your answer.

3. Baker's mother had a strong influence on him as he grew up. Would Germaine Greer ("A Child Is Born") argue that Mrs. Baker was typical of American mothers, or would Greer assert that she was more like a non-Western mother in her influence over her son? How much control has your own mother had over your upbringing? Are you pleased with the amount of influence she has had over you? Explain your answer.

IDEAS FOR DISCUSSION/WRITING

Preparing to Write

Write freely about yourself in relation to your aspirations: What type of person are you? What do you think about? What are your ideals? Your hopes? Your dreams? Your fears? What do you enjoy doing in your spare time? How are you different from other members of your family? Is anyone in your family a model for you? How have members of your immediate family affected your daily life—past and present? Your career goals? How do you anticipate your family will affect your future?

Choosing a Topic

1. Write a narrative essay introducing yourself to your English class. To explain and define your identity, include descriptions of family members whenever appropriate.

2. Write a narrative that helps explain to a friend how you got involved in a current interest. To expand upon your narrative, refer whenever possible to your long-term goals and aspirations.
3. Ten years from now, your local newspaper decides to devote an entire section to people getting started in careers. You are asked to submit the story of how you got involved in your profession (whatever it may be). Write a narrative that might appear in your hometown newspaper ten years from now; be sure to give the article a catchy headline.

GARRISON KEILLOR   (1942 –   )

■ ■ ■

How the Crab Apple Grew

Best known for his creation of the Peabody Award–winning radio program *A Prairie Home Companion*, Garrison Keillor, a native of Anoka, Minnesota, began his career as a radio announcer and producer during his student days at the University of Minnesota. His show, which was broadcast live for thirteen years before it left the air in 1987, featured an eclectic mix of traditional jazz and folk music supplemented by Keillor's rambling, nostalgic, and often hilarious anecdotes about the zany inhabitants of the fictitious small town of Lake Wobegon, Minnesota. Chief among its residents were Father Emil, the local priest who blessed small animals on the lawn of Our Lady of Perpetual Responsibility Church; Dorothy, the garrulous owner of the Chatterbox Cafe; and Dr. Nute, a retired dentist who coaxed trout toward his fishing lure by intoning, "Open wide . . . this may sting a bit." Keillor—a tall, soft-spoken man who often performs in a tuxedo, high-top sneakers, red socks, and red suspenders—even had a pseudosponsor for the show: Powdermilk Biscuits, "a wholewheat treat that gives shy people the strength to do what has to be done." Thus far, Keillor's monologues have spawned a number of short stories published in the *New Yorker* and six books: *Happy to Be Here: Stories and Comic Pieces* (1982), *Lake Wobegon Days* (1985), *Leaving Home* (1987), *We Are Still Married* (1989), *WLT: A Radio Romance* (1992), and *The Book of Guys* (1993). In 1989, he began a new radio variety show called *Garrison Keillor's American Radio Company*, which is currently carried on more than 230 public radio stations across America.

Preparing to Read

Taken from *Leaving Home*, this graceful and humorous story is a masterful demonstration by Keillor of how to write a narrative essay. As you prepare to read this selection, take a few minutes to think about various items in your life (in your backyard, in your

146

house, at school, at a friend's) that have special meaning to you: What are these items? Why is each of them significant? How do other people relate to these items? In what ways do your surroundings tell different stories about you? What items in your life bring complete stories to your mind? What are some of these stories?

■

I t has been a quiet week in Lake Wobegon. It was warm and sunny on Sunday, and on Monday the flowering crab in the Dieners' backyard burst into blossom. Suddenly, in the morning, when everyone turned their backs for a minute, the tree threw off its bathrobe and stood trembling, purple, naked, revealing all its innermost flowers. When you saw it standing where weeks before had been a bare stick stuck in the dirt, you had to stop, it made your head spin.   1

Becky Diener sat upstairs in her bedroom and looked at the tree. She was stuck on an assignment from Miss Melrose for English, a 750-word personal essay, "Describe your backyard as if you were seeing it for the first time." After an hour she had thirty-nine words, which she figured would mean she'd finish at 1:45 P.M. Tuesday, four hours late, and therefore would get an F even if the essay was great, which it certainly wasn't.   2

How can you describe your backyard as if you'd never seen it? If you'd never seen it, you'd have grown up someplace else, and wouldn't be yourself; you'd be someone else entirely, and how are you supposed to know what that person would think?   3

She imagined seeing the backyard in 1996, returning home from Hollywood. "Welcome Becky!" said the big white banner across McKinley Street as the pink convertible drove slowly along, everyone clapping and cheering as she cruised by, Becky Belafonte the movie star, and got off at her old house. "Here," she said to the reporters, "is where I sat as a child and dreamed my dreams, under this beautiful flowering crab. I dreamed I was a Chinese princess." Then a reporter asked, "Which of your teachers was the most important to you, encouraging you and inspiring you?" And just then she saw an old woman's face in the crowd, Miss Melrose pleading, whispering, "Say me, oh please, say me," and Becky looked straight at her as she said, "Oh, there were so many, I couldn't pick out one, they were all about the same,   4 you know. But perhaps Miss—Miss—oh, I can't remember her name—she taught English, I think—Miss Milross? She was one of them. But there were so many."

She looked at her essay. "In my backyard is a tree that has always been extremely important to me since I was six years old when my dad came home one evening with this bag in the trunk and he said, 'Come here and help me plant this'—" 5

She crumpled the sheet of paper and started again. 6

"One evening when I was six years old, my father arrived home as he customarily did around 5:30 or 6:00 P.M. except this evening he had a wonderful surprise for me, he said, as he led me toward the car. 7

"My father is not the sort of person who does surprising things very often so naturally I was excited that evening when he said he had something for me in the car, having just come home from work where he had been. I was six years old at the time." 8

She took out a fresh sheet. "Six years old was a very special age for me and one thing that made it special was when my dad and I planted a tree together in our backyard. Now it is grown and every spring it gives off large purple blossoms. . . ." 9

The tree was planted by her dad, Harold, in 1976, ten years after he married her mother, Marlys. They grew up on Taft Street, across from each other, a block from the ballfield. They liked each other tremendously and then they were in love, as much as you can be when you're so young. Thirteen and fourteen years old and sixteen and seventeen: they looked at each other a lot. She came and sat in his backyard to talk with his mother and help her shell peas but really to look at Harold as he mowed the lawn, and then he disappeared into the house and she sat waiting for him, and of course he was in the kitchen looking out at her. It's how we all began, when our parents looked at each other, as we say, "when you were just a gleam in your father's eye," or your mother's, depending on who saw who first. 10

Marlys was long-legged, lanky, had short black hair and sharp eyes that didn't miss anything. She came over to visit the Dieners every chance she got. Her father was a lost cause, like the Confederacy, like the search for the Northwest Passage. He'd been prayed for and suffered for and fought for and spoken for, by people who loved him dearly, and when all was said and done he just reached for the gin bottle and said, "I don't know what 11 you're talking about," and he didn't. He was a sore embarrassment to Marlys, a clown, a joke, and she watched Harold for evidence that he wasn't similar. One night she dropped in at the Dieners' and came upon a party where Harold, now nineteen, and his friends were drinking beer by the pail. Harold flopped down on his back and put his legs in the air and a pal put a lit match up to Harold's rear end and blue flame came out like a blowtorch, and Marlys went home disgusted and didn't speak to him for two years.

Harold went crazy. She graduated from high school and started   12 attending dances with a geography teacher named Stu Jasperson, who was tall and dark-haired, a subscriber to *Time* magazine, educated at Saint Cloud Normal School, and who flew a red Piper Cub airplane. Lake Wobegon had no airstrip except for Tollerud's pasture, so Stu kept his plane in Saint Cloud. When he was en route to and from the plane was almost the only time Harold got to see Marlys and try to talk sense into her. But she was crazy about Stu the aviator, not Harold the hardware clerk, and in an hour Stu came buzzing overhead doing loops and dives and dipping his wings. Harold prayed for him to crash. Marlys thought Stu was the sun and the moon; all Harold could do was sit and watch her, in the backyard, staring up, her hand shielding her eyes, saying, "Oh, isn't he marvelous?" as Stu performed aerial feats and then shut off the throttle and glided overhead singing "Vaya con Dios" to her. "Yes, he is marvelous," said Harold, thinking, "DIE DIE DIE."

That spring, Marlys was in charge of the Sweethearts Banquet   13 at the Lutheran church. Irene Holm had put on a fancy winter Sweethearts Banquet with roast lamb, and Marlys wanted to top her and serve roast beef with morel mushrooms, a first for a church supper in Lake Wobegon. Once Irene had referred to Marlys's dad as a lush.

Morel mushrooms are a great delicacy. They are found in the   14 wild by people who walk fifteen miles through the woods to get ten of them and then never tell the location to a soul, not even on their deathbeds to a priest. So Marlys's serving them at the banquet would be like putting out emeralds for party favors. It would blow Irene Holm out of the water and show people that even if Marlys's dad was a lush, she was still someone to be reckoned with.

Two men felt the call to go and search for morels: Harold put   15
on his Red Wing boots and knapsack and headed out one
evening with a flashlight. He was in the woods all night. Morels
are found near the base of the trunk of a dead elm that's been
dead three years, which you can see by the way moonlight does-
n't shine on it, and he thought he knew where some were, but
around midnight he spotted a bunch of flashlights behind him, a
posse of morelists bobbing along on his trail, so he veered off and
hiked five miles in the wrong direction to confuse them, and by
then the sun was coming up so he went home to sleep. He woke
at 2:00 P.M., hearing Stu flying overhead, and in an instant he
knew. Dead elms! Of course! Stu could spot them from the air,
send his ground crew to collect them for Marlys, and the
Sweethearts Banquet would be their engagement dinner.

Stu might have done just that, but he wanted to put on a show   16
and land the Cub in Lake Wobegon. He circled around and
around, and came in low to the west of town, disappearing behind the trees. "He's going to crash!" cried Marlys, and they all
jumped in their cars and tore out, expecting to find the young
hero lying bloody and torn in the dewy grass, with a dying poem
on his lips. But there he was standing tall beside the craft, having
landed successfully in a field of spring wheat. They all mobbed
around him and he told how he was going up to find the morels
and bring them back for Marlys.

There were about forty people there. They seemed to enjoy it,   17
so he drew out his speech, talking about the lure of aviation and
his boyhood and various things so serious that he didn't notice
Harold behind him by the plane or notice the people who noticed what Harold was doing and laughed. Stu was too inspired to
pay attention to the laughter. He talked about how he once
wanted to fly to see the world but once you get up in the air you
can see that Lake Wobegon is the most beautiful place of all, a lot
of warm horse manure like that, and then he gave them a big
manly smile and donned his flying cap and scarf and favored
them with a second and third smile and a wave and he turned
and there was Harold to help him into the cockpit.

"Well, thanks," said Stu, "mighty kind, mighty kind." Harold   18
jumped to the propeller and threw it once and twice, and the
third time the engine fired and Stu adjusted the throttle, checked

the gauges, flapped the flaps, fit his goggles, and never noticed the ground was wet and his wheels were sunk in. He'd parked in a wet spot, and then during his address someone had gone around and made it wetter, so when Stu pulled back on the throttle the Cub just sat, and he gave it more juice and she creaked a little, and he gave it more and the plane stood on its head with its tail in the air and dug in.

It pitched forward like the *Titanic*, and the propeller in the 19 mud sounded like he'd eaten too many green apples. The door opened and Stu climbed out, trying to look dignified and studious as he tilted eastward and spun, and Harold said, "Stu, we didn't say we wanted those mushrooms sliced."

Harold went out that afternoon and collected five hundred 20 morel mushrooms around one dead elm tree. Marlys made her mark at the Sweethearts dinner, amazing Irene Holm, who had thought Marlys was common. Harold also brought out of the woods a bouquet of flowering crab apple and asked her to marry him, and eventually she decided to.

The tree in the backyard came about a few years afterward. 21 They'd been married awhile, had two kids, and some of the gloss had worn off their life, and one afternoon, Harold, trying to impress his kids and make his wife laugh, jumped off the garage roof, pretending he could fly, and landed wrong, twisting his ankle. He lay in pain, his eyes full of tears, and his kids said, "Oh poor Daddy, poor Daddy," and Marlys said, "You're not funny, you're ridiculous."

He got up on his bum ankle and went in the woods and got 22 her a pint of morels and a branch from the flowering crab apple. He cut a root from another crab apple and planted the root in the ground. "Look, kids," he said. He sharpened the branch with his hatchet and split the root open and stuck the branch in and wrapped a cloth around it and said, "Now, there, that will be a tree." They said, "Daddy, will that really be a tree?" He said, "Yes." Marlys said, "Don't be ridiculous."

He watered it and tended it and, more than that, he came out 23 late at night and bent down and said, "GROW. GROW. GROW." The graft held, it grew, and one year it was interesting and the next it was impressive and then wonderful and finally it was magnificent. It's the most magnificent thing in the Dieners' backyard.

Becky finished writing 750 words late that night and lay down to sleep. A backyard is a novel about us, and when we sit there on a summer day, we hear the dialogue and see the characters.

UNDERSTANDING DETAILS

1. Where does this narrative essay take place? Describe this particular place in detail. What one word might characterize this setting?
2. Why is Becky worried about this particular assignment?
3. How many false starts does Becky make when she is trying to write this essay? What causes those false starts?
4. Explain the rivalry between Harold and Stu. What do they both want?

ANALYZING MEANING

1. How are the tree and Becky's writing assignment related?
2. Why does Marlys finally marry Harold?
3. What can you learn about writing from Becky's approach to this essay? How does she finally get started? How does she keep her essay going? How does she keep it focused? What truths from this experience can you apply to your own writing?
4. What does Keillor mean when he says, "A backyard is a novel about us, and when we sit there on a summer day, we hear the dialogue and see the characters" (paragraph 23)?

DISCOVERING RHETORICAL STRATEGIES

1. Keillor starts many of his narratives with "It has been a quiet week in Lake Wobegon." What effect does this beginning have on the rest of the essay?
2. What metaphor or comparison does Keillor use to explain in the beginning of his essay that the tree has bloomed? How effective is this opening? Explain your answer.
3. What does this particular crab apple symbolize? Explain your answer in detail.
4. How appropriate is the title of this essay? What are some other possible titles?

MAKING CONNECTIONS

1. Imagine that Paul Roberts ("How to Say Nothing in Five Hundred Words") has just read Keillor's essay about the

courtship of Harold and Marlys Diener. What grade do you think he would give the paper in a college composition class? What comments would he have for its author?

2. Compare and contrast Keillor's technique of recalling the past in this essay with similar recollections in Amy Tan's "The Joy Luck Club," Ray Bradbury's "Summer Rituals," George Orwell's "Shooting an Elephant," or Russell Baker's "The Saturday Evening Post." Which author's technique of historical reporting seems most vivid and convincing to you? Explain why.

3. Throughout his essay, Keillor mentions a number of details that will strike most readers as funny. How is Keillor's use of humor different from that of Bill Cosby ("The Baffling Question"), Jessica Mitford ("Behind the Formaldehyde Curtain"), Judy Brady ("Why I Want a Wife"), or Barbara Ehrenreich ("Stop Ironing the Diapers")? Which of these essays do you find most entertaining? Explain your answer.

IDEAS FOR DISCUSSION/WRITING

Preparing to Write

Write freely about various symbols in your life or your family's life: What are these symbols? What do they represent? Which of the symbols remind you of various relationships within your family? Which of these symbols are positive? Which are negative? Which symbols remind you of important stories about yourself or other family members? Why are these stories important? What makes specific family stories so important?

Choosing a Topic

1. Write a narrative essay introducing yourself to your English class through a special item in your life. To explain and define your identity, include your relationship to this item in your essay.

2. Write a narrative essay that explains how your parents met. What were the highlights of this meeting? Where did it lead? What is their relationship like now?

3. Your school newspaper is running a series of articles on symbols in our lives. You have been asked to submit a narrative essay on the item that best represents you as a student in college. What is this item? How does it represent you? Shape your answers to these questions into a narrative essay.

3

Example

Illustrating Ideas

Citing an example to help make a point is one of the most instinctive techniques we use in communication. If, for instance, you state that being an internationally ranked tennis player requires constant practice, a friend might challenge that assertion and ask what you mean by "constant practice." When you respond "about three hours a day," your friend might ask for more specific proof. At this stage in the discussion, you could offer the following illustrations to support your statement: When not on tour, Steffi Graf practices three hours per day; Pete Sampras, four hours; and André Agassi, two hours. Your friend's doubt will have been answered through your use of examples.

DEFINING EXAMPLES

Well-chosen examples and illustrations are an essay's building blocks. They are drawn from your experience, your observations, and your reading. They help you *show* rather than *tell* what you mean, usually by supplying concrete details (references to what we can see, smell, taste, hear, or touch) to support abstract ideas (such as faith, hope, understanding, and love), by providing specifics ("I like chocolate") to explain generalizations ("I like sweets"), and by giving definite references ("Turn left at the second stoplight") to clarify vague statements ("Turn in a few blocks"). Though illustrations take many forms, writers often find themselves indebted to description or narration (or some combination of the two) in order to supply enough relevant examples to achieve their rhetorical intent.

As you might suspect, examples are important ingredients in producing exciting, vivid prose. Just as crucial is the fact that carefully chosen examples often encourage your readers to feel one way or another about an issue being discussed. If you tell your parents, for instance, that living in a college dormitory is not conducive to academic success, they may doubt your word, perhaps thinking that you are simply attempting to coerce money out of them for an apartment. You can help dispel this notion, however, by giving them specific examples of the chaotic nature of dorm life: the party down the hall that broke up at 2:00 A.M. when you had a chemistry exam that same morning at 8 o'clock; the stereo next door that seems to be stuck on its highest decibel level at all hours of the day and night; and the new "friend" you recently acquired who thinks you are the best listener in the world—especially when everyone else has the good sense to be asleep. After such a detailed and well-documented explanation, your parents could hardly deny the strain of this difficult environment on your studies. Examples can be very persuasive.

The following paragraphs written by a student use examples to explain how he reacts to boredom in his life. As you read this excerpt, notice how the writer shows rather than tells the readers how he copes with boredom by providing exciting details that are concrete, specific, and definite:

> *We all deal with boredom in our own ways. Unfortunately, most of us have to deal with it far too often. Some people actually seek boredom. Being bored means that they are not required to do anything; being boring means that no one wants anything from them. In short, these people equate boredom with peace and relaxation. But for the rest of us, boredom is not peaceful. It produces anxiety.*
>
> *Most people deal with boredom by trying to distract themselves from boring circumstances. Myself, I'm a reader. At the breakfast table over a boring bowl of cereal, I read the cereal box, the milk carton, the wrapper on the bread. (Have you ever noticed how many of those ingredients are unpronounceable?) Waiting in a doctor's office, I will gladly read weekly news magazines of three years ago, a book for five-year-olds, advertisements for drugs, and even the*

physician's odd-looking diplomas on the walls. Have you ever been so bored you were reduced to reading through all the business cards in your wallet? Searching for names similar to yours in the phone book? Browsing through the National Enquirer *while waiting in the grocery line? At any rate, that's my recipe for beating boredom. What's yours?*

THINKING CRITICALLY BY USING EXAMPLE

Working with examples gives you yet another powerful way of processing your immediate environment and the larger world around you. It involves a manner of thinking that is completely different from description and narration. Using examples to think critically means seeing a definite order in a series of specific, concrete illustrations that are related in some way which may or may not be immediately obvious to your readers.

Isolating this rhetorical mode involves playing with related details in such a way that they create various patterns that relay different messages to the reader. Often, the simple act of arranging examples helps both the reader and the writer make sense of an experience or idea. In fact, ordering examples and illustrations in a certain way may give one distinct impression, while ordering them in another way may send a completely different message. Each pattern creates a different meaning and, as a result, an entirely new effect.

With examples, more than with description and narration, patterns need to be discovered in the context of the topic, the writer's purpose, and the writer's ultimate message. Writers and readers of example essays must make a shift from chronological to logical thinking. A writer discussing variations in faces, for example, would be working with assorted memories of people, incidents, and age differences. All of these details will eventually take shape in some sort of statement about faces, but these observations would probably not follow a strictly chronological sequence.

The exercises here will help you experience the mental differences among these rhetorical modes and will also prepare you to make sense of details and examples through careful arrangement and rearrangement of them in your essay. These exercises will continue to give you more information about your mind's abilities and range.

1. For each sentence below, provide two to three examples that would illustrate the generalization:
   a. I really liked (disliked) some of the movies released this year.
   b. Many career opportunities await a college graduate.
   c. Some companies make large sums of money by selling products with the names of professional sports teams on them.
2. Give an example (as specific as possible) of each item listed here: car, pizza, song, musician, event, friend, emotion, vacation, plant.
3. Jot down five examples of a single problem on campus that bothers you. First, arrange these examples in an order that would convince the president of your school that making some changes in this area would create a more positive learning environment. Second, organize your five examples in such a way that they would convince your parents that the learning environment at your current school cannot be salvaged and you should immediately transfer to another school.

READING AND WRITING ESSAYS THAT USE EXAMPLES

A common criticism of college-level writers is that they often base their essays on unsupported generalizations, such as "All sports cars are unreliable." The guidelines discussed in this introduction will help you avoid this problem and use examples effectively to support your ideas.

As you read the essays in this chapter, take time to notice the degree of specificity the writers use to make various points. To a certain extent, the more examples you use in your essays, the clearer your ideas will be and the more your readers will understand and be interested in what you are saying.

Notice also that these writers know when to stop—when "more" becomes too much and boredom sets in for the reader. Most college students err by using too few examples, however, so we suggest that, when in doubt about whether or not to include another illustration, you should go ahead and add it.

How to Read an Essay that Uses Examples

Preparing to Read. Before you begin reading the essays in this chapter, take some time to think about each author's title: What can you infer about Bill Cosby's attitude toward having children from his title "The Baffling Question"? What do you think is Harry Edwards's view of African-American society? In addition, try to discover the writer's audience and purpose at this point in the reading process; scanning the essay and surveying its synopsis in the Rhetorical Table of Contents will provide you with useful information for this task.

Also important as you prepare to read is information about the author and about how a particular essay was written. Most of this material is furnished for you in the biography preceding each essay. From it, you might learn why Jane Goodall is qualified to write about the minds of chimpanzees or why Alleen Pace Nilson published "Sexism in English: A 1990s Update."

Finally, before you begin to read, take time to answer the Preparing to Read questions and to make some associations with the general subject of the essay: What do you want to know about blindness (Harold Krents)? What are some of your opinions on sexism in the English language (Alleen Pace Nilsen)?

Reading. As you first read these essays, record any thoughts that come to mind. Make associations freely with the content of each essay, its purpose, its audience, and the facts about its publication. For example, try to learn why Cosby writes about having children or why Krents titles his essay "Darkness at Noon." At this point, you will probably be able to make some pretty accurate guesses about the audience each author is addressing. Creating a context for your reading—including the writer's qualifications; the essay's tone, purpose, and audience; and the publication data—is an important first step toward being able to analyze your reading material in any mode.

Finally, after you have read an essay in this section once, preview the questions after the selection before you read it again. Let these questions focus your attention for your second reading.

Rereading. As you read the essays in this chapter for a second time, focus on the examples each writer uses to make his or her point: How relevant are these examples to the thesis and purpose of each essay? How many examples do the writers use? Do they vary the length of these examples to achieve different goals? Do the authors use examples their readers can easily identify with and understand? How are these examples organized in each case? Does this arrangement support each writer's purpose? For example, how relevant are Cosby's examples to his central idea? How many examples does Edwards use to make each point? Does Krents vary the length of each of his examples to accomplish different purposes? How does Goodall organize her examples? Does this arrangement help her accomplish her purpose? In what way? Does Nilsen use examples that men as well as women can identify with? How effective are her examples?

As you read, consider also how other rhetorical modes help each writer accomplish his or her purpose. What are these modes? How do they work along with examples to help create a coherent essay?

Last, answering the questions after each essay will help you check your grasp of its main points and will lead you from the literal to the analytical level in preparation for the discussion/writing assignments that follow.

For a thorough summary of reading tasks, you might want to consult the checklists on pages 20–21 of the Introduction.

How to Write an Essay that Uses Examples

Preparing to Write. Before you can use examples in an essay, you must first think of some. One good way to generate ideas is to use some of the prewriting techniques explained in the Introduction (pages 21–23) as you respond to the Preparing to Write questions that appear before the writing assignments for each essay. You should then consider these thoughts in conjunction with the purpose and the audience specified in your chosen writing assignments. Out of these questions should come a number of good examples for your essay.

Writing. In an example essay, a thesis statement or controlling idea will help you begin to organize your paper. (See page 28 for more information on thesis statements.) Examples become the primary method of organizing an essay when they guide the readers from point to point in reference to the writer's thesis statement. The examples you use should always be relevant to the thesis and purpose of your essay. If, for instance, the person talking about tennis players cited the practice schedules of only unknown players, her friend certainly would not be convinced of the truth of her statement about how hard internationally ranked athletes work at their game. To develop a topic principally with examples, you can use one extended example or several shorter examples, depending on the nature and purpose of your assertion. If you are attempting to prove that Americans are more health-conscious now than they were twenty years ago, citing a few examples from your own neighborhood will not provide enough evidence to be convincing. If, however, you are simply commenting on a neighborhood health trend, you can legitimately refer to these local cases. Furthermore, always try to find examples with which your audience can identify so that they can follow your line of reasoning. If you want your parents to help finance an apartment, citing instances from the lives of current rock stars will probably not prove your point because your parents may not sympathize with these particular role models.

The examples you choose must also be arranged as effectively as possible to encourage audience interest and identification. If you are using examples to explain the imaginative quality of Disneyland, for instance, the most logical approach would probably be to organize your essay by degrees (i.e., from least to most imaginative or most to least original). But if your essay uses examples to help readers visualize your bedroom, a spatial arrangement of the details (moving from one item to the next) might be easiest for your readers to follow. If the subject is a series of important events, like graduation weekend, the illustrations might most effectively be organized chronologically. As you will learn from reading the selections that follow, the careful organization of examples leads quite easily to unity and coherence in your essays. *Unity* is a sense of wholeness and interrelatedness that writers achieve by making sure all their sentences are related to the essay's main idea; *coherence* refers to logical development in an essay, with special attention to how well ideas grow out of one another as the essay develops. Unity and coherence produce good writing—and that, of course, helps foster confidence and accomplishment in school and in your professional life.

Rewriting. As you reread your example essays, look closely at the choice and arrangement of details in relation to your purpose and audience:

Have you included enough examples to develop each of your topics adequately?

Are the examples you have chosen relevant to your thesis?

Have you selected examples that your readers can easily understand?

Have you arranged these examples in a logical manner that your audience can follow?

For more detailed information on writing, see the checklists on pages 32–33 of the Introduction.

STUDENT ESSAY: EXAMPLES AT WORK

In the following essay, a student uses examples to explain and analyze her parents' behavior as they prepare for and enjoy their grandchildren during the Christmas holidays. As you read it, study the various examples the student writer uses to convince us that her parents truly undergo a transformation each winter.

Mom and Dad's Holiday Disappearing Act

General topic
Often during the winter holidays, people find surprises: Children discover the secret contents of brightly wrapped packages that have teased them for weeks; cooks are astonished by the wealth of smells and memories their busy kitchens can bring about; workaholics stumble upon the true joy of a few days' rest. My surprise over the past few winters has been the personality transformation my parents go through around mid-December as they change from Dad and Mom into Poppa and Granny. Yes, they become grandparents and are completely different from the people I know the other eleven and a half months of the year.

Details to capture holiday spirit

Background information

Thesis statement

The first sign of my parents' metamorphosis is the delight they take in visiting toy and children's clothing stores. These two people, who usually despise anything having to do with shopping malls, become crazed consumers. While they tell me to budget my money and shop wisely, they are

First point

Examples relevant to thesis

buying every doll, dump truck, and velvet outfit in sight. And this is only the beginning of the holidays!

<u>When my brother's children arrive, Poppa and Granny come into full form. First they throw out all ideas about a balanced diet for the grandkids.</u> While we were raised in a house where everyone had to take two bites of broccoli, beets, or liver (foods that appeared quite often on our table despite constant groaning), the grandchildren never have to eat anything that does not appeal to them. Granny carries marshmallows in her pockets to bribe the littlest ones into following her around the house, while Poppa offers "surprises" of candy and cake to them all day long. Boxes of chocolate-covered cherries disappear while the bran muffins get hard and stale. The kids love all the sweets, and when the sugar revs up their energy levels, Granny and Poppa can always decide to leave and do a bit more shopping or go to bed while my brother and sister-in-law try to deal with their supercharged, hyperactive kids.

<u>Once the grandchildren have arrived, Granny and Poppa also seem to forget all of the responsibility lectures I so often hear in my daily life.</u> If little Tommy throws a fit at a friend's house, he is "overwhelmed by the number of adults"; if Mickey screams at his sister during dinner, he is "developing his own personality"; if Nancy breaks Granny's vanity mirror (after being told twice to put it down), she is "just a curious child." But, if I track mud into the house while helping to unload groceries, I become "careless"; if I scold one of the grandkids for tearing pages out of my calculus book, I am "impatient." If a grand-

Margin notes:

Transition

Second point

Humorous examples (organized from most to least healthy)

Transition

Third point

Examples in the form of comparisons

child talks back to her mother, Granny and Poppa chuckle at her spirit. If I mumble one word about all of this doting, Mom and Dad reappear to have a talk with me about petty jealousies.

When my nieces and nephews first started appearing at our home for the holidays a few years ago, I probably was jealous, and I complained a lot. But now I spend more time simply sitting back and watching Mom and Dad change into what we call the "Incredible Huggers." They enjoy their time with these grandchildren so much that I easily forgive them their Granny and Poppa faults.

I believe their personality change is due to the lack of responsibility they feel for the grandkids: In their role as grandparents, they don't have to worry about sugar causing cavities or temporary failures of self-discipline turning into lifetime faults. Those problems are up to my brother and sister-in-law. All Granny and Poppa have to do is enjoy and love their grandchildren. They have all the fun of being parents without any of the attendant obligations. And you know what? I think they've earned the right to make this transformation—at least once a year.

Margin annotations:
- Transition to conclusion
- Writer's attitude
- Writer's analysis of situation
- Concluding remark
- Specific reference to introduction

Student Writer's Comments

To begin this essay, I listed examples of my parents' antics during the Christmas holidays as parents and as grandparents and then tried to figure out how these examples illustrated patterns of behavior. Next, I scratched out an outline pairing my parents' actions with what I thought were the causes of those actions. But once I sat down to write, I was completely stumped. I had lots of isolated ideas and saw a few patterns, but I had no notion of where this essay was going.

I thought I might put the theory that writing is discovery to the ultimate test and sit down to write out a very rough first draft. I wanted the introduction to be humorous, but I also wanted to maintain a dignified tone (so I wouldn't sound like a whiny kid!). I was really having trouble getting started. I decided to write down *anything* and then come back to the beginning later on. All of the examples and anecdotes were swimming around in my head wanting to be committed to paper. But I couldn't make sense of many of them, and I still couldn't see where I was headed. I found I needed my thesaurus and dictionary from the very beginning; they helped take the pressure off me to come up with the perfect word every time I was stuck. As I neared the middle of the paper, the introduction popped into my head, so I jotted down my thoughts and continued with the flow of ideas I needed for the body of my essay.

Writing my conclusion forced me to put my experiences with my parents into perspective and gave me an angle for revising the body of my essay. But my focus didn't come to me until I began to revise my entire paper. At that point, I realized I had never really tried to analyze how I felt toward my parents or why they acted as they do during the Christmas holidays. I opened the conclusion with "I believe their [my parents] personality change is due to" and sat in one place until I finished the statement with a reason that made sense out of all these years of frustration. It finally came to me: They act the way they do during the holidays because they don't have primary responsibility for their grandkids. It's a role they have never played before, and they are loving it. (Never mind how it is affecting me!) This basic realization led me to new insights into the major changes they go through during the holidays and ended up giving me a renewed appreciation of their behavior. I couldn't believe the sentence I wrote to close the essay: "I think they've earned the right to make this transformation—at least once a year." Holy cow! Writing this essay actually brought me to a new understanding of my parents.

Revising was a breeze. I felt as if I had just been through a completely draining therapy session, but I now knew what I thought of this topic and where my essay was headed. I dropped irrelevant examples, reorganized other details, and tightened up some of the explanations so they set up my conclusion more clearly. Both my parents and I were delighted with the results.

SOME FINAL THOUGHTS ON EXAMPLES

Although examples are often used to supplement and support other methods of development—such as cause/effect, comparison/contrast, and process analysis—the essays in this section are focused principally on examples. A main idea is expressed in the introduction of each, and the rest of the essay provides examples to bolster that contention. As you read these essays, pay close attention to each author's choice and arrangement of examples; then, try to determine which organizational techniques are most persuasive for each specific audience.

BILL COSBY   (1937 –   )

■ ■ ■

The Baffling Question

Comedian, actor, recording artist, and author Bill Cosby is undoubtedly one of America's best-loved entertainers. From his beginnings on the *I Spy* television series through his *Fat Albert* years
and his work on *Sesame Street*, his eight Grammy awards for comedy albums, his commercials for everything from Kodak film to
Jell-O pudding, his portrayal of the affable obstetrician Cliff
Huxtable on his immensely popular *Cosby Show*, and his latest
role in *Cosby Mysteries*, he has retained his public persona of an
honest and trustworthy storyteller intrigued by the ironies in our
everyday lives. "When I was a kid," he has explained, "I always
used to pay attention to things that other people didn't even
think about. I'd remember funny happenings, just little trivial
things, and then tell stories about them later. I found I could
make people laugh, and I enjoyed doing it because it gave me a
sense of security. I thought that if people laughed at what you
said, that meant they liked you." After a series of hit movies in
the 1970s, Cosby returned to prime-time television in 1984 because of his concern about his family's viewing habits: "I got tired
of seeing TV shows that consisted of a car crash, a gunman, and a
hooker talking to a Black pimp. It was cheaper to do a series than
to throw out my family's six television sets." At the peak of its
success, *The Cosby Show* was seen weekly by over sixty million
viewers. Cosby's publications include *You Are Somebody Special*
(1978), *Fatherhood* (1986), *Time Flies* (1988), and *Love and Marriage*
(1989). He lives with his wife, Camille, in Los Angeles, where he
relaxes by playing an occasional game of tennis.

Preparing to Read

The following selection is from one of Cosby's six books,
Fatherhood, which details the joys and frustrations of raising children. Before reading this piece, pause to consider the effect par-

enthood has had or might have on your life: How did/would you make the decision whether to have children? What variables were/would be involved in this decision? What are/would be some of the difficulties involved in raising children? Some of the joys? How did your parents react to you when you were a child? What memories do you have of your own childhood?

S o you've decided to have a child. You've decided to give up 1 quiet evenings with good books and lazy weekends with good music, intimate meals during which you finish whole sentences, sweet private times when you've savored the thought that just the two of you and your love are all you will ever need. You've decided to turn your sofas into trampolines and to abandon the joys of leisurely contemplating reproductions of great art for the joys of frantically coping with reproductions of yourselves.

Why? 2

Poets have said the reason to have children is to give yourself 3 immortality; and I must admit I did ask God to give me a son because I wanted someone to carry on the family name. Well, God did just that and I now confess that there have been times when I've told my son not to reveal who he is.

"You make up a name," I've said. "Just don't tell anybody who 4 you are."

Immortality? Now that I have had five children, my only hope 5 is that they all are out of the house before I die.

No, immortality was not the reason why my wife and I pro- 6 duced these beloved sources of dirty laundry and ceaseless noise. And we also did not have them because we thought it would be fun to see one of them sit in a chair and stick out his leg so that another one of them running by was launched like Explorer I. After which I said to the child who was the launching pad, "Why did you do that?"

"Do what?" he replied. 7

"Stick out your leg." 8

"Dad, I didn't know my leg was going out. My leg, it does that 9 a lot."

If you cannot function in a world where things like this are said, 10 then you better forget about raising children and go for daffodils.

My wife and I also did not have children so they could yell at 11
each other all over the house, moving me to say, "What's the
problem?"

"She's waving her foot in my room," my daughter replied. 12

"And something like that *bothers* you?" 13

"Yes, I don't *want* her foot in my room." 14

"Well," I said, dipping into my storehouse of paternal wisdom, 15
"why don't you just close the door?"

"Then I can't see what she's doing!" 16

Furthermore, we did not have the children because we 17
thought it would be rewarding to watch them do things that
should be studied by the Menninger Clinic.

"Okay," I said to all five one day, "go get into the car." 18

All five then ran to the same car door, grabbed the same han- 19
dle, and spent the next few minutes beating each other up. Not
one of them had the intelligence to say, "Hey, *look*. There are
three more doors." The dog, however, was already inside.

And we did not have the children to help my wife develop 20
new lines for her face or because she had always had a desire to
talk out loud to herself: "Don't tell *me* you're *not* going to do
something when I tell you to move!" And we didn't have children
so I could always be saying to someone, "Where's my change?"

Like so many young couples, my wife and I simply were un- 21
able to project. In restaurants we did not see the small children
who were casting their bread on the water in the glasses the
waiter had brought; and we did not see the mother who was fast-
ing because she was both cutting the food for one child while
pulling another from the floor to a chair that he would use for
slipping to the floor again. And we did not project beyond those
lovely Saturdays of buying precious little things after leisurely
brunches together. We did not see that *other* precious little things
would be coming along to destroy the first batch.

UNDERSTANDING DETAILS

1. According to Cosby, exactly what is "the baffling question"?
   Why is this question "baffling"?
2. If everyone felt as Cosby does about raising children, what
   kinds of people would have children?

3. List three important issues that Cosby believes couples should consider before they have children.

4. From Cosby's point of view, in what important ways do children change a couple's life?

ANALYZING MEANING

1. Why do you think Cosby focuses on the problems children create in a couple's life? What effect does this approach have on his main point?

2. What does Cosby mean when he says, "You've decided . . . to abandon the joys of leisurely contemplating reproductions of great art for the joys of frantically coping with reproductions of yourselves" (paragraph 1)? Whom is he addressing?

3. Following Cosby's logic, why did he and his wife have children? What examples lead you to this conclusion?

4. In what way is the last sentence in this essay a good summary statement? What specific thoughts does it summarize?

DISCOVERING RHETORICAL STRATEGIES

1. How does the first paragraph set the tone for the rest of the essay?

2. Cosby's primary strategy in this essay is irony. That is, he suggests reasons for having children by listing reasons *not* to have children. What effect is this approach likely to have on his readers?

3. How does Cosby use specific examples to create humor? Is his humor effective? Explain your answer.

4. Cosby is a master of choosing vivid examples to make his point. What other rhetorical strategies does Cosby use to develop his essay? Give examples of each.

MAKING CONNECTIONS

1. Compare Bill Cosby's comments about raising children with those made by Germaine Greer in "A Child Is Born." To what extent is the behavior of Cosby's children typically "American" according to Greer's description of Western society?

2. How seriously does Cosby intend his readers to take his "advice" about not having children? Do you see any connection

between his point of view and that expressed by Judy Brady in "Why I Want a Wife"? How do both of these essays work through the rhetorical device of "irony" (that is, saying the opposite of what we really mean)? Which essay is most effective? Explain your answer.

3. Contrast Cosby's rapport with his children with the parent–child relationships depicted in Amy Tan's "The Joy Luck Club," Lewis Sawaquat's "For My Indian Daughter," or Michael Dorris's "The Broken Cord." Which parents do you think love their children most? Why do you believe this is true?

IDEAS FOR DISCUSSION/WRITING

Preparing to Write

Write freely about the art of parenthood: From your observations or experience, what are some of the principal problems and joys of parenthood? How is being a parent different from baby-sitting? What pleasant baby-sitting experiences have you had? What unpleasant experiences? What kind of child were you? What specific memories lead you to this conclusion?

Choosing a Topic

1. Write an essay for the general public explaining one particular problem or joy of parenthood. In your essay, mimic Cosby's humorous approach to the topic. Use several specific examples to make your point.

2. Write an editorial for your local newspaper on your own foolproof techniques for doing one of the following: (a) baby-sitting, (b) raising children, or (c) becoming a model child. Use specific examples to explain your approach.

3. Interview one or two relatives who are older than you; ask them about the type of child you were. Have them recall some particularly memorable details that characterized your behavior. Then, write an essay explaining their predominant impressions of you. Use examples to support these impressions.

HARRY EDWARDS   (1942 –   )

■ ■ ■

Triple Tragedy in Black Society

Harry Edwards is a prominent sports sociologist who has risen from an impoverished childhood in East St. Louis to a professorship in sociology at the University of California at Berkeley. His first book, *The Revolt of the Black Athlete* (1969), effectively challenged the myth of the American sports establishment as a model of racial harmony and ethnic fair play. Edwards next wrote *Sociology in Sports* (1973), an analysis of the many complex issues that affect sports in modern society, and *The Struggle That Must Be* (1980), an autobiography recounting his personal experiences with racism, his organization of the Black Athletes' Protest at the 1968 Olympics, and his predictions about the future of race relations in America. Edwards is most emphatic when describing an athletic system that, he believes, entraps and exploits African-American males by falsely promising them social equality through sports. In addition to performing his academic duties, he currently serves as special assistant to the commissioner of Major League Baseball and as staff consultant and player personnel consultant for the San Francisco 49ers and the Golden State Warriors.

Preparing to Read

"Triple Tragedy in Black Society," which originally appeared in *Ebony* magazine in August 1988, argues that the "obsessive pursuit of sports" among African-American youths prevents them from advancing in other areas of American society. It decries the "talent drain" toward athletics and away from important careers in such fields as medicine, law, politics, and education. As you prepare to read this essay, take a few moments to consider your own observations on the role of African Americans in society today: To what extent does racial discrimination still exist in American society? Have you ever experienced prejudice? Have any of your friends experienced it? Do you think racism exists in sports today? If so, which sports seem most racist? Which are least so? What can be done to relieve racism in the world of sports? In all aspects of American society?

T he single-minded pursuit of sports fame and fortune is today approaching an institutionalized *triple tragedy* in Black society: The tragedy of thousands and thousands of Black youths in obsessive pursuit of sports goals foredoomed to elude the vast and overwhelming majority of them; the tragedy of the personal and cultural underdevelopment that afflicts so many among both successful and unsuccessful Black sports aspirants; and the tragedy of cultural and institutional underdevelopment in Black society overall, partially as a consequence of the *talent drain* toward sports and away from other critically vital areas of occupational and career emphasis (medicine, law, economics, politics, education, the technical fields, etc.).

Our circumstances in sports are inextricably intertwined with the broader Black experience in America. Notwithstanding sports' reputation in Black society for beneficence and for providing extraordinary, if not exemplary, social and economic mobility opportunities, the reality is that in sports, no less than in society, Black advancement has been achieved at the price of persistent, vigilant, intelligent reflection and determined individual and collective struggle. Nowhere is this perspective more clearly evident than when we consider the challenges and prospects confronting Black youths aspiring to sports stardom.

Owing largely to (1) a longstanding, widely held and—at its root—*racist* presumption of innate race-linked Black athletic superiority, to (2) media propaganda about sports as a broadly accessible route to Black social and economic mobility, and finally to (3) a lack of comparably visible, high-prestige Black role models beyond the sports arena, Black families are four times more likely than White families to push their children toward sports-career aspirations—often to the neglect and detriment of other critically important areas of personal and cultural development.

Only *five percent* of high school athletes go on to compete in their sports at the collegiate level—including those who participate in junior college—which is to say that over 95% of all athletes must face the realities of life after sports at the conclusion of their last high-school athletic competition. Of those Black athletes who do attend four-year institutions on athletic scholarships or grants-in-aid, 65 to 75 percent *never* graduate from the schools they represent in sports. Of the 25 to 35 percent who do graduate, an unconscionable proportion graduate in what are for Blacks often less marketable academic majors riddled with "keep 'em eligible" less-competitive "jock courses" of dubious educational value and occupational relevance. What passes for "physical education" and "communications" majors at many colleges are prime examples.

Even in sports where Blacks predominate as athletes, we are routinely passed over as candidates for top coaching and sports-administration jobs—often despite having the combination of both academic preparation in physical education and substantial practical experience at the *assistant* level in major athletic programs. Hence, there are only two Black athletic directors, four Black head football coaches, and fewer than 30 Black head basketball coaches at major Division I, NCAA colleges and universities. There are no Black head baseball coaches at such institutions today. And in the professional ranks, circumstances relative to Black access to top positions are even more dismal. 5

Similarly, notwithstanding Black athletes' preparation in communications, the press box and the broadcast booth remain the most racially segregated corners of the sports arena. Of 664 beat writers in basketball, football, and baseball, only 28 are Black. And those few Blacks who have found their way into the broadcast booths of major television and radio networks have done so owing more to their athletic prominence than to their academic preparation. (For example, Irv Cross at CBS, Ahmad Rashad at NBC, Tom Jackson at ESPN, Bill Russell formerly at WTBS and O. J. Simpson formerly at ABC). 6

What all of this amounts to is a *plantation system* of occupational relationships in sport—one having Whites holding a virtual monopoly on power and decision-making positions, with a few Blacks in mid-level *assistant* positions, and with the majority of Blacks in the lowest level production and labor roles, i.e., that of athlete. In essence, Blacks have advanced from the cotton fields to the football fields, but the structure of occupational relations remains strikingly similar. 7

Of the Black athletes who participate in collegiate football, basketball or baseball, only 1.6 percent ever sign a professional 8 contract—less than *two out of 100*. And within three and a half years, over 60 percent of those who do sign such contracts are out of professional sports, more often than not financially destitute or in debt, and on the street without either the credentials or the skills to make their way productively in our extremely competitive high-tech society.

Despite efforts by a broad array of media, academic, civil rights and sports interests to draw attention to and rectify the tragedies of Black sports involvement, the fact remains that it is Black families and Black athletes who must assume principal responsibility for remedying the situation. It is now undeniable that through a blind belief in the beneficence and accessibility of sports as a socioeconomic mobility vehicle, Black families have unwittingly become accessories to, and major perpetrators of, the tragedies of Black sports involvement. We have, in effect, set up our children for personal and cultural underdevelopment, academic victimization, and athletic exploitation by our encouragement of the primacy of sports achievement over all else. We have then bartered away the services of the more competitive among our children to the highest bidders among collegiate athletic recruiters in exchange for what are typically extremely hollow promises of ethical educational opportunities or, even worse, promises of sports fame, fortune, and *fat city* forever. 9

Black families have the responsibility to inform themselves about the realities of Black sports involvement—its advantages and liabilities, its triumphs and its tragedies. As a culture and as a people, we simply can no longer permit many among our most competitive and gifted youths to sacrifice a wealth of human potential on the altar of athletic aspiration, to put playbooks ahead of textbooks. This does not mean that Blacks should abandon sports, but that we *must* learn to deal with the realities of sports more intelligently and constructively. Black parents must insist upon the establishment and pursuit of high academic standards and personal development goals by their children. And here we must be crystal clear: *our children's allegiance to high goals and standards will be principally established and enforced not on the campus but in the home.* 10

And, finally, it must be stated unequivocally that it is Black athletes themselves who must shoulder a substantial portion of the responsibility for improving Black circumstances and outcomes in 11

American sports. Black athletes must insist upon intellectual discipline no less than athletic discipline among themselves, and upon educational integrity in athletic programs rather than, as is all too often the case, merely seeking the easiest route to maintaining athletic eligibility. If Black athletes fail to take a conscious, active and informed role in changing the course and character of Black sports involvement, nothing done by any other party to this tragic situation is likely to be effective or lasting—if for no other reason than the fact that *a slave cannot be freed against his will.*

In the 1930s, Paul Robeson, Joe Louis and Jesse Owens led 12 the fight for *Black legitimacy* as athletes. In the late 1940s, and into the 1950s, Jackie Robinson, Althea Gibson, Larry Doby, Roy Campanella and others struggled to secure *Black access* to the mainstream of American sports. From the late 1950s through the 1960s and into the 1970s, Jim Brown, Bill Russell, Curt Flood, Tommy Smith and John Carlos, Muhammad Ali and Arthur Ashe fought to secure *dignity and respect for Blacks* in sports. These were not knights in shining armor, but *pony express riders* carrying the burden of the Black struggle in sports over their particular stretches of historical terrain. And both the record books and the history books bear testament to the magnitude of the success of these great forerunners.

But as was stated at the outset, our circumstances in sports are 13 bound up with and deeply rooted in the broader Black experience in America. And so long as these circumstances—commensurate with developments in society at large—are dynamic and ever evolving, our struggle in sports also must be perpetual and *there can be no final victories.*

The challenges confronting Black people in the sports realm, 14 therefore, are but the latest. They will not be the last. The only question is will the next generation of Blacks in sports be able to move ahead and meet the challenges of their own historical era or will they have to first fight battles that we, both individually and collectively, should have fought—and won?

UNDERSTANDING DETAILS

1. What is the "triple tragedy in Black society" that Edwards refers to in this essay? In Edwards's estimation, what has caused the tragedy?

2. What is the "talent drain" Edwards refers to in paragraph 1?

3. In the author's opinion, what is the relationship for African Americans between achievement in sports and in academics?

4. What main examples from the sports world does Edwards cite to support his theory of the "tragedies" caused by the single-minded involvement of African Americans in sports?

ANALYZING MEANING

1. In what ways are sports both a help and a hindrance to the African-American community? How do sports represent "the broader Black experience in America" (paragraph 2)?

2. What are the author's thoughts on the role of racism in athletics? In what ways does he feel the world of athletics reflects the "plantation system" (paragraph 7) of the past? Explain your answer in detail.

3. Which examples in this essay convince you most persuasively that "the single-minded pursuit of sports fame and fortune" (paragraph 1) among African-American youths today is threatening their advancement in society?

4. Where does Edwards believe the remedy to the problem lies? What leads you to this conclusion?

DISCOVERING RHETORICAL STRATEGIES

1. List the author's main points in this essay. Why does he choose to deal with these topics in this particular order?

2. What factual examples does Edwards use to support his main points in paragraphs 4, 5, 6, 7, and 8? Outline these five paragraphs to show how the examples work in his essay.

3. Describe Edwards's intended audience in as much detail as possible. Why do you think he has aimed his essay at this particular group?

4. Besides examples, what other rhetorical strategies does Edwards draw upon to make his statement about racism in professional athletics? Give examples of each.

MAKING CONNECTIONS

1. Imagine that Shelby Steele ("Affirmative Action: The Price of Preference") has just read Edwards's essay. Would he agree or disagree with Edwards's principal argument that African-American athletes are cheating themselves by their "single-minded pursuit" of careers in professional sports? Would Steele,

like Edwards, lay part of the blame on the racism inherent in our society? Explain your answer.

2. Gloria Steinem ("The Politics of Muscle"), Joyce Carol Oates ("On Boxing"), and Edwards all approach sports in different ways. Which author's argument do you find most convincing? To whom should the general public pay most attention? Explain your reasoning.

3. Compare and contrast Edwards's use of examples with the examples provided by Jane Goodall ("The Mind of the Chimpanzee") and/or by Alleen Pace Nilsen ("Sexism in English: A 1990s Update"). Whose argument is most convincing? Explain your answer.

IDEAS FOR DISCUSSION/WRITING

Preparing to Write

Write freely about the response of contemporary society to African Americans: In what areas of our society have African Americans advanced most dramatically? Where has their advancement been least dramatic? Why do you think African Americans have had more success in some areas than in others? How does racism in America prevent African Americans from making social and economic progress? Which aspects of American life are most blatantly racist? Which are least racist? How do you account for this difference?

Choosing a Topic

1. Using many examples to support his argument, Edwards claims in his essay that sports are both a help and a hindrance to African Americans. From your view of the world, write an example essay explaining to your friends one aspect of American life that is both a help and a hindrance to you.

2. As a college student, you see many events every day that could qualify as tragedies if they persisted. Write an essay for your school newspaper entitled "Triple Tragedy in _____." Fill in the blank, and then, through carefully chosen examples, explain to the college community the extent of the problem you have identified.

3. Comedian Dick Gregory has traveled the United States proclaiming that African Americans naively and unwisely use sports as an attempt to escape from reality; Edwards admits that

sports offer some limited opportunities for African Americans, but he argues that American athletics are still ultimately racist in principle. What is your opinion? Should African Americans and other minorities pursue other interests and careers? Direct your comments to the general public, and use examples to support your opinion.

HAROLD KRENTS   (1944 – 1987)

■ ■ ■

Darkness at Noon

Raised in New York City, Harold Krents earned a B.A. and a law degree at Harvard, studied at Oxford University, worked as a partner in a Washington, D.C., law firm, was the subject of a long-running Broadway play, and wrote a popular television movie—all despite the fact that he was born blind. His "1-A" classification by a local draft board, which doubted the severity of his handicap, brought about the 1969 Broadway hit play *Butterflies Are Free* by Leonard Gershe. Krents once explained that he was merely the "prototype" for the central character: "I gave the story its inspiration—the play's plot is not my story; its spirit is." In 1972 Krents wrote *To Race the Wind*, which was made into a CBS-TV movie in 1980. During his career as a lawyer, Krents worked hard to expand legal protection for the handicapped and fought to secure their right to equal opportunity in the business world. He died in 1987 of a brain tumor.

Preparing to Read

In the following article, originally published in the *New York Times* (1978), the author gives examples of different kinds of discrimination he has suffered because of his blindness. As you prepare to read this essay, take a few minutes to think about disabilities or handicaps in general: Do you have a disability? If so, how are you treated by others? How do you feel others respond to your handicap? Do you know someone else who has a disability? How do you respond to that person? How do you think he or she wants to be treated? To what extent do you think disabilities should affect a person's job opportunities? What can be done to improve society's prejudices against the disabled?

B lind from birth, I have never had the opportunity to see 1
myself and have been completely dependent on the image
I create in the eye of the observer. To date it has not been
narcissistic.

There are those who assume that since I can't see, I obviously 2
also cannot hear. Very often people will converse with me at the
top of their lungs, enunciating each word very carefully.
Conversely, people will also often whisper, assuming that since
my eyes don't work, my ears don't either.

For example, when I go to the airport and ask the ticket agent 3
for assistance to the plane, he or she will invariably pick up the
phone, call a ground hostess and whisper: "Hi, Jane, we've got a 76
here." I have concluded that the word "blind" is not used for one
of two reasons: Either they fear that if the dread word is spoken,
the ticket agent's retina will immediately detach, or they are reluctant to inform me of my condition of which I may not have been
previously aware.

On the other hand, others know that of course I can hear, but 4
believe that I can't talk. Often, therefore, when my wife and I go
out to dinner, a waiter or waitress will ask Kit if "*he* would like a
drink" to which I respond that "indeed *he* would."

This point was graphically driven home to me while we were 5
in England. I had been given a year's leave of absence from my
Washington law firm to study for a diploma in law degree at
Oxford University. During the year I became ill and was hospital-
ized. Immediately after admission, I was wheeled down to the X-
ray room. Just at the door sat an elderly woman—elderly I would
judge from the sound of her voice. "What is his name?" the
woman asked the orderly who had been wheeling me.

"What's your name?" the orderly repeated to me. 6

"Harold Krents," I replied. 7

"Harold Krents," he repeated. 8

"When was he born?" 9

"When were you born?" 10

"November 5, 1944," I responded. 11

"November 5, 1944," the orderly intoned. 12

This procedure continued for approximately five minutes at 13
which point even my saint-like disposition deserted me. "Look," I
finally blurted out, "this is absolutely ridiculous. Okay, granted I

can't see, but it's got to have become pretty clear to both of you that I don't need an interpreter."

"He says he doesn't need an interpreter," the orderly reported to the woman. 14

The toughest misconception of all is the view that because I can't see, I can't work. I was turned down by over forty law firms because of my blindness, even though my qualifications included a cum laude degree from Harvard College and a good ranking in my Harvard Law School class. 15

The attempt to find employment, the continuous frustration of being told that it was impossible for a blind person to practice law, the rejection letters, not based on my lack of ability but rather on my disability, will always remain one of the most disillusioning experiences of my life. 16

I therefore look forward to the day, with the expectation that it is certain to come, when employers will view their handicapped workers as a little child did me years ago when my family still lived in Scarsdale. 17

I was playing basketball with my father in our backyard according to procedures we had developed. My father would stand beneath the hoop, shout, and I would shoot over his head at the basket attached to our garage. Our next-door neighbor, aged five, wandered over into our yard with a playmate. "He's blind," our neighbor whispered to her friend in a voice that could be heard distinctly by Dad and me. Dad shot and missed; I did the same. Dad hit the rim; I missed entirely; Dad shot and missed the garage entirely. "Which one is blind?" whispered back the little friend. 18

I would hope that in the near future when a plant manager is touring the factory with the foreman and comes upon a handicapped and nonhandicapped person working together, his comment after watching them work will be, "Which one is disabled?" 19

UNDERSTANDING DETAILS

1. According to Krents, what are three common misconceptions about blind people?
2. What important details did you learn about Krents's life from this essay? How does he introduce this information?
3. In what ways was Krents frustrated in his search for employment? Was he qualified for the jobs he sought? Why or why not?

4. What attitude toward the handicapped does Krents look forward to in the future?

ANALYZING MEANING

1. What does Krents mean when he says that his self-image gained through the eyes of others "has not been narcissistic" (paragraph 1)? Why do you think this is the case?
2. What is Krents's attitude toward his handicap? What parts of his essay reveal that attitude?
3. How do you account for the reactions to his blindness that Krents tells about in this essay? Are you aware of such behavior in yourself? In others?
4. Do you think we will ever arrive at the point in the working world that Krents describes in the last paragraph? How can we get there? What advantages or disadvantages might accompany such a change?

DISCOVERING RHETORICAL STRATEGIES

1. How does Krents organize the three main points in his essay? Why does he put them in this order? What is the benefit of discussing employment last?
2. Krents often offers specific examples in the form of dialogue or spoken statements. Are these effective ways to develop his main points? Explain your answer.
3. Krents establishes a fairly fast pace in this essay as he discusses several related ideas in a small amount of space. How does he create this sense of speed? What effect does this pace have on his essay as a whole?
4. Although the author's dominant rhetorical mode is example in this essay, what other strategies does he use to develop his ideas? Give examples of each of these strategies.

MAKING CONNECTIONS

1. Compare the employment discrimination faced by Krents because of his blindness with the racial and social discrimination suffered by Lewis Sawaquat ("For My Indian Daughter") and Franklin Zimring ("Confessions of an Ex-Smoker"). Which person has been treated most unfairly by society? Explain your answer.

2. How similar is Krents's use of humor to that of Bill Cosby ("The Baffling Question"), Russell Baker ("The Saturday Evening Post"), or Barbara Ehrenreich ("Stop Ironing the Diapers"). Which author do you find most amusing? Why? Is humor used in a different way in Krents's essay than it is in the other two? If so, how?

3. How many examples does Krents use in his essay? Does Krents use more or fewer examples per page than Jane Goodall ("The Mind of the Chimpanzee") or Harry Edwards ("Triple Tragedy in Black Society")? How does the number of examples affect the believability of each author's argument?

IDEAS FOR DISCUSSION/WRITING

Preparing to Write

Write freely about disabilities: If you are disabled, what is your response to the world? Why do you respond the way you do? How does society respond to you? Are you pleased or not with your relationship to society in general? If you are not disabled, what do you think your attitude would be if you were disabled? How do you respond to disabled people? To what extent does your response depend upon the disability? Are you satisfied with your reaction to other people's disabilities? Are you prejudiced in any way against people with disabilities? Do you think our society as a whole demonstrates any prejudices toward the disabled? If so, how can we correct these biases?

Choosing a Topic

1. As a reporter for your campus newspaper, you have been assigned to study and write about the status of services for the disabled on your campus. Is your school equipped with parking for the handicapped? A sufficient number of ramps for wheelchairs? Transportation for the handicapped? Other special services for the handicapped? Interview some disabled students to get their views on these services. Write an example essay for the newspaper, explaining the situation.

2. With your eyes closed, take a walk through a place that you know well. How does it feel to be nearly sightless? What senses begin to compensate for your loss of vision? Write an essay for

your classmates detailing your reactions. Use specific examples to communicate your feelings.

3. Do you have any phobias or irrational fears that handicap you in any way? Write a letter to a friend explaining one of these "handicaps" and your method of coping with it.

JANE GOODALL (1934 –)

■ ■ ■

The Mind of the Chimpanzee

From the age of eight, Jane Goodall knew exactly what she wanted to be when she grew up: a specialist in primate behavior who lived with and studied wild animals in the jungles of Africa. Twenty-six years later, her dream became reality when world-famous anthropologist Louis Leakey rescued her from an obscure secretarial position at the National Museum of Natural History in Nairobi, Kenya, and selected her to research chimpanzee behavior at the Gombe Stream Research Center on the shore of Lake Tanganyika in Tanzania. Soon thereafter, Goodall earned her Ph.D. at Cambridge University, where she was one of only a handful of students ever awarded a doctorate without first completing a baccalaureate degree. A series of stunning discoveries at Gombe—evidence that chimpanzees eat meat, have an extremely sophisticated social hierarchy, and fashion tools out of grass and twigs—brought Goodall to public prominence and forced the scientific establishment to reevaluate the ever-narrowing boundaries between humans and animals. Goodall has written nine books, including *Primate Behavior* (1965), *In the Shadow of Man* (1971), *Chimps* (1989), and *Through a Window: My Thirty Years with the Chimpanzees of Gombe* (1990). She currently serves as scientific director of the Gombe Research Center in Tanzania. In her spare time, she enjoys horseback riding, listening to classical music, and reading.

Preparing to Read

In the following excerpt from *Through a Window*, Goodall describes some of her discoveries in Tanzania as she studied the cognitive abilities of chimpanzees. As you prepare to read this essay, take a few minutes to think about the roles of research and learning in American society today: What value do you place on the process of learning? What are you being forced to learn? What do you want to learn more about? Have you ever studied something on your own? Were you pleased by your discoveries? Do your friends value learning? Do they value the process of education? How are education and learning related?

O ften I have gazed into a chimpanzee's eyes and won- 1 dered what was going on behind them. I used to look into Flo's, she so old, so wise. What did she remember of her young days? David Greybeard had the most beautiful eyes of them all, large and lustrous, set wide apart. They somehow expressed his whole personality, his serene self-assurance, his inherent dignity—and, from time to time, his utter determination to get his way. For a long time I never liked to look a chimpanzee straight in the eye—I assumed that, as is the case with most primates, this would be interpreted as a threat or at least as a breach of good manners. Not so. As long as one looks with gentleness, without arrogance, a chimpanzee will understand, and may even return the look. And then—or such is my fantasy—it is as though the eyes are windows into the mind. Only the glass is opaque so that the mystery can never be fully revealed.

I shall never forget my meeting with Lucy, an eight-year-old 2 home-raised chimpanzee. She came and sat beside me on the sofa and, with her face very close to mine, searched in my eyes—for what? Perhaps she was looking for signs of mistrust, dislike, or fear, since many people must have been somewhat disconcerted when, for the first time, they came face to face with a grown chimpanzee. Whatever Lucy read in my eyes clearly satisfied her for she suddenly put one arm round my neck and gave me a generous and very chimp-like kiss, her mouth wide open and laid over mine. I was accepted.

For a long time after that encounter I was profoundly dis- 3 turbed. I had been at Gombe for about fifteen years then and I was quite familiar with chimpanzees in the wild. But Lucy, having grown up as a human child, was like a changeling, her essential chimpanzeeness overlaid by the various human behaviors she had acquired over the years. No longer purely chimp yet eons away from humanity, she was man-made, some other kind of being. I watched, amazed, as she opened the refrigerator and various cupboards, found bottles and a glass, then poured herself a gin and tonic. She took the drink to the TV, turned the set on, flipped from one channel to another then, as though in disgust, turned it off again. She selected a glossy magazine from the table and, still carrying her drink, settled in a comfortable chair. Occasionally, as she leafed through the magazine she identified something she saw, using the signs of ASL, the American Sign Language used by the deaf. I, of course, did not understand, but my hostess, Jane Temerlin (who was also Lucy's "mother"), translated: "That dog," Lucy commented, pausing at a photo of a small white poodle. She turned the page. "Blue," she declared, pointing then signing as she gazed at a picture of a lady advertising some kind of soap powder and wearing a brilliant blue dress. And finally, after some vague hand movements—perhaps signed mutterings—"This Lucy's, this mine," as she closed the magazine and laid it on her lap. She had just been taught, Jane told me, the use of the possessive pronouns during the thrice weekly ASL lessons she was receiving at the time.

The book written by Lucy's human "father," Maury Temerlin, 4 was entitled *Lucy: Growing Up Human*. And in fact, the chimpanzee is more like us than is any other living creature. There is close resemblance in the physiology of our two species and genetically, in the structure of the DNA, chimpanzees and humans differ by only just over one per cent. This is why medical research uses chimpanzees as experimental animals when they need substitutes for humans in the testing of some drug or vaccine. Chimpanzees can be infected with just about all known human infectious diseases including those, such as hepatitis B and AIDS, to which other non-human animals (except gorillas, orangutans and gibbons) are immune. There are equally striking similarities between humans and chimpanzees in the anatomy and wiring of the brain and nervous system, and—although many scientists have been reluctant to admit to this—in social behavior, intellectual ability, and the emotions. The notion of an evolutionary continuity in physical structure from pre-human ape to modern man has long been morally acceptable to most scientists. That the same might hold good for mind was generally considered an absurd hypothesis—particularly by those who used, and often misused, animals in their laboratories. It is, after all, convenient to believe that the creature you are using, while it may react in disturbingly human-like ways, is, in fact, merely a mindless and, above all, unfeeling, "dumb" animal.

When I began my study at Gombe in 1960 it was not permis- 5
sible—at least not in ethological circles—to talk about an animal's
mind. Only humans had minds. Nor was it quite proper to talk
about animal personality. Of course everyone knew that they *did*
have their own unique characters—everyone who had ever
owned a dog or other pet was aware of that. But ethologists,
striving to make theirs a "hard" science, shied away from the task
of trying to explain such things objectively. One respected ethol-
ogist, while acknowledging that there was "variability between
individual animals," wrote that it was best that this fact be "swept
under the carpet." At that time ethological carpets fairly bulged
with all that was hidden beneath them.

How naive I was. As I had not had an undergraduate science 6
education I didn't realize that animals were not supposed to have
personalities, or to think, or to feel emotions or pain. I had no
idea that it would have been more appropriate to assign each of
the chimpanzees a number rather than a name when I got to
know him or her. I didn't realize that it was not scientific to discuss behavior in terms of motivation or purpose. And no one had
told me that terms such as *childhood* and *adolescence* were uniquely
human phases of the life cycle, culturally determined, not to be
used when referring to young chimpanzees. Not knowing, I
freely made use of all those forbidden terms and concepts in my
initial attempt to describe, to the best of my ability, the amazing
things I had observed at Gombe. . . .

The editorial comments on the first paper I wrote for publica- 7
tion demanded that every *he* or *she* be replaced with *it*, and every
who be replaced with *which*. Incensed, I, in my turn, crossed out
the *its* and *whichs* and scrawled back the original pronouns. As I
had no desire to carve a niche for myself in the world of science,
but simply wanted to go on living among and learning about
chimpanzees, the possible reaction of the editor of the learned
journal did not trouble me. In fact I won that round: The paper
when finally published did confer upon the chimpanzees the dignity of their appropriate genders and properly upgraded them
from the status of mere "things" to essential Being-ness.

However, despite my somewhat truculent attitude, I did want 8
to learn, and I was sensible of my incredible good fortune in
being admitted to Cambridge. I wanted to get my Ph.D., if only
for the sake of Louis Leakey and the other people who had writ-

ten letters in support of my admission. And how lucky I was to have, as my supervisor, Robert Hinde. Not only because I thereby benefited from his brilliant mind and clear thinking, but also because I doubt that I could have found a teacher more suited to my particular needs and personality. Gradually he was able to cloak me with at least some of the trappings of a scientist. Thus although I continued to hold to most of my convictions—that animals had personalities; that they could feel happy or sad or fearful; that they could feel pain; that they could strive towards planned goals and achieve greater success if they were highly motivated—I soon realized that these personal convictions were, indeed, difficult to prove. It was best to be circumspect—at least until I had gained some credentials and credibility. And Robert gave me wonderful advice on how best to tie up some of my more rebellious ideas with scientific ribbon. "You can't *know* that Fifi was jealous," he admonished on one occasion. We argued a little. And then: "Why don't you just say *If Fifi were a human child we would say she was jealous.*" I did.

It is not easy to study emotions even when the subjects are 9 human. I know how I feel if I am sad or happy or angry, and if a friend tells me that he is feeling sad, happy or angry, I assume that his feelings are similar to mine. But of course I cannot know. As we try to come to grips with the emotions of beings progressively more different from ourselves, the task, obviously, becomes increasingly difficult. If we ascribe human emotions to non-human animals we are accused of being anthropomorphic—a cardinal sin in ethology. But is it so terrible? If we test the effect of drugs on chimpanzees because they are biologically so similar to ourselves, if we accept that there are dramatic similarities in chimpanzee and human brain and nervous system, is it not logical to assume that there will be similarities also in at least the more basic feelings, emotions, moods of the two species?

In fact, all those who have worked long and closely with 10 chimpanzees have no hesitation in asserting that chimps experience emotions similar to those which in ourselves we label pleasure, joy, sorrow, anger, boredom, and so on. Some of the emotional states of the chimpanzee are so obviously similar to ours that even an inexperienced observer can understand what is going on. An infant who hurls himself screaming to the ground, face contorted, hitting out with his arms at any nearby object, banging his head, is clearly having a tantrum. Another youngster, who gambols around his mother, turning somersaults, pirouetting and, every so often, rushing up to her and tumbling into her lap, patting her or pulling her hand towards him in a request for tickling, is obviously filled with *joie de vivre*. There are few observers who would not unhesitatingly ascribe his behavior to a happy, carefree state of well-being. And one cannot watch chimpanzee infants for long without realizing that they have the same emotional need for affection and reassurance as human children. An adult male, reclining in the shade after a good meal, reaching benignly to play with an infant or idly groom an adult female, is clearly in a good mood. When he sits with bristling hair, glaring at his subordinates and threatening them, with irritated gestures, if they come too close, he is clearly feeling cross and grumpy. We make these judgments because the similarity of so much of a chimpanzee's behavior to our own permits us to empathize.

It is hard to empathize with emotions we have not experienced. I can imagine, to some extent, the pleasure of a female chimpanzee during the act of procreation. The feelings of her male partner are beyond my knowledge—as are those of the human male in the same context. I have spent countless hours watching mother chimpanzees interacting with their infants. But not until I had an infant of my own did I begin to understand the basic, powerful instinct of mother-love. If someone accidentally did something to frighten Grub or threaten his well-being in any way, I felt a surge of quite irrational anger. How much more easily could I then understand the feelings of the chimpanzee mother who furiously waves her arm and barks in threat at an individual who approaches her infant too closely, or at a playmate who inadvertently hurts her child. And it was not until I knew the numbing grief that gripped me after the death of my second husband that I could even begin to appreciate the despair and sense of loss that can cause young chimps to pine away and die when they lose their mothers. . . .

When first I began to read about human evolution, I learned that one of the hallmarks of our own species was that we, and only we, were capable of making tools. *Man the Toolmaker* was an oft-cited definition—and this despite the careful and exhaustive research of Wolfgang Kohler and Robert Yerkes on the tool-using and tool-making abilities of chimpanzees. Those studies, carried out independently in the early twenties, were received with skepticism. Yet both Kohler and Yerkes were respected scientists, and both had a profound understanding of chimpanzee behavior. Indeed, Kohler's descriptions of the personalities and behavior of the various individuals in his colony, published in his book *The Mentality of Apes*, remain some of the most vivid and colorful ever written. And his experiments, showing how chimpanzees could stack boxes, then climb the unstable constructions to reach fruit suspended from the ceiling, or join two short sticks to make a pole long enough to rake in fruit otherwise out of reach, have become classic, appearing in almost all textbooks dealing with intelligent behavior in non-human animals.

By the time systematic observations of tool-using came from 13 Gombe, those pioneering studies had been largely forgotten. Moreover, it was one thing to know that humanized chimpanzees in the lab could use implements: It was quite another to find that this was a naturally occurring skill in the wild. I well remember writing to Louis about my first observations, describing how David Greybeard not only used bits of straw to fish for termites but actually stripped leaves from a stem and thus *made* a tool. And I remember too receiving the now oft-quoted telegram he sent in response to my letter: "Now we must redefine *tool*, redefine *Man*, or accept chimpanzees as humans."

There were, initially, a few scientists who attempted to write 14 off the termiting observations, even suggesting that I had taught the chimps! By and large, though, people were fascinated by the information and by the subsequent observations of the other contexts in which the Gombe chimpanzees used objects as tools. And there were only a few anthropologists who objected when I suggested that the chimpanzees probably passed their tool-using traditions from one generation to the next, through observations, imitation and practice, so that each population might be expected to have its own unique tool-using culture. Which, incidentally, turns out to be quite true. And when I described how one chimpanzee, Mike, spontaneously solved a new problem by using a tool (he broke off a stick to knock a banana to the ground when he was too nervous to actually take it from my hand), I don't believe there were any raised eyebrows in the scientific community.

Certainly I was not attacked viciously, as were Kohler and Yerkes, for suggesting that humans were not the only beings capable of reasoning and insight.

The mid-sixties saw the start of a project that, along with other similar research, was to teach us a great deal about the chimpanzee mind. This was Project Washoe, conceived by Trixie and Allen Gardner. They purchased an infant chimpanzee and began to teach her the signs of ASL, the American Sign Language used by the deaf. Twenty years earlier another husband and wife team, Richard and Cathy Hayes, had tried, with an almost total lack of success, to teach a young chimp, Vikki, to talk. The Hayes's undertaking taught us a lot about the chimpanzee mind, but Vikki, although she did well in IQ tests and was clearly an intelligent youngster, could not learn human speech. The Gardners, however, achieved spectacular success with their pupil, Washoe. Not only did she learn signs easily, but she quickly began to string them together in meaningful ways. It was clear that each sign evoked, in her mind, a mental image of the object it represented. If, for example, she was asked, in sign language, to fetch an apple, she would go and locate an apple that was out of sight in another room. . . . 15

When news of Washoe's accomplishments first hit the scientific community, it immediately provoked a storm of bitter protest. It implied that chimpanzees were capable of mastering a human language, and this, in turn, indicated mental powers of generalization, abstraction, and concept-formation as well as an ability to understand and use abstract symbols. And these intellectual skills were surely the prerogatives of *Homo sapiens*. Although there were many who were fascinated and excited by the Gardners' findings, there were many more who denounced the whole project, holding that the data was suspect, the methodology sloppy, and the conclusions not only misleading, but quite preposterous. The controversy inspired all sorts of other language projects. And, whether the investigators were skeptical to start with and hoped to disprove the Gardners' work, or whether they were attempting to demonstrate the same thing in a new way, their research provided additional information about the chimpanzee's mind. 16

And so, with new incentive, psychologists began to test the mental abilities of chimpanzees in a variety of different ways; again and again the results confirmed that their minds are uncannily like our own. It had long been held that only humans were 17 capable of what is called "cross–modal transfer of information"—in other words, if you shut your eyes and someone allows you to feel a strangely shaped potato, you will subsequently be able to pick it out from other differently shaped potatoes simply by looking at them. And vice versa. It turned out that chimpanzees can "know" with their eyes what they "feel" with their fingers in just the same way. In fact, we now know that some other non–human primates can do the same thing. I expect all kinds of creatures have the same ability. . . .

The fact that chimpanzees have excellent memories surprised 18 no one. Everyone, after all, has been brought up to believe that "an elephant never forgets" so why should a chimpanzee be any different? The fact that Washoe spontaneously gave the name–sign of Beatrice Gardner, her surrogate mother, when she saw her after a separation of eleven years was no greater an accomplishment than the amazing memory shown by dogs who recognize their owners after separations of almost as long—and the chimpanzee has a much longer life span than a dog. Chimpanzees can plan ahead, too, at least as regards the immediate future. This, in fact, is well illustrated at Gombe, during the termiting season: Often an individual prepares a tool for use on a termite mound that is several hundred yards away and absolutely out of sight.

This is not the place to describe in detail the other cognitive 19 abilities that have been studied in laboratory chimpanzees. Among other accomplishments chimpanzees possess pre–mathematical skills: They can, for example, readily differentiate between *more* and *less*. They can classify things into specific categories according to a given criterion—thus they have no difficulty in separating a pile of food into *fruit* and *vegetables* on one occasion, and, on another, dividing the same pile of food into *large* versus *small* items, even though this requires putting some vegetables with some fruits. Chimpanzees who have been taught a language can combine signs creatively in order to describe objects for which they have no symbol. Washoe, for example, puzzled her caretakers by asking, repeatedly, for a *rock berry*. Eventually it transpired that she was referring to Brazil nuts, which she had encountered for the first time a while before. Another language–trained chimp described a cucumber as a *green banana*, and another referred to an Alka–Seltzer as a *listen drink*. They can even invent signs. Lucy, as she got older, had to be put on a leash for her outings. One day, eager to set off but having no sign for *leash*, she signalled her wishes by holding a crooked index finger to the ring on her collar. This sign became part of her vocabulary. Some chimpanzees love to draw, and especially to paint. Those who have learned sign language sometimes spontaneously label their works, "This [is] apple"—or bird, or sweetcorn, or whatever. The fact that the paintings often look, to our eyes, remarkably unlike the objects depicted by the artists either means that the chimpanzees are poor draftsmen or that we have much to learn regarding ape-style representational art!

People sometimes ask why chimpanzees have evolved such complex intellectual powers when their lives in the wild are so simple. The answer is, of course, that their lives in the wild are not so simple! They use—and need—all their mental skills during normal day-to-day life in their complex society. They are always having to make choices—where to go or with whom to travel. They need highly developed social skills—particularly those males who are ambitious to attain high positions in the dominance hierarchy. Low-ranking chimpanzees must learn deception—to conceal their intentions or to do things in secret—if they are to get their way in the presence of their superiors. Indeed, the study of chimpanzees in the wild suggests that their intellectual abilities evolved, over the millennia, to help them cope with daily life. And now, the solid core of data concerning chimpanzee intellect collected so carefully in the lab setting provides a background against which to evaluate the many examples of intelligent, rational behavior that we see in the wild. . . .

UNDERSTANDING DETAILS

1. Based on Goodall's research, what are some of the main similarities between chimpanzees and humans? The differences?
2. What gave Goodall the idea that animals have unique personalities?
3. Why were Goodall's references to the gender of chimpanzees in published articles a real breakthrough in the scientific world?
4. Explain Project Washoe in your own words.

ANALYZING MEANING

1. In what way was tool-making a focal point of Goodall's research?

2. Why did Goodall become interested in the chimpanzee's mind?
3. How did Goodall discover that chimpanzees could learn ASL? What was the meaning of this discovery?
4. Why do you think Goodall's discoveries about the mind of the chimpanzee have been so important to the scientific community? What do her findings imply about the distinctions between animals and humans?

DISCOVERING RHETORICAL STRATEGIES

1. Explain Goodall's reference in paragraph 1 to "windows" and "glass." How are chimpanzees' eyes like windows?
2. List the author's main points in the essay. Why do you think she chooses to deal with these topics in this particular order?
3. Describe Goodall's intended audience in as much detail as possible. Why do you think she aims her essay at this particular group?
4. Besides the numerous examples that Goodall offers, what other rhetorical strategies does she use to help make her point? Give examples of each of these strategies.

MAKING CONNECTIONS

1. Compare Goodall's observations about primate language use with those advanced by Alleen Pace Nilsen ("Sexism in English: A 1990s Update") about human language use in her survey of sexism in English. What similar methods does each author employ to observe and record the use of language?
2. If Goodall and John McPhee ("The Pines") had a roundtable discussion about America's responsibility to preserve its environment, which of these authors would argue most forcefully for his or her point of view? Why do you think so?
3. The difficulty Goodall had in being accepted as a legitimate primate specialist by the scientific community is similar to the social prejudice exposed elsewhere in this book by Harry Edwards ("Triple Tragedy in Black Society") and Judy Brady ("Why I Want a Wife"). Which type of prejudice would be most difficult to overcome? Could Edwards and Brady learn anything from the way Goodall overcame the prejudice against her research methods? If so, what?

IDEAS FOR DISCUSSION/WRITING

Preparing to Write

Write freely about the role of learning in contemporary society: What are your main interests? Do you have a desire to learn about anything in particular? How do you pursue this desire? What topics are you especially curious about? How do your friends approach learning? How is learning valued in American society today? Do you feel this value is justified? How is learning related to the American education process?

Choosing a Topic

1. As a college student, you see many different people studying various subjects every day. Some people learn best in groups; others need to study alone. Some learn best by hearing the information, others by seeing it. Some vary their study techniques according to subject matter; others study each subject the same way. Write an essay for your school newspaper explaining your observations about the different ways people learn. Use carefully chosen examples to illustrate your observations.

2. You have been asked to respond to a national survey on the role of education in our lives. The organization conducting the survey wants to know the extent to which education has helped or hindered you in achieving your goals. In a well-developed essay written for a general audience, explain the benefits and liabilities of education in your life at present. Use specific examples to develop your essay.

3. In her essay, Goodall outlines the many similarities between the cognitive abilities of chimpanzees and humans. She also implies that chimps should have the protection from exploitation and injury accorded to other intelligent creatures. How do you feel about animal rights? What basic rights should animals have? Does your opinion depend on the type of animal? Should chimpanzees, for example, have more rights than alligators or snails have? How do you feel about using animals in laboratory research to study disease? Direct your comments to the general public, and use several specific examples to support your opinion.

ALLEEN PACE NILSEN   (1936 –   )

■ ■ ■

Sexism in English: A 1990s Update

While researching books written for children, Alleen Pace Nilsen became interested in linguistic sexism. In 1973, she completed a doctoral dissertation at the University of Iowa entitled "The Effect of Grammatical Gender on the Equal Treatment of Males and Females in Children's Literature." With her husband, Donald Nilsen, she has coauthored two books: *Pronunciation Contrasts in English* (1971) and *Semantic Theory: A Linguistic Perspective* (1975). She is also coeditor of *Sexism and Language* (1977), a book-length collection of essays published by the National Council of Teachers of English, and of a textbook entitled *Literature for Young Adults* (1980–1995, now in its fifth edition). Nilsen, whose current scholarly project is a book on the power of names, is a professor of English at Arizona State University, where, in her spare time, she enjoys creating book displays in the English Department. She advises students using *The Prose Reader* to "read their essays out loud to someone they admire and respect— perhaps even love. They can then use this human audience to help revise and improve their work."

Preparing to Read

"Sexism in English: A 1990s Update" is a 1989 revision of an essay on linguistic sexism originally published in *Female Studies VI: Closer to the Ground* (1972), one among a series of volumes sponsored by the Modern Language Association's Commission on the Status of Women. In this interesting and well-written article, Nilsen examines the extent to which the English language reveals and reinforces a cultural bias against women. Before reading this essay, think for a few moments about sexism in general: What evidence of sexual bias—against either women or men—can you cite from your own experience? How is this bias expressed in our language use? What examples of sexism in language can you think of? Why do you believe such sexual stereotyping exists in our culture today?

T wenty years ago I embarked on a study of the sexism in- 1
herent in American English. I had just returned to Ann
Arbor, Michigan, after living for two years (1967–69) in
Kabul, Afghanistan, where I had begun to look critically at the
role society assigned to women. The Afghan version of the *chaderi*
prescribed for Moslem women was particularly confining. Few
women attended the American-built Kabul University where my
husband was teaching linguistics because there were no women's
dormitories, which meant that the only females who could attend were those whose families happened to live in the capital
city. Afghan jokes and folklore were blatantly sexist, for example
this proverb, "If you see an old man, sit down and take a lesson; if
you see an old woman, throw a stone."

But it wasn't only the native culture that made me question 2
women's roles; it was also the American community. Nearly six
hundred Americans lived in Kabul, mostly supported by U.S. taxpayers. The single women were career secretaries, schoolteachers,
or nurses. The three women who had jobs comparable to the
American men's jobs were textbook editors with the assignment
of developing reading books in Dari (Afghan Persian) for young
children. They worked at the Ministry of Education, a large
building in the center of the city. There were no women's re-
strooms, so during their two-year assignment whenever they
needed to go to the bathroom they had to walk across the street
and down the block to the Kabul Hotel.

The rest of the American women were like myself—wives 3
and mothers whose husbands were either career diplomats, employees of USAID [United States Agency for International
Development], or college professors who had been recruited to
work on various contract teams including an education team
from Teachers College, Columbia University, and an agricultural
team from the University of Wyoming. These were the women
who were most influential in changing my way of thinking. We
were suddenly bereft of our traditional roles; some of us became
alcoholics; others got very good at bridge, while others searched
desperately for ways to contribute either to our families or to
the Afghans. The local economy provided few jobs for women
and certainly none for foreigners; we were isolated from former
friends and the social goals we had grown up with. Most of us
had three servants (they worked for $1.00 a day) because the

cook refused to wash dishes and the dishwasher refused to water the lawn or sweep the sidewalks—it was their form of unionization. Occasionally, someone would try to get along without servants, but it was impossible because the houses were huge and we didn't have the mechanical aids we had at home. Drinking water had to be brought from the deep well at the American Embassy, and kerosene and wood stoves had to be stocked and lit. The servants were all males, the highest-paid one being the cook, who could usually speak some English. Our days revolved around supervising these servants. One woman's husband got so tired of hearing her complain about such annoyances as the *bacha* (the housekeeper) stealing kerosene and needles and batteries, and about the cook putting chili powder instead of paprika on the deviled eggs, and about the gardener subcontracting his work and expecting her to pay all his friends, that he scheduled an hour a week for listening to complaints. The rest of the time he wanted to keep his mind clear to focus on his important work with his Afghan counterparts and with the president of the university and the Minister of Education. What he was doing in this country was going to make a difference! In the great eternal scheme of things, of what possible importance would be his wife's trivial troubles with the servants?

These were the thoughts in my mind when we finished our 4 contract and returned in the fall of 1969 to the University of Michigan in Ann Arbor. I was surprised to find that many other women were also questioning the expectations that they had grown up with. In the spring of 1970, a women's conference was announced. I hired a babysitter and attended, but I returned home more troubled than ever. Now that I knew housework was worth only a dollar a day, I couldn't take it seriously, but I wasn't angry in the same way these women were. Their militancy frightened me. Since I wasn't ready for a revolution, I decided I would have my own feminist movement. I would study the English language and see what it could tell me about sexism. I started reading a desk dictionary and making notecards on every entry that seemed to tell something about male and female. I soon had a dog-eared dictionary, along with a collection of notecards filling two shoe boxes.

Ironically, I started reading the dictionary because I wanted to 5 avoid getting involved in social issues, but what happened was that my notecards brought me right back to looking at society. Language and society are as intertwined as a chicken and an egg. The language that a culture uses is telltale evidence of the values and beliefs of that culture. And because there is a lag in how fast a language changes—new words can easily be introduced, but it takes a long time for old words and usages to disappear—a careful look at English will reveal the attitudes that our ancestors held and that we as a culture are therefore predisposed to hold. My notecards revealed three main points. Friends have offered the opinion that I didn't need to read the dictionary to learn such obvious facts. Nevertheless, it was interesting to have linguistic evidence of sociological observations.

Women Are Sexy; Men Are Successful

First, in American culture a woman is valued for the attractive- 6 ness and sexiness of her body, while a man is valued for his physical strength and accomplishments. A woman is sexy. A man is successful.

A persuasive piece of evidence supporting this view is the 7 eponyms—words that have come from someone's name—found in English. I had a two-and-a-half-inch stack of cards taken from men's names, but less than a half-inch stack from women's names, and most of those came from Greek mythology. In the words that came into American English since we separated from Britain, there are many eponyms based on the names of famous American men: *bartlett pear, boysenberry, diesel engine, franklin stove, ferris wheel, gatling gun, mason jar, sideburns, sousaphone, schick test,* and *winchester rifle.* The only common eponyms taken from American women's names are *Alice blue* (after Alice Roosevelt Longworth), *bloomers* (after Amelia Jenks Bloomer), and *Mae West jacket* (after the buxom actress). Two out of the three feminine eponyms relate closely to a woman's physical anatomy, while the masculine eponyms (except for *sideburns,* after General Burnside) have nothing to do with the namesake's body, but instead honor the man for an accomplishment of some kind.

Although in Greek mythology women played a bigger role 8 than they did in the biblical stories of the Judeo-Christian cultures and so the names of goddesses are accepted parts of the language in such place names as Pomona from the goddess of fruit and Athens from Athena and in such common words as *cereal* from Ceres, *psychology* from Psyche, and *arachnoid* from Arachne, the same tendency to think of women in relation to sexuality is seen in the eponyms *aphrodisiac* from Aphrodite, the Greek name for the goddess of love and beauty, and *venereal disease*, from Venus, the Roman name for Aphrodite.

Another interesting word from Greek mythology is *Amazon*.   9 According to Greek folk etymology, the *a* means "without" as in *atypical* or *amoral*, while *mazon* comes from *mazos*, meaning *breast* as still seen in *mastectomy*. In the Greek legend, Amazon women cut off their right breasts so they could better shoot their bows. Apparently, the storytellers had a feeling that for women to play the active, "masculine" role that the Amazons adopted for them-selves, they had to trade in part of their femininity.

This preoccupation with women's breasts is not limited to an-   10 cient stories. As a volunteer for the University of Wisconsin's *Dictionary of American Regional English (DARE)*, I read a western trapper's diary from the 1830s. I was to make notes of any unusual usages or language patterns. My most interesting finding was that he referred to a range of mountains as *The Teats*, a metaphor based on the similarity between the shapes of the mountains and women's breasts. Because today we use the French wording, *The Grand Tetons*, the metaphor isn't as obvious, but I wrote to map-makers and found the following listings: *Nippletop* and *Little Nipple Top* near Mt. Marcy in the Adirondacks, *Nipple Mountain* in Archuleta County, Colorado, *Nipple Peak* in Coke County, Texas, *Nipple Butte* in Pennington, South Dakota, *Squaw Peak* in Placer County, California (and many other locations), *Maiden's Peak* and *Squaw Tit* (they're the same mountain) in the Cascade Range in Oregon, *Mary's Nipple*, near Salt Lake City, Utah, and *Jane Russell Peaks* near Stark, New Hampshire.

Except for the movie star Jane Russell, the women being re-   11 ferred to are anonymous—it's only a sexual part of their body that is mentioned. When topographical features are named after men, it's probably not going to be to draw attention to a sexual part of their bodies but instead to honor individuals for an ac-complishment. For example, no one thinks of a part of the male body when hearing a reference to Pike's Peak, Colorado, or Jackson Hole, Wyoming.

Going back to what I learned from my dictionary cards, I was   12
surprised to realize how many pairs of words we have in which
the feminine word has acquired sexual connotations while the
masculine word retains a serious businesslike aura. For example, a
callboy is the person who calls actors when it is time for them to
go on stage, but a *callgirl* is a prostitute. Compare *sir* and *madam*.
Sir is a term of respect while *madam* has acquired the specialized
meaning of a brothel manager. Something similar has happened
to *master* and *mistress*. Would you rather have a painting by an *old
master* or an *old mistress*?

It's because the word *woman* had sexual connotations, as in   13
"She's his woman," that people began avoiding its use, hence such
terminology as *ladies room, lady of the house*, and *girls' school* or
school for young ladies. Feminists, who ask that people use the term
woman rather than *girl* or *lady*, are rejecting the idea that *woman* is
primarily a sexual term. They have been at least partially successful in that today *woman* is commonly used to communicate gender without intending implications about sexuality.

I found two hundred pairs of words with masculine and femi-   14
nine forms, e.g., *heir–heiress, hero–heroine, steward–stewardess, usher–
usherette*, etc. In nearly all such pairs, the masculine word is considered the base, with some kind of a feminine suffix being added.
The masculine form is the one from which compounds are made,
e.g., from *king–queen* comes kingdom but not *queendom*, from
sportsman–sportslady comes *sportsmanship* but not *sportsladyship*.
There is one—and only one—semantic area in which the masculine word is not the base or more powerful word. This is in the
area dealing with sex and marriage. When someone refers to a *virgin*, a listener will probably think of a female unless the speaker
specifies *male* or uses a masculine pronoun. The same is true for
prostitute.

In relation to marriage, there is much linguistic evidence   15
showing that weddings are more important to women than to
men. A woman cherishes the wedding and is considered a bride
for a whole year, but a man is referred to as a groom only on the
day of the wedding. The word *bride* appears in *bridal attendant,
bridal gown, bridesmaid, bridal shower*, and even *bridegroom*. *Groom*
comes from the Middle English *grom*, meaning "man," and in this
sense is seldom used outside of a wedding. With most pairs of
male/female words, people habitually put the masculine word

first—*Mr. and Mrs., his and hers, boys and girls, men and women, kings and queens, brothers and sisters, guys and dolls,* and *host and hostess*—but it is the *bride and groom* who are talked about, not the *groom and bride.*

The importance of marriage to a woman is also shown by the 16 fact that when a marriage ends in death, the woman gets the title of *widow.* A man gets the derived title of *widower.* This term is not used in other phrases or contexts, but *widow* is seen in *widowhood, widow's peak,* and *widow's walk.* A *widow* in a card game is an extra hand of cards, while in typesetting it is an extra line of type.

How changing cultural ideas bring changes to language is 17 clearly visible in this semantic area. The feminist movement has caused the differences between the sexes to be downplayed, and since I did my dictionary study two decades ago, the word *singles* has largely replaced such sex-specific and value-laden terms as *bachelor, old maid, spinster, divorcee, widow,* and *widower.* And in 1970 I wrote that when a man is called a *professional* he is thought to be a doctor or lawyer, but when people hear a woman referred to as a *professional* they are likely to think of a prostitute. That's not as true today because so many women have become doctors and lawyers that it's no longer incongruous to think of women in those professional roles.

Another change that has taken place is in wedding announce- 18 ments. They used to be sent out from the bride's parents and did not even give the name of the groom's parents. Today, most couples choose to list either all or none of the parents' names. Also it is now much more likely that both the bride and groom's picture will be in the newspaper, while a decade ago only the bride's picture was published on the "Women's" or the "Society" page. Even the traditional wording of the wedding ceremony is being changed. Many officials now pronounce the couple "husband and wife" instead of the old "man and wife," and they ask the bride if she promises "to love, honor, and cherish," instead of "to love, honor, and obey."

Women Are Passive; Men Are Active

The wording of the wedding ceremony also relates to the sec- 19 ond point that my cards showed, which is that women are expected to play a passive or weak role while men play an active or strong role. In the traditional ceremony, the official asks, "Who gives the bride away?" and the father answers, "I do." Some fathers answer, "Her mother and I do," but that doesn't solve the problem inherent in the question. The idea that a bride is something to be handed over from one man to another bothers people because it goes back to the days when a man's servants, his children, and his wife were all considered to be his property. They were known by his name because they belonged to him and he was responsible for their actions and their debts.

The grammar used in talking or writing about weddings as well as other sexual relationships shows the expectation of men playing the active role. Men *wed* women while women *become* brides of men. A man *possesses* a woman; he *deflowers* her; he *performs*; he *scores*; he *takes away* her virginity. Although a woman can *seduce* a man, she cannot offer him her virginity. When talking about virginity, the only way to make the woman the actor in the sentence is to say that "She lost her virginity," but people lose things by accident rather than by purposeful actions, and so she's only the grammatical, not the real-life, actor.

20

The reason that women tried to bring the term *Ms.* into the language to replace *Miss* and *Mrs.* relates to this point. Married women resented being identified only under their husband's names. For example, when Susan Glascoe did something newsworthy, she would be identified in the newspaper only as Mrs. John Glascoe. The dictionary cards showed what appeared to be an attitude on the part of editors that it was almost indecent to let a respectable woman's name march unaccompanied across the pages of a dictionary. Women were listed with male names whether or not the male contributed to the woman's reason for being in the dictionary or in his own right was as famous as the woman. For example, Charlotte Brontë was identified as Mrs. Arthur B. Nicholls, Amelia Earhart as Mrs. George Palmer Putnam, Helen Hayes as Mrs. Charles MacArthur, Jenny Lind as Mme. Otto Goldschmit, Cornelia Otis Skinner as the daughter of Otis Skinner, Harriet Beecher Stowe as the sister of Henry Ward Beecher, and Edith Sitwell as the sister of Osbert and Sacheverell. A very small number of women got into the dictionary without the benefit of a masculine escort. They were rebels and crusaders: temperance leaders Frances Elizabeth Caroline Willard and Carry Nation, women's rights leaders Carrie Chapman Catt and Elizabeth Cady Stanton, birth control educator Margaret Sanger,

21

religious leader Mary Baker Eddy, and slaves Harriet Tubman and Phyllis Wheatley.

Etiquette books used to teach that if a woman had *Mrs.* in 22 front of her name then the husband's name should follow because *Mrs.* is an abbreviated form of *Mistress* and a woman couldn't be a mistress of herself. As with many arguments about "correct" language usage, this isn't very logical because *Miss* is also an abbreviation of *Mistress*. Feminists hoped to simplify matters by introducing *Ms.* as an alternative to both *Mrs.* and *Miss*, but what happened is that *Ms.* largely replaced *Miss* to become a catch-all business title for women. Many married women still prefer the title *Mrs.*, and some resent being addressed with the term *Ms.* As one frustrated newspaper reporter complained, "Before I can write about a woman, I have to know not only her marital status but also her political philosophy." The result of such complications may contribute to the demise of titles, which are already being ignored by many computer programmers who find it more efficient to simply use names; for example, in a business letter: "Dear Joan Garcia," instead of "Dear Mrs. Joan Garcia," "Dear Ms. Garcia," or "Dear Mrs. Louis Garcia."

The titles given to royalty provide an example of how males 23 can be disadvantaged by the assumption that they are always to play the more powerful role. In British royalty, when a male holds a title, his wife is automatically given the feminine equivalent. But the reverse is not true. For example, a *count* is a high political officer, with a *countess* being his wife. The same is true for a *duke* and a *duchess* and a *king* and a *queen*. But when a female holds the royal title, the man she marries does not automatically acquire the matching title. For example, Queen Elizabeth's husband has the title of *prince* rather than *king*, but if Prince Charles would have become king while he was still married to Lady or Princess Diana, she would have been known as the queen. The reasoning appears to be that since masculine words are stronger, they are reserved for true heirs and withheld from males coming into the royal family by marriage. If Prince Philip were called *King Philip*, it would be much easier for British subjects to forget where the true power lies.

The names that people give their children show the hopes and 24 dreams they have for them, and when we look at the differences between male and female names in a culture we can see the cumulative expectations of that culture. In our culture girls often have names taken from small, aesthetically pleasing items, e.g., *Ruby, Jewel,* and *Pearl. Esther* and *Stella* mean "star," *Ada* means "ornament," and *Vanessa* means "butterfly." Boys are more likely to be given names with meanings of power and strength, e.g., *Neil* means "champion," *Martin* is from Mars, the god of war, *Raymond* means "wise protection," *Harold* means "chief of the army," *Ira* means "vigilant," *Rex* means "king," and *Richard* means "strong king."

We see similar differences in food metaphors. Food is a passive   25
substance just sitting there waiting to be eaten. Many people have recognized this and so no longer feel comfortable describing women as "delectable morsels." However, when I was a teenager, it was considered a compliment to refer to a girl (we didn't call anyone a *woman* until she was middle-aged) as a *cute tomato,* a *peach,* a *dish,* a *cookie, sugar,* or *sweetiepie.* When being affectionate, women will occasionally call a man *honey* or *sweetie,* but in general, food metaphors are used much less often with men than with women. If a man is called a *fruit,* his masculinity is being questioned. But it's perfectly acceptable to use a food metaphor if the food is heavier and more substantive than that used for women. For example, pin-up pictures of women have long been known as *cheesecake,* but when Burt Reynolds posed for a nude centerfold, the picture was immediately dubbed *beefcake,* c.f., *a hunk of meat.* That such sexual references to men have come into the general language is another reflection of how society is beginning to lessen the differences between their attitudes toward men and women.

Something similar to the *fruit* metaphor happens with refer-   26
ences to plants. We insult a man by calling him a *pansy,* but it wasn't considered particularly insulting to talk about a girl being a *wallflower,* a *clinging vine,* or a *shrinking violet,* or to give girls such names as *Ivy, Rose, Lily, Iris, Daisy, Camellia, Heather,* and *Flora.* A plant metaphor can be used with a man if the plant is big and strong, for example Andrew Jackson's nickname of *Old Hickory.* Also, the phrases *blooming idiots* and *budding geniuses* can be used with either sex, but notice how they are based on the most active thing a plant can do, which is to bloom or bud.

Animal metaphors also illustrate the different expectations for   27
males and females. Men are referred to as *studs, bucks,* and *wolves*

while women are referred to with such metaphors as *kitten, bunny, beaver, bird, chick,* and *lamb.* In the 1950s we said that boys went *tomcatting,* but today it's just *catting around* and both boys and girls do it. When the term *foxy,* meaning that someone was sexy, first became popular, it was used only for girls, but now someone of either sex can be described as a *fox.* Some animal metaphors that are used predominantly with men have negative connotations based on the size and/or strength of the animals, e.g., *beast, bull-headed, jackass, rat, loan shark,* and *vulture.* Negative metaphors used with women are based on smaller animals, e.g., *social butterfly, mousy, catty,* and *vixen.* The feminine terms connote action, but not the same kind of large-scale action as with the masculine terms.

Women Are Connected with Negative Connotations, Men with Positive Connotations

The final point that my notecards illustrated was how many   28 positive connotations are associated with the concept of masculine, while there are either trivial or negative connotations connected with the corresponding feminine concept. An example from the animal metaphors makes a good illustration. The word *shrew,* taken from the name of a small but especially vicious animal, was defined in my dictionary as "an ill-tempered scolding woman," but the word *shrewd,* taken from the same root, was defined as "marked by clever, discerning awareness" and was illustrated with the phrase "a shrewd businessman."

Early in life, children are conditioned to the superiority of   29 the masculine role. As child psychologists point out, little girls have much more freedom to experiment with sex roles than do little boys. If a girl acts like a *tomboy,* most parents have mixed feelings, being at least partially proud. But if their little boy acts like a *sissy* (derived from *sister*), they call a psychologist. It's perfectly acceptable for a little girl to sleep in the crib that was purchased for her brother, to wear his hand-me-down jeans and shirts, and to ride the bicycle that he has outgrown. But few parents would put a boy baby in a white and gold crib decorated with frills and lace, and virtually no parents would have their little boy wear his sister's hand-me-down dresses, nor would they have their son ride a girl's pink bicycle with a flower-bedecked basket. The proper names given to girls and boys show this same attitude. Girls can have "boy" names—*Cris,*

Craig, Jo, Kelly, Shawn, Teri, Toni, and *Sam*—but it doesn't work the other way around. A couple of generations ago, *Beverly, Frances, Hazel, Marion,* and *Shirley* were common boys' names. As parents gave these names to more and more girls, they fell into disuse for males, and some older men who have these names prefer to go by their initials or by such abbreviated forms as *Haze* or *Shirl*.

When a little girl is told to *be a lady*, she is being told to sit [30] with her knees together and to be quiet and dainty. But when a little boy is told to *be a man*, he is being told to be noble, strong, and virtuous—to have all the qualities that the speaker looks on as desirable. The concept of manliness has such positive connotations that it used to be a compliment to call someone a *he-man*, to say that he was doubly a man. Today many people are more ambivalent about this term and respond to it much as they do to the word *macho*. But calling someone a *manly man* or a *virile man* is nearly always meant as a compliment. *Virile* comes from the Indo-European *vir* meaning "man," which is also the basis of *virtuous*. Contrast the positive connotations of both *virile* and *virtuous* with the negative connotations of *hysterical*. The Greeks took this latter word from their name for *uterus* (as still seen in *hysterectomy*). They thought that women were the only ones who experienced uncontrolled emotional outbursts and so the condition must have something do to with a part of the body that only women have.

Differences between positive male and negative female conno- [31] tations can be seen in several pairs of words which differ denotatively only in the matter of sex. *Bachelor* as compared to *spinster* or *old maid* has such positive connotations that women try to adopt them by using the term *bachelor-girl* or *bachelorette*. *Old maid* is so negative that it's the basis for metaphors: pretentious and fussy old men are called *old maids*, as are the leftover kernels of unpopped popcorn and the last card in a popular children's game.

Patron and *matron* (Middle English for *father* and *mother*) have [32] such different levels of prestige that women try to borrow the more positive masculine connotations with the word *patroness*, literally "female father." Such a peculiar term came about because of the high prestige attached to *patron* in such phrases as *a patron of the arts* or *a patron saint*. *Matron* is more apt to be used in talking about a woman in charge of a jail or a public restroom.

When men are doing jobs that women often do, we apparently   33
try to pay the men extra by giving them fancy titles; for example,
a male cook is more likely to be called a *chef,* while a male seam-
stress will get the title of *tailor.* The armed forces have a special
problem in that they recruit under such slogans as "The Marine
Corps Builds Men!" and "Join the Army! Become a Man." Once
the recruits are enlisted, they find themselves doing much of the
work that has been traditionally thought of as "women's work."
The solution to getting the work done and not insulting anyone's
masculinity was to change the titles as shown below:

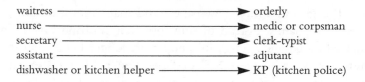

waitress ──────────────▶ orderly
nurse ──────────────▶ medic or corpsman
secretary ──────────────▶ clerk-typist
assistant ──────────────▶ adjutant
dishwasher or kitchen helper ──────────────▶ KP (kitchen police)

Compare *brave* and *squaw.* Early settlers in America truly ad-   34
mired Indian men and hence named them with a word that carried connotations of youth, vigor, and courage. But they used the
Algonquin's name for "woman," and over the years it developed
almost opposite connotations to those of *brave. Wizard* and *witch*
contrast almost as much. The masculine *wizard* implies skill and
wisdom combined with magic, while the feminine *witch* implies
evil intentions combined with magic. Part of the unattractiveness
of both *witch* and *squaw* is that they have been used so often to
refer to old women, something with which our culture is particularly uncomfortable, just as the Afghans were. Imagine my surprise when I ran across the phrases *grandfatherly advice* and *old
wives' tales* and realized that the underlying implication is the
same as the Afghan proverb about old men being worth listening
to while old women talk only foolishness.

Other terms which show how negatively we view old women   35
as compared to young women are *old nag* as compared to *filly, old
crow* or *old bat* as compared to *bird,* and being *catty* as compared to
being *kittenish.* There is no matching set of metaphors for men.
The chicken metaphor tells the whole story of a woman's life. In
her youth she is a *chick.* Then she marries and begins *feathering her
nest.* Soon she begins feeling *cooped up,* so she goes to *hen parties*
where she *cackles* with her friends. Then she has her *brood,* begins
to *henpeck* her husband, and finally turns into *an old biddy.*

I embarked on my study of the dictionary not with the inten- 36
tion of prescribing language change but simply to see what the
language would tell me about sexism. Nevertheless I have been
both surprised and pleased as I've watched the changes that have
occurred over the past two decades. I'm one of those linguists
who believes that new language customs will cause a new generation of speakers to grow up with different expectations. This is
why I'm happy about people's efforts to use inclusive language, to
say *he or she* or *they* when speaking about individuals whose names
they do not know. I'm glad that leading publishers have developed
guidelines to help writers use language that is fair to both sexes,
and I'm glad that most newspapers and magazines list women by
their own names instead of only by their husbands' names and
that educated and thoughtful people no longer begin their business letters with "Dear Sir" or "Gentlemen," but instead use a
memo form or begin with such salutations as "Dear Colleagues,"
"Dear Reader," or "Dear Committee Members." I'm also glad
that such words as *poetess, authoress, conductress*, and *aviatrix* now
sound quaint and old-fashioned and that *chairman* is giving way to
chair or *head, mailman* to *mail carrier, clergyman* to *clergy*, and *stewardess* to *flight attendant*. I was also pleased when the National
Oceanic and Atmospheric Administration bowed to feminist
complaints and in the late '70s began to alternate men's and
women's names for hurricanes. However, I wasn't so pleased to
discover that the change did not immediately erase sexist thoughts
from everyone's mind as shown by a headline about Hurricane
David in a 1979 New York tabloid, "David Rapes Virgin Islands."
More recently a similar metaphor appeared in a headline in the
Arizona Republic about Hurricane Charlie: "Charlie Quits
Carolinas, Flirts with Virginia."

What these incidents show is that sexism is not something 37
existing independently in American English or in the particular
dictionary that I happened to read. Rather, it exists in people's
minds. Language is like an x-ray in providing visible evidence of
invisible thought. The best thing about people being interested
in and discussing sexist language is that as they make conscious
decisions about what pronouns they will use, what jokes they
will tell or laugh at, how they will write their names, or how
they will begin their letters, they are forced to think about the

underlying issue of sexism. This is good, because as a problem that begins in people's assumptions and expectations, it's a problem that will be solved only when a great many people have given it a great deal of thought.

UNDERSTANDING DETAILS

1. What inspired Nilsen's interest in the relationship between language and sex roles?
2. In general terms, what did Nilsen's study of the dictionary tell her about sexism? Explain your answer in detail.
3. What are Nilsen's three main points in this essay? Explain each in your own words, using Nilsen's examples or adding some of your own.
4. What does Nilsen mean at the end of the essay when she says "Language is like an x-ray" (paragraph 37)?

ANALYZING MEANING

1. In paragraph 5, Nilsen claims, "Language and society are as intertwined as a chicken and an egg." She goes on to explain, "The language that a culture uses is telltale evidence of the values and beliefs of that culture." Do you agree or disagree with these statements? Explain your reaction in detail.
2. Which principal examples does the author use to support her theory that the concept of masculinity is generally positive whereas that of femininity is generally negative? Do you agree with this conclusion? Can you think of any examples that argue the contrary position?
3. According to Nilsen, how does the English language describe women as sexy and men as successful? Do you agree with this view? Explain your answer.
4. Based on the author's research, what changes in the language had occurred between 1969 and 1989? What additional linguistic changes can you think of? In what way do these changes reflect our society's view of sex roles?

DISCOVERING RHETORICAL STRATEGIES

1. Describe in as much detail as possible Nilsen's intended audience. Why do you think she aims her essay at this particular group?

2. How does Nilsen organize the examples she chooses to make each major point? Do you think she selected effective examples? Explain your answer.
3. Nilsen's conclusion clearly summarizes her view of the relationship between language and sexism. What are her thoughts on this subject? How does this ending affect you as the reader? What effect does it have on the essay as a whole?
4. This essay progresses most obviously through the use of examples. What other rhetorical strategies support this dominant mode? In what ways do they add to Nilsen's argument?

MAKING CONNECTIONS

1. Using Nilsen's research methods, write down and evaluate all the negative words associated with Native Americans in Lewis Sawaquat's "For My Indian Daughter" and/or all those associated with women in Ray Bradbury's "Summer Rituals."
2. Compare and contrast Nilsen's conclusions about the negative effects of language use on female self-identity with Susan Sontag's insights concerning society's metaphoric depiction of the AIDS virus ("On AIDS").
3. What important parallels do you see between Nilsen's analysis of sexism in language and Judy Brady's explanation of the negative perception of women in "Why I Want a Wife"? Do you think that Brady would agree with Nilsen's conclusions? Explain your answer.

IDEAS FOR DISCUSSION/WRITING

Preparing to Write

Write freely about the interdependence of language and culture: How do you think they affect one another? How is this relationship demonstrated in our society? In what ways can language and culture be separated? How sexist is our language? Our culture? How could these biases be controlled?

Choosing a Topic

1. Write an essay for a college-educated audience based on one of the following statements: "Culture shapes language" or "Language shapes culture." Use carefully selected examples to

prove your point. Keep your audience in mind at all times as you organize and write your essay.

2. Listen to some everyday conversations between men and women. Is there any evidence of sexual bias in these discussions, either against women or against men? Write an example essay for the general public in which you support your observations.

3. Using the multivolume *Oxford English Dictionary*, study the etymology (history) of the following words: *woman, lady, madam, mistress, female, mother, honey, whore, bitch.* Based on your own observations and discussions with friends, do the modern connotations of these words differ significantly from their original dictionary definitions? If so, why? Write an essay explaining to your English class what these words have in common and how each might affect our perceptions of women.

Process Analysis

Explaining Step by Step

Human nature is characterized by the perpetual desire to understand and analyze the process of living well. The best-seller list is always crowded with books on how to know yourself better, how to be assertive, how to become famous, how to avoid a natural disaster, or how to be rich and happy—all explained in three easy lessons. Open almost any popular magazine, and you will find numerous articles on how to lose weight, how elections are run in this country, how to dress for success, how a political rally evolved, how to gain power, or how to hit a successful topspin backhand. People naturally gravitate toward material that tells them how something is done, how something happened, or how something works, especially if they think the information will help them improve their lives in a significant way.

DEFINING PROCESS ANALYSIS

A *process* is a procedure that follows a series of steps or stages; *analysis* involves taking a subject apart and explaining its components in order to better understand the whole. Process analysis, then, explains an action, a mechanism, or an event from beginning to end. It concentrates on either a mental or a physical operation: how to solve a chemistry problem, how to tune up your car, how John F. Kennedy was shot, how the telephone system works. In fact, the explanation of the writing process beginning on page 21 of this book is a good case in point: It divides writing into three interrelated verbal activities and explains how they each work—separately and together.

A process analysis can take one of two main forms: (1) It can give directions, thereby explaining how to do something (directive), or (2) it can give information about how something happened (informative). The first type of analysis gives directions for a task the reader may wish to attempt in the future. Examples include how to make jelly, how to lose weight, how to drive to Los Angeles, how to assemble stereo equipment, how to make money, how to use a microscope, how to knit, how to resuscitate a dying relationship, how to win friends, how to discipline your child, and how to backpack.

The second type of analysis furnishes information about what actually occurred in specific situations. Examples include how Hiroshima was bombed, how certain Hollywood stars live, how the tax system works, how *Forrest Gump* was filmed, how Babe Ruth earned a place in the Baseball Hall of Fame, how gold was first discovered in California, how computers work, how a kibbutz functions, and how the Gulf War began. These subjects and others like them respond to a certain fascination we all have with mastering some processes and understanding the intricate details of others. They all provide us with opportunities to raise our own standard of living, either by helping us directly apply certain processes to our own lives or by increasing our understanding of how our complex twentieth-century world functions.

The following student paragraph analyzes the process of constructing a garden compost pit. Written primarily for people who might wish to make such a pit, this piece is directive rather than informative. Notice in particular the amount of detail the student calls upon to explain each stage of the process and the clear transitions she uses to guide us through her analysis.

> *No garden is complete without a functioning compost pit. Here's a simple, inexpensive way to make your garbage work for you! To begin with, make a pen out of hog wire or chicken wire, four feet long by eight feet wide by four feet high, splitting it down the middle with another piece of wire so that you end up with a structure that looks like a capital "E" on its side. This is a compost duplex. In the first pen, place a layer of soda ash, just sprinkled on the sur-*

face of the dirt. Then, pile an inch or so of leaves, grass clippings, or sawdust on top of the soda ash. You're now ready for the exciting part. Start throwing in all the organic refuse from your kitchen (no meat, bones, or grease, please). After the food is a foot or so deep, throw in a shovelful of steer manure, and cover the entire mess with a thin layer of dirt. Then water it down. Continue this layering process until the pile is three to three-and-a-half feet high. Allow the pile to sit until it decomposes (from one month in warm climates to six months in colder weather). Next, take your pitchfork and start slinging the contents of pen one into pen two (which will land in reverse order, of course, with the top on the bottom and the bottom on the top). This ensures that everything will decompose evenly. Water this down and begin making a new pile in pen one. That's all there is to it! You now have a ready supply of fertilizer for your garden.

THINKING CRITICALLY BY USING PROCESS ANALYSIS

Process analysis embodies clear, careful, step-by-step thinking that takes one of three different forms: chronological, simultaneous, or cyclical. The first follows a time sequence from "first this" to "then that." The second forces you to deal with activities or events that happen or happened at the same time, such as people quietly studying or just getting home from work when the major 1994 earthquake hit Los Angeles. And the third requires you to process information that is continuous, like the rising and setting of the sun. No other thinking pattern will force you to slow down as much as process analysis because the process you are explaining probably won't make any sense if you leave out even the slightest detail.

Good process analysis can truly help your reader see an event in a totally new light. An observer looks at a product already assembled or at a completed event and has no way of knowing without the help of a good process analysis how it got to this final stage. Such an analysis gives the writer or speaker as well as the observer a completely new way of "seeing" the subject in question. Separating process analysis from the other rhetorical modes lets you practice this method of thinking so that you will have a better understanding of the various mental procedures going on in your head. Exercising this possibility in isolation will help you feel its range and its intricacies so that you can become more adept at using it, fully developed, in combination with other modes of thought.

1. List as many examples of each type of process (chronological, simultaneous, and cyclical) that you can think of. Share your list with the class.

2. Write out the process of tying a shoe step by step. Have another person follow your steps exactly to test how well you have analyzed this process.

3. Write a paragraph telling how *not* to do something. Practice your use of humor as a technique for creating interest in the essay by emphasizing the "wrong" way, for example, to wash a car or feed a dog.

READING AND WRITING PROCESS ANALYSIS ESSAYS

Your approach to a process analysis essay should be fairly straightforward. As a reader, you should be sure you understand the author's statement of purpose and then try to visualize each step as you go along. As a writer, you need to adapt the mechanics of the way you normally write to the demands of a process analysis paper, beginning with an interesting topic and a number of clearly explained ideas or stages. As usual, the intended audience determines the choice of words and the degree of detail.

How to Read a Process Analysis Essay

Preparing to Read. Preparing to read a process analysis essay is as uncomplicated as the essay itself. The title of Edwin Bliss's essay in this chapter, "Managing Your Time," tells us exactly what we are going to learn about. Paul Roberts's essay teaches us "How to Say Nothing in Five Hundred Words." Scanning each selection to assess the author's audience will give you an even better idea of what to expect in these essays, while the synopsis of each in the Rhetorical Table of Contents will help focus your attention on its subject.

Also important as you prepare to read these essays are the qualifications of each author to write on this subject: Has he or she performed the task, worked with the mechanism, or seen the event? Is the writer's experience firsthand? When Barbara Ehrenreich tells us to "Stop Ironing the Diapers," is she writing from her personal experience as a mother? What is Jessica

Mitford's experience with mortuaries? How does she know what goes on "Behind the Formaldehyde Curtain"? The biography preceding each essay will help you uncover this information and find out other publication details that will encourage you to focus on the material you are about to read.

Finally, before you begin reading, answer the prereading questions, and then, do some brainstorming on the subject of the essay: What do you want to know about preparing for an interview (Good and Fitzpatrick)? How well do you manage your time, and what do you think you can learn about the subject from Bliss?

Reading. When you read the essays in this chapter for the first time, record your initial reactions to them. Consider the preliminary information you have been studying in order to create a context for each author's composition: Why did Barbara Ehrenreich write "Stop Ironing the Diapers"? What circumstances prompted Mitford's "Behind the Formaldehyde Curtain"? Who do you think is Roberts's target audience in "How to Say Nothing in Five Hundred Words"?

Also determine at this point whether the essay you are reading is directive (explaining how to do something) or informative (giving information about how something happened). This fundamental understanding of the author's intentions, along with a reading of the questions following the essay, will prepare you to approach the contents of each selection critically when you read it a second time.

Rereading. As you reread these process analysis essays, look for an overview of the process at the beginning of the essay so you know where each writer is headed. The body of each essay, then, is generally a discussion of the stages of the process.

This central portion of the essay is often organized *chronologically* (as in Mitford's essay), with clear transitions so that readers can easily follow the writer's train of thought. Other methods of organization are *cyclical*, describing a process that has no clear beginning or end, and *simultaneous* (such as the essays by Good and Fitzpatrick on having a successful interview, by Bliss on organizing one's time, and by Roberts on writing an essay), in which many activities occur at the same time with a clear beginning and end. Most of these essays discuss the process as a whole at some point. During this second reading, you will also benefit from discovering what rhetorical modes each writer uses to support his or her process analysis and why these rhetorical modes work effectively. Do the examples that Good and Fitzpatrick give help explain the process of how to have a good interview? What does Bliss's cause/effect reasoning add to his essay on time management? And how do the descriptions in Mitford's essay on mortuaries heighten the horror of the American mortuary business? How do all the rhetorical modes in each essay help create a coherent whole? After reading each essay for a second time, answer the questions that follow the selection to see if you are understanding your reading material on the literal, interpretive, and analytical levels before you take on the discussion/writing assignments.

For an overview of the entire reading process, you might consult the checklists on pages 20–21 of the Introduction.

How to Write a Process Analysis Essay

Prewriting. As you begin a process analysis assignment, you first need to become as familiar as you can with the action, mechanism, or event you are going to describe. If possible, try to go through the process yourself at least once or twice. If you can't actually carry out the procedure, going through the process mentally and taking notes is a good alternative. Then, try to read something about the process. After all this preparation (and careful consideration of your audience and purpose), you should be ready to brainstorm, freewrite, cluster, or use your favorite prewriting technique (see pages 21–23 of the Introduction) in response to the prewriting questions before you start composing your paper.

Writing. The essay should begin with an overview of the process or event to be analyzed. This initial section should introduce the subject, divide it into a number of recognizable steps, and describe the result once the process is complete. Your thesis in a process essay is usually a purpose statement that clearly and briefly explains your approach to the procedure you will discuss: "Building model airplanes can be divided into four basic steps" or "The American courts follow three stages in prosecuting a criminal case."

Next, the directive or informative essay should proceed logically through the various stages of the process, from beginning to end. The parts of a process usually fall nicely into chronological order, supported by such transitions as "at first," "in the beginning," "next," "then," "after that," and "finally." Some processes, however, are either simultaneous, forcing the writer to choose a more complex logical order for the essay (such as classification), or cyclical, requiring the writer to choose a starting point and then explain the cycle stage by stage. Playing the guitar, for example, involves two separate and simultaneous components that must work together: holding the strings against the frets with the fingers of one hand and strumming with the other hand. In analyzing this procedure, you would probably want to describe both parts of the process and then explain how the hands work together to produce music. An example of a cyclical process would be the changing of the seasons. To explain this concept to a reader, you would need to pick a starting point, such as spring, and describe the entire cycle, stage by stage, from that point onward.

In a process paper, you need to be especially sensitive to your intended audience, or they will not be able to follow your explanation. The amount of information, the number of examples and illustrations, and the terms to be defined all depend on the prior knowledge and background of your readers. A writer explaining to a group of amateur cooks how to prepare a soufflé would take an entirely different approach to the subject than he or she would if the audience were a group of bona fide chefs hoping to land jobs in elegant French restaurants. The professional chefs would need more sophisticated and precise explanations than their recreational counterparts, who would probably find such an approach tedious and complicated because of the extraneous details.

The last section of a process analysis paper should consider the process as a whole. If, for example, the writer is giving directions on how to build a model airplane, the essay might end with a good description or drawing of the plane. The informative essay on our legal system might offer a summary of the stages of judging and sentencing a criminal. And the essay on cooking a soufflé might finish with a photograph of the mouth-watering dish.

Rewriting. In order to revise a process analysis essay, first make sure your main purpose is apparent throughout your paper:

Have you written a directive or an informative essay?

Is your purpose statement clear?

Is your purpose consistent throughout?

Next, you need to determine if your paper is aimed at the proper audience:

Is your vocabulary appropriate for that audience?

At the beginning of the essay, have you given your readers an overview of the process you are going to discuss?

Do you go through the process you are explaining step by step, making sure each phase of the description is comprehensible to your intended audience?

Finally, at the end of the essay, do you help your readers see the process as a complete entity?

The checklists on pages 32–33 will give you further guidelines for writing, revising, and proofreading.

STUDENT ESSAY: PROCESS ANALYSIS AT WORK

The student essay that follows analyzes the process of using a "home permanent" kit. Notice that, once the student gives an overview of the process, she discusses the steps one at a time, being careful to follow a logical order (in this case, chronological) and to use clear transitions. Then, see how the end of the essay shows the process as a whole.

Follow the Simple Directions

Although fickle hairstylists in Paris and Hollywood decide what is currently "in," many romanticists disregard fashion and yearn for a mane of delicate tendrils. Sharing this urge but resenting the cost, I opted for a "home perm" kit. Any literate person with normal dexterity could follow illustrated directions, I reasoned, and the eight easy steps would energize my limp locks in less than two hours. "Before" and "after" photos of flawless models showed the metamorphosis one might achieve. Confidently, I assembled towels, rollers, hair clips, waving lotion, neutralizer, end papers, and a plastic cap. While shampooing, I chortled about my ingenuity and economy.

Purpose statement for informative process analysis

Overview

First step (chronological order)

221

Transition | After towel-drying my hair, I applied the | Second step

gooey, acidic waving lotion thoroughly. Then I wrapped an end paper around a | Third step

parted section and rolled the first curl ("securely but not too tightly"). Despite the reassuring click of the fastened rollers, as I sectioned each new curl the previous one developed its own volition and slowly un-rolled itself. Resolutely, I reapplied waving lotion and rewound—and rewound—each

Transition | curl. Since my hair was already saturated, I regarded the next direction skeptically: "Apply waving lotion to each curl." | Fourth step

Faithfully, however, I complied with the in-structions. Ignoring the fragile state of the

Transition | fastened rollers, I then feigned assurance | Fifth step

and enclosed my entire head in a plastic cap. In forty minutes, chemical magic would occur.

Restless with anticipation, I puttered about the house; while absorbed in small chores, I felt the first few drops of lotion es-cape from the plastic tent. Stuffing wads of cotton around the cap's edges did not help, and the small drops soon became rivulets that left red streaks on my neck and face and splattered on the floor. (Had I overdone the waving lotion?) Ammonia fumes so per-meated each room that I was soon asked to leave. Retreating to the bathroom, I opened the window and dreamed of frivolous new hairstyles.

Transition | Finally, the waving time had elapsed; neutralizing was next. I removed my plastic | Sixth step

cap, carefully heeding the caution: "Do not disturb curlers as you rinse waving lotion from hair." With their usual impudence, however, all the curlers soon bobbed in the sink; undaunted, I continued. "This next step is critical," warned the instructions.

Thinking half-hearted curls were better than no curls at all, I poured the entire bottle of neutralizer on my hair. After a drippy ten-minute wait, I read the next step: "Carefully remove rollers." As this advice was superfluous, I moved anxiously to the finale: "Rinse all solution from your hair, and enjoy your curls."

Transition

Seventh step

Transition

Eighth step

Lifting my head from the sink and expecting visions of Aphrodite, I saw instead Medusa's image in the mirror. Limp question-mark spirals fell over my eyes, and each "curl" ended in an explosion of steel-wool frizz. Reflecting on my ineptitude, I knew why the direction page was illustrated only with drawings. After washing a large load of ammonia-scented towels, I took two aspirin and called my hairdresser. Some repair services are cheap at any price.

Final product

Concluding remark

Student Writer's Comments

Any person with normal dexterity probably *could* do a successful perm! But I sure had trouble. And I decided I wanted to communicate that trouble within my process analysis essay. When I was given this writing assignment, I knew immediately that I wanted to explain how to do a perm. But I didn't know how to handle the humor that had resulted from my misguided attempt to administer a perm to myself. Part of my response to this assignment resides deep within my personality (I'm a closet comedian), but part of it simply has to do with the relationship between me and permanents (actually, anything having to do with cosmetics). But as I started out on this project, I had no idea if I could mold the comedy into a step-by-step analysis of a process.

First, I went to the store and bought a brand-new home perm, so I could review the guidelines step by step. On a piece of paper, I listed the procedures for giving myself a perm. On another sheet of paper, I wrote down any stories or associations I had with each stage of the process. Some of the notes on the second sheet of paper took the form of full paragraphs, others a list of words and phrases, and still others a combination of lists and full sentences. I found myself laughing aloud at some of the memories the home perm directions triggered.

I knew I was writing a directive essay for someone who might actually want to try a home perm. After making my preliminary lists of ideas, I just let my natural sense of humor direct my writing. My overview and purpose statement came easily. Next, I went through the directions one by one, laughing at myself and the process along the way. Before I knew it, I found myself writing, "After washing a large load of ammonia-scented towels, I took two aspirin and called my hairdresser"— the perfect end, or so I thought, to my comedy of errors. I had written the whole first draft from start to finish without once surfacing for air.

When I reread my draft, I realized that the approach I had taken to this process analysis assignment was a satirical one. It allowed me to go through the proper procedure of giving myself a home perm while simultaneously poking fun at myself along the way. As I revised my essay, I tried to exaggerate some of the humorous sections that demonstrated my ineptness or my failure to follow the directions correctly, hoping they would communicate the true ridiculousness of this entire situation. After omitting some details and embellishing others, I came up with the current last sentence of the essay: "Some repair services are cheap at any price." This new concluding remark took the edge off the whiny tone of the previous sentence and brought the essay to an even lighter close than before. I ended up liking the way the humor worked in the essay, because besides accurately capturing my most recent process analysis experience, it made a potentially dull essay topic rather entertaining. My only problem now is that I'm still not sure I got all the frizz out of my hair!

SOME FINAL THOUGHTS ON PROCESS ANALYSIS

In this chapter, a single process dictates the development and organization of each of the essays. Both directional and informational methods are represented here. Notice in particular the clear purpose statements that set the focus of the essays in each case, as well as the other rhetorical modes (such as narration, comparison/contrast, and definition) that are used to help support the writers' explanations.

BARBARA EHRENREICH   (1941 –   )

■ ■ ■

Stop Ironing the Diapers

Barbara Ehrenreich is a respected author, lecturer, and social commentator with opinions on a wide range of topics. After earning a B.A. from Reed College in chemistry and physics and a Ph.D. from Rockefeller University in cell biology, she turned almost immediately to freelance writing, producing a succession of books and pamphlets on a dazzling array of subjects. Early publications examined student uprisings, health care in America, nurses and midwives, poverty, welfare, economic justice for women, and the sexual politics of disease. Her most recent books include *The Hearts of Men: American Dreams and the Flight from Commitment* (1983), *Fear of Falling: The Inner Life of the Middle Class* (1989), and *The Worst Years of Our Lives: Irreverent Notes from a Decade of Greed* (1990)—an indictment of the 1980s that was described by the *New York Times* as "elegant, trenchant, savagely angry, morally outraged, and outrageously funny." Ehrenreich is also well known as a frequent guest on television and radio programs, including *The Today Show, Good Morning America, Nightline, Crossfire,* and *The Phil Donahue Show.* Her many articles and reviews have appeared in the *New York Times Magazine, Esquire,* the *Atlantic Monthly,* the *New Republic, Vogue, Harper's,* and the *Wall Street Journal.* She has been an essayist for *Time* since 1990. Ehrenreich, whose favorite hobby is "voracious reading," lives in Syosset, New York.

Preparing to Read

The following essay, from *The Worst Years of Our Lives,* offers humorous but extremely helpful advice for women who want to raise children and have a career at the same time. As you prepare to read this essay, take a few minutes to think about parenthood: Do your parents both work? Do they enjoy their work? What specific activities did they perform as parents when you were a child? Did you like growing up in your house? Why or why not? If you are a parent now, what characterizes your relationship with your child or children? What activities do you perform as a parent? As a student? Do your children suffer because of your life as a student? In what ways?

I was saddened to read, a few weeks ago, that a group of young 1 women is planning a conference on that ancient question: Is it possible to raise children and have a career at the same time? A group of young *men*—now that would be interesting. But I had thought that among women the issue had been put to rest long ago with the simple retort, Is it possible to raise children *without* having some dependable source of income with which to buy them food, clothing, and Nintendo?

Of course, what the young women are worried about is 2 whether it's possible to raise children *well* while at the same time maintaining one's membership in the labor force. They have heard of "quality time." They are anxious about "missing a stage." They are afraid they won't have the time to nudge their off-springs' tiny intellects in the direction of the inevitable SATs.

And no wonder they are worried: While everything else in 3 our lives has gotten simpler, speedier, more microwavable and user-friendly, child-raising seems to have expanded to fill the time no longer available for it. At least this is true in the trendsetting, postyuppie class, where it is not uncommon to find busy young lawyers breast-feeding until the arrival of molars, reserving entire weekdays for the company of five-year-olds, and feeling guilty about not ironing the diapers.

This is not only silly but dangerous. Except under the most ad- 4 verse circumstances—such as homelessness, unsafe living conditions, or lack of spouse and child care—child-raising was not *meant* to be a full-time activity. No culture on earth outside of mid-century suburban America has ever deployed one woman per child without simultaneously assigning her such major productive activities as weaving, farming, gathering, temple maintenance, and tent building. The reason is that full-time, one-on-one child-raising is not good for women *or* children. And it is on the strength of that anthropological generalization, as well as my own two decades of motherhood, that I offer you my collected tips on *how to raise your children at home in your spare time.*

1. Forget the "stages." The women who are afraid to leave 5
home because they might "miss a stage" do not realize that all
"stages" last more than ten minutes. Sadly, some of them last fifteen years or more. Even the most cursory parent, who drops in
only to change clothes and get the messages off the answering
machine, is unlikely to miss a "stage." Once a "stage" is over—
and let us assume it is a particularly charming one, involving
high-pitched squeals of glee and a rich flow of spittle down the
chin—the best thing you can do is forget it at once. The reason
for this is that no self-respecting six-year-old wants to be reminded that she was once a fat little fool in a high chair; just as
no thirteen-year-old wants to be reminded that she was ever,
even for a moment, a six-year-old.

I cannot emphasize this point strongly enough: the parent 6
who insists on remembering the "stages"—and worse still, bringing them up—risks turning that drool-faced little darling into a
lifelong enemy. I mean, try to see it from the child's point of view:
suppose you were condemned to being two and a half feet tall,
unemployed, and incontinent for an indefinite period of time.
Would you want people reminding you of this unfortunate phase
for the rest of your life?

2. Forget "quality time." I tried it once on May 15, 1978. I 7
know because it is still penciled into my 1978 appointment book.
"Kids," I announced, "I have forty-five minutes. Let's have some
quality time!" They looked at me dully in the manner of rural re-
tirees confronting a visitor from the Census Bureau. Finally, one
of them said, in a soothing tone, "Sure, Mom, but could it be after
Gilligan's Island?"

The same thing applies to "talks," as in "Let's sit down and have 8
a little talk." In response to that—or the equally lame "How's
school?"—any self-respecting child will assume the demeanor of
a prisoner of war facing interrogation. The only thing that works
is *low-quality* time: time in which you—and they—are ostensibly
doing something else, like housework. Even a two-year-old can
dust or tidy and thereby gain an exaggerated sense of self-impor-
tance. In fact, this is the only sensible function of housework, the
other being to create the erroneous impression that you do not
live with children at all.

Also, do not underestimate the telephone as a means of par- 9
ent–child communication. Teenagers especially recognize it as an
instrument demanding full disclosure, in infinite detail, of their
thoughts, ambitions, and philosophical outlook. If you want to
know what's on their minds, call them from work. When you get
home, they'll be calling someone else.

3. Do not overload their intellects. Many parents, mindful of 10
approaching nursery-school entrance exams, PSATs, GREs, and so
forth, stay up late into the night reading back issues of *Scientific
American* and the *Cliff's Notes* for the *Encyclopaedia Britannica*. This
is in case the child should ask a question, such as "Why do horses
walk on their hands?" The *overprepared* parent answers with a
twenty-minute disquisition on evolution, animal husbandry, and
DNA, during which the child slinks away in despair, determined
never to ask a question again, except possibly the indispensable
"Are we there yet?"

The part-time parent knows better, and responds only in vague 11
and elusive ways, letting her voice trail off and her eyes wander to
some mythical landscape, as in: "Well, they don't when they
fight. . . . No, then they rear up. . . . Or when they fly . . . like
Pegasus . . . mmmm." This system invariably elicits a stream of
eager questions, which can then be referred to a more reliable
source.

4. Do not attempt to mold them. First, because it takes too 12
much time. Second, because a child is not a salmon mousse. A
child is a temporarily disabled and stunted version of a larger person, whom you will someday know. Your job is to help them
overcome the disabilities associated with their size and inexperi-
ence so that they get on with being that larger person, and in a
form that you might *like* to know.

Hence the part-time parent encourages self-reliance in all 13
things. For example, from the moment my children mastered
Pidgin English, they were taught one simple rule: Never wake a
sleeping adult. I was mysterious about the consequences, but they
became adept, at age two, at getting their own cereal and hanging
out until a reasonable hour. Also, contrary to widespread
American myth, no self-respecting toddler enjoys having wet and
clammy buns. Nor is the potty concept alien to the one-year-old
mind. So do not make the common mistake of withholding the

toilet facilities until the crisis of nursery-school matriculation forces the issue.

5. Do not be afraid they will turn on you, someday, for being a 14 *lousy parent.* They *will* turn on you. They will also turn on the full-time parents, the cookie-making parents, the Little League parents, and the all-sacrificing parents. If you are at work every day when they get home from school, they will turn on you, eventually, for being a selfish, neglectful careerist. If you are at home every day, eagerly awaiting their return, they will turn on you for being a useless, unproductive layabout. This is all part of the normal process of "individuation," in which one adult ego must be trampled into the dust in order for one fully formed teenage ego to emerge. Accept it.

Besides, a part-time parent is unlikely to ever harbor that most 15 poisonous of all parental thoughts: "What I gave up for you . . . !" No child should have to take the rap for wrecking a grown woman's brilliant career. The good part-time parent convinces her children that they are positive assets, without whose wit and insights she would never have gotten the last two promotions.

6. Whether you work outside the home or not, never tell them 16 *that being a mommy is your "job."* Being a mommy is a relationship, not a profession. Nothing could be worse for a child's self-esteem than to think that you think that being with her is *work*. She may come to think that you are involved in some obscure manufacturing process in which she is only the raw material. She may even come to think that her real mom was switched at birth, and that you are the baby-sitter. Which leads to my final tip:

7. **Even if you are not a part-time parent, even if you** 17 **haven't the slightest intention of entering the wide world of wage earning,** *pretend that you are one.*

UNDERSTANDING DETAILS

1. What is the main idea in this essay?
2. What are Ehrenreich's seven tips on "how to raise your children at home in your spare time" (paragraph 4)?
3. What does Ehrenreich mean when she says that "child-raising seems to have expanded to fill the time no longer available for it" (paragraph 3)?

4. What is the process of "individuation" according to Ehrenreich? What is the dictionary definition of this term?

ANALYZING MEANING

1. Why is the author saddened to find out about a women's conference on combining children and careers? What are the women really worried about?
2. What does guilt have to do with ironing diapers?
3. Why does Ehrenreich say that "full-time, one-on-one child-raising is not good for women *or* children" (paragraph 4)? What does she mean by this statement?
4. According to Ehrenreich, why should you pretend that you are a wage-earning parent?

DISCOVERING RHETORICAL STRATEGIES

1. How would you characterize the tone of this essay? What specific examples bring you to this conclusion?
2. Who do you think is Ehrenreich's audience in this essay? On what do you base your answer?
3. What is Ehrenreich's method of organizing the advice in her essay?
4. Explain Ehrenreich's title. What are some other possible titles?

MAKING CONNECTIONS

1. Imagine that Ehrenreich and Germaine Greer ("A Child Is Born") are having a conversation about the responsibilities of parents in raising their children. Would Greer agree with Ehrenreich's advice? Why or why not? Do you agree with Ehrenreich's advice?
2. Ehrenreich and Edwin Bliss ("Managing Your Time") both give advice along with their explanation of a process. Which essay is easiest to read? Which is most convincing? Explain your answer.
3. If Ehrenreich and Judy Brady ("Why I Want a Wife") were discussing the proper duties of wives and mothers, would they mostly agree or disagree with each other? Explain your answer.

IDEAS FOR DISCUSSION/WRITING

Preparing to Write

Write freely about your favorite daily activities: What roles do you enjoy the most? Why do you enjoy these roles? What activities do you enjoy the most? Why do you enjoy these activities? Do any of the roles you play interfere with the activities you typically participate in? How do you resolve this conflict? What parts of a typical day give you the most satisfaction? Why are they satisfying?

Choosing a Topic

1. Using Ehrenreich's essay as a model, explain what characterizes successful parenthood. Direct your essay to a couple about to have their first child.
2. You have just failed at one of your favorite pastimes. In order to get a laugh, explain to your peers in a well-organized essay how to fail at one of the activities you enjoy.
3. Prepare for your English class a two- to three-minute talk on one of the following topics:

My Favorite Television Show

My Favorite Play

My Favorite Movie

My Favorite Sport

My Favorite Magazine

My Favorite Musical Group

My Favorite Book

My Favorite Concert

My Favorite Quality in My Mother/Father

My Favorite Quality in Myself

EDWIN BLISS (1923 –)

■ ■ ■

Managing Your Time

An internationally known consultant on time-management techniques, Edwin Bliss earned his B.S. and M.S. degrees at the University of Utah, worked as a reporter for the *Columbus Dispatch*, taught journalism at a variety of schools, and was a lobbyist for the National Industrial Council and the U.S. Chamber of Commerce. Not until he became a member of the Washington staff of Senator Wallace F. Bennett, however, did he begin to understand the importance of time management. Since then, Bliss has put his management techniques to work as a consultant for a number of businesses in American and abroad through public seminars sponsored by a company called CareerTrack. "Organizing your time properly is especially important for college students," he claims; "a knowledge of time-management skills can help you avoid writers' block so that you turn your papers in on time." His first book, *Getting Things Done: The ABC's of Time Management*, was published in 1976 (updated and reissued in 1991); his second, *Doing It Now: A Twelve-Step Program for Overcoming Procrastination*, came out in 1983; and his third, *Are Your Employees Stealing You Blind?* (coauthored with Isamu Aoki), appeared in 1993. Bliss currently lives in central California, where he is writing a book on how to operate a small business.

Preparing to Read

In the following essay, which is taken from *Getting Things Done: The ABC's of Time Management*, Bliss offers a number of specific suggestions to help you organize your time more efficiently. Before reading his essay, take a few minutes to think about how you arrange each day: How carefully do you schedule your time? Do you make lists of things you want to do every day? Do you usually accomplish more or less than you wanted to in a typical day? How well do you concentrate on a single activity? Are you able to say *no* to events you don't want to participate in? How much do you procrastinate? Are all aspects of your life in a healthy balance (e.g., work, recreation, school, and family)? If not, what could you do to create a more balanced life for yourself?

I first became interested in the effective use of time when I   1 was an assistant to a U.S. Senator. Members of Congress are faced with urgent and conflicting demands on their time— for committee work, floor votes, speeches, interviews, briefings, correspondence, investigations, constituents' problems, and the need to be informed on a wide range of subjects. The more successful Congressmen develop techniques for getting maximum benefit from minimum investments of time. If they don't, they don't return.

Realizing that I was not one of those who use time effectively,   2 I began to apply in my own life some of the techniques I had observed. Here are ten I have found most helpful.

Plan.   You need a game plan for your day. Otherwise, you'll   3 allocate your time according to whatever happens to land on your desk. And you will find yourself making the fatal mistake of dealing primarily with problems rather than opportunities. Start each day by making a general schedule, with particular emphasis on the two or three major things you would like to accomplish— including things that will achieve long-term goals. Remember, studies prove what common sense tells us: The more time we spend planning a project, the less total time is required for it. Don't let today's busywork crowd planning-time out of your schedule.

Concentrate.   Of all the principles of time management, none   4 is more basic than concentration. People who have serious time-management problems invariably are trying to do too many things at once. The amount of time spent on a project is not what counts: It's the amount of *uninterrupted* time. Few problems can resist an all-out attack; few can be solved piecemeal.

Take Breaks.   To work for long periods without taking a   5 break is not an effective use of time. Energy decreases, boredom sets in, and physical stress and tension accumulate. Switching for a few minutes from a mental task to something physical—isometric exercises, walking around the office, even changing from a sitting position to a standing position for a while—can provide relief.

Merely resting, however, is often the best course, and you 6
should not think of a "rest" break as poor use of time. Not only will being refreshed increase your efficiency, but relieving tension will benefit your health. Anything that contributes to health is good time management.

Avoid Clutter.   Some people have a constant swirl of papers 7
on their desks and assume that somehow the most important matters will float to the top. In most cases, however, clutter hinders concentration and can create tension and frustration—a feeling of being "snowed under."

Whenever you find your desk becoming chaotic, take time out 8
to reorganize. Go through all your papers (making generous use of the wastebasket) and divide them into categories: (1) Immediate action, (2) Low priority, (3) Pending, (4) Reading material. Put the highest priority item from your first pile in the center of your desk, then put everything else out of sight. Remember, you can think of only one thing at a time, and you can work on only one task at a time, so focus all your attention on the most important one. A final point: Clearing the desk completely, or at least organizing it, each evening should be standard practice. It gets the next day off to a good start.

Don't Be a Perfectionist.   There is a difference between striv- 9
ing for excellence and striving for perfection. The first is attainable, gratifying and healthy. The second is often unattainable, frustrating and neurotic. It's also a terrible waste of time. The stenographer who retypes a lengthy letter because of a trivial error, or the boss who demands such retyping, might profit from examining the Declaration of Independence. When the inscriber of that document made two errors of omission, he inserted the missing letters between the lines. If this is acceptable in the document that gave birth to American freedom, surely it would be acceptable in a letter that will be briefly glanced at en route to someone's file cabinet or wastebasket?

Don't Be Afraid to Say No.   Of all the time-saving techniques 10
ever developed, perhaps the most effective is frequent use of the word *no.* Learn to decline, tactfully but firmly, every request that does not contribute to your goals. If you point out that your mo-

tivation is not to get out of work but to save your time to do a better job on the really important things, you'll have a good chance of avoiding unproductive tasks. Remember, many people who worry about offending others wind up living according to other people's priorities.

Don't Procrastinate. Procrastination is usually a deeply rooted 11 habit. But we can change our habits provided we use the right system. William James, the father of American psychology, discussed such a system in his famous *Principles of Psychology*, published in 1890. It works as follows:

1. Decide to start changing as soon as you finish reading this article, while you are motivated. Taking that first step promptly is important.
2. Don't try to do too much too quickly. Just force yourself right now to do one thing you have been putting off. Then, beginning tomorrow morning, start each day by doing the most unpleasant thing on your schedule. Often it will be a small matter: an overdue apology; a confrontation with a fellow worker; an annoying chore you know you should tackle. Whatever it is, do it before you begin your usual morning routine. This simple procedure can well set the tone for your day. You will get a feeling of exhilaration from knowing that although the day is only 15 minutes old, you have already accomplished the most unpleasant thing you have to do all day.

There is one caution: Do not permit any exceptions. William 12 James compared it to rolling up a ball of string; a single slip can undo more than many turns can wind up. Be tough with yourself, for the first few minutes of each day, for the next two weeks, and I promise you a new habit of priceless value.

Apply Radical Surgery. Time-wasting activities are like can- 13 cers. They drain off vitality and have a tendency to grow. The only cure is radical surgery. If you are wasting your time in activities that bore you, divert you from your real goals, and sap your energy, cut them out, once and for all.

The principle applies to personal habits, routines and activities 14 as much as to ones associated with your work. Check your appointment calendar, your extracurricular activities, your reading list, your television viewing habits, and ax everything that doesn't give you a feeling of accomplishment or satisfaction.

Delegate. An early example of failure to delegate is found in 15 the Bible. Moses, having led his people out of Egypt, was so impressed with his own knowledge and authority that he insisted on ruling personally on every controversy that arose in Israel. His wise father-in-law, Jethro, recognizing that this was poor use of a leader's time, recommended a two-phase approach: First, educate the people concerning the laws; second, select capable leaders and give them full authority over routine matters, freeing Moses to concentrate on major decisions. The advice is still sound.

You don't have to be a national leader or a corporate executive 16 to delegate, either. Parents who don't delegate household chores are doing a disservice to themselves and their children. Running a Boy Scout troop can be as time-consuming as running General Motors if you try to do everything yourself. One caution: Giving subordinates jobs that neither you nor anyone else wants to do isn't delegating, it's assigning. Learn to delegate the challenging and rewarding tasks, along with sufficient authority to make necessary decisions. It can help to free your time.

Don't Be a "Workaholic."   Most successful executives I know 17 work long hours, but they don't let work interfere with the really important things in life, such as friends, family and fly fishing. This differentiates them from the workaholic who becomes addicted to work just as people become addicted to alcohol. Symptoms of work addiction include refusal to take a vacation, inability to put the office out of your mind on weekends, a bulging briefcase, and a spouse, son or daughter who is practically a stranger.

Counseling can help people cope with such problems. But for 18 starters, do a bit of self-counseling. Ask yourself whether the midnight oil you are burning is adversely affecting your health. Ask where your family comes in your list of priorities, whether you are giving enough of yourself to your children and spouse, and whether you are deceiving yourself by pretending that the sacrifices you are making are really for them.

Above all else, good time management involves an awareness 19 that today is all we ever have to work with. The past is irretrievably gone, the future is only a concept. British art critic John Ruskin had the word "TODAY" carved into a small marble block that he kept on his desk as a constant reminder to "Do It Now." But my favorite quotation is by an anonymous philosopher:

> Yesterday is a canceled check.
> Tomorrow is a promissory note.
> Today is ready cash. Use it!

UNDERSTANDING DETAILS

1. What are the ten techniques for managing time that Bliss learned from observing successful members of Congress at work? Explain each in your own words.
2. According to Bliss, what is the difference between "delegating" and "assigning" chores (paragraph 16)?
3. What is a "workaholic" (paragraph 17)? What characteristics identify this type of person?
4. Explain Bliss's favorite quotation:

   Yesterday is a canceled check.
   Tomorrow is a promissory note.
   Today is ready cash. Use It!

   What does this saying have to do with time management?

ANALYZING MEANING

1. Why is concentration such an important part of time management? Have you found this to be true in your own experience? Explain your answer.
2. Which of Bliss's guidelines for managing time could you benefit from most? How could it help you? Why do you have trouble in this area?
3. Why does Bliss advise us not to be workaholics? Does this advice conflict with the other guidelines Bliss lists in this essay? Why or why not?
4. In what parts of the essay does Bliss refer to our personal lives? According to the author, how can we balance our personal and professional lives? How realistic are these ideas?

DISCOVERING RHETORICAL STRATEGIES

1. Bliss introduces each new suggestion for managing time as a command and then fully explains each command. How effective is this approach? What effect would headings beginning with present participles have on the essay (e.g., planning, taking breaks, avoiding clutter)?
2. How does Bliss organize his techniques for managing time? Is this order successful? Explain your answer.
3. What is Bliss's general attitude toward time management? In your opinion, is this an efficient attitude toward the subject?

4. What other rhetorical modes does Bliss use to support this process analysis essay? Give examples of each of these modes.

MAKING CONNECTIONS

1. How would William Ouchi ("Japanese and American Workers: Two Casts of Mind") respond to Bliss's essay? Would he agree or disagree with the author's recommendations and conclusions? Do Bliss's suggestions about time management sound more "Japanese" or "American," according to Ouchi's definition of each society's business practices?

2. Bliss's essay analyzing the process of managing our time and Jessica Mitford's essay ("Behind the Formaldehyde Curtain") analyzing funeral customs both try to persuade us to think a certain way as they describe a process. Which essay is more convincing to you? Explain your answer in detail.

3. Pretend that you are Edwin Bliss giving advice to young Russell Baker ("The Saturday Evening Post"), who wants to become a good salesman. Which of Bliss's suggestions should Baker follow most earnestly? Why? Which of these suggestions would be most helpful in your own life?

IDEAS FOR DISCUSSION/WRITING

Preparing to Write

Write freely about various aspects of time management: Do you manage time well from day to day? What benefits can you receive from managing your time better? Can you identify any disadvantages that could result from managing your time better? How can you avoid these problems? Are you a workaholic, or do you strike a good balance between the various aspects of your life? What is the relationship between time management and quality of life?

Choosing a Topic

1. You have been asked by the editor of your campus newspaper to adapt Bliss's suggestions to the life of a student. Write a process analysis essay adjusting Bliss's ten guidelines to a college environment.

2. Interview someone in your class about his or her ability to use time wisely. Use Bliss's guidelines to establish whether the person manages time well. Then, direct a process analysis essay to

this person, briefly evaluating his or her time-management skills and then offering suggestions for improvement.

3. At times, Bliss's approach to time management (do all you can in a day) seems to conflict with the fundamental tenets for leading a quality life (relax and enjoy yourself). Do you think these two aspects of life are incompatible, or are there ways to reconcile the two? Write an essay for your classmates detailing a solution to this dilemma.

JESSICA MITFORD   (1917 –   )

■ ■ ■

Behind the Formaldehyde Curtain

Once called "Queen of the Muckrakers" in a *Time* magazine review, Jessica Mitford has written scathing exposés of the Famous
Writers' School, American funeral directors, television executives,
prisons, a "fat farm" for wealthy women, and many other venera-
ble social institutions. She was born in England into the gentry,
immigrated to the United States, and later became a naturalized
American citizen. After working at a series of jobs, she achieved
literary fame at age forty-six with the publication of *The American
Way of Death* (1963), which relentlessly shatters the image of funeral directors as "compassionate, reverent family-friends-in-
need." Her other major works include *Kind and Unusual
Punishment: The Prison Business* (1973); *Poison Penmanship: The
Gentle Art of Muckraking* (1979), an anthology of Mitford's articles
in The *Atlantic, Harper's*, and other periodicals covering a twenty-
two-year time span; two volumes of autobiography, *Daughters and
Rebels* (1960) and *A Fine Old Madness* (1977); *Faces of Philip: A
Memoir of Philip Toynbee* (1984); *Grace Had an English Heart: The
Story of Grace Darling, Heroine and Victorian Superstar* (1988); and
The American Way of Birth (1992). Superbly skilled in the techniques of investigative reporting, satire, and black humor, Mitford
was described in a *Washington Post* article as "an older, more even-
tempered, better-read Jane Fonda who has maintained her ac-
tivism long past middle age."

Preparing to read

The following essay, taken from *The American Way of Death*, clearly
illustrates the ruthless manner in which Mitford exposes the
greed and hypocrisy of the American mortuary business. As you
prepare to read this article, think for a few minutes about funeral
customs in our society: Have you attended a funeral service recently? Which rituals seemed particularly vivid to you? What
purpose did these symbolic actions serve? What other interesting
customs are you aware of in American society? What purpose do

these customs serve? What public images do these customs have? Are these images accurate? Do you generally approve or disapprove of these customs?

T he drama begins to unfold with the arrival of the corpse 1 at the mortuary.

Alas, poor Yorick! How surprised he would be to see 2 how his counterpart of today is whisked off to a funeral parlor and is in short order sprayed, sliced, pierced, pickled, trussed, trimmed, creamed, waxed, painted, rouged and neatly dressed— transformed from a common corpse into a Beautiful Memory Picture. This process is known in the trade as embalming and restorative art and is so universally employed in the United States and Canada that the funeral director does it routinely, without consulting corpse or kin. He regards as eccentric those few who are hardy enough to suggest that it might be dispensed with. Yet no law requires embalming, no religious doctrine commends it, nor is it dictated by considerations of health, sanitation, or even of personal daintiness. In no part of the world but in Northern America is it widely used. The purpose of embalming is to make the corpse presentable for viewing in a suitably costly container; and here too the funeral director routinely, without first consulting the family, prepares the body for public display.

Is all this legal? The processes to which a dead body may be 3 subjected are after all to some extent circumscribed by law. In most states, for instance, the signature of next of kin must be obtained before an autopsy may be performed, before the deceased may be cremated, before the body may be turned over to a medical school for research purposes; or such provision must be made in the decedent's will. In the case of embalming, no such permission is required nor is it ever sought. A textbook, *The Principles and Practices of Embalming*, comments on this: "There is some question regarding the legality of much that is done within the preparation room." The author points out that it would be most unusual for a responsible member of a bereaved family to instruct the mortician, in so many words, to "*embalm*" the body of a deceased relative. The very term "embalming" is so seldom used that the mortician must rely upon custom in the matter. The author concludes that unless the family specifies otherwise, the act of entrusting the body to the care of a funeral establishment carries with it an implied permission to go ahead and embalm.

Embalming is indeed a most extraordinary procedure, and one 4 must wonder at the docility of Americans who each year pay hundreds of millions of dollars for its perpetuation, blissfully ignorant of what it is all about, what is done, how it is done. Not one in ten thousand has any idea of what actually takes place. Books on the subject are extremely hard to come by. They are not to be found in most libraries or bookshops.

In an era when huge television audiences watch surgical oper- 5 ations in the comfort of their living rooms, when, thanks to the animated cartoon, the geography of the digestive system has become familiar territory even to the nursery school set, in a land where the satisfaction of curiosity about almost all matters is a national pastime, the secrecy surrounding embalming can, surely, hardly be attributed to the inherent gruesomeness of the subject. Custom in this regard has within this century suffered a complete reversal. In the early days of American embalming, when it was performed in the home of the deceased, it was almost mandatory for some relative to stay by the embalmer's side and witness the procedure. Today, family members who might wish to be in attendance would certainly be dissuaded by the funeral director. All others, except apprentices, are excluded by law from the preparation room.

A close look at what does actually take place may explain in 6 large measure the undertaker's intractable reticence concerning a procedure that has become his major *raison d'être*. Is it possible he fears that public information about embalming might lead patrons to wonder if they really want this service? If the funeral men are loath to discuss the subject outside the trade, the reader may, understandably, be equally loath to go on reading at this point. For those who have the stomach for it, let us part the formaldehyde curtain. . . .

The body is first laid out in the undertaker's morgue—or 7 rather, Mr. Jones is reposing in the preparation room—to be readied to bid the world farewell.

The preparation room in any of the better funeral establish- 8 ments has the tiled and sterile look of a surgery, and indeed the embalmer-restorative artist who does his chores there is beginning to adopt the term "dermasurgeon" (appropriately corrupted by some mortician-writers as "demisurgeon") to describe his call-ing. His equipment, consisting of scalpels, scissors, augers, forceps, clamps, needles, pumps, tubes, bowls and basins, is crudely imita-tive of the surgeon's, as is his technique, acquired in a nine- or twelve-month post-high-school course in an embalming school. He is supplied by an advanced chemical industry with a bewil-dering array of fluids, sprays, pastes, oils, powders, creams, to fix or soften tissue, shrink or distend it as needed, dry it here, restore the moisture there. There are cosmetics, waxes and paints to fill and cover features, even plaster of Paris to replace entire limbs. There are ingenious aids to prop and stabilize the cadaver: A Vari-Pose Head Rest, the Edwards Arm and Hand Positioner, the Repose Block (to support the shoulders during the embalming), and the Throop Foot Positioner, which resembles an old-fashioned stocks.

Mr. John H. Eckels, president of the Eckels College of Mortuary Science, thus describes the first part of the embalming procedure: "In the hands of a skilled practitioner, this work may be done in a comparatively short time and without mutilating the body other than by slight incision—so slight that it scarcely would cause serious inconvenience if made upon a living person. It is necessary to remove the blood, and doing this not only helps in the disinfecting, but removes the principal cause of disfigure-ments due to discoloration." 9

Another textbook discusses the all-important time element: "The earlier this is done, the better, for every hour that elapses between death and embalming will add to the problems and complications encountered. . . ." Just how soon should one get going on the embalming? The author tells us, "On the basis of such scanty information made available to this profession through its rudimentary and haphazard system of technical research, we must conclude that the best results are to be obtained if the sub-ject is embalmed before life is completely extinct—that is, before cellular death has occurred. In the average case, this would mean within an hour after somatic death." For those who feel that there is something a little rudimentary, not to say haphazard, about this advice, a comforting thought is offered by another writer. Speaking of fears entertained in early days of premature burial, he points out, "One of the effects of embalming by chemical injec-tion, however, has been to dispel fears of live burial." How true; 10

once the blood is removed, chances of live burial are indeed remote.

To return to Mr. Jones, the blood is drained out through the 11
veins and replaced by embalming fluid pumped in through the
arteries. As noted in *The Principles and Practices of Embalming*,
"every operator has a favorite injection and drainage point—a
fact which becomes a handicap only if he fails or refuses to forsake his favorites when conditions demand it." Typical favorites
are the carotid artery, femoral artery, jugular vein, subclavian vein.
There are various choices of embalming fluid. If Flextone is used,
it will produce a "mild, flexible rigidity. The skin retains a velvety
softness, the tissues are rubbery and pliable. Ideal for women and
children." It may be blended with B. and G. Products Company's
Lyf-Lyk tint, which is guaranteed to reproduce "nature's own
skin texture . . . the velvety appearance of living tissue." Suntone
comes in three separate tints: Suntan; Special Cosmetic Tint, a
pink shade "especially indicated for young female subjects"; and
Regular Cosmetic Tint, moderately pink.

About three to six gallons of a dyed and perfumed solution of 12
formaldehyde, glycerin, borax, phenol, alcohol and water is soon
circulating through Mr. Jones, whose mouth has been sewn together with a "needle directed upward between the upper lip and
gum and brought out through the left nostril," with the corners
raised slightly "for a more pleasant expression." If he should be
bucktoothed, his teeth are cleaned with Bon Ami and coated
with colorless nail polish. His eyes, meanwhile, are closed with
flesh-tinted eye caps and eye cement.

The next step is to have at Mr. Jones with a thing called a 13
trocar. This is a long, hollow needle attached to a tube. It is
jabbed into the abdomen, poked around the entrails and chest
cavity, the contents of which are pumped out and replaced with
"cavity fluid." This done, and the hole in the abdomen sewn up,
Mr. Jones's face is heavily creamed (to protect the skin from
burns which may be caused by leakage of the chemicals), and he
is covered with a sheet and left unmolested for a while. But not
for long—there is more, much more, in store for him. He has
been embalmed, but not yet restored, and the best time to start
the restorative work is eight to ten hours after embalming, when
the tissues have become firm and dry.

The object of all this attention to the corpse, it must be re-   14
membered, is to make it presentable for viewing in an attitude of
healthy repose. "Our customs require the presentation of our
dead in the semblance of normality . . . unmarred by the ravages
of illness, disease or mutilation," says Mr. J. Sheridan Mayer in his
Restorative Art. This is rather a large order since few people die in
the full bloom of health, unravaged by illness and unmarked by
some disfigurement. The funeral industry is equal to the challenge: "In some cases the gruesome appearance of a mutilated or
disease-ridden subject may be quite discouraging. The task of
restoration may seem impossible and shake the confidence of the
embalmer. This is the time for intestinal fortitude and determination. Once the formative work is begun and affected tissues are
cleaned or removed, all doubts of success vanish. It is surprising
and gratifying to discover the results which may be obtained."

The embalmer, having allowed an appropriate interval to   15
elapse, returns to the attack, but now he brings into play the skill
and equipment of sculptor and cosmetician. Is a hand missing?
Casting one in plaster of Paris is a simple matter. "For replace-
ment purposes, only a cast of the back of the hand is necessary;
this is within the ability of the average operator and is quite adequate." If a lip or two, a nose or an ear should be missing, the embalmer has at hand a variety of restorative waxes with which to
model replacements. Pores and skin texture are simulated by stip-
pling with a little brush, and over this cosmetics are laid on. Head
off? Decapitation cases are rather routinely handled. Ragged
edges are trimmed, and head joined to torso with a series of
splints, wires and sutures. It is a good idea to have a little something at the neck—a scarf or a high collar—when time for viewing comes. Swollen mouth: Cut out tissue as needed from inside
the lips. If too much is removed, the surface contour can easily be
restored by padding with cotton. Swollen necks and cheeks are
reduced by removing tissue through vertical incisions made
down each side of the neck. "When the deceased is casketed, the
pillow will hide the suture incisions. . . . As an extra precaution
against leakage, the suture may be painted with liquid sealer."

The opposite condition is more likely to present itself—that of   16
emaciation. His hypodermic syringe now loaded with massage
cream, the embalmer seeks out and fills the hollowed and sunken

areas by injection. In this procedure the backs of the hands and fingers and the under-chin area should not be neglected.

Positioning the lips is a problem that recurrently challenges the   17
ingenuity of the embalmer. Closed too tightly, they tend to give a stern, even disapproving expression. Ideally, embalmers feel, the lips should give the impression of being ever so slightly parted, the upper lip protruding slightly for a more youthful appearance. This takes some engineering, however, as the lips tend to drift apart. Lip drift can sometimes be remedied by pushing one or two straight pins through the inner margin of the lower lip and then inserting them between the two front upper teeth. If Mr. Jones happens to have no teeth, the pins can just as easily be anchored in his Armstrong Face Former and Denture Replacer. Another method to maintain lip closure is to dislocate the lower jaw, which is then held in its new position by a wire run through holes which have been drilled through the upper and lower jaws at the midline. As the French are fond of saying, *il faut souffrir pour être belle.*

If Mr. Jones had died of jaundice, the embalming fluid will   18
very likely turn him green. Does this deter the embalmer? Not if he has intestinal fortitude. Masking pastes and cosmetics are heavily laid on, burial garments and casket interiors are color-correlated with particular care, and Jones is displayed beneath rose-colored lights. Friends will say "How *well* he looks." Death by carbon monoxide, on the other hand, can be rather a good thing from the embalmer's viewpoint: "One advantage is the fact that this type of discoloration is an exaggerated form of a natural pink coloration." This is nice because the healthy glow is already present and needs but little attention.

The patching and filling completed, Mr. Jones is now shaved,   19
washed and dressed. Cream-based cosmetic, available in pink, flesh, suntan, brunette and blond, is applied to his hands and face, his hair is shampooed and combed (and, in the case of Mrs. Jones, set), his hands manicured. For the horny-handed son of toil special care must be taken; cream should be applied to remove ingrained grime, and the nails cleaned. "If he were not in the habit of having them manicured in life, trimming and shaping is advised for appearance—never questioned by kin."

Jones is now ready for casketing (this is the present participle   20
of the verb "to casket"). In this operation his right shoulder

should be depressed slightly "to turn the body a bit to the right and soften the appearance of lying flat on the back." Positioning the hands is a matter of importance, and special rubber positioning blocks may be used. The hands should be cupped slightly for a more lifelike, relaxed appearance. Proper placement of the body requires a delicate sense of balance. It should lie as high as possible in the casket, yet not so high that the lid, when lowered, will hit the nose. On the other hand, we are cautioned, placing the body too low "creates the impression that the body is in a box."

Jones is next wheeled into the appointed slumber room where 21 a few last touches may be added—his favorite pipe placed in his hand or, if he was a great reader, a book propped into position. (In the case of little Master Jones a Teddy bear may be clutched.) Here he will hold open house for a few days, visiting hours 10 A.M. to 9 P.M.

All now being in readiness, the funeral director calls a staff 22 conference to make sure that each assistant knows his precise duties. Mr. Wilber Kriege writes "This makes your staff feel that they are a part of the team, with a definite assignment that must be properly carried out if the whole plan is to succeed. You never heard of a football coach who failed to talk to his entire team before they go on the field. They have drilled on the plays they are to execute for hours and days, and yet the successful coach knows the importance of making even the bench-warming third-string substitute feel that he is important if the game is to be won." The winning of *this* game is predicated upon glass-smooth handling of the logistics. The funeral director has notified the pallbearers whose names were furnished by the family, has arranged for the presence of clergyman, organist, and soloist, has provided transportation for everybody, has organized and listed the flowers sent by friends. In *Psychology of Funeral Service*, Mr. Edward A. Martin points out: "He may not always do as much as the family thinks he is doing, but it is his helpful guidance that they appreciate in knowing they are proceeding as they should. . . . The important thing is how well his services can be used to make the family believe they are giving unlimited expression to their own sentiment."

The religious service may be held in a church or in the chapel 23 of the funeral home; the funeral director vastly prefers the latter arrangement, for not only is it more convenient for him but it affords him the opportunity to show off his beautiful facilities to the gathered mourners. After the clergyman has had his say, the mourners queue up to file past the casket for a last look at the deceased. The family is *never* asked whether they want an open-casket ceremony; in the absence of their instruction to the contrary, this is taken for granted. Consequently, well over 90 percent of all American funerals feature the open casket—a custom unknown in other parts of the world. Foreigners are astonished by it. An English woman living in San Francisco described her reaction in a letter to the writer:

> I myself have attended only one funeral here—that of an elderly fellow worker of mine. After the service I could not understand why everyone was walking towards the coffin (sorry, I mean casket), but thought I had better follow the crowd. It shook me rigid to get there and find the casket open and poor old Oscar lying there in his brown tweed suit, wearing a suntan makeup and just the wrong shade of lipstick. If I had not been extremely fond of the old boy, I have a horrible feeling that I might have giggled. Then and there I decided that I could never face another American funeral—even dead.

The casket (which has been resting throughout the service on a Classic Beauty Ultra Metal Casket Bier) is now transferred by a hydraulically operated device called Porto-Lift to a balloon-tired, Glide Easy casket carriage which will wheel it to yet another conveyance, the Cadillac Funeral Coach. This may be lavender, cream, light green—anything but black. Interiors, of course, are color-correlated, "for the man who cannot stop short of perfection." 24

At graveside, the casket is lowered into the earth. This office, once the prerogative of friends of the deceased, is now performed by a patented mechanical lowering device. A "Life-time Green" artificial grass mat is at the ready to conceal the sere earth, and overhead, to conceal the sky, is a portable Steril Chapel Tent ("resists the intense heat and humidity of summer and the terrific storms of winter . . . available in Silver Grey, Rose or Evergreen"). Now is the time for the ritual scattering of earth over the coffin, as the solemn words "earth to earth, ashes to ashes, dust to dust" are pronounced by the officiating cleric. This can today be accomplished "with a mere flick of the wrist with the Gordon Leak-Proof Earth Dispenser. No grasping of a handful of dirt, no soiled fingers. Simple, dignified, beautiful, reverent! The modern 25 way!" The Golden Earth Dispenser (at $5) is of nickel-plated brass construction. It is not only "attractive to the eye and long wearing"; it is also "one of the 'tools' for building better public relations" if presented as "an appropriate non-commercial gift" to the clergyman. It is shaped something like a saltshaker.

Untouched by human hand, the coffin and the earth are now 26 united.

It is in the function of directing the participants through the 27 maze of gadgetry that the funeral director has assigned to himself his relatively new role of "grief therapist." He has relieved the family of every detail, he has revamped the corpse to look like a living doll, he has arranged for it to nap for a few days in a slumber room, he has put on a well-oiled performance in which the concept of *death* has played no part whatsoever—unless it was inconsiderately mentioned by the clergyman who conducted the religious service. He has done everything in his power to make the funeral a real pleasure for everybody concerned. He and his team have given their all to score an upset victory over death.

UNDERSTANDING DETAILS

1. List the major steps of the embalming process that the author reveals in this essay.
2. Why, according to Mitford, do funeral directors not want to make public the details of embalming? To what extent do you think their desire for secrecy is warranted?
3. Why isn't the permission of a family member needed for embalming? What does this custom reveal about Americans?
4. In what ways has embalming become the undertaker's *raison d'être*? How do American funeral customs encourage this procedure?

ANALYZING MEANING

1. What is Mitford's primary purpose in this essay? Why do you think she has analyzed this particular process in such detail?
2. Explain the title of this essay.
3. Do you think the author knows how gruesome her essay is? How can you tell? What makes the essay so horrifying? How does such close attention to macabre detail help Mitford accomplish her purpose?

4. What does Mitford mean when she argues that the funeral director and his team "have given their all to score an upset victory over death" (paragraph 27)? Who or what is "the team"? Why does Mitford believe death plays no part in American burial customs?

DISCOVERING RHETORICAL STRATEGIES

1. Why does Mitford begin her essay with a one-sentence paragraph? Is it effective? Why or why not?
2. A euphemism is the substitution of a deceptively pleasant term for a straightforward, less pleasant one. In what way is "Beautiful Memory Picture" (paragraph 2) a euphemism? How are we reminded of this phrase throughout the essay? What other euphemisms can you find in this selection?
3. What tone does Mitford establish in the essay? What is her reason for creating this particular tone? What is your reaction to it?
4. What other rhetorical strategies does Mitford use besides gruesome examples and illustrations to make her point? Give examples of each of these different strategies.

MAKING CONNECTIONS

1. Imagine that Stephen King ("Why We Crave Horror Movies") has just read Mitford's essay on funeral customs. According to King, what would be the source of our fascination with these macabre practices? Why do essays like Mitford's both intrigue and repulse us at the same time?
2. Compare and contrast Mitford's use of examples with those used by Paul Roberts ("How to Say Nothing in Five Hundred Words") or Harold Krents ("Darkness at Noon"). How often does each author use examples? What is the relationship between the frequency of examples in each essay and the extent to which you are convinced by the author's argument?
3. Like Alleen Pace Nilsen ("Sexism in English: A 1990s Update"), Mitford seems to argue that the names we assign to people and objects strongly influence our feelings about them. What verbal similarities do you find between referring to an unmarried woman as an *old maid* and calling an area in which a dead body is displayed a *slumber room*? Can you think of mo-

ments in your own life when people have used such linguistic manipulation to influence your opinions on a subject? Explain your answer.

IDEAS FOR DISCUSSION/WRITING

Preparing to Write

Write freely about a particularly interesting custom in America or in another country: Why does this custom exist? What role does it play in the society? What value does it have? What are the details of this custom? In what way is this custom a part of your life? Your family's life? What purpose does it serve for you? Is it worth continuing? Why or why not?

Choosing a Topic

1. In a process analysis essay directed to your classmates, explain a custom you do not approve of. Decide on your tone and purpose before you begin.
2. In a process analysis essay directed to your classmates, explain a custom you approve of. Select a specific tone and purpose before you begin to write.
3. You have been asked to address a group of students at a college of mortuary science. In this role, you have an opportunity to influence the opinion of these students concerning the practice of embalming. Write a well-reasoned lecture to this group arguing either for or against the process of embalming.

PAUL ROBERTS   (1917 – 1967)

■ ■ ■

How to Say Nothing in Five Hundred Words

Paul Roberts was an English professor and specialist in structural linguistics who wrote a number of influential books and articles on language use. Born in San Luis Obispo, California, the author received his B.A. from San Jose State University and his M.A. and Ph.D. from the University of California at Berkeley. He taught English and linguistics for several years at San Jose State and at Cornell University, then became director of languages at the Center of American Studies in Rome, where he lived until his death in 1967. His principal books, familiar to a generation of college students, include *Understanding Grammar* (1954), *Patterns of English* (1956), *Understanding English* (1958), *English Sentences* (1962), and *English Syntax* (1964).

Preparing to Read

The following essay, from *Understanding English*, discusses ways to avoid several common problems faced by beginning college writers. As you prepare to read this article, pause for a moment to consider your own ability in writing: What are your strengths? What types of errors do you commonly make? What have you done in the past to remedy these flaws? Do you have any writing problems for which you have no solutions? What advice would you give to another student who wishes to improve his or her writing?

I t's Friday afternoon, and you have almost survived another 1
week of classes. You are just looking forward dreamily to the
weekend when the English instructor says: "For Monday you
will turn in a five-hundred-word composition on college football."

Well, that puts a good big hole in the weekend. You don't have 2
any strong views on college football one way or the other. You
get rather excited during the season and go to all the home

games and find it rather more fun than not. On the other hand, the class has been reading Robert Hutchins in the anthology and perhaps Shaw's "Eighty-Yard Run," and from the class discussion you have got the idea that the instructor thinks college football is for the birds. You are no fool. You can figure out what side to take.

After dinner you get out the portable typewriter that you got 3 for high school graduation. You might as well get it over with and enjoy Saturday and Sunday. Five hundred words is about two double-spaced pages with normal margins. You put in a sheet of paper, think up a title, and you're off:

Why College Football Should Be Abolished

College football should be abolished because it's bad for the school and also bad for the players. The players are so busy practicing that they don't have any time for their studies.

This, you feel, is a mighty good start. The only trouble is that 4 it's only thirty-two words. You still have four hundred and sixty-eight to go, and you've pretty well exhausted the subject. It comes to you that you do your best thinking in the morning, so you put away the typewriter and go to the movies. But the next morning you have to do your washing and some math problems, and in the afternoon you go to the game. The English instructor turns up too, and you wonder if you've taken the right side after all. Saturday night you have a date, and Sunday morning you have to go to church. (You can't let English assignments interfere with your religion.) What with one thing and another, it's ten o'clock Sunday night before you get out the typewriter again. You make a pot of coffee and start to fill out your views on college football. Put a little meat on the bones.

Why College Football Should Be Abolished

In my opinion, it seems to me that college football should be abolished. 5 The reason why I think this to be true is because I feel that football is bad for the colleges in nearly every aspect. As Robert Hutchins says in his article in our anthology in which he discusses college football, it would be better if the colleges had race horses and had races with one another, because then the horses would not have to attend classes. I firmly agree with Mr. Hutchins on this point, and I am sure that many other students would agree too.

One reason why it seems to me that college football is bad is that it has   6
become too commercial. In the olden times when people played football just
for the fun of it, maybe college football was all right, but they do not play
football just for the fun of it now as they used to in the old days. Nowadays
college football is what you might call a big business. Maybe this is not true
at all schools, and I don't think it is especially true here at State, but certainly
this is the case at most colleges and universities in America nowadays, as Mr.
Hutchins points out in his very interesting article. Actually the coaches and
alumni go around to the high schools and offer the high school stars large
salaries to come to their colleges and play football for them. There was one
case where a high school star was offered a convertible if he would play football for a certain college.

Another reason for abolishing college football is that it is bad for the   7
players. They do not have time to get a college education, because they are
so busy playing football. A football player has to practice every afternoon
from three to six and then he is so tired that he can't concentrate on his
studies. He just feels like dropping off to sleep after dinner, and then the next
day he goes to his classes without having studied and maybe he fails the test.

(Good ripe stuff so far, but you're still a hundred and fifty-one
words from home. One more push.)

Also I think college football is bad for the colleges and the universities   8
because not very many students get to participate in it. Out of a college of
ten thousand students only seventy-five or a hundred play football, if that
many. Football is what you might call a spectator sport. That means that
most people go to watch it but do not play it themselves.

(Four hundred and fifteen. Well, you still have the conclusion, and
when you retype it, you can make the margins a little wider.)

These are the reasons why I agree with Mr. Hutchins that college football   9
should be abolished in American colleges and universities.

On Monday you turn it in, moderately hopeful, and on Friday   10
it comes back marked "weak in content" and sporting a big "D."

This essay is exaggerated a little, not much. The English in-   11
structor will recognize it as reasonably typical of what an assignment on college football will bring in. He knows that nearly half
of the class will contrive in five hundred words to say that college
football is too commercial and bad for the players. Most of the
other half will inform him that college football builds character
and prepares one for life and brings prestige to the school. As he
reads paper after paper all saying the same thing in almost the

same words, all bloodless, five hundred words dripping out of nothing, he wonders how he allowed himself to get trapped into teaching English when he might have had a happy and interesting life as an electrician or a confidence man.

Well, you may ask, what can you do about it? The subject is 12 one on which you have few convictions and little information. Can you be expected to make a dull subject interesting? As a matter of fact, this is precisely what you are expected to do. This is the writer's essential task. All subjects, except sex, are dull until somebody makes them interesting. The writer's job is to find the argument, the approach, the angle, the wording that will take the reader with him. This is seldom easy, and it is particularly hard in subjects that have been much discussed: College Football, Fraternities, Popular Music, Is Chivalry Dead?, and the like. You will feel that there is nothing you can do with such subjects except repeat the old bromides. But there are some things you can do which will make your papers, if not throbbingly alive, at least less insufferably tedious than they might otherwise be.

Avoid the Obvious Content

Say the assignment is college football. Say that you've decided 13 to be against it. Begin by putting down the arguments that come to your mind: It is too commercial, it takes the students' minds off their studies, it is hard on the players, it makes the university a kind of circus instead of an intellectual center, for most schools it is financially ruinous. Can you think of any more arguments, just off hand? All right. Now when you write your paper, *make sure that you don't use any of the material on this list.* If these are the points that leap to your mind they will leap to everyone else's too, and whether you get a "C" or a "D" may depend on whether the instructor reads your paper early when he is fresh and tolerant or late, when the sentence "In my opinion, college football has become too commercial," inexorably repeated, has brought him to the brink of lunacy.

Be against college football for some reason or reasons of your 14 own. If they are keen and perceptive ones, that's splendid. But even if they are trivial or foolish or indefensible, you are still ahead so long as they are not everybody else's reasons too. Be against it because the colleges don't spend enough money on it to make it worthwhile, because it is bad for the characters of the spectators, because the players are forced to attend classes, because the football stars hog all the beautiful women, because it competes with baseball and is therefore un-American and possibly Communist inspired. There are lots of more or less unused reasons for being against college football.

Sometimes it is a good idea to sum up and dispose of the trite   15
and conventional points before going on to your own. This has the advantage of indicating to the reader that you are going to be neither trite nor conventional. Something like this:

> We are often told that college football should be abolished because it has become too commercial or because it is bad for the players. These arguments are no doubt very cogent, but they don't go to the heart of the matter.

Then you go to the heart of the matter.

Take the Less Usual Side

One rather simple way of getting into your paper is to take the   16
side of the argument that most of the citizens will want to avoid. If the assignment is an essay on dogs, you can, if you choose, explain that dogs are faithful and lovable companions, intelligent, useful as guardians of the house and protectors of children, indispensable in police work—in short, when all is said and done, man's best friends. Or you can suggest that those big brown eyes conceal, more often than not, a vacuity of mind and an inconstancy of purpose; that the dogs you have known most intimately have been mangy, ill-tempered brutes, incapable of instruction; and that only your nobility of mind and fear of arrest prevent you from kicking the flea-ridden animals when you pass them on the street.

Naturally personal convictions will sometimes dictate your ap-   17
proach. If the assigned subject is "Is Methodism Rewarding to the Individual?" and you are a pious Methodist, you have really no choice. But few assigned subjects, if any, will fall in this category. Most of them will lie in broad areas of discussion with much to be said on both sides. They are intellectual exercises, and it is legitimate to argue now one way and now another, as debaters do in similar circumstances. Always take the side that looks to you hardest, least defensible. It will almost always turn out to be easier to write interestingly on that side.

This general advice applies where you have a choice of sub- 18
jects. If you are to choose among "The Value of Fraternities" and
"My Favorite High School Teacher" and "What I Think About
Beetles," by all means plump for the beetles. By the time the instructor gets to your paper, he will be up to his ears in tedious
tales about the French teacher at Bloombury High and assertions
about how fraternities build character and prepare one for life.
Your views on beetles, whatever they are, are bound to be a refreshing change.

Don't worry too much about figuring out what the instructor 19
thinks about the subject so that you can cuddle up with him.
Chances are his views are no stronger than yours. If he does have
convictions and you oppose him, his problem is to keep from
grading you higher than you deserve in order to show he is not
biased. This doesn't mean that you should always cantankerously
dissent from what the instructor says; that gets tiresome too. And
if the subject assigned is "My Pet Peeve," do not begin, "My pet
peeve is the English instructor who assigns papers on 'my pet
peeve.' " This was still funny during the War of 1812, but it has
sort of lost its edge since then. It is in general good manners to
avoid personalities.

Slip Out of Abstraction

If you will study the essay on college football [near the begin- 20
ning of this essay], you will perceive that one reason for its appalling dullness is that it never gets down to particulars. It is just a
series of not very glittering generalities: "Football is bad for the
colleges," "it has become too commercial," "football is a big business," "it is bad for the players," and so on. Such round phrases
thudding against the reader's brain are unlikely to convince him,
though they may well render him unconscious.

If you want the reader to believe that college football is bad for 21
the players, you have to do more than say so. You have to display
the evil. Take your roommate, Alfred Simkins, the second-string
center. Picture poor old Alfy coming home from football practice
every evening, bruised and aching, agonizingly tired, scarcely able
to shovel the mashed potatoes into his mouth. Let us see him
staggering up to the room, getting out his econ textbook, peering
desperately at it with his good eye, falling asleep and failing the
test in the morning. Let us share his unbearable tension as

Saturday draws near. Will he fail, be demoted, lose his monthly allowance, be forced to return to the coal mines? And if he succeeds, what will be his reward? Perhaps a slight ripple of applause when the third-string center replaces him, a moment of elation in the locker room if the team wins, of despair if it loses. What will he look back on when he graduates from college? Toil and torn ligaments. And what will be his future? He is not good enough for pro football, and he is too obscure and weak in econ to succeed in stocks and bonds. College football is tearing the heart from Alfy Simpkins and, when it finishes with him, will callously toss aside the shattered hulk.

This is no doubt a weak enough argument for the abolition of   22
college football, but it is a sight better than saying, in three or four variations, that college football (in your opinion) is bad for players.

Look at the work of any professional writer and notice how   23
constantly he is moving from the generality, the abstract statement, to the concrete example, the facts and figures, the illustration. If he is writing on juvenile delinquency, he does not just tell you that juveniles are (it seems to him) delinquent and that (in his opinion) something should be done about it. He shows you juveniles being delinquent, tearing up movie theatres in Buffalo, stabbing high school principals in Dallas, smoking marijuana in Palo Alto. And more than likely he is moving toward some specific remedy, not just a general wringing of the hands.

It is no doubt possible to be *too* concrete, too illustrative or anec-   24
dotal, but few inexperienced writers err this way. For most the soundest advice is to be seeking always for the picture, to be always turning general remarks into seeable examples. Don't say, "Sororities teach girls the social graces." Say, "Sorority life teaches a girl how to carry on a conversation while pouring tea, without sloshing the tea into the saucer." Don't say, "I like certain kinds of popular music very much." Say, "Whenever I hear Gerber Sprinklittle play 'Mississippi Man' on the trombone, my socks creep up my ankles."

Get Rid of Obvious Padding

The student toiling away at his weekly English theme is too   25
often tormented by a figure: five hundred words. How, he asks himself, is he to achieve this staggering total? Obviously by never using one word when he can somehow work in ten.

He is therefore seldom content with a plain statement like 26 "Fast driving is dangerous." This has only four words in it. He takes thought, and the sentence becomes:

> In my opinion, fast driving is dangerous.

Better, but he can do better still:

> In my opinion, fast driving would seem to be rather dangerous.

If he is really adept, it may come out:

> In my humble opinion, though I do not claim to be an expert on this complicated subject, fast driving, in most circumstances, would seem to be rather dangerous in many aspects, or at least so it would seem to me.

Thus four words have been turned into forty, and not an iota of content has been added.

Now this is a way to go about reaching five hundred words, 27 and if you are content with a "D" grade, it is as good a way as any. But if you aim higher, you must work differently. Instead of stuffing your sentences with straw, you must try steadily to get rid of the padding, to make your sentences lean and tough. If you are really working at it, your first draft will greatly exceed the required total, and then you will work it down, thus:

> It is thought in some quarters that fraternities do not contribute as much as might be expected to campus life.
> Some people think that fraternities contribute little to campus life.
> The average doctor who practices in small towns or in the country must toil night and day to heal the sick.
> Most country doctors work long hours.
> When I was a little girl, I suffered from shyness and embarrassment in the presence of others.
> I was a shy little girl.
> It is absolutely necessary for the person employed as a marine fireman to give the matter of steam pressure his undivided attention at all times.
> The fireman has to keep his eye on the steam gauge.

You may ask how you can arrive at five hundred words at this 28 rate. Simple. You dig up more real content. Instead of taking a couple of obvious points off the surface of the topic and then circling warily around them for six paragraphs, you work in and explore, figure out the details. You illustrate. You say that fast driving is dangerous, and then you prove it. How long does it take to stop a car at forty and at eighty? How far can you see at night? What happens when a tire blows? What happens in a head-on collision at fifty miles an hour? Pretty soon your paper will be full of broken glass and blood and headless torsos, and reaching five hundred words will not really be a problem.

Call a Fool a Fool

Some of the padding in freshman themes is to be blamed not 29 on anxiety about the word minimum but on excessive timidity. The student writes, "In my opinion, the principal of my high school acted in ways that I believe every unbiased person would have to call foolish." This isn't exactly what he means. What he means is, "My high school principal was a fool." If he was a fool, call him a fool. Hedging the thing about with "in-my-opinion's" and "it-seems-to-me's" and "as-I-see-it's" and "at-least-from-my-point-of-view's" gains you nothing. Delete these phrases whenever they creep into your paper.

The student's tendency to hedge stems from a modesty that in 30 other circumstances would be commendable. He is, he realizes, young and inexperienced, and he half suspects that he is dopey and fuzzy-minded beyond the average. Probably only too true. But it doesn't help to announce your incompetence six times in every paragraph. Decide what you want to say and say it as vigorously as possible, without apology and in plain words.

Linguistic diffidence can take various forms. One is what we 31 call *euphemism.* This is the tendency to call a spade "a certain garden implement" or women's underwear "unmentionables." It is stronger in some eras than others and in some people than others but it always operates more or less in subjects that are touchy or taboo: death, sex, madness, and so on. Thus we shrink from saying "He died last night" but say instead "passed away," "left us," "joined his Maker," "went to his reward." Or we try to take off the tension with a lighter cliché: "kicked the bucket," "cashed in his chips," "handed in his dinner pail." We have found all sorts of ways to avoid saying *mad*: "mentally ill," "touched," "not quite right upstairs," "feeble-minded," "innocent," "simple," "off his trolley," "not in his right mind." Even such a now plain word as *insane* began as a euphemism with the meaning "not healthy."

Modern science, particularly psychology, contributes many 32 polysyllables in which we can wrap our thoughts and blunt their force. To many writers there is no such thing as a bad schoolboy. Schoolboys are maladjusted or unoriented or misunderstood or in the need of guidance or lacking in continued success toward satisfactory integration of the personality as a social unit, but they are never bad. Psychology no doubt makes us better men and women, more sympathetic and tolerant, but it doesn't make writing any easier. Had Shakespeare been confronted with psychology, "To be or not to be" might have come out, "To continue as a social unit or not to do so. That is the personality problem. Whether 'tis a better sign of integration at the conscious level to display a psychic tolerance toward the maladjustments and repressions induced by one's lack of orientation in one's environment or—" But Hamlet would never have finished the soliloquy.

Writing in the modern world, you cannot altogether avoid 33 modern jargon. Nor, in an effort to get away from euphemism, should you salt your paper with four-letter words. But you can do much if you will mount guard against those roundabout phrases, those echoing polysyllables that tend to slip into your writing to rob it of its crispness and force.

Beware of Pat Expressions

Other things being equal, avoid phrases like "other things 34 being equal." Those sentences that come to you whole, or in two or three doughy lumps, are sure to be bad sentences. They are no creation of yours but pieces of common thought floating in the community soup.

Pat expressions are hard, often impossible, to avoid, because 35 they come too easily to be noticed and seem too necessary to be dispensed with. No writer avoids them altogether, but good writers avoid them more often than poor writers.

By "pat expressions" we mean such tags as "to all practical in- 36 tents and purposes," "the pure and simple truth," "from where I sit," "the time of his life," "to the ends of the earth," "in the twinkling of an eye," "as sure as you're born," "over my dead body," "under cover of darkness," "took the easy way out," "when all is said and done," "told him time and time again," "parted the best of friends," "stand up and be counted," "gave him the best years of her life," "worked her fingers to the bone." Like other clichés, these expressions were once forceful. Now we should use them only when we can't possibly think of anything else.

Some pat expressions stand like a wall between the writer and   37
thought. Such a one is "the American way of life." Many student writers feel that when they have said that something accords with the American way of life or does not they have exhausted the subject. Actually, they have stopped at the highest level of abstraction. The American way of life is the complicated set of bonds between a hundred and eighty million ways. All of us know this when we think about it, but the tag phrase too often keeps us from thinking about it.

So with many another phrase dear to the politician: "this great   38
land of ours," "the man in the street," "our national heritage." These may prove our patriotism or give a clue to our political beliefs, but otherwise they add nothing to the paper except words.

Colorful Words

The writer builds with words, and no builder uses a raw mate-   39
rial more slippery and elusive and treacherous. A writer's work is a constant struggle to get the right word in the right place, to find that particular word that will convey his meaning exactly, that will persuade the reader or soothe him or startle or amuse him. He never succeeds altogether—sometimes he feels that he scarcely succeeds at all—but such successes as he has are what make the thing worth doing.

There is no book of rules for this game. One progresses   40
through everlasting experiment on the basis of ever-widening experience. There are few useful generalizations that one can make about words as words, but there are perhaps a few.

Some words are what we call "colorful." By this we mean that   41
they are calculated to produce a picture or induce an emotion. They are dressy instead of plain, specific instead of general, loud instead of soft. Thus, in place of "Her heart beat," we may write, "Her heart *pounded, throbbed, fluttered, danced.*" Instead of "He sat in his chair," we may say, "He *lounged, sprawled, coiled.*" Instead of

"It was hot," we may say, "It was *blistering, sultry, muggy, suffocating, steamy, wilting.*"

However, it should not be supposed that the fancy word is al- 42
ways better. Often it is as well to write "Her heart beat" or "It was hot" if that is all it did or all it was. Ages differ in how they like their prose. The nineteenth century liked it rich and smoky. The twentieth has usually preferred it lean and cool. The twentieth century writer, like all writers, is forever seeking the exact word, but he is wary of sounding feverish. He tends to pitch it low, to under-state it, to throw it away. He knows that if he gets too colorful, the audience is likely to giggle.

See how this strikes you: "As the rich, golden glow of the sun- 43
set died away along the eternal western hills, Angela's limpid blue eyes looked softly and trustingly into Montague's flashing brown ones, and her heart pounded like a drum in time with the joyous song surging in her soul." Some people like that sort of thing, but most modern readers would say, "Good grief," and turn on the television.

Colored Words

Some words we call not so much colorful as colored—that is, 44
loaded with associations, good or bad. All words—except perhaps structure words—have associations of some sort. We have said that the meaning of a word is the sum of the contexts in which it oc-curs. When we hear a word, we hear with it an echo of all the sit-uations in which we have heard it before.

In some words, these echoes are obvious and discussable. The 45
word *mother*, for example, has for most people, agreeable associa-tions. When you hear *mother* you probably think of home, safety, love, food, and various other pleasant things. If one writes, "She was like a mother to me," he gets an effect which he would not get in "She was like an aunt to me." The advertiser makes use of the associations of *mother* by working it in when he talks about his product. The politician works it in when he talks about himself.

So also with such words as *home, liberty, fireside, contentment, pa-* 46
triot, tenderness, sacrifice, childlike, manly, bluff, limpid. All of these words are loaded with associations that would be rather hard to indicate in a straightforward definition. There is more than a lit-eral difference between "They sat around the fireside" and "They

sat around the stove." They might have been equally warm and happy around the stove, but *fireside* suggests leisure, grace, quiet tradition, congenial company, and *stove* does not.

Conversely, some words have bad associations. *Mother* suggests 47 pleasant things, but *mother-in-law* does not. Many mothers-in-law are heroically lovable and some mothers drink gin all day and beat their children insensible, but these facts of life are beside the point. The point is that *mother* sounds good and *mother-in-law* does not.

Or consider the word *intellectual*. This would seem to be a 48 complimentary term, but in point of fact it is not, for it has picked up associations of impracticality and ineffectuality and general dopiness. So also such words as *liberal, reactionary, Communist, socialist, capitalist, radical, schoolteacher, truck driver, under-taker, operator, salesman, huckster, speculator*. These convey meaning on the literal level, but beyond that—sometimes, in some places—they convey contempt on the part of the speaker.

The question of whether to use loaded words or not depends 49 on what is being written. The scientist, the scholar, try to avoid them; for the poet, the advertising writer, the public speaker, they are standard equipment. But every writer should take care that they do not substitute for thought. If you write, "Anyone who thinks that is nothing but a Socialist (or Communist or capital-ist)," you have said nothing except that you don't like people who think that, and such remarks are effective only with the most naive readers. It is always a bad mistake to think your readers more naive than they really are.

Colorless Words

But probably most student writers come to grief not with 50 words that are colorful or those that are colored but with those that have no color at all. A pet example is *nice*, a word we would find it hard to dispense with in casual conversation but which is no longer capable of adding much to a description. Colorless words are those of such general meaning that in a particular sen-tence they mean nothing. Slang adjectives like *cool* ("That's real cool") tend to explode all over the language. They are applied to everything, lose their original force, and quickly die.

Beware also of nouns of very general meaning, like *circumstances*, 51 *cases, instances, aspects, factors, relationships, attitudes, eventualities*, etc. In most circumstances you will find that those cases of writing which contain too many instances of words like these will in this and other aspects have factors leading to unsatisfactory relationships with the reader resulting in unfavorable attitudes on his part and perhaps other eventualities, like a grade of "D." Notice also what "etc." means. It means "I'd like to make this list longer, but I can't think of any more examples."

UNDERSTANDING DETAILS

1. According to Roberts, what is a writer's principal task? How does this task help introduce the rest of the essay?
2. List the nine guidelines Roberts suggests for good writing, and explain each briefly.
3. Can you give five examples of euphemisms now in current use (without repeating any of the ones Roberts uses)? Why is our society so dependent upon euphemisms? What social function do such words serve?
4. What are "colorful words," "colored words," and "colorless words," according to Roberts? Add five examples of your own to each of the lists in the essay.

ANALYZING MEANING

1. What is the principal purpose of this essay? Does it accomplish its purpose in your opinion? Explain your answer.
2. To what extent do you identify with the college student described by the author at the outset of this essay? In what important ways are you different?
3. According to Roberts, why do students have a tendency to "hedge"? In what ways does hedging detract from the overall effect of an essay? Give an example of hedging from one of your papers. How could you have made the statement more forceful?
4. Does Roberts follow his own suggestions for good writing in this essay? Why or why not? Give examples that illustrate how successfully the author follows his own advice.

DISCOVERING RHETORICAL STRATEGIES

1. How does Roberts organize the elements of his essay? Why does he choose this particular order? Is it effective in achieving his purpose? Why or why not?

2. Describe in some detail Roberts's intended audience. How did you come to this conclusion?

3. Analyze Roberts's use of humor throughout this essay (especially in his last paragraph). How does he raise our awareness regarding language as he makes us laugh at ourselves?

4. Roberts predominantly uses examples to show how to attack a writing task. What other rhetorical strategies does he use to make his point about good writing? Give an example of each of these strategies.

MAKING CONNECTIONS

1. Both Roberts and Garrison Keillor ("How the Crab Apple Grew") give advice about how to write a good essay, though each author delivers his suggestions differently. Compare and contrast how these authors provide advice to their readers. Which essay do you find most convincing? Explain your answer.

2. Read through William Golding's "Thinking as a Hobby," and identify, according to Roberts's definition of the terms, ten "colorful," ten "colored," and ten "colorless" words in Golding's essay. Which category of words could you find most easily? Why? Which of these three types of words does Roberts use most often in his own essay?

3. Which essay in *The Prose Reader* does the best job of following Roberts's advice on how to write a good paper? Examine that essay in detail, explaining how it satisfies the guidelines set up in "How to Say Nothing in Five Hundred Words."

IDEAS FOR DISCUSSION/WRITING

Preparing to Write

Write freely about your own writing weaknesses: What problems do you have to watch out for in your own writing? Do these problems fluctuate with different kinds of assignments (essays, reports, research papers, or business writing)? How do you try to improve upon these weak areas when you find them?

Choosing a Topic

1. One of your friends who is still in high school has asked you for information about college-level English courses. Write to

this friend, using process analysis to explain how to survive freshman composition. Decide on a purpose and a point of view before you begin to write.

2. The student may not be the only one who needs improvement in this essay. The instructor's assignment of "a five-hundred-word composition on college football" does not promise to generate exciting prose. Devise a writing assignment on the topic of college sports that will get students more involved than the original assignment. Include purpose, audience, and writer's role in your directions. Then, write a process analysis essay explaining how to create a well-crafted writing assignment.

3. Using the guidelines Roberts suggests in his article, write an essay analyzing one of your recent papers.

C. EDWARD GOOD   (1945 –   )

WILLIAM FITZPATRICK   (1943 –   )

■ ■ ■

A Successful Interview

Born in Atlanta, Georgia, Edward Good earned his B.A. in economics at the University of North Carolina, Chapel Hill, and his law degree at the University of Virginia. He currently serves as "writer-in-residence" at the law firm of Finnegan, Henderson, Farabow, Garrett, & Dunner in Washington, D.C., which specializes in patent law. His job is to provide continual training seminars in persuasive and effective writing for the firm's legal staff. Good's best-known book, coauthored with William Fitzpatrick, is *Does Your Resume Wear Blue Jeans?* (1985, revised in 1993); a companion edition for the military—*Does Your Resume Wear Combat Boots?*—was published in the same year. Additional publications by Good include *Mightier Than the Sword: Powerful Writing in the Legal Profession* (1987), *Mightier Than the Sword: Powerful Writing in Class and on the Job* (1987), and *Legal Research Without Losing Your Mind* (1993). A self-confessed "ACC basketball nut," Good also relaxes by playing the piano in his spare time. When asked to advise students using *The Prose Reader*, Good counseled them "to struggle mightily to obliterate the verb 'to be' from their writing." Good's coauthor on the following essay, William Fitzpatrick, was born in Hudson, New York, and earned his B.A. at Columbia College in sales management. His current position is Regional Vice President of European Operations for the Academy Life Insurance Company, which is a member of the Providian family of companies. A veteran of twenty-four years in the army, he is also a regular columnist for the *Army, Navy, and Air Force Times* newspapers and the *Military News Services*.

Preparing to Read

Taken from *Does Your Resume Wear Blue Jeans?*, the following essay details the proper way to prepare for a successful job interview. Before reading it, think for a few minutes about your expectations of the interview process: What do you believe is the main purpose of this process? Why do employers conduct interviews? What are they trying to find out? In your opinion, what are the most positive features of the interview process? The most negative features? Why do most job candidates get nervous at interviews? Have you ever been interviewed for a job? Have you interviewed someone else for a job? What differences did you notice in the two roles? Which role did you like better and why?

Y ou've invested a lot of time and effort to get to this point 1
in the job search. You have researched, written, prospected, and planned with the single goal of obtaining an interview. Your search reflects your self-confidence. Confidence is important, and it will help you in presenting your qualifications, but you aren't going to beat out the competition with confidence alone. Interviewing is a complex process that requires careful planning, an organized approach, and a good measure of rehearsal.

Clothes

Your first step in getting ready for the interview is to get 2
yourself into the proper uniform. There is a uniform in corporate America, and in other employment settings, and you really have to comply with the dress standards. If you doubt that, pick up a copy of the annual report of any major company that includes photographs of the executives or the board of directors. See how they are dressed. Those are the people who set the standards for the company. The first rule for interviewing is to remember that the interviewer will judge your appearance based on his or her standards, not yours! It doesn't matter what your impression of stylishness may be. It's the interviewer's standards of taste that matter most.

So your first task is to do some further research. There are 3
some excellent books on the subject of dress, such as *Dress for*

Success. But the best way to find out about dress standards is to go and look. Visit a place where you will find business people in your industry. What you will generally see are people who dress conservatively, and who all dress alike. You might find that the people in your industry do not dress formally. For example, if you seek a position that requires you to work with your hands, such as an equipment operator or a mechanic, don't show up for the interview in a suit. The employer will feel you might not be willing to get in there and get your hands dirty. On the other hand, don't show up in blue jeans, sneakers, and a t-shirt.

Some positions and situations, and some types of firms, may 4 call for a degree of informality for the interview somewhere between those of the manual worker and the business executive. Examples include interviews for graphic artists, computer software designers, writers, and other creative positions. Here there's more leeway, although it's still important to project a reassuring, responsible image. In other words, don't take dumb risks with your wardrobe, and be sensitive to the culture of the industry and even of the particular firm.

You should be able to put together an interview wardrobe for 5 a minimum amount of money. There are many discount clothing stores around if you watch for sales, for both men and women. But if you're faced with the decision to spend a little more money for just the right look or to save some money by buying a cheap suit, always choose the right look. The extra money invested will pay dividends time and time again.

Advance Work

If you've never been to the interview location before, and if 6 you have the time, go there before the interview and check out any possible problems with traffic, directions, and parking. (You might discover in advance that you don't even want the job after you've evaluated potential commute problems.) This reconnaissance will also allow you to time your trip properly on the day of the interview. A friend of ours once had an appointment in downtown Miami in July. He planned his trip to arrive at the place about ten minutes before his appointment, but failed to realize that the closest parking was seven blocks away. He had to park the car and sprint seven blocks through downtown Miami in the heat to get there almost on time. With the heat and humidity, you can imagine how he looked.

Advance Research

Well before the interview, make certain you research the com-   7
pany or organization and, if possible, the interviewers themselves.
My toughest interview was for a judicial fellowship at the
Supreme Court of the United States. The interview panel consisted of several trial and appellate federal judges, the administrative assistant to the chief justice, the retired chairman of the board
of a major steel company, a former dean of Harvard Law School,
and several other heavyweights. To prepare, I researched each
panel member, committing various biographical data to memory.
During the evening before the interview, the nine finalists were
invited to dinner with the panel members. At my table sat the administrative assistant to the chief justice, a Mormon who (I had
learned) had spent his two-year mission in Argentina. At one of
those inevitable lulls in the conversation I turned to him and
asked how he enjoyed his stay in Argentina. His mouth dropped
open and he asked, "How did you know about my mission to
Argentina?" I shot back, "Well, sir, the panel has received a great
deal of information about me, so I thought it only fair that I find
out something about each panel member." At that point, I firmly
believe, I won the fellowship.

You do the same. Visit the company before the interview. Call   8
friends who know something about the company. Get a copy of
the annual report. Do a search on CompuServe or other computer database for any recent stories on the company. Do anything you can to find out vital information, and then make
certain you reveal this knowledge at some point in the interview.
This one trick will work wonders.

Punctuality

You should arrive at the appropriate office at least ten minutes   9
before the appointed time, but not more than fifteen. If you arrive an hour early, as over-achievers tend to do, you will throw
the interview schedule off, and it may work against you. Further,
if you have to sit around the office for any length of time, they
will have a longer period to look at you and consider you an imposition in their day rather than a welcome, timely visitor.

In the Office

If you smoke, leave your cigarettes in the car. Even if the inter- 10
viewer smokes, you should not. It is impossible to maintain eye
contact while you're smoking. Three out of four people are nonsmokers anyway. In fact, you should remove any bulky items from
your pocket, such as keys, papers, or other paraphernalia.

When you arrive, you will probably be asked to fill out a long 11
application for employment. Be sure you bring enough information with you to complete this form. Items such as dates, addresses, and names can be hard to remember. Take your time
with this form and fill it out completely. Don't write, "see resume" in place of data; if the company had wanted only to see
your resume, it would not have asked you to complete the form.
Because resumes differ so greatly, most companies like to use an
application form. It ensures they get all of the information they
need in the format they prefer. If you are prepared and fill out the
form completely, you will again be ahead of the other candidates
who have not read this book.

Assume everyone who has contact with you at the company 12
on the day of the interview may be asked to evaluate you. If an
employment manager is trying to decide between two candidates
for a position and can't make up her mind, the first person she
will ask for an opinion will be her secretary. You can be sure she
is going to give her a candid view of her impressions. Act professional, but not stiff. Be friendly and conversational, but don't talk
too much with the office staff. Be careful not to try to get too
friendly or personal with them; they may go to lunch with you,
but you won't get the job.

Before you're finally ushered in to meet the interviewer, make a 13
last-minute check of your personal appearance. For men, is your tie
straight? Are your socks pulled up tight? Are they the same color?
Lapel pin right-side up? Shoes clean and shined? Hair combed?
Portfolio under the left arm? (Leave the right free for handshakes.)

For women, are your makeup and lipstick okay? Shoes clean 14
and shined? Hosiery okay? Slip showing? Hair neat?

Your Grand Debut

Everything checks out? Okay, go ahead and make your en- 15
trance. Walk straight to the interviewer and offer your hand and a

pleasant smile. Be careful not to make the handshake too firm (you are not applying to be the stand-in for Arnold Schwarzenegger) or too limp. Grasp the other person's hand completely, not just the fingers for one of those dead fish handshakes. If you are wearing a jacket (suit coat), unbutton it before sitting down, then ensure it hangs properly and is not bunched up and gaping open. (Practice sitting down in front of a mirror. See how you appear from the other side of the desk.) Women should be extra careful about the skirt riding up, and men should be mindful of hairy ankles peeking out over the socks.

Now some philosophy: As I said, the conduct of the interview 16 is the responsibility of the interviewer. A skillful interviewer will control all facets of the conversation and guide you through a logical plan in order to uncover specific items of information. Some questions will be directed at gaining data, and others will be used to determine your thought process.

Usually, you will undergo more than one interview. The first 17 will be conducted by human resources professionals who will totally control the direction of the conversation. That's their job, what they are trained to do, and you have little choice but to go with the flow. Second or subsequent interviews are conducted by people who make hiring decisions, but who have little or no training in interview techniques. If you understand the process, sometimes you can take control of the interview and help to guide the interviewer to the proper conclusion—to hire you.

The Interview

The interviewer will most likely take the following steps with 18 you:

Establish Rapport. The interviewer's responsibility is to put 19 you at ease, both physically and emotionally. The more relaxed you are, the more you will trust the interviewer and open up to him or her. Skilled interviewers will not put you in front of a desk. They will put the chair beside the desk so there are no barriers between you or will not use a desk at all. Initial conversation will be about trivial matters such as the weather, parking, or any subject to get you talking.

Determine Your Qualifications. The interviewer has to find 20 out as early as possible if you are technically qualified (on the surface) for the job. Time is valuable, and an interviewer can't waste it on unqualified candidates. The determination is made by a review of the application and your resume. This can turn into a simple yes and no session as the interviewer matches your qualifications against the requirements for the position. During this phase, information is gathered to develop questions later on in the conversation. This technique is called blueprinting.

Explain the Company and the Job. At this point in the interview, the interviewer will try to get you excited about wanting to work for the company. He or she generally will cover job responsibilities and company benefits to interest you even further. 21

Determine Your Suitability. The interviewer now has to determine if you are the best candidate. In many cases this is a subjective judgment based upon impressions of your conduct and your ability to handle the questions posed to you. In this part of the interview you will be asked situational questions, which may or may not be directly related to your future duties. The interviewer may even ask some startling questions to get your response. The technique used is to ask open-ended questions (those that require more than a one-word answer) during this phase, rather than close-ended questions (those that only require a simple yes or no). 22

Conclusion. At this point it is the interviewer's responsibility to review the major points you covered during the interview and get you out of the office in a timely manner. The interviewer should ensure all of your questions have been answered and will generally let you know what the next step is and when a decision will be made. 23

As you can see, an interview is a planned and controlled process. As stated, a trained and skilled interviewer will guide you through the steps and will know exactly how to keep you on track. The managers in the second and subsequent interviews may not follow a planned agenda and may even have trouble staying on track themselves. If you understand what is happening, you can take control. The rules for the interview are based on one theory only. If you were called, you probably are qualified for the job. Your task is to show the company you are the best qualified of the candidates who are competing. Here are some suggestions for doing that. 24

Always Be Positive.   Losers dwell on past losses, winners dwell   25
on future successes. Don't worry about where you have been,
worry about where you're going. Make sure your accomplishments are related to your capabilities.

Listen, Listen, Listen.   Throughout the interview, concentrate   26
to be sure you're really listening to what the interviewer has to
say. It looks very bad when you ask a question the interviewer
just answered.

State Your Qualifications, Not Your Drawbacks.   Tell them what   27
you can do; let them wonder about what you can't do.

Ask Questions.   Be sure to ask intelligent, well-thought-out   28
questions that indicate you are trying to find out what you can
do for the company. Base any statements on proven experience,
not dreams and hopes.

Watch Out for Close-Ended Questions.   Be wary of interview-   29
ers who ask close-ended questions. They probably don't know
what they are doing. If you begin to hear a series of questions
that require only a yes or no, the other candidates are probably
hearing the same questions. If the interviewer asks three candidates the same question and all he gets are three no answers, he
won't be able to distinguish among the three. If all the answers
are the same, he can't make an intelligent choice. Your strategy,
then, is to turn these close-ended questions into open-ended
ones so you can put a few intelligent sentences together. In this
way, you will distinguish yourself from the other yes and no candidates.

Stay Focused.   Concentrate on the conversation at hand. Don't   30
get off on extraneous matters that have nothing to do with the
job or your qualifications.

Don't Get Personal.   Keep personal issues out of the inter-   31
view. Never confide in an interviewer no matter how relaxed and
comfortable you feel. If you feel the urge to bare your soul, your
feelings should tell you the interviewer is very skilled and followed the first step of the interview extremely well.

Rehearse.   Plan some answers to obvious questions. Why did   32
you leave your previous position? Why did you choose your academic major? What are your training and experience going to
do for the company?

Maintain Eye Contact. If you can't look interviewers in the eye, they won't believe your answer. Further, there are no answers written on the ceiling, so if you get in a bind, don't look up for divine guidance. The answer is not on the ceiling. It's in your head. 33

Pause a Moment. Take a moment before each answer to consider what you will say. Don't answer the question in a rush, but reflect a moment to get it straight. 34

Take Notes. If you plan on taking notes, ask first. Some people are uncomfortable when their words are written down. Do not attempt to record the conversation. 35

Multiple Interviewers. If you are interviewed by more than one person, answer all of them equally. Begin with the questioner, let your eyes go to each of the others as you continue your answer, and finally come back to the original questioner. Each of them will then feel you are speaking to him or her alone. 36

Don't Drink, Don't Smoke. In fact, don't ingest anything at all. Although it is polite to accept a proffered cup of coffee or a soft drink, it is not polite to spill it in your lap. You will be nervous, so don't take the chance. Remember, they are merely trying to establish rapport. Besides, you can't maintain eye contact while drinking or eating. 37

Likely Open-Ended Questions. What follows are some properly formulated open-ended questions you may hear later. Get used to the format and prepare answers. Keep them down to a couple of sentences, not thee paragraphs. 38

1. In your relationship with your previous supervisor, would you mind giving an example of how you were alike or not alike?
2. How would you define success?
3. Would you demonstrate some methods you would use to cause a marginal employee to rise to his or her full potential?
4. How can a team atmosphere improve your personal effectiveness?
5. If you were a problem, how would you solve yourself?

After the Interview

When the interview concludes, don't linger, but don't run out the door, either. If the interviewers haven't indicated when a decision will be reached, ask them. This will give them the impression that you might have other offers you are considering. When you get back to 39 your car, take out a professional-looking note card (purchased in advance for just this purpose) and write (in longhand with a roller pen or a fountain pen) a brief thank-you note to all the people in the company who interviewed you. The note should say something like the note shown below.

Thank-you note.

Dear Ms. Jones:

It was a pleasure to meet you, and I appreciate the opportunity to compete for the position of high speed yo-yo operator. The job offers a real challenge, and I am very interested in joining the team. I'll await your decision.

Sincerely,

Joseph D. Ragman

Take the note to the post office and mail it the same day. It is important that the note reach the interviewer the next day. You hope it will hit her desk at the same time she is comparing your resume with other candidates'. You now have the advantage of having at least two documents on her desk with your name on them. It might not help, but it certainly won't hurt. 40

Facing the interview might make you apprehensive, but there is no reason to fear it. It is your real opportunity to get face to face with your product's potential buyer and bring to bear all of your personal selling skills. If you go into the situation with confidence based on preparation and not on ego, you will come out a winner. Take the time to prepare properly. The interview has been your goal thus far in the job search, so it is your stepping stone to future success. Be positive, be enthusiastic, and rely on your experience in communicating with people. 41

UNDERSTANDING DETAILS

1. What are the basic requirements for a good interview?
2. Explain two of the topics you should research before an interview. Why are they important?

3. What is your main responsibility during an interview?
4. What are the interviewer's responsibilities during the interview? What do all of these items have in common?

ANALYZING MEANING

1. Why are clothes such an important aspect of an interview? What do they say about you?
2. What are some of the dangers of drifting off the subject? What may the interviewers think if you do?
3. Why are open-ended questions better than close-ended questions? Give some examples of each.
4. What do Good and Fitzpatrick suggest that you do to distinguish yourself from the other candidates after the interview process? Do you think this is a good idea or not?

DISCOVERING RHETORICAL STRATEGIES

1. How does Good and Fitzpatrick's introduction prepare us for the information that follows? In your opinion, is this an effective beginning to their essay?
2. Who do you think is Good and Fitzpatrick's primary audience? On what information do you base your answer?
3. Good and Fitzpatrick divide their interview guidelines into three major sections: "Clothes," "Advance Work," and "Your Grand Debut." In what ways do these labels help you work through the essay? Do the subtopics fit in with their headings in the essay? Are the headings and subheadings effective? Why or why not?
4. How do the authors organize the specific guidelines for the person being interviewed (paragraphs 25–38)? Is this order effective? Why or why not?

MAKING CONNECTIONS

1. Good and Fitzpatrick's essay is a "directive" process analysis: that is, it explains how to go through the process of preparing for and participating in a job interview. Pick one of the other process analysis essays from this section of the book that illustrates an "informative" approach—how something happened. How are these two essays different from each other in terms of their organization and approach?

2. If William Ouchi ("Japanese and American Workers: Two Casts of Mind") had written an essay similar to Good and Fitzpatrick's on how to prepare for an interview with a Japanese employer, how would it have been different from "A Successful Interview"? In your opinion, what different kinds of questions would Japanese and American interviewers ask? What would be the principal reasons for these differences?

3. Pretend that you want a job working as a secretary for novelist Stephen King ("Why We Crave Horror Movies"). How would you prepare for the interview? What clothes would you wear? What kinds of research would you do in preparing to meet King? What specific strategies might help you get the job?

IDEAS FOR DISCUSSION/WRITING

Preparing to Write

Write freely about various jobs or responsibilities you have had in the past: What were these jobs? Were they all paid positions? How did you get the jobs? In what ways did you distinguish yourself from the other applicants? Which of these jobs did you like the best and why? What did you learn from these various jobs?

Choosing a Topic

1. A popular magazine has asked you to explain to a group of people who might want to apply for this type of work the details of a job you have held. For the magazine, write a process analysis essay on a job of your choice.

2. The editors of this magazine have asked you to revise your essay for a group of people looking for work. This time, the editors want you to persuade their readers to apply for this job. In this case, present your process analysis essay as a sales pitch to the general public, explaining the benefits of this type of work along with your detailed directions for carrying it out.

3. Many jobs teach us specialized skills that help us lead better lives. For your English class, write an essay discussing the relationship between certain types of work and your personal life, citing as often as possible examples from your own experience.

5

Division/Classification

Finding Categories

Both division and classification play important roles in our everyday lives: Bureau drawers separate one type of clothing from another; kitchen cabinets organize food, dishes, and utensils into proper groups; grocery stores shelve similar items together so shoppers can easily locate what they want to buy; school notebooks with tabs help students divide up their academic lives; newspapers classify local and national events in order to organize a great deal of daily information for the general public; and our own personal classification systems assist us in separating what we like from what we don't so that we can have access to our favorite foods, our favorite cars, our favorite entertainment, our favorite people. The two processes of division and classification are so natural to us, in fact, that we sometimes aren't even aware we are using them.

DEFINING DIVISION/CLASSIFICATION

Division and classification are actually mirror images of each other. Division is the basic feature of process analysis, which we studied in the last chapter: It moves from a general concept to subdivisions of that concept or from a single category to multiple subcategories. Classification works in the opposite direction, moving from specifics to a group with common traits or from multiple subgroups to a single, larger, and more inclusive category. These techniques work together in many ways: A college, for example, is *divided* into departments (single to multiple), whereas courses are *classified* by department (multiple to single); the medical field is *divided* into specialties, whereas doctors are *classified* by a single specialty; a cookbook is *divided* into chapters, whereas recipes are *classified* according to type; and athletics is *divided* into specific sports, whereas athletes are *classified* by the sport in which they participate. Division is the separation of an idea or an item into its basic parts, such as a home into rooms, a course into assignments, or a job into various duties or responsibilities; classification is the organization of items with similar features into a group or groups, such as ordering furniture to decorate a dining room, dropping all carbohydrates from your diet, or preferring to date only tall, sun-tanned swimmers.

Classification is an organizational system for presenting a large amount of material to a reader or listener. This process helps us make sense of the complex world we live in by letting us work with smaller, more understandable units of that world. Classification must be governed by some clear, logical purpose (such as focusing on all lower-division course requirements), which will then dictate the system of categories to be used. The plan of organization that results should be as flexible as possible, and it should illustrate the specific relationship to each other of items in a group and of the groups themselves to one another.

As you already know, many different ways of classifying the same elements are possible. If you consider the examples at the outset of this chapter, you will realize that bureau drawers vary from house to house and even from person to person; that no one's kitchen is set up exactly the same way as someone else's; and that grocery stores have similar but not identical systems of food classification. (Think, for instance, of the many different schemes for organizing dairy products, meats, foreign foods, etc.) In addition, your friends probably use a method different from yours to organize their school notebooks; different newspapers vary their presentation of the news; and two professors will probably teach the same course material in divergent ways. We all have distinct and uniquely logical methods of classifying the elements in our own lives.

The following student paragraph about friends illustrates both division and classification. As you read it, notice how the student writer moves back and forth smoothly from general to specific and from multiple to single:

> The word friend *can refer to many different types of relationships. Close friends are "friends" at their very best: people for whom we feel respect, esteem, and, quite possibly, even love. We regard these people and their well-being with kindness, interest, and goodwill; we trust them and will go out of our way to help them. Needless to say, we could all use at least one close friend. Next come "casual friends," people with whom we share a particular interest or activity. The investment of a great amount of time and energy in developing this type of friendship is usually not required, though casual friends often become close friends with the passage of time. The last division of "friend" is most general and is composed of all those individuals whose acquaintance we have made and who feel no hostility toward us. When one is counting friends, this group should certainly be included, since such friendships often develop into "casual" or "close" relationships. Knowing people in all three groups is necessary, however, because all types of friends undoubtedly help us live healthier, happier lives.*

THINKING CRITICALLY BY USING DIVISION/CLASSIFICATION

The thinking strategies of division and classification are the flip sides of each other: Your textbook is *divided* into chapters (one item divided into many), but chapters are *classified* (grouped) into sections or units. Your brain performs these mental acrobatics constantly, but to be as proficient at this method of thinking as possible, you need to be aware of the cognitive activities you go through. Focusing on these two companion patterns of thought will develop your skill in dealing with these complex schemes as it simultaneously increases your overall mental capabilities.

You might think of division/classification as a driving pattern that goes forward and then doubles back on itself in reverse. Division is a movement from a single concept to multiple categories, while classification involves gathering multiple concepts into a single group. Dividing and/or classifying helps us make sense of our subject by using categories to highlight similarities and differences. In the case of division, you are trying to find what differences break the items into separate groups, while, with classification, you let the similarities among the items help you put the material into meaningful categories. Processing your material in this way helps your readers see your particular subject in a new way and often brings renewed insights to both reader and writer.

Experimenting with division and classification is important to your growth as a critical thinker. It will help you process complex information so you can understand more fully your options for dealing with material in all subject areas. Practicing division and classification separate from other rhetorical modes makes you concentrate on improving this particular pattern of thinking before adding it to your expanding arsenal of critical thinking skills.

1. Study the table of contents of a magazine that interests you. Into what sections is the magazine divided? What distinguishing features does each section have? Now study the various advertisements in the same magazine. What different categories would you use to classify these ads? List the ads in each category.

2. Make a chart classifying the English instructors at your school. Explain your classification system to the class.

3. List six to eight major concerns you have about American society. Which of these are most important? Which are least important? Now classify these concerns into two or three distinct categories.

READING AND WRITING DIVISION/ CLASSIFICATION ESSAYS

Writers of division/classification essays must first decide if they are going to break down a topic into many separate parts or group together similar items into one coherent category; a writer's purpose will, of course, guide him or her in this decision. Readers must likewise recognize and understand which of these two parallel operations an author is using to structure an essay. Another important identifying feature of division/classification essays is an explanation (explicit or implicit) of the significance of a particular system of organization.

How to Read a Division/Classification Essay

Preparing to Read. As you approach the selections in this chapter, you should study all the material that precedes each essay so you can prepare yourself for your reading. First of all, what hints does the title give you about what you are going to read? To what extent does Judy Brady reveal in her title her attitude toward women? Who do you think Judith Wallerstein and Sandra Blakeslee's audience is in "Second Chances for Children of Divorce"? Does Judith Viorst's title give us any indication about her point of view in "The Truth About Lying"? Then, see what you can learn from scanning each essay and reading its synopsis in the Rhetorical Table of Contents.

Also important as you prepare to read the essays in this chapter is your knowledge about each author and the conditions under which each essay was written: What does the biographical material tell you about Brady's "Why I Want a Wife"? About the selection from Golding's "Thinking as a Hobby"? Knowing where these essays were first published will give you even more information about each author's purpose and audience.

Finally, before you begin to read, answer the Preparing to Read questions, and then, think freely for a few minutes about the general topic: What do you want to know about the different types of ex-smokers classified in Zimring's essay? What are some different types of lies you have told (Viorst)?

Reading. As you read each essay for the first time, write down your initial reactions to the topic itself, to the preliminary material, to the mood the writer sets, or to a specific incident in the essay. Make associations between the essay and your own experiences.

In addition, create a context for each essay by drawing on the preliminary material you just read about the essay: What are Wallerstein and Blakeslee implying about the relationship between emotional health and divorce, and why do they care about this relationship? What is significant about Zimring's point of view in "Confessions of an Ex-Smoker"? According to Viorst, why are some lies permissible?

Also, in this first reading, notice whether the writers divided (split up) or classified (gathered together) their material to make their point. Finally, read the questions after each essay, and let them guide your second reading of the selection.

Rereading. When you read these division/classification essays a second time, notice how the authors carefully match their dominant rhetorical approach (in this case, division or classification) to their purpose in a clear thesis. What, for example, is Brady's dominant rhetorical approach to her subject? How does this approach further her purpose? What other rhetorical strategies support her thesis? Then, see how these writers logically present their division or classification systems to their readers, defining new categories as their essays progress. Finally, notice how each writer either implicitly or explicitly explains the significance or value of his or her division/classification system. How do Wallerstein and Blakeslee explain their system of organization? And how does Viorst give her organizing principle significance? Now, answer the questions after each essay to check your understanding and to help you analyze your reading in preparation for the discussion/writing topics that follow.

For a more complete survey of reading guidelines, you may want to consult the checklist on pages 20–21 of the Introduction.

How to Write a Division/Classification Essay

Preparing to Write. You should approach a division/classification essay in the same way you have begun all your other writing assignments—with some kind of prewriting activity that will help you generate ideas, such as the Preparing to Write questions featured in this chapter. The prewriting techniques outlined in the Introduction on pages 21–23 can help you approach these questions imaginatively. Before you even consider the selection and arrangement of details, you need to explore your subject, choose a topic, and decide on a specific purpose and audience. The best way to explore your subject is to think about it, read about it, and then write about it. Look at it from all possible angles, and see what patterns and relationships emerge. To choose a specific topic, you might begin by listing any groups, patterns, or combinations you discover within your subject matter. Your purpose should take shape as you form your thesis, and your audience is probably dictated by the assignment. Making these decisions before you write will make the rest of your task much easier.

Writing. As you begin to write, certain guidelines will help you structure your ideas for a division/classification essay:

1. First, declare an overall purpose for your classification.
2. Then, divide the item or concept you are dealing with into categories.
3. Arrange these categories into a logical sequence.

4. Define each category, explaining the difference between one category and another and demonstrating that difference through examples.
5. Explain the significance of your classification system (Why is it worth reading? What will your audience learn from it?).

All discussion in such an essay should reinforce the purpose stated at the beginning of the theme. Other rhetorical modes—such as narration, example, and comparison/contrast—will naturally be used to supplement your classification.

To make your classification as workable as possible, take special care that your categories do not overlap and that all topics fall into their proper places. If, for example, you were classifying all the jobs performed by students in your writing class, the categories of (1) indoor work and (2) outdoor work would probably be inadequate. Most delivery jobs, for example, fall into both categories. At a pizza parlor, a florist, or a gift shop, a delivery person's time would be split between indoor and outdoor work. So you would need to design a different classification system to avoid this problem. The categories of (1) indoor work, (2) outdoor work, and (3) a combination of indoor and outdoor work would be much more useful for this task. Making sure your categories don't overlap will help make your classification essays more readable and more accurate.

Rewriting. As you rewrite your division/classification essays, consider carefully the probable reactions of your readers to the form and content of your paper:

Does your thesis communicate your purpose clearly?

Have you divided your topic into separate and understandable categories?

Are your categories original and unique?

Are these categories arranged logically?

Are the distintions between your categories as clear as possible?

Do you explain the significance of your particular classification system?

More guidelines for writing and rewriting are available on pages 32–33 of the Introduction.

STUDENT ESSAY: DIVISION/CLASSIFICATION AT WORK

The following student essay divides skiers into interesting categories based on their physical abilities. As you read it, notice how the student writer weaves the significance of his study into his opening statement of purpose. Also, pay particular attention to his logical method of organization and clear explanation of categories as he moves with ease from multiple to single and back to multiple again throughout the essay.

People on the Slopes

When I first learned to ski, I was amazed **Subject** by the shapes who whizzed by me and slipped down trails marked only by a black diamond signifying "most difficult," while others careened awkwardly down the "bunny slopes." These skiers, I discovered, **Thesis statement** could be divided into distinct categories— for my own entertainment and for the **Overall purpose** purpose of finding appropriate skiing partners.

First category First are the poetic skiers. They glide down the mountainside silently with what seems like no effort at all. They float from **Definition** side to side on the intermediate slopes, their knees bent perfectly above parallel **Supporting details** skis, while their sharp skills allow them to bypass slower skiers with safely executed turns at remarkable speeds.

Second category The crazy skiers also get down the mountain quickly, but with a lot more noise attending their descent. At every hill, they yell a loud "Yahoo!" and slam their **Definition** skis into the snow. These go-for-broke athletes always whiz by faster than everyone else, and they especially seem to love the **Supporting details (with humor)** crowded runs where they can slide over the backs of other people's skis. I often find crazy skiers in mangled messes at the bot-

287

toms of steep hills, where they are yelling loudly, but not the famous "Yahoo!"

After being overwhelmed by the crazy skiers, I am always glad to find other skiers like myself: the average ones. We are polite on the slopes, concentrate on improving our technique with every run, and ski the beginner slopes only at the beginning of the day to warm up. We go over the moguls (small hills) much more cautiously than the crazy or poetic skiers, but we still seek adventure with a slight jump or two each day. We remain a silent majority on the mountain.

Below us in talent, but much more evident on the mountainside, are what I call the eternal beginners. These skiers stick to the same beginner slope almost every run of every day during their vacation. Should they venture onto an intermediate slope, they quickly assume the snowplow position (a pigeon-toed stance) and never leave it. Eternal beginners weave from one side of the run to the other and hardly ever fall, because they proceed so slowly; however, they do yell quite a bit at the crazies who like to run over the backs of their skis.

Having always enjoyed people-watching, I have fun each time I am on the slopes observing the myriad of skiers around me. I use these observations to pick out possible ski partners for myself and others. Since my mother is an eternal beginner, she has more fun skiing with someone who shares her interests than with my dad, who is a poetic skier with solitude on his mind. After taking care of Mom, I am free to find a partner I'll enjoy. My sister, the crazy skier of the family, just heads for the rowdiest group she can find! As the years go by and my

Margin annotations:
- Transition
- Third category
- Definition
- Supporting details (comparative)
- Transition
- Fourth category
- Definition
- Supporting details
- Transition
- Significance of classification system

Concluding
remarks
> talents grow, I am trusting my perceptions of skier types to help me find the right partner for life on and off the slopes. No doubt watching my fellow skiers will always remain an enjoyable pastime.

Student Writer's Comments

To begin this paper—the topic of which occurred to me as I flew over snow-capped mountains on a trip—I brainstormed. I jotted down the general groups of skiers I believed existed on the slopes and recorded characteristics of each group as they came to me. The ideas flowed quite freely at this point, and I enjoyed imagining the people I was describing. This prewriting stage brought back some great memories from the slopes that cluttered my thinking at times, but in most cases one useless memory triggered two or three other details or skiing stories that helped me make sense of my division/classification system.

I then felt ready to write a first draft but was having a lot of trouble coming up with a sensible order for my categories. So I just began to write. My categories were now clear to me, even though I wanted to work a little more on their labels. And the definitions of each category came quite naturally as I wrote. In fact, the ease with which they surfaced made me believe that I really had discovered some ultimate truth about types of skiers. I also had tons of details and anecdotes to work with from my brainstorming session. When I finished the body of my first draft (it had no introduction or conclusion yet), I realized that every paragraph worked nicely by itself—four separate category paragraphs. But these paragraphs didn't work together yet at all.

As I reworked the essay, I knew my major job was to reorganize my categories in some logical way and then smooth out the prose with transitions that would make the essay work as a unified whole. To accomplish this, I wrote more drafts of this single paper than I can remember writing for any other assignment. But I feel that the order and the transitions finally work now. The essay moves logically from type to type, and I think my transitions justify my arrangement along the way. My overall purpose came to me as I was reorganizing my categories, at which point I was able to write my introduction and conclusion. After I had put my purpose into words, the significance of my division/classification system became clear. I saved it, however, for the conclusion.

The most exciting part of this paper was realizing how often I had used these mental groupings in pairing my family and friends with other skiers. I had just never labeled, defined, or organized the categories I had created. Writing this paper helped me verbalize these categories and ended up being a lot of fun (especially when it was finished).

SOME FINAL THOUGHTS ON DIVISION/CLASSIFICATION

The essays collected in this chapter use division and/or classification as their primary organizing principle. All of these essays show both techniques at work to varying degrees. As you read these essays, you might also want to be aware of the other rhetorical modes that support these division/classification essays, such as description and definition. Finally, pay particular attention to how these authors bring significance to their systems of classification and, as a result, to their essays themselves.

WILLIAM GOLDING   (1911 – 1993)

■ ■ ■

Thinking as a Hobby

Born in Cornwall, England, William Golding attended Oxford University and then followed in his father's footsteps by becoming a schoolteacher. After commanding a rocket-launching ship in the North Atlantic during World War II, he returned to his teaching career and began writing novels, the first of which was his epic allegory on human nature entitled *Lord of the Flies* (1954), which chronicles the degeneration to savagery of a group of British schoolboys stranded on an island during a nuclear war. Rejected by a total of twenty-one publishers before Faber & Faber accepted the manuscript, this brilliant novel was described by its author as "an attempt to trace the defects of society back to the defects of human nature." Golding followed this successful literary debut with a number of other novels, including *The Inheritors* (1955), *Free Fall* (1960), *The Spire* (1964), *Darkness Visible* (1979), *Rites of Passage* (1980), and *Fire Down Below* (1989). Awarded the Nobel Prize for literature in 1983, he preferred to be known as a "craftsman" rather than an "artist." He saw himself as being "like one of the old-fashioned shipbuilders, who conceived the boat in their mind and then, after that, touched every single piece that went into the boat. They were in complete control; they knew it inch by inch, and I think the novelist is very much like that." Prior to his death in 1993, Golding described his hobbies as "thinking, classical Greek, sailing, and archaeology."

Preparing to Read

The following essay, originally published in *Holiday* magazine (August 1961), offers us some important insights into the mind of young William Golding, who depicts himself as a student in grammar school struggling to learn how to think clearly and creatively. Prior to reading this essay, consider your definition of thinking: What constitutes thinking? When do you know you are really thinking clearly? Are there different types of thinking? How is thinking different from feeling? How do you know the difference between these functions? Do thinking and feeling serve separate purposes? What are these purposes?

W hile I was still a boy, I came to the conclusion that there were three grades of thinking; and since I was later to claim thinking as my hobby, I came to an even stranger conclusion—namely, that I myself could not think at all. 1

I must have been an unsatisfactory child for grownups to deal with. I remember how incomprehensible they appeared to me at first, but not, of course, how I appeared to them. It was the headmaster of my grammar school who first brought the subject of thinking before me—though neither in the way, nor with the result he intended. He had some statuettes in his study. They stood on a high cupboard behind his desk. One was a lady wearing nothing but a bath towel. She seemed frozen in an eternal panic lest the bath towel slip down any farther; and since she had no arms, she was in an unfortunate position to pull the towel up again. Next to her, crouched the statuette of a leopard, ready to spring down at the top drawer of a filing cabinet labeled A-AH. My innocence interpreted this as the victim's last, despairing cry. Beyond the leopard was a naked, muscular gentleman, who sat, looking down, with his chin on his fist and his elbow on his knee. He seemed utterly miserable. 2

Some time later, I learned about these statuettes. The headmaster had placed them where they would face delinquent children, because they symbolized to him the whole of life. The naked lady was the Venus of Milo. She was Love. She was not worried about the towel. She was just busy being beautiful. The leopard was Nature, and he was being natural. The naked, muscular gentleman was not miserable. He was Rodin's Thinker, an image of pure thought. It is easy to buy small plaster models of what you think life is like. 3

I had better explain that I was a frequent visitor to the headmaster's study, because of the latest thing I had done or left undone. As we now say, I was not integrated. I was, if anything, disintegrated; and I was puzzled. Grownups never made sense. 4

Whenever I found myself in a penal position before the head-master's desk, with the statuettes glimmering whitely above him, I would sink my head, clasp my hands behind my back and writhe one shoe over the other.

The headmaster would look opaquely at me through flashing 5 spectacles.

"What are we going to do with you?" 6

Well, what *were* they going to do with me? I would writhe my 7 shoe some more and stare down at the worn rug.

"Look up, boy! Can't you look up?" 8

Then I would look up at the cupboard, where the naked lady 9 was frozen in her panic and the muscular gentleman contem-plated the hind-quarters of the leopard in endless gloom. I had nothing to say to the headmaster. His spectacles caught the light so that you could see nothing human behind them. There was no possibility of communication.

"Don't you ever think at all?" 10

No, I didn't think, wasn't thinking, couldn't think—I was sim- 11 ply waiting in anguish for the interview to stop.

"Then you'd better learn—hadn't you?" 12

On one occasion the headmaster leaped to his feet, reached up 13 and plonked Rodin's masterpiece on the desk before me.

"That's what a man looks like when he's really thinking." 14

I surveyed the gentleman without interest or comprehension. 15

"Go back to your class." 16

Clearly there was something missing in me. Nature had en- 17 dowed the rest of the human race with a sixth sense and left me out. This must be so, I mused, on my way back to the class, since whether I had broken a window, or failed to remember Boyle's Law, or been late for school, my teachers produced me one, adult answer: "Why can't you think?"

As I saw the case, I had broken the window because I had 18 tried to hit Jack Arney with a cricket ball and missed him; I could not remember Boyle's Law because I had never bothered to learn it; and I was late for school because I preferred looking over the bridge into the river. In fact, I was wicked. Were my teachers, per-haps, so good that they could not understand the depths of my depravity? Were they clear, untormented people who could direct their every action by this mysterious business of thinking? The whole thing was incomprehensible. In my earlier years, I found even the statuette of the Thinker confusing. I did not believe any of my teachers were naked, ever. Like someone born deaf, but bitterly determined to find out about sound, I watched my teachers to find out about thought.

There was Mr. Houghton. He was always telling me to think. 19 With a modest satisfaction, he would tell me that he had thought a bit himself. Then why did he spend so much time drinking? Or was there more sense in drinking than there appeared to be? But if not, and if drinking were in fact ruinous to health—and Mr. Houghton was ruined, there was no doubt about that—why was he always talking about the clean life and the virtues of fresh air? He would spread his arms wide with the action of a man who habitually spent his time striding along mountain ridges.

"Open air does me good, boys—I know it!" 20

Sometimes, exalted by his own oratory, he would leap from his 21 desk and hustle us outside into a hideous wind.

"Now, boys! Deep breaths! Feel it right down inside you— 22 huge draughts of God's good air!"

He would stand before us, rejoicing in his perfect health, an 23 open-air man. He would put his hands on his waist and take a tremendous breath. You could hear the wind, trapped in the cavern of his chest and struggling with all the unnatural impediments. His body would reel with shock and his ruined face go white at the unaccustomed visitation. He would stagger back to his desk and collapse there, useless for the rest of the morning.

Mr. Houghton was given to high-minded monologues about 24 the good life, sexless and full of duty. Yet in the middle of one of these monologues, if a girl passed the window, tapping along on her neat little feet, he would interrupt his discourse, his neck would turn of itself and he would watch her out of sight. In this instance, he seemed to me ruled not by thought but by an invisible and irresistible spring in his nape.

His neck was an object of great interest to me. Normally it 25 bulged a bit over his collar. But Mr. Houghton had fought in the First World War alongside both Americans and French, and had come—by who knows what illogic?—to a settled detestation of both countries. If either country happened to be prominent in current affairs, no argument could make Mr. Houghton think well of it. He would bang the desk, his neck would bulge still further and go red. "You can say what you like," he would cry, "but I've thought about this—and I know what I think!"

Mr. Houghton thought with his neck.   26

There was Miss Parsons. She assured us that her dearest wish   27
was our welfare, but I knew even then, with the mysterious clairvoyance of childhood, that what she wanted most was the husband she never got. There was Mr. Hands—and so on.

I have dealt at length with my teachers because this was my in-   28
troduction to the nature of what is commonly called thought.
Through them I discovered that thought is often full of unconscious prejudice, ignorance and hypocrisy. It will lecture on disinterested purity while its neck is being remorselessly twisted toward a skirt. Technically, it is about as proficient as most businessmen's golf, as honest as most politicians' intentions, or—to come near my own preoccupation—as coherent as most books that get written. It is what I came to call grade-three thinking, though more properly, it is feeling, rather than thought.

True, often there is a kind of innocence in prejudices, but in   29
those days I viewed grade-three thinking with an intolerant contempt and an incautious mockery. I delighted to confront a pious lady who hated the Germans with the proposition that we should love our enemies. She taught me a great truth in dealing with grade-three thinkers; because of her, I no longer dismiss lightly a mental process which for nine-tenths of the population is the nearest they will ever get to thought. They have immense solidarity. We had better respect them, for we are outnumbered and surrounded. A crowd of grade-three thinkers, all shouting the same thing, all warming their hands at the fire of their own prejudices, will not thank you for pointing out the contradictions in their beliefs. Man is a gregarious animal, and enjoys agreement as cows will graze all the same way on the side of a hill.

Grade-two thinking is the detection of contradictions. I   30
reached grade two when I trapped the poor, pious lady. Grade-two thinkers do not stampede easily, though often they fall into the other fault and lag behind. Grade-two thinking is a withdrawal, with eyes and ears open. It became my hobby and brought satisfaction and loneliness in either hand. For grade-two thinking destroys without having the power to create. It set me

watching the crowds cheering His Majesty the King and asking myself what all the fuss was about, without giving me anything positive to put in the place of that heady patriotism. But there were compensations. To hear people justify their habit of hunting foxes and tearing them to pieces by claiming that the foxes liked it. To hear our Prime Minister talk about the great benefit we conferred on India by jailing people like Pandit Nehru and Gandhi. To hear American politicians talk about peace in one sentence and refuse to join the League of Nations in the next. Yes, there were moments of delight.

But I was growing toward adolescence and had to admit that 31 Mr. Houghton was not the only one with an irresistible spring in his neck. I, too, felt the compulsive hand of nature and began to find that pointing out contradiction could be costly as well as fun. There was Ruth, for example, a serious and attractive girl. I was an atheist at the time. Grade-two thinking is a menace to religion and knocks down sects like skittles. I put myself in a position to be converted by her with an hypocrisy worthy of grade three. She was a Methodist—or at least, her parents were, and Ruth had to follow suit. But, alas, instead of relying on the Holy Spirit to convert me, Ruth was foolish enough to open her pretty mouth in argument. She claimed that the Bible (King James Version) was literally inspired. I countered by saying that the Catholics believed in the literal inspiration of Saint Jerome's *Vulgate*, and the two books were different. Argument flagged.

At last she remarked that there were an awful lot of Methodists, 32 and they couldn't be wrong, could they—not all those millions? That was too easy, said I restively (for the nearer you were to Ruth, the nicer she was to be near to) since there were more Roman Catholics than Methodists anyway; and they couldn't be wrong, could they—not all those hundreds of millions? An awful flicker of doubt appeared in her eyes. I slid my arm round her waist and murmured breathlessly that if we were counting heads, the Buddhists were the boys for my money. But Ruth had *really* wanted to do me good, because I was so nice. She fled. The combination of my arm and those countless Buddhists was too much for her.

That night her father visited my father and left, red-cheeked 33 and indignant. I was given the third degree to find out what had

happened. It was lucky we were both of us only fourteen. I lost
Ruth and gained an undeserved reputation as a potential libertine.

So grade-two thinking could be dangerous. It was in this   34
knowledge, at the age of fifteen, that I remember making a comment from the heights of grade two, on the limitations of grade
three. One evening I found myself alone in the school hall,
preparing it for a party. The door of the headmaster's study was
open. I went in. The headmaster had ceased to thump Rodin's
Thinker down on the desk as an example to the young. Perhaps
he had not found any more candidates, but the statuettes were
still there, glimmering and gathering dust on top of the cupboard.
I stood on a chair and rearranged them. I stood Venus in her bath
towel on the filing cabinet, so that now the top drawer caught its
breath in a gasp of sexy excitement. "A-ah!" The portentous
Thinker I placed on the edge of the cupboard so that he looked
down at the bath towel and waited for it to slip.

Grade-two thinking, though it filled life with fun and excite-   35
ment, did not make for content. To find out the deficiencies of
our elders bolsters the young ego but does not make for personal security. I found that grade two was not only the power to
point out contradictions. It took the swimmer some distance
from the shore and left him there, out of his depth. I decided
that Pontius Pilate was a typical grade-two thinker. "What is
truth?" he said, a very common grade-two thought, but one that
is used always as the end of an argument instead of the beginning. There is a still higher grade of thought which says, "What
is truth?" and sets out to find it.

But these grade-one thinkers were few and far between.   36
They did not visit my grammar school in the flesh though they
were there in books. I aspired to them, partly because I was ambitious and partly because I now saw my hobby as an unsatisfactory thing if it went no further. If you set out to climb a
mountain, however high you climb, you have failed if you cannot reach the top.

I *did* meet an undeniably grade-one thinker in my first year at   37
Oxford. I was looking over a small bridge in Magdalen Deer
Park, and a tiny mustached and hatted figure came and stood by
my side. He was a German who had just fled from the Nazis to
Oxford as a temporary refuge. His name was Einstein.

But Professor Einstein knew no English at that time and I 38
knew only two words of German. I beamed at him, trying word-
lessly to convey by my bearing all the affection and respect that
the English felt for him. It is possible—and I have to make the
admission—that I felt here were two grade-one thinkers standing
side by side; yet I doubt if my face conveyed more than a formless
awe. I would have given my Greek and Latin and French and a
good slice of my English for enough German to communicate.
But we were divided; he was as inscrutable as my headmaster. For
perhaps five minutes we stood together on the bridge, undeniable
grade-one thinker and breathless aspirant. With true greatness,
Professor Einstein realized that any contact was better than none.
He pointed to a trout wavering in midstream.

He spoke: "*Fisch.*" 39

My brain reeled. Here I was, mingling with the great, and yet 40
helpless as the veriest grade-three thinker. Desperately I sought
for some sign by which I might convey that I, too, revered pure
reason. I nodded vehemently. In a brilliant flash I used up half of
my German vocabulary.

"*Fisch. Ja. Ja.*" 41

For perhaps another five minutes we stood side by side. Then 42
Professor Einstein, his whole figure still conveying good will and
amiability, drifted away out of sight.

I, too, would be a grade-one thinker. I was irreverent at the 43
best of times. Political and religious systems, social customs, loyalties and traditions, they all came tumbling down like so many
rotten apples off a tree. This was a fine hobby and a sensible
substitute for cricket, since you could play it all the year round. I
came up in the end with what must always remain the justification for grade-one thinking, its sign, seal and charter. I devised a
coherent system for living. It was a moral system, which was
wholly logical. Of course, as I readily admitted, conversion of
the world to my way of thinking might be difficult, since my
system did away with a number of trifles, such as big business,
centralized government, armies, marriage. . . .

It was Ruth all over again. I had some very good friends who 44
stood by me, and still do. But my acquaintances vanished, taking
the girls with them. Young women seemed oddly contented with
the world as it was. They valued the meaningless ceremony with a
ring. Young men, while willing to concede the chaining sordid-

ness of marriage, were hesitant about abandoning the organizations which they hoped would give them a career. A young man
on the first rung of the Royal Navy, while perfectly agreeable to
doing away with big business and marriage, got as red-necked as
Mr. Houghton when I proposed a world without any battleships
in it.

Had the game gone too far? Was it a game any longer? In   45
those prewar days, I stood to lose a great deal, for the sake of a
hobby.

Now you are expecting me to describe how I saw the folly of   46
my ways and came back to the warm nest, where prejudices are
so often called loyalties, where pointless actions are hallowed into
custom by repetition, where we are content to say we think when
all we do is feel.

But you would be wrong. I dropped my hobby and turned   47
professional.

If I were to go back to the headmaster's study and find the   48
dusty statuettes still there, I would arrange them differently. I
would dust Venus and put her aside, for I have come to love her
and know her for the fair thing she is. But I would put the
Thinker, sunk in his desperate thought, where there were shadows before him—and at his back, I would put the leopard,
crouched and ready to spring.

UNDERSTANDING DETAILS

1. What exactly is Golding classifying in this essay? Explain each
   part of his classification system.
2. What does the author think of each type of thinking he discusses?
3. What characterizes the relationship between Golding and his
   headmaster? What do they learn from each other?
4. Describe the people who represent each of Golding's categories of thinking.

ANALYZING MEANING

1. Why must Golding have been "an unsatisfactory child for
   grownups to deal with" (paragraph 2)? In what ways was
   Golding probably "unsatisfactory"?
2. What did the three statuettes in the headmaster's office represent? Why are they important to Golding's essay?

3. Why do you think so many adults asked Golding, "Why can't you think"?

4. Why does Golding call thinking his "hobby"?

DISCOVERING RHETORICAL STRATEGIES

1. In what ways does Golding use division and classification in this essay? How does he give significance or value to his system of organization? What other rhetorical techniques does he use to accomplish his purpose?

2. What distinctions does Golding make between thinking and feeling in this essay? Do you agree with these distinctions?

3. Through his style, Golding gives the impression that he is detached from his subject and is able to analyze his behavior as well as the behavior of others around him. How does he give his readers this impression? Do you think it is an accurate impression?

4. Why do you think Golding ends his essay with a discussion of the statuettes in the headmaster's office? What effect does this ending create? What is the significance of the new arrangement of the statuettes?

MAKING CONNECTIONS

1. Golding's description of his brief encounter with Einstein, when neither man could speak the other's language, is similar in some ways to Michael Dorris's attempt in "The Broken Cord" to communicate with his son, Adam, who suffers from fetal alcohol syndrome, and to Jane Goodall's experiences with her primates in "The Mind of the Chimpanzee." What would Golding say to Dorris and/or Goodall about the frustrations of miscommunication?

2. Compare and contrast Golding's early years, when he was learning to think clearly, with the same period in the life of Eudora Welty ("Listening"). Which author had a more stable, comfortable upbringing? How was each author influenced by these different circumstances? Whose early years were most like yours?

3. Which of the three stages of thinking does Golding spend most of his time describing? Which the least? Does Judith Viorst ("The Truth About Lying") or Judy Brady ("Why I

Want a Wife") display a similar imbalance in her division/-classification essay? Why does each author emphasize some categories more than others?

IDEAS FOR DISCUSSION/WRITING

Preparing to Write

Write freely about various types of thinking you are aware of: What are these types? How are these types of thinking represented in different kinds of behavior? Why are different types of thinking important to your daily survival? To your progress in school? What type of thinking do you believe will bring you the most success in life? In school? In what ways is thinking different from feeling?

Choosing a Topic

1. Your English teacher has asked about your ability to think critically. Respond to this question by classifying for this teacher all the different types of thinking you do in a typical day—with your main focus on critical thinking. Remember that each thinking task you do should fit into a category. Decide on a point of view before you begin to write.
2. Speculate about the thinking activities of a close friend or relative by analyzing that person's behavior and preferences. Remember that analysis is based on the process of division. Divide this person's behavior and preferences into logical parts; then, study those parts so that you can better understand the person's reasoning techniques. Decide on a purpose and audience before you begin to write.
3. If the mental activities we perform say something about us, analyze yourself by writing an essay that classifies the different mental activities you have carried out in the last week. Discuss your choices as you proceed.

JUDY BRADY   (1937 –   )

■ ■ ■

Why I Want a Wife

Judy Brady is a freelance writer and political activist who was born in San Francisco. She earned a B.F.A. in painting from the University of Iowa, married, raised two daughters, and then returned to San Francisco, where she is now an "ex-wife" who works as a secretary: "I must spend my days working in the corporate world where image has become so much more important than reality. It's crazy-making. My relief comes from doing political work with other people who have found the courage to acknowledge what is really going on and then act accordingly." Strong commitment to the feminist movement has taken her to Cuba for several visits, which have prompted the publication of articles about such diverse topics as abortion, literacy, unions, and the role of women in society. The author now devotes much of her time to the politics of cancer. Her most recent publication is *One in Three: Women with Cancer Confront an Epidemic* (1991), an anthology of poems, stories, and essays that "make accessible through personal testimony the facts of the cancer epidemic in this country." Her advice to students using *The Prose Reader* is to be "brutally honest" in their written work. She insists that "glossy writing, devoid of emotional truth and honesty, is quite useless."

Preparing to Read

The following essay first appeared under the author's married name, Judy Syfers. It was originally published in the preview issue of *Ms.* magazine (Spring 1972) and was later reprinted in the periodical's December 1979 issue. In it, Brady presents a wry, satirical view of woman's conventional social role as a docile servant to her husband. As you prepare to read this article, take a few moments to think about the various roles you play in your life: How many distinct roles do you play? Do you act differently as a student? A friend? A lover? A member of your family? An employee? How does each role make you feel? What different expectations are placed upon you in each of these roles? Who sets these expectations? How clearly are they stated? What happens when you do not fulfill each of these roles properly?

I belong to that classification of people known as wives. I am A Wife. And, not altogether incidentally, I am a mother. 1

Not too long ago a male friend of mine appeared on the scene fresh from a recent divorce. He had one child, who is, of course, with his ex-wife. He is looking for another wife. As I thought about him while I was ironing one evening, it suddenly occurred to me that I, too, would like to have a wife. Why do I want a wife? 2

I would like to go back to school so that I can become economi- 3 cally independent, support myself, and, if need be, support those dependent upon me. I want a wife who will work and send me to school. And while I am going to school I want a wife to take care of my children. I want a wife to keep track of the children's doctor and dentist appointments. And to keep track of mine, too. I want a wife to make sure my children eat properly and are kept clean. I want a wife who will wash the children's clothes and keep them mended. I want a wife who is a good nurturant attendant to my children, who arranges for their schooling, makes sure that they have an adequate social life with their peers, takes them to the park, the zoo, etc. I want a wife who takes care of the children when they are sick, a wife who arranges to be around when the children need special care, because, of course, I cannot miss classes at school. My wife must arrange to lose time at work and not lose the job. It may mean a small cut in my wife's income from time to time, but I guess I can tolerate that. Needless to say, my wife will arrange and pay for the care of the children while my wife is working.

I want a wife who will take care of *my* physical needs. I want a 4 wife who will keep my house clean. A wife who will pick up after my children, a wife who will pick up after me. I want a wife who will keep my clothes clean, ironed, mended, replaced when need be, and who will see to it that my personal things are kept in their proper place so that I can find what I need the minute I need it. I want a wife who cooks the meals, a wife who is a *good* cook. I want a wife who will plan the menus, do the necessary grocery shopping, prepare the meals, serve them pleasantly, and then do the cleaning up while I do my studying. I want a wife who will care for me when I am sick and sympathize with my pain and loss of time from school. I want a wife to go along when our family takes a vacation so that someone can continue to care for me and my children when I need a rest and change of scene.

I want a wife who will not bother me with rambling complaints about a wife's duties. But I want a wife who will listen to me when I feel the need to explain a rather difficult point I have come across in my course of studies. And I want a wife who will type my papers for me when I have written them.

I want a wife who will take care of the details of my social life. When my wife and I are invited out by my friends, I want a wife who will take care of the babysitting arrangements. When I meet people at school that I like and want to entertain, I want a wife who will have the house clean, will prepare a special meal, serve it to me and my friends, and not interrupt when I talk about things that interest me and my friends. I want a wife who will have arranged that the children are fed and ready for bed before my guests arrive so that the children do not bother us. I want a wife who takes care of the needs of my guests so that they feel comfortable, who makes sure that they have an ashtray, that they are passed the hors d'oeuvres, that they are offered a second helping of the food, that their wine glasses are replenished when necessary, that their coffee is served to them as they like it. And I want a wife who knows that sometimes I need a night out by myself.

I want a wife who is sensitive to my sexual needs, a wife who makes love passionately and eagerly when I feel like it, a wife who makes sure that I am satisfied. And, of course, I want a wife who will not demand sexual attention when I am not in the mood for it. I want a wife who assumes the complete responsibility for birth control, because I do not want more children. I want a wife who will remain sexually faithful to me so that I do not have to clutter up my intellectual life with jealousies. And I want a wife who understands that *my* sexual needs may entail more than strict adherence to monogamy. I must, after all, be able to relate to people as fully as possible.

If, by chance, I find another person more suitable as a wife than the wife I already have, I want the liberty to replace my present wife with another one. Naturally, I will expect a fresh, new life; my wife will take the children and be solely responsible for them so that I am left free.

When I am through with school and have a job, I want my wife to quit working and remain at home so that my wife can more fully and completely take care of a wife's duties. 9

My God, who *wouldn't* want a wife? 10

UNDERSTANDING DETAILS

1. How many categories of wifely duties does Brady refer to in this essay? How are they related?
2. How does the author define the term *wife*? Is her portrayal of wives realistic? According to this essay, how do husbands differ from wives?
3. Why does the author want a wife? Explain your answer in some detail.
4. What would be your answer to Brady's question at the end of her essay: "My God, who *wouldn't* want a wife?" (paragraph 10)?

ANALYZING MEANING

1. What is the overall purpose of Brady's essay? How do you know? What clues make this purpose clear?
2. What type of wife does Brady ask for in this essay? What motivates this wife? Where are this person's loyalties? What are this wife's convictions?
3. Is this essay as pertinent today as it was in 1972? From your perspective, how have sexual roles changed since 1972? How are wives' roles today different from your mother's role as a wife?
4. Do you want a "wife"? What qualities would this person have? Explain your answer in detail.

DISCOVERING RHETORICAL STRATEGIES

1. Where in this essay does the author use division? Where does she use classification? Give specific examples. What other rhetorical modes does Brady use in her essay?
2. List the topics of each paragraph in the body of the essay (paragraphs 3–9). What advantages does this order have over other possible arrangements of the same ideas? How would the effect have been altered if Brady had changed the order of these ideas?

3. This essay works principally through parallel structure, in which similar grammatical elements are repeated in a series of phrases or clauses. Look, for example, at the following sentence:

I want *a wife who* is sensitive to my sexual needs,
      a wife who makes love passionately and eagerly when I feel like it,
      a wife who makes sure that I am satisfied (paragraph 7).

The repetitions in this example are italicized, whereas the parallel structures are lined up under each other. Find two other instances of this technique in the essay, and explain how each works. What effect does this rhetorical technique have on you as you read this essay?
4. What point of view does Brady take in her article? What tone results from this point of view? Look up the term *satire* in a literary dictionary, and explain what use Brady is making of this verbal technique.

MAKING CONNECTIONS

1. Imagine a conversation between Judy Brady, Gloria Steinem ("The Politics of Muscle"), and Barbara Ehrenreich ("Stop Ironing the Diapers") in which each author attempts to define the proper role of women in our society. How would these writers differ in their definitions of "a woman's place in America"? What limitations, if any, would each place upon women in today's society? Do you think there should be any limits placed upon what women can do? If so, what should those limits be?
2. Brady and Bill Cosby ("The Baffling Question") both use effective irony (saying the opposite of what they really mean) in their essays. Write out a single sentence explaining each author's main point. What do these authors gain or lose by using irony to express their opinions? Does understanding such essays require more or less reader involvement than reading a non-ironic essay? Explain your answer.
3. To what extent would Alleen Pace Nilsen ("Sexism in English: A 1990s Update") argue that the gender inequities described by Brady are related to the sexism encoded in our language? Would you agree with Nilsen? Explain your answer.

IDEAS FOR DISCUSSION/WRITING

Preparing to Write

Write freely about your own various roles in life: What are some of the major roles you play (e.g., husband, wife, girlfriend, boyfriend, sister, brother, son, daughter, student, friend, employee)? What personal characteristics define the different roles you play? Which of these roles is most comfortable for you? Which is least comfortable? How does each of these roles make you feel about yourself?

Choosing a Topic

1. Use division to explain one of the roles you play in life. Break down the role into its basic parts, and then, discuss those parts in an essay to your English class. Make sure you decide on a purpose and a point of view before you begin to write.
2. Do you feel that husbands are ever categorized or exploited in much the same way as Brady's "wife"? Write an essay entitled "Why I Want a Husband" that presents the other side of the story.
3. Using Brady's ironic method, write an essay for your classmates in which you claim to need something that you could never have.

Judith Wallerstein (1921 –)

Sandra Blakeslee (1943 –)

■ ■ ■

Second Chances for Children of Divorce

Judith Wallerstein grew up in New York City, earned her Ph.D. at Lund University in Sweden, and now lives and works in Marin County, California, where she serves as director of the Center for the Family in Transition. Since 1965, she has taught psychology at the University of California at Berkeley, where she specializes in divorce and its effect on family members. Her first book, *Surviving the Breakup* (coauthored by Joan Kelly, 1980), analyzes the impact of divorce on young children in the family. Her next, *Second Chances: Men, Women, and Children a Decade After Divorce* (1989), is a study of the long-term effects of divorce on teenagers and young adults. Now hard at work on a study of happy marriages, Wallerstein is very concerned about what is happening to the American family. "There's a lot of anger in relationships between men and women today," she explains. "It's always easier to express anger than love." An avid reader, she collects ideas the way "other people collect recipes." She advises college students to read as much as possible: "The first prerequisite a writer must have is a love of reading." Her coauthor on *Second Chances*, Sandra Blakeslee, was born in Flushing, New York, and earned her B.S. degree at Berkeley, where her specialty was neurobiology. She is currently the West Coast science and medicine correspondent for the *New York Times*. A former Peace Corps volunteer in Borneo, she advises students using *The Prose Reader* to travel as much as possible: "You need a wide range of experiences to be a good writer." Blakeslee goes mountain biking and runs in her spare time.

Preparing to Read

In the following essay from *Second Chances*, Wallerstein and Blakeslee classify the psychological tasks children who have suffered through the divorce of their parents must complete to free themselves from the past. As you prepare to read this article, take a few minutes to think about the effects of divorce on yourself or someone you know: How close have you been to a divorce experience? How were people directly associated with the experience affected? What differences did you notice in the way adults and children responded to the same situation? What feelings were most common among the adults? Among the children? Why do you think the divorce rate has been so high during the last fifty years? Do you think this trend will continue, or will it taper off in the next few years?

∎

A t each stage in the life cycle, children and adults face pre- 1 dictable and particular issues that represent the coming together of the demands of society and a biological and psychological timetable. Just as we physically learn to sit, crawl, walk, and run, we follow an equivalent progression in our psychological and social development. Each stage presents us with a sequence of tasks we must confront. We can succeed or fail in mastering them, to varying degrees, but everyone encounters the tasks. They begin at birth and end at death.

Children move upward along a common developmental lad- 2 der, although each goes it alone at his or her own pace. Gradually, as they pass through the various stages, children consolidate a sense of self. They develop coping skills, conscience, and the capacity to give and receive love.

Children take one step at a time, negotiating the rung they 3 are on before they can move up to the next. They may—and often do—falter in this effort. The climb is not steady under the best of circumstances, and most children briefly stand still in their ascent. They may even at times move backward. Such regressions are not a cause for alarm; rather, they may represent an appropriate response to life's stresses. Children who fail one task are not stalled forever; they will go on to the next stage, although they may be weakened in their climb. Earlier failures will not necessarily imperil their capacity as adults to trust a relationship, make a commitment, hold an appropriate job, or be a parent—to make use of their second chances at each stage of development.

I propose that children who experience divorce face an addi- 4
tional set of tasks specific to divorce in addition to the normal
developmental tasks of growing up. Growing up is inevitably
harder for children of divorce because they must deal with psychological issues that children from well-functioning intact families do not have to face.

The psychological tasks of children begin as difficulties, escalate 5
between the parents during the marriage, and continue through
the separation and divorce and throughout the postdivorce years.

TASK: *Understanding the Divorce*

The first and most basic task at the time of separation is for the 6
children to understand realistically what the divorce means in their
family and what its concrete consequences will be. Children, especially very young children, are thrown back on frightening and
vivid fantasies of being abandoned, being placed in foster care, or
never seeing a departed parent again, or macabre fantasies such as a
mother being destroyed in an earthquake or a father being destroyed by a vengeful mother. All of these fantasies and the feelings
that accompany them can be undone only as the children, with
the parents' continuing help, begin to understand the reality and
begin to adjust to the actual changes that the divorce brings.

The more mature task of understanding what led to the mari- 7
tal failure awaits the perspective of the adolescent and young
adult. Early on, most children regard divorce as a serious error,
but by adolescence most feel that their parents never should have
married. The task of understanding occurs in two stages. The first
involves accurately perceiving the immediate changes that divorce
brings and differentiating fantasy fears from reality. The second
occurs later, when children are able at greater distance and with
more mature understanding to evaluate their parents' actions and
can draw useful lessons for their own lives.

TASK: *Strategic Withdrawal*

Children and adolescents need to get on with their own lives 8
as soon as possible after the divorce, to resume their normal activities at school and at play, to get back physically and emotionally
to the normal tasks of growing up. Especially for adolescents who
may have been beginning to spread their wings, the divorce pulls

them back into the family orbit, where they may become consumed with care for siblings or a troubled parent. It also intrudes on their academic and social life, causing them to spend class time preoccupied with worry and to pass up social activities because of demands at home. This is not to say that children should ignore the divorce. Their task is to acknowledge their concern and to provide appropriate help to their parents and siblings, but they should strive to remove the divorce from the center of their own thoughts so that they can get back to their own interests, pleasures, problems, and peer relationships. To achieve this task, children need encouragement from their parents to *remain* children.

TASK: Dealing with Loss

In the years following divorce, children experience two profound losses. One is the loss of the intact family together with the symbolic and real protection it has provided. The second is the loss of the presence of one parent, usually the father, from their daily lives.   9

In dealing with these losses, children fall back on many fantasies to mask their unhappiness. As we have seen, they may idealize the father as representative of all that is lacking in their current lives, thinking that if only he were present, everything would be better.   10

The task of absorbing loss is perhaps the single most difficult task imposed by divorce. At its core, the task requires children to overcome the profound sense of rejection, humiliation, unlovability, and powerlessness they feel with the departure of one parent. When the parent leaves, children of all ages blame themselves. They say, "He left me because I was not lovable. I was not worthy." They conclude that had they been more lovable, worthy, or different, the parent would have stayed. In this way, the loss of the parent and lowered self-esteem become intertwined.   11

To stave off these intensely painful feelings of rejection, children continually try to undo the divorce scenario, to bring their parents back together, or to somehow win back the affection of the absent parent. The explanation "Had he loved me, he would not have left the family" turns into a new concern. "If he loved me, he would visit more often. He would spend more time with me." With this in mind, the children not only are pained at the   12 outset but remain vulnerable, sometimes increasingly, over the years. Many reach out during adolescence to increase contact with the parent who left, again to undo the sad scenario and to rebuild their self-esteem as well.

This task is easier if parents and children have a good relation- 13 ship, within the framework of a good visiting or joint custody arrangement.

Some children are able to use a good, close relationship with 14 the visiting parent to promote their growth within the divorced family. Others are able to acknowledge and accept that the visiting parent could never become the kind of parent they need, and they are able to turn away from blaming themselves. Still others are able to reject, on their own, a rejecting parent or to reject a role model that they see as flawed. In so doing, these youngsters are able to effectively master the loss and get on with their lives.

TASK: Dealing with Anger

Divorce, unlike death, is always a voluntary decision for at least 15 one of the partners in a marriage. Everyone involved knows this. The child understands that divorce is not a natural disaster like an earthquake or tornado; it is caused by the decision of one or both of the parents to separate. Its true cause lies in the parents' failure to maintain the marriage, and someone is culpable.

Given this knowledge, children face a terrible dilemma. They 16 know that their unhappiness has been caused by the very people charged with their protection and care—their parents are the agents of their distress. Furthermore, the parents undertook this role voluntarily. This realization puts children in a dreadful bind because they know something that they dare not express—out of fear, out of anxiety, out of a wish to protect their parents.

Children get angry at their parents, experiencing divorce as in- 17 difference to their needs and perceiving parents sometimes realistically as self-centered and uncaring, as preaching a corrupt morality, and as weak and unable to deal with problems except by running away.

At the same time, children are aware of their parents' needi- 18 ness, weaknesses, and anxiety about life's difficulties. Although children have little understanding of divorce, except when the fighting has been open and violent, they fully recognize how un-happy and disorganized their parents become, and this frightens them very much. Caught in a combination of anger and love, the children are frightened and guilty about their anger because they love their parents and perceive them as unhappy people who are trying to improve their lives in the face of severe obstacles. Their concern makes it difficult even to acknowledge their anger.

A major task, then, for children is to work through this anger, to recognize their parents as human beings capable of making mistakes, and to respect them for their real efforts and their real courage. 19

Cooling of anger and the task of forgiveness go hand in hand with children's growing emotional maturity and capacity to ap-preciate the various needs of the different family members. As anger diminishes, young people are better able to put the di-vorce behind them and experience relief. As children forgive their parents, they forgive themselves for feeling anger and guilt and for failing to restore the marriage. In this way, children can free themselves from identification with the angry or violent parent or with the victim. 20

TASK: Working Out Guilt

Young children often feel responsible for divorce, thinking that their misbehavior may have caused one parent to leave. Or, in a more complicated way, they may feel that their fantasy wish to drive a wedge between their mother and father has been magi-cally granted. Many guilty feelings arise at the time of divorce but dissipate naturally as children mature. Others persist, usually with roots in a profound continuing sense of having caused the un-thinkable—getting rid of one parent so as to be closer to the other. 21

Other feelings of guilt are rooted in children's realization that they were indeed a cause of marital difficulty. Many divorces occur after the birth of a child, and the child correctly compre-hends that he or she really did drive a wedge between the adults. 22

We see another kind of guilt in girls who, in identifying with their troubled mothers, become afraid to surpass their mothers. These young women have trouble separating from their mothers, 23 whom they love and feel sorry for, and establishing their own successful relationships with suitable young men. The children of divorce need to separate from guilty ties that bind them too closely to a troubled parent and to go on with their lives with compassion and love.

TASK: Accepting the Permanence of the Divorce

At first, children feel a strong and understandable need to deny   24
the divorce. Such early denial may be a first step in the coping process. Like a screen that is alternately lowered and raised, the denial helps children confront the full reality of the divorce, bit by bit. They cannot take it in all at once.

Nevertheless, we have learned that five and even ten years   25
after divorce, some children and adolescents refuse to accept the divorce as a permanent state of affairs. They continue to hope, consciously or unconsciously, that the marriage will be restored, finding omens of reconciliation even in a harmless handshake or a simple friendly nod.

In accepting permanence, the children of divorce face a more   26
difficult task than children of bereavement. Death cannot be undone, but divorce happens between living people who can change their minds. A reconciliation fantasy taps deep into children's psyches. Children need to feel that their parents will still be happy together. They may not overcome this fantasy of reconciliation until they themselves finally separate from their parents and leave home.

TASK: Taking a Chance on Love

This is perhaps the most important task for growing children   27
and for society. Despite what life has dealt them, despite lingering fears and anxieties, the children of divorce must grow, become open to the possibility of success or failure, and take a chance on love. They must hold on to a realistic vision that they can both love and be loved.

This is the central task for youngsters during adolescence and   28
at entry into young adulthood. And as we have seen, it is the task on which so many children tragically flounder. Children who lose a parent through death must take a chance on loving with the knowledge that all people eventually die and that death can

take away our loved ones at any time. Children who lose the intact family through divorce must also take a chance on love, knowing realistically that divorce is always possible but being willing nevertheless to remain open to love, commitment, marriage, and fidelity.

More than the ideology of hoping to fall in love and find 29 commitment, this task involves being able to turn away from the model of parents who could not stay committed to each other. While all the young people in our study were in search of romantic love, a large number of them lived with such a high degree of anxiety over fears of betrayal or of not finding love that they were entirely unable to take the kind of chances necessary for them to move emotionally into successful young adulthood.

This last task, taking a chance on love, involves being able to 30 venture, not just thinking about it, and not thinking one way and behaving another. It involves accepting a morality that truly guides behavior. This is the task that occupies children of divorce throughout their adolescence. It is what makes adolescence such a critical and difficult time for them. The resolution of life's tasks is a relative process that never ends, but this last task, which is built on successfully negotiating all the others, leads to psychological freedom from the past. This is the essence of second chances for children of divorce.

UNDERSTANDING DETAILS

1. Name the seven categories into which Wallerstein and Blakeslee divide the psychological growth of the children of divorce. How long will it take most children to perform these tasks?
2. Choose one of these tasks and explain it in your own words.
3. According to Wallerstein and Blakeslee, what is probably the most difficult task that results from divorce? Why do the authors believe this stage is so painful?
4. What did Wallerstein and Blakeslee find out about their subjects' ability to deal with love in their lives?

ANALYZING MEANING

1. In your opinion, which of the emotional tasks that Wallerstein and Blakeslee describe is likely to be most traumatic in a child's

life after a divorce? On what do you base your conclusion?

2. What is the relationship suggested in this essay between the parents' divorce and a child's sense of rejection?

3. In what ways does dealing with all facets of their anger create a problem for children of divorce? Do you know anyone who has worked through such a problem? Explain your answer in detail.

4. How might an understanding of the seven tasks discussed in this essay help people deal more effectively with children affected by divorce?

DISCOVERING RHETORICAL STRATEGIES

1. How do Wallerstein and Blakeslee organize their categories in this essay? Why do they place these tasks in this particular order?

2. What is the authors' general attitude toward divorce? What references in the essay reveal this point of view?

3. Describe the authors' intended audience. What makes you think they are directing their comments to this group?

4. What other rhetorical modes do Wallerstein and Blakeslee use in this essay besides division and classification? How do these other modes support the authors' division/classification system?

MAKING CONNECTIONS

1. Compare and contrast the love and support needed by children of divorce with the love and support provided naturally by the non-Western families described in Germaine Greer's "A Child Is Born." Do children of divorce need anything, according to Wallerstein and Blakeslee, that would not be furnished by a typical non-Western family? If so, what would it be?

2. What are the principal differences between Wallerstein and Blakeslee's prescriptions for how a child can best cope with the death of his or her parents' relationship and the way in which funeral directors in Jessica Mitford's "Behind the Formaldehyde Curtain" help us endure the death of a friend or relative? Which coping mechanisms are the same? Which are different?

3. Wallerstein and Blakeslee divide their essay into seven "tasks" that must be accomplished by children of divorce. Find a division/classification essay in this section of *The Prose Reader* that has more subdivisions. Then, find one that has fewer. How does the number of subdivisions in a division/classification essay affect your ability to understand the author's entire argument? Which of these essays is the easiest to follow? Which is the most difficult? Why?

IDEAS FOR DISCUSSION/WRITING

Preparing to Write

Write freely about your thoughts on divorce and the effects of divorce on others: Do you know anyone who has gone through a divorce? How did the experience affect the couple getting divorced? How did it affect their friends, their relatives, and their children? How do you think the high divorce rate is affecting Americans in general? Why is America's national divorce rate so high? What changes could we make to lower the divorce rate?

Choosing a Topic

1. Assume that you are an expert on the variety and scope of college relationships. In an essay written for your classmates, divide your observations on different types of relationships into categories that will show students the full range of these associations in a college setting.
2. Because you have been involved with divorce in some way, you have been asked to submit to your college newspaper an editorial classifying the various ways in which different types of people react to divorce (husbands, wives, children, friends, and so on). You have been told to pay particular attention to the reactions of college students whose parents are going through or have gone through a divorce.
3. In an essay written for the general public, speculate about the reasons for the high national divorce rate. Use your own experience, interview others, or consult sources in the library to investigate the reasons for this trend. Suggest how we could solve this problem in America.

FRANKLIN ZIMRING (1942 –   )

■ ■ ■

Confessions of an Ex-Smoker

Born in Los Angeles, Franklin Zimring earned his B.A. at Wayne State University and his law degree at the University of Chicago and then served for ten years as the director of the Center for Studies in Criminal Justice at the University of Chicago before moving to his present post as director of the Earl Warren Legal Institute at the University of California at Berkeley. A specialist in legal policy and institutions, he has published a number of books on a wide variety of topics, many of which were coauthored with colleague Gordon Hawkins, including *The Citizen's Guide to Gun Control* (1987), *Social Control of the Drinking Driver* (1988), *Pornography in a Free Society* (1989), *The Scale of Imprisonment* (1991), *The Search for Rational Drug Control* (1992), and *Incapacitation: Penal Confinement and the Restraint of Crime* (1995). His advice to students using *The Prose Reader* is to "listen to your own internal prompter as you write." A great believer in E. M. Forster's famous question "How do I know what I think till I see what I say?," Zimring counsels students to "relax and decide what you really think about a topic, and then express it as clearly and concisely as possible." The author's own relaxation comes from the sport of swimming, to which he confesses a "religious devotion."

Preparing to Read

Originally published in *Newsweek* magazine (20 April 1987), the following article is one in a series of "Mid-Life Memoranda" that Zimring has been writing since 1985. It offers a witty classification of ex-smokers into four distinct groups: zealots, evangelists, the elect, and the serene. As you prepare to read this essay, think for a few moments about your own addictions: Have you ever had any addictions? Were they good addictions or bad? Are any of these addictions still with you? Why are these addictions part of your life? Do you want to change the status of these addictions? Why or why not? What do you think causes people to be addicted to certain substances or behavior? How can we break away from addictions successfully?

—— ∎

Americans can be divided into three groups—smokers, 1 nonsmokers and that expanding pack of us who have quit. Those who have never smoked don't know what they're missing, but former smokers, ex-smokers, reformed smokers can never forget. We are veterans of a personal war, linked by that watershed experience of ceasing to smoke and by the temptation to have just one more cigarette. For almost all of us ex-smokers, smoking continues to play an important part in our lives. And now that it is being restricted in restaurants around the country and will be banned in almost all indoor public places in New York State starting next month, it is vital that everyone understand the different emotional states cessation of smoking can cause. I have observed four of them; and in the interest of science I have classified them as those of the zealot, the evangelist, the elect and the serene. Each day, each category gains new recruits.

Not all antitobacco zealots are former smokers, but a substan- 2 tial number of fire-and-brimstone opponents do come from the ranks of the reformed. Zealots believe that those who continue to smoke are degenerates who deserve scorn not pity and the penalties that will deter offensive behavior in public as well. Relations between these people and those who continue to smoke are strained.

One explanation for the zealot's fervor in seeking to outlaw 3 tobacco consumption is his own tenuous hold on abstaining from smoking. But I think part of the emotional force arises from sheer envy as he watches and identifies with each lung-filling puff. By making smoking in public a crime, the zealot seeks reassurance that he will not revert to bad habits; give him strong social penalties and he won't become a recidivist.

No systematic survey has been done yet, but anecdotal evi- 4 dence suggests that a disproportionate number of doctors who have quit smoking can be found among the fanatics. Just as the most enthusiastic revolutionary tends to make the most enthusiastic counterrevolutionary, many of today's vitriolic zealots include those who had been deeply committed to tobacco habits.

By contrast, the antismoking evangelist does not condemn 5 smokers. Unlike the zealot, he regards smoking as an easily curable condition, as a social disease, and not a sin. The evangelist spends an enormous amount of time seeking and preaching to the unconverted. He argues that kicking the habit is not *that* difficult. After all, *he* did it; moreover, as he describes it, the benefits of quitting are beyond measure and the disadvantages are nil.

The hallmark of the evangelist is his insistence that he never 6 misses tobacco. Though he is less hostile to smokers than the zealot, he is resented more. Friends and loved ones who have been the targets of his preachments frequently greet the resumption of smoking by the evangelist as an occasion for unmitigated glee.

Among former smokers, the distinctions between the evange- 7 list and the elect are much the same as the differences between proselytizing and nonproselytizing religious sects. While the evangelists preach the ease and desirability of abstinence, the elect do not attempt to convert their friends. They think that virtue is its own reward and subscribe to the Puritan theory of predestination. Since they have proved themselves capable of abstaining from tobacco, they are therefore different from friends and relatives who continue to smoke. They feel superior, secure that their salvation was foreordained. These ex-smokers rarely give personal testimony on their conversion. They rarely speak about their tobacco habits, while evangelists talk about little else. Of course, active smokers find such blue-nosed behavior far less offensive than that of the evangelist or the zealot, yet they resent the elect simply because they are smug. Their air of self-satisfaction rarely escapes the notice of those lighting up. For active smokers, life with a member of the ex-smoking elect is less stormy than with a zealot or evangelist, but it is subtly oppressive nonetheless.

I have labeled my final category of former smokers the serene. 8 This classification is meant to encourage those who find the other psychic styles of ex-smokers disagreeable. Serenity is quieter than zealotry and evangelism, and those who qualify are not as self-righteous as the elect. The serene ex-smoker accepts himself and also accepts those around him who continue to smoke. This kind of serenity does not come easily nor does it seem to be an immediate option for those who have stopped. Rather it is a goal, an end stage in a process of development during which some former smokers progress through one or more of the less-than-positive psychological points en route. For former smokers, serenity is thus a positive possibility that exists at the end of the rainbow. But all former smokers cannot reach that promised land.

What is it that permits some former smokers to become   9
serene? I think the key is self-acceptance and gratitude. The fully mature former smoker knows he has the soul of an addict and is grateful for the knowledge. He may sit up front in an airplane, but he knows he belongs in the smoking section in back. He doesn't regret that he quit smoking, nor any of his previous adventures with tobacco. As a former smoker, he is grateful for the experience and memory of craving a cigarette.

Serenity comes from accepting the lessons of one's life. And   10
ex-smokers who have reached this point in their world view have much to be grateful for. They have learned about the potential and limits of change. In becoming the right kind of former smoker, they developed a healthy sense of self. This former smoker, for one, believes that it is better to crave (one hopes only occasionally) and not to smoke than never to have craved at all. And by accepting that fact, the reformed smoker does not need to excoriate, envy or disassociate himself from those who continue to smoke.

UNDERSTANDING DETAILS

1. What are the four categories of reformed smokers that Zimring has observed? What characterizes each type?
2. What is the difference between the "elect" and the "serene" ex-smokers according to the author?
3. What is the general purpose of this division/classification essay?
4. How are becoming "the right kind of former smoker" and "a healthy sense of self" (paragraph 10) related? How do they affect one another?

ANALYZING MEANING

1. How does Zimring portray smokers in this essay? What effect does this attitude have on the rest of the essay?
2. What type of ex-smoker do you think would be most difficult to live with and why?

3. Why do you think many doctors who stop smoking become zealots?

4. Do you agree with Zimring that the key to being a "serene" ex-smoker is "self-acceptance and gratitude" (paragraph 9)? Are these positive qualities in an ex-smoker? Explain your answer in detail.

DISCOVERING RHETORICAL STRATEGIES

1. Who do you think is Zimring's specific audience for this essay? Explain your answer.

2. What do you think is Zimring's purpose in writing this essay? How did you come to this conclusion?

3. Zimring discusses these types of reformed smokers in a specific order. Explain this progression and discuss whether it is effective in achieving Zimring's overall purpose.

4. What rhetorical modes support the author's division/classification? Give examples of each.

MAKING CONNECTIONS

1. Compare Zimring's description of the addictive nature of tobacco with Michael Dorris's account of alcohol addiction in "The Broken Cord." Which substance do you think is most addictive? Explain your answer.

2. Use Zimring's definition of a "zealot" to help analyze essays by Mitchell Lazarus ("Rx for Mathophobia"), Donald Drakeman ("Religion's Place in Public Schools"), and Robert Hughes ("The N.R.A. in a Hunter's Sights"). To what extent are these authors zealots in support of their cause? Which author is most passionate in his opinion? Which is the least? Are you zealous about any particular issue? If so, which one? What is your personal opinion about this issue?

3. Examine Germaine Greer's "A Child Is Born," Jessica Mitford's "Behind the Formaldehyde Curtain," and Judy Brady's "Why I Want a Wife" in order to determine whether any of these authors has reached Zimring's level of "serenity" in life? Which of these writers would you characterize as "zealots"? Which as "evangelists"? Which as "the elect"? What are the principal differences in the approaches of these three authors?

IDEAS FOR DISCUSSION/WRITING

Preparing to Write

Write freely about the role addiction plays in our lives in America: What do you know about addiction in general? What different substances and activities can people be addicted to? How can they break an addiction? What addictions are most dominant in American society? In what ways have you avoided addiction? In what ways are you addicted? What are your worst addictions? What are some of your friends' addictions? What do your addictions say about your personality? What do your friends' addictions say about them? What are some of America's major addictions? How could we alleviate these problems?

Choosing a Topic

1. Your high school graduating class has decided to put together a brochure for students starting high school about substance abuse and addiction. You have been asked to explain addiction and its consequences to this audience. Make your essay as vivid as possible.

2. Pretend that your college newspaper is running a special issue distinguishing between different generations of students. In a coherent essay written for the readers of this newspaper, classify the students of your generation in some logical, interesting fashion. Remember that classification is a rhetorical movement from "many" to "one." Group the members of your generation by some meaningful guidelines or general characteristics that you establish. Be sure to decide on a purpose and a point of view before you begin to write.

3. You have had many different types of friends over the years. Discuss one type of friend by dividing into logical categories the actual behavior of that type of person. Discuss each part of your division, giving examples as frequently as possible. Decide on a purpose and a point of view before you begin to write.

JUDITH VIORST   (1931 –   )

■ ■ ■

The Truth About Lying

A poet, journalist, writer of children's books, and contributing editor of *Redbook* magazine, Judith Viorst reached the top of the *New York Times* best-seller list with *Necessary Losses* (1986), a detailed examination of "the loves, illusions, dependencies, and impossible expectations that all of us have to give up in order to grow." She earned her B.A. at Rutgers University in 1952 and began writing poetry. These early efforts, she claims, were "terrible poems about dead dogs, mostly, . . . the meaning of life, death, pain, lust, and suicide." Her first complete book of poetry, however, entitled *The Village Square* (1965), was quite successful, as were such subsequent volumes as *People and Other Aggravations* (1971), *How Did I Get to Be Forty and Other Atrocities* (1976), *Love and Guilt and the Meaning of Life* (1984), and *Forever Fifty and Other Negotiations* (1989). Additional publications include *The Washington, D.C. Underground Gourmet* (1970), *Yes, Married: A Saga of Love and Complaint* (1972), *Love and Guilt and the Meaning of Life, Etc.* (1979), *Necessary Losses* (1986), *The Good-bye Book* (1988), *Earrings!* (1990), and several books for children. The author lives in Washington with her husband, Milton Viorst (a syndicated political columnist), and their three sons.

Preparing to Read

"The Truth About Lying," originally published in the March 1981 issue of *Redbook* magazine, classifies and describes the different categories of lies we all experience at some point in our lives. As you prepare to read this essay, take a few moments to consider various lies you have told: Under what conditions are you tempted to lie? When have you actually lied? Why did you do so? Can you generalize about the types of lies you habitually tell? Are you irritated when people lie to you? Why or why not? In what circumstances might lying be acceptable? Why?

I 've been wanting to write on a subject that intrigues and 1
challenges me: the subject of lying. I've found it very difficult
to do. Everyone I've talked to has a quite intense and personal but often rather intolerant point of view about what we
can—and can never *never*—tell lies about. I've finally reached the
conclusion that I can't present any ultimate conclusions, for too
many people would promptly disagree. Instead, I'd like to present
a series of moral puzzles, all concerned with lying. I'll tell you
what I think about them. Do you agree?

Social Lies

Most of the people I've talked with say that they find social 2
lying acceptable and necessary. They think it's the civilized way
for folks to behave. Without these little white lies, they say, our
relationships would be short and brutish and nasty. It's arrogant,
they say, to insist on being so incorruptible and so brave that you
cause other people unnecessary embarrassment or pain by com-
pulsively assailing them with your honesty. I basically agree. What
about you?

Will you say to people, when it simply isn't true, "I like your 3
new hairdo," "You're looking much better," "It's so nice to see
you," "I had a wonderful time"?

Will you praise hideous presents and homely kids? 4

Will you decline invitations with "We're busy that night—so 5
sorry we can't come," when the truth is you'd rather stay home
than dine with the So-and-sos?

And even though, as I do, you may prefer the polite evasion of 6
"You really cooked up a storm" instead of "The soup"—which
tastes like warmed-over coffee—"is wonderful," will you, if you
must, proclaim it wonderful?

There's one man I know who absolutely refuses to tell social 7
lies. "I can't play that game," he says; "I'm simply not made that
way." And his answer to the argument that saying nice things to
someone doesn't cost anything is, "Yes, it does—it destroys your
credibility." Now, he won't, unsolicited, offer his views on the
painting you just bought, but you don't ask his frank opinion unless you want *frank*, and his silence at those moments when the
rest of us liars are muttering, "Isn't it lovely?" is, for the most part,
eloquent enough. My friend does not indulge in what he calls

"flattery, false praise and mellifluous comments." When others tell fibs he will not go along. He says that social lying is lying, that little white lies are still lies. And he feels that telling lies is morally wrong. What about you?

Peace-Keeping Lies

Many people tell peace-keeping lies; lies designed to avoid irritation or argument; lies designed to shelter the liar from possible blame or pain; lies (or so it is rationalized) designed to keep trouble at bay without hurting anyone. 8

I tell these lies at times, and yet I always feel they're wrong. I understand why we tell them, but still they feel wrong. And whenever I lie so that someone won't disapprove of me or think less of me or holler at me, I feel I'm a bit of a coward, I feel I'm dodging responsibility, I feel . . . guilty. What about you? 9

Do you, when you're late for a date because you overslept, say that you're late because you got caught in a traffic jam? 10

Do you, when you forget to call a friend, say that you called several times but the line was busy? 11

Do you, when you didn't remember that it was your father's birthday, say that his present must be delayed in the mail? 12

And when you're planning a weekend in New York City and you're not in the mood to visit your mother, who lives there, do you conceal—with a lie, if you must—the fact that you'll be in New York? Or do you have the courage—or is it the cruelty?—to say, "I'll be in New York, but sorry—I don't plan on seeing you"? 13

(Dave and his wife Elaine have two quite different points of view on this very subject. He calls her a coward. She says she's being wise. He says she must assert her right to visit New York sometimes and not see her mother. To which she always patiently replies: "Why should we have useless fights? My mother's too old to change. We get along much better when I lie to her.") 14

Finally, do you keep the peace by telling your husband lies on the subject of money? Do you reduce what you really paid for your shoes? And in general do you find yourself ready, willing and able to lie to him when you make absurd mistakes or lose or break things? 15

"I used to have a romantic idea that part of intimacy was confessing every dumb thing that you did to your husband. But after a couple of years of that," says Laura, "have I changed my mind!" 16

And having changed her mind, she finds herself telling peace- 17
keeping lies. And yes, I tell them too. What about you?

Protective Lies

Protective lies are lies folks tell—often quite serious lies—be- 18
cause they're convinced that the truth would be too damaging.
They lie because they feel there are certain human values that su-
persede the wrong of having lied. They lie, not for personal gain,
but because they believe it's for the good of the person they're
lying to. They lie to those they love, to those who trust them
most of all, on the grounds that breaking this trust is justified.

They may lie to their children on money or marital matters. 19

They may lie to the dying about the state of their health. 20

They may lie about adultery, and not—or so they insist—to 21
save their own hide, but to save the heart and the pride of the
men they are married to.

They may lie to their closest friend because the truth about 22
her talents or son or psyche would be—or so they insist—utterly
devastating.

I sometimes tell such lies, but I'm aware that it's quite pre- 23
sumptuous to claim I know what's best for others to know. That's
called playing God. That's called manipulation and control. And
we never can be sure, once we start to juggle lies, just where
they'll land, exactly where they'll roll.

And furthermore, we may find ourselves lying in order to back 24
up the lies that are backing up the lie we initially told.

And furthermore—let's be honest—if conditions were re- 25
versed, we certainly wouldn't want anyone lying to us.

Yet, having said all that, I still believe that there are times when 26
protective lies must nonetheless be told. What about you?

If your Dad had a very bad heart and you had to tell him some 27
bad family news, which would you choose: to tell him the truth
or lie?

If your former husband failed to send his monthly child- 28
support check and in other ways behaved like a total rat, would
you allow your children—who believed he was simply wonderful—to continue to believe that he was wonderful?

If your dearly beloved brother selected a wife whom you deeply 29
disliked, would you reveal your feelings or would you fake it?

And if you were asked, after making love, "And how was that 30
for you?" would you reply, if it wasn't too good, "Not too good"?

Now, some would call a sex lie unimportant, little more than 31
social lying, a simple act of courtesy that makes all human intercourse run smoothly. And some would say all sex lies are bad
news and unacceptably protective. Because, says Ruth, "a man
with an ego that fragile doesn't need your lies—he needs a psy-
chiatrist." Still others feel that sex lies are indeed protective lies,
more serious than simple social lying, and yet at times they tell
them on the grounds that when it comes to matters sexual,
everybody's ego is somewhat fragile.

"If most of the time things go well in sex," says Sue, "I think 32
you're allowed to dissemble when they don't. I can't believe it's
good to say, 'Last night was four stars, darling, but tonight's performance rates only a half.'"

I'm inclined to agree with Sue. What about you? 33

Trust-Keeping Lies

Another group of lies are trust-keeping lies, lies that involve 34
triangulation, with *A* (that's you) telling lies to *B* on behalf of *C*
(whose trust you'd promised to keep). Most people concede that
once you've agreed not to betray a friend's confidence, you can't
betray it, even if you must lie. But I've talked with people who
don't want you telling them anything that they might be called
on to lie about.

"I don't tell lies for myself," says Fran, "and I don't want to 35
have to tell them for other people." Which means, she agrees, that
if her best friend is having an affair, she absolutely doesn't want to
know about it.

"Are you saying," her best friend asks, "that if I went off with a 36
lover and I asked you to tell my husband I'd been with you, that
you wouldn't lie for me, that you'd betray me?"

Fran is very pained but very adamant. "I wouldn't want to be- 37
tray you, so . . . don't ask me."

Fran's best friend is shocked. What about you? 38

Do you believe you can have close friends if you're not pre- 39
pared to receive their deepest secrets?

Do you believe you must always lie for your friends? 40

Do you believe, if your friend tells a secret that turns out to be 41 quite immoral or illegal, that once you've promised to keep it, you must keep it?

And what if your friend were your boss—if you were perhaps   42
one of the President's men—would you betray or lie for him over, say, Watergate?

As you can see, these issues get terribly sticky.   43

It's my belief that once we've promised to keep a trust, we   44
must tell lies to keep it. I also believe that we can't tell Watergate lies. And if these two statements strike you as quite contradictory, you're right—they're quite contradictory. But for now they're the best I can do. What about you?

Some say that truth will out and thus you might as well tell   45
the truth. Some say you can't regain the trust that lies lose. Some say that even though the truth may never be revealed, our lies pervert and damage our relationships. Some say . . . well, here's what some of them have to say.

"I'm a coward," says Grace, "about telling close people impor-   46
tant, difficult truths. I find that I'm unable to carry it off. And so if something is bothering me, it keeps building up inside till I end up just not seeing them any more."

"I lie to my husband on sexual things, but I'm furious," says   47
Joyce, "that he's too insensitive to know I'm lying."

"I suffer most from the misconception that children can't take   48
the truth," says Emily. "But I'm starting to see that what's harder and more damaging for them is being told lies, is *not* being told the truth."

"I'm afraid," says Joan, "that we often wind up feeling a bit of   49
contempt for the people we lie to."

And then there are those who have no talent for lying.   50

"Over the years, I tried to lie," a friend of mine explained, "but   51
I always got found out and I always got punished. I guess I gave myself away because I feel guilty about any kind of lying. It looks as if I'm stuck with telling the truth."

For those of us, however, who are good at telling lies, for those   52
of us who lie and don't get caught, the question of whether or not to lie can be a hard and serious moral problem. I liked the re- mark of a friend of mine who said, "I'm willing to lie. But just as a last resort—the truth's always better."

"Because," he explained, "though others may completely ac-   53
cept the lie I'm telling, I don't."

I tend to feel that way too.   54

What about you?   55

UNDERSTANDING DETAILS

1. Viorst discusses four types of lies in this essay. Explain each in your own words.
2. What types of lies are most serious? What does the author mean by "serious"?
3. What does Viorst mean by "Watergate lies" in paragraph 44? What is your feeling about this level of trust-keeping lies?
4. According to Viorst, what is the relationship between lying and her self-image?

ANALYZING MEANING

1. In what ways is lying a moral problem?
2. Why do people respond in so many different ways to the issue of lying?
3. In your opinion or experience, what are the principal consequences of lying? Do the negative consequences outweigh the positive, or is the reverse true? Explain your answer in as much detail as possible.
4. How do you feel about lying? Does your opinion vary according to the type of lie you tell? Why? Explain your answer in detail.

DISCOVERING RHETORICAL STRATEGIES

1. In this essay, Viorst works with both division and classification as she arranges lies into several distinct categories. Write down the main subdivisions of her classification system; then, list under each category the examples she cites. How has she organized these categories? Do all her examples support the appropriate classification? How does she give significance or value to this system of classification?
2. Who do you think is Viorst's intended audience? What specific verbal clues in the essay help you reach this conclusion?
3. Notice that the author repeats the question "What about you?" several times. What effect does this repetition have on your response to the essay?

4. What other rhetorical modes besides division/classification does Viorst use to make her point in the essay? Give specific examples to support your answers.

MAKING CONNECTIONS

1. If Judith Viorst read Alleen Pace Nilsen's "Sexism in English: A 1990s Update," how would she classify most of the lies about women contained in the English language? Select five different linguistic "lies," and explain the purpose of each.

2. In "Triple Tragedy in Black Society," Harry Edwards exposes the "lie" that sports provide African American athletes with the opportunity for "social and economic mobility." Would Viorst agree with Edwards that these athletes have been lied to? If so, by whom and for what purpose?

3. How separate and exclusive are Viorst's categories of lies? Could some lies fit within two categories at the same time? Examine Franklin Zimring's "Confessions of an Ex-Smoker" and/or William Golding's "Thinking as a Hobby" to determine if either of these authors' categories overlap in the same way that Viorst's do. Do division/classification essays work better if there is little or no overlap between categories? If so, why?

IDEAS FOR DISCUSSION/WRITING

Preparing to Write

Write freely about various lies you have told in the past: When did you lie? When did you consider lying but told the truth? In what types of situations do you most often resort to lying? Why do you lie in these circumstances? How does lying make you feel? How does telling the truth make you feel? Do you have a general philosophy about lying that you try to follow? If so, what is it?

Choosing a Topic

1. At some time in our lives, we all tell or receive lies as Viorst defines them. Choose a particularly memorable lie (one you either told or received), and classify all your feelings connected with the experience. What did you learn from the situation?

2. You have decided that your future roommate/spouse deserves an honest profile of your personality before you begin living

together. Analyze for him or her some fundamental truths about your character by classifying your reactions to the information in one of the categories in Viorst's essay.

3. Being in school presents a number of potential opportunities for lying. Answers to such questions as "Why is your homework late?" "Why can't you go out this weekend?" and "Why did you miss class yesterday?" can get people *into* or *out* of all sorts of trouble. For a friend of yours still in high school, write an essay offering advice on handling situations such as these. Devise a useful classification system for these school-related dilemmas; then, explain what your experiences have taught you in each case about lying.

6

Comparison/Contrast

Discovering Similarities and Differences

Making comparisons is such a natural and necessary part of our everyday lives that we often do so without conscious effort. When we were children, we compared our toys with those of our friends, we contrasted our height and physical development to other children's, and we constantly evaluated our happiness in comparison with that evidenced by our parents and childhood companions. As we grew older, we habitually compared our dates, teachers, parents, friends, cars, and physical attributes. In college, we learn about anthropology by writing essays on the similarities and differences between two African tribes, about political science by contrasting the Republican and Democratic platforms, about business by comparing annual production rates, and about literature by comparing Shakespeare with Marlowe or Browning with Tennyson. Comparing and contrasting various elements in our lives helps us make decisions, such as which course to take or which house to buy, and it justifies preferences that we already hold, such as liking one city more than another or loving one person more than the next. In these ways and in many others, the skillful use of comparison and contrast is clearly essential to our social and professional lives.

DEFINING COMPARISON/CONTRAST

Comparison and contrast allow us to understand one subject by putting it next to another. Comparing involves discovering likenesses or similarities, whereas contrasting is based on finding differences. Like division and classification, comparison and contrast are generally considered part of the same process, because we usually have no reason for comparing unless some contrast is also involved. Each technique implies the existence of the other. For this reason, the word *compare* is often used to mean both techniques.

Comparison and contrast are most profitably applied to two items that have something in common, such as cats and dogs or cars and motorcycles. A discussion of cats and motorcycles, for example, would probably not be very rewarding or stimulating, because they do not have much in common. If more than two items are compared in an essay, they are still most profitably discussed in pairs: for instance, motorcycles and cars, cars and bicycles, or bicycles and motorcycles.

An analogy is an extended, sustained comparison. Often used to explain unfamiliar, abstract, or complicated thoughts, this rhetorical technique adds energy and vividness to a wide variety of college-level writing. The process of analogy differs slightly from comparison/contrast in three important ways: Comparison/ contrast begins with subjects from the same class and places equal weight on both of them. In addition, it addresses both the similarities and the differences of these subjects. Analogy, conversely, seldom explores subjects from the same class and focuses principally on one familiar subject in an attempt to explain another, more complex one. Furthermore, it deals only with similarities, not with contrasts. A comparison/contrast essay, for example, might study two veterans' ways of coping with the trauma of the Gulf War by pointing out the differences in their methods as well as the similarities. An analogy essay might use the familiar notion of a fireworks display to reveal the chilling horror of the lonely hours after dark during this war: "Nights in the Persian Gulf were similar to a loud, unending fireworks display. We had no idea when the next blast was coming, how loud it would be, or how close. We cringed in terror after dark, hoping the next surprise would not be our own death." In this example, rather than simply hearing about an event, we participate in it through this highly refined form of comparison.

The following student paragraph compares and contrasts married and single life. As you read it, notice how the author compares similar social states and, in the process, justifies her current lifestyle:

> *Recently I saw a bumper sticker that read, "It used to be wine, women, and song, and now it's beer, the old lady, and TV." Much truth may be found in this comparison of single and married lifestyles. When my husband and I used to date, for example, we'd go out for dinner and drinks and then maybe see a play or concert. Our discussions were intelligent, often ranging over global politics, science, literature, and other lofty topics. He would open doors for me, buy me flowers, and make sure I was comfortable and happy. Now, three years later, after marriage and a child, the baby bottle has replaced the wine bottle, the smell of diapers wipes out the scent of roses, and our nights on the town are infrequent, cherished events. But that's OK. A little bit of the excitement and mystery may be gone, but these intangible qualities have given way to a sturdy, dependable trust in each other and a quiet confidence about our future together.*

THINKING CRITICALLY BY USING COMPARISON/CONTRAST

Comparison and contrast are basic to a number of different thought processes. We compare and contrast quite naturally on a daily basis, but all of us would benefit greatly from being more aware of these companion strategies in our own writing. They help us not only in perceiving our environment but also in understanding and organizing large amounts of information.

The basic skill of finding similarities and differences will enhance your ability to create accurate descriptions, to cite appropriate examples, to present a full process analysis, and, of course, to classify and label subjects. It is a pattern of thought that is essential to more complex thinking strategies, so perfecting the ability to use it is an important step in your efforts to improve your critical thinking.

Once again, we are going to practice this strategy in isolation to get a strong sense of its mechanics before we combine it with other rhetorical modes. Isolating this mode will make your reading and writing even stronger than they are now, because the individual parts of the thinking process will be more vigorous and effective, thus making your academic performance more powerful than ever.

1. Find magazine ads that use comparison/contrast to make a point or sell a product. What is the basis of each comparison? How effective or ineffective is each comparison?
2. Compare or contrast the experience of spending time with a special person to another type of experience (e.g., a roller-coaster ride, drowning, sleeping, or a trip across the United States). Be as specific as possible in your comparison.
3. Have you ever been to the same place twice? Think for a moment about how the first and second visits to this place differed? How were they similar? What were the primary reasons for the similarities and differences in your perceptions of these visits?

READING AND WRITING COMPARISON/CONTRAST ESSAYS

Many established guidelines regulate the development of a comparison/contrast essay and should be taken into account from both the reading and the writing perspectives. All good comparative studies serve a specific purpose. They attempt either to examine their subjects separately or to demonstrate the superiority of one over the other. In evaluating two different types of cars, for example, a writer might point out the amazing gas mileage of one model and the smooth handling qualities of the other or the superiority of one car's gas mileage over that of the other. Whatever the intent, comparison/contrast essays need to be clear and logical and to have a precise purpose.

How to Read a Comparison/Contrast Essay

Preparing to Read. As you begin reading this chapter, pull together as much preliminary material as possible for each essay so you can focus your attention and have the benefit of prior knowledge before you start to read. In particular, you are trying to discover what is being compared or contrasted and why. From the title of his essay, can you tell what Bruce Catton is comparing in "Grant and Lee: A Study in Contrasts"? What does William Ouchi's title ("Japanese and American Workers: Two Casts of Mind") suggest to you? From glancing at the essay itself and reading the synopsis in the Rhetorical Table of Contents, what does Joyce Carol Oates's essay try to accomplish?

Also, before you begin to read these essays, try to discover information about the author and about the conditions under which each essay was written. Why is Ouchi qualified to write about Japanese and American workers? Does he reveal his background in his essay? What is Germaine Greer's stand on childbirth customs in the Middle East? To what extent do you expect her opinions on this topic to color her comparison of these customs in the Middle East and America?

Finally, just before you begin to read, answer the Preparing to Read questions, and then, make some free associations with the general topic of each essay: For example, what do you think are some of the similarities and differences in childbirth customs between Third World countries and the Western world (Germaine Greer)? What is your general view on women's bodybuilding (Gloria Steinem)?

Reading. As you read each comparison/contrast essay for the first time, be sure to record your own feelings and opinions. Some of the issues presented in this chapter are highly controversial. You will often have strong reactions to them, which you should try to write down as soon as possible.

In addition, you may want to comment on the relationship between the preliminary essay material, the author's stance in the essay, and the content of the essay itself. For example, what motivated Steinem to write "The Politics of Muscle"? Who is her primary audience? What is Oates's tone in "On Boxing," and how does it further her purpose? Answers to questions such as these will provide you with a context for your first reading of these essays and will assist you in preparing to analyze the essays in more depth on your second reading.

At this point in the chapter, you should make certain you understand each author's thesis and then take a close look at his or her principal method of organization: Is the essay arranged (1) point by point, (2) subject by subject, (3) as a combination of these two, or (4) as separate discussions of similarities and differences between two subjects? (See the chart on page 340 for an illustration of these options.) Last, preview the questions that follow the essay before you read it again.

Rereading. When you read these essays a second time, you should look at the comparison or contrast much more closely than you have up to now. First, look in detail at the writer's method of organization (see the chart on page 340). How effective is it in advancing the writer's thesis?

Next, you should consider whether each essay is fully developed and balanced: Does Catton compare similar items? Does Greer discuss the same qualities of her subjects? Does Ouchi deal with all aspects of the comparison between Japanese and American workers? Is Steinem's treatment of her subjects well balanced? And does Oates give her audience enough specific details to clarify the extent of her comparison? Do all the writers in this chapter use well-chosen transitions so you can move smoothly from one point to the next? Also, what other rhetorical modes support each comparison/contrast in this chapter?

Finally, the answers to the questions after each selection will let you evaluate your understanding of the essay and help you analyze its contents in preparation for the discussion/writing topics that follow.

For a more thorough inventory of the reading process, you should turn to pages 20–21 in the Introduction.

How to Write a Comparison/Contrast Essay

Preparing to Write. As you consider various topics for a comparison/contrast essay, you should answer the Preparing to Write questions that precede the assignments and then use the prewriting techniques explained in the Introduction to generate even more ideas on these topics.

As you focus your attention on a particular topic, keep the following suggestions in mind:

1. Always compare/contrast items in the same category (e.g., compare two professors, but not a professor and a swimming pool).
2. Have a specific purpose or reason for writing your essay.
3. Discuss the same qualities of each subject (if you evaluate the teaching techniques of one professor, do so for the other professor as well).
4. Use as many pertinent details as possible to expand your comparison/contrast and to accomplish your stated purpose.
5. Deal with all aspects of the comparison that are relevant to the purpose.
6. Balance the treatment of the different subjects of your comparison (i.e., don't spend more time on one than on another).
7. Determine your audience's background and knowledge so that you will know how much of your comparison should be explained in detail and how much can be skimmed over.

Next, in preparation for a comparison/contrast project, you might list all the elements of both subjects that you want to compare. This list can then help you give your essay structure as well as substance. At this stage in the writing process, the task may seem similar to pure description, but a discussion of two subjects in relation to one another rapidly changes the assignment from description to comparison.

Writing. The introduction of your comparison/contrast essay should (1) clearly identify your subjects, (2) explain the basis of your comparison/contrast, and (3) state your purpose and the overall limits of your particular study. Identifying your subject is, of course, a necessary and important task in any essay. Similarly, justifying the elements you will be comparing and contrasting creates reader interest and gives your audience some specifics to look for in the essay. Finally, your statement of purpose or thesis (for example, to prove that one professor is superior to another) should include the boundaries of your discussion. You cannot cover all the reasons for your preference in one short essay, so you must limit your consideration to three or four basic categories (perhaps teaching techniques, the clarity of the assignments given, classroom attitude, and grading standards). The introduction is the place to make all these limits known.

You can organize the body of your paper in one of four ways: (1) a point-by-point, or alternating, comparison; (2) a subject-by-subject, or divided, comparison; (3) a combination of these two methods; or (4) a division between the similarities and differences. (See the chart on page 340.)

The point-by-point comparison evaluates both subjects in terms of each category. If the issue, for example, is which of two cars to buy, you might discuss both models' gasoline mileage first; then, their horsepower; next, their ease in handling; and, finally, their standard equipment. Following the second method of organization, subject by subject, you would discuss the gasoline mileage, horsepower, ease in handling, and standard equipment of car A first and then follow the same format for car B. The third option would allow you to introduce, say, the interior design of each car point by point (or car by car) and then to explain the mechanical features of the automobiles (miles per gallon, horsepower, gear ratio, and braking system) subject by subject. To use the last method of organization, you might discuss the similarities between the two models first and the differences second (or vice versa). If the cars you are comparing have similar miles-per-gallon (MPG) ratings but completely different horsepower, steering systems, and optional equipment, you could discuss the gasoline mileage first and then emphasize the differences by mentioning them later in the essay. If, instead, you are trying to emphasize the fact that the MPG ratings of these models remain consistent despite their differences, then reverse the order of your essay.

Methods of Organization

Point by Point*	**Subject by Subject+**
MPG, car A MPG, car B Horsepower, car A Horsepower, car B Handling, car A Handling, car B Equipment, car A Equipment, car B	MPG, car A Horsepower, car A Handling, car A Equipment, car A MPG, car B Horsepower, car B Handling, car B Equipment, car B
*Emphasizes individual points. Is best for long essays. Helpful hint: Use transitions to avoid lists.	+Emphasizes each subject. Is best for short essays. Helpful hint: Use transitions to avoid two separate essays.

Combination	**Similarities/Differences**

Interior, car A
Interior, car B
 	
———
 	
MPG, car A
Horsepower, car A
 	
MPG, car B
Horsepower, car B
	Similarities:
	   MPG, cars A & B
	
	Differences:
	   Horsepower, cars A & B
	   Handling, cars A & B
	   Equipment, cars A & B

When confronted with the task of choosing a method of organization for a comparison/contrast essay, you need to find the pattern that best suits your purpose. If you want single items to stand out in a discussion, for instance, the best choice will be the point-by-point system; it is especially appropriate for long essays but has a tendency to turn into an exercise in listing if you don't pay careful attention to your transitions. If, however, the subjects themselves (rather than the itemized points) are the most interesting feature of your essay, you should use the subject-by-subject comparison; this system is particularly good for short essays in which the readers can retain what was said about one subject while they read about a second subject. Through this second system of organization, each subject becomes a unified whole, an approach to an essay that is generally effective unless the theme becomes awkwardly divided into two separate parts. You must also remember, if you choose this second method of organization, that the second (or last) subject is in the most emphatic position because that is what your readers will have seen most recently. The final two options for organizing a comparison/contrast essay give you some built-in flexibility so that you can create emphasis and attempt to manipulate reader opinion simply by the structure of your essay.

Using logical transitions in your comparison/contrast essays will establish clear relationships between the items in your comparisons and will also move your readers smoothly from one topic to the next. If you wish to indicate comparisons, use such words as *like, as, also, in like manner, similarly*, and *in addition*; to signal contrasts, try *but, in contrast to, unlike, whereas*, and *on the one hand/on the other hand*.

The conclusion of a comparison/contrast essay summarizes the main points and states the deductions drawn from those points. As you choose your method of organization, remember not to get locked into a formulaic approach to your subjects, which will adversely affect the readability of your essay. To avoid making your reader feel like a spectator at a verbal table tennis match, be straightforward, honest, and patient as you discover and recount the details of your comparison.

Rewriting. When you review the draft of your comparison/contrast essay, you need once again to make sure that you communicate your purpose as effectively as possible to your intended audience. Three guidelines previously mentioned should help you accomplish this goal:

Do you identify your subjects clearly?

Do you explain the basis of your comparison/contrast?

Does your thesis clearly state the purpose and overall limits of your particular study?

You will also need to pay close attention to the development of your essay:

Are you attempting to compare/contrast items from the same general category?

Do you discuss the same qualities of each subject?

Do you use as many pertinent details as possible to expand your essay?

Do you deal with all aspects of the topic that are relevant to your purpose?

Do you balance the treatment of the different subjects of your essay?

Did you organize your topic as effectively as possible?

Have you used transitional words and phrases that establish clear relationships?

Does your conclusion contain a summary and analysis of your main points?

For further information on writing and revising your comparison/contrast essays, consult the checklists on pages 32–33 of the Introduction.

STUDENT ESSAY: COMPARISON/CONTRAST AT WORK

The following student essay compares the advantages and disadvantages of macaroni and cheese versus tacos in the life of a harried college freshman. As you read it, notice that the writer states his intention in the first paragraph and then expands his discussion with appropriate details to produce a balanced essay. Also, try to determine what effect he creates by using two methods of organization: first subject by subject, then point by point.

Dormitory Chef

To this day, I will not eat either maca- **Topics**
roni and cheese or tacos. No, it's not be-
Basis of cause of any allergy; it's because during my
comparison freshman year at college, I prepared one or
the other of these scrumptious dishes more
Thesis
times than I care to remember. However, **statement:**
my choice of which culinary delight to **Purpose**
and limits
cook on any given night was not as simple **of compa-**
a decision as one might imagine. **rison**

Paragraph Macaroni and cheese has numerous ad-
on Subject vantages for the dormitory chef. First of **Point 1**
A: Maca-
roni and all, it is inexpensive. No matter how poor **(Price)**
cheese one may be, there's probably enough
change under the couch cushion to buy a
box at the market. All that starch for only
89¢. What a bargain! Second, it can be pre- **Point 2**
(Prepa-
pared in just one pan. This is especially im- **ration)**
portant given the meager resources of the
Point 3 average dorm kitchen. Third, and perhaps
(Odor) most important, macaroni and cheese is
odorless. By odorless, I mean that no one
else can smell it. It is a well-known fact
that dorm residents hate to cook and that
they love nothing better than to wander
dejectedly around the kitchen with big, sad
eyes after someone else has been cooking.
But with macaroni and cheese, no enticing
aromas are going to find their way into the
nose of any would-be mooch.

Paragraph Tacos, on the other hand, are a different **Transition**
on Subject matter altogether. For the dorm cook, the
B: Tacos
most significant difference is obviously the **Point 1**
price. To enjoy tacos for dinner, the adven- **(Price)**
turous dorm gourmet must purchase no
fewer than five ingredients from the market: corn tortillas, beef, lettuce, tomatoes,
and cheese. Needless to say, this is a major

expenditure. Second, the chef must adroitly shuffle these ingredients back and forth among his very limited supply of pans and bowls. And finally, tacos smell great. That wouldn't be a problem if the tacos didn't also smell great to about twenty of the cook's newest—if not closest—friends, who appear with those same pathetic, starving eyes mentioned earlier. When this happens, the cook will be lucky to get more than two of his own creations.

Tacos, then, wouldn't stand much of a chance if they didn't outdo macaroni and cheese in one area: taste. Taste is almost—but not quite—an optional requirement in the opinion of a frugal dormitory hash-slinger. Taste is just important enough so that tacos are occasionally prepared, despite their disadvantages.

But tacos have other advantages besides their taste. With their enticing, colorful ingredients, they even look good. The only thing that can be said about the color of macaroni and cheese is that it's a color not found in nature.

On the other hand, macaroni and cheese is quick. It can be prepared in about ten minutes, while tacos take more than twice as long. And there are occasions—such as final exam week—when time is a scarce and precious resource.

As you can see, quite a bit of thinking went into my choice of food in my younger years. These two dishes essentially got me through my freshman year and indirectly taught me how to make important decisions (like what to eat). But I still feel a certain revulsion when I hear their names today.

Margin notes:
- Point 2 (Preparation)
- Point 3 (Odor)
- Subject B
- Transition
- Subject A
- Paragraph on Point 4: Taste
- Transition
- Paragraph on Point 5: Color
- Subject B
- Subject A
- Transition
- Subject A
- Paragraph on Point 6: Time
- Subject B
- Transition
- Analysis
- Summary
- Concluding statement

Student Writer's Comments

I compare and contrast so many times during a typical day that I took this rhetorical technique for granted. In fact, I had overlooked it completely. The most difficult part of writing this essay was finding two appropriate subjects to compare. Ideally, I knew they should be united by a similarity. So I brainstormed to come up with some possible topics. Then, working from this list of potential subjects, I began to freewrite to see if I could come up with two topics in the same category on which I could write a balanced comparison. Out of my freewriting came this reasoning: Macaroni and cheese and tacos, in reality, are two very different kinds of food from the same category. Proving this fact is easy and wouldn't result in an interesting essay. But their similar property of being popular dorm foods unites the two despite their differences and also gave me two important reasons for writing the comparison: to discover why they are both popular dorm delicacies and to determine which one had more advantages for my particular purposes. In proportion to writing and revising, I spent most of my time choosing my topic, brainstorming, freewriting, and rebrainstorming to make sure I could develop every aspect of my comparison adequately. Most of my prewriting work took the form of two columns, in which I recorded my opinions on the choice between macaroni and cheese versus tacos.

Sitting down to mold my lists into an essay posed an entirely new set of problems. From the copious notes I had taken, I easily wrote the introductory paragraph, identifying my topics, explaining the basis of my comparison/contrast, and stating the purpose and limits of my study (my thesis statement). But now that I faced the body of the essay, I needed to find the best way to organize my opinions on these two dorm foods: Point by point, subject by subject, a combination of these two, or a discussion of similarities and differences?

I wrote my first draft discussing my topics point by point. Even with an occasional joke and a few snide comments interjected, the essay reminded me of a boring game of table tennis with only a few attempts at changing the pace. I started over completely with my second draft and worked through my topics subject by subject. I felt this approach was better, but not quite right yet for my particular purpose and audience. I set out to do some heavy-handed revising.

Discussing my first three points (price, preparation, and odor) subject by subject seemed to work quite well. I was actually satisfied with the first half of my discussion of these two subjects. But the essay really started to get sluggish when I brought up the fourth point: taste. So I broke off my discussion there and rewrote the second half of my essay point by point, dealing with taste, color, and time each in its own paragraph. This change gave my essay the new direction it needed to keep the readers' attention and also offered me some new insights into my comparison. Then, I returned to the beginning of my essay and revised it for readability, adding transitions and making sure the paper now moved smoothly from one point or subject to the next. Finally, I added my final paragraph, including a brief summary of my main points and an explanation of the deductions I had made. My concluding remark ("But I still feel a certain revulsion when I hear their names today.") came to me as I was putting the final touches on this draft.

What I learned from writing this particular essay is that comparison/contrast thinking, more than thinking in other rhetorical modes, is much like a puzzle. I really had to spend an enormous amount of time thinking through, mapping out, and rethinking my comparison before I could start to put my thoughts in essay form. The results are rewarding, but I sure wore out a piece of linoleum on the den floor on the way to my final draft.

SOME FINAL THOUGHTS ON COMPARISON/CONTRAST

The essays in this section demonstrate various methods of organization as well as a number of distinct stylistic approaches to writing a comparison/contrast essay. As you read these selections, pay particular attention to the clear, well-focused introductions; the different logical methods of organization; and the smooth transitions between sentences and paragraphs.

BRUCE CATTON   (1899 – 1978)

■ ■ ■

Grant and Lee: A Study in Contrasts

Bruce Catton was a much-loved and respected historian of the U.S. Civil War, whose many books and articles have brought an "eyewitness" vividness to this crucial period in American development. Believing that history "ought to be a good yarn," Catton saw himself as more of a reporter than a historian, stripping away the romantic glamour of war to reveal with vigor and clarity the reality of this important historical era. A native of Benzonia, Michigan, the author was fascinated during his childhood by stories told by the many Civil War veterans who had returned to his small town. Catton attended Oberlin College, worked for a time as a newspaper reporter, and then turned his attention principally to researching and writing about the Civil War. His most popular and influential book was *A Stillness at Appomattox* (the third part of his *Army of the Potomac* trilogy), which won both the Pulitzer Prize and the National Book Award for history in 1954. Among his many other books are *This Hallowed Ground* (1956), *The Coming Fury* (1961), *Terrible Swift Sword* (1963), *Grant Takes Command* (1969), and *Michigan: A Bicentennial History* (1976). For the last twenty-four years of his life, Catton was also editor of *American Heritage* magazine.

Preparing to Read

The following essay is taken from *The American Story* (1956), a collection of essays by distinguished historians; it examines the similarities and differences between Generals Grant and Lee at the conclusion of the Civil War. As you prepare to read this article, take a few moments to consider heroes in your life: What special qualities turn people into heroic figures? Why do you think some heroes are admired more than others? What historical events bring forth heroes? How does American society act in general toward these people? Why do most of us seem to need heroic figures in our lives?

When Ulysses S. Grant and Robert E. Lee met in the parlor of a modest house at Appomattox Court House, Virginia, on April 9, 1865, to work out the terms for the surrender of Lee's Army of Northern Virginia, a great chapter in American life came to a close, and a great new chapter began.

These men were bringing the Civil War to its virtual finish. To be sure, other armies had yet to surrender, and for a few days the fugitive Confederate government would struggle desperately and vainly, trying to find some way to go on living now that its chief support was gone. But in effect it was all over when Grant and Lee signed the papers. And the little room where they wrote out the terms was the scene of one of the poignant, dramatic contrasts in American history.

They were two strong men, these oddly different generals, and they represented the strengths of two conflicting currents that, through them, had come into final collision.

Back of Robert E. Lee was the notion that the old aristocratic concept might somehow survive and be dominant in American life.

Lee was tidewater Virginia, and in his background were family, culture, and tradition . . . the age of chivalry transplanted to a New World which was making its own legends and its own myths. He embodied a way of life that had come down through the age of knighthood and the English country squire. America was a land that was beginning all over again, dedicated to nothing much more complicated than the rather hazy belief that all men had equal rights and should have an equal chance in the world. In such a land Lee stood for the feeling that it was somehow of advantage to human society to have a pronounced inequality in the social structure. There should be a leisure class, backed by ownership of land; in turn, society itself should be keyed to the land as the chief source of wealth and influence. It would bring forth (according to this ideal) a class of men with a strong sense of obligation to the community; men who lived not to gain advantage for themselves, but to meet the solemn obligations which had been laid on them by the very fact that they were privileged. From them the country would get its leadership; to them it could look for the higher values—of thought, of conduct, of personal deportment—to give it strength and virtue.

Lee embodied the noblest elements of this aristocratic ideal. Through him, the landed nobility justified itself. For four years, the Southern states had fought a desperate war to uphold the ideals for which Lee stood. In the end, it almost seemed as if the Confederacy fought for Lee; as if he himself was the Confederacy . . . the best thing that the way of life for which the Confederacy stood could ever have to offer. He had passed into legend before Appomattox. Thousands of tired, underfed, poorly clothed Confederate soldiers, long since past the simple enthusiasm of the early days of the struggle, somehow considered Lee the symbol of everything for which they had been willing to die. But they could not quite put this feeling into words. If the Lost Cause, sanctified by so much heroism and so many deaths, had a living justification, its justification was General Lee.

Grant, the son of a tanner on the Western frontier, was every- 7 thing Lee was not. He had come up the hard way and embodied nothing in particular except the eternal toughness and sinewy fiber of the men who grew up beyond the mountains. He was one of a body of men who owed reverence and obeisance to no one, who were self-reliant to a fault, who cared hardly anything for the past but who had a sharp eye for the future.

These frontier men were the precise opposites of the tidewater 8 aristocrats. Back of them, in the great surge that had taken people over the Alleghenies and into the opening Western country, there was a deep, implicit dissatisfaction with a past that had settled into grooves. They stood for democracy, not from any reasoned conclusion about the proper ordering of human society, but simply because they had grown up in the middle of democracy and knew how it worked. Their society might have privileges, but they would be privileges each man had won for himself. Forms and patterns meant nothing. No man was born to anything, except perhaps to a chance to show how far he could rise. Life was competition.

Yet along with this feeling had come a deep sense of belong- 9 ing to a national community. The Westerner who developed a farm, opened a shop, or set up in business as a trader could hope to prosper only as his own community prospered—and his community ran from the Atlantic to the Pacific and from Canada down to Mexico. If the land was settled, with towns and highways and accessible markets, he could better himself. He saw his fate in terms of the nation's own destiny. As its horizons expanded, so did his. He had, in other words, an acute dollars-and-cents stake in the continued growth and development of his country.

And that, perhaps, is where the contrast between Grant and Lee   10
becomes most striking. The Virginia aristocrat, inevitably, saw himself in relation to his own region. He lived in a static society which
could endure almost anything except change. Instinctively, his first
loyalty would go to the locality in which that society existed. He
would fight to the limit of endurance to defend it, because in defending it he was defending everything that gave his own life its
deepest meaning.

The Westerner, on the other hand, would fight with an equal   11
tenacity for the broader concept of society. He fought so because
everything he lived by was tied to growth, expansion, and a constantly widening horizon. What he lived by would survive or fall
with the nation itself. He could not possibly stand by unmoved in
the face of an attempt to destroy the Union. He would combat it
with everything he had, because he could only see it as an effort
to cut the ground out from under his feet.

So Grant and Lee were in complete contrast, representing two   12
diametrically opposed elements in American life. Grant was the
modern man emerging; beyond him, ready to come on the stage,
was the great age of steel and machinery, of crowded cities and a
restless burgeoning vitality. Lee might have ridden down from the
old age of chivalry, lance in hand, silken banner fluttering over his
head. Each man was the perfect champion of his cause, drawing
both his strengths and his weaknesses from the people he led.

Yet it was not all contrast, after all. Different as they were—in   13
background, in personality, in underlying aspiration—these two
great soldiers had much in common. Under everything else, they
were marvelous fighters. Furthermore, their fighting qualities
were really very much alike.

Each man had, to begin with, the great virtue of utter tenacity   14
and fidelity. Grant fought his way down the Mississippi Valley in
spite of acute personal discouragement and profound military
handicaps. Lee hung on in the trenches at Petersburg after hope
itself had died. In each man there was an indomitable quality . . .
the born fighter's refusal to give up as long as he can still remain
on his feet and lift his two fists.

Daring and resourcefulness they had, too; the ability to think   15
faster and move faster than the enemy. These were the qualities
which gave Lee the dazzling campaigns of Second Manassas and
Chancellorsville and won Vicksburg for Grant.

Lastly, and perhaps greatest of all, there was the ability, at the 16
end, to turn quickly from war to peace once the fighting was
over. Out of the way these two men behaved at Appomattox
came the possibility of a peace of reconciliation. It was a possibility not wholly realized, in the years to come, but which did, in
the end, help the two sections to become one nation again . . .
after a war whose bitterness might have seemed to make such a
reunion wholly impossible. No part of either man's life became
him more than the part he played in this brief meeting in the
McLean house at Appomattox. Their behavior there put all succeeding generations of Americans in their debt. Two great
Americans, Grant and Lee—very different, yet under everything
very much alike. Their encounter at Appomattox was one of the
great moments of American history.

UNDERSTANDING DETAILS

1. What two conflicting views of American life does the author
   believe these two generals represented?
2. What special qualities of Grant and Lee does Catton contrast
   to achieve his purpose? What qualities does he compare?
3. How did both Grant and Lee respond to progress and change
   in general? Explain your answer in detail.
4. What does Catton imply about the behavior of these two generals at Appomattox Court House? According to this essay,
   why was the encounter of Grant and Lee at Appomattox "one
   of the great moments of American history" (paragraph 16)?

ANALYZING MEANING

1. What is Catton's purpose in this essay? What truths, according
   to the author, needed to be made clear about these two great
   Civil War generals? Why did Catton study similarities as well as
   differences in these two men?
2. What does Catton mean when he says, "Life was competition"
   (paragraph 8) in Grant's philosophy? What aspects of this philosophy do you see in today's society?
3. In what ways were Lee and Grant emblems of the past and the
   future, respectively?
4. About the actions of these men at Appomattox, Catton says,
   "Their behavior there put all succeeding generations of

Americans in their debt" (paragraph 16). What does he mean by this statement? What influences of these two men can we still see in our culture today?

DISCOVERING RHETORICAL STRATEGIES

1. Which of the four main methods of organizing a comparison/contrast essay does Catton use? How many paragraphs does the author spend on each part of his comparison? Why do you think he spends this amount of time on each?
2. What transitional words or phrases does the author use to move from one part of this essay to the next? Give at least three specific examples. Do these devices hold the essay together effectively? Explain your answer.
3. In what ways does the last paragraph of this essay echo the first paragraph? Why is this echoing technique an effective way to end the essay?
4. What other rhetorical strategies besides comparison and contrast does Catton use to achieve his purpose in this essay? Give examples of each strategy.

MAKING CONNECTIONS

1. Like Bruce Catton, Tom Wolfe ("The Right Stuff") describes one particular moment in time, the training of Mercury astronauts, when the world was changed forever. What similarities can you find between these two important events in the history of the United States?
2. First, Catton contrasts Grant and Lee, and then he compares them. How is this structural approach different from the comparison/contrast essays written by Germaine Greer ("A Child Is Born") and William Ouchi ("Japanese and American Workers: Two Casts of Mind")? Which organizational technique do you find most effective? Explain your answer.
3. According to Catton, Grant and Lee each represented "the strengths of two conflicting currents that, through them, had come into final collision" (paragraph 3). Along the same lines, how does an "unfamiliar country" symbolize old age for Malcolm Cowley in "The View from 80"? In other words, how do both authors use symbols to give significance to everyday events?

IDEAS FOR DISCUSSION/WRITING

Preparing to Write

Write freely about heroes and heroines in American society: Name some public figures you respect. Why do you admire them? What qualifies someone as a heroic figure in your opinion? What do most of the heroes and heroines you admire have in common? How are they different? How are history and heroic figures related in your mind?

Choosing a Topic

1. In an essay written for your classmates, compare and/or contrast two famous people in history. As Catton did, try to explain what forces in society these figures represent. Decide on a clear focus and point of view before you begin.
2. Choose two people who have had a significant influence on your life. Then, compare and/or contrast how they have affected you.
3. America has had many new beginnings throughout its history. The time at the end of the Civil War, discussed in this essay, was one of them. Explain to your classmates another new beginning for America. What were the details of this new start? Who were the heroes? Where, when, how, and why did it take place?

■

GERMAINE GREER   (1939 –   )

■ ■ ■

A Child Is Born

Germaine Greer is one of the world's best-known and most controversial feminist authors. Australian by birth, she earned degrees
at the universities of Melbourne and Sydney, then won a scholarship to Cambridge University in England, where she received a
doctorate in Shakespeare. Early jobs as a teacher and a television
actress gave way to a career as a writer and a political activist. Her
first book, *The Female Eunuch* (1970), is a sharply written indictment of women for allowing themselves to be passively stereo-
typed, subjugated, and symbolically castrated by society. *The
Obstacle Race* (1979) followed, a survey of the trials and triumphs
of women painters throughout history. *Sex and Destiny: The
Politics of Human Fertility* (1984) is a well-researched, thorough
investigation into the global politics of human reproduction.
More recent publications include *Shakespeare* (1985), *The
Madwoman's Underclothes* (1986), *Kissing the Rod: An Anthology of
Seventeenth-Century Women's Verse* (1988), *Daddy, We Hardly Knew
You* (1989), and *The Change: Women, Aging and the Menopause*
(1991). Through her books, numerous articles, and television appearances, Greer continues to project a spirited, stimulating, and
intelligent defense of women's rights. She lectures occasionally at
the University of Warwick near her home in Coventry, England,
and describes herself as an "anarchist," an "atheist," and a "super-
groupie" with great affection for jazz and rock music.

Preparing to Read

In the following essay, excerpted from *Sex and Destiny*, Greer
compares the role of children in traditional agricultural societies
with that of children in Western industrialized countries. As you
prepare to read this essay, take a few moments to think about
your own family structure and that of other people you know:
What has happened to the Western family unit over the last fifty
to a hundred years? Does it play a more important or less impor-

tant role in our society? What are the advantages of our society's concept of the "family"? The disadvantages? How do you think our family life differs from that of Eastern cultures? What are the advantages and disadvantages of these two approaches to the family unit? What do you think will be the future role of the family in the Western world?

I n many societies women still go forth from their mother's house at marriage to live with a mother-in-law and the wives of their husband's brothers. It is a truism of anthropology that such women do not become members of their new family until they have borne a child. If we consider that in such societies the marriage was quite likely to have been arranged, it is understandable that the bride, too, longs for the child who will stand in the same intimate relationship to her as she with her own mother. The Western interpretation of such mores is that they are backward, cruel and wrong; it is assumed that the sexual relations between the spouses are perfunctory and exploitative and that all mothers-in-law are unjust and vindictive. At a conference to mark International Women's Day at the U.N. Secretariat in Vienna in 1981, two members of an organization called Amnesty for Women provided the assembled women with a description of typical Muslim marriage which was no more than a coarse ethnocentric libel. The one Muslim woman on the panel, who may have been virtually the only Muslim present, looked up in astonishment to hear the domestic life of her people described in terms of the utmost squalor, but, less willing to divide the consensus than were the speakers, she decided to hold her tongue. One of the greatest difficulties in the way of feminists who are not chauvinistic and want to learn from women who still live within a female society is the tendency of those women to withdraw into silent opposition when participating in international forums conducted in languages which they cannot speak with fluency; women officials of the Sudanese government told me that they had given up going to international conferences, even though the trips were a tremendous treat, because they were tired of being told about their own lives instead of being consulted.

Thus in the West we would regard it as outrageous that a woman could lose her own name and become known as the

355

mother of her firstborn, once she has borne it—although of course most of us do not protest against the sinking of the woman's lineage under her husband's name at marriage. In many traditional societies the relationship between mother and child is more important than the relationship between husband and wife: In some, indeed, the child's relationship with the rest of his family is as important as or even more important than either. Among the fierce Rajputs, a bridegroom leaving to collect his bride "sucks his mother's breast to signify that the highest duty of a Rajput is to uphold the dignity of his mother's milk."

The woman who satisfies the longings of her peers by producing the child they are all anxious to see finds her achievement celebrated in ways that dramatize her success. Among the few first-person accounts of how this works in practice is this one from a young Sylheti woman: 3

> If a girl is lucky, and her parents are alive, she goes to her mother's house for the last few months of her pregnancy and about the first three months of the baby's life. There she gets a lot of love and care. She is asked, "What would you like to eat? What do you fancy?" All the time she is looked after. The whole matter of pregnancy is one of celebration. When the baby is born it is an occasion of joy for the whole family. The naming ceremony is lovely. It is held when the baby is seven days old. A new dress is bought for it and a new sari for the mother. There is feasting and singing until late at night. The women and girls gather and sing songs. Garlands of tumeric and garlic are worn to ward off evil spirits. That's when the name is chosen. . . . The ceremony is held for the birth of a boy or a girl. Of course it is considered better to have a boy, but the birth of a girl is celebrated with the same joy by the women in the family. We sit together eating *pan* and singing. Some of us might be young unmarried girls, others aged ladies of forty or fifty. There are so many jokes, so much laughter. People look so funny eating *pan* and singing. The men don't take much part. They may come and have a look at the baby, but the singing, the gathering together at night—it is all women. The songs are simple songs which are rarely written down. They are about the lives of women in Bengal.

Among the rewards of pregnancy in this case, as in many others, is that the woman gets to go home to visit her mother and sisters; the nostalgic tone of the description, which is clearly tinged with rose, may be the product of the contrast that this young woman finds in England. Another of the Asian women who found a voice in Amrit Wilson's book gives a similarly rosy picture of rearing a child in Bangladesh: 4

In Bangladesh children under the age of five or six are looked after by the whole family. All the children of the joint family are looked after together. They are taken to the pond for a bath perhaps by one daughter-in-law, and she bathes them all. Then they all come in and sit down to eat. Perhaps the youngest daughter-in-law has cooked the meal. Another woman feeds them. As for playing, the children play out of doors with natural objects. Here people say that Asian children don't play with toys. In Bangladesh they don't need toys. They make their own simple things. . . . In the afternoon they love to hear Rupthoka [fairy tales]. Maybe there is a favorite aunt; she tells them these stories. But at night when they get sleepy they always go to their mother and sleep in her embrace. But other women do help a lot; in fact they have such strong relationships with the child that it is not uncommon for them to be called Big Mother or Small Mother.

The system does not always work as well as it does in this account by Hashmat Ara Begum, but it is the ideal that lies behind the common sight of children carrying children in the subcontinent. In the tone of her explanation of the fact that Asian children do not have toys, the strain of confrontation with the industrialized lifestyle can be sensed; deprived of the real Bangladeshi world, Asian children have yet to develop a taste for the expensive surrogate objects with which we placate our children for their lack of human contact. The Asian lifestyle seems austere to consumerist society; to the immigrants, the British lifestyle seems inhuman. Transplanted from their villages to the decaying inner suburbs of dull industrial towns, these women suffer greatly, despite the fact that they have a better chance of bearing healthy children than they had at home. Their misery is not simply explained by their ignorance of the language or the thinly disguised racist hostility that they encounter. Their entire support system has vanished; from never being alone they have moved into a situation of utter solitude, for which their relative affluence cannot compensate. The crisis of childbirth, faced, as it is for all women in the West, without psychological support and involving severe outrage to Muslim modesty, frequently precipitates them into depressed states. (The attitude of medical personnel to these women, based as it is on utter incomprehension of their terror and despair, is a contributory factor.) Amrit Wilson went to visit one such woman, forced into emotional dependence upon a husband who was working long hours to give the family the good life they had come to England to find. "Late, late at night my husband comes home. He loves the babies. He is a good husband, but what can he do? And what can I do? How can I live, sister, how can I live?"

Children in the West, then, are a far greater burden than they are 6
in the countries that these women came from; not only are women
more likely to be dealing with the children alone, but the children
themselves are more demanding than they are in a nonconsumer
society. In the Egyptian village, for example, "there are invariably at
least two grown-up women attending to the rearing of the child.
As the newborn baby, or even any child, has no special cradle, cot
or bed, it always sleeps by its mother or sits on her lap."

The Egyptian baby is not trained in consumer behavior any 7
more than the Bangladeshi baby. In the last hundred years the
consumerism of Western babies has gone ahead by leaps and
bounds. The baby carriage, a relatively modern invention, is the
most expensive item, and, significantly, the one that is paraded before the public; to it are added the baby's layette, crib, cot, diapers,
and the like, all clearly designed for baby's use and therefore instantly obsolescent. Some of the impedimenta, such as bootees and
talcum powder, are completely useless, but most are designed to
keep baby dry, tidy and out of contact, hemmed in from the real
world by bassinet walls or perambulator covers or, most bizarre of
all, the bars of the playpen. The child who has no pram, no crib,
and certainly no room of its own cannot be escaped, especially if it
cannot be put down on the floor, either because precious water
cannot be spared to wash it very often or because it is made of
dirt. Children who are constantly attached to adults obviously
cannot be segregated; they must come into the work place and
into the sleeping place and the patterns of both must be modified
to receive them. Often drudgery separates adults from children, if
they are working on road gangs or construction sites, for example,
but the separation is seen as another of the trials of poverty.

The child's socialization will be carried out in the midst of his 8
kin group; it is not easy to drive the wedge of professional care
into traditional families. There is no need of a play group, because
the play group is right there, nor for that matter of the nursery
school. The noise of children is a constant accompaniment to
daily life, and probably a good deal less fraying to the nerves than
the cacophony of consumer society. Mothers are not so vulnerable to infantile ill temper because they do not have to take sole
responsibility for it. Reward and punishment are doled out according to family practice; mothers don't have to rush to Dr.

Spock to find out how to deal with some particularly antisocial manifestation. The family ethos prevails as it has prevailed for generations, without anxious soul-searching, which is not to say that it is always humane or just, but simply that it is not a cause of internalized tension. The extended family is in many ways a boring and oppressive environment, but it does offer a sense and a context to mothering which two-bedroom ranch houses in the suburbs do not. The children may be grubby, they may be less well-nourished than Western children, but they have a clear sense of the group they belong to, and their own role within it. They will not be found screaming for all the goods displayed in the supermarket (and to make them so scream is the point of the display), until their frantic mothers lose control and bash them, and then compound the injury by poking sweets into their mouths.

The closeness of adults and children in traditional societies is partly a result of the exclusion of women from the public sphere and their generally low levels of literacy, but these disabilities are in part compensated for by the centrality of the household in daily life. There is little in the way of public or commercial amusement; entertainments and celebrations take place in the household and children are included. Men may go to the coffeehouse or the mudhif for their entertainment, but their freedom to do so is not regarded with envy, for women and children are capable of having riotous good fun on their own. Perhaps the most important difference between mothering in traditional societies and mothering in our own is that the traditional mother's role increases in complexity and importance as she grows older. If she is skillful and fortunate enough to keep her sons and her sons' wives as members of her household, she will enjoy their service and companionship as she grows older. She will have time to play with her grandchildren; her flagging pace will match their unsteady steps. As she sinks into feebleness, her sons' wives will assume her responsibilities and care for her until the last. The ideal situation is not inevitable—dispossessed old women can be found begging and dying on the streets of India—but success is possible. The role of matriarch is a positive one which can be worked towards by an intelligent and determined woman. Mistreating daughters-in-law is unlikely to further her aims, because discontented wives are a principal cause of the fissioning of the ex-

9

tended family. Because the household is an essential unit in the production of goods and services, her role as manager of it is a challenging one, beside which the role of the Western housewife seems downright impoverished. Even her absent daughters, whose departure for their husbands' dwelling places caused her such grief, keep close to her in feeling. One of the most remarkable aspects of Elizabeth Warnock Fernea's life as the veiled wife of an American anthropologist in an Iraqi village was the utter certainty of the Iraqi women that she must have been as attached to her mother as they were:

> "Where is your mother?" Kulthum asked. I told her she was in America far away. . . . The women clucked in sympathy.
> "Poor girl," they said, "poor child. . . ."
> "When you have children, you will not feel so alone without your mother," prophesied Kulthum.

When she announced her impending return to America, the 10 women saw only one reason for their going:

> "Ask Mr. Bob to bring your mother, and then you'll never have to leave us and go back to America."

Mrs. Fernea did not volunteer to reveal the truth about the 11 status of mothers in Western society. Eventually the Iraqi women confronted her with it:

> "And is it true," asked Basima, "that in America they put all the old women in houses by themselves, away from their families?"
> I admitted that this was sometimes true and tried to explain, but my words were drowned in the general murmur of disapproval.
> "What a terrible place that must be!"
> "How awful!"
> "And their children let them go?"
> . . . . It had never occurred to me before, but the idea of old people's homes must have been particularly reprehensible to these women whose world lay within the family unit and whose lives of toil and childbearing were rewarded in old age, when they enjoyed repose and respect as members of their children's households.

This discussion of the difference in the role of mothers in 12 highly industrialized bureaucratic communities and in traditional agricultural communities is not meant as a panegyric of the disappearing world, but simply to indicate something of the context in which the birthrate in the developed world has fallen. There is little point in feeling sorry for Western mothers, who are most often as anxious to be freed of their children as their children are to be freed of them. The inhabitants of old people's homes and retirement villages do not sit sobbing and railing against destiny, although they do compete with each other in displaying the rather exiguous proofs of their children's affection. As the recession bites deeper and unemployment rises, more and more adult children are having to remain dependent on their parents, who are lamenting loudly and wondering more vociferously than usual why they let themselves in for such a thankless task as parenting. The point of the contrast is simply to caution the people of the highly industrialized countries which wield such massive economic and cultural sway over the developing world against assuming that one of the things they must rescue the rest of the world from is parenting. Because motherhood is virtually meaningless in our society is no ground for supposing that the fact that women are still defined by their mothering function in other societies is simply an index of their oppression. We have at least to consider the possibility that a successful matriarch might well pity Western feminists for having been duped into futile competition with men in exchange for the companionship and love of children and other women.

UNDERSTANDING DETAILS

1. How do traditional and Western childbearing methods vary? How does Greer account for these differences?
2. What are the main differences and similarities between the roles of mothers in traditional and Western societies? Explain your answer in detail.
3. What is the relationship between consumerism and child rearing in Greer's comparison? What behavior results from this relationship?
4. According to the author, what is the precise difference between the extended family and the nuclear family?

ANALYZING MEANING

1. Of all the examples the author cites in her essay, which one convinces you most effectively that raising children in traditional countries is a more meaningful activity than it is in Western society? Why?

2. Why do you think the extended family has become relatively obsolete in the Western world? In your opinion, what is its future fate in Western society? Explain your reasoning.

3. This essay ends on a fairly negative note. Explain in your own words Greer's last sentence (paragraph 12), and discuss its implications about Western society. In your opinion, is this an effective ending? Why or why not?

4. How are children socialized in traditional societies? What aspects of this process would not be appropriate in a "consumer society"? Explain your answer in detail.

DISCOVERING RHETORICAL STRATEGIES

1. How does the author organize her comparison? Which of the four main types of organization best describes Greer's essay? Is this format a good choice for accomplishing her purpose? Why or why not?

2. Does the author omit or downplay any of the distinctions between Western and traditional child care that might be detrimental to her argument? If so, what are these distinctions?

3. What opinions of her own does Greer reveal about methods of child rearing in the two communities? What references betray these opinions?

4. Why do you think Greer has chosen comparison/contrast to prove her point in this essay? How effective is this technique? What other rhetorical modes does the author use to state her case?

MAKING CONNECTIONS

1. Imagine that Germaine Greer, Bill Cosby ("The Baffling Question"), and Judy Brady ("Why I Want a Wife") are having a conversation about the "rewards" of pregnancy. Compare and contrast Cosby's and Brady's opinions about the trials and tribulations of being pregnant and delivering a baby in the United States with Greer's more optimistic version of what goes on in non-Western societies. Which of these authors would you agree with most? Explain your answer.

2. Based on the information contained in Alleen Pace Nilsen's "Sexism in English: A 1990s Update" and Greer's article, what

do you think the main differences are between the treatment of women in Western and non-Western societies. In which of these societies are women valued more highly? Explain your answer.

3. Just as Greer's article reveals a great deal about American child-raising customs through her comparison with non-Western methods, so does William Ouchi's "Japanese and American Workers: Two Casts of Mind" illustrate a number of problems in the corporate United States by contrasting our work ethic with that of the Japanese. Do Greer and Ouchi identify any of the same flaws in American society? If so, what are they?

IDEAS FOR DISCUSSION/WRITING

Preparing to Write

Write freely about the Western family: What generally constitutes a "family" in the industrialized West? How has its makeup changed over the years? Is the family unit a significant part of our society, or is the individual more important? What facts and observations support your opinion? In what ways do you think the American family will change in the next fifty to a hundred years? In your opinion, will these be positive or negative changes?

Choosing a Topic

1. For your college sociology class, compare the extended family with the nuclear family by discussing the principal advantages and disadvantages of each.

2. As objectively as possible, describe to a friend some of your family's cherished traditions. When possible, compare and/or contrast your family's traditions with those of your friend's family. Give someone you like more insight into yourself by helping the person understand which traditions your family values.

3. You have been asked to make a prediction about the future of the American family for *The Sociological Quarterly*. The readers of this journal are especially interested in whether the family as a group or the family as individuals will become more prominent after the year 2000. Offer your prediction and explain your reasoning in a comparison/contrast essay to be published in this periodical.

WILLIAM OUCHI   (1943 –   )

■ ■ ■

Japanese and American Workers:
Two Casts of Mind

Born in Honolulu, Hawaii, William Ouchi is an internationally known expert on business management—particularly on the relationship between American and Japanese corporations. Ouchi was educated at Williams College, Stanford University, and the University of Chicago; since then, he has taught in business programs at several major American universities, most recently at the Graduate School of Management at UCLA. The author has also served as associate study director for the National Opinion Research Center and as a business consultant for many of America's most successful companies. He has written three books on organization and management: *Theory Z: How American Business Can Meet the Japanese Challenge* (1981) is a thorough analysis of the differences between American and Japanese industrial productivity; *The M-Form Society: How American Teamwork Can Recapture the Competitive Edge* (1984) is the result of a three-year study by a team of sixteen researchers led by Ouchi; and *Organizational Economics* (1986) is a textbook coedited with Jay Barney. Ouchi is currently serving as chief of staff to Los Angeles mayor Richard Riordan. He advises students using *The Prose Reader* to spend plenty of time revising their material. "No one writes a good first draft," he explains. "You must continue to revise your work till you understand exactly what you want to say and you have constructed a group of sentences that say it clearly." Ouchi lives in Santa Monica, California, with his wife and three children.

Preparing to Read

The following essay, excerpted from *Theory Z*, compares and contrasts Japan's collective work ethic with the American spirit of individualism. As you prepare to read this essay, think about your own work ethic: When you study, for example, do you prefer working alone or with a group of people? What kinds of jobs have you held during your life? Did they stress individual or collective behavior? Were you often rewarded for individual achievement, or did you work mostly within a homogeneous group? In what sort of work environment are you most productive? Most satisfied?

P erhaps the most difficult aspect of the Japanese for Westerners to comprehend is the strong orientation to collective values, particularly a collective sense of responsibility. Let me illustrate with an anecdote about a visit to a new factory in Japan owned and operated by an American electronics company. The American company, a particularly creative firm, frequently attracts attention within the business community for its novel approaches to planning, organizational design, and management systems. As a consequence of this corporate style, the parent company determined to make a thorough study of Japanese workers and to design a plant that would combine the best of East and West. In their study they discovered that Japanese firms almost never make use of individual work incentives, such as piecework or even individual performance appraisal tied to salary increases. They concluded that rewarding individual achievement and individual ability is always a good thing.

In the final assembly area of their new plant long lines of young Japanese women wired together electronic products on a piece-rate system: The more you wired, the more you got paid. About two months after opening, the head foreladies approached the plant manager. "Honorable plant manager," they said humbly as they bowed, "we are embarrassed to be so forward, but we must speak to you because all of the girls have threatened to quit work this Friday." (To have this happen, of course, would be a great disaster for all concerned.) "Why," they wanted to know, "can't our plant have the same compensation system as other Japanese companies? When you hire a new girl, her starting wage should be fixed by her age. An eighteen-year-old should be paid more than a sixteen-year-old. Every year on her birthday, she should receive an automatic increase in pay. The idea that any one of us can be more productive than another must be wrong, because none of us in final assembly could make a thing unless all of the other people in the plant had done their jobs right first. To single one person out as being more productive is wrong and is also personally humiliating to us." The company changed its compensation system to the Japanese model.

Another American company in Japan had installed a suggestion 3 system much as we have in the United States. Individual workers were encouraged to place suggestions to improve productivity into special boxes. For an accepted idea the individual received a bonus amounting to some fraction of the productivity savings realized from his or her suggestion. After a period of six months, not a single suggestion had been submitted. The American managers were puzzled. They had heard many stories of the inventiveness, the commitment, and the loyalty of Japanese workers, yet not one suggestion to improve productivity had appeared.

The managers approached some of the workers and asked why 4 the suggestion system had not been used. The answer: "No one can come up with a work improvement idea alone. We work together, and any ideas that one of us may have are actually developed by watching others and talking to others. If one of us was singled out for being responsible for such an idea, it would embarrass all of us." The company changed to a group suggestion system, in which workers collectively submitted suggestions. Bonuses were paid to groups which would save bonus money until the end of the year for a party at a restaurant or, if there was enough money, for family vacations together. The suggestions and productivity improvements rained down on the plant.

One can interpret these examples in two quite different ways. 5 Perhaps the Japanese commitment to collective values is an anachronism that does not fit with modern industrialism but brings economic success despite that collectivism. Collectivism seems to be inimical to the kind of maverick creativity exemplified in Benjamin Franklin, Thomas Edison, and John D. Rockefeller. Collectivism does not seem to provide the individual incentive to excel which has made a great success of American enterprise. Entirely apart from its economic effects, collectivism implies a loss of individuality, a loss of the freedom to be different, to hold fundamentally different values from others.

The second interpretation of the examples is that the Japanese 6 collectivism is economically efficient. It causes people to work well together and to encourage one another to better efforts.

Industrial life requires interdependence of one person on another. But a less obvious but far-reaching implication of the Japanese collectivism for economic performance has to do with accountability.

In the Japanese mind, collectivism is neither a corporate or individual goal to strive for nor a slogan to pursue. Rather, the nature of things operates so that nothing of consequence occurs as a result of individual effort. Everything important in life happens as a result of teamwork or collective effort. Therefore, to attempt to assign individual credit or blame to results is unfounded. A Japanese professor of accounting, a brilliant scholar trained at Carnegie-Mellon University who teaches now in Tokyo, remarked that the status of accounting systems in Japanese industry is primitive compared to those in the United States. Profit centers, transfer prices, and computerized information systems are barely known even in the largest Japanese companies, whereas they are a commonplace in even small United States organizations. Though not at all surprised at the difference in accounting systems, I was not at all sure that the Japanese were primitive. In fact, I thought their system a good deal more efficient than ours.

Most American companies have basically two accounting systems. One system summarizes the overall financial state to inform stockholders, bankers, and other outsiders. That system is not of interest here. The other system, called the managerial or cost accounting system, exists for an entirely different reason. It measures in detail all of the particulars of transactions between departments, divisions, and key individuals in the organization, for the purpose of untangling the interdependencies between people. When, for example, two departments share one truck for deliveries, the cost accounting system charges each department for part of the cost of maintaining the truck and driver, so that at the end of the year, the performance of each department can be individually assessed, and the better department's manager can receive a larger raise. Of course, all of this information processing costs money, and furthermore may lead to arguments between the departments over whether the costs charged to each are fair.

In a Japanese company a short-run assessment of individual performance is not wanted, so the company can save the considerable expense of collecting and processing all of that informa-

7

8

9

tion. Companies still keep track of which department uses a truck how often and for what purposes, but like-minded people can interpret some simple numbers for themselves and adjust their behavior accordingly. Those insisting upon clear and precise measurement for the purpose of advancing individual interests must have an elaborate information system. Industrial life, however, is essentially integrated and interdependent. No one builds an automobile alone, no one carries through a banking transaction alone. In a sense the Japanese value of collectivism fits naturally into an industrial setting, whereas the Western individualism provides constant conflicts. The image that comes to mind is of Chaplin's silent film "Modern Times" in which the apparently insignificant hero played by Chaplin successfully fights against the unfeeling machinery of industry. Modern industrial life can be aggravating, even hostile, or natural: All depends on the fit between our culture and our technology.

The *shinkansen* or "bullet train" speeds across the rural areas of   10
Japan giving a quick view of cluster after cluster of farmhouses surrounded by rice paddies. This particular pattern did not develop purely by chance, but as a consequence of the technology peculiar to the growing of rice, the staple of the Japanese diet. The growing of rice requires construction and maintenance of an irrigation system, something that takes many hands to build. More importantly, the planting and the harvesting of rice can only be done efficiently with the cooperation of twenty or more people. The "bottom line" is that a single family working alone cannot produce enough rice to survive, but a dozen families working together can produce a surplus. Thus the Japanese have had to develop the capacity to work together in harmony, no matter what the forces of disagreement or social disintegration, in order to survive.

Japan is a nation built entirely on the tips of giant, suboceanic   11
volcanoes. Little of the land is flat and suitable for agriculture. Terraced hillsides make use of every available square foot of arable land. Small homes built very close together further conserve the land. Japan also suffers from natural disasters such as earthquakes and hurricanes. Traditionally homes are made of light construction materials, so a house falling down during a disaster will not crush its occupants and also could be quickly and inexpensively

rebuilt. During the feudal period until the Meiji restoration of 1868, each feudal lord sought to restrain his subjects from moving from one village to the next for fear that a neighboring lord might amass enough peasants with which to produce a large agricultural surplus, hire an army and pose a threat. Apparently bridges were not commonly built across rivers and streams until the late nineteenth century, since bridges increased mobility between villages.

Taken all together, this characteristic style of living paints the picture of a nation of people who are homogeneous with respect to race, history, language, religion, and culture. For centuries and generations these people have lived in the same village next door to the same neighbors. Living in close proximity and in dwellings which gave very little privacy, the Japanese survived through their capacity to work together in harmony. In this situation, it was inevitable that the one most central social value which emerged, the one value without which the society could not continue, was that an individual does not matter.

To the Western soul this is a chilling picture of society. Subordinating individual tastes to the harmony of the group and knowing that individual needs can never take precedence over the interests of all is repellent to the Western citizen. But a frequent theme of Western philosophers and sociologists is that individual freedom exists only when people willingly subordinate their self-interests to the social interest. A society composed entirely of self-interested individuals is a society in which each person is at war with the other, a society which has no freedom. This issue, constantly at the heart of understanding society, comes up in every century, and in every society, whether the writer be Plato, Hobbes, or B. F. Skinner. The question of understanding which contemporary institutions lie at the heart of the conflict between automatism and totalitarianism remains. In some ages, the kinship group, the central social institution, mediated between these opposing forces to preserve the balance in which freedom was realized; in other times the church or the government was most critical. Perhaps our present age puts the work organization as the central institution.

In order to complete the comparison of Japanese and American living situations, consider a flight over the United

12

13

14

States. Looking out of the window high over the state of Kansas, we see a pattern of a single farmhouse surrounded by fields, followed by another single homestead surrounded by fields. In the early 1800s in the state of Kansas there were no automobiles. Your nearest neighbor was perhaps two miles distant; the winters were long, and the snow was deep. Inevitably, the central social values were self-reliance and independence. Those were the realities of that place and age that children had to learn to value.

The key to the industrial revolution was discovering that non-human forms of energy substituted for human forms could increase the wealth of a nation beyond anyone's wildest dreams. But there was a catch. To realize this great wealth, non-human energy needed huge complexes called factories with hundreds, even thousands of workers collected into one factory. Moreover, several factories in one central place made the generation of energy more efficient. Almost overnight, the Western world was transformed from a rural and agricultural country to an urban and industrial state. Our technological advance seems to no longer fit our social structure: In a sense, the Japanese can better cope with modern industrialism. While Americans still busily protect our rather extreme form of individualism, the Japanese hold their individualism in check and emphasize cooperation.

UNDERSTANDING DETAILS

1. Describe in your own words the two different philosophies Ouchi is comparing in this essay.
2. What is Ouchi's main point in this essay? Where does he introduce his purpose?
3. According to the author, what is the most difficult aspect of the Japanese business ethic for Westerners to understand?
4. Why does "collectivism" work better for the Japanese than for the Americans? What is its history in Japan? How is it different from Western "individualism"?

ANALYZING MEANING

1. What is Ouchi's personal opinion of the two value systems he is comparing? At what points does he reveal his preference?
2. Why does the author introduce the origins of American and Japanese living conditions?

3. Which set of business values do you prefer after reading Ouchi's comparison? Explain the reasons for your preference.
4. In what ways is the "work organization" the middle ground between automatism and totalitarianism today? Give examples of this observation from your own experience.

DISCOVERING RHETORICAL STRATEGIES

1. How does Ouchi organize this essay? Outline the main points he covers for each subject.
2. Why do you think the author introduces the two anecdotes at the outset of this essay? How do these stories help Ouchi achieve his purpose?
3. Who do you think is the author's intended audience? How much knowledge about these two subjects does he assume they have? What evidence can you give to support your answer?
4. What other rhetorical strategies besides comparison and contrast does Ouchi use to achieve his purpose in this essay? Give examples of each strategy.

MAKING CONNECTIONS

1. Ouchi argues persuasively that geography has played a major role in Japan's orientation toward "collective" values. Scarcity of land and crowded conditions have forced Japanese citizens to work together harmoniously in ways that seem alien to our concept of self-reliance and independence, born on the wide-open American frontier. In what similar ways does geography play a part in the essays by John McPhee ("The Pines"), George Orwell ("Shooting an Elephant"), Jane Goodall ("The Mind of the Chimpanzee"), and Bruce Catton ("Grant and Lee: A Study in Contrasts")?
2. Imagine that Ouchi, Germaine Greer ("A Child Is Born"), and Robert Ramirez ("The Barrio") are having a conversation about the importance of cooperation among people who live close together. What would these authors say are the principal difficulties of achieving such necessary cooperation? What would they say are the main rewards? How "cooperative" is the neighborhood in which you live? Do you wish it were more so? Why or why not?

3. Compare the suggestions made by Ouchi and Edwin Bliss ("Managing Your Time") concerning how American businesses could work more effectively and efficiently. What ideas would you like to share with our business leaders to help make American industry more productive?

IDEAS FOR DISCUSSION/WRITING

Preparing to Write

Write freely about the work ethic that characterizes your immediate environment—at school, at home, or on the job: How do the people in each of these environments feel about one another? How do you feel about them? When are you most productive in these environments? What are the circumstances? Do you work better individually or collectively? Why?

Choosing a Topic

1. Would you prefer to live your social life individually or collectively (as Ouchi defines the two methods)? Explain your preference to a friend, comparing the advantages and disadvantages of both situations. What implications does your preference have? Be sure to make your purpose as clear as possible.
2. Would you rather work in a factory that follows the Japanese or the American method of organization outlined by Ouchi? Explain your preference to your best friend or your immediate supervisor at work. Compare the advantages and disadvantages of both situations. What implications does your preference have? Be sure to make your purpose as clear as possible.
3. *Leisure* magazine has asked you to compare work and leisure from a college student's point of view. Consider the advantages and disadvantages of each. Be sure to decide on a purpose before you begin to write your comparison.

■

GLORIA STEINEM (1934 –)

■ ■ ■

The Politics of Muscle

Once described as a writer with "unpretentious clarity and force-ful expression," Gloria Steinem is one of the foremost organizers and champions of the modern women's movement. She was born in Toledo, Ohio, earned a B.A. at Smith College, and pursued graduate work in political science at the universities of Delhi and Calcutta in India before returning to America to begin a free-lance career in journalism. One of her earliest and best-known articles, "I Was a Playboy Bunny," was a witty exposé of the entire Playboy operation written in 1963 after she had worked under-cover for two weeks in the New York City Playboy Club. In 1968 she and Clay Felker founded *New York* magazine; then, in 1972, they started *Ms.* magazine, which sold out its entire 300,000-copy run in eight days. Steinem's subsequent publications have in-cluded *Outrageous Acts and Everyday Rebellions* (1983), *Marilyn: Norma Jean* (1986), *Bedside Book of Self-Esteem* (1989), and *Moving Beyond Words* (1994). She has also written several television scripts and is a frequent contributor to such periodicals as *Esquire, Vogue, Cosmopolitan, Seventeen*, and *Life*. An articulate and passionate spokesperson for feminist causes, Steinem has been honored nine times by the *World Almanac* as one of the twenty-five most influ-ential women in America.

Preparing to Read

Taken from the author's newest book, *Moving Beyond Words*, "The Politics of Muscle" is actually an introduction to a longer essay entitled "The Strongest Woman in the World," which celebrates the virtues of women's bodybuilding champion Bev Francis. In this introductory essay, Steinem examines the sexual politics of women's weightlifting and the extent to which a "new beauty standard" has begun to evolve because of pioneers in the sport like Francis. As you prepare to read this essay, examine for a few minutes your own thoughts about the associations Americans make with weakness and strength in both men and women: Which sex do you think of as stronger? In America, what does strength have to do with accomplishment? With failure? Do these associations vary for men and women? What does weakness suggest in American culture? Do these suggestions vary for men and women? What are the positive values Americans associate with muscles and strength? With helplessness and weakness? What are the negative values Americans associate with muscles and strength? With helplessness and weakness? What connections have you made from your experience between physical strength and gender roles?

I come from a generation of women who didn't do sports. 1 Being a cheerleader or a drum majorette was as far as our imaginations or role models could take us. Oh yes, there was also being a strutter—one of a group of girls (and we were girls then) who marched and danced and turned cartwheels in front of the high school band at football games. Did you know that big football universities actually gave strutting scholarships? That shouldn't sound any more bizarre than football scholarships, yet somehow it does. Gender politics strikes again.

But even winning one of those rare positions, the stuff that 2 dreams were made of, was more about body display than about the considerable skill they required. You could forget about trying out for them if you didn't have the right face and figure, and my high school was full of girls who had learned to do back flips and twirl flaming batons, all to no avail. Winning wasn't about being the best in an objective competition or achieving a personal best, or even about becoming healthy or fit. It was about *being chosen.*

That's one of many reasons why I and other women of my 3 generation grew up believing—as many girls still do—that the most important thing about a female body is not what it does but how it looks. The power lies not within us but in the gaze of the observer. In retrospect, I feel sorry for the protofeminist gym teachers who tried so hard to interest us in half-court basketball and other team sports thought suitable for girls in my high school, while we worried about the hairdo we'd slept on rollers all night to achieve. Gym was just a stupid requirement you tried to get out of, with ugly gym suits whose very freedom felt odd on bodies accustomed to being constricted for viewing. My blue-collar neighborhood didn't help much either, for it convinced me that sports like tennis or golf were as remote as the country clubs where they were played—mostly by men anyway. That left tap dancing and ballet as my only exercise, and though my dancing school farmed us out to supermarket openings and local night-clubs, where we danced our hearts out in homemade costumes, those events were about display too, about smiling and pleasing and, even during the rigors of ballet, about looking ethereal and hiding any muscles or strength.

My sports avoidance continued into college, where I went 4 through shock about class and wrongly assumed athletics were only for well-to-do prep school girls like those who brought their own lacrosse sticks and riding horses to school. With no sports training to carry over from childhood—and no place to become childlike, as we must when we belatedly learn basic skills—I clung to my familiar limits. Even at the casual softball games where *Ms.* played the staffs of other magazines, I confined myself to cheering. As the *Ms.* No Stars, we prided ourselves on keeping the same lineup, win or lose, and otherwise disobeying the rules of the jockocracy, so I contented myself with upsetting the men on the opposing team by cheering for their female team members. It's amazing how upset those accustomed to conventional divisions can become when others refuse to be divided by them.

In my case, an interest in the politics of strength had come not 5 from my own experience but from observing the mysterious changes in many women around me. Several of my unathletic friends had deserted me by joining gyms, becoming joggers, or discovering the pleasure of learning to yell and kick in self-de-fense class. Others who had young daughters described the unex-pected thrill of seeing them learn to throw a ball or run with a freedom that hadn't been part of our lives in conscious memory. On campuses, I listened to formerly anorexic young women who said their obsession with dieting had diminished when they dis-covered strength as a third alternative to the usual fat-versus-thin dichotomy. Suddenly, a skinny, androgynous, "boyish" body was no longer the only way to escape the soft, female, "victim" bodies they associated with their mothers' fates. Added together, these examples of before-and-after-strength changes were so dramatic that the only male analogues I could find were Vietnam amputees whose confidence was bolstered when they entered marathons in wheelchairs or on artificial legs, or paralyzed accident survivors whose sense of themselves was changed when they learned to play wheelchair basketball. Compared to their handicapped female counterparts, however, even those men seemed to be less transformed. Within each category, women had been less encouraged to develop whatever muscle and skills we had.

Since my old habits of ignoring my body and living inside my 6 head weren't that easy to break, it was difficult to change my nonathletic ways. Instead, I continued to learn secondhand from watching my friends, from reading about female strength in other cultures, and from asking questions wherever I traveled.

Though cultural differences were many, there were political 7 similarities in the way women's bodies were treated that went as deep as patriarchy itself. Whether achieved through law and social policy, as in this and other industrialized countries, or by way of tribal practice and religious ritual, as in older cultures, an individual woman's body was far more subject to other people's rules than was that of her male counterpart. Women always seemed to be owned to some degree as the means of reproduction. And as possessions, women's bodies then became symbols of men's status, with a value that was often determined by what was rare. Thus, rich cultures valued thin women, and poor cultures valued fat women. Yet all patriarchal cultures valued weakness in women. How else could male dominance survive? In my own country, for example, women who "belong" to rich white men are often thinner (as in "You can never be too rich or too thin") than those who "belong" to poor men of color; yet those very different groups of males tend to come together in their belief that women are supposed to be weaker than men; that muscles and strength aren't "feminine."

If I had any doubts about the psychological importance of cul- 8 tural emphasis on male/female strength difference, listening to arguments about equality put them to rest. Sooner or later, even the most intellectual discussion came down to men's supposedly superior strength as a justification for inequality, whether the person arguing regretted or celebrated it. What no one seemed to explore, however, was the inadequacy of physical strength as a way of explaining oppression in other cases. Men of European origin hadn't ruled in South Africa because they were stronger than African men, and blacks hadn't been kept in slavery or bad jobs in the

United States because whites had more muscles. On the contrary, males of the "wrong" class or color were often confined to laboring positions precisely because of their supposedly greater strength, just as the lower pay females received was often rationalized by their supposedly lesser strength. Oppression has no logic—just a self-fulfilling prophecy, justified by a self-perpetuating system.

The more I learned, the more I realized that belief in great 9 strength differences between women and men was itself part of the gender mind-game. In fact, we can't really know what those differences might be, because they are so enshrined, perpetuated, and exaggerated by culture. They seem to be greatest during the childbearing years (when men as a group have more speed and upper-body strength, and women have better balance, endurance, and flexibility) but only marginal during early childhood and old age (when females and males seem to have about the same degree of physical strength). Even during those middle years, the range of difference *among* men and *among* women is far greater than the generalized difference *between* males and females as groups. In multiracial societies like ours, where males of some races are smaller than females of others, judgments based on sex make even less sense. Yet we go right on assuming and praising female weakness and male strength.

But there is a problem about keeping women weak, even in a 10 patriarchy. Women are workers, as well as the means of reproduction. Lower-class women are especially likely to do hard physical labor. So the problem becomes: How to make sure female strength is used for work but not for rebellion? The answer is: Make women ashamed of it. Though hard work requires lower-class women to be stronger than their upper-class sisters, for example, those strong women are made to envy and imitate the weakness of women who "belong" to, and are the means of reproduction for, upper-class men—and so must be kept even *more* physically restricted if the lines of race and inheritance are to be kept "pure." That's why restrictive dress, from the chadors, or full-body veils, of the Middle East to metal ankle and neck rings in Africa, from nineteenth-century hoop skirts in Europe to corsets and high heels here, started among upper-class women and then sifted downward as poor women were encouraged to envy or imitate them. So did such bodily restrictions as bound feet in China, or clitoridectomies and infibulations in much of the Middle East and Africa, both of which practices began with women whose bodies were the means of reproduction for the powerful, and gradually became generalized symbols of feminity. In this country, the self-starvation known as anorexia nervosa is mostly a white, upper-middle-class, young-female phenomenon, but all women are encouraged to envy a white and impossibly thin ideal.

Sexual politics are also reflected through differing emphases on the reproductive parts of women's bodies. Whenever a patriarchy wants females to populate a new territory or replenish an old one, big breasts and hips become admirable. Think of the bosomy ideal of this country's frontier days, or the *zaftig*, Marilyn Monroe–type figure that became popular after the population losses of World War II. As soon as increased population wasn't desirable or necessary, hips and breasts were deemphasized. Think of the Twiggy look that arrived in the 1960s. 11

But whether bosomy or flat, *zaftig* or thin, the female ideal remains weak, and it stays that way unless women ourselves organize to change it. Suffragists shed the unhealthy corsets that produced such a tiny-waisted, big-breasted look that fainting and smelling salts became routine. Instead, they brought in bloomers and bicycling. Feminists of today are struggling against social pressures that exalt siliconed breasts but otherwise stick-thin silhouettes. Introducing health and fitness has already led to a fashion industry effort to reintroduce weakness with the waif look, but at least it's being protested. The point is: Only when women rebel against patriarchal standards does female muscle become more accepted. 12

For these very political reasons, I've gradually come to believe that society's acceptance of muscular women may be one of the most intimate, visceral measures of change. Yes, we need progress everywhere, but an increase in our physical strength could have more impact on the everyday lives of most women than the occasional role model in the boardroom or in the White House. 13

UNDERSTANDING DETAILS

1. According to Steinem, what is "gender politics" (paragraph 1)?
2. In what ways does Steinem equate "winning" with "being chosen" (paragraph 2)? Why is this an important premise for her essay?

3. What does Steinem mean when she says, "Oppression has no logic" (paragraph 8)? Explain your answer in detail.
4. In what ways does "power" lie with the observer rather than within the female?

ANALYZING MEANING

1. Why does Steinem call the female body a "victim" body (paragraph 5)? What did girls' mothers have to do with this association?
2. Do you agree with the author that a woman's body is "far more subject to other people's rules than [is] that of her male counterpart" (paragraph 7)? Explain your answer giving examples from your own experience.
3. What is Steinem implying about the political overtones connected with female weakness and male strength? According to Steinem, why are these judgments so ingrained in American social and cultural mores?
4. What are Steinem's reasons for saying that "society's acceptance of muscular women may be one of the most intimate, visceral measures of change" (paragraph 13)? Do you agree with this statement or not? Explain your reaction in detail.

DISCOVERING RHETORICAL STRATEGIES

1. Who do you think is Steinem's intended audience for this essay? On what do you base your answer.
2. In your opinion, what is Steinem's primary purpose in this essay? Explain your answer in detail.
3. How appropriate is the title of this essay? What would be some possible alternate titles?
4. What rhetorical modes support the author's comparison/contrast? Give examples of each.

MAKING CONNECTIONS

1. To what extent would Alleen Pace Nilsen ("Sexism in English: A 1990s Update") agree with Gloria Steinem's assertion that "the most important thing about a female body is not what it does but how it looks" (paragraph 3)? Do you agree or disagree with this assertion? Give at least three reasons for your opinion.

2. If Steinem is correct that American women have not tradition-ally found power in their muscles, where have they found it? If you were able to ask Barbara Ehrenreich ("Stop Ironing the Diapers"), Judy Brady ("Why I Want a Wife"), or Germaine Greer ("A Child Is Born") this same question, what do you think their answers would be? With whom would you agree most? Explain your answer.

3. How would Nancy Gibbs ("When Is It Rape?") feel about the revolution Steinem describes in women's bodybuilding that is bringing renewed power and strength to women of all ages. To what extent might Gibbs see this trend as an antidote to the epidemic of sex crimes against women?

IDEAS FOR DISCUSSION/WRITING

Preparing to Write

Write freely about the definition and role of strength and weak-ness in American society: What does strength generally mean in American society? What does weakness mean? What associations do you have with both modes of behavior? Where do these asso-ciations come from? What are the political implications of these associations? The social implications? In what ways are strength and weakness basic to the value system in American culture?

Choosing a Topic

1. Compare two different approaches to the process of succeed-ing in a specific job or activity. Develop your own guidelines for making the comparison; then, write an essay for your fel-low students about the similarities and differences you have observed between these two different approaches. Be sure to decide on a purpose and a point of view before you begin to write.

2. Interview your mother and your father about their views on physical strength in their separate family backgrounds. If you have grandparents or step-parents, interview them as well. Then, compare and contrast these various influences in your life. Which of them are alike? Which are different? How have you personally dealt with these similarities and differences? Be sure to decide on a purpose and a point of view before you begin to write.

3. In her essay, Steinem argues that "an increase in our [women's] physical strength could have more impact on the everyday lives of most women than the occasional role model in the boardroom or in the White House" (paragraph 13). Do you agree with the author? Write an essay to be published in your hometown newspaper explaining your views on this issue.

JOYCE CAROL OATES   (1938 –   )

■ ■ ■

On Boxing

A prolific author of short stories, novels, plays, and critical essays, Joyce Carol Oates was born in Lockport, New York. After earning a B.A. from Syracuse University and an M.A. in English from the University of Wisconsin, she taught English and creative writing at the University of Detroit and the University of Windsor (Ontario, Canada) before becoming a professor of English and writer-in-residence at Princeton University. At age twenty-five, she published her first collection of short stories, *By the North Gate* (1963), which prompted praise from reviewers and comparisons with the work of William Faulkner, because both authors wrote about southern pride, rural violence, and fictitious communities "cradled in tradition." Subsequent publications have included *A Garden of Earthly Delights* (1976), *Crossing the Border* (1976), *Angel of Light* (1981), *You Must Remember This* (1987), *On Boxing* (1987), *American Appetites* (1989), *Because It Is Bitter, and Because It Is My Heart* (1990), *Foxfire: Confessions of a Girl Gang* (1993), and *The Sophisticated Cat: An Anthology* (1993). Her most prominent books of literary criticism are *The Edge of Impossibility* (1971), *The Poetry of D. H. Lawrence* (1973), and *New Heaven, New Earth* (1974). Describing herself as an author "who writes in flurries," she nevertheless is "strongly in favor of intelligent, even fastidious revision, which is, or certainly should be, an art in itself. There are pages in recent novels that I've rewritten as many as seventeen times." Oates now lives near Princeton University, where she enjoys playing tennis and practicing the piano.

Preparing to Read

The following essay, taken from *On Boxing*, gives us insight into the sport of boxing by comparing it to "a story—a unique and highly condensed drama without words." Because the comparison is sustained for the entire essay, it is an analogy. As you prepare to read this extended comparison, take a few minutes to think about your favorite sport: Why do you like this sport? Do you usually watch it or participate in it? If you do both, what are the major differences between these two roles? Who are your heroes or heroines in this activity? Why are they your heroes or heroines? Do they serve as role models for you in any other way?

———————————————————————————————— ∎

E ach boxing match is a story—a unique and highly con- 1 densed drama without words. Even when nothing sensational happens: Then the drama is "merely" psychological. Boxers are there to establish an absolute experience, a public accounting of the outermost limits of their beings; they will know, as few of us can know of ourselves, what physical and psychic power they possess—of how much, or how little, they are capable. To enter the ring near-naked and to risk one's life is to make of one's audience voyeurs of a kind: Boxing is so intimate. It is to ease out of sanity's consciousness and into another, difficult to name. It is to risk, and sometimes to realize, the agony of which *agon* (Greek, "contest") is the root.

In the boxing ring there are two principal players, overseen by 2 a shadowy third. The ceremonial ringing of the bell is a summoning to full wakefulness for both boxers and spectators. It sets into motion, too, the authority of Time.

The boxers will bring to the fight everything that is them- 3 selves, and everything will be exposed—including secrets about themselves they cannot fully realize. The physical self, the maleness, one might say, underlying the "self." There are boxers possessed of such remarkable intuition, such uncanny prescience, one would think they were somehow recalling their fights, not fighting them as we watch. There are boxers who perform skillfully, but mechanically, who cannot improvise in response to another's alteration of strategy; there are boxers performing at the peak of their talent who come to realize, mid-fight, that it will not be enough; there are boxers—including great champions—whose careers end abruptly, and irrevocably, as we watch. There has been at least one boxer possessed of an extraordinary and disquieting awareness not only of his opponent's every move and anticipated move but of the audience's keenest shifts in mood as well, for which he seems to have felt personally responsible—Cassius Clay/Muhammad Ali, of course. "The Sweet

Science of Bruising" celebrates the physicality of men even as it dramatizes the limitations, sometimes tragic, more often poignant, of the physical. Though male spectators identify with boxers, no boxer behaves like a "normal" man when he is in the ring and no combination of blows is "natural." All is style.

Every talent must unfold itself in fighting. So Nietzche speaks of 4 the Hellenic past, the history of the "contest"—athletic, and otherwise—by which Greek youths were educated into Greek citizenry. Without the ferocity of competition, without, even "envy, jealousy, and ambition" in the contest, the Hellenic city, like the Hellenic man, degenerated. If death is a risk, death is also the prize—for the winning athlete. . . .

If a boxing match is a story it is an always wayward story, one 5 in which anything can happen. And in a matter of seconds. Split seconds! (Muhammad Ali boasted that he could throw a punch faster than the eye could follow, and he may have been right.) In no other sport can so much take place in so brief a period of time, and so irrevocably.

Because a boxing match is a story without words, this doesn't 6 mean that it has no text or no language, that it is somehow "brute," "primitive," "inarticulate," only that the text is impro- vised in action; the language a dialogue between the boxers of the most refined sort (one might say, as much neurological as psychological: a dialogue of split-second reflexes) in a joint re- sponse to the mysterious will of the audience, which is always that the fight be a worthy one so that the crude paraphernalia of the setting—ring, lights, ropes, stained canvas, the staring on- lookers themselves—be erased, forgotten. (As in the theater or the church, settings are erased by way, ideally, of transcendent action.) Ringside announcers give to the wordless spectacle a narrative unity, yet boxing as performance is more clearly akin to dance or music than narrative.

To turn from an ordinary preliminary match to a "Fight of the 7 Century" like those between Joe Louis and Billy Conn, Joe Frazier and Muhammad Ali, Marvin Hagler and Thomas Hearns is to turn from listening or half-listening to a guitar being idly plucked to hearing Bach's *Well-Tempered Clavier* perfectly exe- cuted, and that too is part of the story's mystery: so much happens so swiftly and with such heart-stopping subtlety you cannot absorb it except to know that something profound is happening and it is happening in a place beyond words.

UNDERSTANDING DETAILS

1. What does Oates mean when she says, "Every talent must unfold itself in fighting" (paragraph 4)? What specifically is she referring to?
2. If boxing is like a story, then what is the "language" of boxing?
3. What is so mysterious about boxing? How does this mystery make boxing profound?
4. According to the author, what secrets are "exposed" in boxing?

ANALYZING MEANING

1. List the primary equations Oates makes throughout her essay. Explain each one in detail.
2. Exactly how does boxing resemble a story? What role do the spectators play in this analogy?
3. Oates says, "In no other sport can so much take place in so brief a period of time, and so irrevocably" (paragraph 5). Do you agree with this statement about boxing? Can you think of an example to disprove this contention? What other sports could be described in this same way?
4. In what ways is boxing "akin to dance or music" (paragraph 6)?

DISCOVERING RHETORICAL STRATEGIES

1. What rhetorical modes does Oates use to support her analogy? How effective are these choices for her purpose?
2. Who do you think is Oates's intended audience? On what evidence do you base your answer?
3. What is the author's attitude toward her subject in this essay? What details in the essay reveal this point of view?
4. Oates uses sentence fragments sporadically throughout this essay (e.g., "The physical self, the maleness, one might say, underlying the 'self,'" paragraph 3). What effect do these fragmented thoughts have on you as the reader? What effect do they create within the essay as a whole?

MAKING CONNECTIONS

Examine Oates's argument that the excitement of a great boxing match happens "in a place beyond words" (paragraph 7) and Steven King's similar assertion in "Why We Crave Horror Movies" that horror films appeal principally to our "base instincts" and our "irrationality." What do these observations have in common? What experiences have you had recently that have happened in a place beyond words?

2. When she compares a boxing match to "a story—a unique and highly condensed drama without words" (paragraph 1), Oates is using metaphor to clarify a topic (in this case, boxing) that may not be familiar to all her readers. In the same fashion, Malcolm Cowley ("The View from 80"), Rita Mae Brown ("Writing as a Moral Act"), Tom Wolfe ("The Right Stuff"), and Susan Sontag ("On AIDS") all use metaphors to help make their prose vivid and understandable to their readers. Who uses metaphors most effectively? Why do you feel this way?

3. Compare and contrast Oates's views on violence with those of Nancy Gibbs ("When Is It Rape?"), Robert Hughes ("The N.R.A. in a Hunter's Sights"), and/or John Langone ("Group Violence"). How would each of these authors define the term *violence*?

IDEAS FOR DISCUSSION/WRITING

Preparing to Write

Write freely about your favorite sport or form of exercise: What other familiar activity does this sport remind you of? What are the parallels between the sport and the activity? Do these parallels help you understand the sport better in any way? Explain your new understanding of the sport. Why do you like this sport more than other sports? How do you feel when you are watching or participating in this sport?

Choosing a Topic

1. For people unfamiliar with the sport you like, compare it to something they know well. Explain as many parallels between the two as you can so that the sport becomes more clearly defined as your essay progresses.

2. Write an analogy essay explaining your attraction to your favorite sport. Why do you like it? How does seeing it or doing it make you feel? Why do you think it affects you this way? What does your commitment to this sport say about you?

3. In an essay written for your peers, explain why you admire one of your sports heroes. Exactly what do you like about this person's performance? In what way is he or she a role model for you? How does this person help you enjoy the sport more?

7

Definition

Limiting the Frame of Reference

Definitions help us function smoothly in a complex world. All effective communication, in fact, is continuously dependent on our unique human ability to understand and employ accurate definitions of a wide range of words, phrases, and abstract ideas. If we did not work from a set of shared definitions, we would not be able to carry on coherent conversations, write comprehensible letters, or respond to even the simplest radio and television programs. Definitions help us understand basic concrete terms (such as automobiles, laser beams, and the gross national product), discuss various events in our lives (such as snow skiing, legal proceedings, and a Cinco de Mayo celebration), and grasp difficult abstract ideas (such as the concepts of democracy, ambition, and resentment). The ability to comprehend definitions and use them effectively helps us keep our oral and written level of communication accurate and accessible to a wide variety of people.

DEFINING DEFINITION

Definition is the process of explaining a word, object, or idea in such a way that the reader (or listener) knows as precisely as possible what we mean. A good definition sets up intellectual boundaries by focusing on the special qualities of a word or phrase that set it apart from other similar words or phrases. Clear definitions always give the writer and the reader a mutual starting point on the sometimes bumpy road to successful communication.

Definitions vary from short, dictionary-length summaries to longer, "extended" accounts that determine the form of an entire essay. Words or ideas that require expanded definitions are usually abstract, complex, or unavoidably controversial; they generally bear many related meanings or many shades of meaning. Definitions can be *objective* (technically precise and generally dry) or *subjective* (colored with personal opinion), and they can be used to instruct or entertain, or to accomplish a combination of these two fundamental rhetorical goals.

In the following excerpt, a student defines "childhood" by putting it into perspective with other important stages of life. Though mostly entertaining, the paragraph is also instructive as the student objectively captures the essence of this phase of human development:

> *Childhood is a stage of growth somewhere between infancy and adolescence. Just as each developmental period in our lives brings new changes and concerns, childhood serves as the threshold to puberty—the time we learn to discriminate between good and bad, right and wrong, love and lust. Childhood is neither a time of irresponsible infancy nor responsible adulthood. Rather, it is marked by duties that we don't really want, challenges that excite us, feelings that puzzle and frighten us, and limitless opportunities that help us explore the world around us. Childhood is a time when we solidify our personalities in spite of pressures to be someone else.*

THINKING CRITICALLY BY USING DEFINITION

Definitions are building blocks in communication that help us make certain we are functioning from the same understanding of terms and ideas. They give us a foundation to work from in both reading and writing. Definitions force us to think about meanings and word associations that make other thinking strategies stronger and easier to work with.

The process of thinking through our definitions forces us to come to some understanding about a particular term or concept we are mentally wrestling with. Articulating that definition helps us move to other modes of thought and higher levels of understanding. Practicing definitions in isolation to get a feel for them is much like separating the skill of peddling from the process of riding a bike. The better you get at peddling, the more natural the rest of the cycling process becomes. The following exercises ask you to practice definitions in a number of different ways. Being more conscious of what definition entails will make it more useful to you in both your reading and your writing.

1. Define one of the concrete words and one of the abstract words listed here in one or two sentences. What were some of the differences between the process you went through to explain the concrete word and the abstract word? What can you conclude from this brief exercise about the differences in defining abstract and concrete words? Concrete: *cattle, book, ranch, water, gum.* Abstract: *freedom, progress, equality, fairness, boredom.*
2. Define the word *grammar.* Consult a dictionary, several handbooks, and maybe even some friends to get their views on the subject. Then, write a humorous definition of grammar that consolidates all these views into a single definition.
3. In what ways can you "define" yourself? What qualities or characteristics are crucial to an understanding of you as a person?

READING AND WRITING DEFINITION ESSAYS

Extended definitions, which usually range from two or three paragraphs to an entire essay, seldom follow a set pattern of development or organization. Instead, as you will see from the examples in this chapter, they draw on a number of different techniques to help explain a word, object, term, concept, or phenomenon.

How to Read a Definition Essay

Preparing to Read. As you begin to read each of the definition essays in this chapter, take some time to consider the author's title and the synopsis of the essay in the Rhetorical Table of Contents: How much can you learn about Nancy Gibbs's topic from her title "When Is It Rape?" What is Rita Mae Brown's attitude toward writing in "Writing as a Moral Act"? What do you sense is the general mood of Susan Sontag's "On AIDS"?

Equally important as you prepare to read is scanning an essay and finding information from its preliminary material about the author and the circumstances surrounding the composition of the essay. What do you think is Robert Ramirez's purpose in his definition of the barrio? And what can you learn about Tom Wolfe and his qualifications for writing "The Right Stuff"?

Last, as you prepare to read these essays, answer the prereading questions before each essay, and then, spend a few minutes thinking freely about the general subject of the essay at hand: What do you want to know from Wolfe about astronaut training in the 1960s? What role does writing play in your life (Brown)? What information do you need about AIDS (Sontag)?

Reading. As you read a definition essay, as with all essays, be sure to record your initial reactions to your reading material. What are some of your thoughts or associations in relation to each essay?

As you get more involved in the essay, reconsider the preliminary material so you can create a context within which to analyze what the writer is saying: What is Gibbs's purpose in writing "When Is It Rape?" Does her tone effectively support that purpose? Who do you think is Ramirez's primary audience? Do you think his essay will effectively reach that group of people? In what ways is Brown qualified to write about the writing process?

Also, determine at this point whether the author's treatment of his or her subject is predominantly objective or subjective. Then, make sure you understand the main points of the essay on the literal, interpretive, and analytical levels by reading the questions that follow.

Rereading. When you read these definition essays for a second time, check to see how each writer actually sets forth his or her definition: Does the writer put each item in a specific category with clear boundaries? Do you understand how the item being defined is different from other items in the same category? Did the author name the various components of the item, explain its etymology (linguistic origin and history), discuss what it is not, or perform a combination of these tasks?

To evaluate the effectiveness of a definition essay, you need to reconsider the essay's primary purpose and audience. If Wolfe is trying to get the general reader to understand the rigors of military flight training, how effective is he in doing so? In like manner, is Gibbs successful in communicating the seriousness of date rape?

Especially applicable is the question of what other rhetorical strategies help the author communicate this purpose. What other modes does Ramirez use to help him define the barrio? Through what other modes does Sontag define AIDS?

For an inventory of the reading process, you can review the guidelines on pages 20–21 of the Introduction.

How to Write a Definition Essay

Preparing to Write. As with other essays, you should begin the task of writing a definition essay by answering the prewriting questions featured in this text and then by exploring your subject and generating other ideas. (See the explanation of various prewriting techniques on pages 21–23 of the Introduction.) Be sure you know what you are going to define and how you will approach your definition. You should then focus on a specific audience and purpose as you approach the writing assignment.

Writing. The next step toward developing a definition essay is usually to describe the general category to which the word belongs and then to contrast the word with all other words in that group. To define *exposition*, for example, you might say that it is a type of writing. Then, to differentiate it from other types of writing, you could go on to say that its main purpose is to "expose," or present information, as opposed to rhetorical modes such as description and narration, which describe and tell stories. In addition, you might want to cite some expository methods, such as example, process analysis, division/classification, and comparison/contrast.

Yet another way to begin a definition essay is to provide a term's etymology. Tracing a word's origin often illuminates its current meaning and usage as well. *Exposition*, for example, comes from the Latin *exponere*, meaning "to put forth, set forth, display, declare, or publish" (*ex* = out; *ponere* = to put or place). This information can generally be found in any good dictionary or in a good encyclopedia.

Another approach to defining a term is to explain what it does *not* mean. *Exposition* is not description or narration; nor is it poetry of any kind. By limiting the readers' frame of reference in these various ways, you are helping to establish a working definition for the term under consideration.

Finally rhetorical methods that we have already studied, such as description, narration, example, process analysis, division/classification, and comparison/contrast, are particularly useful to writers in expanding their definitions. To clarify the term *exposition*, you might **describe** the details of an expository theme, **narrate** a story about the wide use of the term in today's classroom, or **give examples** of assignments that would produce good expository writing. In other situations, you could **analyze** various writing assignments and discuss the **process** of producing an expository essay, **classify** exposition apart from creative writing and then **divide** it into categories similar to the headings of this book, or **compare** and **contrast** it with creative writing. Writers also use definition quite often to support other rhetorical modes.

Rewriting. Reviewing and revising a definition essay is a relatively straightforward task:

Have you chosen an effective beginning for your paper?
Did you create a reasonable context for your definition?
Have you used appropriate rhetorical strategies to develop your ideas?
Will your explanation be clear to your intended audience?
Have you achieved your overall purpose as effectively as possible?

Other guidelines to direct your writing and revising appear on pages 32–33 of the Introduction.

STUDENT ESSAY: DEFINITION AT WORK

In the following essay, a student defines "the perfect yuppie." Notice how the writer puts this term in a category and then explains the limits of that category and the uniqueness of this term within the category. To further inform her audience of the features of "yuppiedom," the student calls on the word's etymology, its dictionary definition, an itemization of the term's basic characteristics, a number of examples that explain those characteristics, and, finally, a general discussion of causes and effects that regulate a yuppie's behavior.

The Perfect Yuppie

Etymology/ dictionary definition

Many people already know that the letters YUP stand for "young urban professional." *Young* in this context is understood to mean thirtyish; *urban* often means suburban; and *professional* means most definitely college-educated. Double the *P* and add an

General category of word being defined

Subject *I* and an *E* at the end, and you get *yuppie*—
that 1980s bourgeois, the marketers' dar-
ling, and the 1960s' inheritance. But let's
not generalize. Not every thirty-year-old

Limitations
set suburban college graduate qualifies as a
yuppie. Nor is every yuppie in his or her
thirties. True yuppiness involves much more
than the words that make up the acronym.

Writer's
credibility Being the little sister of a couple of yups, I
am in an especially good position to define
the perfect yuppie. I watched two develop.

Why the dictionary definition is inadequate

  The essence of yuppiness is generally
new money. In the yuppie's defense, I will
admit that most yuppies have worked hard
for their money and social status.

General character-istic

Cause/
Effect Moreover, the baby boom of which they
are a part has caused a glut of job seekers in
their age bracket, forcing them to be competitive if they want all the nice things re-
tailers have designed for them. But with

General
character-
istic new money comes an interesting combination of wealth, naiveté, and pretentiousness.

  For example, most yuppies worthy of the

Specific
example title have long ago traded in their fringed
suede jackets for fancy fur coats. Although
they were animal rights activists in the 1960s,
they will not notice the irony of this change.
In fact, they may be shameless enough to parade in their fur coats—fashion-show style—
for friends and family. Because of their
"innocence," yuppies generally will not see
the vulgarity of their actions.

Cause/ effect

Specific example

  Because they are often quite wealthy,

General
character-
istic yuppies tend to have a lot of "things."
They are simply overwhelmed by the responsibility of spending all that money. For
example, one yup I know has fourteen pairs
of sunglasses and seven watches. She, her
husband, and their three children own at

Specific example

least twenty collections of everything from Specific example
comic books to Civil War memorabilia.
Most yuppies have so much money that I
often wonder why the word "yuppie" does
not have a dollar sign in it somewhere.

General character-istic Perhaps in an effort to rid themselves of Cause/effect
this financial burden, all good yuppies go to
Europe as soon as possible. Not Germany
or France or Portugal, mind you, but
Europe. They do not know what they are
doing there and thus generally spend much Cause/effect
more money than they need to—but, after
all, no yuppie ever claimed to be frugal.
General character-istic Most important, they bring home slides of
Europe and show them to everyone they
know. A really good yuppie will forget and
show you his or her slides more than once.
Incidentally, when everyone has seen the
slides of Europe twice, the yuppie's next
stop is Australia.

General character-istic A favorite pastime of yuppies is having
wine-tasting parties for their yuppie
friends. At these parties, they must make a Specific example
great to-do about tasting the wine, cupping
their faces over the glass with their palms
(as if they were having a facial), and even
sniffing the cork, for goodness sake. I once
knew a yuppie who did not understand Specific example
that a bottle of wine could not be rejected
simply because he found he "did not like
Specific example that kind." Another enjoyed making a show
of having his wife choose and taste the
wine occasionally, which they both thought
was adorable.

What it is not Some yuppie wanna-be's drive red or
black BMWs, but don't let them fool you.
A genuine, hard-core yuppie will usually
own a gold or silver Volvo station wagon. In General character-istic
this yuppie-mobile, the yuppie wife will
chauffeur her young yupettes to and from

Specific examples

their modeling classes, track meets, ballet, the manicurist, and boy scouts, for the young yuppie is generally as competitive and socially active as his or her parents. On the same topic, one particularly annoying trait of yuppie parents is bragging about their yupettes. You will know yuppies by the fact that they have the smartest, most

General character- istic

talented children in the world. They will show you their kids' report cards, making sure you notice any improvements from last quarter.

Specific example

Perhaps I have been harsh in my por- trayal of the perfect yuppie, and, certainly, I will be accused by some of stereotyping.

Division/ classifica- tion

But consider this: I never classify people as yuppies who do not so classify themselves. The ultimate criterion for being yuppies is that they will always proudly label them- selves as such.

General character- istic and concluding statement

Student Writer's Comments

The most difficult part about writing this definition essay was choosing a topic. I knew it had to be a word or phrase with different shades of meaning, but it also had to be either something I knew more about than the average person or something I had an unusual perspective on. I figured *yuppie* was a good word, not only because it has different meanings for different people, but also because it is an acronym, and acronyms tend to be greater than the sum of their parts.

I started by looking the word up in the dictionary and writ- ing down its etymology (which I later referred to in my open- ing sentence). I then used freewriting to record the various meanings and natural associations I have with the word *yuppie*, which helped me discover relationships between these mean- ings and associations. I felt my mind wandering freely over all aspects of this word as I filled up pages and pages of freewrit- ing. I then felt as if I had enough material to work with, so I began to write a draft of my essay.

I started writing the essay from the beginning, a process that was a real novelty for me. After citing the etymology of my word and placing it in a general category, I explained why the dictionary definition was inadequate. Then, I let the general characteristics I associate with the word take me step by step through the essay. As I wrote, I found myself mentally reorganizing my prewriting notes so that I could stay slightly ahead of my actual writing. I kept looping back and forth into my notes, looking for the next best characters to introduce, then writing, then going back to my notes again. I generated my entire first draft this way and revised the order only slightly in my final draft.

As I reworked my essay before handing it in, I added some humor from my own experience with my older sisters and looked closely at other rhetorical modes I had used to support my definition. Naturally, I had scattered examples throughout my essay and had discussed causes and effects quite openly. I revised my paper to make some of the connections I had had in mind clearer by either adding transitions or explaining the relationships in other words. I found that this process lengthened my essay quite a bit as I revised. I also worked on the essay at this point to bring out a secondary point I had had in mind, which is that some yuppies have lost the 1960s values they once had but often don't even realize it.

I spent the remainder of my time on my conclusion, which I rewrote from scratch four times. I finally ended up directly addressing the classification of yuppies, at which point I stumbled on the ultimate criterion for being a yuppy: "They will always proudly label themselves as such." When I reached this insight, I knew my paper was finished, and I was content with the results. I also realized that rewriting the conclusion so many times had given me a headache, but the pain was worth it.

SOME FINAL THOUGHTS ON DEFINITION

The following selections feature extended definitions whose main purpose is to explain a specific term or idea to their readers. Each essay in its own way helps the audience identify with various parts of its definitions, and each successfully communicates the unique qualities of the term or idea in question. Notice what approaches to definition each writer takes and how these approaches limit the readers' frame of reference in the process of effective communication.

NANCY GIBBS   (1960 –   )

■ ■ ■

When Is It Rape?

Nancy Gibbs, a New York City native, graduated summa cum laude from Yale with a degree in history; she also attended Oxford University, where she studied politics and philosophy while on a prestigious Marshall Scholarship. In 1985, she began working for *Time* magazine, where she was originally assigned to the international section. Two years later, she transferred to business and the economy just in time to help cover the stock market crash of 1987. The following year she became a feature writer, covering such topics as child labor laws, racism on campus, the elderly in America, emergency care, the right to die, homelessness, and the changing doctor-patient relationship. She currently writes on national affairs and domestic policy issues for *Time's* Nation section. Her book *Children of Light* (1985) details the history of Quaker education in the state of New York. A frequent guest on radio and television talk shows, Gibbs is also an active member of the Fifth Avenue Presbyterian Church, where she serves as head of the board of deacons. In her spare time, she enjoys sailing and dancing. Her advice to students using *The Prose Reader* is to "keep writing." "The more you do it," she explains, "the better you get." She also urges student writers to seek out criticism from someone they respect: "Find a writing mentor, and pay attention to what that person tells you."

Preparing to Read

The following essay, originally published in *Time* (June 3, 1991), examines the social, legal, and moral aspects of rape—particularly "date rape"—and its effects on the men and women involved. As you prepare to read Gibbs's definition of date rape, pause a few moments to think about any associations you make with the word *rape*: What is your definition of *rape*? Why might different people have developed different definitions for this word? Why has this topic been so hotly debated on college campuses? What biases do people have in connection with rape? Why do so few rape victims ever report the crime? How successful has our legal system been in dealing with this problem in the past?

B e careful of strangers and hurry home, says a mother to her daughter, knowing that the world is a frightful place but not wishing to swaddle a child in fear. Girls grow up scarred by caution and enter adulthood eager to shake free of their parents' worst nightmares. They still know to be wary of strangers. What they don't know is whether they have more to fear from their friends.

Most women who get raped are raped by people they already know—like the boy in biology class, or the guy in the office down the hall, or their friend's brother. The familiarity is enough to make them let down their guard, sometimes even enough to make them wonder afterward whether they were "really raped." What people think of as "real rape"—the assault by a monstrous stranger lurking in the shadows—accounts for only 1 out of 5 attacks.

So the phrase "acquaintance rape" was coined to describe the rest, all the cases of forced sex between people who already knew each other, however casually. But that was too clinical for headline writers, and so the popular term is the narrower "date rape," which suggests an ugly ending to a raucous night on the town.

These are not idle distinctions. Behind the search for labels is the central mythology about rape: that rapists are always strangers, and victims are women who ask for it. The mythology is hard to dispel because the crime is so rarely exposed. The experts guess— that's all they can do under the circumstances—that while 1 in 4 women will be raped in her lifetime, less than 10% will report the assault, and less than 5% of the rapists will go to jail.

When a story of the crime lodges in the headlines, the myths have a way of cluttering the search for the truth. The tale of Good Friday in Palm Beach landed in the news because it involved a Kennedy, but it may end up as a watershed case, because all the mysteries and passions surrounding date rape are here to be dissected. William Kennedy Smith met a woman at a bar, invited her back home late at night and apparently had sex with her on the lawn. She says it was rape, and the police believed her

1

2

3

4

5

story enough to charge him with the crime. Perhaps it was the bruises on her leg; or the instincts of the investigators who found her, panicked and shaking, curled up in the fetal position on a couch; or the lie-detector tests she passed.

On the other side, Smith has adamantly protested that he is a man falsely accused. His friends and family testify to his gentle nature and moral fiber and insist that he could not possibly have committed such a crime. Maybe the truth will come out in court—but regardless of its finale, the case has shoved the debate over date rape into the minds of average men and women. Plant the topic in a conversation, and chances are it will ripen into a bitter argument or a jittery sequence of pale jokes. **6**

Women charge that date rape is the hidden crime; men complain it is hard to prevent a crime they can't define. Women say it isn't taken seriously; men say it is a concept invented by women who like to tease but not take the consequences. Women say the date-rape debate is the first time the nation has talked frankly about sex; men say it is women's unconscious reaction to the excesses of the sexual revolution. Meanwhile, men and women argue among themselves about the "gray area" that surrounds the whole murky arena of sexual relations, and there is no consensus in sight. **7**

In court, on campus, in conversation, the issue turns on the elasticity of the word *rape*, one of the few words in the language with the power to summon a shared image of a horrible crime. **8**

At one extreme are those who argue that for the word to retain its impact, it must be strictly defined as forced sexual intercourse: a gang of thugs jumping a jogger in Central Park, a psychopath preying on old women in a housing complex, a man with an ice pick in a side street. To stretch the definition of the word risks stripping away its power. In this view, if it happened on a date, it wasn't rape. A romantic encounter is a context in which sex *could* occur, and so what omniscient judge will decide whether there was genuine mutual consent? **9**

Others are willing to concede that date rape sometimes occurs, that sometimes a man goes too far on a date without a woman's consent. But this infraction, they say, is not as ghastly a crime as street rape, and it should not be taken as seriously. The *New York Post*, alarmed by the Willy Smith case, wrote in a recent editorial, "If the sexual encounter, *forced or not*, has been preceded **10** by a series of consensual activities—drinking, a trip to the man's home, a walk on a deserted beach at 3 in the morning—the charge that's leveled against the alleged offender should, it seems to us, be different than the one filed against, say, the youths who raped and beat the jogger."

This attitude sparks rage among women who carry scars received at the hands of men they knew. It makes no difference if the victim shared a drink or a moonlit walk or even a passionate kiss, they protest, if the encounter ended with her being thrown to the ground and forcibly violated. Date rape is not about a misunderstanding, they say. It is not a communications problem. It is not about a woman's having regrets in the morning for a decision she made the night before. It is not about a "decision" at all. Rape is rape, and any form of forced sex—even between neighbors, coworkers, classmates and casual friends—is a crime. 11

A more extreme form of that view comes from activists who see rape as a metaphor, its definition swelling to cover any kind of oppression of women. Rape, seen in this light, can occur not only on a date but also in a marriage, not only by violent assault but also by psychological pressure. A Swarthmore College training pamphlet once explained that acquaintance rape "spans a spectrum of incidents and behaviors, ranging from crimes legally defined as rape to verbal harassment and inappropriate innuendo." 12

No wonder, then, that the battles become so heated. When innuendo qualifies as rape, the definitions have become so slippery that the entire subject sinks into a political swamp. The only way to capture the hard reality is to tell the story. 13

A 32-year-old woman was on business in Tampa last year for the Florida supreme court. Stranded at the courthouse, she accepted a lift from a lawyer involved in her project. As they chatted on the ride home, she recalls, "he was saying all the right things, so I started to trust him." She agreed to have dinner, and afterward, at her hotel door, he convinced her to let him come in to talk. "I went through the whole thing about being old-fashioned," she says. "I was a virgin until I was 21. So I told him talk was all we were going to do." 14

But as they sat on the couch, she found herself falling asleep. "By now, I'm comfortable with him, and I put my head on his shoulder. He's not tried anything all evening, after all." Which is 15 when the rape came. "I woke up to find him on top of me, forcing himself on me. I didn't scream or run. All I could think about was my business contacts and what if they saw me run out of my room screaming rape.

"I thought it was my fault. I felt so filthy, I washed myself over 16 and over in hot water. Did he rape me?, I kept asking myself. I didn't consent. But who's gonna believe me? I had a man in my hotel room after midnight." More than a year later, she still can't tell the story without a visible struggle to maintain her composure. Police referred the case to the state attorney's office in Tampa, but without more evidence it decided not to prosecute. Although her attacker has admitted that he heard her say no, maintains the woman, "he says he didn't know that I meant no. He didn't feel he'd raped me, and he even wanted to see me again."

Her story is typical in many ways. The victim herself may not 17 be sure right away that she has been raped, that she had said no and been physically forced into having sex anyway. And the rapist commonly hears but does not heed the protest. "A date rapist will follow through no matter what the woman wants because his agenda is to get laid," says Claire Walsh, a Florida-based consultant on sexual assaults. "First comes the dinner, then a dance, then a drink, then the coercion begins." Gentle persuasion gives way to physical intimidation, with alcohol as the ubiquitous lubricant. "When that fails, force is used," she says. "Real men don't take no for an answer."

The Palm Beach case serves to remind women that if they go 18 ahead and press charges, they can expect to go on trial along with their attacker, if not in a courtroom then in the court of public opinion. The *New York Times* caused an uproar on its own staff not only for publishing the victim's name but also for laying out in detail her background, her high school grades, her driving record, along with an unattributed quote from a school official about her "little wild streak." A freshman at Carleton College in Minnesota, who says she was repeatedly raped for four hours by a fellow student, claims that she was asked at an administrative hearing if she performed oral sex on dates. In 1989 a man charged with raping at knife-point a woman he knew was acquitted in Florida because his victim had been wearing lace shorts and no underwear.

From a purely legal point of view, if she wants to put her at- 19 tacker in jail, the survivor had better be beaten as well as raped, since bruises become a badge of credibility. She had better have reported the crime right away, before taking the hours-long shower that she craves, before burning her clothes, before curling up with the blinds down. And she would do well to be a woman of shining character. Otherwise the strict constructionist definitions of rape will prevail in court. "Juries don't have a great deal of sympathy for the victim if she's a willing participant up to the nonconsensual sexual intercourse," says Norman Kinne, a prosecutor in Dallas. "They feel that many times the victim has placed herself in the situation." Absent eyewitnesses or broken bones, a case comes down to her word against his, and the mythology of rape rarely lends her the benefit of the doubt.

She should also hope for an all-male jury, preferably composed 20 of fathers with daughters. Prosecutors have found that women tend to be harsh judges of one another—perhaps because to find a defendant guilty is to entertain two grim realities: that anyone might be a rapist, and that every woman could find herself a victim. It may be easier to believe, the experts muse, that at some level the victim asked for it. "But just because a woman makes a bad judgment, does that give the guy a moral right to rape her?" asks Dean Kilpatrick, director of the Crime Victim Research and Treatment Center at the Medical University of South Carolina. "The bottom line is, Why does a woman's having a drink give a man the right to rape her?"

Last week the Supreme Court waded into the debate with a 7- 21 to-2 ruling that protects victims from being harassed on the witness stand with questions about their sexual history. The Justices, in their first decision on "rape shield laws," said an accused rapist could not present evidence about a previous sexual relationship with the victim unless he notified the court ahead of time. In her decision, Justice Sandra Day O'Connor wrote that "rape victims deserve heightened protection against surprise, harassment and unnecessary invasions of privacy."

That was welcome news to prosecutors who understand the re- 22 luctance of victims to come forward. But there are other impediments to justice as well. An internal investigation of the Oakland police department found that officers ignored a quarter of all reports of sexual assaults or attempts, though 90% actually warranted investigation. Departments are getting better at educating officers in handling rape cases, but the courts remain behind. A New York City task force on women in the courts charged that judges and lawyers were routinely less inclined to believe a woman's testimony than a man's.

The present debate over degrees of rape is nothing new: All 23 through history, rapes have been divided between those that mattered and those that did not. For the first few thousand years, the only rape that was punished was the defiling of a virgin, and that was viewed as a property crime. A girl's virtue was a marketable asset, and so a rapist was often ordered to pay the victim's father the equivalent of her price on the marriage market. In early Babylonian and Hebrew societies, a married woman who was raped suffered the same fate as an adulteress—death by stoning or drowning. Under William the Conqueror, the penalty for raping a virgin was castration and loss of both eyes—unless the violated woman agreed to marry her attacker, as she was often pressured to do. "Stealing an heiress" became a perfectly conventional means of taking—literally—a wife.

It may be easier to prove a rape case now, but not much. Until 24 the 1960s it was virtually impossible without an eyewitness; judges were often required to instruct jurors that "rape is a charge easily made and hard to defend against; so examine the testimony of this witness with caution." But sometimes a rape was taken very seriously, particularly if it involved a black man attacking a white woman—a crime for which black men were often executed or lynched.

Susan Estrich, author of *Real Rape*, considers herself a lucky 25 victim. This is not just because she survived an attack 17 years ago by a stranger with an ice pick, one day before her graduation from Wellesley. It's because police, and her friends, believed her. "The first thing the Boston police asked was whether it was a black guy," recalls Estrich, now a University of Southern California law professor. When she said yes and gave the details of the attack, their reaction was, "So, you were really raped." It was an instructive lesson, she says, in understanding how racism and sexism are factored into perceptions of the crime.

A new twist in society's perception came in 1975, when Susan 26 Brownmiller published her book *Against Our Will: Men, Women and Rape.* In it she attacked the concept that rape was a sex crime, arguing instead that is was a crime of violence and power over women. Throughout history, she wrote, rape has played a critical function. "It is nothing more or less than a conscious process of intimidation, by which *all men* keep *all women* in a state of fear."

Out of this contention was born a set of arguments that have 27
become politically correct wisdom on campus and in academic circles. This view holds that rape is a symbol of women's vulnerability to male institutions and attitudes. "It's sociopolitical," insists Gina Rayfield, a New Jersey psychologist. "In our culture men hold the power, politically, economically. They're socialized not to see women as equals."

This line of reasoning has led some women, especially radical- 28
ized victims, to justify flinging around the term rape as a political weapon, referring to everything from violent sexual assaults to inappropriate innuendos. Ginny, a college senior who was really raped when she was 16, suggests that false accusations of rape can serve a useful purpose. "Penetration is not the only form of violation," she explains. In her view, rape is a subjective term, one that women must use to draw attention to other, nonviolent, even nonsexual forms of oppression. "If a woman did falsely accuse a man of rape, she may have had reasons to," Ginny says. "Maybe she wasn't raped, but he clearly violated her in some way."

Catherine Comins, assistant dean of student life at Vassar, also 29
sees some value in this loose use of "rape." She says angry victims of various forms of sexual intimidation cry rape to regain their sense of power. "To use the word carefully would be to be careful for the sake of the violator, and the survivors don't care a hoot about him." Comins argues that men who are unjustly accused can sometimes gain from the experience. "They have a lot of pain, but it is not a pain that I would necessarily have spared them. I think it ideally initiates a process of self-exploration. 'How do I see women?' 'If I didn't violate her, could I have?' 'Do I have the potential to do to her what they say I did?' Those are good questions."

Taken to extremes, there is an ugly element of vengeance at 30
work here. Rape is an abuse of power. But so are false accusations of rape, and to suggest that men whose reputations are destroyed might benefit because it will make them more sensitive is an attitude that is sure to backfire on women who are seeking justice for all victims.

On campuses where the issue is most inflamed, male students are outraged that their names can be scrawled on a bathroom-wall list of rapists and they have no chance to tell their side of the story.

"Rape is what you read about in the *New York Post* about 17 little boys raping a jogger in Central Park," says a male freshman at a liberal-arts college, who learned that he had been branded a rapist after a one-night stand with a friend. He acknowledges that they were both very drunk when she started kissing him at a party and ended up back in his room. Even through his haze, he had some qualms about sleeping with her: "I'm fighting against my hormonal instincts, and my moral instincts are saying, 'This is my friend and if I were sober, I wouldn't be doing this,' " But he went ahead anyway. "When you're drunk, and there are all sorts of ambiguity, and the woman says 'Please, please' and then she says no sometime later, even in the middle of the act, there still may very well be some kind of violation, but it's not the same thing. It's not rape. If you don't hear her say no, if she doesn't say it, if she's playing around with you—oh, I could get squashed for saying it—there is an element of say no, mean yes." 31

The morning after their encounter, he recalls, both students woke up hung over and eager to put the memory behind them. Only months later did he learn that she had told a friend that he had torn her clothing and raped her. At this point in the story, the accused man starts using the language of rape. "I felt violated," he says. "I felt like she was taking advantage of me when she was very drunk. I never heard her say 'No!,' 'Stop!,' anything." He is angry and hurt at the charges, worried that they will get around, shatter his reputation and force him to leave the small campus. 32

So here, of course, is the heart of the debate. If rape is sex without consent, how exactly should consent be defined and communicated, when and by whom? Those who view rape through a political lens tend to place all responsibility on men to make sure that their partners are consenting at every point of a sexual encounter. At the extreme, sexual relations come to resemble major surgery, requiring a signed consent form. Clinical psychologist Mary P. Koss of the University of Arizona in Tucson, who is a leading scholar on the issue, puts it rather bluntly: "It's the man's penis that is doing the raping, and ultimately he's responsible for where he puts it." 33

Historically, of course, this has never been the case, and there   34
are some who argue that it shouldn't be—that women too must
take responsibility for their behavior, and that the whole realm
of intimate encounters defies regulation from on high.
Anthropologist Lionel Tiger has little patience for trendy sexual
politics that make no reference to biology. Since the dawn of
time, he argues, men and women have always gone to bed with
different goals. In the effort to keep one's genes in the gene pool,
"it is to the male advantage to fertilize as many females as possible, as quickly as possible and as efficiently as possible." For the female, however, who looks at the large investment she will have to
make in the offspring, the opposite is true. Her concern is to "select" who "will provide the best set up for their offspring." So, in
general, "the pressure is on the male to be aggressive and on the
female to be coy."

No one defends the use of physical force, but when the coer-   35
cion involved is purely psychological, it becomes hard to assign
blame after the fact. Journalist Stephanie Gutmann is an ardent
foe of what she calls the date-rape dogmatists. "How can you
make sex completely politically correct and completely safe?" she
asks. "What a horribly bland, unerotic thing that would be! Sex
is, by nature, a risky endeavor, emotionally. And desire is a violent
emotion. These people in the date-rape movement have erected
so many rules and regulations that I don't know how people can
have erotic or desire-driven sex."

Nonsense, retorts Cornell professor Andrea Parrot, co-author   36
of *Acquaintance Rape: The Hidden Crime*. Seduction should not be
about lies, manipulation, game playing or coercion of any kind,
she says. "Too bad that people think that the only way you can
have passion and excitement and sex is if there are miscommuni-
cations and one person is forced to do something he or she
doesn't want to do." The very pleasures of sexual encounters should
lie in the fact of mutual comfort and consent: "You can hang from
the ceiling, you can use fruit, you can go crazy and have really
wonderful sensual erotic sex, if both parties are consenting."

It would be easy to accuse feminists of being too quick to clas-   37
sify sex as rape, but feminists are to be found on all sides of the
debate, and many protest the idea that all the onus is on the man.
It demeans women to suggest that they are so vulnerable to coer-

cion or emotional manipulation that they must always be es-
corted by the strong arm of the law. "You can't solve society's ills
by making everything a crime," says Albuquerque attorney Nancy
Hollander. "That comes out of the sense of overprotection of
women, and in the long run that is going to be harmful to us."

What is lost in the ideological debate over date rape is the fact 38
that men and women, especially when they are young, and
drunk, and aroused, are not very good at communicating. "In
many cases," says Estrich, "the man thought it was sex, and the
woman thought it was rape, and they are both telling the truth."
The man may envision a celluloid seduction, in which he is being
commanding, she is being coy. A woman may experience the
same event as a degrading violation of her will. That some men
do not believe a woman's protests is scarcely surprising in a society so drenched with messages that women have rape fantasies
and a desire to be overpowered.

By the time they reach college, men and women are loaded 39
with cultural baggage, drawn from movies, television, music
videos and "bodice ripper" romance novels. Over the years they
have watched Rhett sweep Scarlett up the stairs in *Gone With the
Wind*; or Errol Flynn, who was charged twice with statutory rape,
overpower a protesting heroine who then melts in his arms; or
Stanley rape his sister-in-law Blanche du Bois while his wife is in
the hospital giving birth to a child in *A Streetcar Named Desire*.
Higher up the cultural food chain, young people can read of date
rape in Homer or Jane Austen, watch it in *Don Giovanni* or
Rigoletto.

The messages come early and often, and nothing in the femi- 40
nist revolution has been able to counter them. A recent survey of
sixth- to ninth-graders in Rhode Island found that a fourth of
the boys and a sixth of the girls said it was acceptable for a man
to force a woman to kiss him or have sex if he has spent money
on her. A third of the children said it would not be wrong for a
man to rape a woman who had had previous sexual experiences.

Certainly cases like Palm Beach, movies like *The Accused* and 41
novels like Avery Corman's *Prized Possessions* may force young
people to re-examine assumptions they have inherited. The use of
new terms, like acquaintance rape and date rape, while controversial, has given men and women the vocabulary they need to ex-

press their experiences with both force and precision. This dialogue would be useful if it helps strip away some of the dogmas, old and new, surrounding the issue. Those who hope to raise society's sensitivity to the problem of date rape would do well to concede that it is not precisely the same sort of crime as street rape, that there may be very murky issues of intent and degree involved.

On the other hand, those who downplay the problem should 42 come to realize that date rape is a crime of uniquely intimate cruelty. While the body is violated, the spirit is maimed. How long will it take, once the wounds have healed, before it is possible to share a walk on a beach, a drive home from work, or an evening's conversation without always listening for a quiet alarm to start ringing deep in the back of the memory of a terrible crime?

UNDERSTANDING DETAILS

1. Define the term *date rape* in your own words.
2. What is the central mythology in the American culture about rapists and their victims? Explain it in detail.
3. What are the main differences of opinion between men and women on the issue of date rape?
4. According to most women, when does sex become a crime?

ANALYZING MEANING

1. Explain three of the many ambiguous issues associated with the word *rape*.
2. After Gibbs wrote this essay, William Kennedy Smith was acquitted of the charge of rape in a dramatic case televised for the American public. In what ways does this verdict help us understand "date rape" more clearly? What role did the media play in this understanding?
3. Why is Gibbs not surprised that some men don't believe women's protests? What lessons have these men learned from the media as they were growing up?
4. Exactly what is Gibbs asking when she says, "How long will it take, once the wounds have healed, before it is possible to share a walk on a beach, a drive home from work, or an evening's conversation without always listening for a quiet alarm to start

ringing deep in the back of the memory of a terrible crime?" (paragraph 42)?

DISCOVERING RHETORICAL STRATEGIES

1. What rhetorical techniques explained at the beginning of this chapter does Gibbs use in her definition?
2. Choose from this essay a difference of opinion between men and women, and explain the reasoning at work on each side.
3. Gibbs has to choose her words very carefully in an essay on a subject charged with so many emotional and political ramifications. Choose one paragraph from this essay, and explain how different words would send different messages and associations. Would these changes be for the better or worse, considering Gibbs's intended audience?
4. What rhetorical strategies, besides definition, does Gibbs use in this essay? Give examples of each strategy.

MAKING CONNECTIONS

1. If Nancy Gibbs, Judy Brady ("Why I Want a Wife"), and Germaine Greer ("A Child Is Born") were interviewed, how do you think each author would complete the following sentence: "Women are exploited when _____ ." How would you complete the same sentence? Have you ever been exploited? What were the circumstances? How did you respond?
2. Gibbs strips away the mythology surrounding rape in the same way that Jessica Mitford ("Behind the Formaldehyde Curtain") reveals the morbid reality behind American funeral customs. In what way have these misleading myths kept us from changing public attitudes toward these two controversial issues?
3. Imagine a conversation between Gibbs and Alleen Pace Nilsen ("Sexism in English: A 1990s Update") in which both authors claim that the high incidence of rape in America is understandable, perhaps even predictable, in a culture that devalues women through its daily use of language. What is your reaction to this assertion?

IDEAS FOR DISCUSSION/WRITING

Preparing to Write

Write freely about your reactions to crimes in general: What makes an action a crime? What are the most common crimes in

America today? Has your definition of rape changed since you read this article? Is there a distinction in your mind between "street rape" and "date or acquaintance rape"? If so, what is the difference? Why do you think rape has become such a frequently committed crime? Why is the issue of rape receiving so much attention on college campuses? What other crimes are common occurrences on college campuses?

Choosing a Topic

1. In a coherent essay written for your classmates, define a serious injustice or crime (other than rape) that frequently takes place on college campuses. What type of people usually commit these injustices or crimes? Why do they do so? Why are such activities "unjust" or "criminal"? Before you begin to write, decide on a purpose and point of view.

2. Do you think rape is a sex crime or a "crime of violence and power over women" (paragraph 26), as Susan Brownmiller argues in her book? Discuss this issue in a well-developed essay, and draw your own conclusions from your discussion.

3. Choose one of the definitional techniques explained in the introduction to this chapter, and define the word *crime* in a well-developed, logically organized essay written for the general public. Introduce your main topic at the beginning of your essay; then, explain and illustrate it clearly as your essay progresses. You may use other definition techniques in addition to the controlling one.

ROBERT RAMIREZ   (1949 –   )

■ ■ ■

The Barrio

Robert Ramirez was born and raised in Edinburg, a southern Texas town near the Mexican border in an area that has been home to his family for almost two hundred years. After graduating from the University of Texas–Pan American, he taught freshman composition and worked for a while as a photographer. For the next several years, he was a salesman, reporter, and announcer/anchor for the CBS affiliate station KGBT-TV in Harlingen, Texas. His current job has brought him full circle, back to the University of Texas–Pan American, where he serves as a development officer responsible for alumni fund-raising. He loves baseball and once considered a professional career, but he now contents himself with bike riding, swimming, and playing tennis. A conversion to the Baha'i faith in the 1970s has brought him much spiritual happiness. When asked to give advice to students using *The Prose Reader*, Ramirez responded, "The best writing, like anything else of value, requires a great deal of effort. Rewriting is 90 percent of the process. Sometimes, if you are fortunate, your work can take on a life of its own, and you end up writing something important that astounds and humbles you. This is what happened with 'The Barrio,' which is much better than the essay I originally intended. There's an element of the divine in it, as there is in all good writing."

Preparing to Read

First titled "The Woolen Sarape," Ramirez's essay was written while he was a student at the University of Texas–Pan American. His professor, Edward Simmens, published it in an anthology entitled *Pain and Promise: The Chicano Today* (1972). In it, the author defines the exciting, colorful, and close-knit atmosphere typical of many Hispanic barrios or communities. As you prepare to read this essay, take a few moments to think about a place that is very special to you: What are its physical characteristics? What memories are connected to this place for you? What kinds of people live there? What is the relationship of these people to each other? To people in other places? Why is this place so special to you? Is it special to anyone else?

T he train, its metal wheels squealing as they spin along the silvery tracks, rolls slower now. Through the gaps between the cars blinks a streetlamp, and this pulsing light on a barrio street-corner beats slower, like a weary heartbeat, until the train shudders to a halt, the light goes out, and the barrio is deep asleep. 1

Throughout Aztlán (the Nahuatl term meaning "land to the north"), trains grumble along the edges of a sleeping people. From Lower California, through the blistering Southwest, down the Rio Grande to the muddy Gulf, the darkness and mystery of dreams engulf communities fenced off by railroads, canals, and expressways. Paradoxical communities, isolated from the rest of the town by concrete columned monuments of progress, and yet stranded in the past. They are surrounded by change. It eludes their reach, in their own backyards, and the people, unable and unwilling to see the future, or even touch the present, perpetuate the past. 2

Leaning from the expressway or jolting across the tracks, one enters a different physical world permeated by a different attitude. The physical dimensions are impressive. It is a large section of town which extends for fifteen blocks north and south along the tracks, and then advances eastward, thinning into nothingness beyond the city limits. Within the invisible (yet sensible) walls of the barrio are many, many people living in too few houses. The homes, however, are much more numerous than on the outside. 3

Members of the barrio describe the entire area as their home. It is a home, but it is more than this. The barrio is a refuge from the harshness and the coldness of the Anglo world. It is a forced refuge. The leprous people are isolated from the rest of the community and contained in their section of town. The stoical pariahs of the barrio accept their fate, and from the angry seeds of rejection grow the flowers of closeness between outcasts, not the thorns of bitterness and the mad desire to flee. There is no want to escape, for the feeling of the barrio is known only to its inhabitants, and the material needs of life can also be found here. 4

The *tortillería* fires up its machinery three times a day, produc- 5
ing steaming, round, flat slices of barrio bread. In the winter, the
warmth of the tortilla factory is a wool sarape in the chilly
morning hours, but in the summer, it unbearably toasts every
noontime customer.

The *panadería* sends its sweet messenger aroma down the dimly 6
lit street, announcing the arrival of fresh, hot, sugary *pan dulce*.

The small corner grocery serves the meal-to-meal needs of 7
customers, and the owner, a part of the neighborhood, willingly
gives credit to people unable to pay cash for foodstuffs.

The barbershop is a living room with hydraulic chairs, radio, 8
and television, where old friends meet and speak of life as their
salted hair falls aimlessly about them.

The pool hall is a junior level country club where *'chucos*, 9
strangers in their own land, get together to shoot pool and rap, while
veterans, unaware of the cracking, popping balls on the green felt,
complacently play dominoes beneath rudely hung *Playboy* foldouts.

The *cantina* is the night spot of the barrio. It is the country 10
club and the den where the rites of puberty are enacted. Here the
young become men. It is in the taverns that a young dude shows
his *machismo* through the quantity of beer he can hold, the stories
of *rucas* he has had, and his willingness and ability to defend his
image against hardened and scarred old lions.

No, there is no frantic wish to flee. It would be absurd to leave 11
the familiar and nervously step into the strange and cold Anglo
community when the needs of the Chicano can be met in the
barrio.

The barrio is closeness. From the family living unit, familial re- 12
lationships stretch out to immediate neighbors, down the block,
around the corner, and to all parts of the barrio. The feeling of
family, a rare and treasurable sentiment, pervades and accounts for
the inability of the people to leave. The barrio is this attitude
manifested on the countenances of the people, on the faces of
their homes, and in the gaiety of their gardens.

The color-splashed homes arrest your eyes, arouse your curios- 13
ity, and make you wonder what life scenes are being played out in
them. The flimsy, brightly colored, wood-frame houses ignore no
neon-brilliant color. Houses trimmed in orange, chartreuse, lime
green, yellow, and mixtures of these and other hues beckon the

beholder to reflect on the peculiarity of each home. Passing through this land is refreshing like Brubeck, not narcoticizing like revolting rows of similar houses, which neither offend nor please.

In the evenings, the porches and front yards are occupied with 14 men calmly talking over the noise of children playing baseball in the unpaved extension of the living room, while the women cook supper or gossip with female neighbors as they water the *jardines*. The gardens mutely echo the expressive verses of the colorful houses. The denseness of multicolored plants and trees gives the house the appearance of an oasis or a tropical island hideaway, sheltered from the rest of the world.

Fences are common in the barrio, but they are fences and not 15 the walls of the Anglo community. On the western side of town, the high wooden fences between houses are thick, impenetrable walls, built to keep the neighbors at bay. In the barrio, the fences may be rusty, wire contraptions or thick green shrubs. In either case you can see through them and feel no sense of intrusion when you cross them.

Many lower-income families of the barrio manage to maintain 16 a comfortable standard of living through the communal action of family members who contribute their wages to the head of the family. Economic need creates interdependence and closeness. Small barefooted boys sell papers on cool, dark Sunday mornings, deny themselves pleasantries, and give their earnings to *mamá*. The older the child, the greater the responsibility to help the head of the household provide for the rest of the family.

There are those, too, who for a number of reasons have not 17 achieved a relative sense of financial security. Perhaps it results from too many children too soon, but it is the homes of these people and their situation that numbs rather than charms. Their houses, aged and bent, oozing children, are fissures in the horn of plenty. Their wooden homes may have brick-pattern asbestos tile on the outer walls, but the tile is not convincing.

Unable to pay city taxes or incapable of influencing the city 18 to live up to its duty to serve all the citizens, the poorer barrio families remain trapped in the nineteenth century and survive as best they can. The backyards have well-worn paths to the outhouses, which sit near the alley. Running water is considered a luxury in some parts of the barrio. Decent drainage is usually unknown, and when it rains, the water stands for days, an incubator of health hazards and an avoidable nuisance. Streets, costly to pave, remain rough, rocky trails. Tires do not last long, and the constant rattling and shaking grind away a car's life and spread dust through screen windows.

The houses and their *jardines*, the jollity of the people in an ad-   19
verse world, the brightly feathered alarm clock pecking away at supper and cautiously eyeing the children playing nearby, produce a mystifying sensation at finding the noble savage alive in the twentieth century. It is easy to look at the positive qualities of life in the barrio, and look at them with a distantly envious feeling. One wishes to experience the feelings of the barrio and not the hardships. Remembering the illness, the hunger, the feeling of time running out on you, the walls, both real and imagined, reflecting on living in the past, one finds his envy becoming more elusive, until it has vanished altogether.

Back now beyond the tracks, the train creaks and groans, the   20
cars jostle each other down the track, and as the light begins its pulsing, the barrio, with all its meanings, greets a new dawn with yawns and restless stretchings.

UNDERSTANDING DETAILS

1. Define the barrio in your own words.
2. What is the difference between fences in the barrio and in the Anglo community?
3. In Ramirez's view, what creates "interdependence and closeness" (paragraph 16)? How does this phenomenon work in the barrio?
4. According to Ramirez, why are the houses in the barrio so colorful? What do you think is the relationship between color and happiness in the barrio?

ANALYZING MEANING

1. Why does Ramirez call the people in the barrio "leprous" (paragraph 4)?
2. What does the author mean when he says, "The barrio is closeness" (paragraph 12)? How does this statement compare with the way you feel about your neighborhood? Why can't people leave the barrio?

3. Why might people look at the barrio with "a distantly envious feeling" (paragraph 19)? What other feelings may alter or even erase this sense of envy?

4. In what ways does the barrio resemble the communal living of various social groups in the 1960s?

DISCOVERING RHETORICAL STRATEGIES

1. How does Ramirez use the train to help him define the barrio? In what ways would the essay be different without the references to the train?

2. Ramirez uses metaphors masterfully throughout this essay to help us understand the internal workings of the barrio. He relies on this technique especially in paragraphs 4 through 10. For example, a metaphor that explains how relationships develop in the barrio is "The stoical pariahs of the barrio accept their fate, and from the angry seeds of rejection grow the flowers of closeness between outcasts, not the thorns of bitterness and the mad desire to flee" (paragraph 4). In this garden metaphor, "rejection" is likened to "angry seeds," "closeness between outcasts" to "flowers," and "bitterness" to "thorns." Find four other metaphors in these paragraphs, and explain how the comparisons work. What are the familiar and less familiar items in each comparison?

3. What tone does Ramirez establish in this essay? How does he create this tone?

4. The dominant method the author uses to organize his essay is definition. What other rhetorical strategies does Ramirez use to support his definition?

MAKING CONNECTIONS

1. Compare and contrast the "feeling of family" described by Ramirez with that depicted by Germaine Greer in "A Child Is Born." In which geographic location, the barrio or traditional non-Western cultures, is this feeling the strongest? Why do you think this is so?

2. Ramirez does a wonderful job of creating a sensual experience in his essay as he chronicles the vivid sights, sounds, smells, tastes, and textures of life in the barrio. In the same way, Tom Wolfe ("The Right Stuff") and John McPhee ("The Pines")

appeal to our senses in descriptions of military flight training and a wilderness area in the eastern United States. Which author's prose style do you find most sensual? Explain your answer.

3. While Ramirez defines the "barrio" through description, Nancy Gibbs ("When Is It Rape?") and Susan Sontag ("On AIDS") define their principal topics differently. How do the three authors differ in constructing their definitions? Which technique do you find most persuasive? Explain your answer.

IDEAS FOR DISCUSSION/WRITING

Preparing to Write

Write freely about a place that is special to you: Describe this place from your perspective. Is this place special to anyone else? Describe this place from someone else's perspective. How do these descriptions differ? What characteristics differentiate this place from other places? What makes this place special to you? Use some metaphors to relay to your readers your feelings about certain features of this place. Do you think this place will always be special to you? Why or why not?

Choosing a Topic

1. Ramirez's definition of the barrio demonstrates a difference between an insider's view and an outsider's view of the same location. In an essay for your classmates, define your special place from both the inside and the outside. Then, discuss the similarities and differences between these two points of view.

2. In essay form, define the relationships among the people who are your extended family. These could be people from your neighborhood, your school, your job, or a combination of places. How did these relationships come about? Why are you close to these people? Why are these people close to you? To each other?

3. What primary cultural or social traditions have made you what you are today? In an essay written to a close friend, define the two or three most important traditions you practiced as a child, and explain what effects they had on you.

RITA MAE BROWN (1944 –)

■ ■ ■

Writing as a Moral Act

Born in Hanover, Pennsylvania, Rita Mae Brown earned her B.A. at New York University, a certificate in cinematography at the New York School of Visual Arts, and a Ph.D. at the Institute for Policy Studies in Washington, D.C. She then became politically active as an executive officer in the National Organization for Women and as a founder of the Lesbian Separatist Movement in the early 1970s. Her first novel, *Rubyfruit Jungle* (1973), was turned down by most major publishing houses before being printed by a small feminist press named Daughters, Inc. It was later picked up by Bantam Books and has sold well over a million copies since being published. In describing its controversial central character, one critic wrote, "Imagine, if you will, Huckleberry Finn, only foul-mouthed, female, and lesbian, and you have some idea of Molly Bolt." Brown has defended this unconventional choice of a heroine in the following way: "While American heroes may occasionally be women, they may not be lesbians. Or if they are, they had better be discreet or at least miserable. Not Molly. She is lusty and lewd and pursues sex with gusto." Brown followed this successful literary debut with a number of other novels, including *In Her Day* (1976), *A Plain Brown Rapper* (1976), *Six of One* (1978), *Southern Discomfort* (1982), *High Hearts* (1986), *Bingo* (1988), and *Wish You Were Here* (1990), plus several screenplays, television scripts, and books of poetry. Upset by being labeled merely a "lesbian writer," Brown has explained that "On the page all humans really are created equal. All stories are important. All lives are worthy of concern and description. . . . Incarcerating authors into types is an act of treason against literature and, worse, an assault on the human heart."

Preparing to Read

The following essay, taken from *Starting from Scratch: A Different Kind of Writers' Manual* (1988), argues strongly that people should "write and speak the truth" in life. As you prepare to read this essay, take a few moments to think about the role of language in your life: Do you feel confident about your use of language? Do the right words come to you when you need them? Does language help you get what you want in life? Do you use language appropriately, adjusting your words and explanations to different audiences? When does the use of language rise to the level of literature or art? If language is the basis of our communication, when might the use of language be moral or immoral?

L anguage is decanted and shared. If only one person is left alive speaking a language—the case with some American Indian languages—the language is dead. Language takes two and their multiples. 1

Speaking is a social contract. You and I agree to exchange sounds whose organized noises represent agreed-upon symbols. *Cat* means the same thing to you as it does to me. It doesn't mean a thing to a Portuguese person. You might think of a sleek tiger cat and I might be thinking of a long-haired red cat but we are in sync about the species. If you want to get fancy you could say feline (Latin again) but we're in the same ballpark. 2

Up to this point we are in agreement. We are cooperating as two individuals conceding to civilization. Literacy, or even simple speech, is the starting point of civilization. The unspoken truth is that we are unequal; we are different. If you and I were exactly the same, a pair of identical strangers, we wouldn't need to speak to one another or to write. You'd know what I was thinking and vice versa. All communication rests upon inequality. That's the sheer excitement of it. I don't know what you think. I can't wait to find out. Language is the common thread by which we explore our differences and, if we are both lucky and mature, the thread that will bring us to a form of agreement or at least understanding. 3

Therefore it is imperative that people write and speak the truth. There can be no community if a person is not as good as her/his word. How easy to write that and how hard to put it in practice. You, my reader, whoever you are, know things that will disturb others. You must tell. Camus said, "It is immoral not to tell." 4

Again we can split hairs. A dear friend of mine has put on ten 5 pounds. Do I say, "Gee, Frank, you're fat as a toad" (the truth) or "Frank, you look wonderful." It may be wonderful to see him but he still looks fat. I'll choose to make my friend feel better.

If Frank, involved in a sordid affair with the wife of another 6 friend of mine, asks my opinion, I'll tell him the truth. "Either she leaves him and goes to you or you leave her. Don't mess with married people."

Telling the truth should be simple. Writing the truth should be 7 even easier because you don't have to look your listener/reader in the eye. Writing the truth is far more treacherous. The act of putting words down on paper gives them a glamour and permanence not associated with speech. Writing, to most everyone, is a more serious act than speaking.

Every generation produces those people—writers, composers, 8 plastic artists, and even the re-creative artists—who shatter social convention and tell the truth. They aren't saying "Here I am." They are saying "Here you are." The "you" is both individual and plural. In the case of *Oedipus Rex* or *Crime and Punishment*, this recognition can be horrifying. In the case of *The Birds* or *School for Scandal* it can be deliciously funny.

If this is prevented from happening (as in Stalin's Soviet 9 Union, Hitler's Germany, Botha's South Africa) the civilization begins to die from the inside out. There may be a plethora of books in such nations but they aren't upsetting. They merely entertain. Art must both entertain and provoke.

If people refrain from telling what they know, how long before 10 they actively lie? Is there not a subtle and corrosive connection between withholding the truth and lying? You are as sick as you are secret.

If you don't believe that words will be followed by deeds, how 11 can you trust anyone? How can you form a community? When language no longer corresponds to reality, any form of betrayal and misconduct are to be expected.

Writers are the moral purifiers of the culture. We may not be 12 pure ourselves but we must tell the truth, which is a purifying act. Therefore it is impossible for a real fiction writer to be the mouthpiece for a political cause. A writer should, as should any citizen, cherish his or her political beliefs but that's not the same as being a propagandist.

By political beliefs I am not talking about the American two- 13
party system. The Republican party is a study in unlimited van-
dalism, and the Democratic party presides over the cadaver of
liberalism. The difference between Republicans and Democrats is
the difference between syphilis and gonorrhea. Political beliefs are
stronger than that. The separation of church and state is a political
belief. Affirming or repudiating capital punishment is a political
belief. The desire for a state-controlled economy is not only a political belief, in some nations it's a religion. You get the difference.
Our political parties skate over the political fashions that are current. Opportunism wears many masks.

Since politicians seek to conceal the truth in order to dupe the 14
public, every writer alive is critical of whatever political system
s/he lives in. Not everyone in politics is bad and politics is a necessary evil, *but* politics is never ever about the truth. Politics seeks
to conceal; Art, to reveal.

The severest blasts in Russia or in our own country are di- 15
rected at people the state considers expendable. First, writers get it
because they are potentially dangerous. Scientists run into walls
only if they become critical of the uses of science by the government. If they shut up and continue as the hired help, they're okay.
In our country, we are too sophisticated to put writers in jail. It
looks bad. Also, we are very fortunate in that most of our elected
officials are semi-illiterate, and therefore they don't even know
what we're writing. Should a writer happen to become disturbing
and powerful enough to come to the attention of our civic wor-
thies, then the fur flies. A politician will cite the offending author
and make a stink. His acolytes will press to have the subversive
texts banned from the libraries. (Actually, the acolytes control the
politician. S/he usually responds to their pressure.) Loathsome as
it is, such talk does get into the newspapers, and once publicity at-
taches itself to a book, the sales shoot upward. Bless the narrow-
minded! You can survive that. You'll know when you're really in
dutch when the IRS hounds you. You think a highly placed government official wouldn't stoop that low? You think the IRS is
not a punitive instrument of whatever administration is current?
You also believe in the tooth fairy, don't you?

Communist and fascist nations recognize the power of writers. 16
They imprison them or drive them out of their homeland. The

United States of America, no matter how absurd and contradictory our various administrations, has drawn the line here. When push comes to shove, we defend the First Amendment. Today, in 1987, that Amendment is a political hot potato but I trust it will flourish intact. By defending the First Amendment we are defending writers. Buried in the marrow of our collective bones is the recognition that we must know the truth about ourselves. Even the most bigoted American hates a liar. Despite our economic struggle, far better to be a writer here than elsewhere.

Morality is involved in issues other than lying or withholding   17
information. What happens when the word is substituted for the deed? Some act of faith is always involved in the connection between theory and action. To write and talk and not produce the action is to destroy faith. Once again, community becomes impossible.

The best example I can think of for this phenomenon involves   18
the protest movements of the late 1960's and early 1970's. While the Nazis committed unspeakable acts (I mean unspeakable— they had no word for what they were doing), the New Left and the Women's Movement spoke incessantly but committed few acts. This seems to be a hallmark of leftist politics: the substitution of the word for the deed. Yes, some things got accomplished but compare it to the dedicated raising of money by the New Right and the intelligent daily application of those funds and you quickly grasp the difference.

The New Right has few writers. The New Left was top-heavy   19
with them. From the New Left true fiction writers emerged, leaving behind the restrictions of ideology and moving toward a wider embrace of human experience but, I hope, imbued with a belief in justice, equality, and innovation. To date, not one decent fiction writer has emerged from the New Right.

I was one of those people to emerge from the New Left. I re-   20
call the early days of the movement. The blind were leading the blind with great excitement into walls, into ravines, into the waiting rifles at Jackson and Kent State. These anguished memories are then supplanted with pride; we did help to end a war which was ill-conceived. We wrested a few changes from the system for the nonwhite, and we created the conditions for the removal of a President who may have committed criminal acts. From this

haunted terrain sprang a generation of scribblers. Perhaps the New Right will fool me yet and bring forth fiction writers capable of making us see ourselves as we really are. One thing is certain: That writer or those writers will get clobbered by their former associates. The Right suffers little dissent.

Some writers maintain that they are apolitical. A worm is apolitical; a human being is not. If you live in a political system and do not seek to make it better you are still a product of that system. Your lack of involvement is a political statement. All Art rests on a political foundation but it need not concern itself with politics. **21**

Go back to *The Iliad*. Achilles has plopped his butt in his tent and won't fight. Agamemnon took a damsel awarded to Achilles for his battle prowess. Briseis was her name and Achilles, although in love with Patroclus, a man, wanted the girl. Why not eat your cake and have it too? The Greeks were not as ravaged by sexual definitions as we are. Agamemnon, as head of the armed forces (think of him as Eisenhower during World War II), could take this woman. He had the power but he didn't have the right. Achilles, by our standards, should set aside personal ego and fight for his people. Achilles, by Greek standards, is absolutely right. His first allegiance is to his honor. This conflict between the need of the individual to be sovereign and the need of the community to triumph/survive provides the context for the unfolding drama. *The Iliad* has a political basis but you can read it without giving politics a thought. **22**

Even *Alice's Adventures in Wonderland* rests on a political foundation. It can be read as a glorious fantasy or it can be read as a comment on the powerlessness of a child, of children in society. You don't have to choose—you can read it on many levels, including reading it as a drug trip. **23**

Both *The Iliad* and *Alice in Wonderland* ring true. People read them today with as much pleasure as people derived from them when they were first written. A work lives like that if it is morally true. **24**

You bring to a book your past, your system of beliefs. First, you read a book and answer that book with those beliefs. If you are a student of literature you will study the environment of the writer and then you'll read the book again, setting aside your values. When you've finished the second reading you can engage the **25** writer's beliefs with your own. Reading is an active moral and intellectual exchange. If you aren't reading books that challenge you, you're reading the wrong books.

If you aren't writing books that challenge you, keep writing. It takes years to get there. I know the book I wanted to write, the challenging, lyrical work I dreamed about. You know only the book I wrote. I am acutely aware of the gap between desire and performance. Lash me though you might, you'll never hit me as hard as I hit myself, for only I know the full extent of my failure. 26

Morality shifts. Infanticide was acceptable to the Greeks. It isn't acceptable to us. Your work will reflect your implied faiths and fears. Without your being necessarily conscious of it, your work reflects your society. Here's an example. Since *The Iliad*, Western writers have treated common experience as comic relief. This attitude depends on a clear class structure in which the superior classes, aristocrats, are assumed better than the inferior classes. When the middle classes began to assert themselves, this shifted. Chaucer in *The Canterbury Tales* presents sympathetic middle-class characters. Some are comic and some are not but none of them is heroic. A great revolution took place on the page. This accelerated over time. Shakespeare used all the classes, to his and our great profit. 27

Eventually, middle-class people developed the leisure in which to write and what did they do? They wrote about themselves. As the Industrial Revolution wears on, their literature takes over. The middle-class character is not a king or a landed aristocrat but a lawyer or a doctor perhaps. Chekhov comes to my mind instantly. The tendency to present ordinary people (an assumption in itself—are there ordinary people?) as vaguely comic still exists but it isn't as strict a literary convention as it was for a good two thousand years. 28

When you reject inferiority at the lowest level, you topple the whole structure of dominance. The shift in literature, beginning with Chaucer, reflected real life and, in turn, had an impact upon real life. No longer were kings and queens so important. They were replaced with parliaments or by revolutions. They were replaced on the page. Morally, there's nothing wrong with having a king for your form of government or for your literary hero but as an American I bet you don't write about one. 29

This struggle for literary representation bubbles over the 30
decades. Today, the lower classes, thanks to programs to get them
into colleges, are producing literature. The class in control of the
arts, the middle class, finds itself besieged from below. Not only
are the lower classes becoming literate, nonwhites and non-
Christians have acquired the skills to create English literature.
Stick around—the show is just beginning!

As Shakespeare arrived at a creative imbalance between the 31
passing medieval world and the coming modern world (Bacon,
Newton, Descartes), so we are at a similar overlap between the
nation-state and global interdependence, between men and women, between whites and nonwhites, between the Christian world
and science, the Christian world and the non-Christian world,
between spiritual concerns and material ones. Like Shakespeare we
find ourselves in a time where the future, so thrilling to the non-
rigid, terrifies the rigid. Every action has an equal and opposite
reaction. Every cultural/social push forward is followed by people
organizing to hold back the hands of time. Those men who were
willing to kill you if you thought the earth revolved around the
sun instead of believing Ptolemy are still here. Those people, like
Elizabeth I, who killed their political enemies are here too. Like
Shakespeare, you've got to try to make sense of it. You don't have
to explain it. He didn't. You need to use it, use every bit of it. This
overlap and straining of divergent world views is a gift. Don't ask
to live in tranquil times. Literature doesn't grow there.

UNDERSTANDING DETAILS

1. What does Brown mean when she declares, "Speaking is a social contract" (paragraph 2)?
2. According to Brown, what are some of the consequences
   when language and reality don't correspond?
3. Based on the author's observations, which social class controls
   art? Explain your answer in detail.
4. According to this essay, how are morality and language use related?

ANALYZING MEANING

1. In paragraph 3, Brown says, "all communication rests upon inequality." In what ways is this statement true?

2. Do you agree with Brown's statement that writing is "a more serious act than speaking" (paragraph 7)? Explain your answer.
3. Do you agree that "Politics seeks to conceal; Art, to reveal" (paragraph 14)? Explain your answer.
4. Why does art thrive among "divergent worldviews" (paragraph 31)?

DISCOVERING RHETORICAL STRATEGIES

1. How would you characterize Brown's tone? At what points in the essay does she vary her tone? How does she accomplish these changes in tone?
2. In your opinion, what is Brown's primary purpose in this essay? Explain your answer in detail.
3. Who do you think is Brown's intended audience for this essay? On what do you base your answer?
4. What rhetorical modes support the author's definition? Give examples of each.

MAKING CONNECTIONS

1. Contrast Brown's assertion that "it is imperative that people write and speak the truth" (paragraph 4) with Judith Viorst's argument in "The Truth About Lying" that many different types of lies are not only acceptable but necessary in modern society. Which author is right? With whom do you most agree? Explain your answer.
2. If Brown, Annie Dillard ("When You Write"), and Russell Baker ("The Saturday Evening Post") were panel members discussing the topic of "writing as a moral act," which of these authors would speak most strongly for the necessity of writing the truth? On what do you base your answer?
3. Exactly what is Brown "defining" in her essay? Is her definition easier to understand than those by Robert Ramirez ("The Barrio") or Nancy Gibbs ("When Is It Rape?")? Why or why not?

IDEAS FOR DISCUSSION/WRITING

Preparing to Write

Write freely about language use in your immediate environment: Why do you use language? Is your language at school different in any way from your language at home? Do you find yourself explaining the same idea to different people in different ways? Do you notice any differences in the way you use language in speaking and in writing? Do you and the people you know use language honestly and openly, or do you often disguise what you are trying to say? Does language help or hinder you in accomplishing your current goals?

Choosing a Topic

1. You have been asked to speak at freshman orientation at your college. Your assigned topic is "The Role of Language in a College Student's Life." Using Brown's article as a resource, define *language use* from a student's perspective. (Remember to cite your source whenever necessary.) Supplement your definition with examples of language use from your own experience and observation.

2. For a group of people your own age, define *morality*. In your definition, consider what activities you find moral. Why are they moral? Before you write your essay, limit your subject and settle on a main point of view. Make your purpose clear throughout the essay.

3. Write a letter to one of your past or present instructors about his or her use of language. Does this person's language communicate clearly to a variety of people? Is it interesting to listen to? Is it appropriate, stimulating, provocative? Give examples to support your judgments.

TOM WOLFE   (1931 –   )

■ ■ ■

The Right Stuff

Writer, journalist, painter, and social commentator Thomas Kennerly Wolfe was born in Richmond, Virginia, and began his literary career with a Ph.D. in American Studies from Yale University. He is best known for his contribution to a prose style called the *new journalism*, which features factual writing enlivened by such fiction techniques as in–depth character analysis, expanded dialogue, and detailed descriptions of setting, clothing, and other physical features. Early articles in *Esquire* and The *New York Herald Tribune* led to his first book, *The Kandy-Kolored Tangerine-Flake Streamline Baby* (1965), a collection of twenty-two of his best essays that examine and satirize several 1960s American trends and pop-culture heroes. Wolfe followed soon after with *The Electric Kool-Aid Acid Test* (1968), which tells the story of West Coast novelist Ken Kesey and his group of "Merry Pranksters," and *Radical Chic and Mau Mauing the Flak Catchers* (1970), which in one of its two long essays describes how composer Leonard Bernstein hosted a fund-raising party for the Black Panthers. *The Painted Word* (1975) is an exposé of modern art, whereas *From Bauhaus to Our House* (1981) offers a similar treatment of modern architecture. Wolfe's finest book, according to many critics, is *The Right Stuff* (1979), a brilliantly written study of the early years of the U.S. space program (later made into a movie of the same title). In 1987, he published his first novel, *The Bonfire of the Vanities* (also made into a movie). His most recent book is *Through the Looking Glass* (1992). Wolfe, who now lives in New York City, advises student writers to be patient and persistent in their work. "Sometimes," he explains, "marvelous rushes of words will just fall into place. Other times you just have to put your head in a vise and make them come out."

Preparing to Read

The following essay from *The Right Stuff* attempts to define what it took to succeed in the rigorous naval flight training required of such Mercury astronauts as Scott Carpenter, John Glenn, and

Gus Grissom. As you prepare to read this essay, take a few moments to think about success and failure in general: What marks success in different areas of life for you—at work, at school, at home? What marks failure? How do you feel when you have succeeded at something? When you have failed? Have you ever thought you had succeeded at a task, then realized you were only partway there? What were the circumstances? How did this realization make you feel?

A young man might go into military flight training believing that he was entering some sort of technical school in which he was simply going to acquire a certain set of skills. Instead, he found himself all at once enclosed in a fraternity. And in this fraternity, even though it was military, men were not rated by their outward rank as ensigns, lieutenants, commanders, or whatever. No, herein the world was divided into those who had it and those who did not. This quality, this *it*, was never named, however, nor was it talked about in any way.

As to just what this ineffable quality was . . . well, it obviously involved bravery. But it was not bravery in the simple sense of being willing to risk your life. The idea seemed to be that any fool could do that, if that was all that was required, just as any fool could throw away his life in the process. No, the idea here (in the all-enclosing fraternity) seemed to be that a man should have the ability to go up in a hurtling piece of machinery and put his hide on the line and then have the moxie, the reflexes, the experience, the coolness, to pull it back in the last yawning moment—and then go up again *the next day*, and the next day, and every next day, even if the series should prove infinite—and, ultimately, in its best expression, do so in a cause that means something to thousands, to a people, a nation, to humanity, to God. Nor was there *a test* to show whether or not a pilot had this righteous quality. There was, instead, a seemingly infinite series of tests. A career in flying was like climbing one of those ancient Babylonian pyramids made up of a dizzy progression of steps and ledges, a ziggurat, a pyramid extraordinarily high and steep; and the idea was to prove at every foot of the way up that pyramid that you were one of the elected and anointed ones who had *the right stuff* and could move higher and higher and even—ultimately, God willing, one day—that you might be able to join that special few at the very top, that elite who had the capacity to bring tears to men's eyes, the very Brotherhood of the Right Stuff itself.

None of this was to be mentioned, and yet it was acted out in 3 a way that a young man could not fail to understand. When a new flight (i.e., a class) of trainees arrived at Pensacola, they were brought into an auditorium for a little lecture. An officer would tell them: "Take a look at the man on either side of you." Quite a few actually swiveled their heads this way and that in the interest of appearing diligent. Then the officer would say: "One of the three of you is not going to make it!"—meaning, not get his wings. That was the opening theme, the *motif* of primary training. We already know that one-third of you do not have the right stuff—it only remains to find out who.

Furthermore, that was the way it turned out. At every level in 4 one's progress up that staggeringly high pyramid, the world was once more divided into those men who had the right stuff to continue the climb and those who had to be *left behind* in the most obvious way. Some were eliminated in the course of the opening classroom work, as either not smart enough or not hard-working enough, and were left behind. Then came the basic flight instruction, in single-engine, propeller-driven trainers, and a few more—even though the military tried to make this stage easy— were washed out and left behind. Then came more demanding levels, one after the other, formation flying, instrument flying, jet training, all-weather flying, gunnery, and at each level more were washed out and left behind. By this point easily a third of the original candidates had been, indeed, eliminated . . . from the ranks of those who might prove to have the right stuff.

In the Navy, in addition to the stages that Air Force trainees 5 went through, the neophyte always had waiting for him, out in the ocean, a certain grim gray slab; namely, the deck of an aircraft carrier; and with it perhaps the most difficult routine in military flying, carrier landings. He was shown films about it, he heard lec- tures about it, and he knew that carrier landings were hazardous. He first practiced touching down on the shape of a flight deck painted on an airfield. He was instructed to touch down and gun right off. This was safe enough—the shape didn't move, at least— but it could do terrible things to, let us say, the gyroscope of the soul. *That shape!—It's so damned small!* And more candidates were washed out and left behind. Then came the day, without warning, when those who remained were sent out over the ocean for the first of many days of reckoning with the slab. The first day was always a clear day with little wind and a calm sea. The carrier was so steady that it seemed, from up there in the air, to be resting on pilings, and the candidate usually made his first carrier landing successfully, with relief and even *élan*. Many young candidates looked like terrific aviators up to that very point—and it was not until they were actually standing on the carrier deck that they first began to wonder if they had the proper stuff, after all. In the training film the flight deck was a grand piece of gray geometry, perilous, to be sure, but an amazing abstract shape as one looks down upon it on the screen. And yet once the newcomer's two feet were on it . . . *Geometry*—my God, man, this is a . . . skillet! It *heaved*, it moved up and down underneath his feet, it pitched up, it pitched down, it rolled to port (this great beast *rolled*!) and it rolled to starboard, as the ship moved into the wind and, therefore, into the waves, and the wind kept sweeping across, sixty feet up in the air out in the open sea, and there were no railings whatsoever. This was a *skillet*!—a frying pan!—a short-order grill!—not gray but black, smeared with skid marks from one end to the other and glistening with pools of hydraulic fluid and the occasional jet-fuel slick, all of it still hot, sticky, greasy, runny, virulent from God knows what traumas—still ablaze!—consumed in detonations, explosions, flames, combustion, roars, shrieks, whines, blasts, horrible shudders, fracturing impacts, as little men in screaming red and yellow and purple and green shirts with black Mickey Mouse helmets over their ears skittered about on the surface as if for their very lives (you've said it now!), hooking fighter planes onto the catapult shuttles so that they can explode their afterburners and be slung off the deck in a red-mad fury with a *kaboom*! that pounds through the entire deck—a procedure that seems absolutely controlled, orderly, sublime, however, compared to what he is about to watch as aircraft return to the ship for what is known in the engineering stoicisms of the military as "recovery and arrest." To say that an F-4 was coming back onto this heaving barbecue from out of the sky at a speed of 135 knots . . . that might have been the truth in the training lecture, but it did not begin to get across the idea of what the newcomer saw from the deck itself, because it created the notion that perhaps the plane was gliding in. On the deck one knew differently! As the aircraft came closer and the carrier heaved on into the waves and the plane's speed did not diminish and the deck did not grow steady—indeed, it pitched up and down five or ten feet per greasy heave—one experienced a neural alarm that no lecture could have prepared him for: This is not an *airplane* coming toward me, it is a brick with some poor sonofabitch riding it (*someone much like myself!*), and it is not *gliding*, it is *falling*, a thirty-thousand-pound brick, headed not for a stripe on the deck but for *me*—and with a horrible *smash!* it hits the skillet, and with a blur of momentum as big as a freight train's it hurtles toward the far end of the deck—another blinding storm!—another roar as the pilot pushes the throttle up to full military power and another smear of rubber screams out over the skillet—and this is nominal!—quite okay!—for a wire stretched across the deck has grabbed the hook on the end of the plane as it hit the deck tail down, and the smash was the rest of the fifteen-ton brute slamming onto the deck, as it tripped up, so that it is now straining against the wire at full throttle, in case it hadn't held and the plane had "boltered" off the end of the deck and had to struggle up into the air again. And already the Mickey Mouse helmets are running toward the fiery monster. . . .

And the candidate, looking on, begins to *feel* that great heaving 6 sun-blazing deathboard of a deck wallowing in his own vestibular system—and suddenly he finds himself backed up against his own limits. He ends up going to the flight surgeon with so-called conversion symptoms. Overnight he develops blurred vision or numbness in his hands and feet or sinusitis so severe that he cannot tolerate changes in altitude. On one level the symptom is real. He really cannot see too well or use his fingers or stand the pain. But somewhere in his subconscious he knows it is a plea and a beg-off; he shows not the slightest concern (the flight surgeon notes) that the condition might be permanent and affect him in whatever life awaits him outside the arena of the right stuff.

Those who remained, those who qualified for carrier duty— 7 and even more so those who later on qualified for *night* carrier duty—began to feel a bit like Gideon's warriors. *So many have been left behind!* The young warriors were now treated to a deathly sweet and quite unmentionable sight. They could gaze at length upon the crushed and wilted pariahs who had washed out. They could inspect those who did not have that righteous stuff.

The military did not have very merciful instincts. Rather than   8 packing up these poor souls and sending them home, the Navy, like the Air Force and the Marines, would try to make use of them in some other role such as flight controller. So the washout has to keep taking classes with the rest of his group, even though he can no longer touch an airplane. He sits there in the classes staring at sheets of paper with cataracts of sheer human mortification over his eyes while the rest steal looks at him . . . this man reduced to an ant, this untouchable, this poor sonofabitch. And in what test had he been found wanting? Why, it seemed to be nothing less than *manhood* itself. Naturally, this was never mentioned, either. Yet there it was. *Manliness, manhood, manly courage* . . . there was something ancient, primordial, irresistible about the challenge of this stuff, no matter what a sophisticated and rational age one might think he lived in.

UNDERSTANDING DETAILS

1. According to Wolfe, how did military men going through flight training prove they have "the right stuff"? What is the climax of this proof?
2. Why do only two out of three trainees make it through the training?
3. Who were Gideon's warriors? Why might those who qualify for carrier duty "feel a bit like Gideon's warriors" (paragraph 7)?
4. What does *primordial* mean? What is primordial about "*manliness, manhood, manly courage*" (paragraph 8)?

ANALYZING MEANING

1. Why does Wolfe equate military training with being "enclosed in a fraternity" in paragraph 1? With what else does he compare military training? Give at least three specific examples.
2. Is the necessity of having "the right stuff" limited to men? To pilots? To military training? In what other areas of life is "the right stuff" desirable?

3. To make this essay meaningful, Wolfe relies in part on the reader's identification with the details involved in the astronauts' military training program. To what extent can women identify with this essay? In what ways did you yourself identify with the experiences Wolfe relates? On the basis of your answers to these questions, explain how successfully Wolfe defines "the right stuff" within your frame of reference.

4. Why does Wolfe equate "the right stuff" with manhood and courage at the end of his essay? In what way does this comparison provide an effective conclusion for the essay?

DISCOVERING RHETORICAL STRATEGIES

1. Throughout this essay, Wolfe is attempting to define an abstract subject ("the right stuff") in concrete terms. Divide a piece of paper into two columns. In the first column, list all the various abstractions the author presents; in the other column, list the concrete examples of these qualities that Wolfe discusses. Then, explain the relationships he draws between these two columns and the effects of those relationships on his readers.

2. Wolfe equates a career in flying with climbing an ancient Babylonian pyramid (a ziggurat) "made up of a dizzy progression of steps and ledges" (paragraph 2). In what way does this metaphor bring order and coherence to his essay?

3. Wolfe reaches a climax in his definition of "the right stuff" in paragraph 5 when he describes the details of the carrier landings. How does Wolfe's use of sentence structure (including word choice and length of sentences) and punctuation tell us that this is the climax of the essay?

4. In this essay, Wolfe's primary method of organization is definition. What other rhetorical strategies does the author use to support his definition?

MAKING CONNECTIONS

1. Contrast Wolfe's essay on the training of men with Gloria Steinem's views on the training of women in "The Politics of Muscle." In the 30 years between the original Mercury astronaut program in the 1960s described by Wolfe and the publication of Steinem's essay in 1994, what major social changes

have occurred in women's induction into and training in our armed forces? How do you feel about these changes? Do you approve or disapprove of them? Explain your answer.

2. Compare and contrast Wolfe's "new journalistic" style of writing (see the biography that precedes his essay in *The Prose Reader* for a brief definition of the term) with the equally distinctive but different prose style of John McPhee in "The Pines." Which author's writing seems more vivid to you? Explain why you feel this way.

3. If Wolfe, Susan Sontag ("On AIDS"), Joyce Carol Oates ("On Boxing"), and Malcolm Cowley ("The View from 80") held a discussion on the value of metaphors in writing, which author would probably argue most vehemently for their importance? Which author's metaphors are easiest for you to follow? Whose are most difficult? Why?

IDEAS FOR DISCUSSION/WRITING

Preparing to Write

Write freely about the qualities that constitute success and failure in your immediate environment as a student: How do you know when you succeed? When you fail? How do you feel in each of these different situations? Has success ever turned into failure for you? Has the reverse ever occurred? How important are success and failure in your life as a student? In the lives of your friends? What roles do success and failure play in academia in general? To what extent do these roles prepare us for the "real world"?

Choosing a Topic

1. Write an essay for your classmates defining "the right stuff" for social success in college.

2. Choose an area other than military training and school. Then, use examples to define "the wrong stuff" in that area for members of your composition class.

3. The relationship between college and the "real world" has changed since your parents were in school. Explain to them the current relationship between academic success (or failure) and the job market. What do you think the connections are between doing well in college and having a successful career?

SUSAN SONTAG   (1933 –   )

■ ■ ■

On AIDS

Susan Sontag is a novelist, essayist, screenwriter, and film and theater director who is one of America's foremost social commentators. Born in New York City and raised in Arizona and
California, she studied at the University of California at Berkeley
and the University of Chicago, earning her B.A. degree at the age
of eighteen from the latter. After doing graduate work in philosophy at Harvard, she held a succession of jobs as a teacher and
writer-in-residence at several universities. Her first important
publication was *Against Interpretation, and Other Essays* (1966),
which established Sontag as an influential critic and cultural ana-
lyst. The autobiographical *Trip to Hanoi* (1968) followed, then
Styles of Radical Will (1969). Her prose fiction includes two novels, *The Benefactor* (1963) and *Death Kit* (1967), and a collection of
short stories entitled *I, etcetera* (1978). She has also written and directed four films: *Duet for Cannibals* (1969) and *Brother Carl*
(1971), both made in Sweden; *Promised Lands* (1974), a documentary about Israel; and *Unguided Tour* (1975), based on an earlier
short story. One of Sontag's best-known books is *On Photography*
(1977), a systematic inquiry into the source and meaning of visual
imagery. In this seminal text, the author uses already established
critical tools of literary analysis, linguistics, and philosophy to help
describe the effect of modern art and photography on viewers.
Other recent publications include *Illness as Metaphor* (1977), *Under
the Sign of Saturn* (1980), *AIDS and Its Metaphors* (1988), *The
Volcano Lover: A Romance* (1992), and *Alice in Bed* (1993). Sontag
lives and works in New York City.

Preparing to Read

The following chapter from Sontag's 1988 book *AIDS and Its
Metaphors* examines the figurative language commonly used to describe and define this terrifying disease: The virus "invades" and
"pollutes" our bodies, while in military fashion our immune systems

"mobilize" and "defend" against the "attack of alien cells." As you begin to read this essay, take a few minutes to consider what you know about AIDS: What facts do you have about the disease? Do you know anyone who has AIDS? Anyone who has died from AIDS? How do different people respond to those suffering from the virus? Are you afraid of being infected? Have you altered your behavior in any way because of the threat of contagion? Do you think our government is doing enough to help prevent the spread of this disease and to find a cure? When do you think a cure will be found?

J ust as one might predict for a disease that is not yet fully understood as well as extremely recalcitrant to treatment, the advent of this terrifying new disease, new at least in its epidemic form, has provided a large-scale occasion for the metaphorizing of illness.

Strictly speaking, AIDS—acquired immune deficiency syndrome—is not the name of an illness at all. It is the name of a medical condition, whose consequences are a spectrum of illnesses. In contrast to syphilis and cancer, which provide prototypes for most of the images and metaphors attached to AIDS, the very definition of AIDS requires the presence of other illnesses, so-called opportunistic infections and malignancies. But though not in *that* sense a single disease, AIDS lends itself to being regarded as one—in part because, unlike cancer and like syphilis, it is thought to have a single cause.

AIDS has a dual metaphoric genealogy. As a microprocess, it is described as cancer is: an invasion. When the focus is transmission of the disease, an older metaphor, reminiscent of syphilis, is invoked: pollution. (One gets it from the blood or sexual fluids of infected people or from contaminated blood products.) But the military metaphors used to describe AIDS have a somewhat different focus from those used in describing cancer. With cancer, the metaphor scants the issue of causality (still a murky topic in cancer research) and picks up at the point at which rogue cells inside the body mutate, eventually moving out from an original site or organ to overrun other organs or systems—a domestic subversion. In the description of AIDS the enemy is what causes the disease, an infectious agent that comes from the outside:

1

2

3

The invader is tiny, about one sixteen-thousandth the size of the head of a pin. . . . Scouts of the body's immune system, large cells called macrophages, sense the presence of the diminutive foreigner and promptly alert the immune system. It begins to mobilize an array of cells that, among other things, produce antibodies to deal with the threat. Single-mindedly, the AIDS virus ignores many of the blood cells in its path, evades the rapidly advancing defenders and homes in on the master coordinator of the immune system, a helper T cell. . . .

This is the language of political paranoia, with its characteristic distrust of a pluralistic world. A defense system consisting of cells "that, among other things, produce antibodies to deal with the threat" is, predictably, no match for an invader who advances "single-mindedly." And the science-fiction flavor, already present in cancer talk, is even more pungent in accounts of AIDS—this one comes from *Time* magazine in late 1986—with infection described like the high-tech warfare for which we are being prepared (and inured) by the fantasies of our leaders and by video entertainments. In the era of Star Wars and Space Invaders, AIDS has proved an ideally comprehensible illness:

On the surface of that cell, it finds a receptor into which one of its envelope proteins fits perfectly, like a key into a lock. Docking with the cell, the virus penetrates the cell membrane and is stripped of its protective shell in the process. . . .

Next the invader takes up permanent residence, by a form of alien takeover familiar in science-fiction narratives. The body's own cells *become* the invader. With the help of an enzyme the virus carries with it,

the naked AIDS virus converts its RNA into . . . DNA, the master molecule of life. The molecule then penetrates the cell nucleus, inserts itself into a chromosome and takes over part of the cellular machinery, directing it to produce more AIDS viruses. Eventually, overcome by its alien product, the cell swells and dies, releasing a flood of new viruses to attack other cells. . . .

As viruses attack other cells, runs the metaphor, so "a host of opportunistic diseases, normally warded off by a healthy immune system, attacks the body," whose integrity and vigor have been sapped by the sheer replication of "alien product" that follows the collapse of its immunological defenses. "Gradually weakened by the onslaught, the AIDS victim dies, sometimes in months, but almost always within a few years of the first symptoms." Those who have not already succumbed are described as "under assault, showing the telltale symptoms of the disease," while millions of others "harbor the virus, vulnerable at any time to a final, all-out attack."

Cancer makes cells proliferate; in AIDS, cells die. Even as this 4 original model of AIDS (the mirror image of leukemia) has been altered, descriptions of how the virus does its work continue to echo the way the illness is perceived as infiltrating the society. "AIDS Virus Found to Hide in Cells, Eluding Detection by Normal Tests" was the headline of a recent front-page story in the *New York Times* announcing the discovery that the virus can "lurk" for years in the macrophages—disrupting their disease-fighting function without killing them, "even when the macrophages are filled almost to bursting with virus," and without producing antibodies, the chemicals the body makes in response to "invading agents" and whose presence has been regarded as an infallible marker of the syndrome. That the virus isn't lethal for *all* the cells where it takes up residence, as is now thought, only increases the illness-foe's reputation for wiliness and invincibility.

What makes the viral assault so terrifying is that contamina- 5 tion, and therefore vulnerability, is understood as permanent. Even if someone infected were never to develop any symptoms— that is, the infection remained, or could by medical intervention be rendered, inactive—the viral enemy would be forever within. In fact, so it is believed, it is just a matter of time before something awakens ("triggers") it, before the appearance of "the telltale symptoms." Like syphilis, known to generations of doctors as "the great masquerader," AIDS is a clinical construction, an inference. It takes its identity from the presence of *some* among a long, and lengthening, roster of symptoms (no one has everything that AIDS could be), symptoms which "mean" that what the patient has is this illness. The construction of the illness rests on the invention not only of AIDS as a clinical entity but of a kind of junior AIDS, called AIDS-related complex (ARC), to which people are assigned if they show "early" and often intermittent symptoms of immunological deficit such as fevers, weight loss, fungal infections, and swollen lymph glands. AIDS is progressive, a disease of time. Once a certain density of symptoms is attained, the course of the illness can be swift and brings atrocious suffering. Besides the commonest "presenting" illnesses (some hitherto unusual, at least in a fatal form, such as a rare skin cancer and a rare form of pneumonia), a plethora of disabling, disfiguring, and humiliating symptoms make the AIDS patient steadily more infirm, helpless, and unable to control or take care of basic functions and needs.

The sense in which AIDS is a slow disease makes it more like 6 syphilis, which is characterized in terms of "stages," than like cancer. Thinking in terms of "stages" is essential to discourse about AIDS. Syphilis in its most dreaded form is "tertiary syphilis," syphilis in its third stage. What is called AIDS is generally understood as the last of three stages—the first of which is infection with a human immunodeficiency virus (HIV) and early evidence of inroads on the immune system—with a long latency period between infection and the onset of the "telltale" symptoms. (Apparently not as long as syphilis, in which the latency period between secondary and tertiary illness might be decades. But it is worth noting that when syphilis first appeared in epidemic form in Europe at the end of the fifteenth century, it was a rapid disease, of an unexplained virulence that is unknown today, in which death often occurred in the second stage, sometimes within months or a few years.) Cancer *grows* slowly: It is not thought to be, for a long time, latent. (A convincing account of a process in terms of "stages" seems invariably to include the notion of a normative delay or halt in the process, such as is supplied by the notion of latency.) True, a cancer is "staged." This is a principal tool of diagnosis, which means classifying it according to its gravity, determining how "advanced" it is. But it is mostly a spatial notion: that the cancer advances through the body, traveling or migrating along predictable routes. Cancer is first of all a disease of the body's geography, in contrast to syphilis and AIDS, whose definition depends on constructing a temporal sequence of stages.

UNDERSTANDING DETAILS

1. In what ways do the words *invasion* and *pollution* (paragraph 3) help define AIDS? What two points of view of the disease do these words represent?

2. How is the language of AIDS different from that of cancer? From that of syphilis?
3. Explain the headline Sontag cites in paragraph 4: "AIDS Virus Found to Hide in Cells, Eluding Detection by Normal Tests."
4. In what way is AIDS "a disease of time" (paragraph 5)?

ANALYZING MEANING

1. According to Sontag, what makes the attack of AIDS so "terrifying" (paragraph 5)?
2. Explain all aspects of the two main metaphors Sontag uses to define AIDS (invasion and pollution). How does Sontag's examination of these metaphors help you understand the AIDS virus more specifically?
3. Devise a new metaphor to explain the progress of this disease.
4. Why do you think people turn to metaphor to help them define certain diseases? How do metaphors help us understand AIDS?

DISCOVERING RHETORICAL STRATEGIES

1. How does Sontag use the language of science fiction to define AIDS?
2. What effect does Sontag's use of quotations have on the essay?
3. Sontag uses both comparison/contrast and analogy to define AIDS in this essay. Find an example of each of these rhetorical modes, and explain how it works.
4. What other rhetorical strategies, besides comparison/contrast and analogy, does Sontag use in this essay? Give examples of each.

MAKING CONNECTIONS

1. Contrast Sontag's comments about the "staging" of disease with the various stages children of divorce go through in "Second Chances for Children of Divorce" by Judith Wallerstein and Sandra Blakeslee. To what extent are these stages sequential (that is, does a person always have to go through one stage in order to get to the next)? Name an event in your own life that has happened in stages.
2. Compare Sontag's assertion that the metaphors associated with

AIDS help shape our image of the disease and Alleen Pace Nilsen's ("Sexism in English: A 1990s Update") argument that negative language about women adversely influences their treatment in society. To what extent is each of these authors dealing with the way in which words control our thoughts?

3. Imagine that Sontag has just read Mitchell Lazarus's article "Rx for Mathophobia," in which the author asserts that the fear of mathematics is a "disease" that can be cured by "reality-based" curriculum reform in our nation's schools. Is the language of disease as crucial to Lazarus's argument as it is to Sontag's? Why or why not?

IDEAS FOR DISCUSSION/WRITING

Preparing to Write

Write freely about your current reactions to the AIDS virus: How do you feel about the disease? What should we be doing to control the spread of AIDS? What should we be doing to protect the rights of AIDS victims? To protect the rights of people who do not have AIDS? What do you think the future of the virus in America will be?

Choosing a Topic

1. Choose an ailment other than AIDS (for example, something serious, such as a stroke or heart trouble, or something less threatening, such as the flu or a cold), and write an essay in which you define this illness through an extended comparison.

2. For a medical report prepared by your college or university, define *health* as it relates to college students today. Determine an audience and focus before you begin to write.

3. One feud in connection with the AIDS epidemic in the United States revolves around the civil rights of the AIDS victims versus the rights of people not infected with the virus. Many states are taking actions that require physicians to report AIDS victims to a central agency. Write an editorial for your local newspaper explaining where you stand on this issue and why.

8

Cause/Effect

Tracing Reasons and Results

Wanting to know why things happen is one of our earliest, most basic instincts: Why can't I go out, Mommy? Why are you laughing? Why won't the dog stop barking? Why can't I swim faster than my big brother? These questions, and many more like them, reflect the innately inquisitive nature that dwells within each of us. Closely related to this desire to understand *why* is our corresponding interest in *what* will happen in the future as a result of some particular action: What will I feel like tomorrow if I stay up late tonight? How will I perform in the track meet Saturday if I practice all week? What will be the result if I mix together these two potent chemicals? What will happen if I turn in my next English assignment two days early?

A daily awareness of this intimate relationship between causes and effects allows us to begin to understand the complex and interrelated series of events that make up our lives and the lives of others. For example, trying to understand the various causes of the conflict in the Persian Gulf teaches us about international relations; knowing our biological reactions to certain foods helps us make decisions about what to eat; understanding the interrelated reasons for the outbreak of World War II offers us insight into historical trends and human nature; knowing the effects of sunshine on various parts of our bodies helps us make decisions about how much ultraviolet exposure we can tolerate and what suntan lotion to use; and understanding the causes of America's most recent recession will help us respond appropriately to the next economic crisis we encounter. More than anything else, tracing causes and effects teaches us how to think clearly and react intelligently to our multifaceted environment.

In college, you will often be asked to use this natural interest in causes and effects to analyze particular situations and to discern general principles. For example, you might be asked some of the following questions on essay exams in different courses:

Anthropology: Why did the Mayan culture disintegrate?

Psychology: Why do humans respond to fear in different ways?

Biology: How do lab rats react to caffeine?

History: What were the positive effects of the Spanish–American War?

Business: Why did so many computer manufacturing companies go bankrupt in the early 1980s?

Your ability to answer such questions will depend in large part on your skill at writing a cause/effect essay.

DEFINING CAUSE/EFFECT

Cause/effect analysis requires the ability to look for connections between different elements and to analyze the reasons for those connections. As the name implies, this rhetorical mode has two separate components: cause and effect. A particular essay might concentrate on cause (Why do you live in a dorm?), on effect (What are the resulting advantages and disadvantages of living in a dorm?), or on some combination of the two. In working with causes, we are searching for any circumstances from the past that may have caused a single event; in looking for effects, we seek occurrences that took place after a particular event and resulted from that event. Like process analysis, cause/effect makes use of our intellectual ability to analyze. Process analysis addresses *how* something happens, whereas causal analysis discusses *why* it happened and *what* the result was. A process analysis paper, for example, might explain how to advertise more effectively to increase sales, whereas a cause/effect study would discover that three specific elements contributed to an increase in sales: effective advertising, personal service, and selective discounts. The study of causes and effects, therefore, provides many different and helpful ways for humans to make sense of and clarify their views of the world.

Looking for causes and effects requires an advanced form of thinking. It is more complex than most rhetorical strategies we have studied because it can exist on a number of different and progressively more difficult levels. The most accurate and effective causal analysis accrues from digging for the real or ultimate causes or effects, as opposed to those that are merely superficial or immediate. Actress Angela Lansbury would have been out of work on an episode of the television show *Murder, She Wrote*, for example, if her character had stopped her investigation at the immediate cause of death (slipping in the bathtub) rather than searching diligently for the real cause (an overdose of cocaine administered by an angry companion, which resulted in the slip in the tub). Similarly, voters would be easy to manipulate if they considered only the immediate effects of a tax increase (a slightly higher tax bill) rather than the ultimate benefits that would result (the many years of improved education that our children would receive because of the specialized programs created by such an increase). Only the discovery of the actual reasons for an event or an idea will lead to the logical and accurate analysis of causes and effects important to a basic understanding of various aspects of our lives.

Faulty reasoning assigns causes to a sequence of actions without adequate justification. One such logical fallacy is called *post hoc, ergo propter hoc* ("after this, therefore because of this"): The fact that someone lost a job after walking under a ladder does not mean that the two events are causally related; by the same token, if we get up every morning at 5:30 A.M., just before the sun rises, we cannot therefore conclude that the sun rises *because* we get up (no matter how self-centered we are!). Faulty reasoning also occurs when we oversimplify a particular situation. Most events are connected to a multitude of causes and effects. Sometimes one effect has many causes: A student may fail a history exam because she's been working two part-time jobs, she was sick, she didn't study hard enough, and she found the instructor very boring. One cause may also have many effects. If a house burns down, the people who lived in it will be out of a home. If we look at such a tragic scene more closely, however, we may also note that the fire traumatized a child who lived there, helped the family learn what good friends they had, encouraged the family to double their future fire insurance, and provided the happy stimulus that they needed to make a long-dreamed-of move to another city. One event has thus resulted in many interrelated effects. Building an argument on insecure foundations or oversimplifying the causes or effects connected with an event will seriously hinder the construction of a rational essay. No matter what the nature of the cause/effect analysis, it must always be based on clear observation, accurate facts, and rigorous logic.

In the following paragraph, a student writer analyzes some of the causes and effects connected with the controversial issue of euthanasia. Notice how he makes connections and then analyzes those connections as he consistently explores the immediate and ultimate effects of being able to stretch life beyond its normal limits through new medical technology:

> *Along with the many recent startling advancements in medical technology have come a number of complex moral, ethical, and spiritual questions that beg to be answered. We now have the ability to prolong the life of the human body for a very long time. But what rights do patients and their families have to curtail cruel and unusual medical treatment that stretches life beyond its normal limits? This dilemma has produced a ripple effect in society. Is the extension of life an unquestionable goal in itself, regardless of the quality of that life? Modern scientific technology has forced doctors to reevaluate the exact meaning and purpose of their profession. For example, many medical schools and undergraduate university programs now routinely offer classes on medical ethics—an esoteric and infrequently taught subject only a few years ago. Doctors and scholars alike are realizing that medical personnel alone cannot be expected to decide on the exact parameters of life. In like manner, the judicial process must now evaluate the legal complexities of mercy killings and the rights of patients to die with dignity and without unnecessary medical intervention. The insurance business, too, wrestles with the catastrophic effects of new technology on the costs of today's hospital care. In short, medical progress entails more than microscopes, chemicals, and high-tech instruments. If we are to develop as a thoughtful, just, and merciful society, we must consider*

not only the physical well-being of our nation's patients, but their emotional, spiritual, and financial status as well.

THINKING CRITICALLY BY USING CAUSE/EFFECT

Thinking about causes and effects is one of the most advanced mental activities that we perform. It involves complex operations that we must think through carefully, making sure all connections are reasonable and accurate. Unlike other rhetorical patterns, cause/effect thinking requires us to see specific relationships between two or more items. To practice this strategy, we need to look for items or events that are causally related—that is, one that has caused the other. Then, we can focus on either the causes (the initial stimulus), the effects (the results), or a combination of the two.

Searching out causes and effects requires a great deal of digging that is not necessary for most of the other modes. Cause/effect necessitates the ultimate in investigative work. The mental exertion associated with this thinking strategy is sometimes exhausting, but it is always worth going through when you discover relationships that you never saw before or you uncover links in your reasoning that were previously unknown or obscure to you.

If you've ever had the secret desire to be a private eye or an investigator of any sort, practicing cause/effect reasoning can be lots of fun. It forces you to see relationships among multiple items and then to make sense of those connections. Completing exercises in this skill by itself will once again help you perfect the logistics of cause/effect thinking before you mix and match it with several other thinking strategies.

1. Choose a major problem you see in our society, and list what you think are the main causes of this problem on one side of a piece of paper and the effects on the other side. Compare the two lists to see how they differ. Then, compare and contrast your list with those written by other students.
2. What "caused" you to become a student? What influences led you to this choice at this point in your life? How has being a student affected your life? List several overall effects.
3. List the effects of one of the following: getting a speeding ticket, winning the U.S. Open tennis tournament, graduating from college, or watching TV till the wee hours of the morning.

READING AND WRITING CAUSE/EFFECT ESSAYS

Causal analysis is usually employed for one of three main purposes: (1) to prove a specific point (such as the necessity of stricter gun control), in which case the writer generally deals totally with facts and with conclusions drawn from those facts; (2) to argue against a widely accepted belief (for example, the assertion that cocaine is addictive), in which case the writer relies principally on facts, with perhaps some pertinent opinions; or (3) to speculate on a theory (for instance, why the crime rate is higher in most major cities than it is in rural areas), in which case the writer probably presents hypotheses and opinions along with facts. This section will explore these purposes in cause/effect essays from the standpoint of both reading and writing.

How to Read a Cause/Effect Essay

Preparing to Read. As you set out to read the essays in this chapter, begin by focusing your attention on the title and the synopsis of the essay you are about to read and by scanning the essay itself: What do you think Stephen King is going to talk about in "Why We Crave Horror Movies"? What does the synopsis in the Rhetorical Table of Contents tell you about Michael Dorris's "The Broken Cord" or about Richard Rodriguez's "The Fear of Losing a Culture"?

Also, at this stage in the reading process, you should try to learn as much as you can about the author of the essay and the reasons he or she wrote it. Ask yourself questions like the following: What is King's intention in "Why We Crave Horror Movies"? Who is Mitchell Lazarus's intended audience in "Rx for Mathophobia"? And what is Alice Walker's point of view in "Beauty: When the Other Dancer Is the Self"?

Finally, before you begin to read, answer the prereading questions for each essay and then consider the proposed essay topic from a variety of perspectives: For example, concerning Rodriguez's topic, how important to you is your ethnic or national background? Which segments of American society are most aware of cultural differences? Which the least? Do you have a fear of math? What do you want to know from Lazarus about curing or controlling that fear?

Reading. As you read each essay in this chapter for the first time, record your spontaneous reactions to it, drawing as often as possible on the preliminary material you already know: What do you think of horror movies (King)? Why did Lazarus choose the title he did? What is Dorris suggesting about fetal alcohol babies? Have you experienced an addiction of any kind?

Whenever you can, try to create a context for your reading: What is the tone of Rodriguez's comments about culture? How does this tone help him communicate with his audience? What do you think Walker's purpose is in her essay concerning her childhood accident? How clearly does she get this purpose across to you?

Also, during this reading, note the essay's thesis and check to see if the writer thoroughly explores all possibilities before settling on the primary causes and/or effects of a particular situation; in addition, determine whether the writer clearly states the assertions that naturally evolve from a discussion of the topic. Finally, read the questions following each essay to get a sense of the main issues and strategies in the selection.

Rereading. When you reread these essays, you should focus mainly on the writer's craft. Notice how the authors narrow and focus their material, how they make clear and logical connections between ideas in their essays, how they support their conclusions with concrete examples, how they use other rhetorical modes to accomplish their cause/effect analysis, and how they employ logical transitions to move us smoothly from one point to another. Most important, however, ask yourself if the writer actually discusses the real causes and/or effects of a particular circumstance: What does King say are the primary reasons people crave horror movies? What does Lazarus consider the main causes of mathophobia? What solutions does he offer? What are the primary causes and effects of Walker's childhood injury?

For a thorough outline of the reading process, consult the checklist on pages 20–21 of the Introduction.

How to Write a Cause/Effect Essay

Preparing to Write. Beginning a cause/effect essay requires—as does any other essay—exploring and limiting your subject, specifying a purpose, and identifying an audience. The Preparing to Write questions before the essay assignments, coupled with the prewriting techniques outlined in the Introduction, encourage you to consider specific issues related to your reading. The assignments themselves will then help you limit your topic and determine a particular purpose and audience for your message. For cause/effect essays, determining a purpose is even more important than usual, because your readers can get hopelessly lost unless your analysis is clearly focused.

Writing. For all its conceptual complexity, a cause/effect essay can be organized quite simply. The introduction generally presents the subject(s) and states the purpose of the analysis in a clear thesis. The body of the paper then explores all relevant causes and/or effects, typically progressing either from least to most influential or from most to least influential. Finally, the concluding section summarizes the various cause-and-effect relationships established in the body of the paper and clearly states the conclusions that can be drawn from those relationships.

The following additional guidelines should assist you in producing an effective cause/effect essay in all academic disciplines:

1. Narrow and focus your material as much as possible.
2. Consider all possibilities before assigning real or ultimate causes or effects.
3. Show connections between ideas by using transitions and key words—such as *because, reasons, results, effects*, and *consequences*—to guide your readers smoothly through your essay.
4. Support all inferences with concrete evidence.
5. Be as objective as possible in your analysis so that you don't distort logic with personal biases.
6. Understand your audience's opinions and convictions, so that you know what to emphasize in your essay.
7. Qualify your assertions to avoid overstatement and oversimplification.

These suggestions apply to both cause/effect essay assignments and exam questions.

Rewriting. As you revise your cause/effect essays, ask yourself the following important questions:

Is your thesis stated clearly at the outset of your paper?

Does it include your subject and your purpose?

Do you accomplish your purpose as effectively as possible for your particular audience?

Do you use logical reasoning throughout the essay?

Do you carefully explore all relevant causes and/or effects, searching for the real (as opposed to the immediate) reasons in each case?

Have you organized your discussion in some sequential way?

Have you checked your essay against the guidelines listed above?

Do you state clearly the conclusions that can be drawn from the various cause/effect relationships discussed in your paper?

More specific guidelines for writing and revising your essays appear on pages 32–33 of the Introduction.

STUDENT ESSAY: CAUSE/EFFECT AT WORK

In the following essay, the student writer analyzes the effects of contemporary TV soap operas on young people: Notice that she states her subject and purpose at the beginning of the essay and then presents a combination of facts and opinions in her exploration of the topic. Notice also that, in her analysis, the writer is careful to draw clear connections between her perceptions of the issue and various objective details in an attempt to trace the effects of this medium in our society today. At the end of her essay, look at her summary of the logical relationships she establishes in the body of the essay and her statements about the conclusions she draws from these relationships.

Distortions of Reality

Background Television's contributions to society, positive and negative, have been debated continually since this piece of technology invaded the average American household in the 1950s. Television has brought an unlimited influx of new information, ideas, and cultures into our homes. However, based on my observations of my thirteen-year-old cousin, Katie, and her friends, I think we need to take a closer look at the effects of soap operas on adolescents today. The **Thesis statement** distortions of reality portrayed on these programs are frighteningly misleading and,

452

in my opinion, can be very confusing to young people.

Transition   During the early 1990s, the lifestyle of the typical soap opera "family" has been radically transformed from comfortable pretentiousness to blatant and unrealistic decadence. The characters neither live nor dress like the majority of their viewers, who are generally middle-class Americans. These television families live in large, majestic homes that are flawlessly decorated. The actors are often adorned in beautiful

Concrete examples designer clothing, fur coats, and expensive jewelry, and this opulent lifestyle is sustained by people with no visible means of income. Very few of the characters seem to "work" for a living. When they do, upward mobility—without the benefit of the proper education or suitable training—and a well-planned marriage come quickly.

First distortion of reality

Transition   From this constant barrage of conspicuous consumption, my cousin and her friends seem to have a distorted view of everyday economic realities. I see Katie and her group becoming obsessed with the appearance of their clothes and possessions. I frequently hear them berate their parents'

Concrete examples jobs and modest homes. With noticeable arrogance, these young adolescents seem to view their parents' lives as "failures" when compared to the effortless, luxurious lifestyles portrayed in the soaps.

First effect

Transition   One of the most alluring features of this genre is its masterful use of deception. Conflicts between characters in soap operas are based on secrecy and misinformation.

Concrete examples Failure to tell the truth and to perform honorable deeds further complicates the entangled lives and love affairs of the participants. But when the truth finally comes out and all mistakes and misdeeds become public, the culprits and offenders hardly ever suffer for their actions. In fact, they appear to leave the scene of the crime guilt-free.

Second distortion of reality

Transition Regrettably, Katie and her friends consistently express alarming indifference to this lack of moral integrity. In their daily **Concrete examples** viewing, they shrug off underhanded scenes of scheming and conniving, and they marvel at how the characters manipulate each other into positions of powerlessness or grapple in distasteful love scenes. I can only conclude that continued exposure to this amoral behavior is eroding the fundamental values of truth and fidelity in these kids.

Second effect

Transition Also in the soaps, the powers-that-be conveniently disregard any sense of responsibility for wrongdoing. Characters serve jail terms quickly and in relative comfort. Drug **Concrete examples** or alcohol abuse does not mar anyone's physical appearance or behavior, and poverty is virtually nonexistent. Usually, the wrongdoer's position, wealth, and prestige are quickly restored—with little pain and suffering.

Third distortion of reality

Adolescents are clearly learning that people can act without regard for the harmful effects of their actions on themselves and others when they see this type of behavior go unpunished. Again, I notice the result of this delusion in my cousin. Recently, when a businessman in our community was convicted of embezzling large sums of money from his clients, Katie was outraged because **Concrete examples** he was sentenced to five years in prison, unlike her daytime TV "heartthrob," who had been given a suspended sentence for a similar crime. With righteous indignation, Katie

Third effect

claimed that the victims, many of whom had lost their entire savings, should have realized that any business investment involves risk and the threat of loss. Logic and common sense evaded Katie's reasoning as she insisted on comparing television justice with real-life scruples.

The writers and producers of soap operas argue that the shows are designed to entertain viewers and are not meant to be reflections of reality. Theoretically, this may be true, but I can actually see how these soap operas are affecting my cousin and her crowd. Although my personal observations are limited, I cannot believe they are unique or unusual. Too many young people think that they can amass wealth and material possessions without an education, hard work, or careful financial planning; that material goods are the sole measure of a person's success in life; and that honesty and integrity are not necessarily admirable qualities.

Ultimate effect

Proposed solution

Soap operas should demonstrate a realistic lifestyle and a responsible sense of behavior. The many hours adolescents spend in front of the television can obviously influence their view of the world. As a society, we cannot afford the consequences resulting from the distortions of reality portrayed every day in these shows.

Student Writer's Comments

In general, writing this essay was not as easy as I had anticipated during my prewriting phase. Although I was interested in and familiar with my topic, I had trouble fitting all the pieces together: matching causes with effects, examples with main points, and problems with solutions.

My prewriting activities were a combination of lists and journal entries that gave me loads of ideas and phrasing to work with in my drafts. From this initial thinking exercise, I made an informal outline of the points I wanted to make. I played with the order of these topics for a while and then began to write.

Because I had spent so much time thinking through various causal relationships before I began to write, I generated the first draft with minimal pain. But I was not happy with it. The examples that I had chosen to support various points I wanted to make did not fit as well as they could, and the whole essay was unfocused and scattered. Although all writing requires support and focus, I realized that a cause/effect essay demands special attention to the relationship between specific examples and their ultimate causes and/or effects. As a result, I had to begin again to revise my sprawling first draft.

I spent my first revising session on the very sloppy introduction and conclusion. I felt that if I could tighten up these parts of the essay, I would have a clearer notion of my purpose and focus. I am convinced now that the time I spent on the beginning and ending of my essay really paid off. I rewrote my thesis several times until I finally arrived at the statement in the draft printed here. This final thesis statement gave me a clear sense of direction for revising the rest of my paper.

I then worked through my essay paragraph by paragraph, making sure that the examples and illustrations I cited supported as effectively as possible the point I was making. I made sure that the causes and effects were accurately paired, and I reorganized sections of the essay that didn't yet read smoothly. I put the final touches on my conclusion and handed in my paper—with visions of causes, effects, and soap opera characters still dancing around in my head.

SOME FINAL THOUGHTS ON CAUSE/EFFECT

The essays in this chapter deal with both causes and effects in a variety of ways. As you read each essay, try to discover its primary purpose and the ultimate causes and/or effects of the issue under discussion. Note also the clear causal relationships that each author sets forth on solid foundations supported by logical reasoning. Although the subjects of these essays vary dramatically, each essay exhibits the basic elements of effective causal analysis.

STEPHEN KING   (1947 –   )

■ ■ ■

Why We Crave Horror Movies

"People's appetites for terror seem insatiable," Stephen King once remarked, an insight which may help justify his phenomenal success as a writer of horror fiction since the mid-1970s. His twenty-four books have sold over one hundred million copies, and the movies made from them have generated more income than the gross national product of several small countries. After early jobs as a janitor, a laundry worker, and a high school English teacher in Portland, Maine, King turned to writing full time following the spectacular sales of his first novel, *Carrie* (1974), which focuses on a shy, socially ostracized young girl who takes revenge on her cruel classmates through newly developed telekinetic powers. King's subsequent books have included *The Shining* (1976), *Firestarter* (1980), *Cujo* (1981), *The Dark Tower* (1982), *Christine* (1983), *Pet Sematary* (1983), *Misery* (1987), *The Stand* (1990), *Four Past Midnight* (1990), *The Waste Lands* (1992), and *Delores Claiborne* (1993). Asked to explain why readers and moviegoers are so attracted to his tales of horror, King told a *Chicago Tribune* interviewer that most people's lives "are full of fears—that their marriage isn't working, that they aren't going to make it on the job, that society is crumbling all around them. But we're really not supposed to talk about things like that, and so they don't have any outlets for all those scary feelings. But the horror writer can give them a place to put their fears, and it's OK to be afraid then, because nothing is real, and you can blow it all away when it's over." A cheerful though somewhat superstitious person, King, who now lives in Bangor, Maine, admits to doing most of his best writing during the morning hours. "You think I want to write this stuff at night?" he once asked a reviewer.

Preparing to Read

As you prepare to read this article, consider your thoughts on America's emotional condition: How emotionally healthy are Americans? Were they more emotionally healthy twenty years ago? A century ago? What makes a society emotionally healthy? Emotionally unhealthy? How can a society maintain good health? What is the relationship between emotional health and a civilized society?

I think that we're all mentally ill; those of us outside the asylums only hide it a little better—and maybe not all that much better, after all. We've all known people who talk to themselves, people who sometimes squinch their faces into horrible grimaces when they believe no one is watching, people who have some hysterical fear—of snakes, the dark, the tight place, the long drop . . . and, of course, those final worms and grubs that are waiting so patiently underground.

When we pay our four or five bucks and seat ourselves at tenth-row center in a theater showing a horror movie, we are daring the nightmare.

Why? Some of the reasons are simple and obvious. To show that we can, that we are not afraid, that we can ride this roller coaster. Which is not to say that a really good horror movie may not surprise a scream out of us at some point, the way we may scream when the roller coaster twists through a complete 360 or plows through a lake at the bottom of the drop. And horror movies, like roller coasters, have always been the special province of the young; by the time one turns 40 or 50, one's appetite for double twists or 360-degree loops may be considerably depleted.

We also go to reestablish our feelings of essential normality; the horror movie is innately conservative, even reactionary. Freda Jackson as the horrible melting woman in *Die, Monster, Die!* confirms for us that no matter how far we may be removed from the beauty of a Robert Redford or a Diana Ross, we are still light-years from true ugliness.

And we go to have fun.

Ah, but this is where the ground starts to slope away, isn't it? Because this is a very peculiar sort of fun, indeed. The fun comes from seeing others menaced—sometimes killed. One critic has suggested that if pro football has become the voyeur's version of combat, then the horror film has become the modern version of the public lynching.

It is true that the mythic, "fairy-tale" horror film intends to 7
take away the shades of gray. . . . It urges us to put away our more
civilized and adult penchant for analysis and to become children
again, seeing things in pure blacks and whites. It may be that horror movies provide psychic relief on this level because this invitation to lapse into simplicity, irrationality, and even outright
madness is extended so rarely. We are told we may allow our
emotions a free rein . . . or no rein at all.

If we are all insane, then sanity becomes a matter of degree. If 8
your insanity leads you to carve up women, like Jack the Ripper or
the Cleveland Torso Murderer, we clap you away in the funny *Degrees*
farm (but neither of those two amateur-night surgeons was ever *or levels*
caught, heh-heh-heh); if, on the other hand, your insanity leads *of*
you only to talk to yourself when you're under stress or to pick *insanity*
your nose on your morning bus, then you are left alone to go
about your business . . . though it is doubtful that you will ever be
invited to the best parties.

The potential lyncher is in almost all of us (excluding saints, 9
past and present; but then, most saints have been crazy in their
own ways), and every now and then, he has to be let loose to
scream and roll around in the grass. Our emotions and our fears
form their own body, and we recognize that it demands its own
exercise to maintain proper muscle tone. Certain of these emotional muscles are accepted—even exalted—in civilized society;
they are, of course, the emotions that tend to maintain the status
quo of civilization itself. Love, friendship, loyalty, kindness—these
are all the emotions that we applaud, emotions that have been
immortalized in the couplets of Hallmark cards and in the verses
(I don't dare call it poetry) of Leonard Nimoy.

When we exhibit these emotions, society showers us with pos- 10
itive reinforcement; we learn this even before we get out of diapers. When, as children, we hug our rotten little puke of a sister *Good*
and give her a kiss, all the aunts and uncles smile and twit and *Deed*
cry, "Isn't he the sweetest little thing?" Such coveted treats as *+*
chocolate-covered graham crackers often follow. But if we delib- *coseq.*
erately slam the rotten little puke of a sister's fingers in the door,
sanctions follow—angry remonstrance from parents, aunts and *Bad need*
uncles; instead of a chocolate-covered graham cracker, a spanking. *conseq.*

But anticivilization emotions don't go away, and they demand 11 periodic exercise. We have such "sick" jokes as, "What's the differ-ence between a truckload of bowling balls and a truckload of dead babies?" (You can't unload a truckload of bowling balls with a pitchfork . . . a joke, by the way, that I heard originally from a ten-year-old.) Such a joke may surprise a laugh or a grin out of us even as we recoil, a possibility that confirms the thesis: If we share a brotherhood of man, then we also share an insanity of man. None of which is intended as a defense of either the sick joke or insanity but merely as an explanation of why the best horror films, like the best fairy tales, manage to be reactionary, an-archistic, and revolutionary all at the same time.

The mythic horror movie, like the sick joke, has a dirty job to do. It deliberately appeals to all that is worst in us. It is morbidity unchained, our most base instincts let free, our nastiest fantasies realized . . ., and it all happens, fittingly enough, in the dark. For those reasons, good liberals often shy away from horror films. For myself, I like to see the most aggressive of them—*Dawn of the Dead*, for instance—as lifting a trap door in the civilized forebrain and throwing a basket of raw meat to the hungry alligators swim-ming around in that subterranean river beneath.   12

Why bother? Because it keeps them from getting out, man. It keeps them down there and me up here. It was Lennon and McCartney who said that all you need is love, and I would agree with that.   13

As long as you keep the gators fed.   14

UNDERSTANDING DETAILS

1. Why, in King's opinion, do civilized people enjoy horror movies?
2. According to King, in what ways are horror movies like roller coasters?
3. According to King, how are horror films like public lynchings?
4. What is the difference between "emotions that tend to main-tain the status quo of civilization" (paragraph 9) and "anticivi-lization emotions" (paragraph 11)?

ANALYZING MEANING

1. How can horror movies "reestablish our feelings of essential normality" (paragraph 4)?

2. What is "reactionary, anarchistic, and revolutionary" (paragraph 11) about fairy tales? About horror films?
3. Why does the author think we need to exercise our anticivilization emotions? What are some other ways we might confront these emotions?
4. Explain the last line of King's essay: "As long as you keep the gators fed" (paragraph 14).

DISCOVERING RHETORICAL STRATEGIES

1. What is the cause/effect relationship King notes in society between horror movies and sanity?
2. Why does King begin his essay with such a dramatic statement as "I think that we're all mentally ill" (paragraph 1)?
3. Who do you think is the author's intended audience for this essay? Describe them in detail. How did you come to this conclusion?
4. What different rhetorical strategies does King use to support his cause/effect analysis? Give examples of each.

MAKING CONNECTIONS

1. Apply Stephen King's definition of "horror" to such horrific experiences as rape (Nancy Gibbs, "When Is It Rape?"), caring for a fetal alcohol syndrome child (Michael Dorris, "The Broken Cord"), and/or the preparation of a dead body for its funeral (Jessica Mitford, "Behind the Formaldehyde Curtain"). In what way is each of these events "horrible"? What are the principal differences between watching a horror movie and living through a real-life horror like a rape?
2. In this essay, King gives us important insights into his own writing process, especially into how horror novels and movies affect their audiences. Compare and contrast his revelation of the techniques of his trade with those advanced by Annie Dillard ("When You Write"), Kurt Vonnegut ("How to Write with Style"), or Paul Roberts ("How to Say Nothing in Five Hundred Words"), all of whom are writing about the writing process. Whose advice is most helpful to you? Explain your answer.
3. Compare King's comments about "fear" with similar insights into fear by such other authors as Tom Wolfe ("The Right

Stuff"), Richard Rodriguez ("The Fear of Losing a Culture"), and Alice Walker ("Beauty: When the Other Dancer Is the Self"). How would each of these writers define the term differently? With which author's definition would you be most in agreement? Explain your answer.

IDEAS FOR DISCUSSION/WRITING

Preparing to Write

Write freely about how most people maintain a healthy emotional attitude: How would you define emotional well-being? When are people most emotionally healthy? Most emotionally unhealthy? What do your friends and relatives do to maintain a healthy emotional life? What do you do to maintain emotional health? What is the connection between our individual emotional health and the extent to which our society is civilized?

Choosing a Topic

1. Think of a release other than horror films for our most violent emotions. Is it an acceptable release? Write an essay for the general public explaining the relationship between this particular release and our "civilized" society.
2. If you accept King's analysis of horror movies, what role in society do you think other types of movies play (e.g., love stories, science-fiction movies, and comedies)? Choose one type, and explain its role to your college composition class.
3. Your psychology instructor has asked you to explain your opinions on the degree of sanity or insanity in America at present. In what ways are we sane? In what ways are we insane? Write an essay for your psychology instructor explaining in detail your observations along these lines.

MICHAEL DORRIS   (1945 –   )

■ ■ ■

The Broken Cord

Michael Dorris, a descendant of Modoc American Indians and Irish and French settlers, grew up in Kentucky and Montana. He earned his B.A. at Georgetown University and his Master of Arts degree at Yale and was for many years a professor of anthropology and Native-American Studies at Dartmouth, where he was also head of the Native-American Studies program. His training has been quite eclectic. "I came to cultural anthropology," he has explained, "by way of an undergraduate program in English and classics and a Master's Degree in history of the theater." He has been a Guggenheim Fellow (1978), a Rockefeller Fellow (1985), a member of the Smithsonian Institution Council, a National Endowment for the Humanities consultant, a National Public Radio commentator, and a member of the editorial board of the *American Indian Culture and Research Journal* during his distinguished academic career. His many publications have included *Native Americans: Five Hundred Years After* (1975); a bestselling novel, *A Yellow Raft in Blue Water* (1987); *The Broken Cord* (1989), a work of nonfiction that won the Heartland Prize, the Christopher Medal, and the National Book Critics Circle Award; *Morning Girl* (1992), a book of short stories; and two more novels, *Working Men* (1993) and *Rooms in the House of Stone* (1993). Dorris has also coauthored several books with his wife, Louise Erdrich, including *Route Two and Back* (1991), a collection of travel essays. He advises students using *The Prose Reader* to "work at as many kinds of jobs as possible while they are young and to keep daily journals of their experiences and impressions." The author currently lives and works in Cornish Flat, New Hampshire.

Preparing to Read

The following excerpt from *The Broken Cord* details some of Dorris's frustrations in raising his adopted son, Adam, who suffered from fetal alcohol syndrome until his death in 1991. As you prepare to read this article, take a few moments to think about your own physical and mental growth: What do you know about your birth? How did you develop as a child? Are you reaching your physical and mental potential? How do you know? Are there any barriers between you and this potential? What are they? How can you surmount them? How will you maintain your potential?

A dam's birthdays are, I think, the hardest anniversaries, even 1 though as an adoptive father I was not present to hear Adam's first cry, to feel the aspirated warmth of his body meeting air for the first time. I was not present to count his fingers, to exclaim at the surprise of gender, to be comforted by the hope at the heart of his new existence.

From what I've learned, from the sum of gathered profiles di- 2 vided by the tragedy of each case, the delivery of my premature son was unlikely to have been a joyous occasion. Most fetal alcohol babies emerge not in a tide, the facsimile of saline, primordial, life-granting sea, but instead enter this world tainted with stale wine. Their amniotic fluid literally reeks of Thunderbird or Ripple, and the whole operating theater stinks like the scene of a three-day party. Delivery room staff who have been witness time and again tell of undernourished babies thrown into delirium tremens when the cord that brought sustenance and poison is severed. Nurses close their eyes at the memory. An infant with the shakes, as cold turkey as a raving derelict deprived of the next fix, is hard to forget.

Compared to the ideal, Adam started far in the hole, differently 3 from the child who began a march through the years without the scars of fetters on his ankles, with eyes and ears that worked, with nothing to carry except what he or she collected along the path.

Adam's birthdays are reminders for me. For each celebration 4 commemorating that he was born, there is the pang, the rage, that he was not born whole. I grieve for what he might have, what he should have been. I magnify and sustain those looks of understanding or compassion or curiosity that fleet across his face, fast as a breeze, unexpected as the voice of God—the time he said to me in the car, the words arising from no context I could see, "Kansas is between Oklahoma and Texas." But when I turned in amazement, agreeing loudly, still ready after all these years to discover a buried talent or passion for geography, for anything, that possible person had disappeared.

"What made you say that?" I asked.   5

"Say what?" he answered. "I didn't say anything."   6

The sixteenth birthday, the eighteenth. The milestones. The   7
driver's license, voting, the adult boundary-marker birthdays. The days I envisioned while watching the mail for the response to my first adoption application, the days that set forth like distant skyscrapers as I projected ahead through my years of fatherhood. I had given little specific consideration to what might come between, but of those outstanding days I had been sure. They were the pillars I followed, the oases of certainty. Alone in the cabin in Alaska or in the basement apartment near Franconia while I waited for the definition of the rest of my life to commence, I planned the elaborate cake decorations for those big birthdays, the significant presents I would save to buy. Odd as it may seem, the anticipation of the acts of letting Adam go began before I even knew his name. I looked forward to the proud days on which the world would recognize my son as progressively more his own man. Those were among the strongest hooks that bonded me to him in my imagination.

As each of these anniversaries finally came and went, nothing   8
like I expected them to be, I doubly mourned. First, selfishly, for me, and second for Adam, because he didn't know what he was missing, what he had already missed, what he would miss. I wanted to burst through those birthdays like a speeding train blasts a weak gate, to get past them and back into the anonymous years for which I had made no models, where there were no obvious measurements, no cakes with candles that would never be lit.

It was a coincidence that Adam turned twenty-one as this   9
book neared completion, but it seemed appropriate. On the morning of his birthday, I rose early and baked him a lemon cake, his favorite, and left the layers to cool while I drove to Hanover to pick him up. His gifts were wrapped and on the kitchen table—an electric shaver, clothes, a Garfield calendar. For his special dinner he had requested tacos, and as always I had reserved a magic candle—the kind that keeps reigniting no matter how often it is blown out—for the center of his cake.

I was greeted at Adam's house by the news that he had just had   10
a seizure, a small one this time, but it had left him groggy. I helped
him on with his coat, bent to tie his shoelace, all the while talking
about the fun we would have during the day. He looked out the
window. Only the week before he had been laid off from his dish-
washing job. December had been a bad month for seizures, some
due to his body's adjustment to a change in dosage and some occurring because Adam had skipped taking medicine altogether. The
bowling alley's insurance carrier was concerned and that, combined
with an after-Christmas slump in business, decided the issue. Now
he was back at Hartford for a few weeks while Ken Krambert and
his associates sought a new work placement. I thought perhaps
Adam was depressed about this turn of events, so I tried to cheer
him up as we drove south on the familiar road to Cornish.

"So, Adam," I said, making conversation, summoning the con-   11
ventional words, "do you feel any older? What's good about being
twenty-one?"

He turned to me and grinned. There *was* something good.   12

"Well," he answered, "now the guys at work say I'm old   13
enough to drink."

His unexpected words kicked me in the stomach. They   14
crowded every thought from my brain.

"Adam, you can't," I protested. "I've told you about your birth-   15
mother, about your other father. Do you remember what happened to them?" I knew he did. I had told him the story several
times, and we had gone over it together as he read, or I read to
him, parts of this book.

Adam thought for a moment. "They were sick?" he offered fi-   16
nally. "That's why I have seizures?"

"No, they weren't sick. They died, Adam. They died from   17
drinking. If you drank, it could happen to you." My memory
played back all the statistics about sons of alcoholic fathers and
their particular susceptibility to substance abuse. "It would not
mix well with your medicine."

Adam sniffed, turned away, but not before I recognized the   18
amused disbelief in his expression. He did not take death seriously, never had. It was an abstract concept out of his reach and
therefore of no interest to him. Death was less real than Santa
Claus—after all, Adam had in his album a photograph of himself

seated on Santa Claus's lap. Death was no threat, no good reason to refuse his first drink.

My son will forever travel through a moonless night with only   19
the roar of wind for company. Don't talk to him of mountains, of tropical beaches. Don't ask him to swoon at sunrises or marvel at the filter of light through leaves. He's never had time for such things, and he does not believe in them. He may pass by them close enough to touch on either side, but his hands are stretched forward, grasping for balance instead of pleasure. He doesn't wonder where he came from, where he's going. He doesn't ask who he is, or why. Questions are a luxury, the province of those at a distance from the periodic shock of rain. Gravity presses Adam so hard against reality that he doesn't feel the points at which he touches it. A drowning man is not separated from the lust for air by a bridge of thought—he is one with it—and my son, conceived and grown in an ethanol bath, lives each day in the act of drowning. For him there is no shore.

[Editors' Note: Michael Dorris's son Adam died on September 22, 1991, after being struck by a car as he walked home from work. He was described in his obituary as "a brave, forgiving, and trusting person, gentle of heart and quick to laugh."]

UNDERSTANDING DETAILS

1. Why are Adam's birthdays difficult for Dorris?
2. What are some of the problems Adam was born with?
3. Why will Adam never reach his full potential?
4. In what ways did Dorris feel Adam's birthdays would be "oases of certainty" (paragraph 7)? How did the actual celebrations differ from these expectations?

ANALYZING MEANING

1. Why does Dorris "doubly" mourn (paragraph 8) his son's birthdays? Explain your answer.
2. In what way was "the definition of the rest of [Dorris's] life" (paragraph 7) connected with his son's birthdays?
3. In what way is death like Santa Claus for Adam? Explain your answer.
4. What does Dorris mean when he says "Questions are a luxury" for his son (paragraph 19)?

DISCOVERING RHETORICAL STRATEGIES

1. At what points in this essay does Dorris either directly or indirectly analyze the causes of Adam's behavior? When does he study its effects (on either himself or his son)? Divide a piece of paper in half. List the causes on one side and the effects on the other. Record the paragraph references in each case. Then, discuss the pattern that emerges from your two lists. Does Dorris give more attention to the causes or the effects of Adam's behavior? Why do you think the author develops his essay around this particular emphasis?

2. Dorris uses several comparisons to help his readers understand what raising a fetal alcohol child is like. Look, for example, at paragraph 19, in which he compares Adam's life to "a moonless night" and to "the act of drowning." Find two other vivid comparisons in this essay. What do all these comparisons add to the essay? What effect do they have on the essay as a whole?

3. What tone does Dorris establish in his essay? Describe it in three or four well-chosen words. How does he create this tone? What effect does this particular tone have on you as a reader?

4. What rhetorical strategies does Dorris use to support his cause/effect analysis? Give examples of each.

MAKING CONNECTIONS

1. Contrast Dorris's definition of "addiction" with the definitions in the following essays that discuss other addictive topics: Franklin Zimring's "Confessions of an Ex-Smoker," Kimberly Wozencraft's "Notes from the Country Club," Stephen King's "Why We Crave Horror Movies," and/or Shelby Steele's "Affirmative Action: The Price of Preference." What substance is addictive in these essays? Which addiction do you think would be most difficult to recover from? Explain your answer.

2. Love and concern for a child is the principal topic of Dorris's essay, as it is in Lewis Sawaquat's "For My Indian Daughter," Bill Cosby's "The Baffling Question," Russell Baker's "The Saturday Evening Post," Germaine Greer's "A Child Is Born," and Judith Wallerstein and Sandra Blakeslee's "Second Chances for Children of Divorce." If we were able to get all these authors together in a roundtable discussion about parent-child

relationships, do you think they would agree on any of the issues? If so, what would these areas of agreement be?

3. Birthdays are milestones in Dorris's essay, just as they are for Malcolm Cowley in "The View from 80." What are the principal differences in the ways each author celebrates these birthdays? Why do these differences exist?

IDEAS FOR DISCUSSION/WRITING

Preparing to Write

Write freely about the process of growing up and reaching your potential: What special problems did you experience while growing up? How did you deal with these problems? How did your parents deal with these problems? Do you feel you are heading toward your full potential, or have you already reached it? How do you plan to reach or maintain your potential? What experiences or people have disappointed you mainly because they were not what you expected? What were their shortcomings? Can these shortcomings be remedied? What effects do such shortcomings have on society as a whole?

Choosing a Topic

1. In a conversation with your mother, father, or another close relative, explain what problems you found most difficult as you were growing up, and speculate about the causes of those problems. In dialogue form, record the conversation as accurately as possible. Add an introduction, a conclusion, and an explanation of your discussion in order to mold the conversation into an essay.

2. In the last paragraph of his essay, Dorris implies that his son is slowly drowning in his birth-mother's alcohol abuse. This essay is Dorris's process of grieving about "what [his son] was missing, what he had already missed, what he would miss" (paragraph 8). In an essay of your own, explain something (a process, a person, an event, a relationship, or an activity) that disappointed you mainly because your expectations weren't met. What were the principal reasons for your disappointment? What were the effects of your disappointment? What could have changed the situation?

3. Many forms of addiction and abuse plague our society at present. In an essay written for your composition class, choose one of these problems and speculate on its primary causes and effects in society today. As often as possible, give specific examples to support your observations.

RICHARD RODRIGUEZ   (1944 –   )

■ ■ ■

The Fear of Losing a Culture

Richard Rodriguez was raised in Sacramento, California, the son of industrious working-class Mexican immigrant parents. He attended parochial schools there and later continued his education at Stanford University, Columbia University, London's Warburg Institute, and, finally, the University of California at Berkeley, where he earned a Ph.D. in English Renaissance literature. A writer and journalist, he is now associate editor of the Pacific News Service in San Francisco. In 1982, he received wide critical acclaim for the publication of his autobiography, *Hunger of Memory: The Education of Richard Rodriguez*, which detailed his struggle to succeed in a totally alien culture. A regular contributor to the *Los Angeles Times*, he has also published essays in *New Republic, Time, Harper's, American Scholar, Columbia Forum*, and *College English*. His most recent book is *Mexico's Children: Days of Obligation* (1992), a study of Mexican immigrants in America. Asked to provide advice for students using *The Prose Reader*, Rodriguez explained that "there is no 'secret' to becoming a writer. Writing takes time—and patience, more than anything else. If you are willing to rewrite and rewrite and rewrite, you will become a good writer."

Preparing to Read

The following essay, originally published in *Time* magazine (July 11, 1988), discusses the causes and effects of cultural pride. As you prepare to read this essay, take a few moments to think about culture and assimilation: How would you describe America's culture? Does it have a central core of its own? What are the main features of this American culture? To what extent are Americans threatened by the intrusion of other cultures? What can be gained through assimilation between cultures? What can be lost?

■

What is culture, after all? The immigrant shrugs. Latin 1
Americans initially come to the U.S. with only the
things they need in mind—not abstractions like culture. They need dollars. They need food. Maybe they need to get
out of the way of bullets. Most of us who concern ourselves with
Hispanic-American culture, as painters, musicians, writers—or as
sons and daughters—are the children of immigrants. We have
grown up on this side of the border, in the land of Elvis Presley
and Thomas Edison. Our lives are prescribed by the mall, by the
7-Eleven, by the Internal Revenue Service. Our imaginations
vacillate between an Edenic Latin America, which nevertheless
betrayed our parents, and the repellent plate-glass doors of a real
American city, which has been good to us.

Hispanic-American culture stands where the past meets the 2
future. The cultural meeting represents not just a Hispanic mile-
stone, not simply a celebration at the crossroads. America transforms into pleasure what it cannot avoid. Hispanic-American
culture of the sort that is now in evidence (the teen movie, the
rock song) may exist in an hourglass, may in fact be irrelevant.
The U.S. Border Patrol works through the night to arrest the
flow of illegal immigrants over the border, even as Americans
stand patiently in line for *La Bamba*. While Americans vote to declare, once and for all, that English shall be the official language of
the U.S., Madonna starts recording in Spanish.

Before a national TV audience, Rita Moreno tells Geraldo 3
Rivera that her dream as an actress is to play a character rather
like herself: "I speak English perfectly well. . . . I'm not dying
from poverty. . . . I want to play *that* kind of Hispanic woman,
which is to say, an American citizen." This is an actress talking;
these are show-biz pieties. But Moreno expresses as well a general
Hispanic-American predicament. Hispanics want to belong to
America without betraying the past. Yet we fear losing ground in
any negotiation with America. Our fear, most of all, is of losing
our culture.

We come from an expansive, an intimate, culture that has long 4
been judged second-rate by the U.S. Out of pride as much as affection, we are reluctant to give up our past. Our notoriety in the
U.S. has been our resistance to assimilation. The guarded symbol
of Hispanic-American culture has been the tongue of flame:

Spanish. But the remarkable legacy Hispanics carry from Latin America is not language—an inflatable skin—but breath itself, capacity of soul, an inclination to live. The genius of Latin America is the habit of synthesis. We assimilate.

What Latin America knows is that people create one another 5 when they meet. In the music of Latin America you will hear the litany of bloodlines: the African drum, the German accordion, the cry from the minaret. The U.S. stands as the opposing New World experiment. In North America the Indian and the European stood separate. Whereas Latin America was formed by a Catholic dream of one world, of meltdown conversion, the U.S. was shaped by Protestant individualism. America has believed its national strength derives from separateness, from diversity. The glamour of the U.S. is the Easter promise: You can be born again in your lifetime. You can separate yourself from your past. You can get a divorce, lose weight, touch up your roots.

Immigrants still come for that promise, but the U.S. has wa- 6 vered in its faith. America is no longer sure that economic strength derives from individualism. And America is no longer sure that there is space enough, sky enough, to sustain the cabin on the prairie. Now, as we near the end of the American Century, two alternative cultures beckon the American imagination: the Asian and the Latin American. Both are highly communal cultures, in contrast to the literalness of American culture. Americans devour what they might otherwise fear to become. Sushi will make them lean, subtle corporate warriors. Combination Plate No. 3, smothered in mestizo gravy, will burn a hole in their hearts.

Latin America offers passion. Latin America has a life—big 7 clouds, unambiguous themes, tragedy, epic—that the U.S., for all its quality of life, yearns to have. Latin America offers an undistressed leisure, a crowded kitchen table, even a full sorrow. Such is the urgency of America's need that it reaches right past a fledgling, homegrown Hispanic-American culture for the darker bottle of Mexican beer, for the denser novel of a Latin American master.

For a long time, Hispanics in the U.S. felt hostility. Perhaps be- 8 cause we were preoccupied by nostalgia, we withheld our Latin American gift. We denied the value of assimilation. But as our presence is judged less foreign in America, we will produce a more generous art, less timid, less parochial. Hispanic Americans do not have a pure Latin American art to offer. Expect bastard themes. Expect winking ironies, comic conclusions. For Hispanics live on this side of the border, where Kraft manufactures Mexican-style Velveeta, and where Jack in the Box serves Fajita Pita. Expect marriage. We will change America even as we will be changed. We will disappear with you into a new miscegenation.

Along and across the border there remain real conflicts, real   9
fears. But the ancient tear separating Europe from itself—the Catholic Mediterranean from the Protestant north—may yet heal itself in the New World. For generations, Latin America has been the place, the bed, of a confluence of so many races and cultures that Protestant North America shuddered to imagine it.

The time has come to imagine it.

UNDERSTANDING DETAILS

1. In what way is "culture" an abstraction? Explain your answer.
2. What does Rodriguez mean when he says "Hispanic-American culture stands where the past meets the future" (paragraph 2)?
3. In what ways are Asian and Latin American cultures "communal" whereas America's is "literal" (paragraph 6)?
4. What does Rodriguez claim is the source of the hostility Hispanics have traditionally felt from other Americans?

ANALYZING MEANING

1. To what extent do you think Hispanics can belong to America "without betraying the past" (paragraph 3)? How might they accomplish this?
2. What is the main difference in philosophy between North America and Latin America? Why is assimilation so difficult under these circumstances?
3. What does Rodriguez mean when he says that "people create one another when they meet" (paragraph 5)? Explain your answer in detail.
4. What do North America and Latin America have to offer each other? What can they learn from each other? What does Rodriguez mean in the last sentence of this essay?

DISCOVERING RHETORICAL STRATEGIES

1. According to Rodriguez, the fact that Hispanics sometimes don't easily assimilate into American culture causes some consequences and is the result of others. List the causes of this action in one column and the effects in another. In what way does the question of assimilation become a focal point for the essay?
2. Why does Rodriguez introduce the Asian culture into this essay? How does this reference help further his argument?
3. Rodriguez ends his essay with a one-sentence paragraph. What effect does this ending have on you? Explain your answer.
4. What other rhetorical strategies besides cause and effect does Rodriguez use to support his essay about Hispanic-American assimilation? Give examples of each.

MAKING CONNECTIONS

1. Rodriguez, Robert Ramirez ("The Barrio"), and Peter Salins ("Take a Ticket") all discuss the complex topic of how immigrants can assimilate into a new culture without "betraying their past." Compare and contrast their opinions on this controversial subject; then give your own views on the issue.
2. Rodriguez's image of an "Edenic" former Latin culture is similar to the pleasant memories Tan depicts of Kweilin ("The Joy Luck Club"), John McPhee's vision of an unspoiled wilderness area before the intrusions of civilization ("The Pines"), and Bruce Catton's depiction of Robert E. Lee's tidewater Virginia aristocratic heritage ("Grant and Lee: A Study in Contrasts"). To what extent do you think each of these memories has been warped and changed by the passage of time? How accurate are your own recollections of pleasant events and places from the past?
3. How many different causes does Rodriguez suggest to explain why some Hispanic-Americans resist assimilation into American culture? Contrast the number of causes Rodriguez mentions with the number introduced by Stephen King ("Why We Crave Horror Movies") and Michael Dorris ("The Broken Cord"). How does the number of causes in a cause/effect essay affect your ability to follow the author's argument?

IDEAS FOR DISCUSSION/WRITING

Preparing to Write

Write freely about culture and assimilation: What makes up a culture? In what ways do merging cultures threaten one another? What does assimilation consist of? Why is assimilation between cultures such an emotional issue? What are the ground rules in the process of assimilation? What major cultural changes is our country experiencing at present? In what way are these changes affecting you personally?

Choosing a Topic

1. We all confront assimilation every day in different situations. We may choose to assimilate into a club we want to join but may refuse to make the necessary changes to fit into a fast-moving party scene. For an article in your campus newspaper demonstrating the constant role of assimilation in our lives, explain the causes and/or effects of one time you chose or refused to assimilate. What were the circumstances leading up to your decision? What were the consequences of your decision?

2. America is currently undergoing some dramatic cultural changes. We are rapidly becoming a multiracial, multicultural society. In an essay written for your local newspaper, analyze the causes and effects of some of these changes, and explain how they are affecting you personally.

3. As a foreign-exchange student, you have just arrived in another country to attend college for one year. Naturally, you realize that you must adapt to many new customs and attitudes; however, you will still cling to many of your country's ways. In an essay, explain which of your national traditions you would find most difficult to give up and why. Do you think assimilating into a new culture and still holding on to your beliefs and customs is possible? Explain your reasoning.

MITCHELL LAZARUS   (1942 –   )

■ ■ ■

Rx for Mathophobia

Lawyer and author Mitchell Lazarus is the product of a varied educational background. Canadian by birth, he has a bachelor's degree in electrical engineering from McGill University, an M.S. in the same field from the Massachusetts Institute of Technology, a Ph.D. in psychology from MIT, and a law degree from Georgetown University. "Some people think it's odd having so many degrees," he says, "but I thoroughly enjoyed getting them. Besides, knowledge is never wasted. Back in engineering school, I never dreamed of becoming a lawyer, but now I use the engineering skills every day in my legal practice. And the scientific outlook I picked up doing doctoral research in psychology (on visual perception) gave me a deeper view of the world and enriched my life immeasurably. Sure, it's important to specialize—but it doesn't have to be forever. You can specialize for the time being." This unique educational philosophy has led Lazarus to a number of interesting jobs. He has worked in computer design; taught electrical engineering, mathematics, and psychology at MIT; worked at the Education Development Center in Newton, Massachusetts, where he helped produce *Infinity Factory*, a PBS television series on mathematics; and helped the Children's Television Workshop launch its PBS mathematics series *Square One TV*. He currently practices law in Washington, D.C., specializing in computers and communication. Since the mid-1970s, Lazarus has published over sixty articles and reviews, mostly on education or law, and five books, including *Educating the Handicapped* (1980) and *Goodbye to Excellence: A Critical Look at Minimum Competency Testing* (1981). He lives in Takoma Park, Maryland, where he relaxes with the *London Sunday Times* crossword puzzles and struggles to master ever-more-complicated guitar licks.

Preparing to Read

The following article on "mathophobia," originally published in the *Saturday Review* (June 28, 1975), explains why the fear of mathematics haunts so many Americans. Before you read this essay, think for a moment about some of the fears that affect your life: What are you most afraid of? How and when did this fear start? What effect does it have on your daily life? What other fears do you have? How do you cope with these fears? Do you have any anxieties related to succeeding in school? What are you doing to overcome them?

■

M ost people dislike—or fear—mathematics. Somehow, a 1 vast majority of the population has come to believe that mathematics must be difficult, unpleasant, and mysterious. Even people who are good at mathematics and use it every day are comfortable only to a point. I hold a graduate degree in engineering, and my own mathematics is pretty good, but I still feel uneasy listening to arguments based on mathematics more advanced than I can understand. Yet, I can converse among historians, musicians, philosophers, and others, understanding just as little but feeling much less uncomfortable about it.

Now, my work involves designing new approaches to the 2 teaching of elementary mathematics. And whenever I talk about this work, about sensible ways of handling mathematics education that will appeal to children, the reaction is nearly always the same: "I wish there had been something like that when I was a kid. I always hated math in school!"

Jerrold Zacharias, noted physicist and educator, calls the prob- 3 lem *mathophobia*: a fear of mathematics. Most people will indeed try to avoid mathematical problems, sometimes with the vehemence of an acrophobe avoiding a high place. Both the acrophobe and the mathophobe deny themselves fascinating views and vistas, unnecessarily narrowing their horizons.

Curiously, there has been virtually no formal research con- 4 cerning this very widespread—nearly universal—problem. In the absence of organized data, my colleagues and I have had to fall back on anecdotal evidence. Over the past few years we have discussed mathematics experiences with people in all walks of life.

These were not formal interviews; we have no coded data. Instead, they were casual conversations with friends, acquaintances, and people met in passing. With their help we have tried to construct an etiology of mathophobia and to indicate strategies for its prevention.

For example, many adults say that they liked mathematics 5 "until we did so-and-so in school"—until they were exposed to some topic that seemed particularly difficult. But did the enjoyment of mathematics ever return after the hard topic was past? Almost never. The dislike is usually irreversible.

If one looks at the curricula in use at most schools, this aver- 6 sion is not surprising. The mathematics taught in each grade depends strongly on most of the work done in preceding years: Trouble in any year, for any reason, is nearly certain to spell trouble in all the years to come.

A second factor in the curriculum is the frequent lack of any 7 meaningful connection between school mathematics and the rest of the student's life. Thus the mathematics people *do* learn in school is quickly forgotten; most of us have little use for it after graduation.

Perhaps another element is mathophobia's social acceptability. 8 Even those who are otherwise proud of their education tend to speak up freely about their mathematical ignorance. They can say, "I'm terrible at math," almost with a hint of pride, as if being poor at mathematics somehow is a mark of good taste in failure.

This attitude affects our treatment of children in school. 9 Parents often seem unconcerned about a child's failure in mathematics, as if to say, "Well, I was never good at math in school; so I shouldn't be too upset if Johnny isn't, either." Unfortunately, Johnny is likely to sense this attitude and react accordingly.

Moreover, many teachers are themselves affected by matho- 10 phobia, sometimes admitting that they feel uncomfortable when they teach mathematics. If the teacher is tense and ill at ease with mathematics, such feelings infect the class with the idea that mathematics is hard or unpleasant.

When people withdraw from mathematics, exactly what are 11 they avoiding?

From conversations with many mathophobes, two distinct im- 12 pressions emerge of what mathematics is like. One view equates mathematics with the tedious, boring, exacting routines of school arithmetic. Yet, if total exposure to music over several years were limited to just scales and mechanical exercises, music would be unpleasant, too.

The other popular view of mathematics sees it as the arcane   13
province of a select few geniuses. Someone who feels that mathematics must forever be beyond his or her ken will quite naturally shy away from it and need not hesitate to admit—or even boast of—a distaste for the subject.

In reality arithmetic is always a means to an end, never an end   14
in itself—except in school. Indeed, very few activities call for actual skill in arithmetic nowadays. With computers, elaborate cash registers, and now the small electronic calculators, the mechanics of arithmetic take second place, in practice, to choosing the necessary calculations and the right numbers to work with. Thus, we ask children to spend several years learning difficult, tedious skills that are rapidly coming to be of limited value. In doing so, we inadvertently teach that mathematics is not only hard but also not very useful. Rote arithmetic is a difficult and tedious branch of mathematics—a poor starting point for most students.

The "new math" tried to help by showing why arithmetic re-   15
sults come out the way they do, starting from "basic principles" that typically included set theory and number base. But for a great many students (and their parents), these special topics were at least as confusing as the arithmetic had been.

Parts of the "new math" tried to deemphasize pure arithmetic   16
or at least to set arithmetic in a wider mathematical context. But the "new math" context is that of the professional mathematician: abstract, definitional, axiomatic, and supposedly rigorous. The result is to pull mathematics even farther from its actual uses.

Mathematics does not belong to the professional mathematician   17
alone. It cuts across many other fields of endeavor and touches upon many people's lives. This perspective—mathematics that is useful to people—should be the starting point for a new approach to mathematics education. This alternative builds upon usefulness as a basic ingredient of elementary mathematics. Choice of topics and ways of teaching should center on mathematics as a helpful force in day-to-day life and should take into account the fact that the technology has made longhand arithmetic all but obsolete. Such a program has a twofold aim: to provide the mathematical tools and skills children will find useful and enlightening now and in later life

and to make them comfortable with, and appreciative of, mathematical subject matter. The two aims are very closely related.

The new approach will find its place in the vast middle ground 18 between rote arithmetic and the work of the professional mathematician. It includes, for example, the mathematics of cooking, carpentry, engineering, wallpaper hanging, dressmaking, magazine editing, bartending, storekeeping, and a vast array of other occupations and pastimes. It is the kind of mathematics that grows from real problems and returns in real solutions. It adapts recipes to serve more than the prescribed number of guests, fits bookshelves neatly into alcoves, purchases the right amount of shelf paper, carries the driver from one gasoline pump to the next, and in general helps people through a multitude of ordinary tasks. It also develops the kind of understanding that children will find most useful in their ongoing activities—the kind that will apply to many of their current interests.

The topics stressed should be those with the most direct link 19 between mathematics and the real world—the topics most helpful to people who use mathematics for practical reasons. These include, for example, measurement and estimation, making rough maps and sketching simple graphs, and the performance of quick, approximate arithmetic in our heads—skills that will not get rusty because they will be used constantly by people of all ages.

One important development not covered by conventional cur- 20 ricula would be an appreciation of inexact answers. "Mathematics is an exact science," many teachers say, "and there is only one right answer." Often that statement is worse than wrong. It is constraining and intimidating. Estimations, approximation, rough calculation—all part of mathematics—are often very useful, need not be exact, and can have many "right answers," if a right answer is one to meet our needs. Most of us tried to learn in school how to find that 49×319 works out to be 15,631. Few of us learned to see the problem quickly and roughly as 50×300, which mentally becomes 15,000—close enough for most practical purposes.

A widescale approach to mathematics that stems from realistic 21 situations which children find interesting and which gives them new power to cope with situations outside of school would go a long way toward preventing mathophobia. Mathematics can be a part of everyday life; it need not be special and apart. Most people can read street maps, for example, which involves a lot of mathematics that ordinarily we do not recognize. We understand how an "average family" can have 1.9 children, even though we may joke about it. The concept of odds in betting is clear to most of us, although it is based on quite sophisticated concepts. People who cook know that it is safe to triple recipes for soup, but not for cake.

As an educational issue, reading street maps, for example, is 22 unimportant in itself. But maps involve a number of mathematical ideas that *are* important and general: ratio, proportion, scaling, measuring and estimating length and distance, estimating time, and some geometry. In most curricula nowadays these ideas appear in the abstract if they appear at all. A proportion problem, for example, might appear as: $20/5 = ?/2$. The new approach would stay with the street map—or even better, a student-made map of the classroom—and ask: According to the map, how far is it from the door to the chalkboard? The mathematical issue of proportion is the same, but the map puts the idea in a much more concrete and realistic context. Thus the student can better understand the idea of proportion and how it applies in real situations. Moreover, the "hands-on" experience of making the measurements, sketching the map, and checking the results is a valuable aid in acquiring the concept and contributes to a good "feel" for what proportion is about.

Symbols and abstraction for their own sakes, now very com- 23 mon in mathematics curricula, often strike students as pointless and confusing. As far as possible, all of the concepts presented to students should appear in realistic, familiar contexts. Symbols and abstraction are still important—indeed, are the essence of mathematics—but should serve ends that students can understand. Presentations ought to begin and end with reality in order that students can make sense of the mathematics in between.

Applications have always been a part of mathematics educa- 24 tion, but until now they have played a very minor role. The applications in most textbooks were contrived—transparent excuses for more calculation. Use of applications of primary function, so that calculation serves as the means (rather than the other way around), will impart to school mathematics the pertinence, meaning, and impact that it presently lacks. Children will understand why mathematics is important and worth knowing.

Some students do very well in the "new math," and some even 25
seem to enjoy rote calculation. Students with a knack and a flair for
mathematics will find as much in this approach that captures their
interest as there was in earlier curricula, for here there is a great
deal of room for exploring theoretical relationships and plenty of
opportunity for calculation. The topics are rich and the pedagogy
open-ended. Just as important, however, is the fact that many students who have *not* liked mathematics until now—and these are a
majority—will begin to see a place for mathematics in their own
lives and will start feeling comfortable with mathematical ideas.

Eventually, a curriculum reform on the scale of the "new math" 26
will probably be necessary. The "new math" is not working out
well, and there is a strong national trend away from it. Most educa-
tors seem disinclined to go back to the "old math," seeing that the
arguments against it are still valid. In contrast, the approach outlined here will appeal directly to students' interests and needs and
will provide a strong foundation for more advanced work.

The key to preventing mathophobia is letting mathematics 27
take root in the student's daily life. Reality-based teaching will go
a long way toward solving the national mathematics problem because it will put elementary mathematics into a form that will
make sense to children.

UNDERSTANDING DETAILS

1. According to Lazarus, why are most people afraid of math?
   What are the immediate causes of this fear? The ultimate
   causes?
2. What was wrong with the "new math" in Lazarus's opinion?
3. At what point in the essay does the author begin discussing solutions to mathophobia? What solutions does the author propose?
4. In what ways is arithmetic "always a means to an end" (paragraph 14)?

ANALYZING MEANING

1. Explain the title of this essay. How effective is it in your opinion? Can you suggest an alternate title?
2. How do we currently imply to children that mathematics isn't
   very useful? What suggestions does Lazarus have for changing

this message? Do you think these ideas will help curtail mathophobia? Explain your answer in detail.

3. What does Lazarus mean when he comments on "the frequent lack of any meaningful connection between school mathematics and the rest of the student's life" (paragraph 7)? Do you think math in grade school and high school should be more relevant to everyday life? What other subjects should be made more relevant? At what academic levels?

4. According to Lazarus, why would "an appreciation of inexact answers" (paragraph 20) be an important development in mathematics? Do you agree with the author's reasoning on this issue? Why or why not?

DISCOVERING RHETORICAL STRATEGIES

1. At what points in the essay does the author explore causes? When does he consider effects? Is this balance between causes and effects appropriate to the essay's purpose? Why or why not?

2. How has Lazarus organized the characteristics of mathophobia? Why does he discuss the characteristics in this manner?

3. Who do you think is Lazarus's intended audience? Describe them in detail. How did you come to this conclusion?

4. What other rhetorical strategies, besides cause and effect, does Lazarus use to advance his proposal for "reality-based" mathematics in the schools?

MAKING CONNECTIONS

1. Both Mitchell Lazarus and William Golding ("Thinking as a Hobby") discuss ways in which schools and teachers can traumatize students. What are the different types of traumas and phobias mentioned by each author, and how could schools avoid inflicting them on students? Have you ever been traumatized by an experience at school? What happened? How did you get over it?

2. Like Lazarus, Donald Drakeman ("Religion's Place in Public Schools") argues that our nation's schools should make some important changes in the way they deal with today's students. While Lazarus believes that more "reality-based" math should be taught, Drakeman argues that students should be allowed to

meet for religious purposes on school property, just as they do for such nonreligious activities as cheerleading and band practice. Which author presents his case most persuasively? Explain your answer.

3. Does Lazarus blame a single cause for "mathophobia," or does he identify multiple causes? How many causes are identified by Stephen King ("Why We Crave Horror Movies") or Richard Rodriguez ("The Fear of Losing a Culture") in their cause/effect essays? Do multiple causes make a cause/effect essay easier or more difficult to understand? Why

IDEAS FOR DISCUSSION/WRITING

Preparing to Write

Write freely about any fears that you have: Does any particular type of schoolwork frighten you? Any people? Any activities? Any specific situations? Why do you think these various fears haunt you? How do you cope with these problems? Are you content with your solutions?

Choosing a Topic

1. A college counselor has asked all students at your college to explain what frightens them most. What is your response to this question? Write an essay for the counselor explaining in detail your greatest fear. Cover both the causes and the effects of your fear. (This fear does not have to be related to school matters.)

2. Your college mathematics instructor wants to know if you are afraid of math. In a detailed essay written for this instructor, explain why you are or are not frightened by this subject. What events/attitudes/teachers have played a part in developing your feelings toward mathematics? Has your attitude toward math become more positive or negative over the past five years?

3. Is mathophobia the only academic anxiety that strikes today's students? What about "writer's phobia"? How do you feel about writing essays and papers? What events/attitudes/teachers have shaped this feeling? What effects does this attitude have on your performance as a writer? Address those questions in an essay designed for your composition instructor. (Now don't panic. Take a deep breath. . . .)

ALICE WALKER   (1944 –   )

■ ■ ■

Beauty: When the Other Dancer Is the Self

Born in Eatonton, Georgia, and educated at Spelman College
and Sarah Lawrence University, Alice Walker is best known for
her Pulitzer Prize-winning novel *The Color Purple* (1983), which
was later made into an immensely popular movie of the same
title. The book details a young African American woman's search
for self-identity within a world contaminated by racial prejudice
and family crisis. Although many critics have argued that the
work "transcends culture and gender," Walker's focus on the
racial and ethnic climate of the Deep South is crucial to the
novel's success and importance. The author has explained that
"the Black woman is one of America's greatest heroes," though
she has been denied credit for her accomplishments and "oppressed beyond recognition." Most of Walker's other novels and
collections of short stories echo the same theme, and most share
the "sense of affirmation" featured in *The Color Purple* that over-
comes the anger and social indignity suffered by so many of her
characters. The author's many other publications include *In Love
and Trouble: Stories of Black Women* (1973), *Meridian* (1976), *You
Can't Keep a Good Woman Down* (1981), *In Search of Our Mothers'
Gardens* (1983), *Living by the Word* (1988), *To Hell with Dying*
(1988), *The Temple of My Familiar* (1989), and *Possessing the Secret
of Joy* (1992). Walker has been a professor and writer-in-residence at Wellesley College, the University of Massachusetts, the
University of California at Berkeley, and Brandeis University.
She is also a member of the Board of Trustees of Sarah Lawrence
University. Walker currently lives in San Francisco.

Preparing to Read

The following essay, from *In Search of Our Mothers' Gardens*, focuses on young Alice Walker's reaction to being blinded in one
eye as a result of an accident with a BB gun. As you begin to
read this essay, take a few minutes to consider the role of physi-

cal appearance in our lives: Do you find that you often judge people based on their physical appearance? Do you feel that people judge you based on your appearance? What other characteristics play a part in your judgment of others? How important are good looks to you? Why do they carry this importance for you? What specific people affect the way you feel about yourself? Do you want more control over your own self-esteem? How can you gain this control?

I t is a bright summer day in 1947. My father, a fat, funny man with beautiful eyes and a subversive wit, is trying to decide which of his eight children he will take with him to the county fair. My mother, of course, will not go. She is knocked out from getting most of us ready: I hold my neck stiff against the pressure of her knuckles as she hastily completes the braiding and then beribboning of my hair. 1

My father is the driver for the rich old white lady up the road. Her name is Miss Mey. She owns all the land for miles around, as well as the house in which we live. All I remember about her is that she once offered to pay my mother thirty-five cents for cleaning her house, raking up piles of her magnolia leaves, and washing her family's clothes, and that my mother—she of no money, eight children, and a chronic earache—refused it. But I do not think of this in 1947. I am two and a half years old. I want to go everywhere my daddy goes. I am excited at the prospect of riding in a car. Someone has told me fairs are fun. That there is room in the car for only three of us doesn't faze me at all. Whirling happily in my starchy frock, showing off my biscuit-polished patent-leather shoes and lavender socks, tossing my head in a way that makes my ribbons bounce, I stand, hands on hips, before my father. "Take me, Daddy," I say with assurance; "I'm the prettiest!" 2

Later, it does not surprise me to find myself in Miss Mey's shiny black car, sharing the back seat with the other lucky ones. Does not surprise me that I thoroughly enjoy the fair. At home that night I tell the unlucky ones all I can remember about the merry-go-round, the man who eats live chickens, and the teddy bears, until they say: that's enough, baby Alice. Shut up now, and go to sleep. 3

It is Easter Sunday, 1950. I am dressed in a green, flocked, scal- 4
loped-hem dress (handmade by my adoring sister, Ruth) that has
its own smooth satin petticoat and tiny hot-pink roses tucked into
each scallop. My shoes, new T-strap patent leather, again highly
biscuit-polished. I am six years old and have learned one of the
longest Easter speeches to be heard that day, totally unlike the
speech I said when I was two: "Easter lilies / pure and white /
blossom in / the morning light." When I rise to give my speech I
do so on a great wave of love and pride and expectation. People in
the church stop rustling their new crinolines. They seem to hold
their breath. I can tell they admire my dress, but it is my spirit,
bordering on sassiness (womanishness), they secretly applaud.

"That girl's a little *mess*," they whisper to each other, pleased. 5

Naturally I say my speech without stammer or pause, unlike 6
those who stutter, stammer, or, worst of all, forget. This is before
the word "beautiful" exists in people's vocabulary, but "Oh, isn't
she the *cutest* thing!" frequently floats my way. "And got so much
sense!" they gratefully add . . . for which thoughtful addition I
thank them to this day.

It was great fun being cute. But then, one day, it ended. 7

I am eight years old and a tomboy. I have a cowboy hat, cowboy 8
boots, checkered shirt and pants, all red. My playmates are my
brothers, two and four years older than I. Their colors are black and
green, the only difference in the way we are dressed. On Saturday
nights we all go to the picture show, even my mother; Westerns are
her favorite kind of movie. Back home, "on the ranch," we pretend
we are Tom Mix, Hopalong Cassidy, Lash LaRue (we've even
named one of our dogs Lash LaRue); we chase each other for
hours rustling cattle, being outlaws, delivering damsels from distress.
Then my parents decide to buy my brothers guns. These are not
"real" guns. They shoot "BBs," copper pellets my brothers say will
kill birds. Because I am a girl, I do not get a gun. Instantly I am rel-
egated to the position of Indian. Now there appears a great distance
between us. They shoot and shoot at everything with their new
guns. I try to keep up with my bow and arrows.

One day while I am standing on top of our makeshift 9
"garage"—pieces of tin nailed across some poles—holding my

bow and arrow and looking out toward the fields, I feel an incredible blow in my right eye. I look down just in time to see my brother lower his gun.

Both brothers rush to my side. My eye stings, and I cover it 10 with my hand. "If you tell," they say, "we will get a whipping. You don't want that to happen, do you?" I do not. "Here is a piece of wire," says the older brother, picking it up from the roof; "say you stepped on one end of it and the other flew up and hit you." The pain is beginning to start. "Yes," I say. "Yes, I will say that is what happened." If I do not say this is what happened, I know my brothers will find ways to make me wish I had. But now I will say anything that gets me to my mother.

Confronted by our parents we stick to the lie agreed upon. 11 They place me on a bench on the porch and I close my left eye while they examine the right. There is a tree growing from underneath the porch that climbs past the railing to the roof. It is the last thing my right eye sees. I watch as its trunk, its branches, and then its leaves are blotted out by the rising blood.

I am in shock. First there is intense fever, which my father tries 12 to break using lily leaves bound around my head. Then there are chills: my mother tries to get me to eat soup. Eventually, I do not know how, my parents learn what has happened. A week after the "accident" they take me to see a doctor. "Why did you wait so long to come?" he asks, looking into my eye and shaking his head. "Eyes are sympathetic," he says. "If one is blind, the other will likely become blind too."

This comment of the doctor's terrifies me. But it is really how 13 I look that bothers me most. Where the BB pellet struck there is a glob of whitish scar tissue, a hideous cataract, on my eye. Now when I stare at people—a favorite pastime, up to now—they will stare back. Not at the "cute" little girl, but at her scar. For six years I do not stare at anyone, because I do not raise my head.

Years later, in the throes of a mid-life crisis, I ask my mother and 14 sister whether I changed after the "accident." "No," they say, puzzled. "What do you mean?"

What do I mean? 15

I am eight, and, for the first time, doing poorly in school, 16 where I have been something of a whiz since I was four. We have just moved to the place where the "accident" occurred. We do not know any of the people around us because this is a different county. The only time I see the friends I knew is when we go back to our old church. The new school is the former state penitentiary. It is a large stone building, cold and drafty, crammed to overflowing with boisterous, ill-disciplined children. On the third floor there is a huge circular imprint of some partition that has been torn out.

"What used to be here?" I ask a sullen girl next to me on our   17
way past it to lunch.

"The electric chair," says she.   18

At night I have nightmares about the electric chair and about   19
all the people reputedly "fried" in it. I am afraid of the school,
where all the students seem to be budding criminals.

"What's the matter with your eye?" they ask, critically.   20

When I don't answer (I cannot decide whether it was an "acci-   21
dent" or not), they shove me, insist on a fight.

My brother, the one who created the story about the wire,   22
comes to my rescue. But then brags so much about "protecting"
me, I become sick.

After months of torture at the school, my parents decide to   23
send me back to our old community, to my old school. I live with
my grandparents and the teacher they board. But there is no room
for Phoebe, my cat. By the time my grandparents decide there *is*
room, and I ask for my cat, she cannot be found. Miss Yarborough,
the boarding teacher, takes me under her wing and begins to teach
me to play the piano. But soon she marries an African—a
"prince," she says—and is whisked away to his continent.

At my old school there is at least one teacher who loves me.   24
She is the teacher who "knew me before I was born" and bought
my first baby clothes. It is she who makes life bearable. It is her
presence that finally helps me turn on the one child at the school
who continually calls me "one-eyed bitch." One day I simply
grab him by his coat and beat him until I am satisfied. It is my
teacher who tells me my mother is ill.

My mother is lying in bed in the middle of the day, something I   25
have never seen. She is in too much pain to speak. She has an ab-
scess in her ear. I stand looking down on her, knowing that if she

dies, I cannot live. She is being treated with warm oils and hot bricks held against her cheek. Finally a doctor comes. But I must go back to my grandparents' house. The weeks pass but I am hardly aware of it. All I know is that my mother might die, my father is not so jolly, my brothers still have their guns, and I am the one sent away from home.

"You did not change," they say.   26

Did I imagine the anguish of never looking up?   27

I am twelve. When relatives come to visit I hide in my room. My   28
cousin Brenda, just my age, whose father works in the post office and whose mother is a nurse, comes to find me. "Hello," she says. And then she asks, looking at my recent school picture, which I did not want taken, and on which the "glob," as I think of it, is clearly visible, "You still can't see out of that eye?"

"No," I say, and flop back on the bed over my book.   29

That night, as I do almost every night, I abuse my eye. I rant   30
and rave at it, in front of the mirror. I plead with it to clear up before morning. I tell it I hate and despise it. I do not pray for sight. I pray for beauty.

"You did not change," they say.   31

I am fourteen and baby-sitting for my brother Bill, who lives in   32
Boston. He is my favorite brother and there is a strong bond between us. Understanding my feelings of shame and ugliness he and his wife take me to a local hospital, where the "glob" is removed by a doctor named O. Henry. There is still a small bluish crater where the scar tissue was, but the ugly white stuff is gone. Almost immediately I become a different person from the girl who does not raise her head. Or so I think. Now that I've raised my head I win the boyfriend of my dreams. Now that I've raised my head I have plenty of friends. Now that I've raised my head classwork comes from my lips as faultlessly as Easter speeches did, and I leave high school as valedictorian, most popular student, and *queen*, hardly believing my luck. Ironically, the girl who was voted most beautiful in our class (and was) was later shot twice through the chest by a male companion, using a "real" gun, while she was pregnant. But that's another story in itself. Or is it?

"You did not change," they say.   33

It is now thirty years since the "accident." A beautiful journalist   34
comes to visit and to interview me. She is going to write a cover
story for her magazine that focuses on my latest book. "Decide
how you want to look on the cover," she says. "Glamorous, or
whatever."

Never mind "glamorous," it is the "whatever" that I hear.   35
Suddenly all I can think of is whether I will get enough sleep the
night before the photography session: if I don't, my eye will be
tired and wander, as blind eyes will.

At night in bed with my lover I think up reasons why I should   36
not appear on the cover of a magazine. "My meanest critics will
say I've sold out," I say. "My family will now realize I write scan-
dalous books."

"But what's the real reason you don't want to do this?" he asks.   37

"Because in all probability," I say in a rush, "my eye won't be   38
straight."

"It will be straight enough," he says. Then, "Besides, I thought   39
you'd made your peace with that."

And I suddenly remember that I have.   40

I remember.   41

I am talking to my brother Jimmy, asking if he remembers anything unusual about the day I was shot. He does not know I consider that day the last time my father, with his sweet home
remedy of cool lily leaves, chose me, and that I suffered and raged
inside because of this. "Well," he says, "all I remember is standing
by the side of the highway with Daddy, trying to flag down a car.
A white man stopped, but when Daddy said he needed somebody to take his little girl to the doctor, he drove off."

I remember.   42

I am in the desert for the first time. I fall totally in love with it.
I am so overwhelmed by its beauty, I confront for the first time,
consciously, the meaning of the doctor's words years ago: "Eyes
are sympathetic. If one is blind, the other will likely become blind
too." I realize I have dashed about the world madly, looking at
this, looking at that, storing up images against the fading of the
light. *But I might have missed seeing the desert!* The shock of that
possibility—and gratitude for over twenty-five years of sight—
sends me literally to my knees. Poem after poem comes—which
is perhaps how poets pray.

ON SIGHT

I am so thankful I have seen
The Desert
And the creatures in the desert
And the desert Itself.

The desert has its own moon
Which I have seen
With my own eye.
There is no flag on it.

Trees of the desert have arms
All of which are always up
That is because the moon is up
The sun is up
Also the sky
The stars
Clouds
None with flags.

If there were flags, I doubt
the trees would point.
Would you?

But mostly, I remember this: 43
I am twenty-seven, and my baby daughter is almost three. Since
her birth I have worried about her discovery that her mother's eyes
are different from other people's. Will she be embarrassed? I think.
What will she say? Every day she watches a television program
called "Big Blue Marble." It begins with a picture of the earth as it
appears from the moon. It is bluish, a little battered-looking, but
full of light, with whitish clouds swirling around it. Every time I
see it I weep with love, as if it is a picture of Grandma's house. One
day when I am putting Rebecca down for her nap, she suddenly
focuses on my eye. Something inside me cringes, gets ready to try
to protect myself. All children are cruel about physical differences,
I know from experience, and that they don't always mean to be is
another matter. I assume Rebecca will be the same.

But no-o-o-o. She studies my face intently as we stand, her in-   44
side and me outside her crib. She even holds my face maternally
between her dimpled little hands. Then, looking every bit as serious and lawyerlike as her father, she says, as if it may just possibly

have slipped my attention: "Mommy, there's a *world* in your eye." (As in, "Don't be alarmed, or do anything crazy.") And then, gently, but with great interest: "Mommy, where did you *get* that world in your eye?"

For the most part, the pain left then. (So what, if my brothers 45 grew up to buy even more powerful pellet guns for their sons and to carry real guns themselves. So what, if a young "Morehouse man" once nearly fell off the steps of Trevor Arnett Library because he thought my eyes were blue.) Crying and laughing I ran to the bathroom, while Rebecca mumbled and sang herself off to sleep. Yes indeed, I realized, looking into the mirror. There *was* a world in my eye. And I saw that it was possible to love it: that in fact, for all it had taught me of shame and anger and inner vision, I *did* love it. Even to see it drifting out of orbit in boredom, or rolling up out of fatigue, not to mention floating back at attention in excitement (bearing witness, a friend has called it), deeply suitable to my personality, and even characteristic of me.

That night I dream I am dancing to Stevie Wonder's song 46 "Always" (the name of the song is really "As," but I hear it as "Always"). As I dance, whirling and joyous, happier than I've ever been in my life, another bright-faced dancer joins me. We dance and kiss each other and hold each other through the night. The other dancer has obviously come through all right, as I have done. She is beautiful, whole and free. And she is also me.

UNDERSTANDING DETAILS

1. What time frame in the author's life does this essay cover?
2. What is the focal point of the essay? What activities lead up to this "accident"? What are the long-term effects of this "accident"?
3. In what ways does Walker think her life changed after she was shot in the eye?
4. Describe the author's relationship with her brothers—before and after the accident.

ANALYZING MEANING

1. Why is Walker devastated by the scar tissue in her eye? Which bothers her more—the scar tissue or the blindness? Explain your answer.

2. Which of the people introduced in the essay (other than her family members) mean the most to her? List them in order of importance. Then, explain why each is important in this cause/effect essay.
3. List the changes that Walker mentions in her actions and personality. Then, analyze these changes by discussing their causes and effects.
4. Why is Rebecca's declaration "Mommy, there's a *world* in your eye" (paragraph 44) so important to the author? What changes in Walker result from this particular encounter with her daughter?

DISCOVERING RHETORICAL STRATEGIES

1. Why do you think Walker wrote this essay? What was she trying to accomplish by writing it?
2. How does Walker use blank spaces between her paragraphs? In what ways does this spacing contribute to her essay?
3. Why does Walker put the sentences "It was fun being cute. But then, one day, it ended" (paragraph 7) by themselves in italics?
4. Explain the emotional ups and downs in the essay. How does Walker's language change in each case?

MAKING CONNECTIONS

1. Walker's essay centers on a single momentous event, the blinding of her right eye, that affected her life from the instant it happened. In the following essays, similarly significant events shape the lives of the principal characters: Ray Bradbury's "Summer Rituals," George Orwell's "Shooting an Elephant," and Michael Dorris's "The Broken Cord." Compare and contrast the extent to which any of these events influences the characters involved.
2. One of Walker's primary themes involves the eventual acceptance of who we are in life. Locate the same theme in Malcolm Cowley's "The View from 80," Lewis Sawaquat's "For My Indian Daughter," or Richard Rodriguez's "The Fear of Losing a Culture"; then, decide which of these authors seems most content with his or her own self-image. Why do you think this is true?

3. The relationship between Walker's original injury and the shyness and insecurity that result from it imply a negative cause/effect connection. Find an essay in this section of the book that implies a positive connection between a cause and its effect. How are the two essays different? How are they the same?

IDEAS FOR DISCUSSION/WRITING

Preparing to Write

Write freely about your self-esteem and the role of self-esteem in the life of college students: How important is self-esteem to you personally? To your academic performance? What affects your self-esteem most? Why do these events affect you? Do they help or hinder your self-esteem? What elements affect the self-esteem of other students you know? Of friends of yours? Of relatives? What effects have you observed in college students that result from low self-esteem? In friends? In relatives? How do you control your self-esteem? Do you recommend this method to others?

Choosing a Topic

1. Low self-esteem can cause a number of serious problems in different aspects of college students' lives. Conduct a study of the causes and effects of low self-esteem in the lives of several students at your school. Write an essay for the college community explaining these causes and effects.

2. Your campus newspaper is printing a special issue highlighting the psychological health of different generations of college students. Interview some people who represent a generation other than your own. Then, characterize an earlier generation of students (i.e., people older than yourself) for the newspaper. In essay form, introduce the features you have discovered, and then discuss their causes and effects.

3. Some people believe self-esteem is a result of peer groups; others say that it is a result of one's family environment. What do you think? *Time* magazine is soliciting student reactions on this issue and has asked for your opinion. Where do you stand on this question? Give specific examples that support your opinion. Respond in essay form.

9

Argument and Persuasion

Inciting People to Thought or Action

Almost everything we do or say is an attempt to persuade. Whether we dress up to impress a potential employer or argue openly with a friend about an upcoming election, we are trying to convince various people to see the world our way. Some aspects of life are particularly dependent upon persuasion. Think, for example, of all the television, magazine, and billboard ads we see urging us to buy certain products or of the many impassioned appeals we read and hear on such controversial issues as school prayer, abortion, gun control, and nuclear energy. Religious leaders devote their professional lives to convincing people to live a certain way and believe in certain religious truths, whereas scientists and mathematicians use rigorous logic and natural law to convince us of various hypotheses. Politicians make their living persuading voters to elect them and then support them throughout their terms of office. In fact, anyone who wants something from another person or agency, ranging from federal money for a research project to a new bicycle for Christmas, must use some form of persuasion to get what he or she desires. The success or failure of this type of communication is easily determined: If the people being addressed change their actions or attitudes in favor of the writer or speaker, the attempt at persuasion has been successful.

DEFINING ARGUMENT AND PERSUASION

The terms *argument* and *persuasion* are often used interchangeably, but one is actually a subdivision of the other. Persuasion names a purpose for writing. To persuade your readers is to convince them to think, act, or feel a certain way. Much of the writing you have been doing in this book has persuasion as one of its goals: A description of an African tribe has a "dominant impression" you want your readers to accept; in an essay comparing various ways of celebrating Thanksgiving, you are trying to convince your readers to believe that these similarities and differences actually exist; and in writing an essay exam on the causes of the Vietnam war, you are trying to convince your instructor that your reasoning is clear and your conclusions sound. In a sense, some degree of persuasion propels all writing.

More specifically, however, the process of persuasion involves appealing to one or more of the following: to reason, to emotion, or to a sense of ethics. An *argument* is an appeal predominantly to your readers' reason and intellect. You are working in the realm of argument when you deal with complex issues that are debatable; opposing views (either explicit or implicit) are a basic requirement of argumentation. But argument and persuasion are taught together because good writers are constantly blending these three appeals and adjusting them to the purpose and audience of a particular writing task. Although reason and logic are the focus of this chapter, you need to learn to use all three methods of persuasion as skillfully as possible to write effective essays.

An appeal to reason relies upon logic and intellect and is usually most effective when you are expecting your readers to disagree with you in any way. This type of appeal can help you change your readers' opinions or influence their future actions through the sheer strength of logical validity. If you wanted to argue, for example, that pregnant women should refrain from smoking cigarettes, you could cite abundant statistical evidence that babies born to mothers who smoke have lower birth weights, more respiratory problems, and a higher incidence of sudden infant death syndrome than the children of nonsmoking mothers. Because smoking clearly endangers the health of the unborn child, reason dictates that mothers who wish to give birth to the healthiest possible babies should avoid smoking during pregnancy.

Emotional appeals, however, attempt to arouse your readers' feelings, instincts, senses, and biases. Used most profitably when your readers already agree with you, this type of essay generally validates, reinforces, and/or incites in an effort to get your readers to share your feelings or ideas. In order to urge our lawmakers to impose stricter jail sentences for alcohol abuse, you might describe a recent tragic accident involving a local twelve-year-old girl who was killed by a drunk driver as she rode her bicycle to school one morning. By focusing on such poignant visual details as the condition of her mangled bike, the bright blood stains on her white dress, and the anguish on the faces of parents and friends, you could build a powerfully persuasive essay that would be much more effective than a dull recitation of impersonal facts and nationwide statistics.

An appeal to ethics, the third technique writers often use to encourage readers to agree with them, involves cultivating a sincere, honest tone that will establish your reputation as a reliable, qualified, experienced, well-informed, and knowledgeable person whose opinions on the topic under discussion are believable because they are ethically sound. Such an approach is often used in conjunction with logical or emotional appeals to foster a verbal environment that will result in minimal resistance from its readers. Ed McMahon, Johnny Carson's congenial announcer on the *Tonight Show* for many years and the host of *Star Search*, is an absolute master at creating this ethical, trustworthy persona as he coaxes his television viewers to purchase everything from dog food to beer. In fact, the old gag question "Would you buy a used car from this man?" is our instinctive response to all forms of attempted persuasion, whether the salesperson is trying to sell us Puppy Chow or gun control, hair spray or school prayer. The more believable we are as human beings, the better chance we will have of convincing our audience.

The following student paragraph is directed primarily toward the audience's logical reasoning ability. Notice that the writer states her assertion and then gives reasons to convince her readers to change their ways. The student writer also brings both emotion and ethics into the argument by choosing her words and examples with great precision.

Have you ever watched a pair of chunky thighs, a jiggling posterior, and an extra-large sweatshirt straining to cover a beer belly ~~emotion~~
and thought, "Thank God I don't look like that! I'm in pretty

good shape . . . for someone my age." Well, before you become too smug and self-righteous, consider what kind of shape you're really in. Just because you don't look like Shamu the Whale doesn't mean you're in good condition. What's missing, you ask? Exercise. You can diet all day, wear the latest slim-cut designer jeans, and still be in worse shape than someone twice your age if you don't get a strong physical workout at least three times a week. Exercise is not only good for you, but it can also be fun—especially if you find a sport that makes you happy while you sweat. Your activity need not be expensive: Jogging, walking, basketball, tennis, and handball are not costly, unless you're seduced by the glossy sheen of the latest sporting fashions and accessories. Most of all, however, regular exercise is important for your health. You can just as easily drop dead from a sudden heart attack in the middle of a restaurant when you're slim and trim as when you're a slob. Your heart and lungs need regular workouts to stay healthy. So do yourself a favor and add some form of exercise to your schedule. You'll feel better and live longer, and your looks will improve, too!

THINKING CRITICALLY BY USING ARGUMENT AND PERSUASION

Argument and persuasion require you to present your views on an issue through logic, emotion, and good character in such a way that you convince an audience of your point of view. This rhetorical mode comes at the end of this book because it is an extremely complex and sophisticated method of reasoning. The more proficient you become in this strategy of thinking and presenting your views, the more you will get what you want out of life (and out of school). Winning arguments means getting the pay raises you need, the refund you deserve, and the grades you've worked so hard for.

In a successful argument, your logic must be flawless. Your conclusions should be based on clear evidence, and your evidence must be organized in such a way that it builds to an effective, convincing conclusion. You should constantly have your purpose and audience in mind as you build your case; at the same time, issues of emotion and good character should support the flow of your logic.

Exercising your best logical skills is extremely important to all phases of your daily survival—in and out of the classroom. Following a logical argument in your reading and presenting a logical response to your course work are the hallmarks of a good student. Right now, put your best logic forward and work on your reasoning and persuasive abilities in the series of exercises below. Isolate argument and persuasion from the other rhetorical strategies so that you can practice it and strengthen your ability to argue by itself before you combine it with other methods.

1. Bring to class two magazine ads—one ad that tries to sell a product and another that tries to convince the reader that a particular action or product is wrong or bad (unhealthy, misinterpreted, politically incorrect, etc.). How does each ad appeal to the reader's logic? How does the advertiser use emotion and character in his or her appeal?

2. Think of a recent book you have read. How could you persuade a friend either to read or not to read this book?

3. Fill in the following blanks: The best way to _____ is to _____ (For example, "The best way to lose weight is to exercise.") Then, list ways you might use to persuade a reader to see your point of view in this statement.

READING AND WRITING PERSUASIVE ESSAYS

Although persuasive writing can be approached essentially in three different ways—logically, emotionally, and/or ethically—our stress in this chapter is on logic and reason, because they are at the heart of most college writing. As a reader, you will see how various forms of reasoning and different methods of organization affect your reaction to an essay. Your stand on a particular issue will control the way you process information in argument and persuasion essays. As you read the essays in this chapter, you will also learn to recognize emotional and ethical appeals and the different effects they create. In your role as writer, you need to be fully aware of the options available to you as you compose. Although the basis of your writing will be logical argument, you will see that you can learn to control your readers' responses to your essays by choosing your evidence carefully, organizing it wisely, and seasoning it with the right amount of emotion and ethics—depending on your purpose and audience.

How to Read Persuasive Essays

Preparing to Read. As you prepare to read the essays in this chapter, spend a few minutes browsing through the preliminary material for each selection: What does Donald Drakeman's title, "Religion's Place in Public Schools," prepare you for? What can you learn from scanning Ellen Goodman's essay, "Putting In a Good Word for Guilt," and reading its synopsis in the Rhetorical Table of Contents?

Also, you should bring to your reading as much information as you can from the authors' biographies: Why do you think Shelby Steele writes about affirmative action? Does he have the proper qualifications to teach us about "The Price of Preference"? What is the source of Donald Drakeman's interest in "Religion's Place in Public Schools"? For the essays in this chapter that present two sides of an argument, what biographical details prepare us for each writer's stand on the issue? Who were the original audiences for these pro and con arguments?

Last, before you read these essays, try to generate some ideas on each topic so that you can take the role of an active reader. In this text, the Preparing to Read questions will prepare you for this task. Then, you should speculate further on the general subject of the essay: How do you think affirmative action is working nationally? What would you change about America's approach to this controversial topic? What would you continue? What do you want to know from Robert Hughes about gun control? Which side of this issue are you on? On what do you base your current opinion?

Reading. Be sure to record your spontaneous reactions to the persuasive essays in this chapter as you read them for the first time: What are your opinions on each subject? Why do you hold these opinions? Be especially aware of your responses to the essays representing opposing viewpoints at the end of the chapter; know where you stand in relation to each side of the issues here.

Use the preliminary material before an essay to help you create a framework for your responses to it: Who was Drakeman's primary audience when his essay was first published? In what ways is the tone of his essay appropriate for that audience? Why is Steele so interested in affirmative action? What motivated Hughes to publish his arguments on gun control? Which argument do you find most convincing?

Your main job at this stage of reading is to determine each author's primary assertion or proposition (thesis statement) and to create an inquisitive environment for thinking critically about the essay's ideas. In addition, take a look at the questions after each selection to make sure you are picking up the major points of the essay.

Rereading. As you reread these persuasive essays, notice how the writers integrate their appeals to logic, to emotion, and to ethics. Also, pay attention to the emphasis the writers place on one or more appeals at certain strategic points in the essays: How does Goodman integrate these three appeals in "Putting In a Good Word for Guilt"? Which of these appeals does she rely on to help bring her essay to a close? How persuasive is her final appeal? What combination of appeals does Peter Salins use in "Take a Ticket"? In what way does the tone of his writing support what he is saying? How does he establish the tone?

Also, determine what other rhetorical strategies help these writers make their primary points. How do these strategies enable each writer to establish a unified essay with a beginning, a middle, and an end?

Then, answer the questions after each reading selection to make certain you understand the essay on the literal, interpretive, and analytical levels in preparation for the discussion/writing assignments that follow.

For a list of guidelines for the entire reading process, see the checklists on pages 20–21 of the Introduction.

How to Write Persuasive Essays

Preparing to Write. The first stage of writing an essay of this sort involves, as usual, exploring and then limiting your topic. As you prepare to write your persuasive paper, first try to generate as many ideas as possible—regardless of whether they appeal to logic, emotion, or ethics. To do this, review the prewriting techniques in the Introduction and answer the Preparing to Write questions. Then, choose a topic. Next, focus on a purpose and a specific audience before you begin to write.

Writing. Most persuasive essays should begin with an assertion or a proposition stating what you believe about a certain issue. This thesis should generally be phrased as a debatable statement, such as, "If individual states reinstituted the death penalty, Americans would notice an immediate drop in violent crimes." At this point in your essay, you should also justify the significance of the issue you will be discussing: "Such a decline in the crime rate would affect all our lives and make this country a safer place in which to live."

The essay should then support your thesis in a variety of ways. This support may take the form of facts, figures, examples, opinions by recognized authorities, case histories, narratives/anecdotes, comparisons, contrasts, or cause/effect studies. This evidence is most effectively organized from least to most important when you are confronted with a hostile audience (so that you can lead your readers through the reasoning step by step) and from most to least important when you are facing a supportive audience (so that you can build on their loyalty and enthusiasm as you advance your thesis). In fact, you will be able to engineer your best support if you know your audience's opinions, feelings, and background before you write your essay, so that your intended "target" is as clear as possible. The body of your essay will undoubtedly consist of a combination of logical, emotional, and ethical appeals—all leading to some final summation or recommendation.

The concluding paragraph of a persuasive essay should restate your main assertion (in slightly different terms from those in your original statement) and should offer some constructive recommendations about the problem you have been discussing (if you haven't already done so). This section of your paper should clearly bring your argument to a close in one final attempt to move your audience to accept or act on the viewpoint you present. Let's look more closely now at each of the three types of appeals used in such essays: logical, emotional, and ethical.

To construct a *logical* argument, you have two principal patterns available to you: inductive reasoning or deductive reasoning. The first encourages an audience to make what is called an "inductive leap" from several particular examples to a single, useful generalization. In the case of the death penalty, you might cite a number of examples, figures, facts, and case studies illustrating the effectiveness of capital punishment in various states, thereby leading up to your firm belief that the death penalty should be reinstituted. Used most often by detectives, scientists, and lawyers, the process of inductive reasoning addresses the audience's ability to think logically by moving them systematically from an assortment of selected evidence to a rational and ordered conclusion.

In contrast, deductive reasoning moves its audience from a broad, general statement to particular examples supporting that statement. In writing such an essay, you would present your thesis statement about capital punishment first and then offer clear, orderly evidence to support that belief. Although the mental process we go through in creating a deductive argument is quite sophisticated, it is based on a three-step form of reasoning called the *syllogism*, which most logicians believe is the foundation of logical thinking. The traditional syllogism has

A major premise:	All humans fear death.
A minor premise:	Criminals are humans.
A conclusion:	Therefore, criminals fear death.

As you might suspect, this type of reasoning is only as accurate as its original premises, so you need to be careful with the truth of the premises as well as with the logical validity of your argument.

In constructing a logical argument, you should take great care to avoid the two types of fallacies in reasoning found most frequently in lower-division college papers: giving too few examples to support an assertion and citing examples that do not represent the assertion fairly. If you build your argument on true statements and abundant, accurate evidence, your essay will be effective.

Persuading through *emotion* necessitates controlling your readers' instinctive reactions to what you are saying. You can accomplish this goal in two different ways: (1) by choosing your words with even greater care than usual and (2) by using figurative language whenever appropriate. In the first case, you must be especially conscious of using words that have the same general denotative (or dictionary) meaning but bear decidedly favorable or unfavorable connotative (or implicit) meanings. For example, notice the difference between *slender* and *scrawny, patriotic* and *chauvinistic,* or *compliment* and *flattery.* Your careful attention to the choice of such words can help readers form visual images with certain positive or negative associations that subtly encourage them to follow your argument and adopt your opinions. Second, the effective use of figurative language—especially similes and metaphors—makes your writing more vivid, thus triggering your readers' senses and encouraging them to accept your views. Both of these techniques will help you manipulate your readers into the position of agreeing with your ideas.

Ethical appeals, which establish you as a reliable, well-informed person, are accomplished through (1) the tone of your essay and (2) the number and type of examples you cite. Tone is created through deliberate word choice: Careful attention to the mood implied in the words you use can convince your readers that you are serious, friendly, authoritative, jovial, or methodical—depending on your intended purpose. In like manner, the examples you supply to support your assertions can encourage readers to see you as experienced, insightful, relaxed, or intense. In both of these cases, winning favor for yourself will usually also gain approval for your opinions.

Rewriting. To rework your persuasive essays, you should play the role of your readers and impartially evaluate the different appeals you have used to accomplish your purpose:

Is your thesis statement clear?

Is the main thrust of your essay argumentative (an appeal to reason)?

Which of your supporting details appeal to emotion? To ethics?

Will the balance of these appeals effectively accomplish your purpose with your intended audience?

Does your conclusion restate your argument, make a recommendation, and bring your essay to a close?

You should also look closely at the way your appeals work together in your essay:

When you use logic, is that section of your paper arranged through either inductive or deductive reasoning?

Is that the most effective order to achieve your purpose?

In appealing to the emotions, have you chosen your words with proper attention to their denotative and connotative effects?

Have you used figurative language whenever appropriate?

And in your ethical appeals, have you created the right tone for your essay?

Is it suitable for your purpose and your audience?

Have you chosen examples carefully to support your thesis statement?

Any additional guidance you may need as you write and revise your persuasive essays is furnished on pages 32–33 of the Introduction.

STUDENT ESSAY: ARGUMENT AND PERSUASION AT WORK

The following student essay uses all three appeals to make its point about the power of language in shaping our view of the world. First, the writer sets forth her character references (ethical appeal) in the first paragraph, after which she presents her thesis and its significance in paragraph 2. The support for her thesis is a combination of logical and emotional appeals, heavy on the logical, as the writer moves her paragraphs from general to particular in an effort to convince her readers to adopt her point of view and adjust their language use accordingly.

The Language of Equal Rights

Up front, I admit it. I've been a card-carrying feminist since junior high school. I want to see an Equal Rights Amendment to the U.S. Constitution, equal pay for equal—and comparable—work, and I go dutch on dates. Furthermore, I am quite prickly on the subject of language. I'm one of those women who bristles at terms like *lady doctor* (you know they don't mean a gynecologist), *female policeman* (a paradox), and *mankind* instead of *humanity* (are they really talking about me?).

Ethical appeal

Emotional appeal

Many people ask "How important are mere words, anyway? You know what we really mean." A question like this ignores the symbolic and psychological importance of language. What words "mean" can go beyond what a speaker or writer consciously intends, reflecting personal and

Assertion or thesis statement

cultural biases that run so deep that most of the time we aren't even aware they exist. "Mere words" are incredibly important: They are our framework for seeing and understanding the world.

Significance of assertion

Logical appeal

Man, we are told, means woman as well as man, just as *mankind* supposedly stands for all of humanity. In the introduction of a sociology textbook I recently read, the author was anxious to demonstrate his awareness of the controversy over sexist language and to assure his female readers that, despite his use of noninclusive terms, he was not forgetting the existence or importance of women in society. He was making a conscious decision to continue to use *man* and *mankind* instead of *people, humanity*, etc., for ease of expression and aesthetic reasons. "Man" simply sounds better, he explained. I flipped through the table of contents and found "Man and Society," "Man and Nature," "Man and Technology," and, near the end, "Man and Woman." At what point did *Man* quit meaning people and start meaning men again? The writer was obviously unaware of the answer to this question, because it is one he would never think to ask. Having consciously addressed the issue only to dismiss it, he reverted to form.

Examples organized deductively

Emotional appeal

Logical appeal

The very ambiguity of *man* as the generic word for our species ought to be enough to combat any arguments that we keep it because we all "know what it means" or because it is both traditional and sounds better. And does it really sound all that much better, or are we just more used to it, more comfortable? Our own national history proves that we can be comfortable with a host of words and attitudes that

Examples organized deductively

strike us as unjust and ugly today. A lot of white folks probably thought that Negroes were getting pretty stuffy and picky when they began to insist on being called blacks. After all, weren't there more important things to worry about, like civil rights? But black activists recognized the emotional and symbolic significance of having a name that was parallel to the name that the dominant race used for itself—a name equal in dignity, lacking that vaguely alien, anthropological sound. After all, whites were called *Caucasians* only in police reports, textbooks, and autopsies. *Negro* may have sounded better to people in the bad old days of blatant racial bigotry, but we adjusted to the word *black* and have now moved on to African American, and more and more people of each race are adjusting to the wider implications and demands of practical, as well as verbal labels.

Emotional appeal

In a world where *man* and *human* are offered as synonymous terms, I don't think it is a coincidence that women are still vastly underrepresented in positions of money, power, and respect. Children grow up learning a language that makes maleness the norm for anything that isn't explicitly designated as female, giving little girls a very limited corner of the universe to picture themselves in. Indeed, the language that nonfeminists today claim to be inclusive was never intended to cover women in the first place. "One man, one vote" and "All men are created equal" meant just that. Women had to fight for decades to be included even as an afterthought; it took constitutional amendments to convince the government and the courts that women are human, too.

Logical appeal

Examples organized deductively

Conclusion/   The message is clear. <u>We have to start</u>
restatement <u>speaking about people, not men, if we are</u>
<u>going to start thinking in terms of both</u>
<u>women and men.</u> A "female man" will
<u>never be the equal of her brother.</u>

Student Writer's Comments

The hardest task for me in writing this essay was trying to come up with a topic! The second hardest job was trying to be effective without getting preachy, strident, or wordy. I wanted to persuade an audience that would no doubt include the bored, the hostile, and the indifferent, and I was worried about losing their attention.

I chose my topic after several prewriting sessions that generated numerous options for me to write about. I stumbled on the idea of sexist language in one of these sessions and then went on to generate new material on this particular topic. Eventually satisfied that I had enough ideas to stay with this topic, I doubled back and labeled them according to each type of appeal.

Even before I had written my thesis, I had a good idea of what I wanted to say in this essay. I began working from an assertion that essentially remained the same as I wrote and revised my essay. It's more polished now, but its basic intention never changed.

To create my first draft, I worked from my notes, labeled by type of appeal. I let the logical arguments guide my writing, strategically introducing emotional and ethical appeals as I sensed they would be effective. I appealed to ethics in the beginning of the essay to establish my credibility, and I appealed to the readers' emotions occasionally to vary my pace and help my argument gain momentum. I was fully aware of what I was doing when I moved from one appeal to another. I wrote from a passionate desire to change people's thinking about language and its ability to control our perceptions of the world.

Next, I revised my entire essay several times, playing the role of different readers with dissimilar biases in each case. Every time I worked through the essay, I made major changes in the introduction and the conclusion as well. At this point, I paid special attention to the denotation, connotation, and tone of my words (especially highly charged language) and to the examples I had chosen to support each point I decided to keep in my argument. Though I moved a lot of examples around and thought of better ones in some cases, I was eventually happy with the final product. I am especially pleased with the balance of appeals in the final draft.

SOME FINAL THOUGHTS ON ARGUMENT AND PERSUASION

As you can tell from the selections that follow, the three different types of persuasive appeals usually complement each other in practice. Most good persuasive essays use a combination of these methods to achieve their purposes. Good persuasive essays also rely on various rhetorical modes we have already studied—such as example, process analysis, division/classification, comparison/contrast, definition, and cause/effect—to advance their arguments. In the following essays, you will see a combination of appeals at work and a number of different rhetorical modes furthering the arguments.

DONALD DRAKEMAN   (1953 –   )

■ ■ ■

Religion's Place in Public Schools

Donald Drakeman describes himself as a business executive and corporate lawyer with a "therapeutic" interest in church–state affairs. He was born in Camden, New Jersey, and earned a B.A. degree in religion from Dartmouth College, a Ph.D. in religion from Princeton University, and a law degree from Columbia University. He is currently president of a company named Medarex, which uses biotechnology to treat cancer and other diseases. Drakeman has published a number of articles on religion in public schools, religious cults, and First Amendment rights. His two books are titled *Church and State in American History: The Burden of Religious Pluralism* (coedited with John F. Wilson, 1988) and *Church–State Constitutional Issues: Making Sense of the Establishment Clause* (1991). Drakeman lives in Princeton, New Jersey, where he enjoys teaching part time at Princeton University, playing squash, practicing the trumpet, and spending time with his family. When asked for permission to publish the following essay in *The Prose Reader*, the author replied, "If you are including my article as an example of good writing, I am honored. If my piece is representative of poor writing, please send me a copy of your book so that I may improve."

Preparing to Read

In the following essay, originally published in the *Christian Century* magazine in May 1984, Drakeman logically and carefully presents his opinions concerning the appropriate role of religion in the public schools. As you prepare to read his suggestions on this controversial topic, take a few moments to focus your own thoughts on the subject: What do you think the proper relationship should be between religion and education? Does your opinion depend on whether the schools in question are public or private? Grade schools, high schools, or colleges? What is the role of education in American life? Of religion? Why do you think these topics are so controversial in America today?

R ecently I represented the New Jersey Council of 1 Churches in a federal lawsuit challenging New Jersey's "moment-of-silence" legislation—a law requiring public-school teachers to provide a minute of silence at the beginning of the school day for students to engage in "contemplation or introspection."

The American Civil Liberties Union immediately sued to have 2 the law declared unconstitutional on the grounds that it was designed to bring back prayer into the public schools—something the U.S. Supreme Court had outlawed 20 years ago. There was a great deal of evidence showing that the New Jersey legislators wanted to return prayer to the classroom, but had left the word out of the bill in hopes of avoiding the court's pronouncements. To the surprise of many, the New Jersey Council of Churches, an interdenominational Christian body, intervened in the case as a "friend of the court" to oppose the law.

At the same time, religious and civil liberties groups have been 3 in a quandary over what to do about cases involving students who want to meet for religious purposes during noninstructional times at the public schools. Two federal appellate courts have declared such practices unconstitutional, saying that they are not qualitatively different from the school-sponsored prayers held unconstitutional in the 1960s. The issue remains open, however, and it is not clear—at least to me—that a mandatory moment of silence (or prayer) is the same thing as permitting students to elect a religious activity in place of the chess club or debating team.

Once again in American history, the public schools are at the 4 intersection of church and state (or, perhaps more accurately, religion and government). This issue of when and where students may pray at school not only raises thorny questions of constitutional interpretation, but also asks us how we should relate our Christian faith to a world that has been called secular, amoral, modern, postmodern and even anti-Christian. Or, as ethicist Paul Ramsey has eloquently put it, "How shall we sing the Lord's song in a pluralistic land?"

To try to come to terms with this problem, we will need to   5
look briefly at its legal dimensions, since the Constitution has set
the parameters within which we must act, and then to relate the
constitutional issues to the role of the Christian in our society.

The language of the Constitution is deceptively simple. The fed-   6
eral government and the states may not make laws "respecting an
establishment of religion or prohibiting the free exercise thereof."
In two famous cases in the early '60s, the United States Supreme
Court declared that school-sponsored prayer and Bible reading in
the public schools violate the Constitution's establishment clause.
These decisions brought a shower of public wrath upon the court.
Many religious leaders feared that a godless, atheistic empire would
soon take the place of the Christian republic that has been built on
a foundation of faith and Scripture. The governors of every state
but New York called for a constitutional amendment reversing the
court's decisions, and the justices soon became the Grinches that
stole Christmas from our children's school pageants.

Subsequently, the Supreme Court struck down a Kentucky law   7
requiring that the Ten Commandments be posted in public-school
classrooms, and other federal courts have outlawed school-sponsored
grace before meals, student-led classroom prayer, and mandatory
moments of silence. In each case, the courts have tried to follow the
Supreme Court's conclusion that religious activities supported and
sponsored by the schools are contrary to the Constitution even if
the activities are "nondenominational" and voluntary.

Thus, the primary constitutional issues are (1) Is the activity *re-*   8
ligious, and (2) Is it supported and sponsored by the school? Or, as
the Supreme Court has expressed it: Does the state's action have a
clearly secular purpose? Does it have a primary effect that neither
advances nor inhibits religion? And does it avoid excessive government entanglement with religion? Each of these tests must be
met for an action of the government to be constitutional.

Three federal courts have already decided that the moment-   9
of-silence laws are unconstitutional. The evidence for these findings is compelling, despite legislative efforts to use neutral
language such as "introspection," "contemplation" or "medita-
tion" to avoid having the bill appear to be clearly religious. In
every case, the moment-of-silence bills have evolved within the
context of returning prayer to the classroom. Not only is the moment of silence directly within the long tradition of commencing

the school day with a prayer (a practice still found in many schools despite Supreme Court pronouncements), but it is also legislatively designed to be a religious activity. In every state that has recently enacted a moment-of-silence law, the floor debate has been almost exclusively devoted to the topic of putting prayer, and religion generally, back into the minds and hearts of our public-school students. Only then, posit our lawmakers, will America return to its former days of glory.

Faced with this evidence of the legislators' religious intent 10 (which is enough, under Supreme Court precedents, to invalidate the moment-of-silence laws), lawyers defending the laws have created a variety of after-the-fact secular rationales for commencing the school day with a quiet moment. These arguments simply do not work; legislative history cannot so easily be rewritten. But, more important, the public cannot help but see the moment of silence as morning prayer. In many schools, most of the parents and teachers alike must have begun their own school days by saying prayers or reading the Bible. The moment-of-silence laws cannot be evaluated without taking into account this cultural fact that will unavoidably give a religious coloring to an ostensibly neutral law.

Although the moment-of-silence laws run afoul of the establish- 11 ment clause, does it necessarily follow that we, as Christians, should oppose religion in the schools? After all, many religious groups are calling for a constitutional amendment that would permit teachers and students to lead prayers in public-school classrooms.

The crux of this issue is whether we think the state should 12 have the power to favor one religion (or type of religion) over another. By having a time set aside for prayer during the part of the school day when teachers have virtually total control over their students, the schools are putting their imprimatur on those religions that believe in prayer. Moreover, if we admit that the state, through its schools, may regulate religion by encouraging prayer, we are tacitly giving it the authority to regulate the exercise of our religion by excluding, limiting, or defining the kinds of prayer in which we, or our children, may engage.

As our nation becomes increasingly diverse and secular, the 13 likelihood that school-supported religious activities will correspond with the students' particular beliefs will diminish. Most of those who support school prayer hope for a return to the "Judeo-Christian" prayers of our educational past. But what if in some schools prayers are addressed instead to Shiva, the Ayatollah Khomeini, or Sun Myung Moon? For all of us, believers and nonbelievers alike, the safest course is to keep the schools out of the religion business.

Now that I have taken prayer out of the schools, I would like to put it back in under different auspices. Many public schools, particularly at the junior and senior high school levels, have non-instructional periods during which students are free to choose from among a variety of activities—sports, service clubs, language societies, and the like. In a number of communities, voluntary student religious groups have sought to meet during these activity periods. As I noted earlier, several federal courts have made no distinction between these requests and legislative attempts to bring back school-sponsored prayer. I think they are wrong.   14

During the instructional portion of the school day, teachers have almost complete control over the students' activities. Inserting prayer during those parts of the day clearly runs contrary to the mandates of the Constitution. But when students are asked to select from a wide variety of extracurricular activities, the school's role changes dramatically. No longer the domineering ruler of the students' every move, it becomes the host for a great number of (theoretically) socially enriching activities. To deny students the opportunity to meet for religious purposes is to say that religion cannot stand as an equal with football, debating, cheerleading, and the classics club. It is to single out religion as the one activity always inappropriate within the schools.   15

Even if we agree that voluntary, student-initiated religious groups may meet during noninstructional periods, will our present Constitution countenance it, or must we join those calling for a constitutional amendment? Fortunately, the Constitution provides ample support for allowing such student groups. While our government may not "establish" religion, it may not prohibit the free exercise of religion or restrict the free speech of its citizens (including students). When the school prescribes prayer, it is establishing religion; when it proscribes prayer, it is prohibiting students from freely exercising their religions.   16

Although there is some element of religious establishment when a school allows students to meet for religious purposes, the state support of religion is minimal. If the meetings are truly voluntary, the school must only exercise the basic supervision neces-   17 sary to ensure that the students do not damage themselves or public property. On balance, this degree of "establishment" is insignificant compared to the detrimental impact on religious exercise and speech if students are told that they may elect any activity but prayer and discuss any subject but God.

There is no question that the public schools are important purveyors of our culture and its fundamental values. Teachers have control over our children for a vast portion of their formative and impressionable years. Precisely for this reason we must be particularly concerned about the schools' interaction with our faith and the faith of others. We must urge the schools to let religion compete on an equal footing with secular extracurricular activities. But at the same time, we must be wary of any attempt to make the schools transmitters of religious beliefs and practices. It is the place of churches and families to guide us in the ways of faith. The schools must not be given the power to tell our children when, where, or how to pray.

18

UNDERSTANDING DETAILS

1. What does Drakeman mean when he says, "Once again in American history, the public schools are at the intersection of church and state" (paragraph 4)?
2. What are the main constitutional issues surrounding the relationship between public schools and religion? Explain these issues in your own words.
3. Why does Paul Ramsey call America "a pluralistic land" (paragraph 4)? What effect might this feature of American life have on the role of prayer in the public schools?
4. What does the author feel the appropriate role of religion in the public schools should be?

ANALYZING MEANING

1. What does the author mean when he refers to the "establishment clause" (paragraph 6) of the Constitution? What connotations does this phrase bear for you?
2. Do you think Drakeman's analysis of the relevant issues is accurate? Explain your answer in detail.
3. Why is religion's place in public schools such an important, controversial issue?

4. Do you agree or disagree with Drakeman's opinions on the place of religion in public schools? Have you had any experiences that confirm your point of view?

DISCOVERING RHETORICAL STRATEGIES

1. This essay appeared in a periodical called *The Christian Century*. With this in mind, who do you think is Drakeman's intended audience? Describe them in detail. How might this audience have affected the author's choice of evidence in this particular argument?
2. Is the author's reasoning primarily inductive or deductive? Give one example from the essay to support your answer. Why do you think Drakeman relies so heavily upon an appeal to logic in this essay?
3. The author occasionally uses emotional and ethical appeals to support his logic. When does he invoke our emotions in this essay? Our sense of ethics? What other rhetorical modes does he use to further his argument?
4. What additional rhetorical strategies does Drakeman use to develop his argument? Give examples of each.

MAKING CONNECTIONS

1. Both Drakeman and Shelby Steele ("Affirmative Action: The Price of Preference") discuss the law as a remedy for social injustice. Which author's argument do you find most convincing? Explain your answer.
2. Analyze the balance in Drakeman's essay between logical, emotional, and ethical appeals. How is this balance different from that found in Robert Hughes's "The N.R.A. in a Hunter's Sights"? Which author uses more of an emotional appeal? Who uses more logic? Who appeals most to reputation? In what way does the mixture of appeals in each of these essays affect how convincing they are to you?
3. Like Drakeman, Germaine Greer ("A Child Is Born") analyzes the value of religion and religious ceremony in society. Since religion is so dominant in non-Western cultures, do you think Greer would argue that it should be dominant in our American culture as well—even in our schools? Argue from

Greer's point of view that American schools should allow students the opportunity to meet for religious purposes.

IDEAS FOR DISCUSSION/WRITING

Preparing to Write

Write freely about your view of the role of religion in the public schools: What role should religion play in our lives? How, when, and where should religion be taught? What role should school play in our lives? What subjects should American high schools be allowed to teach? What subjects should they exclude? Should education and religion merge at any one point? Under what conditions? What are the advantages of combining the two? The disadvantages? What are the advantages of separating the two? The disadvantages?

Choosing a Topic

1. In a letter addressed to the U.S. Supreme Court, answer one or more of the questions Drakeman poses in paragraph 8 of his essay as they relate to school prayer. Keep in mind that the judges, after reading your response, will be clarifying once again their interpretation of the establishment clause of the Constitution.

2. In a letter to your representative in the state legislature, argue for or against Drakeman's plan to allow religious groups to meet during noninstructional periods of the school day.

3. Your old high school has asked you to present to the current senior class your views on whether organized prayer should be included as part of the public school day. Explain your stand as thoroughly as possible using the background Drakeman furnishes in his essay.

ELLEN GOODMAN   (1941 –   )

■ ■ ■

Putting In a Good Word for Guilt

Ellen Goodman is a nationally syndicated columnist and associate editor of the *Boston Globe*, who frequently pens newspaper columns on such topics as feminism, child rearing, divorce, alternative lifestyles, and gardening. Although Goodman once appealed principally to women, her essays now interest readers of both sexes who are, in the words of *New York Times* critic John Leonard, "full of gratitude for having been introduced to a witty and civilized human being in a vulgar and self-pitying decade." Born in Newton, Massachusetts, and educated at Radcliffe College, Goodman began her career in journalism as a researcher and reporter at *Newsweek* magazine, then moved to the *Detroit Free Press* as a feature writer. In 1967, she was hired as a feature writer and "At Large" columnist by the *Boston Globe*. Her first book was *Turning Points* (1979), which examines how men and women have reacted to the changes brought on by the feminist movement. Other publications include five collections of her best newspaper columns: *Close to Home* (1979), *At Large* (1981), *Keeping in Touch* (1985), *Making Sense* (1989), and *Value Judgments* (1993). In 1980, Goodman's reputation as a first-rate journalist was confirmed when she was awarded the Pulitzer Prize for distinguished commentary. Syndicated now in more than 300 newspapers throughout the country, Goodman lives in Brookline, Massachusetts.

Preparing to Read

The following essay, originally written for *Redbook* magazine (June 1982), suggests that we all need a certain amount of therapeutic guilt in our lives. Before you read this essay, take a few moments to think about your own perceptions of guilt: Are there different types of guilt? How often do you feel guilty? What are the usual reasons? What general feelings do you associate with the word *guilt*? Are these associations generally positive or negative?

What value might guilt have in our lives? What problems might it cause? Do you consider yourself guilt-free, overly guilty, or somewhere in the middle? What brings you to this conclusion about yourself? Are you content with this feature of your personality? Why or why not? ∎

Feeling guilty is nothing to feel guilty about. Yes, guilt can 1 be the excess baggage that keeps us paralyzed unless we dump it. But it can also be the engine that fuels us. Yes, it can be a self-punishing activity, but it can also be the conscience that keeps us civilized.

Not too long ago I wrote a story about that amusing couple 2 Guilt and the Working Mother. I'll tell you more about that later. Through the mail someone sent me a gift coffee mug carrying the message "I gave up guilt for Lent."

My first reaction was to giggle. But then it occurred to me 3 that this particular Lent has been too lengthy. For the past decade or more, the pop psychologists who use book jackets rather than couches all were busy telling us that I am okay, you are okay, and whatever we do is okay.

In most of their books, guilt was given a bad name—or rather, 4 an assortment of bad names. It was a (1) Puritan (2) Jewish (3) Catholic hangover from our (1) parents (2) culture (3) religion. To be truly liberated was to be free of guilt about being rich, powerful, number one, bad to your mother, thoughtless, late, a smoker or about cheating on your spouse.

There was a popular notion, in fact, that self-love began by 5 slaying one's guilt. People all around us spent a great portion of the last decade trying to tune out guilt instead of decoding its message and learning what it was trying to tell us.

With that sort of success, guilt was ripe for revival. Somewhere 6 along the I'm-okay-you're-okay way, many of us realized that, in fact, I am not always okay and neither are you. Furthermore, we did not want to join the legions who conquered their guilt en route to new depths of narcissistic rottenness.

At the deepest, most devastating level, guilt is the criminal in 7 us that longs to be caught. It is the horrible, pit-of-the-stomach sense of having done wrong. It is, as Lady Macbeth obsessively knew, the spot that no one else may see . . . and we can't see around.

To be without guilt is to be without a conscience. Guilt-free 8 people don't feel bad when they cause pain to others, and so they go on guilt-freely causing more pain. The last thing we need more of is less conscience.

Freud once said, "As regards conscience, God has done an un- 9 even and careless piece of work, for a large majority of men have brought along with them only a modest amount of it, or scarcely enough to be worth mentioning."

Now, I am not suggesting that we all sign up for a new guilt 10 trip. But there has to be some line between the accusation that we all should feel guilty for, say, poverty or racism and the assertion that the oppressed have "chosen" their lot in life.

There has to be something between puritanism and hedonism. 11 There has to be something between the parents who guilt-trip their children across every stage of life and those who offer no guidance, no—gulp—moral or ethical point of view.

At quite regular intervals, for example, my daughter looks up 12 at me in the midst of a discussion (she would call it a lecture) and says: "You're making me feel guilty." For a long time this made me, in turn, feel guilty. But now I realize that I am doing precisely what I am supposed to be doing: instilling in her a sense of right and wrong so that she will feel uncomfortable if she behaves in hurtful ways.

This is, of course, a very tricky business. Guilt is ultimately the 13 way we judge ourselves. It is the part of us that says, "I deserve to be punished." But we all know people who feel guilty just for being alive. We know people who are paralyzed by irrational guilt. And we certainly don't want to be among them, or to shepherd our children into their flock.

But it seems to me that the trick isn't to become flaccidly 14 nonjudgmental, but to figure out whether we are being fair judges of ourselves. Karl Menninger once wrote that one aim of psychiatric treatment isn't to get rid of guilt but "to get people's guilt feelings attached to the 'right' things."

In his book *Feelings*, Willard Gaylin quotes a Reverend 15 Tillotson's definition of guilt as "nothing else but trouble arising in our mind from our consciousness of having done contrary to what we are verily perswaded [sic] was our Duty."

We may, however, have widely different senses of duty. I had   16
lunch with two friends a month ago when they both started talking about feeling guilty for neglecting their mothers. One, it
turned out, worried that she didn't call "home" every day; the
other hadn't even chatted with her mother since Christmas.

We are also particularly vulnerable to feelings of duty in a time   17
of change. Today an older and ingrained sense of what we should
do may conflict with a new one. In the gaps that open between
what we once were taught and what we now believe grows a rich
crop of guilt.

Mothers now often tell me that they feel guilty if they are   18
working and guilty if they aren't. One set of older expectations,
to be a perfect milk-and-cookies supermom, conflicts with another, to be an independent woman or an economic helpmate.

But duty has its uses. It sets us down at the typewriter, hustles   19
us to the job on a morning when everything has gone wrong,
pushes us toward the crying baby at 3 A.M.

If guilt is a struggle between our acceptance of shoulds and   20
should nots, it is a powerful and intensely human one. Gaylin
writes, "Guilt represents the noblest and most painful of struggles.
It is between us and ourselves." It is better to struggle with ourselves than give up on ourselves.

This worst emotion, in a sense, helps bring out the best in us.   21
The desire to avoid feeling guilty makes us avoid the worst sort of
behavior. The early guilt of a child who has hurt a younger sister
or brother, even when no one else knows, is a message. The adult
who has inflicted pain on an innocent, who has cheated, lied,
stolen, to get ahead of another—each of us has a list—wakes up
in the middle of the night and remembers it.

In that sense guilt is the great civilizer, the internal command-   22
ment that helps us choose to be kind to each other rather than to
join in a stampede of me-firsts. "If guilt is coming back," said
Harvard Professor David Riesman, who wrote *The Lonely Crowd*,
"one reason is that a tremendous surge of young people overpowered the adults in the sixties. You might say the barbarians
took Rome. Now there are more adults around who are trying to
restore some stability."

Guilt is the adult in each of us, the parent, the one who up-   23
holds the standards. It is the internal guide against which we
argue in vain that "everybody else is doing it."

We even wrestle with ethical dilemmas and conflicts of con- 24
science so that we can live with ourselves more comfortably. I
know two people who were faced with a crisis about their infi-
delities. One woman resolved the triangle she was in by ending
her marriage. The other ended her affair. In both cases, it was the
pain that had motivated them to change.

It is not easy to attach our guilt to the right things. It is never 25
easy to separate right from wrong, rational guilt from neurotic
guilt. We may resolve one by changing our view of it and another
by changing our behavior.

In my own life as a working mother, I have done both half 26
a dozen times. When my daughter was small and I was working, I worried that I was not following the pattern of the good
mother, my mother. Only through time and perspective and
reality did I change that view; I realized that my daughter
clearly did not feel neglected and I clearly was not uncaring.
Good child care, love, luck and support helped me to resolve
my early guilt feelings.

Then again, last winter I found myself out of town more than 27
I was comfortable with. This time I changed my schedule instead
of my mind.

For all of us, in the dozens of daily decisions we make, guilt is 28
one of the many proper motivations. I am not saying our lives are
ruled by guilt. Hardly. But guilt is inherent in the underlying
question: "If I do that, can I live with myself?"

People who don't ask themselves that question, people who 29
never get no for an answer, may seem lucky. They can, we
think, be self-centered without self-punishment, hedonistic
without qualms. They can worry about me–first and forget
about the others.

It is easy to be jealous of those who go through life without a 30
moment of wrenching guilt. But envying the guiltless is like envying a house pet. Striving to follow their lead is like accepting a
catatonic as your role model. They are not the free but the antisocial. In a world in which guilt is one of the few emotions experienced only by human beings, they are, even, unhuman.

Guilt is one of the most human of dilemmas. It is the claim of 31
others on the self, the recognition both of our flaws and of our
desire to be the people we want to be.

UNDERSTANDING DETAILS

1. Which two sides of the argument about guilt does Goodman present in the first paragraph of her essay? Which side does she end up favoring? How can we predict from the first paragraph that she is going to take that side?
2. What does the author mean when she states that "guilt was given a bad name" (paragraph 4)?
3. Explain in your own words the middle ground the author is seeking between guiltlessness and neurotic guilt. Give examples to support your answer.
4. According to Goodman, how are guilt and conscience related?

ANALYZING MEANING

1. Goodman quotes Karl Menninger as saying that one aim of psychiatric treatment isn't to get rid of guilt but " 'to get people's guilt feelings attached to the "right" things' " (paragraph 14). What explanations of this statement does the author offer? What examples does she cite to help us understand it? What does this statement have to do with being "fair judges of ourselves" (paragraph 14)?
2. To what degree can our sense of duty differ from someone else's? Give examples of this range of difference from your own experience.
3. Why does the author mention working mothers in connection with guilt?
4. In what ways can guilt serve as "the great civilizer" (paragraph 22)?

DISCOVERING RHETORICAL STRATEGIES

1. To what extent does the author convince you that guilt can play a valuable role in our lives? What types of appeals does she use to accomplish this purpose? Where does she use these appeals? Be as specific as possible in answering this question.
2. Characterize Goodman's original audience for this essay. Can you make any assumptions about its sexual, ethnic, and economic demographics? Support your answer with specific references to the essay.
3. How would you describe Goodman's tone in this essay? What particular words and phrases help her establish that tone? What effect does this tone have on you as a reader?

4. What principal rhetorical strategies does Goodman use to support her statement about guilt? Give examples of each.

MAKING CONNECTIONS

1. Goodman's essay about guilt is similar in many respects to Judith Viorst's "The Truth About Lying." In fact, Viorst's essay could easily have been titled "Putting In a Good Word for Lying." Compare and contrast the various ways in which these authors try to convince us that lying and guilt are necessary, perhaps even admirable, ingredients in our lives.

2. Examine the uses and abuses of guilt in the following essays: Rita Mae Brown's "Writing as a Moral Act," Alice Walker's "Beauty: When the Other Dancer Is the Self," Russell Baker's "The Saturday Evening Post," and/or Michael Dorris's "The Broken Cord."

3. If Goodman, Stephen King ("Why We Crave Horror Movies"), John Langone ("Group Violence"), and Barbara Ehrenreich ("Stop Ironing the Diapers") were having a roundtable discussion about "normal" behavior, how would each of these authors define that term? What do you think "normal" behavior is?

IDEAS FOR DISCUSSION/WRITING

Preparing to Write

Write freely about the advantages and disadvantages of guilt: From your experience, what is the principal value of guilt? Has guilt ever helped you accomplish something important or worthwhile? Has it ever hindered you from accomplishing something? Has the feeling of guilt ever been extremely uncomfortable for you? How often do you feel guilty? Why do you think you developed this particular ethical stance? Are you content with your "guilt quotient"?

Choosing a Topic

1. Do you agree or disagree with Goodman's main assertion that guilt can be "the conscience that keeps us civilized" (paragraph 1)? Write an argumentative essay to the same *Redbook* audience Goodman addressed supporting or refuting this proposition.

2. What stages do you go through to complete a writing assignment? Does guilt play any part in your composing process? If so, does it help or hinder your work? Write an essay for your classmates arguing for or against the value of guilt in reference to writing. Use concrete examples to support your argument.

3. Should children be forced to say, "I'm sorry"? Does this practice help them develop a conscience? What is the best way to develop an appropriate guilt quotient in children? *Parents* magazine wants to know your opinion on this issue. Write an article for the readers of this magazine focusing on the difference between inducing necessary guilt and emotionally abusing children.

SHELBY STEELE   (1946 –   )

■ ■ ■

Affirmative Action: The Price of Preference

Born in Chicago, Shelby Steele earned his B.A. at Coe College in Iowa, his M.A. at Southern Illinois University, and his Ph.D. at the University of Utah. An early succession of articles in *Harper's*, the *American Scholar*, the *Washington Post*, the *New Republic*, and the *New York Times Book Review* earned him a National Magazine Award in 1989. One of his essays on race relations was selected for inclusion in *The Best American Essays of 1989*. His most well-known publication, however, is *The Content of Our Character: A New Vision of Race in America*, a controversial best-seller that won the National Book Critics Circle Award in 1991. In it, the author examines his own life as a middle-class African American in a world where both blacks and whites have become trapped into seeing "color before character." He argues that social policies designed to lessen racial differences have instead made these diversities much greater and that the posture of "victimization" adopted by many members of his own race has detracted from rather than enhanced the movement toward cultural equality. His advice to students using *The Prose Reader* is concise and helpful: "Use simple, concrete, Anglo-Saxon words; avoid jargon, colloquialisms, and the passive voice. Try to give clarity and immediacy to your work by writing about emotions and events you know from your own experience." For many years a professor of English at San Jose State University in California, Steele is now working on his next book. In his infrequent spare time, he enjoys swimming, jogging, and reading.

Preparing to Read

In the following chapter from *The Content of Our Character*, Steele argues that affirmative action programs, however well intentioned and fairly administered, demoralize and stigmatize blacks as "inferior" to their white counterparts in society. The net result is a culture of "victimization" that seeks to exploit rather than overcome past racial injustices. As you prepare to read this essay, take a few moments to think about your own views on affirmative action: Exactly how does this concept work? How effective is it in your community? In your job? In your school? In what ways has affirmative action affected you directly? From your perspective, what are the principal advantages of affirmative action? The disadvantages? How much longer do you think it will be necessary in America?

I n a few short years, when my two children will be applying to college, the affirmative action policies by which most universities offer black students some form of preferential treatment will present me with a dilemma. I am a middle-class black, a college professor, far from wealthy, but also well-removed from the kind of deprivation that would qualify my children for the label "disadvantaged." Both of them have endured racial insensitivity from whites. They have been called names, have suffered slights, and have experienced firsthand the peculiar malevolence that racism brings out in people. Yet, they have never experienced racial discrimination, have never been stopped by their race on any path they have chosen to follow. Still, their society now tells them that if they will only designate themselves as black on their college applications, they will likely do better in the college lottery than if they conceal this fact. I think there is something of a Faustian bargain in this.

Of course, many blacks and a considerable number of whites would say that I was sanctimoniously making affirmative action into a test of character. They would say that this small preference is the meagerest recompense for centuries of unrelieved oppression. And to these arguments other very obvious facts must be added. In America, many marginally competent or flatly incompetent whites are hired every day—some because their white skin suits the conscious or unconscious racial preference of their employer. The white children of alumni are often grandfathered into elite universities in what can only be seen as a residual benefit of historic white privilege. Worse, white incompetence is always an individual matter, while for blacks it is often confirmation of ugly stereotypes. The Peter Principle was not conceived with only

1

2

blacks in mind. Given that unfairness cuts both ways, doesn't it only balance the scales of history that my children now receive a slight preference over whites? Doesn't this repay, in a small way, the systematic denial under which their grandfather lived out his days?

So, in theory, affirmative action certainly has all the moral sym- 3 metry that fairness requires—the injustice of historical and even contemporary white advantage is offset with black advantage; preference replaces prejudice, inclusion answers exclusion. It is reformist and corrective, even repentant and redemptive. And I would never sneer at these good intentions. Born in the late forties in Chicago, I started my education (a charitable term in this case) in a segregated school and suffered all the indignities that come to blacks in a segregated society. My father, born in the South, only made it to the third grade before the white man's fields took permanent priority over his formal education. And though he educated himself into an advanced reader with an almost professorial authority, he could only drive a truck for a living and never earned more than ninety dollars a week in his entire life. So yes, it is crucial to my sense of citizenship, to my ability to identify with the spirit and the interests of America, to know that this country, however imperfectly, recognizes its past sins and wishes to correct them.

Yet good intentions, because of the opportunity for innocence 4 they offer us, are very seductive and can blind us to the effects they generate when implemented. In our society, affirmative action is, among other things, a testament to white goodwill and to black power, and in the midst of these heavy investments, its effects can be hard to see. But after twenty years of implementation, I think affirmative action has shown itself to be more bad than good and that blacks—whom I will focus on in this essay— now stand to lose more from it than they gain.

In talking with affirmative action administrators and with 5 blacks and whites in general, it is clear that supporters of affirmative action focus on its good intentions while detractors emphasize its negative effects. Proponents talk about "diversity" and "pluralism"; opponents speak of "reverse discrimination," the unfairness of quotas and set-asides. It was virtually impossible to find people outside either camp. The closest I came was a white male manager at a large computer company who said, "I think it amounts to reverse discrimination, but I'll put up with a little of that for a little more diversity." I'll live with a little of the effect to gain a little of the intention, he seemed to be saying. But this only makes him a halfhearted supporter of affirmative action. I think many people who don't really like affirmative action support it to one degree or another anyway.

I believe they do this because of what happened to white and 6 black Americans in the crucible of the sixties when whites were confronted with their racial guilt and blacks tasted their first real power. In this stormy time white absolution and black power co-alesced into virtual mandates for society. Affirmative action be-came a meeting ground for these mandates in the law, and in the late sixties and early seventies it underwent a remarkable escala-tion of its mission from simple antidiscrimination enforcement to social engineering by means of quotas, goals, timetables, set-asides, and other forms of preferential treatment.

Legally, this was achieved through a series of executive orders 7 and EEOC [Equal Employment Opportunity Commission] guidelines that allowed racial imbalances in the workplace to stand as proof of racial discrimination. Once it could be assumed that discrimination explained racial imbalances, it became easy to justify group remedies to presumed discrimination, rather than the normal case-by-case redress for proven discrimination. Preferential treatment through quotas, goals, and so on is designed to correct imbalances based on the assumption that they always indicate discrimination. This expansion of what constitutes dis-crimination allowed affirmative action to escalate into the busi-ness of social engineering in the name of anti-discrimination, to push society toward statistically proportionate racial representa-tion, without any obligation of proving actual discrimination.

What accounted for this shift, I believe, was the white mandate 8 to achieve a new racial innocence and the black mandate to gain power. Even though blacks had made great advances during the sixties without quotas, these mandates, which came to a head in the very late sixties, could no longer be satisfied by anything less than racial preferences. I don't think these mandates in themselves were wrong, since whites clearly needed to do better by blacks and blacks needed more real power in society. But, as they came together in affirmative action, their effect was to distort our understanding of racial discrimination in a way that allowed us to offer the remediation of preference on the basis of mere color rather than actual injury. By making black the color of preference, these mandates have reburdened society with the very marriage of color and preference (in reverse) that we set out to eradicate. The old sin is reaffirmed in a new guise.

But the essential problem with this form of affirmative action 9 is the way it leaps over the hard business of developing a formerly oppressed people to the point where they can achieve proportionate representation on their own (given equal opportunity) and goes straight for the proportionate representation. This may satisfy some whites of their innocence and some blacks of their power, but it does very little to truly uplift blacks.

A white female affirmative action officer at an Ivy League uni- 10 versity told me what many supporters of affirmative action now say: "We're after diversity. We ideally want a student body where racial and ethnic groups are represented according to their proportion in society." When affirmative action escalated into social engineering, diversity became a golden word. It grants whites an egalitarian fairness (innocence) and blacks an entitlement to proportionate representation (power). *Diversity* is a term that applies democratic principles to races and cultures rather than to citizens, despite the fact that there is nothing to indicate that real diversity is the same thing as proportionate representation. Too often the result of this on campuses (for example) has been a democracy of colors rather than of people, an artificial diversity that gives the appearance of an educational parity between black and white students that has not yet been achieved in reality. Here again, racial preferences allow society to leapfrog over the difficult problem of developing blacks to parity with whites and into a cosmetic diversity that covers the blemish of disparity—a full six years after admission, only about 26 percent of black students graduate from college.

Racial representation is not the same thing as racial develop- 11 ment, yet affirmative action fosters a confusion of these very different needs. Representation can be manufactured; development is always hard-earned. However, it is the music of innocence and power that we hear in affirmative action that causes us to cling to it and to its distracting emphasis on representation. The fact is that after twenty years of racial preferences, the gap between white and black median income is greater than it was in the seventies. None of this is to say that blacks don't need policies that ensure our right to equal opportunity, but what we need more is the development that will let us take advantage of society's efforts to include us.

I think that one of the most troubling effects of racial prefer- 12
ences for blacks is a kind of demoralization, or put another way, an enlargement of self-doubt. Under affirmative action the quality that earns us preferential treatment is an implied inferiority. However this inferiority is explained—and it is easily enough explained by the myriad deprivations that grew out of our oppression—it is still inferiority. There are explanations, and then there is the fact. And the fact must be borne by the individual as a condition apart from the explanation, apart even from the fact that others like himself also bear this condition. In integrated situations where blacks must compete with whites who may be better prepared, these explanations may quickly wear thin and expose the individual to racial as well as personal self-doubt.

All of this is compounded by the cultural myth of black inferi- 13
ority that blacks have always lived with. What this means in practical terms is that when blacks deliver themselves into integrated situations, they encounter a nasty little reflex in whites, a mindless, atavistic reflex that responds to the color black with alarm. Attributions may follow this alarm if the white cares to indulge them, and if they do, they will most likely be negative—one such attribution is intellectual ineptness. I think this reflex and the attributions that may follow it embarrass most whites today; therefore, it is usually quickly repressed. Nevertheless, on an equally atavistic level, the black will be aware of the reflex his color triggers and will feel a stab of horror at seeing himself reflected in this way. He, too, will do a quick repression, but a lifetime of such stabbings is what constitutes his inner realm of racial doubt.

The effects of this may be a subject for another essay. The 14
point here is that the implication of inferiority that racial preferences engender in both the white and black mind expands rather than contracts this doubt. Even when the black sees no implication of inferiority in racial preferences, he knows that whites do, so that—consciously or unconsciously—the result is virtually the

same. The effect of preferential treatment—the lowering of normal standards to increase black representation—puts blacks at war with an expanded realm of debilitating doubt, so that the doubt itself becomes an unrecognized preoccupation that undermines their ability to perform, especially in integrated situations. On largely white campuses, blacks are five times more likely to drop out than whites. Preferential treatment, no matter how it is justified in the light of day, subjects blacks to a midnight of self-doubt and so often transforms their advantage into a revolving door.

metaphors 2

Another liability of affirmative action comes from the fact that   15
it indirectly encourages blacks to exploit their own past victimization as a source of power and privilege. Victimization, like implied inferiority, is what justifies preference, so that to receive the benefits of preferential treatment one must, to some extent, become invested in the view of one's self as a victim. In this way, affirmative action nurtures a victim-focused identity in blacks. The obvious irony here is that we become inadvertently invested in the very condition we are trying to overcome. Racial preferences send us the message that there is more power in our past suffering than our present achievements—none of which could bring us a *preference* over others.

When power itself grows out of suffering, then blacks are en-   16
couraged to expand the boundaries of what qualifies as racial oppression, a situation that can lead us to paint our victimization in vivid colors, even as we receive the benefits of preference. The same corporations and institutions that give us preference are also seen as our oppressors. At Stanford University minority students—some of whom enjoy as much as $15,000 a year in financial aid—recently took over the president's office demanding, among other things, more financial aid. The power to be found in victimization, like any power, is intoxicating and can lend itself to the creation of a new class of super-victims who can feel the pea of victimization under twenty mattresses. Preferential treatment rewards us for being underdogs rather than for moving beyond that status—a misplacement of incentives that, along with its deepening of our doubt, is more a yoke than a spur.

But, I think, one of the worst prices that blacks pay for prefer-   17
ence has to do with an illusion. I saw this illusion at work recently in the mother of a middle-class black student who was

going off to his first semester of college. "They owe us this, so don't think for a minute that you don't belong there." This is the logic by which many blacks, and some whites, justify affirmative action—it is something "owed," a form of reparation. But this logic overlooks a much harder and less digestible reality, that it is impossible to repay blacks living today for the historic suffering of the race. If all blacks were given a million dollars tomorrow morning it would not amount to a dime on the dollar of three centuries of oppression, nor would it obviate the residues of that oppression that we still carry today. The concept of historic reparation grows out of man's need to impose a degree of justice on the world that simply does not exist. Suffering can be endured and overcome; it cannot be repaid. Blacks cannot be repaid for the injustice done to the race, but we can be corrupted by society's guilty gestures of repayment.

Affirmative action is such a gesture. It tells us that racial preferences can do for us what we cannot do for ourselves. The corruption here is in the hidden incentive *not* to do what we believe preferences will do. This is an incentive to be reliant on others just as we are struggling for self-reliance. And it keeps alive the illusion that we can find some deliverance in repayment. The hardest thing for any sufferer to accept is that his suffering excuses him from very little and never has enough currency to restore him. To think otherwise is to prolong the suffering.   18

Several blacks I spoke with said they were still in favor of affirmative action because of the "subtle" discrimination blacks were subject to once on the job. One photojournalist said, "They have ways of ignoring you." A black female television producer said, "You can't file a lawsuit when your boss doesn't invite you to the insider meetings without ruining your career. So we still need affirmative action." Others mentioned the infamous "glass ceiling" through which blacks can see the top positions of authority but never reach them. But I don't think racial preferences are a protection against this subtle discrimination; I think they contribute to it.   19

In any workplace, racial preferences will always create two-tiered populations composed of preferreds and unpreferreds. This division makes automatic a perception of enhanced competence for the unpreferreds and of questionable competence for the pre-   20 ferreds—the former earned his way, even though others were given preference, while the latter made it by color as much as by competence. Racial preferences implicitly mark whites with an exaggerated superiority just as they mark blacks with an exaggerated inferiority. They not only reinforce America's oldest racial myth but, for blacks, they have the effect of stigmatizing the already stigmatized.

I think that much of the "subtle" discrimination that blacks 21 talk about is often (not always) discrimination against the stigma of questionable competence that affirmative action delivers to blacks. In this sense, preferences scapegoat the very people they seek to help. And it may be that at a certain level employers impose a glass ceiling, but this may not be against the race so much as against the race's reputation for having advanced by color as much as by competence. Affirmative action makes a glass ceiling virtually necessary as a protection against the corruptions of preferential treatment. This ceiling is the point at which corporations shift the emphasis from color to competency and stop playing the affirmative action game. Here preference backfires for blacks and becomes a taint that holds them back. Of course, one could argue that this taint, which is, after all, in the minds of whites, becomes nothing more than an excuse to discriminate against blacks. And certainly the result is the same in either case—blacks don't get past the glass ceiling. But this argument does not get around the fact that racial preferences now taint this color with a new theme of suspicion that makes it even more vulnerable to the impulse in others to discriminate. In this crucial yet gray area of perceived competence, preferences make whites look better than they are and blacks worse, while doing nothing whatever to stop the very real discrimination that blacks may encounter. I don't wish to justify the glass ceiling here, but only to suggest the very subtle ways that affirmative action revives rather than extinguishes the old rationalizations for racial discrimination.

In education, a revolving door; in employment, a glass ceiling. 22

I believe affirmative action is problematic in our society be- 23 cause it tries to function like a social program. Rather than ask it to ensure equal opportunity we have demanded that it create parity between the races. But preferential treatment does not teach skills, or educate, or instill motivation. It only passes out entitlement by color, a situation that in my profession has created an un-realistically high demand for black professors. The social engineer's assumption is that this high demand will inspire more blacks to earn Ph.D.'s and join the profession. In fact, the number of blacks earning Ph.D.'s has declined in recent years. A Ph.D. must be developed from preschool on. He requires family and community support. He must acquire an entire system of values that enables him to work hard while delaying gratification. There are social programs, I believe, that can (and should) help blacks *develop* in all these areas, but entitlement by color is not a social program; it is a dubious reward for being black.

It now seems clear that the Supreme Court, in a series of re-   24 cent decisions, is moving away from racial preferences. It has dis-allowed preferences except in instances of "identified discrimination," eroded the precedent that statistical racial imbal-ances are *prima facie* evidence of discrimination, and in effect granted white males the right to challenge consent decrees that use preference to achieve racial balances in the workplace. One civil rights leader said, "Night has fallen on civil rights." But I am not so sure. The effect of these decisions is to protect the consti-tutional rights of everyone rather than take rights away from blacks. What they do take away from blacks is the special entitle-ment to more rights than others that preferences always grant. Night has fallen on racial preferences, not on the fundamental rights of black Americans. The reason for this shift, I believe, is that the white mandate for absolution from past racial sins has weakened considerably during the eighties. Whites are now less willing to endure unfairness to themselves in order to grant spe-cial entitlements to blacks, even when these entitlements are justi-fied in the name of past suffering. Yet the black mandate for more power in society has remained unchanged. And I think part of the anxiety that many blacks feel over these decisions has to do with the loss of black power they may signal. We had won a cer-tain specialness and now we are losing it.

But the power we've lost by these decisions is really only the   25 power that grows out of our victimization—the power to claim special entitlements under the law because of past oppression. This is not a very substantial or reliable power, and it is important that we know this so we can focus more exclusively on the kind of development that will bring enduring power. There is talk now that Congress will pass new legislation to compensate for these new limits on affirmative action. If this happens, I hope that their focus will be on development and anti-discrimination rather than entitlement, on achieving racial parity rather than jerry-building racial diversity.

I would also like to see affirmative action go back to its original   26
purpose of enforcing equal opportunity—a purpose that in itself disallows racial preferences. We cannot be sure that the discriminatory impulse in America has yet been shamed into extinction, and I believe affirmative action can make its greatest contribution by providing a rigorous vigilance in this area. It can guard constitutional rather than racial rights and help institutions evolve standards of merit and selection that are appropriate to the institution's needs yet as free of racial bias as possible (again, with the understanding that racial imbalances are not always an indication of racial bias). One of the most important things affirmative action can do is to define exactly what racial discrimination is and how it might manifest itself within a specific institution. The impulse to discriminate *is* subtle and cannot be ferreted out unless its many guises are made clear to people. Along with this there should be monitoring of institutions and heavy sanctions brought to bear when actual discrimination is found. This is the sort of affirmative action that America owes to blacks and to itself. It goes after the evil of discrimination itself, while preferences only sidestep the evil and grant entitlement to its *presumed* victims.

But if not preferences, then what? I think we need social poli-   27
cies that are committed to two goals: the educational and economic development of disadvantaged people, regardless of race, and the eradication from our society—through close monitoring and severe sanctions—of racial, ethnic, or gender discrimination. Preferences will not deliver us to either of these goals, since they tend to benefit those who are not disadvantaged—middle-class white women and middle-class blacks—and attack one form of discrimination with another. Preferences are inexpensive and carry the glamour of good intentions—change the numbers and the good deed is done. To be against them is to be unkind. But I think the unkindest cut is to bestow on children like my own an undeserved advantage while neglecting the development of those

disadvantaged children on the East Side of my city who will likely never be in a position to benefit from a preference. Give my children fairness; give disadvantaged children a better shot at development—better elementary and secondary schools, job training, safer neighborhoods, better financial assistance for college, and so on. Fewer blacks go to college today than ten years ago; more black males of college age are in prison or under the control of the criminal justice system than in college. This despite racial preferences.

The mandates of black power and white absolution out of   28
which preferences emerged were not wrong in themselves. What was wrong was that both races focused more on the goals of these mandates than on the means to the goals. Blacks can have no real power without taking responsibility for their own educational and economic development. Whites can have no racial innocence without earning it by eradicating discrimination and helping the disadvantaged to develop. Because we ignored the means, the goals have not been reached, and the real work remains to be done.

UNDERSTANDING DETAILS

1. Why does specifying his children's race on their college applications present a problem for Steele?
2. According to Steele, what is fair about affirmative action?
3. Why does Steele think affirmative action is "more bad than good" (paragraph 4)?
4. According to Steele, what are the principal negative consequences of affirmative action? Explain each in your own words.

ANALYZING MEANING

1. What does Steele mean when he says, "*Diversity* is a term that applies democratic principles to races and cultures rather than to citizens" (paragraph 10)?
2. In Steele's opinion, what is the difference between "racial representation" and "racial development" (paragraph 11)? Why is affirmative action not closing this gap?
3. How do racial preferences "mark whites with an exaggerated superiority just as they mark blacks with an exaggerated inferi-

ority" (paragraph 20)? What is the relationship in Steele's mind between the "implied inferiority" of affirmative action and "personal self-doubt" (paragraph 12) in the African-American community?

4. Steele argues that preferential treatment based on race perpetuates the revolving door in education and the glass ceiling in employment? Give examples from your own experience to support or refute this claim.

DISCOVERING RHETORICAL STRATEGIES

1. In paragraph 22, Steele uses the metaphors of "a revolving door" and "a glass ceiling" to help illustrate the problems of preferential treatment. Explain these two images in as much detail as you can. How effective are they in making Steele's points?

2. What is the dominant type of appeal (see pages 504–506 of the chapter introduction) that Steele uses in this essay? What parts of Steele's argument are most persuasive to you? Why do you think they are persuasive?

3. Who do you think is Steele's intended audience? Describe them in detail.

4. Which different rhetorical strategies does Steele use to develop his argument? Give examples of each.

MAKING CONNECTIONS

1. Both Steele and Harry Edwards ("Triple Tragedy in Black Society") argue that African Americans should take more responsibility in solving problems within their culture, though Edwards seems to lay more blame on white prejudice than Steele does. Examine each essay for indications of how the authors feel about this issue. To what extent do you feel that problems within African-American society are caused by white racism?

2. Discuss the relative balance of the logical, emotional, and ethical appeals in the essays by Steele, Goodman ("Putting In a Good Word for Guilt"), and/or Peter Salins ("Take a Ticket"). Which author uses logic most? Who relies most heavily on emotion? And whose ethical appeal is the strongest? What do

the dominance of these appeals have to do with the subject matter of each essay?

3. In his essay, Steele refers to affirmative action as "social engineering." Explain what you feel the author means by this phrase, and then locate and examine the same concept in essays by Donald Drakeman ("Religion's Place in Public Schools"), Robert Hughes ("The N.R.A. in a Hunter's Sights"), and/or Rita Mae Brown ("Writing as a Moral Act").

IDEAS FOR DISCUSSION/WRITING

Preparing to Write

Write freely about your thoughts on affirmative action: In what areas does affirmative action work most effectively? In what areas does it work less well? What are the main social consequences of affirmative action? Are you directly affected by affirmative action in any way? Have you witnessed or experienced any discrimination in hiring? What solutions do you propose to solve the problem of discrimination in the job market? How might these solutions be implemented?

Choosing a Topic

1. In paragraph 16 of this essay, Steele claims, "Preferential treatment rewards us for being underdogs rather than for moving beyond that status." Direct an essay to your classmates in which you agree or disagree with this statement. Be sure to explain your reasoning carefully.

2. In your opinion, how serious is racial or sexual discrimination at your school or at your job? How is it manifested? Who suffers most from this discrimination? In a coherent essay, persuade your friends that discrimination is or is not a serious social evil at your school or your workplace.

3. In an essay written for a group of employers, present a proposal other than affirmative action for controlling discrimination in the workplace. Explain the details of its implementation and its projected long-term effects.

ROBERT HUGHES   (1938 –   )

■ ■ ■

The N.R.A. in a Hunter's Sights

Born and educated in Sydney, Australia, Robert Hughes refers to himself as "a journalist who has had the good luck never to be bored by his subject." He has been *Time* magazine's art critic for over twenty years, and he has published such books as *Recent Australian Paintings* (1961), *The Art of Australia* (1966), *The New Generation* (1966), and *Heaven and Hell in Western Art* (1968). His best-known book, *The Shock of the New* (1980), was adapted from his eight-hour PBS television series of the same title. In his preface, he explains that "Art no longer acts on us in the same way that it did on our grandparents. I want to see why." The resulting examination of modern art and its effects on its audience has won much praise from art scholars, who variously described it as "brilliant," "provocative," "brash," "electric," and "elegant." According to *Saturday Review* critic John Canaday, it is "the best book to date on twentieth-century art." In 1987, Hughes published *The Fatal Shore*, a long and fascinating history of the dramatic origins of his native country. This international bestseller, which won several prestigious literary awards for nonfiction, is being made into a movie. Hughes has also written more than twenty television documentaries for Australian television and the BBC, including two seventy-five-minute programs on the artists Caravaggio and Rubens, plus recent books entitled *Nothing If Not Critical* (1990), *Barcelona* (1992), and *Culture of Complaint* (1993).

Preparing to Read

The following essay, which first appeared in *Time* (April 3, 1989), examines America's constitutional "right" to bear arms and argues strenuously for the licensing of firearms. As you prepare to read Hughes's thoughts on this controversial topic, focus your attention on the subject: Where do you stand on the issue of gun control? Do you favor minimal government control, total control, or a compromise between these positions? How did you arrive at this opinion? What arguments best support your views? Do you own a gun? Does anyone in your family? To what extent does this ownership (or lack of ownership) affect your views? Has your opinion on gun control changed over the years? In what ways? What caused the change?

L ike George Bush and thousands of other people, I am a 1 Small White Hunter. Which means that, two or three times a year, one scrambles into one's brush pants and jacket, pulls on a pair of snake boots and goes ambling off on a sedate horse with friends and dogs in pursuit of quail in a pine forest in southern Georgia. Or spends cold predawn hours in a punt on Long Island Sound, or a damp blind on a California marsh, waiting for the gray light to spread and the ducks to come arrowing in.

I have done this at intervals most of my life, ever since I was 2 eleven years old in Australia and my father first issued me a single-shot .22 and two bullets and told me to bring back one rabbit. I hope to keep doing it as long as I can walk and see.

I don't shoot deer anymore; the idea of large-game trophy hunt- 3 ing repels me. But I have never thought there was anything wrong with killing as much small game in one day as I and a few friends could eat in the evening—no more than that and always within the limits. On a good day I can break 24 targets out of 25 at trapshooting, and 22 or so at skeet, which is O.K. for an art critic.

In short, I am supposed—if you believe the advertisements of 4 the National Rifle Association—to be exactly the kind of person whose rights the N.R.A. claims to want to protect. Why, then, have I never joined the N.R.A.? And why do I think of this once omnipotent though now embattled lobby as the sportsman's embarrassment and not his ally?

The answer, in part, goes back to the famous Second 5 Amendment of the American Constitution, which the N.R.A. keeps brandishing like Holy Writ. "A well-regulated militia, being necessary to the security of a free State," it reads, "the right of the people to keep and bear arms shall not be infringed."

The part the N.R.A. quotes is always the second half. The first 6 half is less convenient because it undermines the lobby's propaganda for universal weaponry.

The Founding Fathers, in their wisdom—and more pointedly, 7
their experience—distrusted standing armies. They associated
British ones with tyranny and lacked the money and manpower
to create their own. Without a citizens' militia, the Revolution
would have failed. Does the Constitution let you have the second
half of the Second Amendment, the right to keep and bear arms,
without the first part, the intended use of those arms in the exercises and, when necessary, the campaigns of a citizens' militia to
which the gun owner belongs—as in Switzerland today? That is
still very much a subject for legal debate.

The constitutional framers no more had in mind the socially 8
psychotic prospect of every Tom, Dick, and Harriet with a barn-
ful of MAC-10s, Saturday night specials, and AK-47s than, in
writing the First Amendment, they had in mind the protection of
child-porn video, which did not exist in the 18th century either.
Nowhere does the Constitution say the right to bear arms means
the right to bear any or all arms. *Which* arms is the real issue. At
present, firepower has outstripped the law's power to contain it
within rational limits.

Where the N.R.A. has always revealed its nature as a paranoid 9
lobby, a political anachronism, is in its rigid ideological belief that
any restriction on the private ownership of *any* kind of hand-held
gun leads inexorably to *total* abolition of *all* gun ownership—that,
if today the U.S. Government takes the Kalashnikov from the
hands of the maniac on the school playground, it will be coming
for my Winchester pump tomorrow. There is no evidence for this
absurd belief, but it remains an article of faith. And it does so because the faith is bad faith: the stand the N.R.A. takes is only
nominally on behalf of recreational hunters. The people it really
serves are gun manufacturers and gun importers, whose sole interest is to sell as many deadly weapons of as many kinds to as many
Americans as possible. The N.R.A. never saw a weapon it didn't
love. When American police officers raised their voices against the
sale of "cop-killer" bullets—Teflon-coated projectiles whose sole
purpose is to penetrate body armor—the N.R.A. mounted a
campaign to make people believe this ban would infringe on the
rights of deer hunters, as though the woods of America were full
of whitetails in Kevlar vests. Now that the pressure is on to restrict
public ownership of semiautomatic assault weapons, we hear the

same threadbare rhetoric about the rights of hunters. No serious hunter goes after deer with an Uzi or an AK-47; those weapons are not made for picking off an animal in the woods but for blowing people to chopped meat at close-to-medium range, and anyone who needs a banana clip with 30 shells in it to hit a buck should not be hunting at all. These guns have only two uses: you can take them down to the local range and spend a lot of money blasting off 500 rounds an afternoon at silhouette targets of the Ayatollah, or you can use them to off your rivals and create lots of police widows. It depends on what kind of guy you are. But the N.R.A. doesn't care—underneath its dumb incantatory slogans ("Guns don't kill people; people kill people"), it is defending both guys. It helps ensure that cops are outgunned right across America. It preaches hunters' rights in order to defend the distribution of weapons in what is, in effect, a drug-based civil war.

But we who love hunting have much more to fear from the   10
backlash of public opinion caused by the N.R.A.'s pigheadedness than we do from the Government. Sensible hunters see the need to follow the example of other civilized countries. All fireable guns should be licensed; delays and stringent checks should be built into their purchase, right across the board; and some types, including machine guns and semiautomatic assault weapons, should not be available to the civilian public at all. It is time, in this respect, that America enter the 20th century, since it is only a few years away from the 21st.

UNDERSTANDING DETAILS

1. Characterize in your own words the author's attitude toward the use of firearms.
2. What does Hughes see as the real issue involved in the interpretation of the Second Amendment to the Constitution?
3. Why does Hughes find the N.R.A. an embarrassment to gun enthusiasts?
4. What is Hughes's recommended compromise concerning gun legislation?

ANALYZING MEANING

1. Why does Hughes call the N.R.A. "paranoid" (paragraph 9)? Do you agree or disagree with him?

2. In what ways does the N.R.A. serve the interests of gun manufacturers and importers?
3. According to the author, how does the N.R.A. misuse the Second Amendment of the U.S. Constitution? Do you agree with Hughes's analysis of this section of the Constitution?
4. Why does Hughes refer to the N.R.A.'s statement "Guns don't kill people; people kill people" as a "dumb incantatory slogan" (paragraph 9)? Do you agree with this statement? Why or why not?

DISCOVERING RHETORICAL STRATEGIES

1. Explain the title of this essay. What exactly is the author referring to?
2. Is the author's reasoning primarily inductive or deductive? Give one example from the essay to support your answer. Why do you think Hughes relies so heavily on an appeal to logic in this essay?
3. The author occasionally uses emotional and ethical appeals to support his logical argument. When does he invoke our emotions in this essay? Our sense of ethics?
4. What other rhetorical strategies does Hughes use to further his argument? Give examples of each.

MAKING CONNECTIONS

1. Compare and contrast the extent to which Hughes and Shelby Steele ("Affirmative Action: The Price of Preference") strive to establish an ethical appeal (or an appeal to their own reputations) in each of their essays. How does each author set up his appeal? How important is this appeal to the argument that each author pursues?
2. Both Hughes and Donald Drakeman ("Religion's Place in Public Schools") refer to the law in their essays. Which author relies most heavily on legal reasoning in his argument? Why do you think this is so?
3. In addition to Hughes, the following authors discuss guns and violence in their essays: George Orwell ("Shooting an Elephant"), Bruce Catton ("Grant and Lee: A Study in Contrasts"), Nancy Gibbs ("When Is It Rape?"), and Alice

Walker ("Beauty: When the Other Dancer Is the Self"). If all these authors were involved in a roundtable discussion on violence in our society, which ones would probably be in favor of some form of gun control? Examine the essays and locate the clues that helped you arrive at your opinion.

IDEAS FOR DISCUSSION/WRITING

Preparing to Write

Write freely about your views on gun control: What are the main issues involved in the question of gun control? Where do you stand on these issues? What role does the Constitution play in your reasoning? Do you think different rules should apply to different types of guns, such as handguns, machine guns, and semi-automatic weapons? Do you own a gun? Should everyone be allowed to own and carry a gun for self-defense? Do you know people who own guns? What are their opinions on gun control? Should there be any limits on gun ownership?

Choosing a Topic

1. Your local newspaper is soliciting community opinions on gun control. The editors of the paper want to know your stand on the issue and the reasons behind your position. In a well-organized essay, explain your thoughts on this controversial issue.
2. In a letter to the editor of your local newspaper, play the opposing side, and take issue with one of the points you made in your response to topic 1.
3. In the last paragraph of his essay, Hughes proposes a compromise plan on the issue of gun control. What do you think of this solution? Respond to Hughes's ideas in an essay written for the readers of *Time* magazine. Be sure to address all three parts of Hughes's proposal.

PETER SALINS   (1938 –   )

■ ■ ■

Take a Ticket

Peter Salins is currently Director of the Graduate Program in Urban Planning at Hunter College in New York and a senior fellow at the Manhattan Institute for Public Policy, a conservative "think tank" in New York City. The educational experience that prepared him for these prestigious positions was varied and eclectic: a B.A. in architecture, an M.A. in regional planning, and a Ph.D. in social science and planning, all of which were earned at Syracuse University. This combined background in architecture and social science gave him an "architectural sensitivity" that informs his writing and helps him move "in an orderly way from one space to another" in his essays. "The written word," he advises students using *The Prose Reader*, "should work together with other words like the foundation, frame, mortar, and bricks of a building. Essays should solve intellectual problems in the same way that buildings solve architectural ones." In addition, students should "make certain their essays have a central argument." They should "keep their writing simple and to the point and try to develop their concepts in interesting ways." Among Salins's many publications are *The Ecology of Housing Destruction* (1980), *Housing America's Poor* (1987), *New York Unbound* (1988), and *Scarcity by Design* (1992).

Preparing to Read

The following essay, originally published in the *New Republic* on December 27, 1993, contains a well-researched, carefully reasoned analysis of the current immigration situation in America. Before you read this essay, think about your views on immigration: Are you pleased with the past U.S. immigration policies? What changes would you make in these practices? What other ideas do you have about immigration? Do you think families should be reunited through immigration? What general limitations or restrictions should be put on immigration to the

United States? What are your greatest fears about immigration? Your greatest hopes for immigration?

---∎

The trouble with the immigration debate of the past year 1 or so is that much of it is simply unreal. Intellectuals have been arguing over abstractions, while the insecurities of ordinary Americans have been inflamed by prejudice and misinformation. Those both for and against immigration behave as if it were politically conceivable that the United States might drastically cut immigration again, as we did in the 1920s, and as if our borders could be effectively sealed if we chose to do so. In spite of resurgent nativism, any proposal to sharply curtail legal immigration would meet massive resistance across the political spectrum—from liberals who see open immigration as a basic ingredient of the universalist American idea to conservatives attached to free markets and open international borders. If it came to a vote in Congress, a bipartisan proimmigration alliance would emerge even stronger than the one behind NAFTA [North American Free Trade Agreement], using the same arguments (the long-term economic benefits of immigration outweighing its short-term stresses, the politics of fear versus the politics of hope, etc.). Buttressing the argument would be our proven inability to stem illegal immigration, because any reduction in the quota of legal immigrants almost certainly would be offset by an increase in illegal immigration—an unsettling prospect for most Americans, but especially for the nativists.

So rather than contesting the volume of immigrants, we might 2 re-examine how we actually allocate immigration in a world where the number of potential immigrants vastly exceeds the most generous quota we could tolerate, and how we treat immigrants once they get here. But first, a few facts to reassure ourselves about the benign nature of immigration. To begin with, America is not being inundated with immigrants. While the volume has risen steadily since the national origins quota system was scrapped in 1965, the rate of immigration relative to the nation's base population is far below historic levels. Due in large part to the amnesty of 1.5 million illegal aliens as part of the Immigration Reform and Control Act of 1986 (Simpson-

Rodino), the average rate of legal immigration in the 1981 to 1990 period reached a post-Depression high of 3.1 percent per 1,000 U.S. residents. This rate is below that of every decade from 1830 to 1930, and is about the same as the long-term immigration rate since American independence. Moreover, the percentage of foreign-born in the U.S. population has fallen from 8.8 percent in 1940 to 6.8 percent today.

As important as the volume of immigration is its geography. Most immigrants remain near America's gateways at the perimeter of the country. The greatest number, nearly 40 percent of the total since 1987, live in Southern California, with other large cohorts in New York City, south Florida, Texas and Chicago. Most of the rest can be found in a handful of urban areas on the east and west coasts. Most Americans do not live near immigrants. This suggests either that the new nativism is confined to the peripheral immigrant bastions or that some nativists don't need to meet immigrants to dislike them. 3

Another critical fact: immigrants have been moving to—and staying in—America's cities, filling a vacuum left by native urban households that have been fleeing to the suburbs for more than forty years. Until a new surge of immigration into New York in the 1980s, the city had been losing population—nearly a million from 1970 to 1980. Since 1980 New York is the only city east of the Mississippi to gain population. Wherever they have settled, immigrants have reclaimed inner-city neighborhoods that had fallen into a state of advanced decay. True, poor blacks and other native minorities moved to these zones of white abandonment first, but at unviably low densities, and with households whose poverty and pathology only exacerbated their devastation. 4

In spite of their growing presence in American cities, immigrants have not displaced the native minority poor in the labor force. Hypothetically, the low-wage, low-skill work done by the least skilled immigrants in these ethnic enclaves might otherwise have employed native blacks or Puerto Ricans. But most of these jobs didn't exist before the immigrants came, and most native workers would have spurned them even if they had. As a matter of fact, recent studies show that the unemployment rates of blacks living in or near immigrant enclaves actually fell, following the immigrant influx. Immigrant labor also does not appreciably lower 5 native workers' wages very much. A study by LaLonde and Topel estimates that when immigrant participation in a local labor market doubles, the wages of young blacks in general may fall by 4 percent or less, and those of other minorities are unaffected.

How about the indirect economic impact of immigration, on 6 state and local government budgets, that California's Governor Pete Wilson is so concerned about? All these immigrant children require an education and, at $5,000 per child—thousands more than their parents' local tax contribution—they have filled up the inner-city schools. Here, too, the burden looks greater in the abstract than in reality. Frankly, these inner-city school systems—in New York, Chicago, Miami and L.A.—were dying before the immigrants came. With declining populations, the districts still absorbed a large amount of public funds, without much to show for them. Just as with the cities' dying neighborhoods, the immigrants rescued the schools, not only from bankruptcy, but also irrelevance.

What about that most frightening of the nightmare scenarios 7 promoted by the immigration alarmists: that America will become—God help us—a *nonwhite nation*. Of course, the proper response to this hobgoblin should be: So what? But even those who secretly harbor misgivings about a radical change in the country's racial profile can relax, because the vanishing white majority scare is vastly overblown. The two largest immigrant groups are Hispanic and Asian. Now, Hispanic is not a racial category at all; it's a linguistic one. Even the newer label for this group—Latino—is not racial, it's geographic. Whatever the label, the Latino cohort is very racially mixed, from as white as any Northern European to darker than most native blacks. The vast majority, however, including most Mexicans, have a mixed racial background, and—not that it matters—don't look very different from Americans of Southern European descent, and classify themselves as white in surveys. The same is increasingly the case for Asians.

The truth is, the immigration scare does not reflect a genuine 8 problem, it reflects a genuine panic. The panic is brought on by economic dislocation, which is all too easily laid at the door of immigrants. That is not to say there should not be an immigration debate. On the contrary, it is long overdue. The debate should be not about how many, but rather who, and how, they should be let into the country. Categorical preferences built into the current immigration policy exacerbate both the geographic and ethnic concentration of immigrants, adding to the burden of their assimilation, and pouring fuel on the nativist fires. It's time it was overhauled.

The liberalization of immigration legislated in 1965 was supposed to end the Northern European bias of the nativist-inspired national origins quota system of 1925. The reforms certainly succeeded in that respect, redirecting immigration from Northern Europe to Latin America and Asia. But, at the same time, the preference categories of the current law have perpetuated the root bias of a national origins system, only with a new set of favored nationalities. The largest preference categories under present immigration policy promote "family reunification." This means that once a nationality gains a significant demographic foothold in the United States, it has a vested claim on the immigration quota roughly in proportion to its share of the foreign-born population: exactly the concept that animated the old national origins system. Indeed, the family preferences were written into the 1965 law primarily to reassure the nativists that the national origins idea was not being scrapped entirely. Since the new law's inception, around 70 percent of all legal immigrants have been admitted under one or another family reunification preference category. And with the amnesty provision of the Simpson-Rodino law, the preference has been effectively extended to millions of illegal immigrants as well.

The primary beneficiaries of immigration's family reunification tilt have been Mexicans. Since 1981 more than 30 percent of all legal immigrants to the United States have come from Mexico. The fact that Mexicans account for only 18 percent of all legal immigration since 1965 proves that the national origins bias of family reunification increases over time. Family preferences have also insured that what remains of the pool of legal entrants is dominated by other Latin Americans and Asians from just a few countries: the Philippines, China, Korea and India. The Simpson-Rodino amnesty of 2.5 million illegals, the vast majority of them Mexicans, has further intensified the nationality biases of family reunification, and has been a major factor in provoking a nativist backlash.

The question we failed to ask in these matters is: Why family? The truth is, the family preference violates the underlying rationale of immigration. The United States has historically welcomed immigrants, to a much greater extent than any other modern society, for a number of reasons. Cynics say it did so because some of its most powerful industries needed cheap labor. Sure, but this need could have been filled by merely admitting "guest workers" as the Europeans do. There has been a deeply idealistic aspect to most Americans' acceptance of immigrants. Americans believe in starting over and giving people with ambition and determination, at home and abroad, the opportunity to do so. Americans also realize, intuitively, that immigrants have the ability to recharge the national batteries, supplying new skills, new perspectives, new cultural attributes, that can make the country a more successful and cosmopolitan nation. It was because the national origins immigration quotas violated these basic precepts that the old system was scrapped in 1965. Well, the current system is coming to violate them even more, with nationality biases greater than those of the old system, and mostly because of the family bias.

The other favored set of foreigners are those admitted under 12 refugee and asylum preferences, who account for 15 percent of all immigrants during the last decade. Refugee and asylum preferences have a solid justification, given all the repressive regimes in the world, but they have been seriously compromised by our foreign policy biases. When both Nicaragua and El Salvador were in turmoil during the 1980s, Nicaraguans fleeing a Communist dictatorship were accepted as refugees, while Salvadorans fleeing right-wing death squads were not. Likewise, Cubans were admitted as refugees from the time Castro took power, while no dictator is bloody enough for Haitians to be welcomed. And since most Third World autocracies are also poor, every refugee/asylum case involves a judgment call as to whether its motivation is economic or political.

So there are good reasons to change the preference system. 13 How to do it? There are some who would replace the family-based preferences with ones favoring high levels of skill or education, like Canada does. But such a "designer immigration" bias is not only unfair—vesting the privilege of American immigration in precisely those who have been the most privileged in their native lands—it is not even especially helpful to the economy. Our real labor needs—notwithstanding popular perceptions and high unemployment rates among unskilled natives—are at the bottom of the labor market, mainly in services. And the labor market's demand for skilled professionals is amply met by the large number of foreign students who stay and work here after their graduation and by immigrants admitted on other than skill preferences.

Why not, instead of unfair family rules and unnecessary skills 14 rules, adopt a policy that effectively makes admission to the United States a matter of "first-come, first-served." Of the roughly 700,000 legal (nonamnesty) immigration slots we make available in a typical year, perhaps 150,000 could be reserved for the spouses or minor children of U.S. residents—a much reduced preference for the reunification of nuclear families, and perhaps 75,000 could be set aside for refugees. The other 475,000 could be available for applicants from any nation on earth. How might such a system work? Subject to an annual global cap, applications for immigration would be reviewed and approved in the order they were received at designated centers in each country. To avoid having the immigrant pool swamped by applicants from the most populous countries (with 40 percent of the world's population, China and India might dominate such a system) perhaps no country's annual quota should exceed some percentage of the total. However it were fleshed out, the objective of such a first-come, first-served concept would be to offer immigration to the most highly motivated candidates, from a maximally diverse set of backgrounds, selected by the fairest and most objective of procedures.

The United States has not made a mistake by admitting mil- 15 lions of immigrants since the law was changed in 1965. Indeed, America's liberal immigration policy is one of our proudest public accomplishments. But America's liberal immigration policy is more likely to find continued acceptance among most Americans and keep the nativists at bay if the immigration preference system is changed to assure a fairer and more nationally diverse pool of immigrants. So let's not turn our backs on one of the most successful American ideas. Let's get it right.

UNDERSTANDING DETAILS

1. What is the focus of this essay? Where does Salins state this focus?

2. What approach does Salins think the United States should take toward immigration?
3. What do the nativists fear about unchecked immigration?
4. What does Salins mean by "the politics of fear" and "the politics of hope" (paragraph 1)? In what ways are they opposed to one another?

ANALYZING MEANING

1. Explain the distinction that Salins makes between the "abstract" and the "real."
2. Why do most Americans believe in and continue to support the concept of immigration? How does immigration reflect their own beginnings in the United States?
3. Do you see the family reunification issue as a problem within the larger issue of immigration? Explain your answer in detail.
4. Why is an increase in illegal immigration "an unsettling prospect for most Americans" (paragraph 1)? Why does Salins add "but especially for the nativists" (paragraph 1)?

DISCOVERING RHETORICAL STRATEGIES

1. Why do you think Salins begins his essay with statistics about the rate of immigration? Is this an effective start? Explain your answer.
2. Salins explains in paragraph 2 that he is going to present some facts to prove "the benign nature of immigration." How does he group these facts? In what order does he present his categories? Are you convinced by his discussion? Explain your answer.
3. Who do you think is Salins's intended audience? On what do you base this conclusion?
4. Describe the tone of this essay? Is it well chosen for its audience? Explain your answer.

MAKING CONNECTIONS

1. Both Salins and Richard Rodriguez ("The Fear of Losing a Culture") argue for the concept of immigration, though each gives different reasons for his opinion. Compare and contrast why the two authors believe so strongly in the privilege of immigration to America.

2. What kind of balance does Salins achieve in his essay between logical, emotional, and ethical appeals? Contrast this balance with that reached by Robert Hughes in "The N.R.A. in a Hunter's Sights." Which author relies more on logic? Who uses emotion more? And whose essay has the strongest ethical appeal? What is the relationship between the balance of appeals in each essay and the author's topic?

3. Imagine that Ellen Goodman ("Putting In a Good Word for Guilt") has just read Salins's article. Argue, as if you were speaking for Goodman, that the United States ought to feel guilty about its present stand on immigration. Then, propose a compromise solution that not only would address all the problems mentioned by Salins but would also constructively use our current national guilt over the situation.

IDEAS FOR DISCUSSION/WRITING

Preparing to Write

Write freely about your feelings on immigration in general: Is immigration a positive or negative force? When is it positive? When is it negative? What causes immigration to be positive or negative? What are your views on immigration to the United States? Why is it such a controversial topic at this point in American history? What can the United States do to solve its immigration problems? Does a solution seem likely to you?

Choosing a Topic

1. As a movie reviewer, you have been commissioned to evaluate a movie that deals with immigration in some way. What is the movie saying about immigration? In what ways does this message represent the opinions of American society as a whole?

2. In an essay written for *Time* magazine, you have been asked to respond directly to Salins's article. Do you think Salins's approach to immigration is reasonable? Give specific examples to support your argument.

3. Research and describe the immigration practices of another country. Explain how the country's views on immigration are carried out in specific practice. Give as many examples as possible to support your explanation.

OPPOSING VIEWPOINTS

■ ■ ■

TV Violence

The next two essays debate the benefits and liabilities of television in our current society. The first essay, by Carl Cannon, argues that study after study shows that televised sex and violence have done irreparable harm to the American psyche over the years, particularly to our children, who have absorbed an immense amount of cartoon violence during their formative years. Cannon is a native San Franciscan who earned a B.A. in journalism from the University of Colorado and since then has worked at several different newspapers, including the *San Diego Union*, the *San Jose Mercury News*, and the *Baltimore Sun*, where he is currently on the editorial staff. Over the years, he has won a number of prestigious awards, including a Pulitzer Prize, which he shared with the staff of the *Mercury News* for its reporting on the Loma Prieta earthquake (1989) and a Bernard Nover Prize for his investigation into child molestation by members of the clergy (1988). Cannon advises students using *The Prose Reader,* "There's no substitute for knowing what you're writing about. You can't write well unless you have something to say, and you won't have something to say unless you have thoroughly researched your topic." In his spare time, Cannon enjoys fishing for trout and playing baseball in an over-thirty league.

John Leonard argues that most of the shows on TV are pretty dull after all and that TV's negative effect on viewers has been grossly exaggerated by a number of so-called scientific studies that are ultimately inconclusive. Leonard attended Harvard University from 1956 to 1958 and then received his B.A. degree from the University of California at Berkeley in 1962. Later, he worked in various capacities for the *New York Times, Esquire Magazine, Life, Newsweek*, and *Vanity Fair* before moving to CBS, where he is currently media critic for the *News Sunday Morning* program. His six books include *The Naked Martini* (1964), *Cry Baby of the Western World* (1969), *Black Conceit* (1973), and a collection of essays entitled *The Last Innocent White Man in America* (1993).

Preparing to Read

Both of the following articles were first published in the May–June 1994 issue of the *Utne Reader*. Before you begin to read these essays, think about TV violence and its consequences in American society: How would you define TV violence? Are there any advantages to watching violence on TV? What are the disadvantages of watching violence on TV? Does your opinion about TV violence vary depending on the age of the viewer? What is your personal opinion of TV violence? What do you think are the social consequences of TV violence? Do you think TV affects people's behavior in any way? How might we control these consequences?

CARL CANNON (1955 –   )

■ ■ ■

Honey, I Warped the Kids

T im Robbins and Susan Sarandon implore the nation to   1
treat Haitians with AIDS more humanely. Robert
Redford works for the environment. Harry Belafonte
marches against the death penalty. Actors and producers seem to
be constantly speaking out for noble causes far removed from
their lives. But in the one area over which they have control—the
excessive violence in the entertainment industry—Hollywood
activists remain silent.

The first congressional hearings on the effects of TV violence   2
took place in 1954. Although television was still relatively new, its
extraordinary marketing power was already evident. The tube was
teaching Americans what to buy and how to act, not only in advertisements, but in dramatic shows, too.

Everybody from Hollywood producers to Madison Avenue ad   3
men would boast about this power—and seek to use it on dual
tracks: to make money and to remake society along better lines.

Because it seemed ludicrous to assert that there was only one   4
area—the depiction of violence—where television did not influence behavior, the TV industry came up with this theory: Watching
violence is cathartic. A violent person might be sated by watching a
murder.

The notion intrigued social scientists, and by 1956 they were   5
studying it in earnest. Unfortunately, watching violence turned
out to be anything but cathartic.

In the 1956 study, one dozen 4-year-olds watched a "Woody   6
Woodpecker" cartoon that was full of violent images. Twelve other
preschoolers watched "Little Red Hen," a peaceful cartoon.
Afterward, the children who watched "Woody Woodpecker" were
more likely to hit other children, verbally accost their classmates,
break toys, be disruptive, and engage in destructive behavior during
free play.

For the next 30 years, researchers in all walks of the social sci- 7
ences studied the question of whether television causes violence.
The results have been stunningly conclusive.

"There is more published research on this topic than on al- 8
most any other social issue of our time," University of Kansas
Professor Aletha C. Huston, chair of the American Psychological
Association's Task Force on Television and Society, told Congress
in 1988. "Virtually all independent scholars agree that there is evidence that television can cause aggressive behavior."

There have been some 3,000 studies of this issue—85 of them 9
major research efforts—and they all say the same thing. Of the 85
major studies, the only one that failed to find a causal relationship
between TV violence and actual violence was paid for by NBC.
When the study was subsequently reviewed by three independent
social scientists, all three concluded that it actually did demonstrate a causal relationship.

Some highlights from the history of TV violence research: 10

• In 1973, when a town in mountainous western Canada was 11
wired for TV signals, University of British Columbia researchers
observed first- and second-graders. Within two years, the incidence of hitting, biting, and shoving increased 160 percent.

• Two Chicago doctors, Leonard Eron and Rowell 12
Heusmann, followed the viewing habits of a group of children
for 22 years. They found that watching violence on television is
the single best predictor of violent or aggressive behavior later in
life, ahead of such commonly accepted factors as parents' behavior, poverty, and race.

"Television violence affects youngsters of all ages, of both gen- 13
ders, at all socioeconomic levels and all levels of intelligence," they
told Congress in 1992. "The effect is not limited to children who
are already disposed to being aggressive and is not restricted to
this country."

• In 1988, researchers Daniel G. Linz and Edward Donnerstein 14
of the University of California, Santa Barbara, and Steven Penrod
of the University of Wisconsin studied the effects on young men
of horror movies and "slasher" films.

They found that depictions of violence, not sex, are what de- 15
sensitizes people. They divided male students into four groups.
One group watched no movies, a second watched nonviolent X-

rated movies, a third watched teenage sexual-innuendo movies, and a fourth watched the slasher films *Texas Chainsaw Massacre, Friday the 13th, Part 2, Maniac,* and *Toolbox Murders.*

All the young men were placed on a mock jury panel and 16 asked a series of questions designed to measure their empathy for an alleged female rape victim. Those in the fourth group measured lowest in empathy for the specific victim in the experiment—and for rape victims in general.

The anecdotal evidence is often more compelling than the sci- 17 entific studies. Ask any homicide cop from London to Los Angeles to Bangkok if TV violence induces real-life violence and listen carefully to the cynical, knowing laugh.

Ask David McCarthy, police chief in Greenfield, Massa- 18 chusetts, why 19-year-old Mark Branch killed himself after stabbing an 18-year-old female college student to death. When cops searched his room they found 90 horror movies, as well as a machete and a goalie mask like those used by Jason, the grisly star of *Friday the 13th.*

Or ask Sergeant John O'Malley of the New York Police 19 Department about a 9-year-old boy who sprayed a Bronx office building with gunfire. The boy explained to the astonished sergeant how he learned to load his Uzi-like firearm: "I watch a lot of TV."

Numerous groups have called, over the years, for curbing TV 20 violence: the National Commission on the Causes and Prevention of Violence (1969), the U.S. Surgeon General (1972), the National Institute of Mental Health (1982), and the American Psychological Association (1992) among them.

During that time, cable television and movie rentals have made 21 violence more readily available while at the same time pushing the envelope for network television. But even leaving aside cable and movie rentals, a study of TV programming from 1967 to 1989 showed only small ups and downs in violence, with the violent acts moving from one time slot to another but the overall violence rate remaining pretty steady—and pretty similar from network to network.

"The percent of prime-time programs using violence remains 22 more than seven out of ten, as it has been for the entire 22-year period," researchers George Gerbner of the University of

Pennsylvania Annenberg School of Communication and Nancy Signorielli of the University of Delaware wrote in 1990. For the past 22 years, they found, adults and children have been entertained by about 16 violent acts, including two murders, in each evening's prime-time programming.

They also discovered that the rate of violence in children's   23
programs is three times the rate in prime-time shows. By the age of 18, the average American child has witnessed at least 18,000 simulated murders on television.

But all of the scientific studies and reports, all of the wisdom of   24
cops and grief of parents have run up against Congress' quite proper fear of censorship. For years, Democratic Congressman Peter Rodino of New Jersey chaired the House Judiciary Committee and looked at calls for some form of censorship with a jaundiced eye. At a hearing five years ago, Rodino told witnesses that Congress must be a "protector of commerce."

"Well, we have children that we need to protect," replied   25
Frank M. Palumbo, a pediatrician at Georgetown University Hospital and a consultant to the American Academy of Pediatrics. "What we have here is a toxic substance in the environment that is harmful to children."

Arnold Fege of the national PTA added, "Clearly, this commit-   26
tee would not protect teachers who taught violence to children. Yet why would we condone children being exposed to a steady diet of TV violence year after year?"

JOHN LEONARD   (1939 –   )

■ ■ ■

Why Blame TV?

L ike a warrior-king of Sumer, daubed with sesame oil,   1
gorged on goat, hefting up his sword and drum, Senator
Ernest Hollings looked down November 23 from a ziggurat to intone, all over the op-ed page of the *New York Times*: "If
the TV and cable industries have no sense of shame, we must take
it upon ourselves to stop licensing their violence-saturated programming."

Hollings, of course, is co-sponsor in the Senate, with Daniel   2
Inouye, of a ban on any act of violence on television before, say,
midnight. Never mind whether this is constitutional, or what it
would do to the local news. Never mind, either, that in Los
Angeles last August, in the International Ballroom of the Beverly
Hilton, in front of 600 industry executives, the talking heads—a
professor here, a producer there, a child psychologist and a network veep for program standards—couldn't even agree on a definition of violence. (Is it only violent if it hurts or kills?) And they
disagreed on which was worse, a "happy" violence that sugarcoats
aggressive behavior or a "graphic" violence that at least suggests
consequences. (How, anyway, does television manage somehow
simultaneously to *desensitize* and to *incite*?) Nor were they really
sure what goes on in the dreamy heads of our children as they
crouch in the dark to commune with the tube while their parents, if they have any, aren't around. (*Road Runner*? Beep-beep.)
Nor does the infamous scarlet V "parent advisory" warning even
apply to cartoons, afternoon soaps, or Somalias.

Never mind, because everybody agrees that watching televi-   3
sion causes anti-social behavior, especially among the children of
the poor; that there seems to be more violent programming on
the air now than there ever was before; that *Beavis and Butt-head*
inspired an Ohio 5-year-old to burn down the family trailer; that
in the blue druidic light of television we will have spawned generations of toadstools and triffids.

In fact, there is less violence on network television than there 4
used to be; because of ratings, it's mostly sitcoms. The worst stuff
is the Hollywood splatterflicks; they're found on premium cable,
which means the poor are less likely to be watching. Everywhere
else on cable, not counting the court channel or home shopping
and not even to think about blood sports and Pat Buchanan, the
fare is innocent to the point of stupefaction (Disney, Discovery,
Family, Nickelodeon). That Ohio trailer wasn't even wired for
cable, so the littlest firebird must have got his MTV elsewhere in
the dangerous neighborhood. (And kids have been playing with
matches since, at least, Prometheus. I recall burning down my
very own bedroom when I was 5 years old. The fire department
had to tell my mother that the evidence pointed to me.) Since
the '60s, according to statistics cited by Douglas Davis in *The Five
Myths of Television Power*, more Americans than ever before are
going out to eat in restaurants, see films, plays, and baseball games,
visit museums, travel abroad, jog, even *read*. Watching television,
everybody does *something else* at the same time. While our children are playing with their Adobe Illustrators and Domark Virtual
Reality Toolkits, the rest of us eat, knit, smoke, dream, read magazines, sign checks, feel sorry for ourselves, think about Hillary,
and plot shrewd career moves or revenge.

Actually watching television, unless it's C-Span, is usually more 5
interesting than the proceedings of Congress. Or what we read in
hysterical books like Jerry Mander's *Four Arguments for the
Elimination of Television*, or George Gilder's *Life After Television*, or
Marie Winn's *The Plug-In Drug*, or Neal Postman's *Amusing
Ourselves to Death*, or Bill McKibben's *The Age of Missing
Information*. Or what we'll hear at panel discussions on censorship,
where right-wingers worry about sex and left-wingers worry
about violence. Or just lolling around an academic deepthink-
tank, trading mantras like "violence profiles" (George Gerbner),
"processed culture" (Richard Hoggart), "narcoleptic joys"
(Michael Sorkin), and "glass teat" (Harlan Ellison).

Of *course* something happens to us when we watch television; 6
networks couldn't sell their millions of pairs of eyes to advertising
agencies, nor would ad agencies buy more than $21 billion worth
of commercial time each year, if speech (and sound, and motion)
didn't somehow modify action. But what happens is far from
clear and won't be much clarified by lab studies, however longi-

tudinal, of habits and behaviors isolated from the larger feedback loop of a culture full of gaudy contradictions. The only country in the world that watches more television than we do is Japan, and you should see its snuff movies and pornographic comic books; but the Japanese are pikers compared with us when we compute per capita rates of rape and murder. Some critics in India tried to blame the recent rise in communal violence there on a state-run television series dramatizing the *Mahabharata*, but not long ago they were blaming Salman Rushdie, as in Bangladesh they have decided to blame the writer Taslima Nasrin. No Turk I know of attributes skinhead violence to German TV. It's foolish to pretend that all behavior is mimetic, and that our only model is Spock or Brokaw. Or Mork and Mindy. Why, after so many years of *M*A*S*H*, weekly in prime time and nightly in reruns, aren't all of us out there hugging trees and morphing dolphins? Why, with so many sitcoms, aren't all of us comedians?

But nobody normal watches television the way congressmen, 7 academics, symposiasts, and Bill McKibben do. We are less thrilling. For instance:

On March 3, 1993, a Wednesday, midway through the nine- 8 week run of *Homicide* on NBC, in an episode written by Tom Fontana and directed by Martin Campbell, Baltimore detectives Bayliss (Kyle Secor) and Pembleton (Andre Braugher) had 12 hours to wring a confession out of "Arab" Tucker (Moses Gunn) for the strangulation and disemboweling of an 11-year-old girl. In the dirty light and appalling intimacy of a single claustrophobic room, with a whoosh of wind sound like some dread blowing in from empty Gobi spaces, among maps, library books, diaries, junk food, pornographic crime-scene photographs, and a single black overflowing ashtray, these three men seemed as nervous as the hand-held cameras—as if their black coffee were full of jumping beans, amphetamines, and spiders; as if God himself were jerking them around.

Well, you may think the culture doesn't really need another 9 cop show. And, personally, I'd prefer a weekly series in which social problems are solved through creative nonviolence, after a Quaker meeting, by a collective of vegetarian carpenters. But in a single hour, for which Tom Fontana eventually won an Emmy, I learned more about the behavior of fearful men in small rooms than from any number of better-known movies, plays, and novels on the topic by the likes of Don DeLillo, Mary McCarthy, Alberto Moravia, Heinrich Böll, and Doris Lessing.

This, of course, was an accident, as it usually is when those of 10 us who watch television like normal people are startled in our expectations. We leave home expecting, for a lot of money, to be exalted, and almost never are. But staying put, slumped in an agnosticism about sentience itself, suspecting that our cable box is just another bad-faith credit card enabling us to multiply our opportunities for disappointment, we are ambushed in our lethargy. And not so much by "event" television, like Ingmar Bergman's *Scenes from a Marriage*, originally a six-hour miniseries for Swedish television; or Marcel Ophuls' *The Sorrow and the Pity*, originally conceived for French television; or Rainer Werner Fassbinder's *Berlin Alexanderplatz*, commissioned by German television; or *The Singing Detective*; or *The Jewel in the Crown*. On the contrary, we've stayed home on certain nights to watch television, the way on other nights we'll go out to a neighborhood restaurant, as if on Mondays we ordered in for laughs, as on Fridays we'd rather eat Italian. We go to television—message center, mission control, Big Neighbor, electronic Elmer's glue-all—to look at Oscars, Super Bowls, moon shots, Watergates, Pearlygates, ayatollahs, dead Kings, dead Kennedys; and also, perhaps, to experience some "virtual" community as a nation. But we also go because we are hungry, angry, lonely, or tired, and television is always there for us, a 24-hour user-friendly magic box grinding out narrative, novelty, and distraction, news and laughs, snippets of high culture, remedial seriousness and vulgar celebrity, an incitement and a sedative, a place to celebrate and a place to mourn, a circus and a wishing well.

And suddenly Napoleon shows up, like a popsicle, on *Northern* 11 *Exposure*, while Chris on the radio is reading Proust. Or *Roseanne* is about lesbianism instead of bowling. Or *Picket Fences* has moved on, from serial bathers and elephant abuse to euthanasia and gay-bashing.

Kurt Vonnegut on Showtime! David ("Masturbation") Mamet 12 on TNT! Norman Mailer wrote the TV screenplay for *The Executioner's Song*, and Gore Vidal gave us *Lincoln* with Mary Tyler Moore as Mary Todd. In just the past five years, if I hadn't been watching television, I'd have missed *Tanner '88*, when Robert Altman and Garry Trudeau ran Michael Murphy for president of the United States; *My Name Is Bill W.*, with James Woods as the founding father of Alcoholics Anonymous; *The Final Days*, with Theodore Bikel as Henry Kissinger; *No Place Like Home*, where there wasn't one for Christine Lahti and Jeff Daniels, as there hadn't been for Jane Fonda in *The Dollmaker* and Mare Winningham in *God Bless the Child; Eyes on the Prize*, a home movie in two parts about America's second civil war; *The Last Best Year*, with Mary Tyler Moore and Bernadette Peters learning to live with their gay sons and HIV; *Separate but Equal*, with Sidney Poitier as Thurgood Marshall; and *High Crimes and Misdemeanors*, the Bill Moyers special on Irangate and the scandal of our intelligence agencies; Graham Greene, John Updike, Philip Roth, Gloria Naylor, Arthur Miller, and George Eliot, plus Paul Simon and Stephen Sondheim. Not to mention—guiltiest of all our secrets—those hoots without which any popular culture would be as tedious as a John Cage or an Anaïs Nin, like Elizabeth Taylor in *Sweet Bird of Youth* and the Redgrave sisters in a remake of *Whatever Happened to Baby Jane?*

What all this television has in common is narrative. Even net-   13
work news—which used to be better than most newspapers before the bean counters started closing down overseas bureaus and the red camera lights went out all over Europe and Asia and Africa—is in the storytelling business. And so far no one in Congress has suggested banning narrative.

Because I watch all those despised network TV movies, I know   14
more about racism, ecology, homelessness, gun control, child abuse, gender confusion, date rape, and AIDS than is dreamt of by, say, Katie Roiphe, the Joyce Maynard of Generation X, or than Hollywood has ever bothered to tell me, especially about AIDS. Imagine, Jonathan Demme's *Philadelphia* opened in theaters around the country well after at least a dozen TV movies on AIDS that I can remember without troubling my hard disk. And I've learned something else, too:

We were a violent culture before television, from Wounded   15
Knee to the lynching bee, and we'll be one after all our children have disappeared by video game into the pixels of cyberspace. Before television, we blamed public schools for what went wrong with the Little People back when classrooms weren't overcrowded in buildings that weren't falling down in neighborhoods that didn't resemble Beirut, and whose fault is that? *The A-Team?*

We can't control guns, or drugs, and each year two million American women are assaulted by their male partners, who are usually in an alcoholic rage, and whose fault is that? *Miami Vice?* The gangs that menace our streets aren't home watching Cinemax, and neither are the sociopaths who make bonfires, in our parks, from our homeless, of whom there are at least a million, a supply-side migratory tide of the deindustrialized and dispossessed, of angry beggars, refugee children, and catatonic nomads, none of them traumatized by *Twin Peaks.* So cut Medicare, kick around the Brady Bill, and animadvert Amy Fisher movies. But children who are loved and protected long enough to grow up to have homes and respect and lucky enough to have jobs don't riot in the streets. Ours is a tantrum culture that measures everyone by his or her ability to produce wealth, and morally condemns anybody who fails to prosper, and now blames Burbank for its angry incoherence. Why not recessive genes, angry gods, lousy weather? The mafia, the zodiac, the *Protocols of the Elders of Zion?* Probability theory, demonic possession, Original Sin? George Steinbrenner? Sunspots?

UNDERSTANDING DETAILS

1. What are Cannon ("Honey, I Warped the Kids") and Leonard ("Why Blame TV?") saying about TV violence in these two essays?
2. What arguments can you think of to add to both sides of this question?
3. Why is Congress's fear of censorship in conflict with the research that shows watching violence on TV can elicit aggressive behavior (Cannon)? Explain this conflict.
4. According to Leonard, how do we "experience some 'virtual' community as a nation" (paragraph 10) by watching TV?

ANALYZING MEANING

1. Which side of this particular argument is most convincing to you? Which examples or statistics persuade you most effectively? Explain your reaction to these two positions on the issue of TV violence.
2. Do you agree with Cannon that violence should be reduced in children's TV programs? Explain your answer.

3. Do you agree with Leonard that America is "a tantrum culture that measures everyone by his or her ability to produce wealth, and morally condemns anybody who fails to prosper" (paragraph 15)? Explain your answer.
4. How might the views in these two essays be reconciled? Can you recommend a compromise between them?

DISCOVERING RHETORICAL STRATEGIES

1. Who do you think is the intended audience for each of these essays? Are there any important differences between these audiences in your opinion?
2. These two authors make their points with completely different writing voices. Describe the tone or mood of each essay, and explain whether you think that particular voice was most effective for the author's purpose.
3. How does the organization of the two essays differ? What is the general organizing principle in each case?
4. What other rhetorical strategies does each essay use to make its point? Give examples of each strategy.

MAKING CONNECTIONS

1. The debate between Leonard and Cannon over television violence is similar in many respects to debates over gun control (Robert Hughes, "The N.R.A. in a Hunter's Sights"), affirmative action (Shelby Steele, "Affirmative Action: The Price of Preference"), and religion in the public schools (Donald Drakeman, "Religion's Place in Public Schools"). Examine the arguments by each of these authors, and determine which essay uses the strongest emotional appeal. Why do you think this is the case?
2. Cannon's principal argument, that television violence "desensitizes" viewers to the adverse consequences of real violence, is similar to Alleen Pace Nilsen's assertion, in "Sexism in English: A 1990s Update," that a constant barrage of negative language concerning women leads us to devalue the accomplishments of females in our society. How does each author illustrate the long-term effects of such conditioning? Which essay do you find more convincing? Explain your answer.

3. Compare and contrast Cannon's argument with that in "Why We Crave Horror Movies" by Stephen King, who asserts that horror films are cathartic because they permit us to purge, or "exorcise," socially unacceptable emotions from our collective psyche. With which of these authors do you most agree? Explain your answer.

IDEAS FOR DISCUSSION/WRITING

Preparing to Write

Write freely about your views on TV violence: Do you think Americans should take an active role in controlling violence on TV? What do you think should be done? On what level (federal, state, or local)? What is your general view of TV violence? Does it have an appropriate place in TV schedules? In what ways might censorship help the situation? In what ways might it make the situation worse?

Choosing a Topic

1. Because TV is such an important part of students' lives today, the topic of TV viewing has become a crucial issue in our public schools. You have been asked to serve on a committee to make recommendations for TV viewing for children of different ages. In preparation for the first meeting, you are to write an essay making and justifying your recommendations for each age group.

2. How far should censorship be allowed to go? Should censorship come into play at any point in regulating TV? Should censorship be used to protect any group of people? Does your view conflict in any way with our constitutional right to freedom of speech? In an essay written for your peers, argue for or against putting limits on certain programs.

3. In an essay written for a group of TV executives from different networks, present a proposal for controlling TV violence. Explain the details of your proposal's implementation and its likely effects.

OPPOSING VIEWPOINTS

■ ■ ■

Freedom of the Press

The following two essays debate the limits of freedom of the press in America. The first, by former New York governor Mario Cuomo, argues that this freedom must be unlimited because the press plays an important role in watching our government and keeping our citizens well informed so that they can function effectively in our democratic society. Before he became governor of New York (1983–1994), Cuomo went to St. John's College, where he earned his B.A. in Latin American studies and his law degree. Later, he worked as an attorney in a law firm and as a professor at St. John's Law School and then became secretary of state and later lieutenant governor of the State of New York. He is currently in private legal practice in New York City. His publications include *Diaries of Mario M. Cuomo: The Campaign for Governor* (1984), *Lincoln on Democracy* (1990), and *The Forest Hills Controversy* (1992).

John Merrill, who argues that freedom of the press needs some limits to protect us from the excesses of unethical journalists, has a B.A. in history and English from Delta State University, an M.A. in journalism from Louisiana State University, an M.A. in philosophy from the University of Missouri, and a Ph.D. in mass communications from the University of Iowa. Currently a professor emeritus of journalism at the University of Missouri, he has published twenty-two books, among them *The Imperative of Freedom* (1974), *Existential Journalism* (1977), and *The Legacy of Wisdom* (1995). His advice to students using *The Prose Reader* is that "writing is a lonely activity, but it can be very rewarding when you see the results of your hard work." He admits that he often has to reread one of his many books to find out what he thinks about a particular topic.

Preparing to Read

Cuomo's essay originally appeared as "Preserving Freedom of the Press" in *USA Today Magazine*, Vol. 116 (January 1988), while Merrill's article was first published under the title "Needed: An Ethical Press" in *The World and I* (February 1988). Before you begin to read these essays, think for a minute about your opinion of the media: Do you believe the press does an accurate job of reporting information to the public? How could it do a better job? What are its main flaws? Do you think the press should have total freedom? Do you think it should be limited in any way? In what ways? Do you think the press is always as ethical as it should be? How do you interpret the reference to "freedom . . . of the press" in the First Amendment of the Constitution?

MARIO CUOMO   (1932 –   )

■ ■ ■

Freedom of the Press Must Be Unlimited

The more I learn about government and especially about 1
democracy, the more deeply convinced I become that one
of our greatest strengths as a people is our right to full and
free expression. No people have benefited more from the gift of
free speech and a free press. Never before in history has the gift
been so generously given or so fully used. From the very launching
of our nation, these freedoms were regarded as essential protections
against official repression.

When the geniuses who designed this wonderful ship of state 2
came to draw the blueprints, they remembered Britain and other
lands which had discouraged criticism of government and public
officials, declaring it defamatory and seditious. The Founding
Fathers considered that to be one of the worst parts of British
tyranny. They were convinced that much of the struggle for
American freedom would be the struggle over a free press. So, they
were careful to provide that the right of free expression, through a
free press, would be preserved in their new nation, especially inso-
far as the press dealt with government and public officials. They
declared that right of free expression in the First Amendment to
the Constitution and wrote it in the simplest, least ambiguous language they could fashion: "Congress shall make no law respecting
an establishment of religion, or prohibiting the free exercise
thereof, or abridging the freedom of speech or of the press. . . ."

Having provided for the right of free speech for the whole cit- 3
izenry, they went further and provided separately for "freedom of
. . . the press"; as broadly as possible, not tentatively, not embroi-
dered with nuances, not shrouded and bound up in conditions,
but plainly and purely.

Gambling on Liberty

The Founding Fathers knew precisely what they were dealing 4
with. The press of their time was not only guilty of bad taste and

inaccuracy, it was partisan, reckless, sometimes vicious, and, indeed, the Founding Fathers were themselves often at the point end of the press sword.

In view of that experience, they might have written amend- 5 ments that never mentioned freedom of the press, or they might have tried to protect against an imperfect press like the one they dealt with—with conditions, qualifications, requirements, and penalties—but they did not. They knew the dangers. They knew that broad freedoms inevitably would be accompanied by some abuse and even harm to innocent people. Knowing all the odds, they chose to gamble on liberty.

The gamble has made us all rich. Over all, the press has been a 6 force for good—educating our people, guarding our freedom, watching our government—challenging it, goading it, revealing it, forcing it into the open. Teapot Dome, the Pentagon Papers, Watergate, the revelations of corruption in New York City—these are all examples of disclosures that might never have occurred were it not for our free press. The press' insistence on forcing the White House to begin to tell the truth about the Iranian arms transaction is a dramatic reminder of how the press works incessantly to assure our liberty by guaranteeing our awareness. Less dramatically, the work of revelation by the press goes on day after day at all levels of government, all over the nation.

Surely, the preservation of this extraordinary strength is worth 7 our eternal vigilance. That is why I believe it is appropriate to consider the matter of freedom of the press now, at this moment. It appears to me—and to others as well—that we are approaching a time when shifts in our law seriously may dilute the protection of the press and thereby weaken the fabric of this society.

Our Constitution is not self-executing; it must be interpreted 8 and applied by the Supreme Court. In effect, no matter how plain the language of the great document may appear to the rest of us, the Constitution will say what the Supreme Court says it says. The dimensions of the right to a free press are therefore in the care and at the mercy of the Supreme Court.

In recent decades, the Court has dealt often with the First 9 Amendment and most of the time has expanded its reach, culminating in the landmark protection of the press in the case of *New York Times v. Sullivan* in 1964. *Sullivan* said that, notwithstanding the fact that the press was inaccurate, even negligent, and the inaccuracy substantially damaged a public figure, there would be no liability on the part of the press. Only if the press were guilty of actual malice—that is, a deliberate falsification or conduct that evinced a reckless disregard—could there be a recovery.

This protection obviously was designed to free the press from   10
the chilling—maybe paralyzing—effect of huge damage awards as a consequence of inaccuracy in trying to report the truth. Some believed this was too much protection; they called it a license to defame, an invitation to dangerous, harmful carelessness. However, some—I among them—thought it was good and necessary policy, good and necessary law; that gamble the Founders took was still a good one.

Changing Interpretations

Supreme Court law, however, is not static or permanent; it   11
changes. In 1985, Justice Byron R. White, who joined the majority in *Sullivan*, announced that he had become convinced the Court had struck "an improvident balance" in 1964. He urged that a better approach would be to return to much less protective common-law standards of liability. In a 1986 case, Justice William H. Rehnquist indicated that he too would like to revisit *Sullivan* with an eye to the possibility of overruling it. . . .

Conservatives generally seem to sense this is a good time to   12
strike. Some recently have proposed making simple "negligence" the standard for responsibility for injurious inaccuracy. What would it do to a small newspaper, magazine, or station to be subjected to a multi-million-dollar verdict, because a jury discovered its reporter did not make what the jury considered to be a reasonable search, perhaps in the library, perhaps through clips, perhaps seeking out witnesses; perhaps checking their stories, checking out their references, going to experts?

There is considerable other evidence to suggest that the courts   13
are moving gradually, but consistently, away from *Sullivan* and toward less protection for the press. Floyd Abrams, a noted attorney and expert on the First Amendment, says the *Sullivan* principles are now under "sustained attack."

One more point about the Supreme Court: putting aside its   14
somewhat esoteric legal jurisdiction, the truth is that the Court is

a living institution. Its nine members are subject to the same public events that affect and instruct you and me. Their decisions to some extent reflect changing circumstances in the world around them or changing ideas about what is reasonable or wise.

This means that, when trying to predict a change in First 15
Amendment rulings, the quality of the press as perceived by the public is a relevant factor. In the *Federalist Papers*, Alexander Hamilton asked: "What is the liberty of the press? . . . Its security, whatever fine declarations may be inserted in any constitution respecting it, must altogether depend on public opinion and on the general spirit of the people and the government."

This is still true today. A press regarded by the public as reckless 16
invites the attention of the Supreme Court and tempts it to perform corrective judicial surgery. That is what Mr. Dooley meant when he said, "Th' Supreme Coort follows th' iliction returns."

This raises a number of questions: What is the public percep- 17
tion of the press today? Is it regarded as less than perfect? If so, how specifically?

Official Criticism

It might be worth noting here that, in earlier times, many of 18
our leading public officials were among the press' harshest critics. Today, the press is apt to refer to a public official who criticizes the media as "Nixonian." If, however, presidential labels are appropriate, the media might just as fairly call its critics "Washingtonian," "Jeffersonian," "Lincolnian," "Taftian," "Wilsonian," "Rooseveltian," "Kennedyesque," or "Johnsonian."

For example, George Washington called the press "infamous 19
scribblers." Thomas Jefferson wrote: "Even the least informed of the people have learnt that nothing in a newspaper is to be believed."

Theodore Roosevelt added action to his vitriol. He had Joseph 20
Pulitzer and his *New York World* indicted for criminal libel after the newspaper charged corruption in connection with the digging of the Panama Canal.

William Howard Taft found one paper so bad as to be "intolera- 21
ble." He told his assistant not to show him *The New York Times*. "I don't think reading the *Times* will do me any good and would only be provocative in me of . . . anger and contemptuous feeling."

Woodrow Wilson lost his conciliatory disposition in dealing 22
with the press. He said, "The real trouble is that the newspapers
get the real facts but do not find them to their taste and do not
use them as given them, and in some of the newspaper offices,
news is deliberately invented."

The Best Evidence

The truth is that criticism of the press by its natural targets— 23
public officials, governors, presidents—however illustrious, is not
necessarily good evidence of the press' imperfection. Indeed, it
can be argued that it is the best evidence of the press' effectiveness.

The press' job is to find the whole truth, especially that part of 24
it which is forgotten, ignored, deliberately concealed, or distorted
by public officials. The better the press does its job, the more
likely future generations will be reading colorful condemnations
of reporters and commentators by today's politicians, and the
more likely that the historical record will be truthful and accurate.

I think I understand this as a public official myself. Although I 25
believe I have been treated very well by the press overall, from
time to time I have had occasion to make my own criticisms of
some members of the press and their coverage in particular cases.
The response has revealed that politicians are not the only ones
who are sensitive.

Of much more concern to the press than criticism from me and 26
other public officials should be the criticism that comes from candid, thoughtful members of the press itself. Recently, it has been
harsh indeed. What is worse is that the public at large appears to
agree.

Harper's Magazine observed in 1985 that, when the 27
Westmoreland case hit the headlines, a "flood" of commentary
from the press ensued. Editorial writers noted that the press was
"widely maligned, criticized, abused, and worst of all,
'distrusted.'" They pointed to numerous polls and "the public's
conspicuous failure to be outraged when reporters were barred
from Grenada." *Harper's* continued, "Though Americans ritually
intone their devotion to the 'freedom of the press,' they delight in
repeating another prized national dictum: 'Don't believe what
you read in the papers.'"

The press itself attributes much of this public disfavor to its 28
own curable defects. Thus, "pack journalism" is a frequently heard
complaint, citing the press' dependence on one another, forging a
uniform point of view so as to avoid embarrassing differences,
written as though every statement previously made by any reporter is indisputable, and the clannish locking of arms against
critics from the outside. As Hodding Carter said in 1985, "We are
very, very good at pitching and very, very bad at catching. . . .
The press appears to be paranoid when facing criticism itself."

Tom Wicker adds a larger and more substantive complaint. He 29
feels the media generally is too prone to promote what it believes
is easiest for people to accept and in the process fails to cover significant issues adequately.

The criticism that is set out here easily could be offset with 30
generous accolades from sources equally credible. That is not the
point. No one is more eager than I to proclaim how successfully
the press has done its job over the last couple of hundred years, or
how much better government might do its job. Still, we must recognize the fact that this nation currently is debating—in the place
where we make the rules, the Court—whether or not to limit
the freedom of the press despite its good record of 200 years.

The possibility of limitation is a real one. I believe it requires 31
that we admit the media's confessions of imperfection and what
appears to be a disconcertingly serious loss of public favor that
could encourage restrictions of First Amendment rights.

The first thing we must do is sound the alert and make it clear 32
that we are facing a real threat of restriction of the constitutional
freedom of the press. That is not easy. The drift of the Supreme
Court does not get reported in the morning headlines. It is an
elusive subject to which we must direct attention. Then, we must
hope—and we can not be sure it will work—that the reaction
will affect, for the better, both the press and the courts. . . .

Freedom and Responsibility

Let me offer you what I believe is an opportunity for all the 33
media to make a contribution to the forming of public policy in
this nation: Cover the public issues more thoroughly. Cover campaigns even more extensively. Cover state and local government

more deeply, not just press events created by candidates or public officials. . . .

The press is about finding the truth and telling it to the peo- 34
ple. In pursuit of that, I am making a case for the broadest possible freedom of the press. However, with that great gift comes great responsibility. The press—print and electronic—has the power to inform, but that implies the power to distort. The press can lead our society toward a more mature and discriminating understanding of the process by which we choose our leaders, make our rules, and construct our values, or it can encourage people to despise our systems and avoid participating in them. The press can teach our children a taste for violence, encourage a fascination with perversity and inflicted pain, or it can show them a beauty they have not known. The press can make us wiser, fuller, surer, and sweeter than we are.

One of the miracles of this democracy is that all of us—both 35
the press and the public—are free to make the choices. We must work to keep it that way, to keep the miracle alive.

JOHN MERRILL   (1924 –   )

■ ■ ■

Freedom of the Press Must Be Limited

J ournalists in the United States who enjoy bashing everything 1
and everybody in sight are beginning to get growing
amounts of their own medicine. The spotlight of criticism is
being focused on them and the media they serve.

As the media grow in power and as they cling to their self-des- 2
ignation as a "watchdog on government" and other self-enhanc-
ing labels, they increasingly indulge in what many people
consider irresponsible or unethical practices. In their mad rush to
meet deadlines and what they see as their prime responsibility "to
let the people know," American journalists have been pushing
ethics out of the picture and enthroning expediency and self-interest. Many critics would contend that "ethical journalism" in
today's world is really oxymoronic.

Whether ethics and journalism are contradictory terms or not, 3
it must be said that a considerable degree of unethical activity exists in the press. And often this activity is poorly reported, if at all,
because of the press's natural self-interest and its capacity for controlling the news and having the last word.

Certainly the American media must be commended for their 4
alertness to governmental and social immorality and questionable
activities. Such media attention does, no doubt, help to keep society "honest" and "careful"—at least to a certain degree. But the
media also need to look to their own houses; they themselves
must have a greater resolve to be ethical—if for no other reason
than to improve their negative image among a skeptical public. . . .

The Press as "Watchdog"

The "adversarial relationship" between press and government is 5
an important consideration for the press. It may well be a myth, as
some say, but it is a very important one to journalists. It is a responsibility, in the press's own journalistic dogma, that forces the news

establishment of the country to act as a watchdog on government. Many of the ethical problems of the press spring from the assumption that the press must be a check on government, be a critic of government, keep the government honest, and so on. This prompts the press to dig and probe, snipe and snoop; it causes the press to speculate, and to deal in innuendo in its attempt to unearth corruption in high places and to explain the misdeeds of others.

This concept is responsible for the press's accentuating the 6 negative in government matters, seldom revealing positive activities or trends. Of course, the press could stress the positive, defend government positions, and have a partnership relationship with the government; it has no constitutional mandate to do otherwise. Only its own self-assigned duty has generated this adversarial relationship to government.

Many of the press's modern critics see such a self-assigned duty 7 as another instance of press arrogance that often pushes the journalists into unethical areas where damage is done to the whole social fabric, and where many good potential public servants are dissuaded from participation in the governmental arena due to the persistent and prying minions of the press.

This "watchdog" attitude of the press fosters—or creates—the 8 idea that government is necessarily and inherently evil and must be checked. And, in this game, the press has set itself up as the institution that must keep the government honest. Today, as an increasing number of voices are asking who checks the checker, the press falls back on its constitutional freedom guarantee, and when all the rhetoric is done, the answer from the press is essentially this: *Nobody checks the checker.* The press is free and autonomous.

Such a perspective is filled with danger, especially when signif- 9 icant numbers of journalists are unconcerned with ethics. And there is no real evidence to show that journalists are any less evil and need less careful scrutiny than government employees. But, say the journalists, the press is "free" and this is paramount in the United States.

Confusion over Freedom

One reason the press is confused about ethics is that it is con- 10 fused about its freedom, which it sees as endangered if it puts too much emphasis on its "responsibilities." Talk of responsibility leads to obligations and duties, say the press people, and therefore tends to restrict press freedom. So the journalists always get back to stressing *press freedom* and deemphasizing *press responsibility*. The result is that this deep antipathy to the concept of "social responsibility" keeps journalists from giving much continuing and serious thought to ethics.

What journalists should do is recognize that the concept of "press freedom" can just as easily include the freedom to be positive as negative, and that it can include the freedom of the press to be an ally or apologist for government as well as an adversary. In fact, when the press convinces itself that it is an adversary or watchdog vis-à-vis government, it thereby restricts its own freedom by accepting a very limited role. This "adversary dogma," interestingly, is not even consistent with libertarian theory, and it would seem that journalists who talk about "press freedom" would cease being tied to this "adversary role."   11

A Know-It-All Press

Press people say that their negative approach to news is natural, and that the people want such news. Anyway, how can the people put their house in order if they do not know that it is out of order? The fact is that journalists, by and large, see themselves as a kind of permanent, relentless opposition to government. They must watch government carefully; they must protect the people from government crimes and excesses. But does every grin and every act of every politician contribute anything important to the public understanding? What about news balance? It means little if the journalist is mainly concerned about pouring out every scrap of information. Where is the balanced overview that tries to correct distortions resulting from all these bits and pieces of disjointed "news"? It is not to be found, for the press is dedicated to its specious formula of accentuating the negative and watchdogging ("hounding"?) the government. . . .   12

Never, however, does it seem that the press asks itself this basic question: Where does the press get this directive? The answer, of course, is that it has no such mandate, except that which it constantly whispers in its own ears. Maybe the press should remember that, after all, the people at least elect government officials (or some of them); the people never elect an editor, an anchorperson, a news director, a publisher, or a reporter.   13

The People's "Right to Know"

The other journalistic shibboleth that impinges on press ethics   14
and seems so dear to the heart of media people is "the people's
right to know." In any discussion about press ethics or press responsibility, this sacred tenet is dragged out to support almost any
journalistic tactic. After all, the story goes, the people have a right
to know this or that and we, the journalists, must see to it that
they do. This "right to know" concept is fraught with semantic
and logical implications, and is one that causes many anxious moments for journalists (and government officials, too) who think seriously about ethics.

Do Journalists Represent the Public?

Many media people, obviously not comfortable with the right   15
granted them in the First Amendment, feel they must justify their
activities vis-à-vis government by appealing to a people's right to
know. This justification goes something like this: We're not really
getting this information for ourselves; we're getting it for the
people who have a right to know it. Therefore, you people in
government are obligated to give it to us because we are representatives of the people. (Isn't this rather strange? Many of us
thought that government officials were the representatives of the
people, and the journalists were private-sector, profit-making employees of capitalistic enterprises and not representatives of anybody except publishers and other media owners and managers.)

Perhaps more fundamental is this question: Where do the peo-   16
ple get this "right to know"? Much has been written on this subject, but little has been resolved. Perhaps one can infer such a
"right" from the free-press clause of the Bill of Rights. It would
certainly have to be inferred, for nowhere is such a right specified. Some persons, admitting the lack of a constitutional right to
know, insist that it is a "natural" right. At any rate, if there is such
a right to know, then the press needs to rethink its own position,
for it is abridging this "right" every single day. And it is abridging
it in the name of editorial self-determination or "press freedom."

Journalists constantly decide what they will and will not publish;   17
they arbitrarily determine what the public will or will not know.
They call this reporting and editing, of course. Certainly they do
not call it news management—they reserve that term for govern-

mental activities. But it really is news management; in fact, news management is what journalism is all about. Journalists know this, of course, but talk about and advocate a "people's right to know."

Such concepts as the "watchdog function" of the press (adver- 18 sarial role) and the "people's right to know," well entrenched in the traditional dogma of American journalism, evidence a considerable confusion in the minds of journalists about the nature of press freedom. And this leads to difficulty in developing any kind of consistent journalistic ethics. Little wonder there is so much ethical confusion—in fact, a kind of ethical vacuum—in American journalism. The basic philosophical foundation stones are not very solid and the mortar holding them together is rapidly turning to powder.

The press looks at ethics from a vested-interest and relativistic 19 perspective, shying away from any absolutes and relegating ethics to particular times, circumstances, and problems. Journalists, by and large, conceive of ethics as prudential actions in certain circumstances that will achieve some preconceived plan of theirs— such as getting information from a source. What they often do is to engage in trying to attain their ends and then justifying or rationalizing the means they use. The philosopher Immanuel Kant would not have considered this ethics at all. Journalism conferences show that, almost without exception, participants shy away from absolutes and the Kantian emphasis on "duty to principle," preferring instead to embrace relativistic and personal morality where any option they choose can be justified as the ethical one.

There seems to be no will today for the press to break through 20 self-serving platitudes and gain any real insight into the ethical issues that beg to be dealt with. No common standards exist for normative press ethics. Absolutes are shunned, and everything beyond a strictly personal or individualized ethics is seen as endangering diversity and, by extension, journalistic freedom.

A Competitive Profession

Ethical decisions confront the journalist at every turn. Most 21 often the journalist looks on his decision making as "professional" or institutional and deals with it as such—rather than approaching it from a truly ethical perspective. "It's newsworthy; so we'll print it." This is an example of considering journalism from a pragmatic or professional perspective instead of going to the ethical level. "If we don't print it, some other medium will," journalists often say. "It's the policy of our newspaper to do it, so we do it," the standard excuse goes. Competition, not ethics, too often determines editorial decisions.

This journalistic reflex action is understandable for several rea-   22
sons. Beyond the fact that American journalists are highly institutionalized, routinized creatures of habit, they are part of a highly competitive, capitalistic enterprise; as such they are largely concerned with doing what "works" best. Secondly, they are suspicious of "social ethics" or any group-imposed rules or system of restraints that might cause them to lose their sense of identity and freedom. And lastly, and probably most important of all, journalists know very little and appear uninterested in learning about philosophical ethics. In other words, they appear not to have what Kant would call the "will to be ethical." Journalistic pragmatism has taken precedence over journalistic ethics. Too often journalists, engulfed as they are in the daily routine of habit, tradition and pragmatism, leave the business of morality—personal and social—to theologians and academics.

The press, for its part, is so protective of its traditional idea of   23
individualism and pluralism that it resists anything that might result in standardization or conformity—even codes of ethics and news councils are often suspect. Such a situation is probably still basically in place, but evidence exists that things are changing, that journalists are becoming more serious about ethics and are merging their concern for pragmatism with a recognition that such a concern is not contradictory to ethics. Perhaps this long-time dedication to pragmatism is the very machine that will move the press toward a higher morality. Now they may be seeing that "ethics is the best policy" for long-term success. . . .

Across the country people are beginning to talk about the use   24
of anonymous sources, inaccurate quotes, unbalanced stories, biased and false statements in news stories, shocking and even gruesome photographs, gossip masquerading as news, political bias in the news, and a large number of other questionable practices. Press people themselves are becoming more conscious of ethical problems: Do we print the name of the rape victim? What about the name of the accused rapist? Do we really believe in full-dis-

closure reporting—in the people's right to know? Or do we place ethics above such full-disclosure reporting? What really are our responsibilities, and to whom are they owed? Do the ends (such as getting the story) really justify the means? Any means, which means? Such questions, and many others, are presently being taken seriously by journalists.

Doing the Right Thing

It may be that the time has not yet come for a journalistic rev- 25
olution in ethics. The day of the Kantian "will to be ethical" may still be over the horizon, but there are indications that ethical consciousness is rising in the press and considerable soul-searching about the right thing to do is now mingling with concern about such traditional shibboleths as the people's right to know and the press as a watchdog on government.

Many journalists are recognizing at long last that their calling is 26
a public trust as well as a business and that the press is a powerful ethical force in society, relegating to them an important responsibility. The thought has finally struck home that maybe, just maybe, the people have just as much a right not to know as to know certain things, and that the press can point out positive and helpful facts about government as well as negative and harmful ones.

UNDERSTANDING DETAILS

1. What are the main arguments of Cuomo ("Freedom of the Press Must Be Unlimited") and Merrill ("Freedom of the Press Must Be Limited")? Explain the principal disagreement between these two points of view.
2. What arguments can you think of to add to both sides of this essay?
3. What are the main reasons Cuomo insists that the press needs its freedom?
4. What are the main problems that Merrill identifies concerning freedom of the press?

ANALYZING MEANING

1. Which side of this particular argument is most convincing to you? Which examples or statistics persuade you most effectively?

2. Do you agree with Cuomo or Merrill about the freedom of the press? Explain your answer.
3. Do you agree with Cuomo that freedom and responsibility are intricately related? Explain your answer.
4. How might the views in these two essays be reconciled? Can you recommend a compromise between the two?

DISCOVERING RHETORICAL STRATEGIES

1. Who do you think is the intended audience for each of these essays? Are there any important differences between these audiences in your opinion?
2. Describe the tone or mood of each essay and explain whether you think that particular voice was the most effective for the author's purpose.
3. How does the organization of the two essays differ? What is the general organizing principle in each case?
4. What other rhetorical strategies does each essay use to make its point? Give examples of each strategy.

MAKING CONNECTIONS

1. Imagine that Mario Cuomo, John Merrill, Russell Baker ("The Saturday Evening Post"), Judith Viorst ("The Truth About Lying"), Rita Mae Brown ("Writing as a Moral Act"), and Nancy Gibbs ("When Is It Rape?") were having a round-table discussion about the topic of freedom of the press. Which authors would be most strongly in favor of total freedom? Who would probably agree with Merrill that some limits should be placed on journalistic freedom? Which side would you agree with? Explain your answer.
2. Examine the balance between logical, emotional, and ethical appeals in each essay. Which author relies most heavily on logic? Which on emotion? Whose ethical appeal is strongest? Which essay is most convincing to you? Why? Does your tendency to agree with this essay have anything to do with its balance among the three appeals? Explain your answer.
3. Cuomo and Merrill discuss law as a remedy to social problems in the same way that the following other authors do: Donald Drakeman ("Religion's Place in Public Schools"), Shelby Steele ("Affirmative Action: The Price of Preference"), and

Robert Hughes ("The N.R.A. in a Hunter's Sights"). In which of these essays is the law portrayed as a device for solving problems? In which has the law itself become a problem? Pick one of these essays, and explain your own feelings on whether the law has been a help or a hindrance concerning the issue discussed.

IDEAS FOR DISCUSSION/WRITING

Preparing to Write

Write freely about your opinion of the media: What do you think of the media in general? In your opinion, is any one form of media more accurate, reliable, or interesting than another? On what do you base this judgment? What do you think are the main motives of the press in reporting information to the public? What guidelines do you think it follows in reporting the news? What form of media do you rely on most for the news? Why do you rely on this form? What does ethics have to do with freedom of the press?

Choosing a Topic

1. Your school newspaper has been charged with unethical reporting, and the school administration is considering whether to limit its freedom. The president of the college is soliciting opinions, and you decide to send your suggestions in essay form to the president. Justify your opinions as thoroughly as possible.

2. The media are a vital part of our lives today. In what ways do they affect the morals and values of our society? Of us individually? How much freedom should the media be allowed to have? In an essay written for your peers, write a set of guidelines for keeping the media ethical. Explain the details of these guidelines.

3. Choose an important national or international event from the recent past, and analyze the media's coverage of that event. Consider newspapers, TV newscasts, *Time, Newsweek*, and so on as sources of information. How did the coverage of these media vary? Now that the event has passed, are you aware that any of these sources were more accurate than others? More interesting? More ethical? Present a summary of your findings and your conclusions in an essay addressed to your classmates.

10

Documented Essays

Reading and Writing from Sources

We use sources every day in both informal and formal situations. We explain the source of a phone message, for example, or we refer to an instructor's comments in class. We use someone else's opinion in an essay, or we quote an expert to prove a point. We cite sources both in speaking and in writing through summary, paraphrase, and direct quotation. Most of your college instructors will ask you to write papers using sources so they can see how well you understand the course material. The use of sources in academic papers requires you to understand what you have read and to integrate this reading material with your own opinions and observations—a process that requires a high level of skill in thinking, reading, and writing.

DEFINING DOCUMENTED ESSAYS

Documented essays provide you with the opportunity to perform sophisticated and exciting exercises in critical thinking; they draw on the thinking, reading, and writing abilities you have built up over the course of your academic career, and they often require you to put all the rhetorical modes to work at their most analytical level. Documented essays demonstrate the process of analytical thinking at its best in different disciplines.

In the academic world, documented essays are also called *research papers*, *library papers*, and *term papers*. Documented essays are generally written for one of three reasons: (1) to **report**, (2) to **interpret**, or (3) to **analyze**.

The most straightforward, uncomplicated type of documented essay **reports** information, as in a survey of problems that children have in preschool. The second type of documented essay both presents and **interprets** its findings. It examines a number of different views on a specific issue and weighs these views as it draws its own conclusions. A topic that falls into this category would be whether children who have attended preschool are more sociable than those who have not. After considering evidence on both sides, the writer would draw his or her own conclusions on this topic. A documented essay that **analyzes** a subject presents a hypothesis, tests the hypothesis, and analyzes or evaluates its conclusions. This type of essay calls for the most advanced form of critical thinking. It might look, for example, at the reasons preschool children are more or less socially flexible than nonpreschool children. At its most proficient, this type of writing requires a sophisticated degree of evaluation that forces you to judge your reading, evaluate your sources, and ultimately scrutinize your own reasoning ability as the essay takes shape.

Each of these types of documented essays calls for a higher level of thinking, and each evolves from the previous category. In other words, interpreting requires some reporting, and analyzing draws on both reporting and interpreting.

In the following paragraph, a student reports, interprets, analyzes, and uses sources to document the problem of solid waste in America. Notice how the student writer draws her readers into the essay with a commonly used phrase about America and then questions the validity of its meaning. The student's opinions give shape to the paragraph, while her use of sources helps identify the problem and support her contentions.

"America the Beautiful" is a phrase used to describe the many wonders of nature found throughout our country. America's natural beauty will fade, however, if solutions to our solid waste problems are not discovered soon. America is a rich nation socially, economically, and politically. But these very elements may be the cause of Americans' wastefulness. Americans now generate approximately 160 million tons of solid waste a year—3 1/2 pounds per person per day. We live in a consumer society where convenience, ready-

to-use, and throwaway are words that spark the consumer's attention *(Cook 60). However, many of the products associated with these words create a large part of our problem with solid waste (Grossman 39). We are running out of space for our garbage. The people of America are beginning to produce responses to this problem. Are we too late? A joint effort between individuals, businesses, government industries, and local, state, and federal governments is necessary to establish policies and procedures to combat this waste war. The problem requires not one solution, but a combination of solutions involving technologies and people working together to provide a safe and healthy environment for themselves and future generations.*

READING AND WRITING DOCUMENTED ESSAYS

Reading and writing documented essays involves the skillful integration of two complex operations: research and writing. Reading documented essays critically means understanding the material and evaluating the sources as you proceed. Writing documented essays includes reading and understanding sources on the topic you have chosen and then combining this reading with your own conclusions. The two skills are, essentially, mirror images of one another.

How to Read Documented Essays

Preparing to Read. You should approach a documented essay in much the same way that you approach any essay. First, take a few minutes to look at the preliminary material for each selection: What can you learn from scanning John Langone's essay, "Group Violence," and from reading its synopsis in the Rhetorical Table of Contents? What does Adela de la Torre's title, "Key Issues in Latina Health: Voicing Latina Concerns in the Health Financing Debate," prepare you to read?

Also, you should learn as much as you can from the authors' biographies: What is Langone's interest in group violence? What biographical details prepare us for his approach to this topic? Who was the original audience for Langone's essay? What is Adela de la Torre's background? Does she have the proper qualifications to write about Latina health?

Another important part of preparing to read a documented essay is surveying the sources cited. Turn to the end of the essay, and look at the sources. What publications does Langone draw from? Are these books and magazines well respected? Do you recognize any of the authorities de la Torre quotes?

Last, before you read these essays, try to generate some ideas on each topic so you can participate as fully as possible in your reading. The Preparing to Read questions will get you ready for this task. Then, try to speculate further on the topic of each essay: Why has group violence gained so much momentum in the United States? How do you think group violence differs from acts of violence performed by individuals? What do you want to know from de la Torre about Latina health issues? Why do you think this topic has become an important social issue in America?

Reading. As you react to the material in this chapter, you should respond to both the research and the writing. Record your responses as you read the essay for the first time: What are your reactions to the information you are reading? Are the sources appropriate? How well do they support the author's main points?

Use the preliminary material before each essay to help you create a framework for your responses to it: What motivated Langone to publish his argument on group violence? Do you find it convincing? Who was de la Torre's primary audience when her essay was first published? In what ways is the tone of her essay appropriate for that audience?

Your main job at this stage is to determine each author's primary assertion (thesis statement), note the sources the author cites to support this thesis, and begin to ask yourself questions about the essay so you can respond critically to your reading. In addition, take a look at the questions after each selection to make certain you are comprehending the major ideas of the essay.

Rereading. As you reread these documented essays, take some time to become aware of the difference between fact and opinion, to weigh and evaluate the evidence brought to bear on the arguments, to consider the sources the writers use, to judge the interpretation of the facts cited, to determine what the writers omitted, and to confirm your own views on the issues at hand. All these skills demand the use of critical thinking strategies at their most sophisticated level.

You need to approach this type of argument with an inquiring mind, asking questions and looking for answers as you read the essays. Be especially conscious of the appeals (logical, emotional, and ethical) at work in each essay (see Chapter 9), and take note of other rhetorical strategies that support each author's main argument.

Also, be aware of your own thought processes as you sort facts from opinions. Know where you stand personally in relation to each side of the issues here.

For a list of guidelines for the entire reading process, see the checklists on pages 20–21 of the Introduction.

How to Write Documented Essays

Preparing to Write. Just as with any writing assignment, you should begin the task of writing a documented essay by exploring and limiting your topic. In this case, however, you draw on other sources to help you with this process. You should seek out both primary and secondary sources related to your topic. **Primary sources** are works of literature, historical documents, letters, diaries, speeches, eyewitness accounts, and your own experiments, observations, and conclusions; **secondary sources** explain and analyze information from other sources. Any librarian can help you search for both types of sources related to your topic.

After you have found a few sources on your general topic, you should scan and evaluate what you have discovered so you can limit your topic further. Depending on the required length of your essay, you want to find a topic broad enough to be researched, established enough so that you can find sources on it in the library, and significant enough to demonstrate your abilities to grapple with ideas and draw conclusions. The Preparing to Write questions can help you generate and focus your ideas.

Once you have established these limitations, you might try writing a tentative thesis. At this point, asking a question and attempting to find an answer are productive. But you should keep in mind that your thesis is likely to be revised several times as the range of your knowledge changes and as your paper takes different turns while you research and write. Then, decide on a purpose and audience for your essay.

Once your tentative thesis is formed, you should read your sources for ideas and take detailed notes on your reading. These notes will probably fall into one of four categories: (1) *summary*— a condensed statement of someone else's thoughts or observations; (2) *paraphrase*—a restatement in your own words of someone else's ideas or observations; (3) *direct quotations from sources*; or (4) *a combination of these forms.* Be sure to make a distinction in your notes between actual quotes and paraphrases or summaries. Also, record the sources of all your notes—especially of quoted, summarized, and paraphrased material—which you may need to cite in your essay.

As you gather information, you should consider keeping a "research journal" where you can record your own opinions, interpretations, and analyses in response to your reading. This journal should be separate from your notes on sources and is the place where you can make your own discoveries in relation to your topic by jotting down thoughts and relationships among ideas you are exposed to, by keeping a record of sources you read and others you want to pursue, by tracking and developing your own ideas and theories, and by clarifying your thinking on an issue.

Finally, before you write your first draft, you might want to write an informal working outline for your own information. Such an exercise can help you check the range of your coverage and the order and development of your ideas. With an outline, you can readily see where you need more information, less information, or more solid sources. Try to be flexible, however. This outline may change dramatically as your essay develops.

Writing. Writing the first draft of a documented essay is your chance to discover new insights and to find important connections between ideas that you may not be aware of yet. This draft is your opportunity to demonstrate that you understand the issue at hand and your sources on three increasingly difficult levels— literal, interpretive, and analytical; that you can organize your material effectively; that you can integrate your sources (in the form of summaries, paraphrases, or quotations) with your opinions; and that you can document (that is, cite) your sources.

To begin this process, look again at your thesis statement and your working outline, and adjust them to represent any new discoveries you have made as you read your sources and wrote in your research journal. Then, organize your research notes and information in some logical fashion.

When you begin to draft your paper, write the sections of the essay that you feel most comfortable about first. Throughout the essay, feature your own point of view and integrate summaries, paraphrases, and quotations from other sources into your own analysis. Each point you make should be a section of your paper consisting of your own conclusion and your support for that conclusion (in the form of facts, examples, summaries, paraphrases, and quotations). Remember that the primary reason for doing such an assignment is to let you demonstrate your ability to synthesize material, draw your own conclusions, and analyze your sources and your own reasoning.

A documented paper usually blends three types of material:

1. *Common knowledge, such as the places and dates of events (even if you have to look them up).*
   EXAMPLE: Neil Armstrong and Edwin Aldrin first walked on the moon on July 20, 1969.
2. *Your own thoughts and observations.*
   EXAMPLE: Armstrong and Aldrin's brief walk on the moon's surface was the beginning of a new era in the U.S. space program.
3. *Someone else's thoughts and observations.*
   EXAMPLE: President Richard Nixon reacted to the moonwalk in a telephone call to the astronauts: "For one priceless moment in the history of man all the people on this earth are truly one—one in their pride in what you have done and one in our prayers that you will return safely to earth."

Of these three types of information, you must document or cite your exact source only for the third type. Negligence in citing your sources, whether purposeful or accidental, is called *plagiarism*, which comes from a Latin word meaning "kidnapper." Among student writers, plagiarism usually takes one of three forms: (1) using words from another source without quotation marks; (2) using someone else's ideas in the form of a summary or paraphrase without citing your source; and (3) using someone else's term paper as your own.

Avoiding plagiarism is quite simple: You just need to remember to acknowledge the sources of ideas or wording that you are using to support your own contentions. Acknowledging your sources also gives you credit for the reading you have done and for the ability you have developed to use sources to support your observations and conclusions.

Documentation styles vary from discipline to discipline. Ask your instructor about the particular documentation style he or she wants you to follow. The most common styles are the Modern Language Association (MLA) style, used in humanities courses, and the American Psychological Association (APA) style, used in behavioral sciences and science courses. (See any writing handbook for more details on documentation formats.)

Even though documentation styles vary somewhat from one discipline to another, the basic concept behind documentation is the same in all disciplines: You must give proper credit to other writers by acknowledging the sources of the summaries, paraphrases, and quotations that you use to support the topics in your documented paper. Once you grasp this basic concept and accept it, you will have no trouble avoiding plagiarism.

Rewriting. To rewrite your documented essay, you should play the role of your readers and impartially evaluate your argument and the sources you have used as evidence in that argument. To begin with, revise your thesis to represent all the discoveries you made as you wrote your first draft. Then, look for problems in logic throughout the essay; you might even develop an outline at this point to help evaluate your reasoning:

Are the essay's assertions clear?

Are they adequately supported?

Does your argument flow smoothly?

Are other points of view recognized and examined?

Does the organization of your paper further your assertions/argument?

Are all explanations in your paper clear?

Have you removed irrelevant material?

Have you added information to underdeveloped portions of your paper?

Next, look carefully at specific words and sentences:

Do the words say what you mean?

Do your supporting sentences clearly amplify your main ideas?

Then, check your documentation style:

Is your source material (either summarized, paraphrased, or quoted) presented fairly and accurately?

Have you rechecked the citations for all the sources in your paper?

Do you introduce the sources in your paper when appropriate?

Are your sources in the proper format according to your instructor's guidelines (MLA, APA, or another)?

Then, proofread carefully. Finally, prepare your paper to be submitted to your instructor:

Does your title page follow the assignment's regulations?

Have you prepared your paper with the proper margins?

Are your page numbers in the proper place?

If you have tables and abstracts in your paper, have you consulted the instructor and followed the appropriate rules?

Have you prepared an alphabetical list of your sources for the end of your paper?

Have you followed all your instructor's directions?

Any additional guidance you may need as you write and revise your documented essays is furnished on pages 32–33 of the Introduction.

STUDENT ESSAY: DOCUMENTATION AT WORK

The following student essay uses documented sources to support its conclusions and observations about our eating habits today. First, the writer creates a profile of carnivorous species in contrast to human beings. She then goes on to discuss the harsh realities connected with eating meat. After recognizing and refuting some opposing views, this student writer ends her paper with her own evaluation of the situation and a list of some famous vegetarians. Throughout the essay, the student writer carefully supports her principal points with summaries, paraphrases, and quotations from other sources. Notice that she uses the MLA documentation style and closes the paper with an alphabetical list of "Works Cited."

Food for Thought

The next time you sit down to a nice steak dinner, pause for a moment to consider whether you are biologically programmed to eat meat. Unlike carnivores, such as lions and tigers, with claws and sharp front teeth allowing them to tear and eat raw flesh, humans are omnivores, with fingers that can pluck fruits and grains and flat teeth that can grind these vegetable foods. To digest their meals, carnivores have an acidic saliva and a very strong hydrochloric acid digestive fluid. In contrast, we humans have an alkaline saliva, and our digestive fluids are only one-tenth as potent as those of carnivores. Moreover, carnivores have an intestinal tract barely three times their body length, which allows for faster elimination of rotting flesh; humans have an intestinal tract eight to twelve times our body length, better enabling us to digest plant nutrients. These marked physiological distinctions clearly suggest that carnivorous animals and humans are adapted to very different kinds of foods (Diamond and Diamond, *Fit for Life II* 239). What happens, then, when we eat flesh? The effects of a meat-based diet are far-reaching: massive suffering of the animals killed and eaten, a myriad of diseases in humans, and a devastating effect on world ecology.

The atrocities committed daily to provide meat should be enough to make a meat-based diet completely unconscionable. According to Peter Singer, of People for the Ethical Treatment of Animals (PETA), every year several hundred million cattle, pigs, and sheep and 3 billion chickens are slaughtered to provide food for hu-

Margin notes:

Background information

Common knowledge

Common knowledge

Paraphrase of secondary source

Citation (MLA form)

Thesis

Student's first conclusion

Summary of secondary source

mans (*Animal Liberation* 92). That is equal to 6,278 animals every minute of every day—and those are just the ones that make it to the slaughterhouse. Over 500,000 animals die in transit each year (Singer, *Animal Liberation* 150).

Support for conclusion #1

A slaughterhouse is not a pretty sight. Anywhere from 50 to 90 percent of the cattle are slaughtered in a "kosher" manner (Robbins 142). "Kosher" sounds innocent enough, but what it actually means is that the animal must be "healthy and moving" at the time of death. This requires the animals to be fully conscious as "a heavy chain is clamped around one of their rear legs; then they are jerked off their feet and hang upside down" for anywhere from two to five minutes, usually twisting in agony with a broken leg, while they are moved down the conveyer belt to be slaughtered (Robbins 140–41).

Paraphrase of secondary source (fact)

Summary of secondary source

The pain doesn't start at the time of slaughter, however, for most of these animals, but rather at birth. An in-depth look at the animal most slaughtered by people, the chicken, reveals particularly horrendous treatment. Chickens are used in two ways: for their flesh and for their eggs. For egg manufacturers, the one-half million male chicks born every day are useless, so they are immediately thrown into garbage bags and left to suffocate. When you consider the life of their female counterparts, however, perhaps such brutal treatment is a blessing (Robbins 54).

Student's opinion

Examples to support opinion

Paraphrase of secondary source (opinion)

Chickens naturally belong to a flock with a specific pecking order. They seem to enjoy open spaces to stretch their wings as they scratch around, dust-bathe, and build nests for their eggs (Singer, *Animal Liberation*

Paraphrase of secondary source (facts)

599

Para-
phrase of
secondary
source
(facts)
109). Today, however, chickens are housed in wire-mesh cages suspended over a trench to collect droppings. The typical cage is 12 by 18 inches, holding four or five hens for their entire productive life, which is at least a year or more (Mason in Singer, *Defense* 91). This overcrowding results in such high levels of stress that the hens resort to pecking each other's feathers out and to canni-
balism (Singer, *Animal Liberation* 98). Rather than incur the expense of increasing space to alleviate these conditions, chicken farm-
ers have routinely adopted the practice of debeaking the hens by slicing a hot knife through their highly sensitive beak tissue (Singer, *Animal Liberation* 99). Another result of this overcrowding is that the hens' toe-
nails get tangled in the bottom wires of the cages; after some time the flesh grows onto the wire. The solution to this problem has become to cut off the chick's toes within a day or two of birth (Robbins 61). Conditions for other farm animals are equally despicable (Singer, *Defense*).

Analysis
from
secondary
source

Para-
phrase of
secondary
sources
(facts)

Para-
phrase of
secondary
source
(opinion)

While we would like to assume the ani-
mals we eat are healthy at the time of butchering, this is often not the case. Most veal calves, for example, are near death from anemia when sent to the butcher (Diamond and Diamond, *Fit for Life II* 238). Inspections have revealed leukosis (cancer) in 90 percent of the chickens (Robbins 67), pneumonia rates of 80 percent and stomach ulcers of 53 percent in pigs (Robbins 94). Salmonellosis is found in 90 percent of the chickens dressed and ready to be purchased (Robbins 303).

Student's
opinion

Examples
from
secondary
sources

How can the factory farming industry justify its behavior? The answer boils down to money, for factory farming has become

Student's
opinion

an incredibly huge business, and meat producers can't afford to be sentimental. As shown by USDA Economic Indicators for the Farm Sector, in 1988 the United States had cash receipts totaling over $150 billion **Para-** from farm marketing (*State Financial* **phrase of** *Summary* 151) and nearly $80 billion from **secondary** **sources** livestock and livestock products (153). As **(fact)** Fred Haley, head of a poultry farm with nearly 250,000 hens, has stated, "The object of producing eggs is to make money. When **Quotation** we forget this objective, we have forgotten **from** **secondary** what it is all about" (qtd. in Robbins 67). **source**

Cattle auctioneer Henry Pace has a similar comment about the treatment of cattle: **Quotation** "We believe we can be most efficient by **from** not being emotional. We are a business, not **secondary** **source** a humane society, and our job is to sell merchandise at a profit. It's no different from selling paper clips or refrigerators" (qtd. in Robbins 104).

Student's Even if we, like the industry leaders, **second** could turn a cold heart to the plight of our **conclusion** fellow creatures, we would still find many reasons to warrant a vegetarian diet, beginning with our own health. Recapping just a few of the hundreds of studies that link diet to disease, we might consider the following:

Para- —A study of nearly 90,000 American **Support** **phrase of** women published in the *New England* **for second** **secondary** **conclusion** **sources** *Journal of Medicine* reports that daily pork, **(facts)** lamb, or beef eaters have a 250 percent greater likelihood of developing colon cancer than people who consume these foods once a month or less ("Red Meat Alert").

—The *Journal of the American Medical Association* stated that a vegetarian diet could prevent 97 percent of coronary occlusions (Robbins 247).

—Scientists now routinely screen cattle workers for BIV, a disease that "shares about 35 percent of its genetic makeup with HIV," the human AIDS retrovirus ("Cattle's Link with AIDS" 19).

Other equally shocking residual health problems associated with a meat diet are also being documented. For instance, people tend to think that vegetarians are at high risk for pesticide poisoning, but ac-

Summary of secondary source cording to the EPA's *Pesticides Monitoring Journal*, most pesticides in the American diet come from foods originating from animals. Studies have shown that 95 to 99 percent of toxic chemicals in the American diet come from meat, fish, and animal products (Robbins 315). These same pesticides are ending up in the milk of lactating mothers. A similar study in the *New England Journal of Medicine* showed that the breast milk of vegetarian mothers has contamination levels only 1 to 2 percent of the average (Robbins 345). Not only does vegetarian breast milk have strikingly lower levels of contamination, it also has higher levels of essential elements, such as selenium (Debski et al. 215).

Paraphrase of secondary sources (facts)

Student's question But don't we need a lot of protein to be strong and healthy? The RDA for protein is 56 grams (just under 2 ounces) per day (Diamond and Diamond, *Fit for Life* 88). People seem to think that meat is the best (or the only) way to get protein, but think about this: Some of the world's strongest animals—elephants, horses, and gorillas— eat principally fruits, grain, or grass (Diamond, *Fit for Life* 89–90). Lest you believe that humans must eat meat to be strong and healthy, consider the following: Edwin Moses, undefeated in the 400-meter

Paraphrase of secondary source (fact)

Paraphrase of secondary source (fact)

hurdles for eight years, is a vegetarian; Andreas Cahling, 1980 Mr. International Body Builder, is a vegetarian (Robbins 160–61); and Dave Scott, Ironman Triathlon winner four times (no one else has won it more than once), is a vegetarian (Robbins 158). In study after study, the consumption of protein is linked not with health but with such illnesses as heart disease, hypertension, various forms of cancer, arthritis, and osteoporosis (Diamond and Diamond, *Fit for Life* 87).

Examples that answer protein question

The effects of meat diets go beyond causing human disease and death. Perhaps the most frightening legacy being left by America's dietary ritual is just now being realized, and that is the profound ecological impact factory farming is having on our planet. Every five seconds, one acre of forest is cleared in America, and one estimate is that 87 percent is cleared for either livestock grazing or growing livestock feed (Robbins 361). According to Christopher Uhl of the Pennsylvania State University Department of Biology and Geoffrey Parker of the Institute of Ecosystem Studies, 55 square feet of forest in Central America is lost for each hamburger eaten (642).

Forests are not all that we are sacrificing. Local governments are constantly calling for water conservation, yet over 50 percent of all water used in America goes into grain production for livestock (Robbins 367). According to one study, the water required to feed a meat eater for one day is 4,000 gallons, but it is only 1,200 gallons for a lacto-ovo (dairy and egg eating) vegetarian and 300 gallons for a vegan (one who consumes no animal-derived products) (Robbins 367). Not only is the vast amount of water wasted

603

through a meat-based diet outrageous, but the added cost of controlling animal waste must also be taken into account. One cow produces sixteen times as much waste as one human (Robbins 372), and cattle waste produces ten times the water pollution that human waste does (Robbins 373).

Student's opinion A third loss is even more serious than the losses of forests and water. This year, 60 million people will die of starvation, yet in America, we feed 80 percent of our corn and 95 percent of our oats to farm animals. The feed given to cattle alone, excluding pigs and chickens, would feed double the population of humans worldwide (Robbins 352). Three and one-quarter acres of farmland are needed to provide meat for one person per year. A lacto-ovo vegetarian can be fed from just one-half acre per year; a vegan needs only one-sixth of an acre. This means twenty vegans can eat a healthy diet for the same acreage needed to feed just one meat eater. Cutting our meat habit by only 10 percent would provide enough food for all of the 60 million people worldwide who will starve this year (Robbins 352–353).

Paraphrase of secondary sources (facts)

As John Robbins, who relinquished his inheritance of the largest ice cream company in America, Baskin-Robbins, said, "We live in a crazy time, when people who make food choices that are healthy and compassionate are often considered weird, while people are considered normal whose eating habits promote disease and are dependent on enormous suffering" (305).

Quotation from secondary source

With all the devastation the average American diet is creating, we must begin to take responsibility for the consequences of our actions. Let us follow in the footsteps

Student's final remarks

of such famous vegetarians as Charles Darwin, Leonardo da Vinci, Albert Einstein, Sir Isaac Newton, Plato, Pythagoras, Socrates, and Tolstoy (Parham 185). Every time we sit down to eat, we can choose either to contribute to or to help put an end to this suffering and destruction. Only one move matters, and that is the one we make with our forks.

Works Cited

Alphabetical list of sources

Modern Language Association form

"Cattle's Link with AIDS." *New Scientist* 8 Oct. 1987:19.

Debski, Bogdan, et al. "Selenium Content and Glutathione Peroxidase Activity of Milk from Vegetarian and Nonvegetarian Women." *Journal of Nutrition* 119 (1989):215–20.

Diamond, Harvey, and Marilyn Diamond. *Fit for Life*. New York: Warner, 1985.

———. *Fit for Life II, Living Health*. New York: Warner, 1987.

Parham, Barbara. *What's Wrong with Eating Meat?* Denver: Ananda Marga, 1981.

"Red Meat Alert." *New Scientist* 22/29 Dec. 1990.

Robbins, John. *Diet for a New America*. Walpole: Stillpoint, 1987.

Singer, Peter. *Animal Liberation: A New Ethics for Our Treatment of Animals*. New York: Hearst, 1975.

———, ed. *In Defense of Animals*. New York: Basil Blackwell, 1985.

State Financial Summary, 1988. Washington: Economic Indicators for the Farm Sector, 1988.

Uhl, Christopher, and Geoffrey Parker. "Our Steak in the Jungle." *Bio Science* 36 (1986):642.

Student Writer's Comments

From the moment this essay was assigned, I knew my topic would be vegetarianism, because I felt the key to a convincing argument was to select a topic I was passionate about. Since I was undertaking the task of speaking out against the time-honored American tradition of eating meat, I knew I needed to approach the topic in as nonthreatening a manner as possible. I wanted to be graphic as I appealed to the emotions, concerns, and ethics of my audience, so that my message would not easily be forgotten, but I had to strike a careful balance, so that I would not alienate my readers by appearing preachy, accusatory, or unduly crude.

I began the process of writing this paper by going to the library every chance I had (between classes, during lunch, and at night before I went home) and collecting information on the horror stories connected with eating meat. (I had been a loyal vegetarian for years and actually wanted some concrete information on some of the choices I had made in my own eating habits.) I found plenty of horror stories, but I also uncovered some counterarguments that I hadn't been aware of. I was fascinated by the information—both facts and opinions—that I was discovering. But the material wasn't taking any shape at all yet; the only common denominator was the general topic and my interest level.

I was taking notes on notecards, so I had filled quite a stack of cards when I stopped to reread all my material to see if I could put it into any coherent categories. Happily, my notes fell quite naturally into three divisions: (1) the overwhelming cruelty to the animals that we kill and eat, (2) the diseases resulting from eating animals, and (3) the effect of this type of slaughter on world ecology. After this exercise, I could see right away that I had enough material on the suffering of the animals killed for human consumption, and my material in this area was from well-known, reputable sources. My notes on world ecology would be sufficient as well with a few more library sessions, but I had to do some serious investigation on the topic of human diseases in reference to meat eaters or else drop the topic altogether. I had some stray notes that didn't fit any of these categories, but I decided to worry about those later. I tried my hand at a thesis statement, which I think had been floating around in my head for days. Then, I wrote the paper topic by topic over a period of several days. I didn't attempt the introduction and the conclusion until I began to rewrite. As I composed the essay, I was especially aware of the types of material I had to support each of my topics. I had a good distribution of summaries, paraphrases, and quotations and had remembered to keep careful notes on my sources, so I put my source and page numbers into my first draft. I also had several examples for each of my topics and a good blend of facts and opinions.

When I rewrote, I kept in mind that I would be successful in arguing my case only if my words caused the readers to make a change, however small, in their own behavior. I reworked my research paper several times as I played different readers with various biases, during which time I paid special attention to word choice and sentence structure.

Overall, writing this paper gave me a great deal of pleasure. I feel even stronger in my determination to be a vegetarian, and now I have some concrete reasons (and their sources!) for my natural instincts.

SOME FINAL THOUGHTS ON DOCUMENTED ESSAYS

The two essays that follow offer vigorous exercises in critical thinking. They both use a combination of the three different types of persuasive appeals we studied in Chapter 9 (logical, emotional, and ethical) and draw on a wealth of rhetorical modes that we have studied throughout the book. In the first essay, John Langone illustrates the APA documentation format as he dissects and analyzes the notion of mob violence. In the next essay, on Latina health issues, Adela de la Torre uses sources to support her thesis in favor of increased government support of health services for Latin Americans in the United States; it demonstrates the MLA documentation style. As you read these essays, be aware of the combination of appeals at work, the various rhetorical modes each author uses to further his or her argument, and the way each author uses sources to support the topics within the argument.

JOHN LANGONE   (1929 –   )

■ ■ ■

Group Violence

The fifteen books written by scientist/journalist John Langone since the mid-1960s have ranged over a fascinating array of topics, including violence, suicide, death and dying, aging, sex education, mental illness, genetic manipulation, drug abuse, and medical ethics. He grew up in Cambridge, Massachusetts, in a family of scientists and spent a great deal of time in the biology and physiology laboratories at Harvard University, where two of his uncles worked. Although he remained interested in science, he pursued educational and employment opportunities that took him in the direction of journalism. Following a B.S. at Boston University, Langone held several newspaper jobs before becoming Rhode Island bureau chief for United Press International, science editor at the *Boston Herald*, and then senior editor of *Discover* magazine. He is currently associate editor for medical news at *Time* magazine. Three academic fellowships have helped the author bring together his dual interests in journalism and science: a Kennedy Fellowship in medical ethics at Harvard, a Fulbright Scholarship at the University of Tokyo Medical School, and a journalism fellowship at the Center for Advanced Study in the Behavioral Sciences at Stanford. Langone describes himself as "a compulsive writer who has been nurtured in the deadline world of daily newspaper and wire service reporting." His latest book, *Superconductivity: The New Alchemy* (1989), examines the far-reaching implications of research in superconductors—materials that transport electricity without substantial loss of energy. In his private life, the author enjoys gardening, playing ice hockey, reading Shakespeare, and listening to music—particularly Mozart and Liszt.

Preparing to Read

The following essay, taken from *Violence: Our Fastest Growing Public Health Problem* (1984), analyzes the basic causes of mob psychology; its citations and bibliography illustrate proper APA (American

Psychological Association) documentation form. Before you read Langone's article, take a few minutes to think about violence in general: How would you define a "violent" action? How many different types of violent acts can you think of? What are the major similarities among these acts? What do individual violence and group violence have in common? How are they different? How could we control violence in America more effectively than we do now?

V iolence can be done by individuals with their own pri- 1 vate motives, and by individuals working for the motives of a special group. Many times, when one person assaults another it is for highly personal reasons: A drug dealer murders an undercover agent to escape arrest, a woman kills a lover who has been cheating on her to punish him and the other woman, an irate employee murders the manager who fired him, a young man provokes a brawl to prove he is tough, a woman is raped because her attacker was once spurned by a high school girlfriend and now hates all women.

But quite often, individuals commit violent acts not only to sat- 2 isfy themselves, but also to gain some benefit for a group of people. They may belong to a lynch mob that takes the law into its own hands and executes a suspect before he or she has had a fair trial; they may be members of a secret society of misguided zealots that uses violence to intimidate; they may be participants in a family feud, a private war waged for generations to avenge the death of one of its members long ago; they may be political terrorists who use violence to force change, or to call attention to their cause, or to avenge some real or imagined or long-past insult or wrong. Some people may not even be members of the group for whom they commit violence: A hired assassin, for instance, might not be at all concerned with the philosophy or actions of the world leader he has been paid to eliminate, nor have any personal grudge against him. But whether such hired killers formally belong to an organization is not all that important; their reasons for maiming and killing are usually to further the aims of that group.

Let us begin our discussion of group violence by looking at 3 what psychologists call crowd behavior, popularly known as mob psychology. Certainly, there are no formal membership requirements, no dues to be paid, to join a lynch mob or a student riot.

Unlike some of the other forms of group violence to be discussed later, mob violence is often unplanned and unorganized; a mob's members lose their ability to think rationally, so intent are they on acting as one; its leadership generally depends on who can shout the loudest or who is strong enough to get to the front of the crowd fastest. Moreover, a mob generally breaks up rather quickly once its purpose has been achieved. Says one sociology textbook, "In crowd behavior, irrational as it always is, the impulse to follow a suggested course of action is obeyed at once; whereas, in any form of rational behavior, there is always delay enough to permit comparisons and evaluations" (Sutherland & Woodward, 1940, p. 317).

Experts in mob psychology say the anatomy of a riot begins 4 with a precipitating event, a trigger. This may be the arrest of someone the crowd believes to be innocent or a scapegoat; an assault on a white by a black or vice versa; a simple official act, like the dedication of a statue of a controversial figure; the parking of a foreign car near an automobile factory that suffered high unemployment because of foreign-car imports; or merely the announcement that a state has approved the construction of a nuclear power plant.

As word of the triggering event spreads, the crowd becomes 5 angrier; finally, violence erupts, escalating from shouting and occasional rock throwing to open street war as the rioters clash with police, others in authority, or those who oppose their views. Such a situation has been compared to the outbreak of a disease epidemic. Dr. John P. Spiegel, who headed the Lemberg Center for the Study of Violence at Brandeis University, once said of mass violence, "You just can't ignore it, isolate it, or hope that it will cure itself" ("Is Mass Violence," 1967, p. 48).

Often, the common hostility of a crowd has been festering for 6 some time and is not just a sudden eruption. If, for instance, a hostile mob has gathered at a civil rights parade, the concerted action taken when some incident or person ignites the violence is the result of a long-standing racial conflict shimmering in each member of the crowd. Matters are obviously made much worse, and the mob becomes more inflamed, if whatever it is that provokes the riot has not been dealt with fairly, or at all, by authorities.

A mob generally behaves in ways that its individual members 7 would shun if alone: Few members of a riotous crowd would, for

example, stand alone in front of a policeman and shout obsceni-
ties at him; nor would many people break a store window in
broad daylight and help themselves to a television set or a wristwatch; and it is highly unlikely that mob members would, acting
alone, attempt to crash a gate at a navy base to protest the docking of a nuclear submarine. It is the *gathering* of individuals, with
their strong, shared feeling, that gives the individuals within the
group their sense of courage and power, and allows each to release impulses usually kept under control. Wartime and periods of
insurrection contain proof of that. For example, on Easter
Monday in 1282, on the island of Sicily, a riot broke out after a
French soldier insulted a Sicilian woman in front of a church at
the hour of evening worship, or vespers; in what came to be
known as the Sicilian Vespers, the riot swelled to a political revolt
against the Angevin French who ruled the island, and virtually
the entire French population was murdered. In Nanking, China,
during World War II, drunken Japanese soldiers and sailors slaughtered 150,000 Chinese and raped some 5,000 women in an outbreak of mob brutality that seems almost inconceivable.

Mob action, like the violence it spawns, is not new. Dissent has   8
a long history, and mobs have gathered since at least the early
Roman days—when loud protests were lodged even then against
the high cost of living—to air economic, political, and social
grievances, or to vent their anger against other groups. In China
in 1900, for example, a branch of a sect known as the White
Lotus—also   called   Boxers—rose   up   against   foreigners.
Missionaries were murdered, a German official was assassinated,
and later some two hundred foreigners were driven to seek
refuge in the British legation. They were besieged by the Boxers
for two months and were finally rescued by an expedition of soldiers from America, Great Britain, France, Germany, Russia, and
Japan. A few years later, on January 22, 1905, Russian peasant
workers marched on Saint Petersburg to present a petition to the
czar. They were attacked by the czar's troops and hundreds of unarmed workers were killed.

In the United States, mobs turned against immigrants, espe-   9
cially Orientals and Irish Catholics, in the 1800s. Native-born
Americans, fearful that the immigrants would gain political
power, and angry that they were taking jobs for cheaper pay, regularly attacked the immigrants in the streets. During the same pe-

riod, bloody labor riots erupted in cities across the United States, and many lives were lost. In 1886, for instance, there was the celebrated Haymarket riot in Chicago. It occurred when police tried to break up a labor protest meeting organized by anarchists—people who believe that all forms of government are unnecessary and undesirable. Someone threw a bomb, killing seven policemen and wounding seventy other people. A few years later, during the so-called Homestead strike at the Carnegie Steel Company plant in Pennsylvania, an armed clash took place between workers and detectives hired by the company; a number of men were killed, and soon after, the state militia had to be sent in to restore order.

Even today, workers are sometimes set upon. In 1983, when a   10
group of independent truckers went on strike, thousands of trucks that defied the strike and kept on rolling were damaged by rocks thrown from bridges, by nails spread on the highways, and by gunfire. Many drivers were injured and one was killed.

Race has also been a factor in mob violence. During World   11
War I (1914–1918), many blacks took jobs in defense factories. The whites were afraid that the blacks would take their jobs and move into white neighborhoods. Several violent incidents occurred—the worst in East Saint Louis in 1917 when some forty blacks and ten whites were killed during a riot. Similar racial violence broke out after World War II (1939–1945) and has continued through the years. Among the worst in recent years were the riots in the Watts section of Los Angeles in 1965 and in Newark and Detroit in 1967.

In the sixties and seventies, mob violence was common during   12
the student protests against the war in Vietnam (1957–1975). In one of the largest such demonstrations, thousands of young people gathered in Chicago during the 1968 Democratic National Convention and battled with police in the streets. Around the same time, militant black students regularly resorted to violence to back up demands for more Afro-American history and culture courses in their colleges.

But of all this mob violence, the two incidents that stand out   13
in recent years, perhaps for the emotional impact they had on Americans, were the tragic student deaths at Kent State University in Ohio in 1970 and the riot at Attica state prison in New York the following year. The two events were unrelated—the Kent State incident came during demonstrations against

President Nixon's decision to send U.S. forces into Cambodia, and the Attica uprising stemmed from charges that inmates, most of them black, had been mistreated by white guards. But both places have become unofficial national monuments to the tragic consequences of confrontation.

The Kent State incident began with students throwing rocks, 14 bricks, and bottles at National Guardsmen and guardsmen firing tear gas. Then, some of the guardsmen knelt and pointed rifles at demonstrators, who shouted, "Shoot, shoot, shoot!" The kneeling guardsmen did not fire. But moments later, it happened. "I heard the first shot," one account quoted a guardsman as saying. "I had my rifle at my shoulder, not sighting, just at my shoulder. I had my finger on the trigger and fired when the others did. I just didn't think about it. It just happened. How can you think at a time like that? Right after the first shot, it sounded like everyone squeezed off one round, like at the range, drawn out. I fired once. I just closed my eyes and shot. I didn't aim at anyone in particular. I just shot at shoulder level toward the crowd." An estimated sixty shots were fired, and thirteen seconds later, when it was over, four of the student demonstrators had been killed, nine wounded. Two reporters who were there that day wrote, "Most of the victims were dressed in bell-bottoms and flowered Apache shirts, and most had Rolling Stone haircuts. Some carried books. The guardsmen wore battle helmets, gas masks, fatigues, and combat boots. The two sides looked, to each other, like the in-habitants of different worlds. . . . Blood shimmered on the grass. Bullet holes marked the trees. A generation of college students said they had lost all hope for the System and the future" (Eszterhas & Roberts, 1970, pp. 8, 163).

The Attica incident was just as chaotic. The revolt involved 15 some one thousand prisoners, who held thirty-eight guards and civilian workers hostage for four days. Faced with the possibility that the convicts would carry out threats to kill the hostages, New York Governor Nelson Rockefeller ordered state troopers to storm the facility. In the assault, which included use of a tear-gas-spraying helicopter, thirty-two prisoners and nine guards and employees were killed. Rockefeller, who had turned down a request that he personally visit the prison during the revolt, defended the action, saying, "There was no alternative but to go in." Adding to the depth of the tragedy were reports that many of the hostages

had died of bullet wounds, rather than by knife attacks from convicts—an indication that, as commonly happens in scenes of mob
violence, some people were killed unintentionally. Shortly after the
riot was quelled, Rockefeller acknowledged that it was possible
state troopers had killed some of the hostages. "If you recreate the
circumstances of that situation—where the troopers had instructions to shoot the executioners who had been assigned to each of
the prisoners [a reference to convicts menacing hostages] and who
were standing there with a knife at his throat—then you add to
that the helicopter coming in with the gas, and the effect of the
gas—which first creates a cloud and then has an effect on the individual—you have a scene of chaos that is one in which accidents
can very well happen" (New York Times, 1971, p. 1).

Both the Kent State tragedy and the awful ending to the Attica   16
revolt raise questions about how much force should be used to
put down a disturbance. Often, as has been seen, the mob itself
loots and burns and kills; other times, however, it is the authorities who lose control and riot. The Boston Massacre of March 5,
1770, is a familiar example of such a situation, and one that is
sometimes used when the events at Kent State are being discussed. The stationing of British soldiers in Boston in 1768 had
provoked a good deal of anger among the citizens. Matters came
to a head when more troops were sent to the city to protect customs commissioners. A mob of men and boys, led by a black
named Crispus Attucks, began throwing missiles at the soldiers,
who responded by firing into the crowd, killing five. Some witnesses regarded the unfortunate incident as a lawless affair that
discredited both soldiers and the crowd; others have seen it as a
historically significant event, an important preliminary to the
American Revolution. Whatever it was, it lends substance to the
old expression that a policeman's lot is not a happy one. "Police
often vacillate between brutal suppression and inaction," said Dr.
Spiegel. "If they use excessive force, they encourage the use of
counterforce. If they do nothing, they encourage rioters and loot-
ers" ("Is Mass Violence," 1967, p. 48).

The Kent State and Attica incidents may also make it some-   17
what easier to justify the violent explosion of a mob. Many people become angered after being maltreated, as at Attica, or
provoked, as were the guardsmen at Kent State, and it is quite

natural, although perhaps wrong, to lash out occasionally at the people believed responsible. When nobody listens to a complaint that appears to be legitimate, when nobody tries to rectify a bad situation, a violent act is perhaps the only way left to focus attention on the wrong and help get something done about it.

References

Eszterhas, J., & Roberts, M. (1970). *Thirteen seconds: Confrontations at Kent State.* New York: Dodd, Mead.

Farrell, W. E. (1971, September 16). Governor defends order to quell Attica uprising; appoints chief of inquiry. *New York Times*, pp. 1, 48.

Is mass violence an epidemic disease? (1967, September 1). *Medical World News*, pp. 48–52.

Sutherland, R., & Woodward, J. (1940). *Introductory sociology.* Philadelphia: Lippincott.

UNDERSTANDING DETAILS

1. What characterizes "mob violence" (paragraph 3) according to Langone?
2. How can individuals lose their sense of right and wrong when they are part of a mob? What types of behavior may take place? What causes these changes in behavior?
3. What would qualify as a "precipitating event" or a "trigger" (paragraph 4) for group violence?
4. What role does race frequently play in group violence?

ANALYZING MEANING

1. What are the main differences between group and individual violence? Do these differences give you any clues for controlling either type of violence?
2. According to Langone, what generally gives groups their "sense of courage and power" (paragraph 7)? How would you define *courage* and *power* in this context? What are the consequences of this courage and power?
3. The Kent State and Attica revolts came at approximately the same time in America's history. What were the similarities and differences between these two examples of group violence?
4. This essay was written before the violent outbreak in Los Angeles following the verdict in the first Rodney King trial. From your memory of that event, how did the violence start,

and at what point did it take on a life of its own? Does this chain of events support Langone's theories of mob violence?

DISCOVERING RHETORICAL STRATEGIES

1. Which events cited by Langone convince you most clearly that group violence exhibits characteristics different from acts of individual violence?
2. How does Langone organize his essay? List his main topics in the order in which he presents them. What effect does this order have on the reader? What different effects could be produced by changing the order of these topics?
3. Who do you think is Langone's intended audience? How did you come to this conclusion?
4. What main rhetorical modes does Langone use to state his case? Give examples of each.

MAKING CONNECTIONS

1. Compare and contrast Langone's insights into group violence with those expressed by George Orwell in "Shooting an Elephant." Which author do you think describes group violence most accurately? Explain your answer.
2. Compare Langone's use of statistics and documentation with that of Adela de la Torre ("Key Issues in Latina Health"). Which author uses statistics and documentation most effectively? Which essay seems most convincing to you? Does the credibility of this essay have anything to do with the author's use of statistics and documentation?
3. Langone and Nancy Gibbs ("When Is It Rape?") both discuss the reasons that America is such a violent nation. Which reasons do these two authors agree on? Which are mentioned solely by one author? Can you think of any reasons not mentioned by either author? If so, what are they?

IDEAS FOR DISCUSSION/WRITING

Preparing to Write

Write freely about violence in general: What characterizes acts of violence? When, in your opinion, is violence justified? When is it not justified? How should group violence be handled once it breaks out? Why do you think violence is so out of control in America? How much force against violent acts is warranted in your opinion? At what point does control of violence become brutality?

Choosing a Topic

1. Langone says, "When nobody listens to a complaint that appears to be legitimate, when nobody tries to rectify a bad situation, a violent act is perhaps the only way left to focus attention on the wrong, and help get something done about it" (paragraph 17). Do you agree or disagree with this statement? Explain your reaction in a clearly reasoned argumentative essay. Cite Langone's selection whenever necessary.

2. What do you think the role of the police should be in controlling group violence? Use Langone's article as one of your sources, and then read further on the subject in the library. Find specific incidences of crime and violence to support your argument. (The riot following the Rodney King trial might be a good source of information.) Next, write a clear, well-documented argumentative essay explaining your opinion on this issue. Organize your paper clearly and present your suggestions logically, using proper documentation (citations and bibliography) to clarify your point of view.

3. Use additional library sources to study the circumstances at Kent State and at Attica prison. Then, referring to Langone's explanation of "the anatomy of a riot" (paragraph 4), write a well-documented essay analyzing the similarities and differences between these two situations.

■

ADELA DE LA TORRE   (1954 –   )

■ ■ ■

Key Issues in Latina Health: Voicing Latina Concerns in the Health Financing Debate

Adela de la Torre's diverse and interesting educational background has led her to California State University at Long Beach, where she is currently a professor in the Health Care Administration Department and the chair of Chicano and Latino Studies. Following two degrees at the University of California at Berkeley—a B.S. in the political economy of natural resources and a Ph.D. in agricultural and resource economics—she did postdoctoral training at the Medical School of the University of California at San Francisco. Her principal academic fields are now health care finance, Hispanic health, and immigration. Her most recent publication is *Building with Our Hands: New Directions in Chicana Studies* (coauthored in 1993 with Beatrice M. Pesquera). She also writes a regular political column for the *Los Angeles Times*, which, she says, has generated lots of "interesting mail." A marathon runner in her spare time (with four appearances in the Los Angeles Marathon under her belt), she now lives in Los Angeles "with a husband, two kids, and a dog." Asked to give advice to students using *The Prose Reader*, de la Torre replied that "writing must be a daily activity" and that "students should read constantly in order to become good writers." Committed to issues of racial and ethnic harmony, the author insists that "writing forces us all to be civil in a very human way."

Preparing to Read

Taken from an anthology entitled *Chicana Critical Issues* (1993), the following essay argues strongly for a reevaluation of Latina health care, including increased access to physicians, improved insurance plans, and major policy shifts within governmental agencies. Its citations and bibliography illustrate proper MLA (Modern Language Association) documentation form. As you prepare to read this article, take a few minutes to think about health care issues in the United States: What group of people has a fairly good health care plan? Why is this segment of the population the most protected? Should it be? What specific populations in the United States are omitted from health care programs? Does the country as a whole have any responsibility for the uninsured? The under-insured? Do you think the state or federal government should take any responsibility for this second group? Should the state or federal government put any pressure on employers to require health insurance coverage? Where could the money for these changes in health care coverage come from?

■

Demographic Trends: Implications for Latina Health

L atinos in the United States represent a rapidly growing and 1 diverse population. According to the recent census, there are over twenty-two million Latinos comprised of several subgroups: Mexican-origin/Chicano, Puerto Rican, Cuban, and other Central and South American groups. As a result of geographic proximity, as well as political and economic forces, the Mexican-origin population comprises the bulk of the Latino population in the United States. Over sixty percent of Latinos in the U.S. are of Mexican-origin, twelve percent are Puerto Rican, and about five percent Cuban (Ginzberg 22–23). Latinos are the fastest growing group in the United States due to both relatively higher fertility rates and their high rates of immigration.

Concentrations of Latinos in various states, i.e., Mexican ori- 2 gin in the Southwest, Cubans in Florida, and Puerto Ricans in New York, not only reflect patterns of network migration, but also magnify the problems and concerns facing these various groups. For example, in states such as California and Texas, where about one-quarter of the residents are of Mexican origin, in-equities in health or education affecting Mexicanos/Chicanos will be of greater significance in policy deliberations and forma-tion. Another critical component in the demographic Latino pro-file is the increased feminization of poverty. The breakdown of the two-parent household, as well as the legacy of the Reagan ad-ministration's attack on social welfare programs targeted for the poor and working poor, has disproportionately affected minority groups, particularly Latinas. According to one study: "In the

Southwest, more women became head of households between 1970 and 1980. Over forty percent of all Chicana and Black female headed families were poor in 1980, whereas only eighteen percent of White female headed households in the Southwest were poor" (de la Torre and Rochin 8).

Although poverty measures generally focus on income and   3
earning, "it is also a social condition apparent by such indicators as housing, schooling, nutrition, and medical care" (Gordon-Bradshaw 247–48). In the United States, no social indicator is more sensitive to economic status than access to health care. As private health insurance is largely determined by employment status, workers who work part-time, are self-employed, are in sectors such as agriculture, personal services, sales or who work for small businesses are the least likely to have health insurance coverage (Council on Scientific Affairs 249). Unfortunately, many Latinas/Chicanas fall within this status, thus limiting their access to private health insurance, and subsequently, influencing the observed health status problems. Access to health care for Latinas not only is a problem of financial constraints but also reflects limited access to regular and routine medical care (Furino and Munoz 256). Thus, both financing and the delivery of care play pivotal roles in describing the access problems facing Latinas. Only within the context of access to care can the significance of the health status problems facing Latinas be understood and [can] strategies to ameliorate their specific health problems be appropriately developed and delivered.

Latina Health Status Issues: An Overview

In general, the Latino population is relatively youthful. Whereas   4
the general population exhibits an aging pattern with fertility levels below a steady state of reproduction, the Latino population exhibits a relatively high fertility rate: for the United States general population the fertility rate is about 65/1000 live births, compared to 97/1000 live births for Hispanics. A typical pattern observed of Latinas, is that they give birth at younger ages and have on average more children than the general population (Council on Scientific Affairs 248). Given the relatively higher fertility rates for Latinas, an obvious need is access to prenatal and postpartum care, as well as to family planning information.

Several studies that focus on health behaviors and access to   5 care of Latinas observe that these women underutilize such services. According to one study: "Excluding Cubans, sixty percent of Hispanics initiate prenatal care in the first trimester, compared with eighty percent of Whites. Hispanics are three times as likely as non-Hispanics to receive no prenatal care. Among the subgroups, Puerto Ricans received prenatal care later and less often" (Council of Scientific Affairs 249).

Underutilization of health services by Latinas, particularly 6 those services, such as prenatal care, that are comparatively better financed by the public sector than other outpatient services, is a major concern for many public health advocates because of the increased risk associated with insufficient prenatal care for low-income women (Braveman et al. 511). Although Latinas underutilize prenatal care, birth outcomes for specific subpopulations, such as Mexican-Americans, are relatively good. It has been suggested that surprisingly positive birth outcomes for certain Latina subpopulations can be attributed to low levels of acculturation and recent immigrant status (Furino and Munoz 256). Despite their lower social class, the positive health behaviors of recently immigrated Latinas with respect to alcohol, drug, and cigarette use influence the observed birth outcomes. That is, studies of recent immigrant Latinas, particularly Mexican-origin Latinas, suggest relatively low levels of alcohol, tobacco, and drug abuse during pregnancy. However, there are no guarantees that such behaviors will be replicated over time, particularly as these women become more incorporated into the dominant culture and greater economic pressures are placed on their families.

Although low-risk health behaviors are critical in reducing 7 maternal and infant morbidity and mortality, without appropriate health screening, increased adverse health outcomes are possible. Early detection of disease and appropriate diagnosis and treatment result not only in cost savings, but also generally more successful outcomes. It is within this context of health screening and high-risk health behaviors that Latinas become a highly vulnerable population.

Recent epidemiological studies on cancer have indicated that 8 Hispanic women have twice the rate of invasive cervical cancer of White non-Hispanic women (Council on Scientific Affairs 250). Early detection through relatively low-cost Pap smears and intervention requires Latinas to be adequately screened and to maintain continuity of care. Both criteria, although necessary for low-cost prevention and treatment, are lacking due to limited access to care and inadequate knowledge and/or perception of the danger of the disease (Ginzberg 25). Other diseases of which Latinas are at higher risk, and that could benefit from better access to regular and continuous care, are type II diabetes (there is a higher incidence for both Puerto Rican and Mexican-American origin women) and obesity. Approximately one-third of Mexican-American and Puerto Rican women are obese. The occurrence of type II diabetes is approximately two to three times that in the non-Hispanic population (Ginzberg 25). Moreover this often strikes a younger age group and leads to complications if not immediately treated. Obesity has long been associated with increased risk of cardio-vascular disease and other health problems. Early intervention with proper nutritional counseling and improved diet and exercise greatly reduces the risk from this disease.

A final area that has become of increasing concern to the public has been the increase in AIDS transmission within the Latino population. This particular problem is of increasing concern when examining the transmission of pediatric AIDS. A recent study in New York City concluded that forty percent of all AIDS patients under thirteen were Latino (Perales 121). Although over fifty percent of the AIDS transmission can be traced to intravenous [IV] drug abuse in New York City, sexual transmission of the disease within the Latino population cannot be dismissed as a critical factor. Unfortunately, AIDS transmission within Latino subgroups has been viewed disproportionately as a problem of the Puerto Rican community due to a high rate of IV drug abuse and limited research on other Latino subgroups. However, a recent study by Gonzalez-Block and Hayes-Bautista suggests that the incidence of AIDS among Latinos in the United States may increase due to Mexican nationals who enter the migrant stream to the United States and who are at risk for the disease. According to their study of AIDS in Mexico: "It is among the blue collar workers and the non-specialized urban service employees where AIDS is growing at the fastest rate, thus propagating more rapidly precisely among the social groups that are most likely to migrate to the U.S." (Gonzalez-Block and Hayes-Bautista 6).

The major transmission category of the disease for the Mexican-origin population can be attributed to homosexual and bisexual contact among men. However, a recent study of Los Angeles County concluded that the largest percentage of pediatric AIDS cases in the county are Latino children. Thus Latinas, although not highlighted statistically as the major problem in the AIDS epidemic, become central in their role as pregnant mothers at risk, transmitting the disease to their infants in utero (County of Los Angeles, Department of Health Services 1995).

Many of the aforementioned health problems of Latinas become problematic and costly if not diagnosed early and promptly treated and monitored. In particular, as this population is primarily young and of child-bearing age, health programs targeted at family planning, prenatal and postpartum care, and gynecological screening for sexually transmitted diseases and cervical cancer merit consideration so as to reduce morbidity and mortality rates. Early treatment, periodic screening, and continuity of care for Latinas will shift the delivery of services from the more difficult and costly end stages of a disease to a more cost-effective and managed-care solution.   11

Access to Care: Employment Limits to Health Insurance

The health problems faced by Latinas are less symptomatic of unique biological features of these women; rather they reflect their class and occupational position. With the exception of AIDS, early intervention and treatment should rapidly reduce morbidity and mortality rates associated with the diseases that are problematic for Latinas. Thus, improved access to health care is critical in improving health outcomes and maintaining preventative health care measures.   12

Access to health care can be broadly defined by the factors that facilitate the use of medical services. Health insurance or financing for health care, maintenance of continuity of care at a regular site of health care delivery, and type of delivery site all are critical factors in enabling individuals to seek and obtain health care. For Latinos, issues such as level of acculturation have also been factored into studies addressing use of health care services (Solis et al. 11).   13

Given the poverty status of Latinas and their occupational location in the labor force, lack of health insurance has become the key factor in limiting their access to care. Although it has been argued that the employment and occupational position of Latinas mirrors their level of educational attainment and immi-   14 grant status, they also fill a critical void as a low-skilled, low-cost labor force for small industrial enterprises in ethnic communities, particularly in the Southwest (Torres and de la Torre 267). For Latinas, who are often concentrated within the small business labor markets, health insurance is virtually nonexistent, or at best insignificant, for maintaining preventative health care practices. Unfortunately, the relatively high costs for small businesses to provide affordable health insurance to their employees provide little incentive for these employers to seek employee health insurance. There is little likelihood of this situation changing as small employers must compete in a relatively unfavorable small-group health insurance market where employee premiums are higher. Bias toward employing low-risk employees by small businesses and insurers results in the overall lower health care costs of these employees. A recent study by the U.S. General Accounting Office suggests that the small insurance market premiums for small companies often are based on age, sex, and health status of employees. "The average premium costs for women in their twenties can be nearly twice as high as those for men of the same age, partly because of the costs associated with pregnancy and partly because of generally higher use of services" (U.S. General Accounting Office, "Employer Based Health Insurance" 32). Given the relatively youthful age profile of Latinas and their higher fertility rates, small businesses are faced with a potentially higher fringe benefit package for their employees if they choose to provide health insurance to these women. Forcing these employers to provide employee health insurance in the current small insurance market is tantamount to providing them with a license to discriminate against Latinas in employment in order to reduce their health care premium costs. Finally, given the low rate of unionization in the small business sector and the inability of the Federal government to successfully jumpstart the economy and stimulate growth in states such as California, employee-initiated demands for health care insurance coverage are unlikely in the short run, since jobs, rather than health insurance, become the more critical issue. Therefore, under the current voluntary health insurance market system, there is little impetus for reform in the small business sector.

Policy Alternatives: Viable Financing Options

Clearly, the health insurance problems facing Latinas are sympto- 15
matic of the greater malaise facing the health care sector. Latinas
are among the over thirty-seven million Americans who are
uninsured due to the lack of adequate and viable financing mechanisms for the care of the poor and the working poor (Kern and
Bresch 32). However, not all states share the burden of the uninsured in equal numbers, nor do all ethnic/racial groups propor-
tionately share the same levels of uninsured status. Most of the
uninsured in the United States live in approximately twelve states.
"One third of the uninsured are in three states—Florida, Texas,
and California—representing almost twelve million people. A
huge percentage of these are not just illegal aliens (or "undocu-
mented workers"), but simply poor people" (U. S. General
Accounting Office, "Significant Gaps" 17). The three states with
the largest number of uninsured in the United States also have
significant Latina/o populations. Not surprising, then, is the eth-
nic/racial breakdown of the United States uninsured population.
The largest proportion of uninsured of any group is Latinos: one-
third of all Latinos are uninsured; followed by Blacks, one-fifth of
all Blacks: and Whites, one-seventh of all Whites (U. S. General
Accounting Office, "Significant Gaps" 11).

Given the disproportionate representation of Latinas in the 16
ranks of the uninsured, it is incumbent upon them to enter the
health policy debates targeted to reform the current financing
system. Reforms of the present financing system are currently
being debated at both Federal and state levels. Strategies developed by various constituency groups, for example, insurance
companies, physicians, employers, etc., are molding the future financing reform programs; yet with the exception of a few
Hispanic public health interest groups, the Latina voice is not
present. (An example of such a group would be COSSMHO,
National Coalition of Hispanic Health and Human Services
Organization, in Washington, D.C.) Yet, input into what is financed and how it is financed will directly affect both the health
and employment status of these women.

It is within the context of the current health policy debates 17
that two reform mechanisms will be assessed. Although this discussion does not exhaust the array of suggestions for financing re-

form, these two policy recommendations, Medicaid expansion and state-level financing reform, are the most "popular" mechanisms to tackle the problem of the uninsured. In the former case, i.e., Medicaid expansion, specific suggestions concerning reform of the Medicaid law that would address the special needs of the Latina population will be developed. In the latter case, state reform, while not explicitly focusing on the unique needs of Latinas, will focus on the common ground they share with other uninsured groups and examine one proposed state solution, the Universal New York Health Care (UNY-Care) model.

Without question, in our pluralistic health care delivery system, the key to access to services is adequate financing for services rendered. Policy recommendations to improve access and delivery of services have little relevance without recommendations for current and future financing. In the short run a micro-incremental approach may prove to be the most effective in addressing this specific problem (Schlesinger and Kronebusch 94–95). At the Federal level, Medicaid expansion, which allows for subsidizing individual and employer "buy-ins," may assist in reducing the number of uninsured working poor (Schlesinger and Kronebusch 108). However, for Latinas a speedier and useful alternative to the "buy-in" approach would be an expansion of eligibility and reimbursement policies targeted to working poor and poor women. In the short run, this could assist in addressing the inadequate financing issue for needed preventative and screening services that do not result from pregnancy, but may affect future gynecological and obstetric needs of these clients. 18

In 1986, SOBRA [The Sixth Omnibus Budget Reconciliation Act] expansion of Medicaid increased the availability of pregnancy-related health services for working-poor pregnant women (Barber-Madden and Kotch 803). Unfortunately, many Latinas do not seek care or use their entitled services until they become aware of the services, their pregnancy is verified, and their eligibility is determined (Solis et al. 11). Prenatal care is therefore unnecessarily delayed during the critical first trimester of pregnancy. A solution to this problem is to expand eligibility to include working-poor women of child-bearing age for obstetrical and gynecological services, to encourage continuous use of low-cost preventative and diagnostic services, and to ensure early entry into prenatal programs. Using the same eligibility cri- 19 teria developed under the SOBRA expansion of 1986, women at risk of pregnancy or of child-bearing age would be entitled to yearly gynecological screening. This would include not only Pap smears, screening for diabetes and AIDS, but also pregnancy screening. Using the existing EPSDT Program (Early Pregnancy Screening and Detection and Treatment Program), targeted to children up to eighteen years of age and required by all Medicaid programs for preventative care (well-care as opposed to sick-care), and expanding the availability of care for working poor women, i.e., using 185 percent of poverty level as a basis for determining eligibility for this Medicaid screening program, would be a policy alternative that would allow for building or augmenting an existing Medicaid program. Given that EPSDT is required for all Medicaid programs, all states would be required to provide the augmented benefits for working-poor women under the more inclusive eligibility requirements. Currently, Medicaid programs for nonpregnant women and medically indigent programs vary across states with varying eligibility criteria. Although states such as New York are relatively generous in providing health services for the poor, states such as Texas are not and require more rigorous poverty standards for eligibility for their Medicaid program. Therefore, given the disparity in eligibility requirements across states, a federally mandated program will ensure greater access in those states that are less generous with their Medicaid benefits (National Coalition of Hispanic Health and Human Services Organization 1).

A second alternative to expanding Medicaid benefits, which is 20 often criticized as a costly alternative for states due to the Federal-state cost-sharing nature of the program, is to examine a state-mandated program that will deal directly with the uninsured and underinsured individuals in the state. This alternative, although a more radical and macro-incremental approach to transforming the financing of health care at the state level, may provide states with greater control over containing costs and delivering services (Schlesinger and Kronebusch 93–94). For states such as California and New York, where Medicaid cost-sharing with the Federal government is relatively high, federally imposed expansion is not as attractive, given the current state deficit crises in these states. For Latinas, as well as for other poor and working-poor groups, such an approach should increase the array of primary and preventative low-cost health services and minimize the need to develop piecemeal strategies from various state and Federal funding sources to obtain adequate access to care. Clearly, in the states with large numbers of uninsured, the political climate is ripe for state reform proposals that provide cost-effective coverage and provide needed services to the uninsured. Specific models that address universal financing and/or develop subsidies and risk pools for small businesses at the state level may be the most practical mechanism for tackling the uninsured problem in these states and, if successful, may serve as a blueprint for future Federal financing models.

The New York model, Universal New York Health Care 21 (UNY-Care), would develop a single-payer framework, while combining and retaining existing payers. Ultimately, a major goal would be to reduce the waste from the considerable transaction costs resulting from the current multiple-payer system through the creation of an independent public-benefit corporation with a board of governors selected jointly by the governor and the legislature. By standardizing accounts, insuring speedy reimbursement, and simplifying billing for hospitals and physicians, costs should be substantially reduced. Combined with enhancing the efficiency of the current multiple-payer system is the ultimate goal of expanding employment-based insurance, subsidizing insurance for the working poor, children, minorities and the unemployed, and providing a system that will promote universal access to care for all New York residents. Approximately twelve and one-half percent of the state's population is uninsured. In order to significantly reduce this number, UNY-Care would do the following: (1) streamline and expand job-based insurance; (2) purchase publicly subsidized health insurance for unemployed individuals; and (3) subsidize insurance for those whose income falls 200 percent below the poverty level on a sliding-scale basis. Financing for these benefits would require reliance on a payroll tax for those employers who could not meet UNY-Care standards for health insurance. Employers offering coverage for the first time would be eligible for substantial subsidies for the first four years and could avoid offering coverage to part-time employees by payment of the payroll tax. In addition to setting up a universal financing system for all New York residents, as the single buyer for care, UNY-Care will be able to use its monopoly power to control costs and budgets. This will allow for better long-run planning, given the availability of all sources of revenue, and assist in curtailing the current double-digit inflation rates evident in the medical sector (Beauchamp and Rouse 641).

There is no doubt that the UNY-Care model will be closely 22 scrutinized by other states with large numbers of uninsured and underinsured. From an access perspective, this model, in the long run, will provide comprehensive care to Latinas, the poor, and other working poor. From a broader health policy perspective, it provides the beginning of a broader blueprint for structural reform of the health care system, with the subsequent risks of altering other arenas of the economy, such as employment in small enterprises. A critical element in the viability of this proposal will be to balance the competing interests, i.e., private insurers, small businesses, physicians, hospital providers, and workers, to insure that the trade-offs for universal entitlement to health care truly merit such a reform.

Conclusion

Currently, at both state and Federal levels, the crisis of the 23 uninsured and underinsured is being debated. This issue is of immediate relevance to the Latina population as they are disproportionately represented within the ranks of the uninsured and underinsured and will certainly slide through any cracks in the new health safety net. The health status problems they face reflect both the demographic and occupational location of many of these women, who could easily benefit from micro and/or macro incremental change in the financing of health care. Although an array of health policy proposals is currently being debated in major states, such as California and Texas, there is a glaring lack of the Latina voice in setting this critical agenda. Two policy recommendations, one using the existing Federal Medicaid policy and the other introducing an innovative state single-payer financing system to ensure universal access are assessed in light of the health needs of Latinas. Expansion of the Medicaid entitlement program EPSDT is one example of a short-run strategy that would allow for selective diagnostic screening and early treatment of Latinas of child-bearing age. Indeed, any attempt to introduce these women to early and continuous care will in the long run net lower health care costs associated with decreased morbidity and mortality rates from specific "Latina" health problems and complications from unmonitored pregnancies.

The second macro approach, the UNY-Care model, offers a more comprehensive approach to health care reform, tackling the areas of universal access and cost containment. Here a synthesis of concerns that affect Latinas, the poor and working poor, and actors in the health arena unifies to minimize the zero-sum nature of this proposal. A critical caveat here is to recognize that the employment effects of such reform may disproportionately impact Latinas and that safeguards to ensure their employment stability must be considered in the final development and implementation of small business subsidies. No doubt the time is right for such reform; so is the time for Latinas to voice their concern and their agenda.

Works Cited

Barber-Madden, Rosemary, and Jonathan Kotch. "Maternity Care Financing: Universal Access to Universal Care." *Journal of Health Politics Policy and Law* 15 (Winter 1990): 797–814.

Beauchamp, Dan E., and Ronald L. Rouse. "Universal New York Health Care: A Single-Payer Strategy Linking Cost Control and Universal Access." *The New England Journal of Medicine* 323 (September 1990): 640–44.

Braveman, Paula, et al. "Adverse Outcomes and Lack of Health Insurance Among Newborns in an Eight-County Area of California, 1982–1986." *The New England Journal of Medicine* 321 (1989): 508–12.

Council on Scientific Affairs. "Hispanic Health in the United States." *Journal of the American Medical Association* 265 (1991):248–252.

County of Los Angeles, Department of Health Services. *AIDS: Cumulative Advanced AIDS 1982–1995.* March 31, 1995. Tables 2,9.

de la Torre, Adela, and Refugio Rochin. "Hispanic Poor and the Effects of Immigration Reform." *Chicano Law Review* 10 (1990): 1–13.

Furino, Antonio, and Eric Munoz. "Health Status Among Hispanics: Major Themes and New Priorities" *Journal of the American Health Association* 265 (1991): 255–57.

Ginzberg, Eli. "Access of Health Care for Hispanics." In *Health Policy and the Hispanic*, ed. Antonio Furino. Boulder: Westview Press, 1992.

Gonzalez-Block, Miguel A., and David E. Hayes-Bautista. "AIDS: The Silent Threat to Bi-National Security." Working paper, UC-

Mexus Conference on Bi-National Security Issues. Los Angeles: University of California, 1990.

Gordon-Bradshaw, Ruth H. "A Social Essay on Special Issues Facing Poor Women of Color." *Women and Health* 12 (1987): 243–59.

Kern, Rosemary, and Jack E. Bresch. "Systemic Health Care Reform: Is It Time?" *Health Progress* 71 (January–February 1990): 32–44.

National Coalition of Hispanic Health and Human Services Organization (COSSMHO). "Executive Summary." *And Access for All: Medicaid and Hispanics.* Washington D.C. (1990):1.

Perales, Cesar A. " Social Services for People with AIDS: The State Perspective." *The AIDS Patient: An Action Agenda.* Eds. David E. Rogers and Eli Ginsberg. Boulder: Westview Press, 1988. 116–26.

Schlesinger, Mark, and Karl Kronebusch. "The Failure of Prenatal Care Policy for the Poor." *Health Affairs* (Winter 1990): 91–113.

Solis, Julia M. et al. "Acculturation, Access to Care, and Use of Preventative Services by Hispanics: Findings from HHANES 1982–84." *American Journal of Public Health* 80 (December 1990 Supplement): 11–19.

Torres, Rodolfo D., and Adela de la Torre. "Latinos in the U.S. Political Economy: Income Inequality and Policy Alternatives." *Hispanics in the Labor Force: Issues and Policies.* Eds. Edwin Melendez et al. New York: Plenum Press, 1991. 265–287.

U.S. General Accounting Office. "Employer Based Health Insurance: High Costs, Wide Variation Threaten System." September 1992. GAO-HRD–92–125:32.

U. S. General Accounting Office. "Significant Gaps in Hispanic Access to Health Care." Statement of Eleanor Chelimsky, Assistant Comptroller General, Before the House Select Committee on Aging and the Congressional Hispanic Caucus. September 19, 1991. GAO-PEMD–92–6:11.

UNDERSTANDING DETAILS

1. What does de la Torre mean when she talks about the "increased feminization of poverty" (paragraph 2)?

2. According to the author, why are Latinas such a highly vulnerable population as far as their health is concerned? What are the main health risks to this population?

3. What is the key factor that is preventing many Latinas from getting adequate health care? What do health insurance and employment status have to do with one another in reference to Latinas?

4. What are de la Torre's two proposals for financing health care for Latinas? Explain each in detail.

ANALYZING MEANING

1. What do you think de la Torre's main purpose was in writing this essay?
2. Why are most Latinas currently not covered by health insurance plans?
3. Who do you think should be responsible for the health care of the poor and the unemployed? Explain your answer.
4. Why is Latina health care such an important issue in the Latino community?

DISCOVERING RHETORICAL STRATEGIES

1. Who do you think is de la Torre's main audience? How did you come to this conclusion?
2. The author begins her appeal with demographic trends and follows with an overview of Latina health-status issues. Is this an effective beginning for what de la Torre is trying to accomplish? Explain your answer.
3. What information in this essay is most persuasive to you? Least persuasive?
4. What tone does the author establish by citing statistics and referring to other sources in her essay?

MAKING CONNECTIONS

1. Essays by both Adela de la Torre and Alice Walker ("Beauty: When the Other Dancer Is the Self") focus on the problem of delivering health care to poor, rural, isolated minority groups. Which of the prescriptions for health care reform mentioned in de la Torre's essay would have been helpful to Walker when she was injured as a child? Do you have ideas for health care reform not mentioned by de la Torré? If so, what are they?
2. Compare and contrast the way de la Torre uses statistics and documentation in her argument with the use of this technique by John Langone ("Group Violence"). Which author gives us this information most skillfully? Explain your answer.
3. Examine the balance in de la Torre's essay among logical, emotional, and ethical appeals. Then, compare and contrast it with the balance in essays by Donald Drakeman ("Religion's Place in Public Schools") and Robert Hughes ("The N.R.A. in a Hunter's Sights"). Which author uses the most logic? Who uses

emotion most? And whose ethical appeal is strongest? Which author do you find most convincing? Explain your answer.

IDEAS FOR DISCUSSION/WRITING

Preparing to Write

Write freely about your view on health care coverage in the United States: Who should be responsible for providing health care? In your opinion, should all people (employed and unemployed) receive health care? What are your reasons for this opinion? Why is health care so important to some people? (What does health care represent to some people? Why is health care only a practical issue for others?) What do you think the role of the state government should be in providing health care? The federal government? Employers? In your opinion, is universal health care coverage more of a political or a social issue?

Choosing a Topic

1. Design a feasible solution to the health care problem in the United States. Then, using de la Torre's essay as your main source, write an argumentative essay presenting the problem as you understand it and offering a detailed solution to it. Cite de la Torre's essay whenever necessary.

2. What do you think the role of government should be in America's health care crisis? Use de la Torre's article as one of your sources; then, read further on the subject in the library. Next, write a clear, well-documented argument on what American government might do to help solve this serious social problem. Organize your paper clearly, and present your suggestions logically, using proper documentation (citations and bibliography) to support your position.

3. Choose a category of the health problems of another ethnic group and research it further in the library. Then, write a well-documented argument explaining the seriousness or lack of seriousness of the health care problem in the United States by discussing or analyzing in depth the consequences you have discovered.

11

Essays on Thinking, Reading, and Writing

In each of the preceding chapters, we have examined a single rhetorical mode in order to focus attention on how writers use that pattern to organize their thoughts. In this final chapter, five essays on the topics of thinking, reading, and writing demonstrate a combination of rhetorical modes at work in each selection.

Our primary purpose in this text has been to show how thinking, reading, and writing work together as fine machinery to help all of us function as intelligent and productive human beings. Our introduction discusses the relationship of thinking, reading, and writing; the text itself illustrates the crucial interdependence of these skills; and this last chapter concludes the book by presenting essays by some of America's best writers on such related topics as listening, reading fiction, understanding the writing process, writing "with style," and using word processors.

These essays are intended for you to read and enjoy, letting your mind run freely through the material as you recall in a leisurely way what you have learned in this text. They bring together the theoretical framework of this text as they illustrate how thinking, reading, and writing inform each other and work interdependently to make meaning. And they integrate the rhetorical patterns in such a way that each essay is a complex blend of the various rhetorical modes discussed in the preceding chapters—a perfect summary of the topics and strategies you have been working with throughout this text.

EUDORA WELTY   (1909 –   )

■ ■ ■

Listening

I learned from the age of two or three that any room in our   1
house, at any time of day, was there to read in, or to be read
to. My mother read to me. She'd read to me in the big bedroom in the mornings, when we were in her rocker together,
which ticked in rhythm as we rocked, as though we had a cricket
accompanying the story. She'd read to me in the diningroom on
winter afternoons in front of the coal fire, with our cuckoo clock
ending the story with "Cuckoo," and at night when I'd got in my
own bed. I must have given her no peace. Sometimes she read to
me in the kitchen while she sat churning, and the churning
sobbed along with *any* story. It was my ambition to have her read
to me while *I* churned; once she granted my wish, but she read
off my story before I brought her butter. She was an expressive
reader. When she was reading "Puss in Boots," for instance, it was
impossible not to know that she distrusted *all* cats.

It had been startling and disappointing to me to find out that   2
story books had been written by *people*, that books were not natural wonders, coming up of themselves like grass. Yet regardless of
where they came from, I cannot remember a time when I was
not in love with them—with the books themselves, cover and
binding and the paper they were printed on, with their smell and
their weight and with their possession in my arms, captured and
carried off to myself. Still illiterate, I was ready for them, committed to all the reading I could give them.

Neither of my parents had come from homes that could afford   3
to buy many books, but though it must have been something of a
strain on his salary, as the youngest officer in a young insurance
company, my father was all the while carefully selecting and ordering away for what he and Mother thought we children should
grow up with. They bought first for the future.

Besides the bookcase in the livingroom, which was always   4
called "the library," there were the encyclopedia tables and dictio-

nary stand under windows in our diningroom. Here to help us grow up arguing around the diningroom table were the Unabridged Webster, the Columbia Encyclopedia, Compton's Pictured Encyclopedia, the Lincoln Library of Information, and later the Book of Knowledge. And the year we moved into our new house, there was room to celebrate it with the new 1925 edition of the Britannica, which my father, his face always deliberately turned toward the future, was of course disposed to think better than any previous edition.

In "the library," inside the mission-style bookcase with its 5 three diamond-latticed glass doors, with my father's Morris chair and the glass-shaded lamp on its table beside it, were books I could soon begin on—and I did, reading them all alike and as they came, straight down their rows, top shelf to bottom. There was the set of Stoddard's Lectures, in all its late nineteenth-century vocabulary and vignettes of peasant life and quaint beliefs and customs, with matching halftone illustrations: Vesuvius erupting, Venice by moonlight, gypsies glimpsed by their campfires. I didn't know then the clue they were to my father's longing to see the rest of the world. I read straight through his other love-from-afar: the Victrola Book of the Opera, with opera after opera in synopsis, with portraits in costume of Melba, Caruso, Galli-Curci, and Geraldine Farrar, some of whose voices we could listen to on our Red Seal records.

My mother read secondarily for information; she sank as a he- 6 donist into novels. She read Dickens in the spirit in which she would have eloped with him. The novels of her girlhood that had stayed on in her imagination, besides those of Dickens and Scott and Robert Louis Stevenson, were *Jane Eyre, Trilby, The Woman in White, Green Mansions, King Solomon's Mines*. Marie Corelli's name would crop up but I understood she had gone out of favor with my mother, who had only kept *Ardath* out of loyalty. In time she absorbed herself in Galsworthy, Edith Wharton, above all in Thomas Mann of the *Joseph* volumes.

St. Elmo was not in our house; I saw it often in other houses. This 7 wildly popular Southern novel is where all the Edna Earles in our population started coming from. They're all named for the heroine, who succeeded in bringing a dissolute, sinning roué and atheist of a lover (St. Elmo) to his knees. My mother was able to forgo it.

But she remembered the classic advice given to rose growers on how to water their bushes long enough: "Take a chair and *St. Elmo.*"

To both my parents I owe my early acquaintance with a 8 beloved Mark Twain. There was a full set of Mark Twain and a short set of Ring Lardner in our bookcase, and those were the volumes that in time united us all, parents and children.

Reading everything that stood before me was how I came 9 upon a worn old book without a back that had belonged to my father as a child. It was called *Sanford and Merton.* Is there anyone left who recognizes it, I wonder? It is the famous moral tale written by Thomas Day in the 1780s, but of him no mention is made on the title page of *this* book; here it is *Sanford and Merton in Words of One Syllable* by Mary Godolphin. Here are the rich boy and the poor boy and Mr. Barlow, their teacher and interlocutor, in long discourses alternating with dramatic scenes—danger and rescue allotted to the rich and the poor respectively. It may have only words of one syllable, but one of them is "quoth." It ends with not one but two morals, both engraved on rings: "Do what you ought, come what may," and "If we would be great, we must first learn to be good."

This book was lacking its front cover, the back held on by strips 10 of pasted paper, now turned golden, in several layers, and the pages stained, flecked, and tattered around the edges; its garish illustrations had come unattached but were preserved, laid in. I had the feeling even in my heedless childhood that this was the only book my father as a little boy had had of his own. He had held onto it, and might have gone to sleep on its coverless face: He had lost his mother when he was seven. My father had never made any mention to his own children of the book, but he had brought it along with him from Ohio to our house and shelved it in our bookcase.

My mother had brought from West Virginia that set of 11 Dickens; those books looked sad, too—they had been through fire and water before I was born, she told me, and there they were, lined up—as I later realized, waiting for *me.*

I was presented, from as early as I can remember, with books of 12 my own, which appeared on my birthday and Christmas morning. Indeed, my parents could not give me books enough. They must have sacrificed to give me on my sixth or seventh birthday—it was after I became a reader for myself—the ten-volume set of *Our*

Wonder World. These were beautifully made, heavy books I would lie down with on the floor in front of the diningroom hearth, and more often than the rest volume 5, *Every Child's Story Book*, was under my eyes. There were the fairy tales—Grimm, Andersen, the English, the French, "Ali Baba and the Forty Thieves"; and there was Aesop and Reynard the Fox; there were the myths and legends, Robin Hood, King Arthur, and St. George and the Dragon, even the history of Joan of Arc; a whack of *Pilgrim's Progress* and a long piece of *Gulliver*. They all carried their classic illustrations. I located myself in these pages and could go straight to the stories and pictures I loved; very often "The Yellow Dwarf" was first choice, with Walter Crane's Yellow Dwarf in full color making his terrifying appearance flanked by turkeys. Now that volume is as worn and backless and hanging apart as my father's poor *Sanford and Merton*. The precious page with Edward Lear's "Jumblies" on it has been in danger of slipping out for all these years. One measure of my love for *Our Wonder World* was that for a long time I wondered if I would go through fire and water for it as my mother had done for Charles Dickens; and the only comfort was to think I could ask my mother to do it for me.

I believe I'm the only child I know of who grew up with this treasure in the house. I used to ask others, "Did you have *Our Wonder World*?" I'd have to tell them *The Book of Knowledge* could not hold a candle to it. 13

I live in gratitude to my parents for initiating me—and as early as I begged for it, without keeping me waiting—into knowledge of the word, into reading and spelling, by way of the alphabet. They taught it to me at home in time for me to begin to read before starting to school. I believe the alphabet is no longer considered an essential piece of equipment for traveling through life. In my day it was the keystone to knowledge. You learned the alphabet as you learned to count to ten, as you learned "Now I lay me" and the Lord's Prayer and your father's and mother's name and address and telephone number, all in case you were lost. 14

My love for the alphabet, which endures, grew out of reciting it but, before that, out of seeing the letters on the page. In my own story books, before I could read them for myself, I fell in love with various winding, enchanted-looking initials drawn by Walter Crane at the heads of fairy tales. In "Once upon a time," 15

an "O" had a rabbit running it as a treadmill, his feet upon flowers. When the day came, years later, for me to see the *Book of
Kells*, all the wizardry of letter, initial, and word swept over me a
thousand times over, and the illumination, the gold, seemed a part
of the word's beauty and holiness that had been there from the
start.

DONALD HALL   (1928 –   )

■ ■ ■

To Read Fiction

When we learn to read fiction, we acquire a pleasure and 1
a resource we never lose. Although literary study is impractical in one sense—few people make their living reading books—in another sense it is almost as practical as breathing. Literature records and embodies centuries of human thought and feeling, preserving for us the minds of people who lived before us, who were like us and unlike us, against whom we can measure our common humanity and our historical difference. And when we read the stories of our contemporaries they illuminate the world all of us share.

When we read great literature, something changes in us that 2
stays changed. Literature remembered becomes material to think with. No one who has read *The Death of Ivan Ilych* well is quite the same again. Reading adds tools by which we observe, measure, and judge the people and the properties of our universe, we understand the actions and motives of others and of ourselves.

In the fable of the ant and the grasshopper, the wise ant 3
builds his storehouse against winter and prospers; the foolish grasshopper saves nothing and perishes. Anyone who dismisses the study of literature on the ground that it will not be useful—to a chemist or an engineer, to a foreman or an X-ray technician—imitates the grasshopper. When we shut from our lives everything except food and shelter, part of us starves to death. Food for this hunger is music, painting, film, plays, poems, stories, and novels. Much writing in newspapers, magazines, and popular novels is not literature, if we reserve that word for work of high quality. This reading gives us as little nourishment as most television and most fast food. For the long winters and energetic summers of our lives, we require the sustenance of literature.

Reading fiction old and new—taking into ourselves the work 4
of nineteenth-century Russian, contemporary English, Irish, and

especially American storytellers—we build a storehouse of knowledge and we entertain ourselves as well. But to take pleasure and understanding from fiction we have to learn how to read it. No one expects to walk up to a computer and be able to program it without first learning something about computers. For some reason—perhaps because we are familiar with words from childhood and take them for granted—we tend to think that a quick glance at the written word should reward us, and that if we do not take instant satisfaction the work is beyond us, or not worth it, or irrelevant or boring. But all our lives, in other skills, we have needed instruction and practice—to be able to ride a bicycle, drive a car, play guitar, shoot baskets, typewrite, dance.

The knowledge we derive from literature can seem confusing. 5 Equally great works may contradict each other in the generalizations we derive from them. One work may recommend solitude, another society. One may advise us to seize the moment, another to live a life of contemplation. Or, two good readers may disagree about the implication of a work and each argue convincingly, with detailed references to the writing, in support of contrary interpretations. A complex work of fiction cannot be reduced to a simple, correct meaning. In an elementary arithmetic text, the answers may be printed in the back of the book. There are no answers to be printed in the back of . . . any collection of literature.

Such nebulousness, or ambiguity, disturbs some students. After 6 an hour's class discussion of a short story, with varying interpretations offered, they want to know "But what *does* it mean?" We must admit that literature is inexact, and its truth is not easily verifiable. Probably the story means several things at once, and not one thing at all. This is not to say, however, that it means anything that anybody finds in it. Although differing, equally defensible opinions are common, error is even more common.

When we speak of truth in the modern world, we usually 7 mean something scientific or tautological. Arithmetic contains the truth of tautology; two and two make four because our definitions of *two* and *four* say so. In laboratories we encounter the truth of statistics and the truth of observation. If we smoke cigarettes heavily, it is true that we have one chance in four to develop lung cancer. When we heat copper wire over a Bunsen burner, the flame turns blue.

But there is an older sense of truth, in which statements appar- 8
ently opposite can be valid. In this older tradition, truth is dependent on context and circumstance, on the agreement of sensible
men and women—like the "Guilty" or "Not guilty" verdict of a
jury. Because this literary (or philosophical, or legal, or historical)
truth is inexact, changeable, and subject to argument, literature
can seem nebulous to minds accustomed to arithmetical certainty.

Let me argue this: If literature is nebulous or inexact; if it is 9
impossible to determine, with scientific precision, the value or the
meaning of a work of art, *this inexactness is the price literature pays
for representing whole human beings.* Human beings themselves, in
their feelings and thoughts, in the wandering of their short lives,
are ambiguous and ambivalent, shifting mixtures of permanence
and change, direction and disorder. Because literature is true to
life, true to the complexities of human feeling, different people
will read the same work with different responses. And the storyteller's art will sometimes affirm that opposite things are both
true *because they are.* Such a condition is not tidy; it is perhaps re-
grettable—but it is human nature.

What's Good, What's Bad

The claims I make for fiction are large: that it alters and en- 10
larges our minds, our connections with each other past and present, our understanding of our own feelings. These claims apply
to excellent literature only. This . . . suggests that some fiction is
better than other fiction, and that some narratives are not literature at all. Even if judgments are always subject to reversal, even if
there is no way we can be certain of being correct, evaluation
lives at the center of literary study.

When I was nineteen, I liked to read everything: science fic- 11
tion, Russian novels, mystery stories, great poems, adventure magazines. Then for six months after an accident, sentenced to a
hospital bed and a body cast, I set myself a reading list, all serious
books I had been thinking about getting to. Of course there was
a background to this choice: I had been taught by a good teacher
who had directed and encouraged and stimulated my reading. I
read through Shakespeare, the Bible in the King James version,
novels by Henry James and Ernest Hemingway and William
Faulkner. Toward the end of six months, taking physical therapy, I

hurried to finish the books I had assigned myself; I looked forward to taking a vacation among private detectives and adventurers of the twenty-fourth century. I thought I would take a holiday of light reading.

When I tried to read the light things, I experienced one of 12 those "turning points in life" we are asked to describe in freshman composition. I remember the dismay, the abject melancholy that crept over me as I realized—restless, turning from book to book in search of entertainment—that these books bored me; that I was ruined for life, that I would never again lose myself to stick-figure characters and artificial suspense. Literature ruined me for light reading. . . .

I don't mean to say that I was able to give reasons why Fyodor 13 Dostoyevsky's novel about a murder was better than Agatha Christie's or why Aldous Huxley's view of the future, though less exciting, was more satisfying than *Astounding Science Fiction*'s. But I began a lifetime of trying to figure out why. What *is* it that makes Chekhov so valuable to us? The struggle to name reasons for value—to evaluate works of art—is lifelong, and although we may never arrive at satisfactory explanations, the struggle makes the mind more sensitive, more receptive to the next work of literature it encounters. And as the mind becomes more sensitive and receptive to literature, it may become more sensitive and receptive to all sorts of things.

ANNIE DILLARD   (1945 –   )

■ ■ ■

When You Write

When you write, you lay out a line of words. The line 1
of words is a miner's pick, a woodcarver's gouge, a
surgeon's probe. You wield it, and it digs a path you
follow. Soon you find yourself deep in new territory. Is it a dead
end, or have you located the real subject? You will know tomorrow, or this time next year.

You make the path boldly and follow it fearfully. You go where 2
the path leads. At the end of the path, you find a box canyon. You
hammer out reports, dispatch bulletins.

The writing has changed, in your hands, and in a twinkling, 3
from an expression of your notions to an epistemological tool.
The new place interests you because it is not clear. You attend. In
your humility, you lay down the words carefully, watching all the
angles. Now the earlier writing looks soft and careless. Process is
nothing; erase your tracks. The path is not the work. I hope your
tracks have grown over; I hope birds ate the crumbs; I hope you
will toss it all and not look back.

The line of words is a hammer. You hammer against the walls 4
of your house. You tap the walls, lightly, everywhere. After giving
many years' attention to these things, you know what to listen
for. Some of the walls are bearing walls; they have to stay, or
everything will fall down. Other walls can go with impunity; you
can hear the difference. Unfortunately, it is often a bearing wall
that has to go. It cannot be helped. There is only one solution,
which appalls you, but there it is. Knock it out. Duck.

Courage utterly opposes the bold hope that this is such fine 5
stuff the work needs it, or the world. Courage, exhausted, stands
on bare reality: This writing weakens the work. You must demol-
ish the work and start over. You can save some of the sentences,
like bricks. It will be a miracle if you can save some of the paragraphs, no matter how excellent in themselves or hard-won. You

can waste a year worrying about it, or you can get it over with now. (Are you a woman, or a mouse?)

The part you must jettison is not only the best-written part; it 6 is also, oddly, that part which was to have been the very point. It is the original key passage, the passage on which the rest was to hang, and from which you yourself drew the courage to begin. Henry James knew it well, and said it best. In his preface to *The Spoils of Poynton*, he pities the writer, in a comical pair of sentences that rises to a howl: "Which is the work in which he hasn't surrendered, under dire difficulty, the best thing he meant to have kept? In which indeed, before the dreadful *done*, doesn't he ask himself what has become of the thing all for the sweet sake of which it was to proceed to that extremity?"

So it is that a writer writes many books. In each book, he in- 7 tended several urgent and vivid points, many of which he sacrificed as the book's form hardened. "The youth gets together his materials to build a bridge to the moon," Thoreau noted mournfully, "or perchance a palace or temple on the earth, and at length the middle-aged man concludes to build a wood-shed with them." The writer returns to these materials, these passionate subjects, as to unfinished business, for they are his life's work.

KURT VONNEGUT (1922 –   )

■ ■ ■

How to Write with Style

Newspaper reporters and technical writers are trained to reveal almost nothing about themselves in their writings. This makes them freaks in the world of writers, since almost all of the other ink-stained wretches in that world reveal a lot about themselves to readers. We call these revelations, accidental and intentional, elements of literary style. 1

These revelations are fascinating to us as readers. They tell us what sort of person it is with whom we are spending time. Does the writer sound ignorant or informed, crazy or sane, stupid or bright, crooked or honest, humorless or playful—? And on and on. 2

When you yourself put words on paper, remember that the most damning revelation you can make about yourself is that you do not know what is interesting and what is not. Don't you yourself like or dislike writers mainly for what they choose to show you or make you think about? Did you ever admire an empty-headed writer for his or her mastery of the language? No. 3

So your own winning literary style must begin with interesting ideas in your head. Find a subject you care about and which you in your heart feel others should care about. It is this genuine caring, and not your games with language, which will be the most compelling and seductive element in your style. 4

I am not urging you to write a novel, by the way—although I would not be sorry if you wrote one, provided you genuinely cared about something. A petition to the mayor about a pothole in front of your house or a love letter to the girl next door will do. 5

Do not ramble, though. 6

As for your use of language: Remember that two great masters of our language, William Shakespeare and James Joyce, wrote sentences which were almost childlike when their subjects were most profound. "To be or not to be?" asks Shakespeare's Hamlet. The longest word is three letters long. Joyce, when he was frisky, could put together a sentence as intricate and glittering as a 7 necklace for Cleopatra, but my favorite sentence in his short story "Eveline" is this one: "She was tired." At that point in the story, no other words could break the heart of a reader as those words do.

Simplicity of language is not only reputable, but perhaps even 8 sacred. The Bible opens with a sentence well within the writing skills of a lively fourteen-year-old: "In the beginning God created the heavens and the earth."

It may be that you, too, are capable of making necklaces for 9 Cleopatra, so to speak. But your eloquence should be the servant of the ideas in your head. Your rule might be this: If a sentence, no matter how excellent, does not illuminate my subject in some new and useful way, scratch it out. Here is the same rule paraphrased to apply to storytelling, to fiction: Never include a sentence which does not either remark on character or advance the action.

The writing style which is most natural for you is bound to 10 echo speech you heard when a child. English was the novelist Joseph Conrad's third language, and much that seems piquant in his use of English was no doubt colored by his first language, which was Polish. And lucky indeed is the writer who has grown up in Ireland, for the English spoken there is so amusing and musical. I myself grew up in Indianapolis, Indiana, where common speech sounds like a band saw cutting galvanized tin, and employs a vocabulary as unornamental as a monkey wrench.

In some of the more remote hollows of Appalachia, children 11 still grow up hearing songs and locutions of Elizabethan times. Yes, and many Americans grow up hearing a language other than English, or an English dialect a majority of Americans cannot understand.

All these varieties of speech are beautiful, just as the varieties of 12 butterflies are beautiful. No matter what your first language, you should treasure it all your life. If it happens not to be standard English, and if it shows itself when you write standard English, the result is usually delightful, like a very pretty girl with one eye that is green and one that is blue.

I myself find that I trust my own writing most, and others 13 seem to trust it most, too, when I sound most like a person from Indianapolis, which is what I am. What alternatives do I have? The one most vehemently recommended by teachers has no doubt been pressed on you, as well: that I write like cultivated Englishmen of a century or more ago.

I used to be exasperated by such teachers, but am no more. I 14 understand now that all those antique essays and stories with which I was to compare my own work were not magnificent for their datedness or foreignness, but for saying precisely what their authors meant them to say. My teachers wished me to write ac-curately, always selecting the most effective words, and relating the words to one another unambiguously, rigidly, like parts of a machine. The teachers did not want to turn me into an Englishman after all. They hoped that I would become under-standable—and therefore understood.

And there went my dream of doing with words what Pablo 15 Picasso did with paint or what any number of jazz idols did with music. If I broke all the rules of punctuation, had words mean whatever I wanted them to mean, and strung them together hig-gledy-piggledy, I would simply not be understood. So you, too, had better avoid Picasso-style or jazz-style writing, if you have something worth saying and wish to be understood.

If it were only teachers who insisted that modern writers stay 16 close to literary styles of the past, we might reasonably ignore them. But readers insist on the very same thing. They want our pages to look very much like pages they have seen before.

Why? It is because they themselves have a tough job to do, and 17 they need all the help they can get from us. They have to identify thousands of little marks on paper, and make sense of them im-mediately. They have to *read*, an art so difficult that most people do not really master it even after having studied it all through grade school and high school—for twelve long years.

So this discussion, like all discussions of literary styles, must fi- 18 nally acknowledge that our stylistic options as writers are neither numerous nor glamorous, since our readers are bound to be such imperfect artists. Our audience requires us to be sympathetic and patient teachers, ever willing to simplify and clarify—whereas we would rather soar high above the crowd, singing like nightingales.

That is the bad news. The good news is that we Americans are 19 governed under a unique Constitution, which allows us to write whatever we please without fear of punishment. So the most meaningful aspect of our styles, which is what we choose to write about, is unlimited.

Also: We are members of an egalitarian society, so there is no 20 reason for us to write, in case we are not classically educated aristocrats, as though we were classically educated aristocrats.

For a discussion of literary style in a narrower sense, in a more 21 technical sense, I commend to your attention *The Elements of Style* by William Strunk, Jr., and E. B. White (Macmillan, 1979). It contains such rules as this: "A participial phrase at the beginning of a sentence must refer to the grammatical subject," and so on. E. B. White is, of course, one of the most admirable literary stylists this country has so far produced.

You should realize, too, that no one would care how well or 22 badly Mr. White expressed himself, if he did not have perfectly enchanting things to say.

WILLIAM ZINSSER   (1922 –   )

■ ■ ■

Writing with a Word Processor

Writing is a deeply personal process, full of mystery and surprise. No two people go about it in exactly the same way. We all have little devices to get us started, or to keep us going, or to remind us of what we think we want to say, and what works for one person may not work for anyone else. The main thing is to get something written—to get the words out of our heads. There is no "right" method. Any method that will do the job is the right method for you.

It helps to remember that writing is hard. Most non-writers don't know this; they think that writing is a natural function, like breathing, that ought to come easy, and they're puzzled when it doesn't. If you find that writing is hard, it's because it *is* hard. It's one of the hardest things that people do. Among other reasons, it's hard because it requires thinking. You won't write clearly unless you keep forcing yourself to think clearly. There's no escaping the question that has to be constantly asked: What do I want to say next?

So painful is this task that writers go to remarkable lengths to postpone their daily labor. They sharpen their pencils and change their typewriter ribbon and go out to the store to buy more paper. Now these sacred rituals, as IBM would say, have been ob- soleted.

When I began writing this article on my word processor I did- n't have any idea what would happen. Would I be able to write anything at all? Would it be any good? I was bringing to the ma- chine what I assumed were wholly different ways of thinking about writing. The units massed in front of me looked cold and sterile. Their steady hum reminded me that they were waiting. They seemed to be waiting for information, not for writing. Maybe what I wrote would also be cold and sterile.

I was particularly worried about the absence of paper. I knew that I would only be able to see as many lines as the screen would hold—twenty lines. How could I review what I had already written? How could I get a sense of continuity and flow? With paper it was always possible to flick through the preceding pages to see where I was coming from—and where I ought to be going. Without paper I would have no such periodic fix. Would this be a major hardship?

The only way to find out was to find out. I took a last look at my unsharpened pencils and went to work. 6

My particular hang-up as a writer is that I have to get every paragraph as nearly right as possible before I go on to the next paragraph. I'm somewhat like a bricklayer: I build very slowly, not adding a new row until I feel that the foundation is solid enough to hold up the house. I'm the exact opposite of the writer who dashes off his entire first draft, not caring how sloppy it looks or how badly it's written. His only objective at this early stage is to let his creative motor run the full course at full speed; repairs can always be made later. I envy this writer and would like to have his metabolism. But I'm stuck with the one I've got. 7

I also care how my writing looks while I'm writing it. The visual arrangement is important to me: the shape of the words, of the sentences, of the paragraphs, of the page. I don't like sentences that are dense with long words, or paragraphs that never end. As I write I want to see the design that my piece will have when the reader sees it in type, and I want that design to have a rhythm and a pace that will invite the reader to keep reading. O.K., so I'm a nut. But I'm not alone; the visual component is important to a large number of people who write. 8

One hang-up we visual people share is that our copy must be neat. My lifelong writing method, for instance, has gone like this. I put a piece of paper in the typewriter and write the first paragraph. Then I take the paper out and edit what I've written. I mark it up horribly, crossing words out and scribbling new ones in the space between the lines. By this time the paragraph has lost its nature and shape for me as a piece of writing. It's a mishmash of typing and handwriting and arrows and balloons and other directional symbols. So I type a clean copy, incorporating the changes, and then I take that piece of paper out of the typewriter and edit it. It's better, but not much better. I go over it with my pencil again, making more changes, which again make it too 9 messy for me to read critically, so I go back to the typewriter for round three. And round four. Not until I'm reasonably satisfied do I proceed to the next paragraph.

This can get pretty tedious, and I have often thought that there   10
must be a better way. Now there is. The word processor is God's gift, or at least science's gift, to the tinkerers and the refiners and the neatness freaks. For me it was obviously the perfect new toy. I began playing on page 1—editing, cutting and revising—and have been on a rewriting high ever since. The burden of the years has been lifted.

Mostly I've been cutting. I would guess that I've cut at least as   11
many words out of this article as the number that remain. Probably half of those words were eliminated because I saw that they were unnecessary—the sentence worked fine without them. This is where the word processor can improve your writing to an extent that you will hardly believe. Learn to recognize what is clutter and to use the DELETE key to prune it out.

How will you know clutter when you see it? Here's a device I   12
used when I was teaching writing at Yale that my students found helpful; it may be a help here. I would put brackets around every component in a student's paper that I didn't think was doing some kind of work. Often it was only one word—for example, the useless preposition that gets appended to so many verbs (order up, free up), or the adverb whose meaning is already in the verb (blare loudly, clench tightly), or the adjective that tells us what we already know (smooth marble, green grass). The brackets might surround the little qualifiers that dilute a writer's authority (a bit, sort of, in a sense), or the countless phrases in which the writer explains what he is about to explain (it might be pointed out, I'm tempted to say). Often my brackets would surround an entire sentence—the sentence that essentially repeats what the previous sentence has said, or tells the reader something that is implicit, or adds a detail that is irrelevant. Most people's writing is littered with phrases that do no new work whatever. Most first drafts, in fact, can be cut by fifty percent without losing anything organic. (Try it; it's a good exercise.)

By bracketing these extra words, instead of crossing them out, I   13
was saying to the student: "I may be wrong, but I think this can go and the meaning of the sentence won't be affected in any way.

But *you* decide: Read the sentence without the bracketed material and see if it works." In the first half of the term, the students' papers were festooned with my brackets. Whole paragraphs got bracketed. But gradually the students learned to put mental brackets around their many different kinds of clutter, and by the end of the term I was returning papers to them that had hardly any brackets, or none. It was always a satisfying moment. Today many of those students are professional writers. "I still see your brackets," they tell me. "They're following me through life."

You can develop the same eye. Writing is clear and strong to   14
the extent that it has no superfluous parts. (So is art and music and dance and typography and design.) You will really enjoy writing on a word processor when you see your sentences growing in strength, literally before your eyes, as you get rid of the fat. Be thankful for everything that you can throw away.

I was struck by how many phrases and sentences I wrote in   15
this article that I later found I didn't need. Many of them hammered home a point that didn't need hammering because it had already been made. This kind of overwriting happens in almost everybody's first draft, and it's perfectly natural—the act of putting down our thoughts makes us garrulous. Luckily, the act of editing follows the act of writing, and this is where the word processor will bail you out. It intercedes at the point where the game can be won or lost. With its help I cut hundreds of unnecessary words and didn't replace them.

Hundreds of others were discarded because I later thought of a   16
better word—one that caught more precisely or more vividly what I was trying to express. Here, again, a word processor encourages you to play. The English language is rich in words that convey an exact shade of meaning. Don't get stuck with a word that's merely good if you can find one that takes the reader by surprise with its color or aptness or quirkiness. Root around in your dictionary of synonyms and find words that are fresh. Throw them up on the screen and see how they look.

Also learn to play with whole sentences. If a sentence strikes   17
you as awkward or ponderous, move your cursor to the space after the period and write a new sentence that you think is better. Maybe you can make it shorter. Or clearer. Maybe you can make it livelier by turning it into a question or otherwise altering

its rhythm. Change the passive verbs into active verbs. (Passive verbs are the death of clarity and vigor.) Try writing two or three new versions of the awkward sentence and then compare them, or write a fourth version that combines the best elements of all three. Sentences come in an infinite variety of shapes and sizes. Find one that pleases you. If it's clear, and if it pleases you and expresses who you are, trust it to please other people. Then delete all the versions that aren't as good. Your shiny new sentence will jump into position, and the rest of the paragraph will rearrange itself as quickly and neatly as if you had never pulled it apart.

Another goal that the word processor will help you to achieve   18
is unity. No matter how carefully you write each sentence as you assemble a piece of writing, the final product is bound to have some ragged edges. Is the tone consistent throughout? And the point of view? And the pronoun? And the tense? How about the transitions? Do they pull the reader along, or is the piece jerky and disjointed? A good piece of writing should be harmonious from beginning to end in the voice of the writer and the flow of its logic. But the harmony usually requires some last-minute patching.

I've been writing a book by the bricklayer method, slowly and   19
carefully. That's all very well as far as it goes—at the end of every chapter the individual bricks may look fine. But what about the wall? The only way to check your piece for unity is to go over it one more time from start to finish, preferably reading it aloud. See if you have executed all the decisions that you made before you started writing.

One such decision is in the area of tone. I decided, for in-   20
stance, that I didn't want my book to be a technical manual. I'm not a technician; I'm a writer and an editor. The book wouldn't work if I expected the reader to identify with the process of mastering a new technology. He would have to identify with me. The book would be first of all a personal journey and only parenthetically a manual. I knew that this was a hybrid form and that its unities would never be wholly intact. Still, in going over each finished chapter I found places where the balance could be improved—where instructional detail smothered the writer and his narrative, or, conversely, where the writer intruded on the procedures he was trying to explain. With a word processor it was easy

to make small repairs—perhaps just a change of pronoun and verb—that made the balance less uneven.

The instructional portions of the book posed a problem of 21 their own—one that I had never faced before. My hope was to try to explain a technical process without the help of any diagrams or drawings. Would this be possible? It would be possible only if I kept remembering one fundamental fact: Writing is linear and sequential. This may seem so obvious as to be insulting: Everybody knows that writing is linear and sequential. Actually everybody doesn't know. Most people under thirty don't know. They have been reared since early childhood on television—a kaleidoscope of visual images flashed onto their brain—and it doesn't occur to them that sentence B must follow sentence A, and that sentence C must follow sentence B, or all the elegant sentences in the world won't add up to anything but confusion.

I mention this because word processors are going to be widely 22 used by people who need to impart technical information: matters of operating procedure in business and banking, science and technology, medicine and health, education and government, and dozens of other specialized fields. The information will only be helpful if readers can grasp it quickly and easily. If it's muddy they will get discouraged or angry, or both, and will stop reading.

You can avoid this dreaded fate for your message, whatever it 23 is, by making sure that every sentence is a logical sequel to the one that preceded it. One way to approach this goal is to keep your sentences short. A major reason why technical prose becomes so tangled is that the writer tries to make one sentence do too many jobs. It's a natural hazard of the first draft. But the solution is simple: See that every sentence contains only one thought. The reader can accommodate only one idea at a time. Help him by giving him only one idea at a time. Let him understand A before you proceed to B.

In writing this article, I was eager to explain the procedures 24 that I had learned, and I would frequently lump several points together in one sentence. Later, editing what I had written, I asked myself if the procedure would be clear to someone who was puzzling through it for the first time—someone who hadn't struggled to figure the procedure out. Often I felt that it wouldn't be clear. I was giving the reader too much. He was being asked to picture himself taking various steps that were single and sequential, and that's how he deserved to get them.

I therefore divided all troublesome long sentences into two 25 short sentences, or even three. It always gave me great pleasure. Not only is it the fastest way for a writer to get out of a quagmire that there seems to be no getting out of; I also like short sentences for their own sake. There's almost no more beautiful sight than a simple declarative sentence. This article is full of simple declarative sentences that have no punctuation and that carry one simple thought. Without a word processor I wouldn't have chopped as many of them down to their proper size, or done it with so little effort. This is one of the main clarifying jobs that your machine can help you to perform, especially if your writing requires you to guide the reader into territory that is new and bewildering.

Not all my experiences, of course, were rosy. The machine had 26 disadvantages as well as blessings. Often, for instance, I missed not being able to see more than twenty lines at a time—to review what I had written earlier. If I wanted to see more lines I had to "scroll" them back into view.

But even this wasn't as painful as I had thought it would be. I 27 found that I could hold in my head the gist of what I had written and didn't need to keep looking at it. Was this need, in fact, still another writer's hang-up that I could shed? To some extent it was. I discovered, as I had at so many other points in this journey, that various crutches I had always assumed I needed were really not necessary. I made a decision to just throw them away and found that I could still function. The only real hardship occurred when a paragraph broke at the bottom of the screen. This meant that the first lines of the paragraph were on one page and the rest were on the next page, and I had to keep flicking the two pages back and forth to read what I was writing. But again, it wasn't fatal. I learned to live with it and soon took it for granted as an occupational hazard.

Glossary of Useful Terms

Numbers in parentheses indicate pages in the text where the term is defined and/or examples are given.

Abstract (154, 257–258) nouns, such as *truth* or *beauty*, are words that are neither specific nor definite in meaning; they refer to *general* concepts, qualities, and conditions that summarize an entire category of experience. Conversely, *concrete* terms, such as *apple, crabgrass, computer,* and *French horn,* make precise appeals to our senses. The word *abstract* refers to the logical process of abstraction, through which our minds are able to group together and describe similar objects, ideas, or attitudes. Most good writers use abstract terms sparingly in their essays, preferring instead the vividness and clarity of *concrete* words and phrases.

Allusion is a reference to a well-known person, place, or event from life or literature. In "Summer Rituals," for example, Ray Bradbury alludes to Herman Melville's great novel *Moby Dick* when he describes an old man who walks on his front porch "like Ahab surveying the mild mild day."

Analogy (334) is an extended *comparison* of two dissimilar objects or ideas.

Analysis (2, 16, 17, 214, 590) is examining and evaluating a topic by separating it into its basic parts and elements and studying it systematically.

Anecdote (100) is a brief account of a single incident.

Argumentation (497–512) is an appeal predominantly to *logic* and reason. It deals with complex issues that can be debated.

Attitude (106, 506) describes the narrator's personal feelings about a particular subject. In "Triple Tragedy in Black Society," Harry Edwards expresses anger and disgust at the manner in which African American athletes are routinely exploited by the American sports establishment. *Attitude* is one component of *point of view*.

Audience (27, 38, 43–44, 220, 221, 501, 503–507) refers to the person or group of people for whom an *essay* is written.

Cause and effect (444–456) is a form of *analysis* that examines the causes and consequences of events and ideas.

Characterization (107) is the creation of imaginary yet realistic persons in fiction, drama, and *narrative* poetry.

Chronological order (27, 101, 106, 159–160, 219) is a sequence of events arranged in the order in which they occurred. George Orwell follows this natural time sequence in his *narrative essay* "Shooting an Elephant."

Classification (280–290) is the analytical process of grouping together similar subjects into a single category or class; *division* works in the opposite fashion, breaking down a subject into many different subgroups. In "The Truth About Lying," Judith Viorst classifies lies into several distinct categories.

Clichés (261–262) are words or expressions that have lost their freshness and originality through continual use. For example, "busy as a bee," "pretty as a picture," and "hotter than hell" have become trite and dull because of overuse. Good writers avoid clichés through vivid and original phrasing.

Climactic order (159–160) refers to the *organization* of ideas from one extreme to another—for example, from least important to most important, from most destructive to least destructive, or from least promising to most promising.

Cognitive skills (2–4) are mental abilities that help us send and receive verbal messages.

Coherence (160) is the manner in which an *essay* "holds together" its main ideas. A coherent *theme* will demonstrate such a clear relationship between its *thesis* and its logical structure that readers can easily follow the *argument*.

Colloquial expressions (264–265) are informal words, phrases, and sentences that are more appropriate for spoken conversations than for written *essays*.

Comparison (333–346) is an *expository* writing technique that examines the similarities between objects or ideas, whereas *contrast* focuses on differences.

Conclusions (31, 504) bring *essays* to a natural close by summarizing the argument, restating the *thesis*, calling for some specific action, or explaining the significance of the topic just discussed. If the *introduction* states your thesis in the form of a question to be answered or a problem to be solved, then your *conclusion* will be the final "answer" or "solution" provided in your paper. The *conclusion* should be approximately the same length as your *introduction* and should leave your reader satisfied that you have actually "concluded" your discussion rather than simply run out of ideas to discuss.

Concrete: See *abstract*.

Conflict is the struggle resulting from the opposition of two strong forces in the plot of a play, novel, or short story.

Connotation and Denotation (264–265, 505) are two principal methods of describing the meanings of words. *Connotation* refers to the wide array of positive and negative associations that most words naturally carry with them, whereas *denotation* is the precise, literal *definition* of a word that might be found in a dictionary. Alleen Pace Nilsen's "Sexism in English: A 1990s Update" examines the extent to which words such as *mistress, queen, matron*, and *old maid* betray antifeminist *connotations* that far outweigh their *denotative* definitions. See Judy Brady's "Why I Want a Wife" for further examples.

Content and Form (30, 32) are the two main components of an *essay*. *Content* refers to the subject matter of an essay, whereas its *form* consists of the graphic symbols that communicate the subject matter (word choice, spelling, punctuation, paragraphing, etc.).

Contrast: See *comparison*.

Deduction (505) is a form of logical reasoning that begins with a *general* assertion and then presents specific details and *examples* in support of that *generalization*. *Induction* works in reverse by offering a number of *examples* and then concluding with a *general* truth or principle.

Definition (388–397) is a process whereby the meaning of a term is explained. Formal definitions require two distinct operations: (1) finding the *general* class to which the object belongs and (2) isolating the object within that class by describing how it differs from other elements in the same category. Nancy Gibbs ("When Is It Rape?"), for example, defines rape as a crime (general class) and then differentiates it from other crimes (isolation) by explaining ways in which it is unique.

Denotation: See *connotation*.

Description (37–50) is a mode of writing or speaking that relates the sights, sounds, tastes, smells, or feelings of a particular experience to its readers or listeners. Good descriptive writers, such as those featured in Chapter 1, are particularly adept at receiving, selecting, and expressing sensory details from the world around them. Along with *persuasion, exposition,* and *narration, description* is one of the four dominant types of writing.

Development (27–30) concerns the manner in which a *paragraph* of an *essay* expands on its topic.

Dialect is a speech pattern typical of a certain regional location, race, or social group that exhibits itself through unique word choice, pronunciation, and/or grammatical *usage*. See John McPhee's "The Pines," in which Fred and Bill, two residents of a wilderness area in southern New Jersey, speak in a discernible dialect.

Dialogue is a conversation between two or more people, particularly within a novel, play, poem, short story, or other literary work.

Diction (27, 262–265, 505–506) is word choice. If a vocabulary is a list of words available for use, then good *diction* is the careful selection of those words to communicate a particular subject to a specific *audience*. Different types of *diction* include formal (scholarly books and articles), informal (*essays* in popular magazines), *colloquial* (conversations between friends, including newly coined words and expressions), *slang* (language shared by certain social groups), *dialect* (language typical of a certain region, race, or social group), technical (words that make up the basic vocabulary of a specific area of study, such as medicine or law), and obsolete (words no longer in use).

Division: See *classification.*

Documented essay (589–607) is a research or library paper that integrates *paraphrases, summaries,* and quotations from secondary sources with the writer's own insights and conclusions. Such *essays* normally include references within the paper and, at the end, a list of the books and articles cited.

Dominant impression (40, 42, 43) in *descriptive* writing is the principal effect the author wishes to create for the *audience.*

Editing (31–32, 33) is an important part of the *rewriting* process of an *essay* that requires writers to make certain their work observes the conventions of standard written English.

Effect: See *cause and effect.*

Emphasis (101, 503) is the stress given to certain words, phrases, sentences, and/or *paragraphs* within an *essay* by such methods as repeating important ideas; positioning *thesis* and *topic sentences* effectively; supplying additional details or *examples*; allocating more space to certain sections of an *essay*; choosing words carefully; selecting and arranging details judiciously; and using certain mechanical devices, such as italics, underlining, capitalization, and different colors of ink.

Essay is a relatively short prose composition on a limited topic. Most *essays* are five hundred to one thousand words long and focus on a clearly definable question to be answered or problem to be solved. Formal *essays*, such as Germaine Greer's "A Child Is Born," are generally characterized by seriousness of *purpose*, logical *organization*, and dignity of language; informal *essays*, such as Garrison Keillor's "How the Crab Apple Grew," are generally brief, humorous, and more loosely structured. *Essays* in this textbook have been divided into nine traditional *rhetorical* types, each of which is discussed at length in its chapter introduction.

Etymology (392) is the study of the origin and development of words.

Evidence (498, 501, 504, 590) is any material used to help support an *argument*, including details, facts, *examples*, opinions, and expert testimony. Just as a lawyer's case is won or lost in a court of law because of the strength of the evidence presented, so, too, does the effectiveness of a writer's *essay* depend on the *evidence* offered in support of its *thesis statement*.

Example (154–165) is an illustration of a *general* principle or *thesis statement*. Harold Krents's "Darkness at Noon," for instance, gives several different examples of prejudice against handicapped people.

Exposition is one of the four main *rhetorical* categories of writing (the others are *persuasion, narration,* and *description*). The principal *purpose* of expository prose is to "expose" ideas to your readers, to explain, define, and interpret information through one or more of the following modes of exposition: *example, process analysis, division/classification, comparison/contrast, definition,* and *cause/effect*.

Figurative language (44–45, 505) is writing or speaking that purposefully departs from the literal meanings of words to achieve a particularly vivid, expressive, and/or imaginative image. When, for example, Joyce Carol Oates refers to a boxing match as a story, she is using *figurative language*. Other principal figures of speech include *metaphor, simile, hyperbole, allusion,* and *personification*.

Flashback (106) is a technique used mainly in *narrative* writing that enables the author to present scenes or conversations that took place prior to the beginning of the story.

Focus (25–28) is the concentration of a *topic* on one central point or issue.

Form: See *content*.

Formal essay: See *essay*.

Free association (22–25) is a process of generating ideas for writing through which one thought leads randomly to another.

General (154–155, 257–258) words are those that employ expansive categories, such as *animals, sports, occupations,* and *clothing*; *specific* words are more limiting and restrictive, such as *koala, lacrosse, computer programmer,* and *bow tie*. Whether a word is *general* or *specific* depends at least somewhat on its context: *Bow tie* is more *specific* than *clothing*, yet less *specific* than "the pink and green striped bow tie Aunt Martha gave me last Christmas." See also *abstract.*

Generalization (154–155, 157, 505) is a broad statement or belief based on a limited number of facts, *examples*, or statistics. A product of inductive reasoning, generalizations should be used carefully and sparingly in *essays.*

Hyperbole, the opposite of *understatement*, is a type of *figurative language* that uses deliberate exaggeration for the sake of emphasis or comic effect (e.g., "hungry enough to eat 20 chocolate eclairs").

Hypothesis (449, 590) is a tentative theory that can be proved or disproved through further investigation and *analysis.*

Idiom refers to a grammatical construction unique to a certain people, region, or class that cannot be translated literally into another language.

Illustration (154–155) is the use of *examples* to support an idea or *generalization.*

Imagery (43–44) is *description* that appeals to one or more of our five senses. See, for example, Malcolm Cowley's description in "The View from 80" of one of the pleasures of old age: "simply sitting still, like a snake on a sun-warmed stone, with a delicious feeling of indolence that was seldom attained in earlier years." Imagery is used to help bring clarity and vividness to descriptive writing.

Induction: See *deduction.*

Inference (504–505) is a *deduction* or *conclusion* derived from *specific* information.

Informal essay: See *essay.*

Introduction (31) refers to the beginning of an *essay*. It should identify the subject to be discussed, set the limits of that discussion, and clearly state the *thesis* or general *purpose* of the paper. In a brief (five-paragraph) essay, your *introduction* should be only one *paragraph*; for longer papers, you may want to provide longer introductory sections. A good *introduction* will generally catch the *audience's* attention by beginning with a quotation, a provocative statement, a personal *anecdote*, or a stimulating question that somehow involves its readers in the topic under consideration. See also *conclusion*.

Irony (169) is a figure of speech in which the literal, *denotative* meaning is the opposite of what is stated. Judy Brady's "Why I Want a Wife" is heavily ironic: What she really wants is for women to be treated as equals to men.

Jargon (260–261) is the special language of a certain group or profession, such as psychological jargon, legal jargon, or medical jargon. When jargon is excerpted from its proper subject area, it generally becomes confusing or meaningless, as in "I have a latency problem with my backhand" or "I hope we can interface tomorrow night after the dance."

Levels of thought (1–2) is a phrase that describes the three sequential stages at which people think, read, and write: literal, interpretive, and analytical.

Logic (498, 503–506) is the science of correct reasoning. Based principally on *inductive* or *deductive* processes, logic establishes a method by which we can examine *premises* and *conclusions*, construct *syllogisms*, and avoid faulty reasoning.

Logical fallacy (505) is an incorrect conclusion derived from faulty reasoning. See also *post hoc, ergo propter hoc* and *non sequitur*.

Metaphor (44–45, 505–506) is an implied *comparison* that brings together two dissimilar objects, persons, or ideas. Unlike a *simile*, which uses the words *like* or *as*, a *metaphor* directly identifies an obscure or difficult subject with another that is easier to understand. In George Orwell's "Shooting an Elephant," for example, the author metaphorically describes the great beast as having a "preoccupied grandmotherly air"—a vivid comparison that should be of great help to those of us more familiar with grandmothers than with mad elephants.

Mood (106, 506) refers to the atmosphere or *tone* created in a piece of writing. The mood of Harry Edwards's "Triple Tragedy in Black Society," for example, is intense and serious; of Jessica Mitford's "Behind the Formaldehyde Curtain," sarcastic and derisive; and of Ellen Goodman's "Putting In a Good Word for Guilt," good-humored and sympathetic.

Narration (100–112) is storytelling: the recounting of a series of events, arranged in a particular order and delivered by a narrator to a specific *audience* with a clear *purpose* in mind. Along with *persuasion, exposition,* and *description,* it is one of the four principal types of writing.

Non sequitur (504–505) from a Latin phrase meaning "it does not follow," refers to a *conclusion* that does not logically derive from its *premises.*

Objective (38, 42) writing is detached, impersonal, and factual; *subjective* writing reveals the author's personal feelings and *attitudes.* Judith Wallerstein and Sandra Blakeslee's "Second Chances for Children of Divorce" is an *example* of *objective* prose, whereas Amy Tan's "The Joy Luck Club" is essentially *subjective* in nature. Most good college-level *essays* are a careful mix of both approaches, with lab reports and technical writing toward the *objective* end of the scale and personal *essays* in composition courses at the *subjective* end.

Organization (27, 30–31, 102–103, 106–107, 159–161, 219–221, 503–506) refers to the order in which a writer chooses to present his or her ideas to the reader. Five main types of *organization* may be used to develop *paragraphs* or *essays:* (1) *deductive* (moving from *general* to *specific*), (2) *inductive* (from *specific* to *general*), (3) *chronological* (according to time sequence), (4) *spatial* (according to physical relationship in space), and (5) *climactic* (from one extreme to another, such as least important to most important).

Paradox is a seemingly self-contradictory statement that contains an element of truth. In "The View from 80," Malcolm Cowley paradoxically declares that the Ojibwa Indians were "kind to their old people" by killing them when they became decrepit.

Paragraphs are groups of interrelated sentences that develop a central topic. Generally governed by a *topic sentence,* a *paragraph* has its own *unity* and *coherence* and is an integral part of the logical *development* of an *essay.*

Parallelism (306) is a structural arrangement within sentences, *paragraphs*, or entire *essays* through which two or more separate elements are similarly phrased and developed. Look, for example, at Judy Brady's "Why I Want a Wife": "I want a wife who will plan the menus, do the necessary grocery shopping, prepare the meals, serve them pleasantly, and then do the cleaning up while I do my studying."

Paraphrase (593–594) is a restatement in your own words of someone else's ideas or observations.

Parody is making fun of a person, an event, or a work of literature through exaggerated imitation.

Person (44–45, 106) is a grammatical distinction identifying the speaker or writer in a particular context: first person (I or we), second person (you), and third person (he, she, it, or they). The *person* of an *essay* refers to the voice of the narrator. See also *point of view*.

Personification is *figurative language* that ascribes human characteristics to an abstraction, animal, idea, or inanimate object. Consider, for example, Robert Ramirez's description in "The Barrio" of the bakery that "sends its sweet messenger aroma down the dimly lit street, announcing the arrival of fresh, hot, sugary *pan dulce*."

Persuasion (497–511) is one of the four chief forms of *rhetoric*. Its main purpose is to convince a reader (or listener) to think, act, or feel a certain way. It involves appealing to reason, to emotion, and/or to a sense of ethics. The other three main *rhetorical* categories are *exposition, narration*, and *description*.

Point of view (44–45, 106) is the perspective from which a writer tells a story, including *person, vantage point*, and *attitude*. Principal *narrative* voices are first-person, in which the writer relates the story from his or her own vantage point ("When I pulled the trigger, I did not hear the bang or feel the kick"); omniscient, a third-person technique in which the narrator knows everything and can even see into the minds of the various characters; and concealed, a third-person method in which the narrator can see and hear events but cannot look into the minds of the other characters.

Post hoc, ergo propter hoc (446–447), a Latin phrase meaning "after this, therefore because of this," is a *logical fallacy* confusing *cause and effect* with *chronology*. Just because Irving wakes up every morning before the sun rises doesn't mean that the sun rises because Irving wakes up.

Premise (504–506) is a proposition or statement that forms the foundation of an *argument* and helps support a *conclusion*. See also *logic* and *syllogism*.

Prereading (5–9, 19–20) is thoughtful concentration on a topic before reading an *essay*. Just as athletes warm up their physical muscles before competition, so, too, should students activate their "mental muscles" before reading or writing essays.

Prewriting (21–27, 32), which is similar to *prereading*, is the initial stage in the composing process during which writers consider their topics, generate ideas, narrow and refine their *thesis statements*, organize their ideas, pursue any necessary research, and identify their *audiences*. Although *prewriting* occurs principally, as the name suggests, "before" an *essay* is started, writers usually return to this "invention" stage again and again during the course of the writing process.

Process analysis (214–224) one of the seven primary modes of *exposition*, either gives directions about how to do something (directive) or provides information on how something happened (informative).

Proofreading (32, 33) an essential part of *rewriting*, is a thorough, careful review of the final draft of an *essay* that ensures that all errors have been eliminated.

Purpose (27, 40, 43–44, 501, 506) in an *essay* refers to its overall aim or intention: to entertain, inform, or persuade a particular *audience* with reference to a specific topic (to persuade readers of the *Christian Century*, for example, that religion should be taken out of instructional periods in America's high schools, as Donald Drakeman argues in "Religion's Place in Public Schools"). See also *dominant impression*.

Refutation is the process of discrediting the *arguments* that run counter to your *thesis statement*.

Revision (30–31, 32–33), meaning "to see again," takes place during the entire writing process as you change words, rewrite sentences, and shift *paragraphs* from one location to another in your *essay*. It plays an especially vital role in the *rewriting* stage of the composing process.

Rewriting (30–32, 32–33) is a stage of the composing process that includes *revision, editing*, and *proofreading*.

Rhetoric is the art of using language effectively.

Rhetorical questions are intended to provoke thought rather than bring forth an answer. See, for example, Shelby Steele's *rhetorical questions* in "Affirmative Action: The Price of Preference": "Given that unfairness cuts both ways, doesn't it only balance the scales of history that my children now receive a preference over whites? Doesn't this repay, in a small way, the systematic denial under which their grandfather lived out his days?"

Rhetorical strategy or mode is the plan or method whereby an *essay* is organized. Most writers choose from methods discussed in this book, such as *narration, example, comparison/contrast, definition*, and *cause/effect*.

Sarcasm is a form of *irony* that attacks a person or belief through harsh and bitter remarks that often mean the opposite of what they say. See, for example, Jessica Mitford's sarcastic praise of the funeral director in "Behind the Formaldehyde Curtain": "He has relieved the family of every detail, he has revamped the corpse to look like a living doll, he has arranged for it to nap for a few days in a slumber room, he has put on a well-oiled performance in which the concept of *death* has played no part whatsoever. . . . He has done everything in his power to make the funeral a real pleasure for everybody concerned." See also *satire*.

Satire is a literary technique that attacks foolishness by making fun of it. Most good satires work through a "fiction" that is clearly transparent. Judy Brady claims she wants a wife, for example, yet she obviously does not; she simply uses this satiric "pose" to ridicule the stereotypical male view of wives as docile, obedient creatures who do everything possible to please their husbands.

Setting refers to the immediate environment of a *narrative* or *descriptive* piece of writing: the place, time, and background established by the author.

Simile (44, 505–506) is a *comparison* between two dissimilar objects that uses the words *like* or *as*. See, for example, Ray Bradbury's description of the women in "Summer Rituals," who appear "like ghosts hovering momentarily behind the door screen." See also *metaphor*.

Slang (264–265) is casual conversation among friends; as such, it is inappropriate for use in formal and informal writing, unless it is placed in quotation marks and introduced for a specific *rhetorical* purpose: "Hey dude, ya know what I mean?" See also *colloquial expressions*.

Spatial order (101,160) is a method of *description* that begins at one geographical point and moves onward in an orderly fashion. See, for example, the opening of John McPhee's "The Pines," which first describes the front yard of Fred Brown's house, then moves through the vestibule and into the kitchen, and finally settles on Fred himself, who is seated behind a porcelain-topped table in a room just beyond the kitchen.

Specific: See *general*.

Style is the unique, individual way in which each author expresses his or her ideas. Often referred to as the "personality" of an *essay*, *style* is dependent on a writer's manipulation of *diction*, sentence structure, *figurative language, point of view, characterization, emphasis, mood, purpose, rhetorical strategy*, and all the other variables that govern written material.

Subjective: See *objective*.

Summary (593–594) is a condensed statement of someone else's thoughts or observations.

Syllogism (504–505) refers to a three-step *deductive argument* that moves logically from a major and a minor *premise* to a *conclusion*. A traditional example is "All men are mortal. Socrates is a man. Therefore, Socrates is mortal."

Symbol refers to an object or action in literature that metaphorically represents something more important than itself. In George Orwell's "Shooting an Elephant," the stricken beast symbolizes the British Empire, which, despite its immense size, is dying in influence throughout the world.

Synonyms are terms with similar or identical *denotative* meanings, such as *aged, elderly, older person,* and *senior citizen.*

Syntax describes the order in which words are arranged in a sentence and the effect that this arrangement has on the creation of meaning.

Thesis statement or thesis (27–28) is the principal *focus* of an *essay*. It is usually phrased in the form of a question to be answered, a problem to be solved, or an assertion to be argued. The word *thesis* derives from a Greek term meaning "something set down," and most good writers find that "setting down" their thesis in writing helps them tremendously in defining and clarifying their topic before they begin to write an outline or a rough draft.

Tone (106, 506) is a writer's *attitude* or *point of view* toward his or her subject. See also *mood*.

Topic sentence is the central idea around which a *paragraph* develops. A *topic sentence* controls a *paragraph* in the same way a *thesis statement* unifies and governs an entire *essay*. See also *induction* and *deduction*.

Transition (106) is the linking together of sequential ideas in sentences, *paragraphs*, and *essays*. This linking is accomplished primarily through word repetition, pronouns, parallel constructions, and such transitional words and phrases as *therefore, as a result, consequently, moreover,* and *similarly*.

Understatement, the opposite of *hyperbole*, is a deliberate weakening of the truth for comic or emphatic purpose. Commenting, for example, on the great care funeral directors take to make corpses look lifelike for their funerals, Jessica Mitford explains in

"Behind the Formaldehyde Curtain," "This is a rather large order, since few people die in the full bloom of health."

Unity (160) exists in an *essay* when all ideas originate from and help support a central *thesis statement.*

Usage (32, 33) refers to the customary rules that govern written and spoken language.

Vantage point (44–45, 106) is the frame of reference of the narrator in a story: close to the action, far from the action, looking back on the past, or reporting on the present. See also *person* and *point of view.*

CREDITS

Productions, Inc. Used by permission of Bantam Books, a division of Bantam Doubleday Dell Publishing Group, Inc.

p. 429   Tom Wolfe, "The Right Stuff," from *The Right Stuff*, by Tom Wolfe. Copyright © 1979 by Tom Wolfe. Reprinted by permission of Farrar, Straus & Giroux, Inc.

p. 437   Susan Sontag, "On AIDS," from *AIDS and Its Metaphors*, by Susan Sontag. Copyright © 1988, 1989, by Susan Sontag. Reprinted by permission of Farrar, Straus & Giroux, Inc.

p. 457   Stephen King, "Why We Crave Horror Movies," from *Playboy* magazine, 1982. © Stephen King. Reprinted by permission. All other rights reserved.

p. 463   Michael Dorris, "The Broken Cord," excerpt from *The Broken Cord*, by Michael Dorris. Copyright © 1989 by Michael Dorris. Reprinted by permission of HarperCollins Publishers.

p. 471   Richard Brokers Rodriguez, "The Fear of Losing a Culture," *Time* July 11, 1988. Copyright © 1988 by Richard Rodriguez. Reprinted by permission of Georges Borchardt, Inc. and the author.

p. 477   Mitchell Lazarus, "Rx for Mathophobia," *Saturday Review*, June 28, 1975. Reprinted by permission.

p. 486   Alice Walker, "Beauty: When The Other Dancer Is The Self," from *In Search Of Our Mother's Gardens: Womanist Prose*, copyright © 1983 by Alice Walker, reprinted by permission of Harcourt Brace & Company.

p. 512   Donald Drakeman, "Religion's Place in Public Schools," *The Christian Century*, May 2, 1984. Copyright 1984 Christian Century Foundation. Reprinted by permission.

p. 520   Ellen Goodman, "Putting In a Good Word for Guilt," *Redbook*, June 1982. Copyright © 1982 The Boston Globe/Washington Post Writers Group. Reprinted with permission.

p. 528   Shelby Steele, "Affirmative Action: The Price of Preference," from *The Content of Our Character*, copyright © 1990 by Shelby Steele. Reprinted with permission from St. Martin's Press, Inc., New York, NY.

p. 542   Robert Hughes, "The N.R.A. in a Hunter's Sights," *Time*, April 3, 1989. Copyright © 1989 The Time Inc. Magazine Company. Reprinted by permission.

p. 548   Peter Salins, "Take A Ticket," from *The New Republic*. Copyright 1993 by Peter Salins. Reprinted by permission of Peter Salins and *The New Republic*.

p. 559   Carl Cannon, "Honey, I Warped The Kids," from *Mother Jones*. Copyright 1993 by Carl Cannon. Reprinted by permission.

p. 563   John Leonard, "Why Blame TV?", from *The Nation*, December 27, 1993. Copyright 1993 by *The Nation*. Reprinted by permission of *The Nation*.

p. 573   Mario Cuomo, "Freedom Of The Press Must Be Unlimited," from *USA Today*. Reprinted by permission.

p. 580   John Merrill, "Freedom of The Press Must Be Limited." This article appeared in the *February 1988* issue and is reprinted with permission from *The World & I*, a publication of *The Washington Times Corporation*, copyright © 1988.

p. 608   John Langone, "Group Violence," from *Violence: Our Fastest Growing Public Health Problem*, by John Langone. Copyright © 1984 by John Langone. Reprinted by permission of Little, Brown and Company.

p. 618   Adela de la Torre, "Key Issues In Latina Health: Voicing Latina Concerns In The Health Financing Debate." from *Chicana Critical Issues*, edited by Mujeres Activas en Letras y Cambio Social, published by Third Woman Press, Berkeley, Calif. Copyright 1993 by Adela de la Torre. Reprinted by permission.

p. 635   Eudora Welty, "Listening," from *One Writer's Beginnings*, 1983, 1984, by Eudora Welty. Reprinted by permission of Harvard University Press.

Credits

Index of Authors
and Titles

677